STRATEGIC ASIA 2008–09

STRATEGIC ASIA 2008–09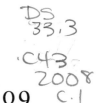

CHALLENGES
AND CHOICES

Edited by

Ashley J. Tellis, Mercy Kuo, and Andrew Marble

With contributions from

Richard K. Betts, Dennis C. Blair, Elizabeth Economy, Evelyn Goh, Rory Medcalf,
Polly Nayak, T.J. Pempel, George Perkovich, Jonathan D. Pollack,
Eugene B. Rumer, Teresita C. Schaffer, S. Frederick Starr, and Michael D. Swaine

NBR THE NATIONAL BUREAU *of* ASIAN RESEARCH
Seattle and Washington, D.C.

THE NATIONAL BUREAU *of* ASIAN RESEARCH

Published in the United States of America by
The National Bureau of Asian Research, Seattle, WA, and Washington, D.C.
www.nbr.org

This material is based upon work supported in part by the Department of Energy (National Nuclear Security Administration) under Award Number DE-FG52-03SF22724.

This report was prepared as an account of work sponsored by an agency of the United States Government. Neither the United States Government nor any agency thereof, nor any of their employees, makes any warranty, express or implied, or assumes any legal liability or responsibility for the accuracy, completeness, or usefulness of any information, apparatus, product, or process disclosed, or represents that its use would not infringe privately owned rights. Reference herein to any specific commercial product, process, or service by trade name, trademark, manufacturer, or otherwise does not constitute or imply its endorsement, recommendation, or favoring by the United States Government or any agency thereof. The views and opinions of authors expressed herein do not necessarily state or reflect those of the United States Government or any agency thereof.

NBR makes no warranties or representations regarding the accuracy of any map in this volume. Depicted boundaries are meant as guidelines only and do not represent the views of NBR or NBR's funders.

Publisher's Cataloging-In-Publication Data
(Prepared by The Donohue Group, Inc.)

Challenges and choices : edited by Ashley J. Tellis, Mercy Kuo, and Andrew Marble ; with contributions from Richard K. Betts ... [et al.]
    p. : ill., maps ; cm. -- (Strategic Asia, 1933-6462 ; 2008-09)
    Based upon work supported in part by the Department of Energy (National Nuclear Security Administration) under Award Number DE-FG52-03SF22724.
    Includes bibliographical references and index.
    ISBN-13: 978-0-9713938-9-9
    ISBN-10: 0-9713938-9-3

    1. Asia--Politics and government--1945- 2. Asia--Economic conditions. 3. Asia--Commercial policy. 4. Asia--Defenses. 5. Asia--Strategic aspects. 6. Asia--Foreign economic relations--United States. 7. United States--Foreign economic relations--Asia. 8. National security--Asia. I. Tellis, Ashley J. II. Kuo, Mercy. III. Marble, Andrew. IV. National Bureau of Asian Research (U.S.) V. Series: Strategic Asia, 1933-6462 ; 2008-09

DS33.3 .C43 2008
320.95

Design and publishing services by The National Bureau of Asian Research

Cover design by Stefanie Choi

Printed in Canada

The paper used in this publication meets the minimum requirement of the American National Standard for Information Sciences—Permanence of Paper for Printed Library Materials, ANSI Z39.48-1992.

Contents

Strategic Asia: Regional Studies

Strategic Asia: Special Studies

Strategic Asia: Indicators

Preface

Richard J. Ellings

Strategic Asia 2008–09: Challenges and Choices is the eighth in the series of annual assessments produced by NBR's Strategic Asia Program. In the context of a U.S. presidential election year, the timeliness of this year's volume underscores the elemental decisions on Asia facing the next U.S. president. The last eight years have witnessed dramatic, transformative forces that have propelled the emergence of Asia as the new global center of gravity. China's growth trajectory and Asia's market magnetism are raising the stakes of competition for capital, capabilities, and capacity-building. For the new U.S. administration, policymakers, and analysts, understanding the impact of a more Asia-centric world on vital U.S. interests requires assessing how the United States might engage Asian powers in ways conducive to global economic growth and political stability.

This year's volume seeks to illuminate the complex variables and vectors fueling Asia's growing influence and how they factor into current and alternative policy options for the incoming U.S. administration. In contrast to previous volumes, the content of this year's book is presented within the framework of a U.S. presidential leadership transition and the impending changes that such a transfer of power entails. Deciding how to marshal the components of national power for the next phase of U.S. relations with key Asian states will be critical.

Foremost on the Asia policy agenda will be China and India. The United States' relationships with both countries have grown stronger, though uncertainties persist with each. The most enduring of U.S.-China issues is Taiwan. Although the Taiwan Strait remains a potential flashpoint in spite of the election of Nationalist Ma Ying-jeou in March 2008, China and Taiwan are forging a less confrontational, and probably more stable, relationship. This should bode well for U.S.-China diplomacy. On the other hand, U.S.-China trade relations will likely become increasingly complex as the din of protectionists is apt to grow louder in either country as economies weaken. Similarly, uncertainties persist in U.S.-India relations. Although India has become a key U.S. strategic partner in the region, New Delhi will most likely continue to pursue an independent foreign policy. At the same time, China and India are increasingly competitive in areas where others, including most notably the United States, have held a preeminent position. India and China are rapidly catching up to or, in some sectors, surpassing the United States in manufacturing especially and to a lesser extent in innovation and services trade. In the international arena, a decline in U.S. supremacy in these areas could have an impact on U.S. trade and security interests; on the domestic front, it may affect U.S. economic growth and employment rates.

Amid these developments fueled by globalization, the American public has become increasingly vested in U.S. policy toward Asia. Americans now come into contact with Asian states on a daily basis through exposure to the plethora of Asian goods and services in the U.S. market, the strength of Asian liquidity in global capital markets, Asian immigrants and visitors, and the endless stream of media coverage on the region. Debating U.S. policy toward Asian states is no longer the reserve of foreign policy specialists and government officials; Asia's global reach has been parlayed into the discourse of local politics across the United States. If not carefully managed, American public opinion could easily exacerbate U.S. policymakers' ability to implement sound foreign policy toward Asia. The 2007 pet food and toy scare and subsequent legislation on product quality standards for imports is but one example of the American populace shaping U.S. foreign policy toward Asia.

The new U.S. administration will also need to be prepared to handle potential crises in Asia stemming from unstable regimes, the threat of terrorism, efforts to acquire WMD, heightened competition for natural resources, and nontraditional security concerns. Ending the nuclear crisis in North Korea will likely require a long-term solution that will in essence define the region's security architecture and may resuscitate regime change in the North. Managing Iran's growing orientation toward Asia and the ongoing Iranian nuclear imbroglio remains a strategic imperative. This is as much an Asian issue as an Atlantic one. Price increases in oil and other natural resources have accentuated tension over disputed claims and have fostered deeper economic linkages between energy supplier states such as Iran, Russia, and Kazakhstan, on the one hand, and oil dependent countries such as China, India, and Japan, on the other. Additionally, water security may become a global security concern as water shortages and poor water quality increasingly threaten transnational food security, public health, and economic growth in China and elsewhere.

Despite these challenges, Asia also offers increasing opportunities for the United States. Vast increases in global trade, brought about in part by open economic development in Asia, have contributed to a dynamic, innovative international economy—a point soon forgotten in the present climate of protectionism in the United States. The benefit for much of the world has been growth with low inflation. Through effective policies at home and in Asia, the United States can continue to benefit from the positive changes unfolding across the region, facilitating Asia's further integration into the global economy and encouraging Asia's acceptance of a greater share of global responsibilities.

The National Bureau of Asian Research developed the Strategic Asia Program to fulfill three objectives: (1) to provide the best possible understanding of the current strategic environment in Asia; (2) to look forward five years, and in some cases beyond, to contemplate the region's future; and (3) to establish a record of data and assessment for those interested in understanding the changes taking place in the Asian strategic landscape.[1]

With these objectives in mind, *Strategic Asia 2008–09: Challenges and Choices* is designed to complement our existing work in the series, broaden the current political debate to include issues related to Asia, and provide U.S. decisionmakers with the most authoritative information and analysis possible. Through a collection of country, regional, and special studies, this volume discusses significant political patterns and developments within key Asian states and the relevant role the United States has played. Based on the results of this rigorous analysis, alternate policy options for the next U.S. administration are assessed in the hope that identifying the potential consequences of these options in the region will assist U.S. decisionmakers in their efforts to craft an effective new policy toward Asia. A companion website provides free access to the comprehensive Strategic Asia database, which contains a wealth of indicators for Asian demographic, trade, communication, and financial trends; measures of states' economic and military capabilities; and information on political and energy dynamics. Drawing together data from disparate sources, the database allows users to compare these statistics across a range of years, countries, and indicators,

---

[1] The Strategic Asia Program considers as "Asia" the entire eastern half of the Eurasian land mass and the arc of offshore islands in the western Pacific. This vast expanse can be pictured as an area centered on China and consisting of four distinct subregions arrayed clockwise around it: Northeast Asia (including the Russian Far East, the Korean Peninsula, and Japan), Southeast Asia (including both its mainland and maritime components), South Asia (including India and Pakistan, and bordered to the west by Afghanistan), and Central Asia (Kazakhstan, Kyrgyzstan, Tajikistan, Turkmenistan, Uzbekistan, and southern Russia). The Strategic Asia Program also tracks significant developments across the Asia-Pacific to the United States and Canada.

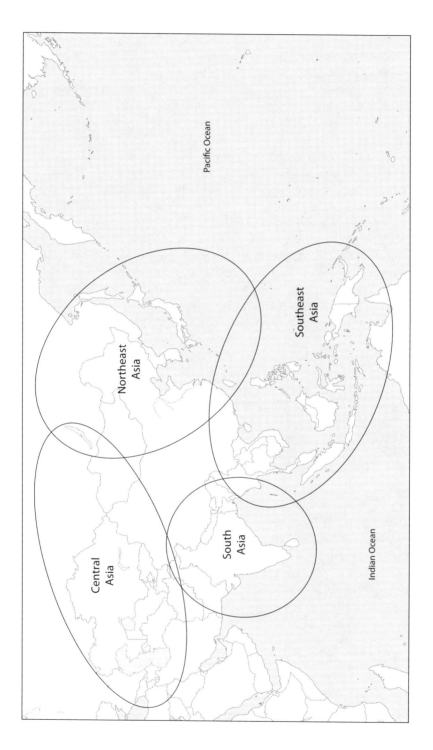

providing an invaluable resource to illustrate and assess the momentous changes underway in Asia.

Acknowledgments

This year's volume of *Strategic Asia* represents a new undertaking for NBR. The volume includes the same rigorous, independent analysis that has characterized previous volumes, but with an impending U.S. presidential transition, more explicitly discusses U.S. policy options than previous volumes of *Strategic Asia*. Making this transition in the research design, while producing the same high quality publication, would not have been possible without the energy, dedication, and hard work of NBR staff and associates that undergird all of NBR's projects.

I am deeply appreciative of the program's two senior advisors—General (ret.) John Shalikashvili, former Chairman of the Joint Chiefs of Staff, and the program's founding research director Aaron Friedberg, Professor of Politics at Princeton University and former Deputy National Security Advisor to the Vice President. Their sage guidance and generous support of the Strategic Asia Program as well as many other research initiatives across NBR serves as the bedrock of our institution. Admiral Dennis Blair, U.S. Navy (ret.), the inaugural Shalikashvili Chair in National Security Studies, contributed a chapter to this year's volume and is playing an important advisory role to the Strategic Asia Program.

In his fifth year as the Strategic Asia Research Director, Ashley Tellis provided the intellectual agenda and research direction for this year's volume. Ashley deserves special thanks for his masterful, analytical leadership and long-standing commitment to the program. In NBR's own internal transition, Michael Wills, now NBR's Director of Research and Operations, passed the mantle of Strategic Asia Program Director to Mercy Kuo, who managed the multiple facets of producing the book and raised the program's research standard to an even higher level. As the NBR Editor, Andrew Marble's thorough care and editorial flourish enhanced the overall quality of the book and ensured its accessibility across multiple readerships. In the research, writing, and editing processes, Ashley, Mercy, and Andrew worked closely with the authors to produce a cogent and comprehensive compilation of analysis on Asia.

I also want to acknowledge the indispensable role that NBR staff played behind the scenes. Collaborating closely with Ashley, Mercy, and Andrew, Stephanie Renzi, Strategic Asia Program Manager, provided vital research, logistical, and production support for this year's publication and applied her deft multi-tasking skills in planning and managing the book launch events in Washington, D.C. Members of NBR's editorial team—Jessica Keough, Managing Editor, Sandra Marble, Online Content and Publications Outreach Coordinator, and Joshua Ziemkowski, NBR Fellow—worked tirelessly with Andrew on the extensive structural and technical editing of the volume. Jannette Whippy contributed her design dexterity in laying out the entire volume and Executive Summary. Programmer Ben Andrews provided ongoing IT support and helped maintain the Strategic Asia online database.

Much of the leg-work undertaken in the Strategic Asia Program has relied on the intellectual and creative talents of this year's Next Generation fellows and program associates. Next Generation Fellows (2007–08) Andrew David and Michael Cognato made key contributions to the book. Andrew coordinated with Stephanie in compiling the appendix, and Michael lent his sharp structural editing eye to the drafts and collaborated with Stephanie in fine-tuning the format of the Executive Summary. NBR interns Ivan Szpakowski, Marc Miller, and Daniel Alderman also provided invaluable assistance with the appendix, index, Executive Summary, and database as well as with research assistance for the scholars. In addition, Next Generation Fellow (2008–09) Matthew Boswell assisted with editing and proofreading.

I am also deeply indebted to many other individuals who have dedicated their time and resources to the Strategic Asia Program throughout the year. Our Board of Directors, in particular its Chairman George Russell, have served as core supporters of and advisors to all of NBR's projects. With their guidance, we have worked to integrate our research initiatives to address timely policy issues in more meaningful ways. Senior Vice Presidents Brigitte Allen and Karolos Karnikis have worked tirelessly to sustain the development of the Strategic Asia Program.

Members of our Washington, D.C., office have played an increasingly vital role in the production and dissemination of the *Strategic Asia* volume. Having expanded their office in the early months of this year, they are more poised than ever to share NBR's research with our nation's policymakers. As Director of the Washington, D.C., office and Vice President of Political and Security Affairs, Roy Kamphausen leads NBR's outreach efforts, regularly interfaces with key leaders, and effectively integrates NBR's political and security research projects, the Strategic Asia Program being one of them. The Strategic Asia Program team has highly valued Roy's unflagging support at every stage of the book production process. Meredith Miller, the new Director of Congressional Outreach, and Raelyn Campbell, Director of Corporate Relations, also provided support with outreach efforts. Special thanks to Tim Cook, Assistant Director of Political and Security Affairs and of the Washington, D.C., office, who provided research assistance to

Admiral Blair in preparing his special study on military power projection in Asia. Sincere thanks to Deborah Cooper, NBR's Washington, D.C., Office Manager, who provided superb logistical support for many of the Strategic Asia meetings and events in Washington, D.C.

This year's top-tier team of leading experts on Asia, international relations, and foreign policy adeptly executed their charge to assess the major challenges and choices facing the new U.S. president in charting the next phase of U.S. engagement with Asia. I would like to express my deepest appreciation to the authors for their hard work, dedication, and flexibility in meeting NBR's tight deadlines and requirements—a difficult feat for which they deserve much credit. These authors join a list of more than seventy other leading specialists who have written for the series, adding their unique perspectives on the region. The anonymous reviewers, both scholarly specialists and government experts, deserve acknowledgement for providing rigorous substantive and structural evaluations of the draft chapters. Their insightful critiques contributed to the high quality of this year's book.

Finally, I would like to extend my heartfelt gratitude to Strategic Asia's cornerstone sponsors—the National Nuclear Security Administration at the U.S. Department of Energy and the Lynde and Harry Bradley Foundation. Their generous support and long-standing commitment have helped sustain the overall prestige and impact of this unique program and enabled the program to expand readership of the book.

Richard J. Ellings
President
The National Bureau of Asian Research
August 2008

STRATEGIC ASIA 2008–09

OVERVIEW

EXECUTIVE SUMMARY

This chapter explores the means through which the U.S. can maintain its position as global leader amid a changing international landscape, particularly in Asia.

MAIN ARGUMENT:
Although the current international system is characterized by the continued dominance of the U.S., in the distant horizon there are new competitors, such as China, poised to lay the foundations for gradually eclipsing U.S. primacy over time. The principal task facing the next administration is thus to consolidate U.S. hegemony by redefining the nation's global role, renewing its strength, and recovering its legitimacy. Successful resolution of these challenges would empower Washington in its dealings with both Asia and the rest of the world.

POLICY IMPLICATIONS:
- U.S. efforts in three areas will reaffirm the country's role as global leader: supporting a durable framework for international trade, maintaining unqualified military supremacy, and ensuring the delivery of certain public goods, such as peace and security, freedom of navigation, and a clean environment.

- The renewal of traditional U.S. economic might requires policies that favor growth and innovation, increased capital and labor pools, and sustained pursuit of total factor productivity.

- Legitimacy is an important facet of U.S. power that has eroded over the last eight years. The U.S. can secure legitimacy for future political acts by shaping world opinion through a combination of decisiveness, cultivation of key allied support, and attentiveness to the views of others.

Preserving Hegemony: The Strategic Tasks Facing the United States

Ashley J. Tellis

The U.S. experience of hegemony in global politics is still very young. Although the United States entered the international system as a great power early in the twentieth century, its systemic impact was not felt until World War II and, soon thereafter, its power was constrained by the presence of another competitor, the Soviet Union. Only after the demise of this challenger in 1991 has the United States been liberated in the exercise of its hegemonic power but—as has become quite evident in the past two decades—this application of power, although potent in its impact when well exercised, is also beset by important limitations. In any event, the now significant, century-long, involvement of the United States in international politics as a great power tends to obscure the reality of how short its hegemonic phase has actually been thus far.

This hegemony is by no means fated to end any time soon, however, given that the United States remains predominant by most conventional indicators of national power. The character of the United States' hegemonic behavior in the future will thus remain an issue of concern both within the domestic polity and internationally. Yet the juvenescence of the U.S. "unipolar moment," combined with the disorientation produced by the September 11 attacks, ought to restrain any premature generalization that the imperial activism begun by the Clinton administration, and which the Bush administration took to its most spirited apotheosis, would in some way come to define the permanent norm of U.S. behavior in the global system. In all probability, it is much more likely that the limitations on U.S.

Ashley J. Tellis is Senior Associate at the Carnegie Endowment for International Peace and Research Director of the Strategic Asia Program at NBR. He can be reached at <atellis@carnegieendowment.org>.

power witnessed in Afghanistan and Iraq will produce a more phlegmatic and accommodating United States over the longer term, despite the fact that the traditional U.S. pursuit of dominance—understood as the quest to maintain a preponderance of power, neutralize threatening challengers, and protect freedom of action, goals that go back to the foundations of the republic—is unlikely to be extinguished any time soon.[1]

Precisely because the desire for dominance is likely to remain a permanent feature of U.S. geopolitical ambitions—even though how it is exercised will certainly change in comparison to the Bush years—the central task facing the next administration will still pertain fundamentally to the issue of U.S. power. This concern manifests itself through the triune challenges of: redefining the United States' role in the world, renewing the foundations of U.S. strength, and recovering the legitimacy of U.S. actions. In other words, the next administration faces the central task of clarifying the character of U.S. hegemony, reinvigorating the material foundations of its power, and securing international support for its policies.

The challenge of comprehensively strengthening U.S. power at this juncture, when the United States is still in the early phase of its unipolar role in global politics, arises importantly from the fact that the hegemony it has enjoyed since 1991 represents a "prize" deriving from victory in intense geopolitical competition with another great power. The historical record suggests that international politics can be unkind to such victors over the long term. A careful scrutiny of the hegemonic cycles since 1494 confirms quite clearly that power transitions at the core of the global system often occur because successes in systemic struggles—of which the Cold War is but one example—can irreparably weaken otherwise victorious hegemonies. The annals of the past actually corroborate the surprising proposition that no rising challenger, however capable, has ever succeeded, at least thus far, in supplanting any prevailing hegemony through cold or hot war. Over the centuries, Spain, France, Germany, Japan, and the Soviet Union all tried in different ways but failed.[2]

This reassuring fact notwithstanding, hegemonic transitions still occurred regularly in international politics, a reality that points to two critical insights about succession struggles in the international system—

---

[1] For insightful overviews of the enduring U.S. desire for dominance, especially through the use of military force, see Robert Kagan, *Dangerous Nation* (New York: Knopf, 2006); Fred Anderson and Andrew Clayton, *The Dominion of War: Empire and Liberty in North America, 1500–2000* (New York: Penguin Books, 2005); Melvyn P. Leffler, *A Preponderance of Power: National Security, the Truman Administration, and the Cold War* (Stanford: Stanford University Press, 1992); and Geoffrey Perret, *A Country Made by War: From the Revolution to Vietnam—The Story of America's Rise to Power* (New York: Random House, 1989).

[2] This and the next two paragraphs are based on the discussion in Michael D. Swaine and Ashley J. Tellis, *Interpreting China's Grand Strategy* (Santa Monica: RAND, 2000), 218–29.

which is a subject that ought to be of great significance to the United States and its allies as well as to its adversaries. First, struggles for hegemony in global politics are rarely limited to dyadic encounters between states. These struggles involve not only the existing hegemon and the rising challenger as the preeminent antagonists—roles that many expect will be played respectively by the United States and China over the long term—but also the entire cast of international characters, including non-state actors involved in economic processes, and the nature of their involvement in the competition become relevant to the succession process. Thus, the nature of the alliances orchestrated and managed by the United States (and possibly China as well) in the future, the relationship between state entities and the global economic system, and the relative burdens borne by every actor involved in this contest become relevant to the outcome.

Second, and equally importantly, who wins in the ensuing struggle—whether that struggle is short or long, peaceful or violent—is as important as by how much. This is particularly relevant because the past record unerringly confirms that the strongest surviving state in the winning coalition usually turns out to be the new primate after the conclusion of every systemic struggle. Both Great Britain and the United States secured their respective ascendancies in this way. Great Britain rose through the wreckage of the wars with Louis XIV and with Napoleon. The United States did so through the carnage of the hot wars with Hitler and Hirohito, finally achieving true hegemony through the detritus of the Cold War with Stalin and his successors. If the United States is to sustain this hard-earned hegemony over the long term, while countering as necessary a future Chinese challenge should it emerge, Washington will need to amass the largest differential in power relative not only to its rivals but also to its friends and allies. Particularly in an era of globalization, this objective cannot be achieved without a conscious determination to follow sensible policies that sustain economic growth, minimize unproductive expenditures, strengthen the national innovation system, maintain military capabilities second to none, and enjoin political behaviors that evoke the approbation of allies and neutral states alike.

The successful pursuit of such policies will enable the United States to cope more effectively with near-term challenges as well, including the war on terrorism and managing threatening regional powers, and will ineluctably require—to return full circle—engaging the central tasks identified earlier as facing the new U.S. administration. These tasks involve the need to satisfactorily define the character of desirable U.S. hegemony, the need for sound policies that will renew the foundations of U.S. strength, and the need to recover the legitimacy of U.S. purposes and actions. What is clearly implied is that the principal burdens facing the next U.S. president transcend Asia writ large. The success of these pursuits, however, will inevitably impact Asia in desirable ways, even as the resolution of several specifically Asian problems—including those highlighted in this volume—would invariably contribute to the conclusive attainment of these larger encompassing goals.

Meeting Foundational Goals

Discharging Hegemonic Responsibilities

The widespread perception both within the United States and internationally that the Bush administration applied U.S. power in an excessively heavy-handed fashion will compel the new administration to define—either explicitly or implicitly—its own vision of how U.S. hegemony ought to be exercised. Many critics have argued that the exercise of hegemony during the past eight years has been particularly dangerous because U.S. actions under George W. Bush have "brazenly undermined Washington's long-held commitment to international law, its acceptance of consensual decisionmaking, its reputation for moderation, and its identification with the preservation of peace."[3] Whether or not this criticism is justified in its details, its focus at least appears to be misplaced because it centers on what Marx might have called the "superstructure" rather than the "base" or the core tasks associated with any successful hegemony.

The first task that any effective hegemony must accomplish is the production of order in the international system. Because interstate competition, including violent contestation, is the customary order of things in an "anarchic"[4] environment, the success of any hegemony is measured primarily by how it can use the acutely unequal distribution of power connoted by the fact of hegemony to preserve a modicum of peace between at least the major powers in the international system and perhaps others of lesser consequence as well. The hegemonic state preserves such order not out of altruism or a philosophical preference for the preservation of peace but because of self-interest. Major wars in the international system are invariably disruptive events: they can undermine the hegemonic state's interests in the regions wherein they occur, threaten its allies, disturb the peaceful

---

[3] See, for instance, Robert W. Tucker and David C. Hendrickson, "The Sources of American Legitimacy," *Foreign Affairs* 83, no. 6 (November/December 2004): 18–32, http://www. foreignaffairs.org/20041101faessay83603/robert-w-tucker-david-c-hendrickson/the-sources-of-american-legitimacy.html.

[4] The term "anarchic" here is used in the sense elaborated in Kenneth N. Waltz, *Theory of International Politics* (New York: McGraw-Hill, 1979).

environment necessary for trade and commerce, and generate alterations in the local balance of power that could produce either new regional or global challengers down the line. For all these reasons, preserving order has always been the most important task facing any hegemonic power.[5]

The second task confronting a hegemonic state today is preserving a durable framework for international trade and commerce. The natural condition in competitive political environments is for states to emphasize autarkic policies that limit economic interdependence. These approaches are intended to minimize the national vulnerability arising from the specialization that would ensure among countries that remained political adversaries. The fear that some states would gain more than their partners in various trading interactions further dampens the propensity to expand trade. The normal consequence of rivalrous international politics, therefore, is a shallow international division of labor and consequently reduced specialization and depressed growth relative to a vibrant and open trading system. The presence of a hegemonic state is necessary to liberate states from such immiserization. Through its superior capabilities, the hegemonic power can ensure that states would not use either the advantages conferred by specialization or the gains derived from trade to accumulate and apply the military instruments that could threaten the security of other states. In so doing, the hegemonic state mitigates the security dilemmas that would otherwise confront critical trading partners and as a result creates conditions for sustaining an open trading system that increases, first and foremost, its own economic growth and the welfare of its own citizenry and, as a derivative consequence, growth and welfare in other nations as well.[6]

The third task facing any hegemonic state is to make the "supernormal" contributions that lead to the adequate production of certain collective goods necessary to the health of the global system. Collective goods are, by definition, non-rivaled and non-excludable; that is, they can be consumed by all—once made available—irrespective of whether any of the consumers have contributed to their production. Thus, the natural tendency in any egotistical social system is for public goods to be underproduced. This is because rational maximizers, all calculating that they can enjoy the collective good for free even if they do not pay for it, usually seek to "free

---

[5] For an extended discussion, see George Modelski and William R. Thompson, *Seapower in Global Politics, 1494–1993* (Basingstoke: Macmillan, 1988).

[6] For a survey of these themes, see Robert Gilpin, *The Political Economy of International Relations* (Princeton: Princeton University Press, 1987); and Robert Gilpin, *Global Political Economy: Understanding the International Economic Order* (Princeton: Princeton University Press, 2001). For extensions and critiques, see Robert O. Keohane, *After Hegemony: Cooperation and Discord in the World Political Economy* (Princeton: Princeton University Press, 2005); and Joseph M. Greico, "Anarchy and the Limits of Cooperation: A Realist Critique of the Newest Liberal Institutionalism," *International Organization* 42, no. 3 (August 1998): 485–507.

ride" by withholding their own contributions in the hope that somebody else may bear the costs of producing it. The aggregation of such individually rational behaviors usually results in the underproduction of many collective goods such as freedom of navigation, regional peace and security, and a clean environment. This conclusion holds true unless a hegemonic state— that is, some "privileged" entity that is inconvenienced more by the absence of the public good than the costs to produce it—makes a supernormal contribution to underwriting its production not as an act of altruism but out of sheer self-interest.[7]

Since a successful hegemony is one that discharges these three tasks efficaciously, how the United States has performed in regard to its global role over the last eight years ought to be judged not so much by its supposed commitment to international law, consensual decisionmaking, or moderate behavior. Rather, the United States ought to be judged by its capacity, intention, and willingness to implement those critical tasks essential to global stability in a foundational sense. By the standards of the three tasks above, it is possible to argue that the Bush administration has not done as badly as its most vociferous critics allege. The United States has successfully maintained regional security in many critical quadrants of the globe. The administration has sustained geopolitical relationships with major states such as Russia on an even keel (sort of) and has successfully juggled (at least thus far) the competing challenges of integrating a rising power such as China while effectively balancing against its potential to disrupt Asian stability. The United States has managed to keep key alliance partners such as Japan and South Korea reasonably reassured, while developing strong ties with new emerging states such as India, and has attempted (although haphazardly and after much hesitation) to resolve important disputes involving the Middle East, North Korea, Libya, and the like. This conclusion may be justifiably challenged in its details in many instances, particularly when measured against the bar of whether Washington could have done better. What is more important for purposes of analysis, however, is that U.S. success be judged not against superficial political realities but rather against the key structural tasks associated with successful hegemony.[8]

As for the first task of maintaining peace and stability, the most radical criticism that could be mounted of the administration's record concerns, of course, George W. Bush's decision to invade Iraq. Internationally, this

[7] Mancur Olson, Jr., *The Logic of Collective Action: Public Goods and the Theory of Groups* (Cambridge: Harvard University Press, 1965).

[8] For one useful survey of Bush's achievements, at least in Asia, see Victor D. Cha, "Winning Asia: Washington's Untold Success Story," *Foreign Affairs* 86, no. 6 (November/December 2007): 98–113; and Michael J. Green, "The Iraq War and Asia: Assessing the Legacy," *Washington Quarterly* 31, no. 2 (Spring 2008): 181–200.

decision has been viewed as an effort by Washington to impose its will in pursuit of naked self-interest rather than to mitigate some generally accepted threat to global order. The virtue of this decision will continue to be debated by historians; what can be said simply at this juncture is that the failures associated with this effort have made the wisdom and the legitimacy of the original decision to invade even more problematic. Even if ultimately concluded successfully, the war in Iraq will remain an important case that tests the issue of how hegemony is to be exercised. True, hegemonic powers have always waged wars against equals or weaker states when necessary in their self-interest, and it is indeed desirable that such wars be waged whenever possible with international support. The key question, however, is whether it is reasonable to expect a hegemonic state to be forever bound by the constraints of *ex ante* foreign approval. This question is made even more complicated by the fact that global, or even majoritarian international, approval is a somewhat slippery thing because acquiescence, if not approval, often arises *ex post* if the hegemonic state enjoys a speedy and a reasonably permanent success in war. Successors to Bush will, therefore, have to face questions that will not go away so long as the United States remains a hegemonic power: how and when should force be applied and to what degree should international consensus be pursued as a precondition to the use of force, given that decisions about war and peace will ultimately always be grounded in the pursuit of self-interest.

The Bush administration also appears to have done reasonably well, at least at first sight, in regard to maintaining an open international economic system. The administration upheld the postwar U.S. commitment to a liberal international order, despite a number of worrisome issues. Foremost among these were the uncertainties associated with China's political and military rise in Asia, the sometimes heavy-handed Russian re-entry into international politics as a raw material-exporting state, the steep rise in energy and food grain prices, and the increasing domestic U.S. disenchantment with globalization and the country's deteriorating national and foreign balances. Washington's political commitment to sustaining an open trading system, however, has resulted in its resisting protectionist pressures at home, contributing to the spread of development benefits in major developing countries such as China and India, and maintaining stable expectations that international trade will continue at relatively high levels well into the prospective future.[9]

---

[9] For an overview of the contemporary U.S. policy debates on the international trading order, see Wayne M. Morrison and William H. Cooper, "The Future Role of U.S. Trade Policy: An Overview," Congressional Research Service, CRS Report, RS22914, July 14, 2008, available at http://opencrs.com/document/RS22914.

Where the administration has been less than successful, at the time of this writing, has been in expanding the international economic system dramatically as it had sought through the successful conclusion of the Doha round.[10] This failure, which hopefully can be mitigated in the future, arose largely from another disappointment: the administration's decision not to offer significant cuts in U.S. farm subsidies despite rising food prices—a product of domestic politics—while simultaneously demanding more extensive access for U.S. agricultural products in foreign markets. Washington has attempted to circumvent—not confront—this conundrum by negotiating preferential trade agreements (PTA) with various states to create in effect multiple micro-systems of free trade among consenting partners. This attempt at "freeing trade on a discriminatory basis"[11] has been justified as a transitory, back door strategy of forcing the desirable expansion of the global trading system in the face of failures in multilateral negotiations. But such efforts, though apparently successful, also come at high costs. They produce undesirable international diversion effects involving a shift in trade flows from cheaper non-partner sources to more expensive preferential partners, thus reducing the gains in welfare all around, even as they prolong the domestic distortions in agricultural pricing that increase the welfare costs to U.S. consumers as well.

Most importantly, from the perspective of preserving a well-ordered international system, the strategy of negotiating multiple PTAs indicates a failure of the United States to exert hegemonic leadership. Despite the presence of committed free traders at the helm, the administration was unable to summon leadership of the kind that would, both by force of example and through the demand for reciprocity, lead the international system toward a more uniform, non-discriminatory expansion of global trade—an enlargement upon which the United States' own continued political dominance, global competitiveness, and increased welfare all depend. Bush's successor will, therefore, be confronted with the strategic decision of whether to persist with existing policy, which yields only modest private benefits but produces significant collective costs, or shift toward a truly hegemonic strategy that involves leading the global trading system toward a new equilibrium, which while being beneficial to the United States also turns out to be advantageous to all.

The Bush administration has also done reasonably well in regard to sustaining the traditional U.S. contribution toward the production of

[10] Stephen Castle and Mark Landler, "After 7 Years, Talks Collapse on World Trade," *New York Times*, July 30, 2008.

[11] This argument has been made most trenchantly in Jagdish Bhagwati, *Termites in the Trading System: How Preferential Agreements Undermine Free Trade* (New York: Oxford University Press, 2008).

collective goods. U.S. successes here have been most conspicuous in the realm of international security, less so in the arenas of climate change and protecting the environment. Since the United States enjoys the sharpest asymmetries in military capability, it is not surprising that those contributions to global public goods ensuing from U.S. military superiority have been the easiest to make and are also the most enduring. Three critical contributions in this regard are worth mentioning. The U.S. system of alliances and its emerging network of friends in Asia—all underwritten by the assurance of superior military power—have been critical to preventing any disorderly balancing within the continent in response to rising Chinese power. The continuing stability of the global energy market in an era of rising prices is also ensured by U.S. military advantages, which push states in the direction of peacefully diversifying sources and realizing energy economies through other means than through predatory political solutions. The continuing ability of the international economic system to flourish is owed largely to the U.S. military's ability to police the commons in a way that makes any unilateral efforts by other states at controlling it both expensive and unproductive. While it is possible, perhaps even likely, that all the major Asian powers in the years ahead will develop contingency plans to shift to alternative strategies in each of these issue areas, these states are unlikely to succumb to any pressures for change as long as U.S. military capability in Asia and globally is viewed as sufficiently robust.[12]

The major arenas requiring a review of current policy subsist in the realm of the environment and climate change. The Bush administration chose not to play the role of a "privileged" contributor to resolving the collective action problems associated with climate change because of the arguably high costs to the U.S. economy.[13] While these costs are significant, especially if borne unilaterally, the real question facing Bush's successor fundamentally revolves around opportunity. The crux is whether the pressure for a significant U.S. contribution to mitigating climate change, even if unilateral, can be viewed as an opening to engineer a new wave of technological innovation—innovation that potentially could restructure the U.S. (and perhaps the global) economy and, more importantly, could create new "leading sectors" that would increase the technological advantage

---

[12] See the discussion in Stephen M. Walt, "American Primacy: Its Prospects and Pitfalls," *Naval War College Review* LV, no. 2 (Spring 2002): 9–28.

[13] For one useful overview, see "Kyoto Protocol and Beyond: The High Economic Cost to the United States," DRI-WEFA, 2002, http://www.accf.org/pdf/EcoImpact-GHG-US.PDF. For a more detailed analysis, see "Impacts of the Kyoto Protocol on U.S. Energy Markets and Economic Activity," Energy Information Administration, SR/OIAF/98-03, 1998, http://www.eia.doe.gov/oiaf/kyoto/kyotorpt.html.

the United States enjoys relative to both its allies and its adversaries.[14] A conscious decision to contribute asymmetrically toward mitigating global climate change would exploit the explosive innovative capacity inherent in American capitalism through deliberate public policy decisions. The new clusters of innovation that would emerge from the attempt to move away from fossil fuels as the motor of economic activity would likely produce a new Kondratieff wave in the global economy—the beneficial consequence of which would be the renewal of U.S. primacy in international politics.

Smart decisions in regard to resolving transnational collective action problems of the kind represented by climate change, then, hold the potential for settling more than simply dilemmas pertaining to the production of public goods. Rather, by contributing to the reinvigoration of the U.S. economy itself, these decisions could lay the foundation for a more durable consolidation of U.S. hegemony. Building such a foundation is particularly crucial at a time when new great powers, such as China, having slowly exploited their comparative advantage of lower labor costs and having steadily mastered existing technologies, could lay the foundations for gradually usurping U.S. primacy over time. The choices made by Bush's successors in regard to the production of critical non-military public goods could thus become the spearhead of revolutionary economic change that creates new leading sectors, fortifies the U.S. position as the world's lead economy, and entrenches U.S. hegemony for a new long cycle in international politics.

Buttressing Material Foundations

Even as the next administration faces up to the challenge of redefining the character of U.S. hegemony in a structural sense—through the manner in which it produces order, upholds the global economy, and provides public goods—it will also be confronted simultaneously with the task of renewing U.S. strength or, in other words, refurbishing the material foundations of U.S. power. The success of the United States as a hegemonic entity derives intimately from its exceptional military capabilities, which in turn are products of a nimble and innovative economic system that thus far has managed to produce both power and plenty without agonizing trade-offs. Even though the United States has for the last several decades grown at a much slower rate in comparison to the fastest-growing developing countries such as China—a not surprising fact because poor countries

---

[14] A path-breaking discussion on the critical role of "leading sectors" in maintaining hegemonic leadership can be found in George Modelski and William R. Thompson, *Leading Sectors and World Powers: The Coevolution of Global Politics and Economics* (Columbia: University of South Carolina Press, 1996).

experience increasing returns to scale in the early phases of their growth cycles—U.S. power derives, at least as a first cut, from the enormous strength of its economy when measured in absolute and relative terms. Since the U.S. economy is so huge, even modest growth rates contribute to an ever-expanding national product, which then pays for both the nation's domestic needs and its international interests.

The sustenance of U.S. hegemony over time, however, requires that the United States maintain a steady rate of economic growth and certainly one that is superior to the secular growth rate of its competitors. The emphasis on secular growth rates is important to preclude any facile extrapolations between the currently high growth rates of developing countries like China and the lower growth rates of mature economies like the United States. Thus, as the Chinese economy develops over time, it is reasonable to expect that the iron constraints of diminishing returns will depress its currently high rates of growth. Consequently, the prospects facing the United States and China—or any other state—is best judged not by a comparison of current growth rates but rather by a more sophisticated assessment of their secular growth trends that takes into account multiple factors such as capital accumulation, labor force growth, and technological change.

The task of reinvigorating U.S. power is, therefore, driven by the necessity of doing whatever it takes to maintain the highest possible growth rates over the long term. This objective has acquired some urgency for two reasons. In all likelihood, the international system appears to be in the early stages of a new long cycle in international politics, one that, though characterized by the unchallenged dominance of the United States, is also likely to see the rise of new competitors such as China over the distant horizon.[15] Further, the emerging reality of globalization, coupled with the information technology revolution, suggests that the United States as well as the global economy may be on the cusp of a dramatic transformation where new forces that enable growth and productivity will confront the older entropic challenges of natural resource depletion and environmental decay. If the United States is to successfully dominate this emerging long cycle in international politics, its economic system will have to maintain the capacity for the highest secular rates of growth possible with minimum negative externalities relative to its peers. Bush's successors will be faced with the challenge of making the necessary course corrections required to set the U.S. economy on such a path given the burdens imposed by the ongoing

[15] For a more involved discussion, see Modelski and Thompson, *Leading Sectors and World Powers*, 65–104. For a sophisticated retrospective, see Joshua S. Goldstein, *Long Cycles: Prosperity and War in the Modern Age* (New Haven: Yale University Press, 1988).

wars in Afghanistan and Iraq, rising raw materials and energy costs, and the serious national budget deficits as well as the negative balance of payments.

Whether the United States can overcome these challenges will depend greatly on the nature of its public policies and how these affect the fundamental components of the growth process. Effective policies would focus on maintaining high levels of capital formation, ensuring the availability of an adequate labor force of sufficient quality, sustaining technological progress, increasing the efficiency with which these inputs are productively combined, and limiting the adverse consequences of any other problematic political decisions on growth.

It is now almost a truism that increasing the stock of capital is critical to sustaining high levels of economic growth because, other things being equal, the greater the amount of capital relative to labor, the more productive the latter can be in the creative process. Increasing capital stock therefore became the Holy Grail in traditional economic theory. Capital formation in principle derives from the rate of savings in an economy which, together with foreign borrowing, determines the national rate of investment. Compared to many fast-growing developing countries, the United States has been an abysmally lower saver. From 1960 to roughly 1980, the U.S. savings rate remained stable at about 11%, dropping steadily until it reached about 1% in 2005 before crossing into negative range in 2006—the first time that has happened since 1932–33, when the United States struggled with the huge job contraction brought by the Great Depression. In contrast, India's savings rate is roughly about 25%, South Korea's and Japan's savings rate varies typically from the high 20s to the mid-30s, and China's savings rate is a staggering 50%.[16]

The United States can sustain domestic economic growth amid such poor savings rates only because it has benefited from large injections of foreign capital. The willingness of foreigners to underwrite U.S. overconsumption over long periods of time—some 55 years and counting—is no doubt a tribute to the attractiveness of the United States as an investment destination. However, it has been made possible equally by the domestic strategies pursued by several important creditors who, having suppressed internal consumption in order to generate high rates of national savings, now choose to invest in the United States either because it provides superior rates of return or greater safety in comparison to some other alternatives. The external deficits sustained by the United States can, therefore, persist for a long time to come so long as these core conditions—the attractiveness

---

[16] Barry P. Bosworth, "United States Saving in a Global Context," testimony before the Senate Committee on Finance, Washington, D.C., April 6, 2006, http://www.brookings.edu/testimony/20 06/0406macroeconomics_bosworth.aspx.

of the U.S. economy coupled with excessive foreign liquidity—continue to hold. In fact, it is reasonable to argue that Washington enjoys the better end of the bargain because it is trading paper IOUs—its currency—for real assets created within the United States as a result of foreign lending.

But such a condition nonetheless creates long-term challenges from the perspective of enhancing national power. For starters, such a strategy will be more and more difficult to sustain as more baby boomers in the United States move into retirement and as U.S. creditors shift to alternative strategies of fueling their own national growth, such as increased domestic consumption. Even if the latter shift does not occur abruptly—which could cause a genuine crisis in the global economy—the current strategy results in a significant short- to medium-term loss of U.S. control over the dollar's value even as it contributes to an overvalued dollar. As a result, it becomes more difficult for U.S.-based firms to enlarge their export markets. Most problematically, however, the excessive U.S. dependence on foreign borrowings raises the specter that U.S. security policy, particularly in Asia, will be unduly compromised by the reliance on creditors, such as China, who are simultaneously its incipient geopolitical rivals. Washington's continuing ability to protect its strategic interests, therefore, necessitates reduced reliance on foreign borrowing over time, which in turn requires an economic strategy that focuses on financing growing U.S. consumption through increased personal incomes rather than relying on cheap foreign lending.[17] In this context, rationalizing taxation policy and exploiting other fiscal instruments to spur new investments in infrastructure and advanced technologies remains critical.

If the next president thus has his work cut out for him in regard to strengthening capital formation for long-term growth, equally important tasks remain with respect to ensuring the availability of an effective labor force. With the world's third largest population, it might be imagined that the United States enjoys a capacity to fuel economic growth through labor force improvements for a long time to come. The quality of life enjoyed by the U.S. population as measured by per capita income is obviously very high—with beneficial consequences for economic growth and productivity—but this population, compared to that of many emerging powers, is progressively aging. The 0–19 age group of the U.S. population in 1950, for example, consisted of about 34% of the total U.S. population, with the 20–64 age group constituting almost 58%, and the 65+ age group

---

[17] For an excellent discussion of these issues, see Stephen D. Cohen, "The Superpower as Super-Debtor: Implications of Economic Disequilibria for U.S.-Asian Relations," in *Strategic Asia 2006–07: Trade, Interdependence, and Security*, ed. Ashley J. Tellis and Michael Wills (Seattle: The National Bureau of Asian Research, 2006), 29–63.

constituting about 8%—a classic Christmas tree–like population pyramid designed to fuel national economic expansion. By 2050 this Christmas tree–like pyramid is projected to become virtually rectangular, with the 0–19 cohort constituting 26% of the population, the 20–64 group coming in at a little more than 53%, and the 65+ cohort constituting well over 20% of the total population.[18]

The changing demographic profile of the United States, with the relative compression of the most productive segments of the population, highlights three important challenges that the next president will have to confront from the perspective of protecting U.S. well-being and long-term growth.

First, the challenges of dealing with an aging population will demand solutions to critical programs like Social Security, Medicare, and Medicaid, which are saddled with problems of solvency that implicate tricky issues of intergenerational equity. While public policy solutions to these programs must be found, any proposed plans will have to satisfy current and prospective retirees without subverting the larger structure of social incentives that has made the United States such a rich and productive country.

Second, the prospective thinning of the most productive cohort within the U.S. economy, and the changed dependency ratios that are triggered thereby, renews attention to the issue of immigration. The reputation of the United States as a country that welcomes immigrants has always been a safety valve from the perspective of maintaining an effective labor force: immigrants can quickly mitigate the deficits in labor force growth and, depending on their skill sets, can do so with minimal disruption to the existing social fabric. Unfortunately, in recent years, thanks both to the tragedy of September 11 and the vicissitudes of domestic politics, the United States has been unable to devise a rational immigration policy that serves the national interests. Further delays in crafting such a policy will exact a high price because the slowdown in the import of immigrant labor (and skilled immigrant labor, in particular) will depress the contribution that labor as a factor of production can make to GNP growth. This is especially worrisome at a time when productivity is likely to fall as the economy absorbs the gains deriving from the IT investments of the 1980s.

Third, the issue of the quality of the future U.S. labor force is also critical. There is a substantial body of evidence demonstrating that, important as physical capital is for national growth, the quality and quantity of human

---

[18] See Laura B. Shrestha, *The Changing Demographic Profile of the United States,* Congressional Research Service, CRS Report for Congress, RL32701, May 5, 2006.

capital available may be even more important.[19] The importance of education is particularly significant in this regard, and the next administration will have to face up to multiple challenges. Among the more prominent are issues relating to the quality of U.S. primary and secondary education, the still conspicuous weakness in science and mathematics training in the school system, and the relatively small number of U.S. citizens receiving advanced training in the physical and engineering sciences. All these issues taken together have an important bearing on whether the United States will be able to maintain its technological edge over time and, by implication, its political hegemony relative to other rising powers.

Although classical growth theory argued the primacy of increasing capital and labor as inputs to the growth process (since land was constant in quantity and entrepreneurship was treated as exogenous), modern economics has invariably emphasized the importance of technological change as a critical driver of long-term growth. Because the iron law of diminishing returns applies to capital accumulation as well, early neoclassical economics postulated the possibility of a "steady state," a hypothetical point where even an increase in capital would not produce further growth. The creation of new technology, however, provided one solution to escape from the tyranny of the steady state. Contemporary growth theory concludes that technology—with its intrinsic links to both human capital and entrepreneurship—is in fact another "endogenous" factor of production, like physical capital and labor, in the growth process.[20] There is in fact little doubt at a policy level that the technological innovativeness of the United States has been a major contributor to its growth as a world power, even if it had been traditionally difficult to prove the difference that technology made as a factor of production to the national product. In any event, there is widespread consensus today that the superior velocity of technical change in the United States across the spectrum from civilian to military endeavors remains the key to its global superiority and must be maintained.

Maintaining U.S. technological leadership, however, requires sustaining, if not improving, what is already the best national innovation system in the world. The majority of U.S. innovations, however, are incremental ones. These innovations, which derive from the marginal improvements in goods,

---

[19] This insight is systematically developed in Theodore W. Schultz, *Investing in People: The Economics of Population Quality* (Berkeley: University of California Press, 1981); and in endogenous growth theory by Paul Romer, Robert Lucas, and Robert Barro. See, for example, Paul M. Romer, "The Origins of Endogenous Growth," *Journal of Economic Perspectives* 8, no. 1 (Winter 1994), 3–22; Paul M. Romer, "Human Capital And Growth: Theory and Evidence," National Bureau of Economic Research, Working Paper no. 3173, November 1989; and Robert E. Lucas, "Ideas and Growth," National Bureau of Economic Research, Working Paper, no. 14133, June 2008.

[20] Robert E. Lucas, Jr., *Lectures on Economic Growth* (Cambridge: Harvard University Press, 2002).

organization, and markets that are constantly occurring in response to the pressures of a competitive marketplace, undoubtedly contribute to most of the economic growth that occurs routinely. So long as this rate of change is superior to that occurring in other countries, the United States will maintain its current lead over other states. What will decisively advantage Washington in the great-power game and allow it to enjoy higher secular growth rates relative to others, however, is not incremental innovation but rather the generation of new leading sectors arising from radical innovations. Such innovations are the kinds that produce what Joseph Alois Schumpeter once described as the "gales of creative destruction" that are caused when revolutionary transformations make obsolete old inventories, ideas, skills, organizations, technologies, and equipment.[21]

Such innovations are fundamentally science driven and in the United States are incubated as much in the private sector as through government-funded research and development. The changing trends, however, deserve careful notice. Increasingly it appears that autonomous private-sector investments account for much smaller shares of critical innovations in contrast to collaborations involving spin-offs from universities and federal laboratories. Furthermore, the number of innovations that derive from federal funding has increased dramatically. These facts suggest that the task of the next administration will therefore be to at least sustain, if not increase, the level of public funding for science and technology and to improve the policy framework to assist the transformation of advanced research into breakthrough products that can rapidly reach the market.[22] The United States does very well in basic research and invention, as evidenced by the country's patent rankings internationally. It does equally well in producing and distributing new technologies efficiently thanks to its highly dexterous private-sector system. What it does least effectively is bridging these two bookends by enabling efficacious early–state technology development when novel and innovative ideas have to overcome extraordinarily high business and technical risks before they can be transformed into end-products that can be manufactured en masse and distributed through conventional means in the national and global marketplace. Improving the nation's capacity to sustain early–state technology development for radical innovations would be the best single step that could be taken to improve the contribution

[21] Joseph A. Schumpeter, *The Theory of Economic Development* (Edison: Transaction Books, 1982).

[22] Fred Block and Matthew R. Keller, "Where Do Innovations Come From? Transformations in the U.S. National Innovation System, 1970–2006," Information Technology and Innovation Foundation, July 2008, 1–22.

technology makes to GNP growth and, in the process, sustain the U.S. lead over its geopolitical competitors.[23]

While reinvigorating the material foundations of U.S. national power will require adopting policies that permit the growth of national output at the highest possible rate over time—and increasing the quantity and quality of capital, labor, and technology remains important in this context—other intervening variables are also relevant. The most important intervening variable from an economist's perspective is improving the efficiency with which the "inputs" to the production process—or the total factor productivity in economic jargon—are combined. From the perspective of strengthening U.S. power at this juncture, however, another more properly political task also confronts the new administration: determining the future of the current wars in Iraq and Afghanistan because of the burdens they impose on the United States. A brief comment on each of these issues is appropriate.

The United States has enjoyed a remarkable resurgence in productivity since the mid-1990s. The sources of this productivity growth are still contested, with some studies attributing it to the IT investments of the earlier decade and others suggesting that changes in the labor market performance might be responsible.[24] Irrespective of which hypothesis is correct, the issue of note is that U.S. productivity growth has appeared to be slowing since about 2005, at a time when most emerging markets appear to be performing impressively on average. Maintaining productivity growth is obviously important because it enables the United States to increase national output without having to increase the inputs injected into the production process. It is also critical because it remains the best means of increasing standards of living in the long run: since total factor productivity growth is always equal to the weighted average of real wages plus real payments to capital, increased growth enables raising real wages without reducing the returns to capital.

If the issue of maintaining productivity growth constitutes the transforming element in the economic realm, bringing the wars in Afghanistan and Iraq to a happy conclusion could be conceived as its political counterpart. Success here would liberate the U.S. economy to

---

[23] Lewis M. Branscomb and Philip E. Auerswald, "Between Invention and Innovation: An Analysis of the Funding for Early-Stage Technology Development," NIST GCR 02-841, Report to the Advanced Technology Program, National Institute of Standards and Technology, U.S. Department of Commerce, March 6, 2003.

[24] For an example of the different views, see Dale W. Jorgenson, Mun S. Ho, and Kevin J. Stiroh, "Will the U.S. Productivity Resurgence Continue?" *Current Issues in Economics and Finance* 10, no. 13 (2004): 1–7; and Barry P. Bosworth and Jack E. Triplett, "What's New About the New Economy? IT, Economic Growth and Productivity," 2002, http://www.brookings.edu/papers/2000/1020healthcare_bosworth.aspx.

focus on resolving those more pressing domestic problems that inhibit the growth of U.S. strength. Expanding investments in national infrastructure, defeating poverty, restoring fiscal discipline, and expanding the range of opportunity for the U.S. citizenry would be among the problems that could be addressed more easily if a satisfactory conclusion to these twin conflicts could be realized. This will be, however, among the most difficult, yet urgent, challenges facing Bush's successor. If current trends continue, it appears as if the United States will steadily reduce its involvement in Iraq irrespective of whether Senator John McCain or Senator Barack Obama becomes the next president. A number of factors—the steep and rising costs of the war, the public exhaustion with its course, the undermining of all the original rationales for the conflict, and the steadily increasing human toll in combat operations—seem to be coagulating to compel a substantial U.S. withdrawal from Iraq in the not too distant future. The recent improvements in the security situation in that country, coupled with the election of an indigenous government that now seeks for its own domestic reasons to minimize the U.S. presence, will increase the pressure for reduced U.S. involvement, especially given the financial relief that such withdrawal seems to promise (even if it is ultimately belied).

A comparable departure from Afghanistan is unlikely—and unnecessary. First, the scale of U.S. military involvement in Afghanistan is modest in comparison to Iraq, and the financial burdens of this war far more manageable as well. While a drawdown from Iraq will likely result in increased U.S. allocations of personnel and equipment to Afghanistan, such a diversion is not only justified by the origins of this mission but, more importantly, will require only modest increases for success. The biggest challenge in this regard may well be how the United States manages Pakistan rather than any operational or fiscal constraints in regard to completing the Afghan mission. In any event, appropriately altering the character of U.S. military involvement in these two wars to minimize the burdens while still protecting core interests will be essential, if the larger task of strengthening U.S. power for the long term is to be sustained.

Any discussion about reinvigorating the material foundations of U.S. power would be incomplete without a reference, however brief, to the obvious—and, in a competitive political system, to the most important—manifestations of that power: military capabilities. There is little doubt that the United States today and for the foreseeable future will continue to possess unparalleled military capabilities. No other state maintains armed forces of the size, quality, reach, depth, and diversity as those of the United States. Yet for all this potency, the next president will be confronted by difficult decisions in regard to the character of the U.S. military, starting first and foremost with budgetary challenges. Since September 11, the total obligational authority of the U.S. Department of Defense has increased by some 60%, not counting the Bush administration's periodic supplemental requests to finance the current wars. Although this expenditure level will not be reduced drastically, it is quite clear that the pace of growth seen in recent years cannot be sustained. The inevitable paring of U.S. defense expenditures that must be expected in the future will then collide with the major recapitalization requirements necessary to maintain the potency of the armed services over the long term. The steep cost growth of major weapons systems—such as the F-22 air dominance fighter, the Littoral Combat Ship and the DDG 1000 destroyer, and the Armed Reconnaissance Helicopter—only exacerbates this problem. And the increased burdens exacted by health care and other current personnel costs on the procurement and research, development, test, and evaluation (RDT&E) budget—those components that underwrite the present and prospective combat capabilities of the force—make the trade-offs facing defense decisionmakers even more difficult.[25]

Above all else, however, is the structural problem associated with the need to maintain dramatically different kinds of combat capabilities for purposes of maintaining hegemonic order. The necessity of being able to quickly dominate the conventional battlefield against prospective regional adversaries requires complex joint and combined-arms capabilities spanning the air, land, sea, space, cyber, and possibly nuclear realms. A global power like the United States must be able to summon this "full spectrum dominance" in more than one theater simultaneously. Protecting the homeland, U.S. allies, and the U.S. armed forces against WMD across the continuum from deterrence to consequence management requires an entirely different set of capabilities. Although having receded considerably, the risk of major nuclear war involving the great powers has not passed sufficiently into irrelevance as to justify the disbandment of extant U.S. strategic capabilities. Defeating radical terrorist groups, conducting irregular warfare, and undertaking stability operations under varying conditions of threat all demand manpower-intensive capabilities involving diverse intelligence assets, Special Forces, and army and Marine Corps units. If the demand for these elements is seen to increase in what is currently an interlude in great-power competition, then the issues pertaining to the appropriate size of U.S. land forces, the lift capabilities required to transport them to extended battlefields, and the technologies required to defend them

---

[25] See the discussion in Richmond L. Lloyd, ed., *A Nation at War: Reconciling Ends and Means*, William B. Ruger Chair of National Security Economics Papers, no. 1 (Newport: Naval War College, 2005).

against lethal anti-personnel weapons all become subjects for budgetary competition. Finally, the necessity of hedging against the rise of a new great-power competitor, most likely China, will also demand advanced maritime and aerospace forces of great reach, endurance, and lethality, not to mention other capabilities that permit the United States to dominate the electromagnetic, cyber, and nuclear spectrums.[26]

Developing a force architecture that services all these diverse objectives simultaneously, while remaining within a more modest defense budget than is currently the case, will tax the ingenuity of the next president. Whatever the solutions finally devised, they will be made incomparably easier to implement if the nation can focus on the fundamental challenges outlined earlier—namely increasing the size of the capital and labor pools, engendering new waves of radical technological innovation, increasing total factor productivity, and in general creating an environment favorable to growth at home in conjunction with sensibly managing the nation's affairs abroad.

While clarifying the nature of the United States' hegemonic role in the world and renewing the foundations of U.S. strength remain the most important tasks facing the next administration, these efforts will be less than efficacious if they are not accompanied by a determination to achieve the third foundational task: restoring the legitimacy of U.S. power. It is almost universally agreed that Washington's legitimacy has been eroded during the last eight years. Although many see this erosion to be a product of the Bush administration's "unilateralism," others perceive it to be the result of excesses associated with what may have otherwise been defensible policies. Still others view it as deriving from a betrayal of the deepest American values, as manifested through the constriction of civil liberties at home and the examples of Guantanamo and Abu Ghraib abroad.

While there is perhaps some truth in every one of these perceptions, the problem of legitimacy is at its core a vexatious one that cannot be easily resolved. The challenge here arises from the fact that U.S. power will always be used, at least in the final analysis, to serve the United States' own interests rather than the interests of some larger collective such as the international system. Ideally, of course, any self-interested exercise of power by the United States would also simultaneously serve some perceptible global interest, if not directly and intentionally, then at least as a positive externality. When such a convergence arises, the tension that may otherwise exist between U.S. self-interest and global collective interest is attenuated, and the relevant

[26] Ashton B. Carter, "Defense Management Challenges in the Post-Bush Era," in *Defense Strategy and Forces: Setting Future Directions,* Economics Papers 3, ed. Richmond M. Lloyd (Newport: Naval War College, 2008).

U.S. actions may enjoy the benefits of legitimacy. Unfortunately, however, there is no way to assure that such a felicitous situation will always obtain. In fact, it is far more likely, in a competitive universe populated by self-regarding states, that almost every U.S. action—including the use of force—will distress some state or another. It is simply unreasonable to expect the United States, or for that matter any other great power, to resolve this problem by pledging always to use force either solely in pursuit of collective interests or only after the creation of an appropriate international consensus. However desirable these solutions may be, they ought not to be expected in an "anarchic" international system without increasing the risks to U.S. sovereignty and the protection of U.S. national interests.[27] The challenge of securing international legitimacy for U.S. actions, especially those relating to the use of force, will therefore be an enduring one, and the structural difficulties involved in this effort can only be mitigated, never eliminated.

How is the United States to proceed then in such circumstances? Three rules derived from Machiavellian politics might offer a way out. First, succeed quickly. The success of political action, especially if decisive and characterized by resolution, often can transform what may have been initially axiologically questionable decisions into at least tolerated acts. Success by itself, of course, cannot guarantee that contested actions would garner legitimacy ex post, but failure almost certainly ensures that such initiatives would be loathed, perhaps enduringly. Consequently, for example, if the Bush administration's war against Iraq was managed more competently, the deleterious impact of its problematic origins might have been mitigated.

Second, keep your friends close. However controversial the character of political actions may be—especially in regard to the use of force in circumstances other than direct self-defense—it makes sense for the United States to make the investment in securing collective support. Though it is desirable that such support be extensive, that may not always be possible. Hence, in certain circumstances, who supports the United States is as important as how many. Constructing "coalitions of the willing" that consist of minor and insignificant states will not increase the legitimacy of controversial U.S. actions but rather, by inviting derision, will actually detract from the grudging acquiescence that might have otherwise accrued to successful action undertaken unilaterally. In the context of contentious decisions regarding the use of force, above all else, what seems most fatal to legitimacy is to lose the support of the major powers, especially those known to be one's friends and allies. Thus, for example, if the Bush administration

---

[27] See the discussion in Ivo Daalder and Robert Kagan, "America and the Use of Force: Sources of Legitimacy," Stanley Foundation, May 2007.

had enjoyed the support of its own democratic alliance partners in the lead-up to the war in Iraq, the political circumstances surrounding this war might have turned out to be quite different.

Third, a decent regard for the opinions of mankind is always desirable. While the United States as a hegemonic power cannot be expected to be bound by the approval of others, being deaf to the views of others will neither ease the obstacles confronting its policy preferences nor strengthen its standing in the system over which it presides. Whether it can be formalized or not, the views, expectations, and interests of other states define the objective constraints surrounding all U.S. decisions in regard to high politics. Thus, attention to these compulsions not only increases the chances of successfully implementing critical decisions but also forewarns of pitfalls that must be avoided. In this context, the relationship between the United States and the opinions of mankind is not merely unidirectional, with the latter pressing upon the former; rather, Washington should be as much an active shaper of these opinions as it invariably becomes a target of them. The two instruments of critical consequence are classical diplomacy—which pertains to the engagement between countries behind closed doors—and public diplomacy—which pertains to the arts of shaping mass and elite opinion outside of the United States. Both skills, which Washington had perfected during the Cold War, appear to have atrophied disastrously. U.S. diplomacy today often consists predominantly of stating positions and then restating positions, rather than engaging creatively in an exchange of considerations. The U.S. Foreign Service also is under-strength, relative to the tasks that need to be accomplished. During the Cold War, U.S. public diplomacy successfully conveyed the magnificent diversity of the United States through independent organizations such as the United States Information Agency, the Voice of America, and Radio Free Europe/Radio Liberty (which were not subservient to the administration of the day). By contrast, U.S. public diplomacy has now degenerated into a pedestrian propaganda mill that is neither effective nor credible.

The next administration will therefore have its hands full tackling the myriad tasks necessary to restore the legitimacy of U.S. power. In beginning this effort, however, it should recognize two important realities. First, however egregious the Bush administration's failures were in this regard, the fundamental problem about legitimacy is one that is rooted in a complex interaction between U.S. self-interests, a competitive international system, and the asymmetric global distribution of power. Second, while it is certainly possible to do better than the current administration has in managing this issue, all efforts at striking a new course will rapidly come to grief if this elemental tension is not appreciated.

The United States and Asia

The foregoing discussion should have amply demonstrated the truth of the proposition advanced earlier: the principal challenges facing the next administration transcend Asia, but their successful resolution would empower Washington in its dealings with the continent, even as progress on some key Asian issues—for example, the wars in Afghanistan and Iraq and the nonproliferation threats posed by North Korea and Iran—would produce a virtuous feedback that enhances U.S. power. This volume, *Strategic Asia 2008–09: Challenges and Choices,* surveys the critical issues in Asia that will confront the next president as he takes office at the end of George W. Bush's tumultuous two terms. The last eight years have seen great changes in Asia, many of them a consequence of U.S. policies, but many others owing to different independent causes. The chapters in this book take stock of transformations that have occurred in various Asian countries and subregions with an eye to informing the incoming administration about the big challenges, dilemmas, and decisions facing the United States in regard to Strategic Asia.

In any election year, it will not be surprising to find many attempts at regional assessment similar to the one undertaken in this book. At a substantive level, however, this volume aims to distinguish itself by the approach taken in the country studies and regional studies chapters. These chapters take into account not only the impact of past U.S. actions but also the consequences of other variables—such as system-structural effects, economic performance, domestic political change, ideological ferment, and military challenges—to account for the condition of the country or the region as the new administration will find it. To accomplish this task in a coherent way, authors of those chapters have sought to engage the following issues systematically.

- What are the grand strategies or core national objectives of the country or the key countries in the region that are the subjects of analysis?

- What is the state of the country or region at the end of the Bush administration after the last eight years of U.S. policy and other independent factors are taken into account? Specifically, how have the following variables affected the grand strategy of the subject country (or the countries in the region) and contributed toward the key challenges that national leaders face at this moment in history?

  - the global war on terrorism and its effects

- the political and economic rise of China, and, where relevant, India, as part of the evolving change in the Asian balance of power

- the phenomenon of globalization and economic integration

- key domestic political changes, including issues of internal stability, governance, and ideology, as well as economic transformations occurring within a country or region

- dimensions of regional stability as they relate to local or continental inter-state conflict, arms races, alliance formation, and WMD

- critical issues pertaining to collective goods that impact the country or the region such as energy, the environment, climate, and public health

- any other country- or region-specific issues that bear on strategic stability or critical U.S. national security interests

• Against this backdrop, first, what are the core issues and policies pursued either by the country or region or pertinent to the country or region insofar as these issues affect the United States or U.S. strategic interests? Second, how has the United States responded, and with what success, to these policy choices in the context of the seven structural issues discussed earlier and Washington's own strategic objectives? And third, if appropriate, what are the alternative U.S. strategies that can be envisaged and what are the advantages and limitations of each alternative?

• Finally, what are the implications of the analysis for change in existing U.S. policies both in terms of goals and strategies?

The analyses that follow suggest that the United States, while certainly doing well in Asia by many measures, nonetheless is confronted by major challenges in Asia that span the gamut of U.S. foreign policy: winning the war on terrorism and the struggle against Islamist terrorism—issues that implicate Afghanistan, Iraq, Pakistan, India, Bangladesh, Australia, and the Central and Southeast Asian states; preventing further proliferation and the use of WMD—an issue that implicates the Korean Peninsula, China, Japan, Iran, Pakistan, and India; managing the rise of new (or returning) great powers without undermining the existing U.S.-dominated global order—an issue that implicates China, India, Russia, Japan, Australia, and Southeast Asia; assuring the requisite level of public goods, especially stable access to energy, a clean environment, and mitigating global climate change—an issue that implicates Russia, China, India, Japan, Central Asia, the Gulf states, and the Southeast Asian tigers; and controlling regional rivalries and the threats of armed conflict among critical dyads—an issue that implicates North and South Korea, China and Taiwan, China and Japan, China and India, China and Russia, China and the various Southeast Asian states, and Iran and the Gulf states.

Many of these issues find reflection in Richard Betts' wide-ranging and theoretically informed assessment of the key challenges facing the United States in Asia. Betts points to the fact that the next president will have no choice but to attend to the incomplete tasks of winning the war on terrorism in South Asia and managing nuclear proliferation at opposite ends in Northeast Asia and in the Persian Gulf. Betts nonetheless holds that the key strategic challenge for the United States over the long term will be coping with the rise of China, which could be the single most disequilibrating event in international politics. Whether the next administration will have either the energy or the resources to attend to this issue remains to be seen, since the backlog of unfinished business on other fronts is so deep and enervating. Betts argues that the twin facts of rising economic interdependence and the United States' own liberal instincts further suggest that U.S. strategy toward a rising China for the foreseeable future will likely be a conflicted one, an uncomfortable marriage of elements of the realist and the liberal traditions—at least until China's own geopolitical intentions become clearer or some crisis, such as over Taiwan, suddenly unfolds. What makes the challenge of managing China even more problematic, at least in the near term, Betts notes astutely, is the fact that new regional crises elsewhere are certain to emerge and, in all probability, will precipitate U.S. military interventions in areas no one really anticipates today—that at any rate has been the unbroken record of the postwar period. Surveying the multiple challenges the United States faces in the region, Betts concludes—consistent with the larger arguments made in this overview—that protecting the U.S. position in Asia requires emphatically "changes in economic policy and performance" at home.

Eugene Rumer's chapter assesses the challenges posed to the United States by Russian resurgence in Asia. Almost given up for dead, Russia has staged a comeback of sorts in international politics largely on the strength of rising commodity and energy prices. This revival, however, is far more fragile than Moscow's blustering might suggest because Russia confronts serious and still unresolved problems relating to demography, infrastructure, the industrial base, and military capability. In comparison to China, for example, Russia's trajectory could not be more sharply in contrast. These facts notwithstanding, the Russian recuperation has resulted in a new determination by Moscow to assert its influence along its periphery and in Europe more generally. This intention obviously collides with the U.S. and Western European commitment to expand the North Atlantic Treaty Organization (NATO) further, with the resulting conflict exacerbating other disagreements over Iran, energy and pipelines issues, and the direction of Russian domestic politics. Because the United States and Russia still share important common interests—including those related to nuclear stability, managing the rise of China, and controlling Iran's nuclear ambitions—Rumer convincingly argues that Washington ought to stay engaged with Russia, despite all the frustrations. The United States certainly does not enjoy the luxury of ignoring Russia and there is good reason to believe that U.S.-Russian relations can be much better than they currently are. In an effort to achieve such an improvement, Rumer advances the sensible idea that the issue of NATO enlargement—one of the biggest thorns in the bilateral relationship—warrants major reassessment not with the intent of reversing the current policy but to re-evaluate the priority assigned to NATO enlargement in U.S. policy. A similar argument could be made with respect to democratization in Russia. As Henry Kissinger has argued so cogently, at a time when Russia itself is struggling with new arrangements of governance, an "assertive intrusion into what Russians consider their own sense of self runs the risk of thwarting both geopolitical and moral goals."[28]

Today there can be little doubt that China and its future, and especially the character of its relationship with the United States, remain the most critical issues in global geopolitics. As Michael Swaine's chapter in this volume points out, not only has Beijing experienced a remarkable growth in its national power and diplomatic influence during the last eight years, but Sino-U.S. relations also subsist on a far more even keel than appeared to be possible at the beginning of the Bush administration. U.S.-China relations have improved as a result of a combination of events: the tragic convulsions of September 11, Chen Shui-bian's ham-handed efforts at pushing the independence envelope in Taiwan, the administration's need for Chinese cooperation in restraining the DPRK's nuclear program, deepening Sino-U.S. economic ties, and Beijing's own nimble shifts in international behavior. Yet, as Swaine perceptively points out, this increasingly cooperative relationship hides a deep-seated and fundamentally corrosive distrust because the continuing growth in Chinese national power presages a consequential power transition that could end up dethroning the United States as the reigning hegemon in global politics. Understandably, the fear that this could be the inevitable outcome of current trends leads Washington to hedge against the growth in Chinese power, and the fear that

---

[28] Henry A. Kissinger, "Finding Common Ground with Russia," *Washington Post,* July 8, 2008.

this hedging could mutate into active attempts at constraining the expansion of Chinese capabilities over time leads Beijing to, in turn, prepare for the worst eventualities. The mordant consequences of the security dilemma, then, portend a far more difficult bilateral relationship than appears to be the case right now. Swaine argues that avoiding the worst outcome requires the United States to fashion "sophisticated policy approaches toward Beijing that enhance the incentives for positive-sum outcomes." But what remains to be seen is whether even such sagacious undertakings—which require "persistent efforts to [simultaneously] deter, dissuade, reassure, and enmesh"—will suffice to overcome the fundamental antagonism between these two states at the ontological level of competitive international politics. Meanwhile, the best the two countries can do is to seek to deepen their ties across the board, remain engaged with one another, attempt to clarify why constructive relations are in their mutual interest, and resist the temptation to demonize the other.

If there is any state in Asia that is most affected by the rise in Chinese power, it is Japan. T.J. Pempel's chapter in this volume describes a Japan that—while being extremely attentive to this challenge and to a lesser degree the threat posed by the DPRK—reassuringly still views its alliance relationship with the United States as its first line of defense. Although Tokyo has engaged in a steady modernization of its already formidable conventional air and naval capabilities during the last decade and has, with U.S. encouragement, sought to expand its international role through among others institutional innovations at home, Japan has nonetheless moved gingerly thus far. Japan has remained intent on protecting its national security through implementing greater interoperability with the U.S. military, seeking a gradual redefinition of its own role in the context of larger global responsibilities, and aiming to develop some core defense industrial capabilities. Pempel argues that Tokyo has nevertheless sought to anchor its strategic interests in a vision of "comprehensive security" that includes energy, food, health, and environmental concerns in addition to national defense. Pempel notes that the principal near-term challenge will be to reassure Japan that the United States will remain a steadfast ally cognizant of Japanese interests in regard to issues such as the abductees, Taiwan, and China even as Washington seeks to pursue its other interests with Pyongyang and Beijing. He expects that resolving the explicitly bilateral issues pertaining to U.S. forces in Japan, advanced weapons sales, and the like will strengthen the foundations of reassurance as will engaging Tokyo on the other issues such as energy security and climate change. Finally, he concludes that Washington's ability to maintain positive relations with both China and Japan would reduce the temptation for each to view the other as a threat, but he acknowledges the difficulties in getting the balance right given the perpetual fears in Tokyo of being either entrapped or abandoned by the United States.

Jonathan Pollack's masterly survey of developments on the Korean Peninsula centers on one often overlooked strategic fact: that the United States today, for the first time in recent history, has become central to the destinies of both North and South Korea, despite the overwhelming differences in the nature of their political systems, their levels of achievement, and their future trajectories in regard to national success. Both states are no doubt tied in complex ways to other regional powers such as Russia, China, and Japan. The Korean states' relations with the United States, however, have indeed become pivotal to their ability to achieve current national goals—survival for North Korea and increased autonomy for South Korea—because of their preference, as Pollack phrases it, "to deal with one another, if at all, through their separate ties with the United States." The United States, thus, remains the fulcrum on which the success of both North Korea's denuclearization and South Korea's quest for a successful international role hinges. Yet, as Pollack points out, while Washington supports each of these objectives in different ways, crafting successful policies has always been a challenge because of the volatility of domestic politics in South Korea, the idiosyncrasies of North Korea's leadership, the complexity of intra-Korean relations, the interests of other geographically proximate great powers, and the transformations that have been underway in the bilateral U.S.-South Korean relationship for some time now. Consequently, despite the presence of a formal alliance, Pollack warns against easily assuming an automatic congruence in U.S. and South Korean policy goals, which for the foreseeable future will be challenged by the difficult tasks of completing the denuclearization of North Korea and assisting that state to evolve in more normal directions, while preserving stability on the peninsula in the face of rapidly evolving South Korean demands for change.

Rory Medcalf's chapter on Australia's strategic transition assumes special contemporary relevance because Canberra has traditionally been a steadfast U.S. ally globally—as evidenced most recently by its decision to support the U.S. invasion of Iraq during the first term of the Bush administration. The rise of China and its growing economic links with the Asia-Pacific region, especially with Australia, have raised questions, however, about whether the customary Australian support for the United States would survive in the event of a Beijing-Washington clash of interests, for example, in Taiwan or elsewhere. Medcalf presents a penetrating analysis of Australia's dilemmas, which reflect those of many other Asian states that profit from growing interdependence with China. He suggests that any U.S. policy will come to grief very quickly if it compels the United States' Asian partners to make hard choices between Washington and Beijing in circumstances where their security is not threatened directly by China. Equally importantly—and with significant implications for the United States—Medcalf notes that Canberra remains far less concerned than Washington is by the rise of Chinese power. On the face of it, such a response should not be surprising. On one hand, this response reflects the magnetic pull exercised by adroit Chinese diplomacy and the payoffs associated with maintaining profitable economic relations with Beijing. On the other hand, it demonstrates that middle powers in the international system are likely to be less threatened by the emergence of a new rising power than by the reigning hegemon (particularly if the rising power offers a variety of political and economic benefits). This is because the risks to the prevailing hegemon are always more acute in the context of any prospective power transition. The need for a subtle U.S. policy in Asia in the face of such realities is, therefore, imperative. To its credit, the Bush administration managed to pursue a more sophisticated policy in Asia than elsewhere, but even this does not seem to have mitigated the mixed feelings that Medcalf reports the Australian public increasingly harbors about the bilateral alliance. A willingness to listen to Australian concerns may go some way in remedying this slide, but Canberra's own changing interests suggest that the traditional image of Australia as the most allied of U.S. allies may well be a thing of the past.

While U.S. relations with most other Asian powers during the last eight years have been characterized by greater continuity than change, precisely the opposite is true as far the principal powers of South Asia are concerned. During the tenure of George W. Bush, both India and U.S.-Indian relations changed dramatically and for the better. After many decades of stagnation, India is finally set upon a path of high growth that will make it a major global power in time, even as it has successfully managed the twin tasks of keeping a diverse country together while maintaining a flourishing democracy. Teresita Schaffer's chapter on India confirms the resilience of the country's success but flags the serious vulnerabilities arising from still unresolved problems of equity, burdensome dependence on foreign sources for energy, and—most problematic of all—being surrounded by states that are in varying degrees of decay and failure. Managing these threats successfully depends in some measure on the quality of India's external economic and political relationships. Schaffer reports that India has been remarkably successful in balancing a complex set of ties with various countries that sometimes are at odds among themselves. In this context, the transformation of U.S.-Indian ties, which has occurred thanks to the actions of George W. Bush, Atal Bihari Vajpayee, and Manmohan Singh, not only has bilateral significance but also has rather important implications for the emerging balance of power in Asia. The chief challenge to this relationship in the years ahead will be reconciling U.S. expectations of India with New Delhi's obsession with "strategic autonomy." This task can be successful, Schaffer concludes, if both countries develop common approaches on issues where their interests already converge and if the United States can find ways to accommodate Indian aspirations in regard to regional integration and particularly global governance.

While India's evolution remains the bright spot in South Asia, the terrain covered in Polly Nayak's chapter—Pakistan and Bangladesh—evokes only unremitting and remitting gloom respectively. Both Pakistan and Bangladesh are fragile and dysfunctional states. While Islamabad presides over a flailing, if not a failing, polity, Dhaka mercifully is in a better position. If Bangladesh can surmount its problems of governance, caused mainly by the weakness of its key political parties and problematic civil-military relations, its otherwise reasonably impressive economic and developmental gains could enable the government to oversee a successful state. The usurpationist role played by the Bangladesh Army, however, does not bode well for long-term stability, and the succor offered by the country's military and intelligence services to radical Islamist fundamentalist groups, in order to strengthen the former's power in domestic politics, could presage down the line exactly the kinds of problems now witnessed in Pakistan. Nayak concludes, somewhat consolingly, that Bangladesh's problems seem likely to grow slowly enough to be manageable, but that this conclusion hinges on continued U.S. engagement and particularly generous foreign aid for a country that has been traditionally a friend of the United States. In contrast, Nayak's prognosis for Pakistan is much more gloomy. Although committed Islamists remain only a small proportion of its population, Pakistan's battered political institutions, self-serving and often predatory military, and unsavory history of breeding radical Islamist terrorist groups have now all combined to create a state that cannot exercise sovereignty over important parts of its own territory from which major threats to regional and global security emerge. Nayak's tale here is indeed tragic because the U.S. war on terrorism, in principle, should have assisted Pakistan in combating these problems. The manner in which Washington implemented its engagement with Islamabad—betting excessively on a military regime to deliver against al Qaeda while refraining from pushing it to make a clean break with all terrorist groups even while giving short shrift to rebuilding civilian institutions—only appears to have made things worse. The current—and unenviable—outcome is that the civilian and the military arms of the

Pakistani state seem paralyzed in regard to both the war on terrorism and the larger task of governance.

Even more than the states of South Asia, Evelyn Goh's survey of the Southeast Asian world suggests a strong and unwavering demand for the right kind of U.S. presence and engagement with the region. Given the area's proximity to a rising China—which attracts even as it unsettles—Southeast Asian dependence on the United States for deterrence and reassurance is likely to remain high, irrespective of what Washington's other failings might be. Goh emphasizes, however, that although the region would welcome renewed, but not overbearing, U.S. attention, key regional states are nonetheless focused on diversifying their "strategic dependencies" to include increased engagement with China. Their aim is to enmesh China while reaching out to other major regional actors, such as Japan and India, in an effort to balance the growth of Chinese influence. Mindful of the recent successes of Chinese diplomacy, this Southeast Asian interest in diversification is likely to increase further and though the regional states benefit from a strong offshore U.S. military presence, their ability to transparently support U.S. policies, especially when controversial, is nonetheless limited by the large Muslim populations that reside in many of these states. The best recipe for continuing U.S. success in Southeast Asia, Goh concludes, consists of maintaining a strong offshore military presence capable of maintaining hegemonic order should this be threatened, without either pursuing the "outright containment of China" or leveling burdensome demands in the individual bilateral relationships with key states, while continuing to participate in regional institutions.

S. Frederick Starr's insightful analysis of Central Asia suggests that the key distinguishing feature of this region is the presence of infirm states still struggling to complete the nation-building project in an environment marked by the presence of stronger powers and a major ongoing conflict. These challenges are particularly stressful in Central Asia for two reasons. First, the countries in question are still remarkably young, having received their independence only recently with the fall of the Soviet Union. Second, the one major development that could open the doors for an economic integration with South Asia—peace in Afghanistan—does not appear to be on the anvil. The latter handicap is particularly burdensome because it offers the region an escape from excessive dependence on either Russia or China and thereby presents a means of protecting the independence of these states vis-à-vis their most powerful immediate neighbors. While U.S. policy toward the region enjoyed early successes, the unbalanced focus on democratization produced some reverses along the way. Starr cogently argues that the best way to ensure the long-range development of Central Asia is to win the war in Afghanistan because that would resolve the problems of transit and access as well as eliminate the major source of extremist Islam in one go. If the conflict in Iraq defined the Bush administration, assuring that the war in Afghanistan is finally successful will likely become among the most important preoccupations of its successor. As Starr succinctly phrases it, "the alternative to success is ominous, imposing costs in many areas besides the purely financial." Restoring equilibrium in U.S. relations with Central Asia will become important in this context as well. Toward that end, deepening economic ties with the region's states; pursuing balanced and "mutually reinforcing" policies toward them; coordinating with key partners such as Japan, India, and the United Kingdom; and staying the course consistently over the long term will become key ingredients of a successful U.S. policy.

This volume includes three special studies on different issues of current relevance. The vexatious problem of dealing with Iran's nuclear ambitions remains the focus of one special study. Unlike last year's volume, which examined the domestic determinants of Iran's nuclear decisionmaking, the present study by George Perkovich surveys the choices that the United States has for reversing Tehran's nuclear course. If the objective of international efforts should be terminating Iran's capacity to enrich uranium—because mastering this capability would put Tehran within easy reach of producing a simple but effective nuclear device—the bad news is that there are few good options for doing so. Perkovich notes that fostering regime change or pursuing military operations, primarily air attacks, would only make the Iranian regime more obdurate in is determination to acquire a real, as opposed to a potential, nuclear capability. Permitting limited enrichment, or enrichment under international safeguards, is appealing as a means of avoiding confrontation with Tehran but brings Iran ever closer to the bomb and only creates conditions that beg Tehran to break out in the event of a crisis. A broad and direct strategic dialogue between the United States and Iran may seem attractive as a means of conveying reassurance, but there is no guarantee that Tehran will not pocket this initiative and up the ante by demanding more. Even if such a dialogue is successful, however, it is not certain whether Tehran under the current dispensation would agree to suspension of enrichment as the end product of this process. The cold reality is that Iran abundantly appreciates that the current U.S. ability to coerce it into terminating its nuclear program is minimal—not because degrading its capabilities is technically infeasible, but because the costs of such actions would be very high. Tehran also recognizes that the international community would prefer the absence of an Iranian nuclear program but that individual states are simply not prepared to undertake the necessary burdens associated with collective action to achieve this end. Consequently, Perkovich suggests that the best near-term solution is to withdraw all the carrots currently offered to Iran and essentially wait it out by implementing long-term sanctions until Iran changes course—holding the country in the meanwhile to its commitment not to build nuclear weapons. Given the paucity of options at this juncture, this approach should at least be debated because it could well become, in different packaging, the position the international community eventually gravitates toward in its efforts to control the Iranian nuclear problem.

Another special study, also on an important issue of national security, is Admiral Dennis Blair's innovative and systematic assessment of power projection capabilities in Asia. The economic capabilities of the major Asian states are increasing rapidly, and the fears that such capabilities could be transformed into military instruments have not abated. Blair's study reaches the reassuring conclusion that the power projection capabilities—the military instruments able to apply power at distance with some persistence— of the major Asian states such as China, Japan, and India are still limited and, to the degree that they are increasing, are most likely to be deployed in coalition operations cooperatively. Blair's chapter is important for another analytical reason: it remains perhaps the best recent effort to systematically unpack the components encompassed by the term "power projection," which originated as, and still predominantly remains, essentially a naval concept. By decomposing the concept into its constituent parts, the chapter provides a useful framework to judge the changes in power projection capabilities that may occur in Asia over time. A transparent elucidation of the term, as found in Blair's chapter, should also lay the foundations for a more intensive debate over the political aims of various Asian great powers and the likelihood that their long-term objectives (insofar as can be discerned or hypothesized) would either require the creation of such capabilities for the effective exercise of power or permit them to successfully secure influence through other kinds of military instruments. In any event, the key policy insight deriving from Blair's chapter is that the United States is currently blessed with extraordinary capacities for globe-girding reach and so long as U.S. policymakers make the prudent marginal investments required to sustain this superiority, they can contribute toward prolonging the "Asian miracle" by sustaining the hegemonic peace that precludes the regional states from having to produce order through their own military exertions.

The third special study in this volume focuses on a much neglected but critically important issue: water. Although ordinarily treated as a matter of low politics, the emerging era of water scarcity in Asia could easily transform the issue into one of high politics—particularly if major water diversion schemes of the kind currently contemplated by upper riparian states such as China and India provoke conflicts with neighboring states. Elizabeth Economy's chapter on this subject is critical because it first elucidates the immensity of the challenge posed by water security to Asia's emerging giants, China and India. The most immediate consequence of the growing demands for water amid the emerging scarcities could be internal unrest, with external conflict becoming an extended consequence if states lapse into the temptation of seeking unilateral solutions to protecting their access to water. Access to water (or the lack thereof) in Asia will also be affected by the larger issue of global climate change. Consequently, the opposite problems of flooding and droughts, with all their associated social dislocations, will demand new attention on the part of the major Asian states. Economy argues convincingly that the emerging water crisis in Asia offers the United States a tremendous opportunity to exert its soft power by aiding the region in developing strategies for water management, mediating in situations where inter-state disputes are likely, and by leading the formation of a new consensus on mitigating climate change. Besides all the advantages ensuing from the resulting global approbation for U.S. leadership, Washington would also have made a tangible contribution to advancing human security in some of the most populous and fastest-growing regions of the world.

Conclusion

Taken together, the studies presented in this volume convey clearly the diversity of the challenges that will face the United States in Asia. When assessed synoptically, however, the U.S. position in the continent can be seen to be still remarkably strong. The most critical near-term challenges remain bringing the current wars in Afghanistan and Iraq and the ongoing struggle against radical Islamist movements to a successful conclusion, while managing the threats of proliferation in North Korea and Iran. Although the United States has not yet mustered a winning solution to the Iranian challenge, one can at least hope that the other outstanding problems will meet satisfactory endings either through the current policies or through some modification of them. The most important longer-term challenge, however, will be coping with the rise of China because this event portends the possibility of a consequential power transition at the core of the global system and, by implication, the displacement of U.S. hegemony. Preparations for dealing with this prospect cannot be postponed interminably and, in fact, a major challenge for the next administration will be finding the resources—material, ideational, organizational, and temporal—necessary to address this issue even as it is engulfed by the demands of resolving the plethora of other challenges that will absorb its attention in the short term.

To make things more difficult, the United States will not enjoy the luxury of having a single grand organizing concept such as containment to guide its efforts in meeting this challenge. The Bush administration did formulate a sensible alternative approach, that of maintaining "a balance of power that favors freedom,"[29] but unfortunately, due to distractions, never either systematically elucidated the concept or defended its logic relative to other competitors. The next administration will need to do better. But the incoming president will soon discover that so long as maintaining strategic advantage remains the enduring goal of the United States, there will be no alternative, at least in the near term, to pursuing policies that embody subtlety, agility, and endurance—and that the chances of success accruing to these approaches improve greatly if the country can redefine its role, renew its strength, and recover its legitimacy effectively.

---

[29] Condoleezza Rice, "A Balance of Power That Favors Freedom" (Walter B. Wriston lecture to the Manhattan Institute, New York, October 1, 2002), http://www.manhattan-institute.org/html/wl2002.htm.

STRATEGIC ASIA 2008–09

COUNTRY STUDIES

EXECUTIVE SUMMARY

This chapter evaluates U.S. policy toward Asia and suggests policy options for the next administration.

MAIN ARGUMENT:

- A new president will inevitably focus first on the Middle East and the war on terrorism and second on North Korea's nuclear weapons, but relations with major powers in Asia are ultimately more important.

- The future of Chinese power is the overriding issue for the U.S., yet policymakers remain ambivalent over optimistic and pessimistic models that stress economic interests and the balance of military power, respectively.

- The constant pressure to address immediate concerns in North Korea and Pakistan will challenge the development of long-term strategy in Asia.

POLICY IMPLICATIONS:

There is no need for immediate major revision of strategies toward Asia, but a few changes of course could buffer policy against long-term risks:

- Washington would benefit from maintaining the U.S.-Japan alliance and expanding security relations with India while remaining mindful of the need for Pakistani cooperation against the Taliban and al Qaeda.

- Revising U.S. military strategy to rely on air power in the early phase of a war on the Korean Peninsula would allow removal of the U.S. ground forces that provoke negative public sentiment and undercut the basis of the alliance.

- Toning down pressure on Moscow and reducing U.S. involvement in Central Asia may assist in discouraging strategic Russian-Chinese cooperation against Washington.

- Clarifying but limiting plans for defense of Taiwan could reduce chances of Chinese miscalculation in a crisis and limit U.S. liability.

The United States and Asia

Richard K. Betts

The biggest challenges facing the United States in Asia are in the longer term and will come from evolving conditions in the balance of power. The principal unresolved question here is whether (and how) the United States will accommodate the rise of China or strive to keep the prerogatives of primacy in East Asia to which Washington has become accustomed. Although U.S. political leaders may not be forced to confront the question directly for a long time, trends could bring the issue to the fore in the 2013 presidential term—or a catalytic event could do so even sooner.

With few exceptions, the immediate strategic issues are not pressing and can be managed more or less without significant departures from long-standing policies. The exceptions, the two pressing strategic questions on Asia, come from the fringes of the continent: North Korea in the east, where a weak, poor country manages to exert tremendous leverage on the world's only superpower, and Pakistan in the west, where Asia bleeds into the maelstrom of the Middle East. These two nations will inevitably preoccupy official strategists, given that dealing with near-term problems always crowds out long-term planning. As long as nuclear weapons use in these peripheral areas can be prevented, however, relations with the major powers in Asia are ultimately more important.

U.S. strategy for managing the national security aspects of the relationship with Japan—one of the United States' most important allies—does not need revision. A firm U.S. commitment to defend Japan, and Tokyo's subsidization of the basing costs for doing so, should remain the essence of the strategy. The main challenge is to fend off demands that Japan do more to share U.S. military burdens in Asia. Such calls might have made

Richard K. Betts is the Arnold A. Saltzman Professor and Director of the Saltzman Institute of War and Peace Studies at Columbia University. He can be reached at <rkb4@columbia.edu>.

sense during the Cold War, given the magnitude of the Soviet threat. Today, however, the material benefits would be outweighed by the political and diplomatic disruption that would follow were Japan to become a militarily "normal" country.

Given its size and new economic dynamism, India should naturally be more important to the United States than it has been in the past. Washington's approach to dealing with New Delhi also requires no drastic change. Moves to improve relations with India face fewer complications as U.S. relations with Pakistan have worsened. The awkward but viable triangular relationship Washington maintained with New Delhi and Islamabad during the Musharraf government's cooperation in the war against al Qaeda and the Taliban will become less complicated if the new Pakistani government makes a separate peace with those enemies. In the more hopeful eventuality that Islamabad continues to cooperate on counterterrorism with the United States, there is still reason to move further in U.S.-Indian security relations. If the Pakistani government and army continue to develop the view that India now poses less a threat than does internal decay, state failure, and terrorism, U.S. cooperation with New Delhi will become less of a problem. U.S. policy should strengthen outreach to the moderate middle of Pakistani society and encourage the country's authorities to focus on domestic stability. Meanwhile, the United States should expand ties with India to the extent that the domestic political situation in India permits. In any case, dealing with Pakistan—seeking renewed support in counterterrorism campaigns and preventing the government's radicalization or collapse—will be at the top of the new administration's agenda for the near term.

Russia is regaining importance in the global power game, but Russia's posture toward Europe is of more concern to the United States than are its dealings with Asia. In regard to Asia, Russia's significance will depend on whether the country's relations with China move more decisively toward either opposition or alliance.

China is the dominant concern for U.S. policy and the only potential source of conflict that could lead to major war. Such conflict is by no means inevitable. Developing a strategy to keep the danger low, however, may require modification of U.S. objectives. Conventional wisdom mistakenly relies on projecting the current status quo indefinitely into the future and implicitly assumes that China's priorities and demands will not change as its power position changes. Few if any rising powers in history have blithely continued to accept indefinitely a status with fewer prerogatives than were exercised by the previously dominant power, and it would be reckless to assume that China will break with precedent. Contrary to conventional wisdom, the United States can strive either to control the strategic equation in Asia or to reduce the odds of conflict with China. It will be a historically unusual achievement, however, if Washington manages to do both.

The first of the following sections discusses the evolution and implications of the balance of power in Asia. The second section explains why China must be the focus of U.S. strategy and presents contrasting assumptions over what measures will keep China peaceful. The third section looks at potential changes in U.S. security policy toward several parts of the region, and the final section lays out reasons for the United States to adjust in advance to long-term developments rather than coast forward with policies that have succeeded so far.

Context for Strategic Adjustment: System Structure and Trends

Since September 11, U.S. policy in Asia has been dominated by economic, political, and counterterrorism interests but has placed little emphasis on conventional military issues. The economic problems of greatest relevance to U.S. national security policy are the effects of U.S. budget and trade deficits combined with dependence on China to help fund the U.S. debt. The solutions to these problems lie more in U.S. domestic politics and decisions on hard choices at home than in negotiations with Asian powers. Issues of Asian security policy are currently refracted through U.S. preoccupation with political instability, war, and terrorism in the Middle East. U.S. concern with suppressing movements like Jemaah Islamiyah in Indonesia or the Moro Islamic Liberation Front in the Philippines is more a matter of the war on terrorism than of U.S. strategy toward Asia.

This distraction from Asia is abetted both by the surface stability of most of the region (apart from North Korea) and by the easing of relations between the United States and the People's Republic of China (PRC) after September 11. There has been no impetus to force basic reconsideration of strategy in the region east of Pakistan. Questions of how to deal with a full-grown China in the future lie beyond the short-term horizons of the highest level policymakers. Recent elections seem to have reversed trends of worsening relations both between Taipei and Beijing and between Seoul and Washington. Developments in Asia are not likely to force a shift of focus away from the Middle East during the four years of the next U.S. administration—aside from aspects of the Afghanistan-Pakistan imbroglio linking this region to Asia and from the regime in Pyongyang, which continues to fight far above its weight. Distraction from the remainder of Asia while resting on an assumption of continuity, however, is a recipe for surprise. The biggest shocks to U.S. national security policy since

World War II have often come from countries barely on the radar screens of leaders in Washington (for example, Korea in 1950, Afghanistan in 1979, and Kuwait in 1990).

The United States presides globally but operates regionally. The world is unipolar, but U.S. power is fractionated, stretched across many regions. Thus, particular regions are multipolar, requiring Washington to adapt to the local balance of power and collaborate with other states or groups to achieve its goals. In Europe, Washington depends on the North Atlantic Treaty Organization (NATO) alliance. In Iraq, the United States tried to resolve a military problem mostly alone and found U.S. forces stretched to the breaking point. In Asia, Washington depends both on formal alliances with Japan, South Korea, and Australia and on varying degrees of cooperation from India, Russia, China, and middle powers of the region.

There are several main trends in the Asian balance of power:

- The United States dominates the Pacific, and China dominates the mainland.

- Japan is an economic great power and potentially a military great power; the United States and Japan remain in a steady-state alliance.

- Russia, recently down but not out, is returning to balance of power politics though is not yet firmly aligned with any other major states in Asia.

- China and India are on trajectories toward increasing dominance of East and South Asia and toward greater diplomatic and economic roles beyond their respective regions.

- North Korea remains utterly weak in conventional terms but retains tremendous strategic leverage because of Pyongyang's diplomatic chutzpah and capacity to set off devastating events.

Table 1 presents data on changes in power since the Cold War. Although some of the changes are distorted by the imprecision of the data—variations in exchange rates, and soft or disputed data for Russia, China, and North Korea—it is worth considering what this data suggests regarding the evolution of economic power and military potential in Asia since the end of the Cold War.

- The United States is in a class by itself in both economic and military dimensions of power, although this power is mortgaged to areas of the world besides Asia.

- The United States devotes two to three times as much of its national resources to military power as do most of the countries of Asia.

TABLE 1 Change in power and potential since the Cold War

	GDP ($b)		Military budget ($b)		Military budget (% of GDP)	
	1990	2007	1990	2007	1990	2007
United States	5,423.4	13,700.0	291.4	622.0	5.4	4.5
Soviet Union	2,042.7	–	116.7	–	5.7	–
Russia	–	2,000.0	–	33.0	–	1.7
Japan	2,971.2	4,560.0	28.7	43.7	1.0	1.0
China	363.8	3,350.0	6.1	46.7/122.0[a]	1.7	1.4 / 3.7[a]
Taiwan	160.7	379.0	8.7	9.6	5.4	2.5
South Korea	239.8	971.0	10.6	26.9	4.4	2.8
North Korea	47.9	–	5.2	2.3[b]	10.9	–
Australia	300.8	792.0	7.0	19.9	2.3	2.5
Singapore	33.6	155.0	1.6	7.2	4.9	4.7
India	283.3	1,209.0	9.3	28.5	3.3	2.4
Pakistan	39.7	144.0	2.9	4.5	7.3	3.2

SOURCE: International Institute for Strategic Studies, *The Military Balance 1991–92* (London: Brassey's, 1991); International Institute for Strategic Studies, *The Military Balance 2007* (London: Routledge, 2007); and International Institute for Strategic Studies, *The Military Balance 2008* (London: Routledge, 2008).

NOTE: Data is in current U.S. dollars, not adjusted for inflation.

[a] Indicates data was calculated first by exchange rate and second by purchasing power parity.

[b] Indicates data is an estimate for 2006 (data for 2007 was not available).

- China's investment in military power has grown at a tremendous rate as the nation's resources have increased and, at recent growth rates, will continue to outpace that of other major states in the region.
- Taiwan's military spending, which has declined in real terms, now accounts for less than half the proportion of GDP that it did in 1990.
- India's military spending dramatically outpaced Pakistan's, which is now little more than 15% of its rival's spending.
- India's military spending was a third higher than China's at the end of the Cold War but is now little more than half of China's at best.
- China's and India's military spending has skyrocketed since the Cold War, while Japan's has remained constant and Russia's declined.

- By conventional measures, South Korea spends nearly ten times as much on the military as North Korea does. South Korea's forces are qualitatively superior, but North Korea still leads in some quantitative indices of deployed forces.[1]

These trends in the distribution of military power are seldom on the minds of U.S. policymakers, outside of the Department of Defense. Political leaders in Asia are even more focused on economic matters. China will feel encircled if other Asian governments were to collaborate energetically with Washington. Japan, India, and Russia would likely make greater individual efforts militarily if they were to go separate ways. In the absence of strategic collaboration among these countries, however, Washington will find itself in a situation of regional bipolarity with China—in which the United States rules the seas and China dominates the East Asian mainland.

In a worse case, Beijing and Moscow would align against Washington and Tokyo while New Delhi kept to the sidelines. Russia and China have ample reasons for mutual distrust and could return to the days of the late Cold War when they both had better relations with Washington than with each other. Nevertheless, China and Russia have moved closer to each other since the Cold War.[2] Both states have also become more vulnerable to U.S. nuclear striking power and share a common interest in opposing U.S. deployment of ballistic missile defenses.[3] Unbridled NATO expansion, U.S. criticism of Moscow's backsliding on democratization, and abrogation of the ABM Treaty have given ample incentive for Russia to subordinate conflicts of interest with China to the two countries' common interest in resisting

---

[1] Both countries have roughly the same number of reserve military personnel but in recent years North Korea's active duty total (the number more relevant to potential surprise attack) has been approximately 60% higher than South Korea's (1,106,000 compared to 687,000). South Korea's active force has declined in absolute numbers by almost 10% from 1990 (dropping from 750,000). In air power the trend is reversed: North Korea had almost twice as many combat aircraft as South Korea in 1990 (732 compared to 405) but only a slight edge in 2007 (590 compared to 555). Over this period North Korea's number of main battle tanks remained at 3,500, while South Korea's supply increased from 1,550 to 2,330. See International Institute for Strategic Studies, *The Military Balance 1991–92* (London: Brassey's, 1991), 167–70; and International Institute for Strategic Studies, *The Military Balance 2008* (London: Routledge, 2008): 387–91.

[2] Patrick E. Tyler, "Russia and China Sign 'Friendship' Pact," *New York Times,* July 17, 2001, A1, A8.

[3] Keir A. Lieber and Daryl G. Press, "U.S. Nuclear Primacy and the Future of the Chinese Deterrent," *China Security* (Winter 2007): 66–67, 74–75.

Western domination.[4] The one significant adjustment of U.S. strategy that would help avoid such an alignment would be to soft-pedal pressure against Russia in Europe—most notably by halting initiatives to carry NATO expansion into Ukraine, the heartland of the former Soviet Union. This soft-pedaling does not mean subordinating NATO policy to hypothetical developments in another region. Asian interests simply complement other good reasons to avoid provoking dangerous Russian reactions in Europe.

Any of these strategic combinations in Asia would comport with the natural drift of U.S. military policy. These potential combinations provide the United States with a rationale for retaining a strong navy and air force and relying on offshore fire-power rather than on occupation of territory on the ground—priorities that the exacting counterinsurgency campaigns in Iraq and Afghanistan have put in doubt.

China Central

The two general sets of assumptions that are contending to drive U.S. policy on Asia are not grand strategies but grand concepts about the logic of international relations derived from intuitive theories or myths. The applications of these grand concepts focus on China even though there are other large, prosperous, or well-armed countries in the region. This does not mean that China is the only important country in economic, political, or military terms, but that it is the most important country in the region. Japan will remain the most vital U.S. ally, India will be increasingly important, and Russia has bounced back into the major leagues of world politics, yet none of these countries poses the potential challenge to U.S. prerogatives in Asia that China does. This situation will be more evident with every passing day unless (as is quite possible) economic, demographic, or internal political developments derail China's ascent.[5] If China continues on its current trajectory, however, U.S. security relationships with the other major countries in the region will hinge in large part on their effect on the course

---

[4] After communism's collapse, liberals in Russia had hoped to orient the country in an "Atlanticist" direction but lost ground to "Eurasianism." Russian disputes with Japan over the Kurile Islands (known as the Northern Territories in Japan) also limited options for alignment with the West. Meanwhile, Russia and China resolved most of their border disputes and have undertaken significant trade in arms. See Yong Deng, "Remolding Great Power Politics: China's Strategic Partnerships with Russia, the European Union, and India," *Journal of Strategic Studies* 30, no. 4–5 (August–October 2007): 870–72, 874–76. For a more skeptical view of the potential for the two countries' collaboration, see Jennifer Anderson, *The Limits of Sino-Russian Strategic Partnership*, Adelphi Paper 315 (London: Oxford University Press, 1997).

[5] For various risks to China's growth, see the U.S. National Intelligence Council (NIC), *Mapping the Global Future: Report of the National Intelligence Council's 2020 Project,* NIC 2004-13 (Washington, D.C.: NIC, December 2004), 52. See also Susan L. Shirk, *China: Fragile Superpower: How China's Internal Politics Could Derail Its Peaceful Rise* (New York: Oxford University Press, 2007).

of relations between the United States and China because Washington will need more assistance in handling Beijing.

The first set of assumptions, which is optimistic and driven by the primacy of economics, derives from liberal theories that emphasize the pacifying effect of economic globalization and participation in international institutions.[6] This view could be called the institutional model. Under this model, maximizing economic and diplomatic interaction will promote political liberalization and prevent a rising China from becoming a threat. China will be defanged by integration in a web of interdependence, vested interests, and peace-inducing institutions because it will have too much to lose from conflict and too much to gain from cooperation. The PRC will be weaned from mercantilist approaches to securing energy and raw materials, and nationalism will remain under control. Creeping democratization will eventually make China a partner in the worldwide "democratic peace." Optimism is underwritten by the strategically risk-averse character of Chinese policy to date.

Although nominally global, the international norms and institutions crucial to this vision of taming China are essentially those developed by the rich and previously dominant states of the West. U.S. observers thinking in this vein tend to assume that China will be domesticated by the norms and behavior that cosmopolitan elites now see as the natural order of things. In their view, Western preferences for world order are universal and will limit the future importance of military power relationships. In this complex of liberal assumptions it is the West that manages China's rise. Washington need not resist that rise and need only tutor China on its natural self-interest.

The darker second set of assumptions comes out of the realist tradition and could be called the power politics model. This view assumes that politics has a life of its own and that the interests of some countries can prove irreconcilable. Observers in this vein see ambition and muscular demands for change as the natural by-product of increased economic and military clout. This orientation is pessimistic if Washington's aim is to control the international system but is less alarming if Washington finds eventual Chinese dominance in the East Asian region to be acceptable. It is almost certain, however, that Chinese dominance—at least outside the

---

[6] G. John Ikenberry, "The Rise of China and the Future of the West," *Foreign Affairs* 87, no. 1 (January/February 2008): 23–37. For cautious examples of institutionalist optimism, see James Shinn, ed., *Weaving the Net: Conditional Engagement with China* (New York: Council on Foreign Relations, 1996); and David Shambaugh, "China Engages Asia: Reshaping the Regional Order," *International Security* 29, no. 3 (Winter 2004/05): 64–99. For a constructivist version of the optimistic prognosis, see Alastair Iain Johnston, *Social States: China in International Institutions* (Princeton: Princeton University Press, 2008).

realm of economics—will not be acceptable to Washington and other Asian capitals. In any case, the main idea behind the power politics model is that China will not be managed politically and militarily but will chart its own course. The PRC will bend to other powers as long as China is weaker than they are, but only that long. As China grows, Beijing will become less and less patient with what it considers to be simmering injustices or unfair constraints and double standards and will grow more insistent on getting what it sees as China's rights. The country is not yet powerful enough to indulge this natural urge but is getting there fast. Thus, the United States needs to contain and deter China. There are only two other alternatives: in a resurgence of classical balance-of-power politics Japan, Russia, and India could collaborate to contain China, or all major states could concede, leaving China unchallenged as the dominant power shaping the rules of the game in Asia.[7]

China may never reach a level of power that would enable it to dominate Asia, but a security-minded U.S. policy cannot bank on such failure. Moreover, the power politics perspective sees risks from movement in either direction from the status quo. On the one hand, if China continues to prosper, the country will become a superpower, with its power uncompromised and primed to influence other countries in the directions Beijing considers sensible. If China falters and suffers economic reverses, on the other hand, internal political turmoil could result, with destabilizing effects on the rest of the region. A venerable theory sees revolution as most likely when progress and rising expectations are dashed by a downturn.[8] China has a revolutionary tradition as well as a formal ideology that, though now dormant, is available to be reactivated to legitimize rebellion. Alternatively, government or ascendant political groups could promote nationalist expansion as a diversion from domestic disorder.

There is no U.S. grand strategy that embodies either the institutional or the power politics model consistently. Indeed, as a practical matter, the messy democratic process in the United States does not produce any strategy in the coherent sense in which intellectuals think of the word.

---

[7] John J. Mearsheimer, *The Tragedy of Great Power Politics* (New York: W.W. Norton & Company, 2001), 386–96; David Hale, "China's Growing Appetites," *National Interest,* no. 76 (Summer 2004): 137–47; and Warren I. Cohen, "China's Rise in Historical Perspective," *Journal of Strategic Studies* 30, nos. 4–5 (August–October 2007): 683–704, which on p. 703 concludes: "Historically, a strong China has brutalized the weak—and there is no reason to expect it to act differently in the future, to behave any better than other great powers have in the past." For milder versions of the pessimistic view, see Aaron L. Friedberg, "The Future of U.S.-China Relations: Is Conflict Inevitable?" *International Security* 30, no. 2 (Fall 2005): 7–45; and Richard K. Betts and Thomas J. Christensen, "China: Getting the Questions Right," *National Interest,* no. 62 (Winter 2000/01): 17–29.

[8] Alexis de Tocqueville, *The Old Regime and the French Revolution,* trans. Stuart Gilbert (New York: Doubleday, 1955), part 3, chap. 4; and J.C. Davies, "Toward a Theory of Revolution," *American Sociological Review* 27, no. 1 (February 1962): 6.

The frequent turnover of administrations, each of which feels the need to distinguish itself from the last, intensifies discontinuity and reduces official declarations of strategy to glittering generalities and laundry lists of desirable objectives. So far the U.S. approach toward Asia has been an indecisive amalgam of both the models described. Policymakers, whose responsibilities differ from those of theorists, have proven adept at synthesizing the contrasting models by promoting conciliation while hedging against potential conflict. Yet even seemingly pragmatic ad hoc adjustments reflect one of the grand concepts more than the other, and thus more often confront hard choices in one dimension while deflecting them in the other.

Optimistic proponents of the institutional model can point to the broad canvas of mutual economic interests and how security disputes to date have been successfully finessed. The strength of this view is in accounting for the largest proportion of interactions over time; the optimistic approach provides the best bet for how problems will be handled in any given year. The weakness of this view is in failing to provide solutions for the rare but crucial exceptions, the once-in-a-generation crises that can trigger war. With luck the institutional model could work indefinitely. Banking on luck, however, is a risky choice for a president who wants to avoid strategic surprise.

U.S. strategy toward major powers other than China poses fewer difficulties. The United States has clear objectives in regard to Japan, Russia, India, and middle powers such as South Korea, Indonesia, and Pakistan. The trade-offs required to pursue these objectives are manageable, even in the case of Pakistan (as long as events inside that country do not get out of hand). The closest thing to U.S. grand strategy in Asia is a commitment to a hub-and-spoke pattern of bilateral security connections. For over half a century this approach has stood in stark contrast to arrangements in Europe, which hinge on multilateral political and military institutions, especially NATO.

This crucial difference precludes confidence in the institutional model for strategic management. There is no NEATO, SATO, or neo-SEATO in the works to replicate NATO's vital functions in securing the long peace in Europe.[9] The pretensions of other multilateral organs in Asia—such as the ASEAN Regional Forum (ARF)—to deal with security concerns have

---

[9] The acronyms stand for a hypothetical Northeast Asia Treaty Organization, South Asia Treaty Organization, and a reborn Southeast Asia Treaty Organization. The latter was formed in 1955 but never functioned meaningfully and was disbanded in 1975, the year that the Vietnam War ended.

proved weak.[10] Yet the optimistic argument rests on the benefits to be derived from the fantastic web of Western institutions, even though the multilateral mechanisms that apply in Asia do not address military security. For example, John Ikenberry, a proponent of this model, says nothing about what U.S. military policy should be in the region, dismisses the whole dimension of analysis with the facile assumption that mutual nuclear deterrence precludes major war, and asserts with breathtaking confidence that "war-driven change has been abolished as a historical process."[11]

China is central but is not everything. Many smaller powers matter. Vietnam at long last is growing as a trading partner. Although accommodating well to Chinese power in the decades since the two nations fought a small war, Vietnam is in a delicate geographic position on land and has conflicting interests in the disputed islands of the South China Sea (or as the Vietnamese call it, the Eastern Sea).[12] The Philippines and Indonesia are heavily involved in the U.S. war against al Qaeda and its affiliates. Singapore, though a small city-state, is extraordinarily efficient, supportive of U.S. presence, and is the only country in Asia that takes the need for national military power as seriously as does the United States (see Table 1). Cultivating a relationship with Singapore makes perfect strategic sense for Washington, although opposition to Singapore's authoritarian political system compromises the relative importance of the strategic interest.[13] Australia is the United States' closest ally in the region near Southeast Asia and could play a more significant role in an expansive U.S. strategy for Asia. Some commentators have proposed rebasing U.S. forces from Okinawa and Korea in more hospitable Australia, but if those units are not primarily oriented to the defense of Japan and South Korea—in which case they should stay close to where they are—it is not clear why those forces should be sent far to the south rather than home to the United States. It is hard to envision a scenario in which the U.S. military would be employed in a serious way in Australia's neighborhood. Moreover, given that Canberra does not share Washington's ambivalence over China's growth, there is no guarantee that military policies toward China will remain congruent.[14]

---

[10] David Martin Jones and Michael L. R. Smith, "Making Process, Not Progress: ASEAN and the Evolving East Asian Regional Order," *International Security* 32, no. 1 (Summer 2007): 148–84.

[11] Ikenberry, "The Rise of China," 31.

[12] Richard K. Betts, "Vietnam's Strategic Predicament," *Survival* 37, no. 3 (Autumn 1995): 61–81.

[13] Michael Leifer, *Singapore's Foreign Policy: Coping with Vulnerability* (London: Routledge, 2000), 98–108.

[14] Rod Lyon and William T. Tow, "The Future of the U.S.-Australian Security Relationship," *Asian Security* 1, no. 1 (2005): 43–45.

For a strategy of the first order, the major states in East and South Asia would remain the first priority for U.S. attention. For both material and moral reasons, India should play a much larger role in U.S. foreign policy than it ever has in the past. Given India's rapid growth and vibrant high tech sector, trade between the two countries is increasingly important.[15] As a non-aligned nuclear weapons power, India's military potential cannot be ignored. As the world's largest democracy, India has a natural political affinity with the United States. Despite these powerful forces for cooperation, however, Indo-U.S. relations have long remained a second-order concern for Washington. During the Cold War, Indian neutrality (and de facto tilt toward Moscow) eliminated not only the option but the incentive for the United States to develop intimate relations and mechanisms of cooperation in the manner that Washington did with NATO allies and Japan. Today cooperation has grown but is still limited. Both New Delhi and Washington seek to avoid provoking Beijing by the appearance of an encircling entente. Additionally, Indo-U.S. cooperation has been limited by domestic political controversy over the extent and conditions of cooperation on matters of nuclear energy and arms.

Until the last year of the Bush administration, the answer to whether the United States would choose to align with Pakistan or India was "yes." That is, Washington had chosen both countries but in different contexts. The United States simply did not take sides in the security issue of most interest to the two states: their mutual antagonism. More recently, however, Washington lost much leverage in Pakistan as the country's political and military leaders retreated from the war against the Taliban and al Qaeda. Islamabad may rejoin the fight in a vigorous way but if not, the U.S. position in Afghanistan will be in jeopardy. If Pakistan deteriorates into a failed or radicalized state with unsure control of a nuclear arsenal, a dire situation will become catastrophic.

Key Issues and Strategic Adjustments

The natural pressure on political leaders to focus on immediate problems, rather than on a serious grand strategy, is even more extreme for the new president who does not come out of the preceding administration and who lacks any prior experience in the executive branch. This situation makes for an uphill battle to prevent strategy from emerging through drift. It also makes what strategy does exist all the more hostage to the grand

---

[15] On India's belated but impressive economic development, see Arvind Panagariya, *India: The Emerging Giant* (New York: Oxford University Press, 2008), especially chaps. 6, 12–14.

concepts or myths in the minds of the president's advisors. There is a risk of excessive faith in either of the contrasting political myths: that economic globalization will necessarily subordinate military competition or that nothing ever really changes in international relations and that conflict and war must inevitably re-emerge. The first myth risks either vulnerability to predatory powers that reject the liberal logic or the tragedy of a security dilemma in which mutual fears generate conflict that both parties would prefer to avoid. The second myth risks becoming a self-fulfilling prophecy by provoking a spiral of military competition that more relaxed policies might avoid. Of the two, however, the first concept is the shakier basis for security in Asia, although Asian economic development has made many in the foreign policy establishment accept the myth as a matter of faith. The stability that characterizes Asia resembles the stability of real estate on the San Andreas Fault. Asia may not collapse into apocalyptic conflict, just as California may not fall into the sea. Yet something short of such a catastrophe but still very disturbing is likely to occur eventually. Asia has several fault-lines running deeper than those involving great powers on any other continent: cleavages between North and South Korea, China and Taiwan, India and Pakistan, and India and China. The odds that any single one of these fault-lines will not rupture in coming years may be high; the odds that every single one of them will not explode, indefinitely, are lower.

From the first days in office the new administration will inevitably worry most over Iraq, followed closely by Pakistan and Afghanistan. Preventing the Taliban and al Qaeda from re-establishing secure bases is at the top of U.S. foreign policy priorities. These challenges in the region are tied in turn to Iran, where the new president will need to make a basic strategic choice about whether to emphasize coercion or to wait for a Thermidor in the Iranian Revolution that might finally take hold, allowing negotiation and rapprochement. Barring dramatic provocation by Tehran, the new president has the political room for maneuver to revisit the period right after September 11 when Iran cooperated impressively with the United States against the Taliban. Any such initiative would have to be packaged carefully to avoid either encouraging expectations of great results or the appearance of preemptive concession, not least because the risk of negotiation figured in controversies between the candidates during the U.S. election.

This western end of the continent is also tied to Central Asia, a region U.S. national security planners ignored during the Cold War when most of the area was part of the Soviet Union. Since 2001, however, Central Asia has figured more importantly, as a staging area for the U.S. retaliation against the Taliban in Afghanistan and for subsequent operations in the war on terrorism. Former secretary of defense Donald Rumsfeld gave Central Asia new importance in his plan to draw down U.S. forces in the traditional bastion of Europe and sprinkle them around the globe in a new system of small "lily-pad" bases. This shift thrust the United States into collaboration with some odious local regimes. The plan's strategic logic was also dubious, especially if experiences in Iraq and Afghanistan make U.S. leaders more abstemious in the foreign interventions that would be the main rationale for bases in these countries.

U.S. plans to edge back from military involvement in Uzbekistan and neighboring countries should be measured, not precipitous, and considered case by case in light of the effects on the worldwide campaign against al Qaeda and affiliates. If, and only if, retrenchment in Central Asia could be done without opening another base of operations for terrorists or risking international access to the region's energy supplies, five modest strategic benefits might result. In ascending order of importance, retrenchment would marginally reduce the overstretch of U.S. military resources, lessen the number of political relationships that make U.S. human rights policy appear hypocritical to many, mitigate the negative effects of NATO expansion and ease relations with Moscow, give China an avenue for diplomatic and political advance that does not rub up against U.S. power, and leave a front where Moscow and Beijing have no reason to focus on strategic collaboration against the United States and more incentives to compete with each other.[16] Retrenchment would naturally have downsides. For example, direct U.S. influence over governments in Central Asia would decline, and risks that a more muscular Russia could coerce those countries back into Moscow's orbit would increase. Additionally, if aid were cut off entirely, local cooperation in counterterrorism might drop—although the local governments have independent interests in keeping al Qaeda elements out. On balance, however, one timely strategic adjustment for the new administration, if managed carefully, could be to put Central Asia as firmly as possible back where it was before September 11: at the bottom of the radar screen of U.S. national security.

U.S. domestic politics ensures that near-term Asia policy will focus on trade issues. The weakness of the U.S. economy, however, as well as dependence on China to help finance the U.S. national debt, limits the new administration's leverage. In this context, a successful strategy probably cannot be straightforward. The next administration first will need a domestic political strategy that eases the contradiction between the foreign

---

[16] On Russia-China relations and Central Asia, see Michael Clarke, "'Making the Crooked Straight': China's Grand Strategy of 'Peaceful Rise' and Its Central Asian Dimension," *Asian Security* 4, no. 2 (May 2008): 133.

policy elite's uniform devotion to free trade and the demands from the losing segments of the population for protection. The second trick will be to coax Asian countries into more favorable economic arrangements for the United States despite a dwindling kit of applicable carrots and sticks.

To reduce the worrisome dependence on Chinese purchase of U.S. national debt, to make U.S. exports more attractive abroad, or to increase U.S. competiveness with China as investors in the region, Americans would need to make hard choices on taxation, government spending, and private saving. Americans agree in principle on the need to make such choices but not on what the choices should actually be. One obvious tension in goals is between economic interests and the expansive vision of military primacy to which many Americans remain attached. Limiting U.S. military spending to the proportion of GDP allocated by our allies in the region would eliminate the national budget deficit altogether, but this is a choice that no significant political constituency in the United States has been ready to make.

In the medium range—perhaps carrying over into a second term of the administration—traditional security issues are more likely to re-emerge. What is most predictable, however, is that the greatest crisis will occur somewhere we do not currently predict. After all, who would have guessed in 1945 that the six wars the United States would fight in the following 60 years would be in Korea, Vietnam, Yugoslavia, Afghanistan, and Iraq? Or that the United States would teeter on the brink of war with the Soviet Union over events in Cuba and with China over the obscure islands of Quemoy and Matsu? Except for Vietnam and the 2003 invasion of Iraq, practically no one would have predicted any of these wars or crises even shortly before they occurred. If the next acute crisis the United States faces in Asia is in Myanmar, Uzbekistan, the Senkaku/Diaoyutai Islands, or in a place no ordinary American has yet heard of, we should not be surprised—but we will be.

Though a readiness to bounce back from surprise is important, predictable problem areas, such as Kashmir, Korea, or Taiwan, also could erupt. Planning for crises in more predictable areas should be easier. Kashmir and other flashpoints between India and Pakistan are dangerous for the United States—even if not directly involved—because of the potential for nuclear escalation, which would dramatically affect security policies everywhere in the world. Stronger U.S. efforts to aid both contenders technically in securing the safety of their nuclear arsenals would make sense. Although the United States has enjoyed some success in encouraging détente, U.S. diplomatic, political, or military leverage on the long-standing enmity between India and Pakistan is limited. As long as the United States provides aid to Pakistan, Washington should have tangible influence. Such leverage, however, is sure to be used disproportionally to encourage cooperation on counterterrorism rather than to force Pakistani accommodation with India.

Korea is more directly under U.S. influence. The peninsula presents two interlocking problems that are already evident but have not yet ignited. One is North Korea's nuclear program. Diplomatic deals to handle this problem, though elusive and imperfect, are less unsatisfactory than the alternatives. In the worst case, arms control diplomacy will fail permanently, Pyongyang will be unconstrained, and the North Koreans will try to use a small stockpile of weapons to coerce Washington, Tokyo, and Seoul. The least unsatisfactory solution in that case is to rely on deterrence and call Pyongyang's bluff. Preventive war, along the lines of the invasion of Iraq in 2003, is too risky an alternative and could cause exactly what such action is meant to prevent—leaving aside the danger of provoking China or of coping with calamitous results in attempting to occupy, pacify, stabilize, feed, and rehabilitate North Korea. Avoiding the perils of entanglement on the ground by attacking North Korea's known nuclear facilities from the air alone would be no better. There could be no assurance that the stockpile of existing weapons or hidden facilities for building more had been located; thus, destroying known targets would not eliminate the threat. An attack on North Korea's nuclear facilities would provoke Pyongyang to retaliate without preventing it from rebuilding nuclear capacity.[17]

The second Korean problem is the erosion of the U.S.–Republic of Korea (ROK) alliance. The elections that installed more conservative leadership in Seoul appear to have reversed the trend, so this problem might not appear significant when the new U.S. administration begins. The underlying problem, however, could be reactivated whenever tides in South Korean politics shift again. The problem was the wide divergence of U.S. and South Korean policies and public attitudes toward North Korea in the years prior to the most recent election. Seoul's Sunshine Policy, which provided massive aid to North Korea with no reciprocal concessions of consequence, amounted to appeasement in the eyes of many observers in Washington. At the same time, disturbingly high percentages of South Koreans in opinion polls blamed the conflict between the two Koreas more on the U.S. presence than on Pyongyang. Such opinions were concentrated disproportionately in the younger generation, suggesting that the divergence could grow wider over time. By the early part of this decade, it was no longer ridiculous to envision a scenario of conflict between the United States and North Korea

---

[17] For the complete argument about the ineffectiveness of preventive attack, see Richard K. Betts, "The Osirak Fallacy," *National Interest*, no. 83 (Spring 2006): 22–25.

in which a plurality of South Korean opinion might side with Pyongyang rather than Washington—an untenable situation when the only purpose of the U.S.-ROK alliance is for the United States to guard the ROK against North Korea. For the moment, however, the U.S. position seems more secure again. Some Americans believe that the repositioning of military forces outside Seoul may reduce popular resentment of the U.S. presence in the country, but it is unclear just how much such incremental change will matter. As long as Americans have a high profile in South Korea, the risk of political divergence forced by public alienation will remain.

The next U.S. president, if open to a bolder alternative, should consider a revised military strategy designed to achieve the following goals:

- sapping some of the popular South Korean resentment of the U.S. presence in the country

- reducing costs and allowing reallocation of defense resources to other areas such as the Middle East and Southwest Asia, where the war in Iraq has stretched the U.S. Army perilously thin

- preserving ample capacity to defend South Korea in the event of war

The revised strategy would withdraw U.S. ground forces from South Korea while leaving stockpiles of equipment behind to allow rapid reinforcement in a crisis. This would remove a large part of the visible U.S. presence and the particular units most prone to cause public outrage (such as that which occurred when a tank ran over two schoolgirls in 2002). To compensate militarily, U.S. plans would shift to reliance on air power for direct combat involvement in the initial phase of war until ground forces could return to the peninsula.

President Jimmy Carter planned a strategy quite like this one at the beginning of his administration. Such a strategy was a bad idea at the time and thankfully was abandoned. Today, however, more than thirty years later, four considerations make this strategy less risky. First, the danger that a strong U.S. presence in South Korea could be strategically counter-productive is higher now than it was during the Cold War. Second, the substitutability of air power for ground forces was militarily much riskier thirty years ago. The maturation of precision-guided munitions and the experience of the Persian Gulf War in 1991 make clear that air attacks are devastating against any mechanized units on the ground that move. Though it remains difficult for aircraft to destroy enemy armor that is dug in and hidden, the mission is easy when tanks are exposed in attack mode. Third, the Cold War is over. North Korea long ago lost the military aid it received from Moscow and Beijing and the country's huge forces are worrisome but threadbare. Fourth, with the Cold War over, the implications of the potential conquest of South Korea for the worldwide balance of power and U.S. security are less important. There is no longer good reason for Washington to bear the main responsibility for funding and manning the defense of South Korea when the ROK is astronomically richer and more populous than its adversary in the north. South Korea's current level of military effort, in terms of percentage of GDP devoted to military expenditures, is little more than half that of the United States.

If mistakenly characterized as retreat, a new U.S. strategy such as this would alarm Korean conservatives and feed North Korean hubris. The change would have to be done in active collaboration with Seoul and with plenty of rhetoric and actions that bolster the credibility of the explanation that the move is a shift toward strategic efficiency rather than a change of commitment toward military disengagement. The new posture would be analogous to the U.S. military infrastructure in Kuwait in the years between the two wars against Iraq—practical preparation for war without obtrusive presence in peacetime. One element of credible reassurance would be instituting visible practice exercises of reinforcement in which U.S. ground force units fly into the country, break out stored equipment, and move to wartime positions to test and improve the speed with which U.S. power can be brought back in the event of war. The exercises would be similar to NATO's annual REFORGER (Reinforcement of Germany) exercises during the Cold War. If such military practice infuriates Pyongyang, as annual exercises have in the past, all the better for deterrence of the adversary and reassurance of the ally.

The main potential flashpoint for the United States in East Asia is Taiwan. U.S. interest in preventing the island's forcible incorporation with the PRC is an artifact both of history, dating to the outbreak of the Korean War, and of human rights policy, which has been high on most U.S. presidents' agendas for the past three decades. Otherwise, the only strategic interest in defending Taiwan would be if conflict with mainland China were probable for other reasons—a situation U.S. leaders should still want to avoid. In fact, it is precisely the U.S. commitment to Taiwan that would provide the one plausible cause for a U.S.-China war.

Given historic U.S. sponsorship of Taiwan's autonomy, some observers see commitment to the island's defense as a test of general U.S. credibility. Any backtracking would feed perceptions of U.S. decline in Asia—even in countries that will not join Washington to defend the island. Yet this commitment became unclear after the 1972 Shanghai Communiqué and 1978 diplomatic derecognition and was reinvigorated only after 1996. The U.S. president has an interest in not resolving the ambiguity decisively, given that both firm commitment and definite disengagement pose significant costs, but maintaining ambiguity increases risks of miscalculation on either side of the Taiwan Strait.

As with the Grand National Party victory in Korea, the Kuomintang victory in Taiwan's elections eased the risk that the independence movement could provoke a crisis with Beijing. Public opinion and politicians in Taiwan may well prove careful enough to avoid letting preferences for national status override security.[18] Conflict over the island's autonomy still appears to be a longer-term danger if one at all. In this context, focusing on the contingency of a crisis over Taiwan can seem alarmist. It is foolhardy, however, to assume that rapid reversal of circumstances is impossible when control of the situation does not rest with any one country but depends on governments and interest groups in three different capitals: Taipei, Beijing, and Washington. Even though the probability of inadvertent provocation, miscalculation, or escalation of a dispute is low, the gravity of the consequences makes the contingency a high priority. This is the only plausible contingency, apart from Korea, that poses the risk of war with a nuclear-armed power. China's growing capacity to raise the military costs of U.S. intervention increases the risk of escalation from a conventional engagement. China scholar Avery Goldstein concludes that "the Taiwan case offers the strongest evidence confirming the pessimistic predictions of power transition theory."[19]

The instinct of a harried new administration likely will be to leave the Taiwan question on the back burner. There will be no incentive to focus attention on the problem as long as nothing happens. The path of least resistance is to hope that the issue will remain quiescent until economic ties, rising stakes in cooperation, political softening in Beijing, and skillful diplomacy eventually converge to engineer a peaceful *modus vivendi*. This scenario is favored by the optimistic institutional model of coping with China's rise. Optimists, however, leave quite vague exactly how China and Taiwan would agree to unite and implicitly plan as though the current situation of de facto independence for the island can endure indefinitely. The pessimistic power politics model, in contrast, expects Beijing's patience with the status quo to diminish with time, eventually forcing either capitulation by Taipei or military confrontation to make the island conform de facto to its *de jure* status.

---

[18] Brett V. Benson and Emerson M.S. Niou, "Public Opinion, Foreign Policy, and the Security Balance in the Taiwan Strait," *Security Studies* 14, no. 2 (April–June 2005): 274–89.

[19] Avery Goldstein, "Power Transitions, Institutions, and China's Rise in East Asia: Theoretical Expectations and Evidence," *Journal of Strategic Studies* 30, nos. 4–5 (August–October 2007): 675.

The Long Range—Perhaps Sooner Than We Think

It would be heroic for a U.S. president to concentrate attention on long-term prospects in foreign policy before outside pressure forces choice. Although Richard Nixon initiated a bold grand strategy of détente with Moscow and Beijing, he did so under the pressure of rising Soviet military power, frustration with the long war in Vietnam, and the American public's loss of faith in military activism. The experience in Iraq may ultimately have a similar effect. Nothing comparable to the Vietnam War, however, yet provides an incentive to fix an Asian policy that so far does not seem broken.

In Pakistan or North Korea, where the danger that threats may erupt at any time is recognized, no good options for guarding against such risks other than those already being pursued appear evident or within U.S. control. In regard to both Islamabad and Pyongyang, Washington is all too painfully aware of the limits of U.S. leverage, the emptiness of strategies that rely on persuasion without inducement, and the risks of counter-productive effects from military confrontation. In regard to India, where more attention to the strategic relationship seems warranted, the potential benefits are high but the cost of inattention still remains low. The United States has a natural interest in allying with a rising great power, especially one with even more reason to worry over China. India's wariness of alliance as well as U.S. support for Pakistan limit the intensity of cooperation for now. Moreover, unconditional U.S. support could implicate the United States in Indian initiatives that could raise the risk of war with Pakistan.[20] By the same token, given India's growing strength and traditional resistance to subordinate relations with outside powers, the United States can do little to prevent New Delhi from going its own way on regional matters. The logical course is to continue cultivating U.S.-Indian strategic cooperation while not expecting consistent coordination.

In regard to Japan, the vital importance of bilateral security agreements is clear. The main issue is whether Tokyo should continue to keep a military profile, oriented toward direct defense of the home islands, that is lower than normal for a great economic power or become a full, conventional U.S. military partner that is expected to operate jointly in the event of war. On this issue, a focus on the long-term yields the same answer as maintaining the status quo.

The ideal would be to encourage Japan to expand its purely defensive military capacity but avoid developing capabilities and doctrines

---

[20] Walter C. Ladwig III, "A Cold Start for Hot Wars? The Indian Army's New Limited War Doctrine," *International Security* 32, no. 3 (Winter 2007/08).

that could be interpreted as offensive. This ideal, however, cannot be attained. In practice, creating truly modern military capabilities with no offensive potential—either in inherent operational capability or in the eyes of suspicious opponents—is next to impossible. Constraints on the development of Japanese military power are anachronistic by normal standards, but it is not in the diplomatic or strategic interest of the United States for China and the two Koreas to believe that Japan is becoming a normal great power. A Japanese military build-up would be likely to trigger a classic security dilemma in the region. The best compromise would be to avoid a visible ratcheting up of Japan's naval collaboration and to channel growing military energies toward more vigorous participation in multilateral peacekeeping operations. Encouraging a division of labor in which U.S. forces are expected to do the heavy lifting while allies focus on peacekeeping and humanitarian intervention is an idea some have promoted in regard to NATO as well.[21]

In regard to China, there is tension between what makes sense as long as relations are not under great stress and what adjustments are implied by a future world in which China is a superpower. Will there be a "hegemonic transition" in Asia's future in the form theorized by Robert Gilpin, with a clash between a rising China and a United States unwilling to cede leadership?[22] It would be unusual for a U.S. administration to face this question before being compelled by events to do so. Nevertheless, prodding movement in the right direction is worth some effort. Optimists rest too easily on deductive logic and intuitive economic determinism rather than on historical cases that suggest a peaceful hegemonic transition would be unusual. Both conservatives and liberals, moreover, have too much confidence that the benign intent of the United States is obvious to others. Leaders in both U.S. political parties share a conviction that the country has the right and responsibility to deploy military power abroad to keep peace and good order—a prerogative they would never concede to China. Most political leaders have a tin ear for Chinese resentment of double standards. For example, Secretary of Defense Rumsfeld asked what innocent explanation there could be for China's rapid increases in military spending and weapon procurement, despite the fact that the level of Chinese armament is far below that of the United States.

Figuring out a way to engineer the politico-military aspects of peaceful transition reduces the odds of unanticipated conflict and raises the likelihood that Washington as much as Beijing can drive the process.

---

[21] John Hillen, "Superpowers Don't Do Windows," *Orbis* 41, no. 2 (Spring 1997): 241–58.

[22] Robert Gilpin, *War and Change in World Politics* (New York: Cambridge University Press, 1981), chap. 5.

As a practical matter, moving forward depends on a synthesis of the two basic models, optimistic and pessimistic—a synthesis that also focuses on the one contradiction underlying the current policy trend: the difference between China's generally accommodating strategic behavior, which Washington has taken for granted since Nixon's rapprochement, and the behavior to expect in the future when Beijing has less to lose from insisting on its preferences. The optimistic institutional model assumes that China's preferences will be the same as those of the West. This assumption relies, however, on the economic determinism behind the myth: the faith that political disputes will be subordinated to economic interest.

Policy seldom conforms faithfully to any one theory, and it is possible to combine the most compelling parts of the institutional and power politics visions. As Thomas Christensen has pointed out, for example, aspects of U.S. policy that Beijing perceived as attempts at containment prompted Chinese leaders to undertake conciliatory multilateral diplomacy toward India and other countries to preempt development of an anti-PRC coalition.[23] As time passes, the condition for combining both approaches satisfactorily may be U.S. willingness to give up the prerogatives of primacy that Washington has come to take for granted (as reflected notably in Rumsfeld's double standard for how much military power China and the United States could legitimately require). It is difficult to imagine a conscious decision to renounce U.S. primacy in the region that would not provoke a negative domestic reaction. If Washington decides to stop claiming the lead role, the risk would grow that China would not settle for amicable multipolarity but would strive for outright hegemony. Successfully combining the imperatives of the institutional and power politics models would depend on an uncharacteristic divestment of status by the United States as well as exceptional Chinese restraint.

Managing this dilemma will require more statesmanship on all sides than has been commonly found in international politics since Bismarck. That the preservation of peace in Asia might require giving up primacy is a price not recognized or admitted by many in the U.S. foreign policy establishment. If China's rise does not falter, however, there is no reason to expect that Beijing will continue to defer to Washington's leadership or preferences for regional political arrangements—especially regarding Taiwan, where Washington cannot count on military support from any of its allies.

Most other countries and many U.S. observers as well reject the notion that the United States should "contain" China. Yet what does containment

---

[23] Thomas J. Christensen, "Fostering Stability or Creating a Monster? The Rise of China and U.S. Policy toward East Asia," *International Security* 31, no. 1 (Summer 2006): 116–17, 121–22.

mean other than preventing expansion? Containment does not mean roll back. If defending Taiwan is not containment, what is? The question of whether and how far Beijing should be expected to extend political and military influence without challenge remains unresolved. For liberals wedded to the institutional model, this question is not relevant, because traditional power relationships do not matter in a positive-sum world where exchange rather than exploitation is the rule. According to this model, institutions channel governments' aims and interests, and military coercion becomes unnecessary and outmoded. Yet what empirical grounds are there for believing that a superpower China will not emulate the United States' approach to this institutional order? That is, why should Beijing not assume that its own preferences for proper order should be universal and that smaller nations on China's periphery should conform to its notions of proper behavior? In short, why should we expect the PRC to act with more political restraint in Asia than Washington traditionally has in the Western Hemisphere? If China decides to stabilize its border areas by intervening—as the United States often has in Latin America—U.S. foreign policy managers will see such behavior not as emulation but as aggression. Although the new U.S. president need not accept China's rights in international politics as equal to those of the United States, the next administration would do well to understand why leaders in Beijing could decide to act on that principle.

The most recent purveyor of the institutional solution, John Ikenberry, does not deny that there will be a major power transition; indeed, he assumes that China will surpass the United States. Yet Ikenberry believes this change need not matter. The argument rests on the notion that the Western institutional system in which China is to be enmeshed is not dominated by one country and therefore does not challenge Chinese national interests. Thus, integration in this system can make the power transition between Beijing and Washington benign.[24] Ikenberry, however, does not discuss how disputes over territory, sovereignty, and rebellion will be handled by the Western institutional system, which is primarily a set of economic arrangements. Above all, there is one word that does not appear in Ikenberry's article on coping with the rise of Chinese power, a word whose absence is thunderous: Taiwan.

China can complete its rise without tangling militarily with the United States if Washington does not challenge China's core national security interests. Intervening in the final resolution of China's civil war by defending Taiwan, however, would constitute just such a challenge. U.S. leaders downplay the importance of Taiwan to the PRC because

---

[24] Ikenberry, "The Rise of China," 30.

Beijing has regularly subordinated reunification to other interests. Yet Beijing has made quite clear that reunification is merely a question of when, not whether.

The new U.S. administration will have a choice over which way to tilt plans and rhetoric on this subject. For many years after the normalization of relations with Beijing, Washington maintained a stance of strategic ambiguity, keeping U.S. commitment to military protection of Taiwan unclear. After 1996 this ambiguity decreased, most evidently in President Bush's statement that the United States would do "whatever it takes" to defend the island.[25] In the interest of longer-term flexibility on how to handle a superpower China, there would be some benefit in re-establishing ambiguity (assuming that explicit repudiation of any defense commitment is not an option).

The danger in ambiguity, however, is that in particular circumstances Beijing might think it could get away with an attack, whereas Washington would decide to fight when the actual attack shocked the president. The United States has a record of innocently misleading other countries about whether it would counter their actions militarily. In 1950, for example, Secretary of State Dean Acheson's speech at the National Press Club excluded Korea from the U.S. defense perimeter in the Pacific; when North Korea invaded the South six months later, however, President Truman went to war. In 1990 Ambassador April Glaspie gave Saddam Hussein a green light to invade Kuwait when she conveyed Washington's view that the United States did not have a stake in the dispute, then when the invasion occurred President Bush reconsidered and went to war. Were a similar situation to occur over Taiwan, the risks would be higher than in the previous cases because China possesses nuclear weapons.

Though flexibility has advantages, the danger mentioned above recommends more clarity regarding the extent and limits of the U.S. commitment to defending Taiwan. In practical terms U.S. policy in recent years has been to defend Taiwan as long as it is a rebellious province but not if it becomes an independent country. Reinforcing dual deterrence, against moves toward independence by Taiwan and against military action by the mainland, makes good strategic sense to foreign policy elites. If such a policy becomes a subject for broad public discussion, however, it is likely to strike normal Americans as bizarre. This policy is not likely to penetrate public consciousness unless a crisis brings it to the fore. Thus, public support for such a policy might falter just when needed most. Unless the president is willing to declare that the United States will not defend

---

[25] Bush made this statement in an interview with ABC News in 2001. See Tony Karon, "Why Bush Comments Set Off a Diplomatic Scramble," *Time*, April 25, 2001.

Taiwan—a reasonable position in terms of realpolitik, but political suicide in the U.S. domestic arena—the risk in maintaining a policy that seems to defy common sense is worth taking. Backing down from war with the PRC would be damaging to U.S. credibility and honor but preferable to stepping into combat in a situation where one side or the other would find escalation to be the price of avoiding defeat. In a game of chicken with China, the stakes are more important to Beijing than to Washington. There is no reason for confidence that the PRC would back down to avoid collision before the United States does, and thus no reason for confidence that a U.S.-China war in the Taiwan Strait would remain conventional.

There is no low-cost solution to the Taiwan problem for the United States. To avoid the opposing risks of abandoning Taiwan or blundering into a nuclear war, the next president might consider a variant of a strategy that is a compromise but clearer than what has existed so far. First, such a policy would declare that the United States opposes forcible reunification under present circumstances but would have no stake in the conflict if the PRC becomes a genuine democracy. Although such a declaration is not likely to affect political developments in China, it would be as much of an incentive to democratize as anything else Washington can do. Second, the policy would make clear that if the current regime in Beijing attacks or, more likely, blockades Taiwan, the United States would not initiate combat operations against PRC forces. Instead, the United States would provide accelerated yet limited military and other support to Taiwan. Such support could include new weapons transfers, resupply of arms and ammunition, and tactical intelligence. U.S. ships could also deliver as much food and other needed civilian goods as possible. Third, the policy would establish that the U.S. Navy would not fire the first shot against Chinese forces but would respond if PRC submarines attack U.S. ships running the blockade. This policy would not protect other countries' ships from PRC submarines, and thus would not relieve the economic duress on Taiwan. The policy would, however, avoid the United States beginning a shooting war between two major nuclear powers.[26] By establishing that the United States would help Taiwan resist the PRC but would not fire the first shots, this policy would highlight that Beijing would have the last clear chance to avoid war with the United States. Although reducing flexibility and ambiguity in such a manner is dangerous because it boxes Washington in, this approach may be the only way to minimize the danger of miscalculation and unanticipated escalation in a crisis. A move of this sort should not be an immediate priority

[26] See Michael C. Grubb, "Merchant Shipping in a Chinese Blockade of Taiwan," *Naval War College Review* 60, no. 1 (Winter 2007): 81–102.

for the U.S. president facing a plateful of other problems; such a move could become more attractive, however, if Sino-U.S. relations deteriorate.

Such potential adjustments in strategy would not decisively solve the dilemma between abandoning or risking war over Taiwan. The alternatives, however, seem no better: retaining the current degree of ambiguity about U.S. defense of Taiwan abets miscalculation; avoiding the risk of war with China by abandoning any commitment to defend Taiwan is not realistic given U.S. domestic politics; and precipitating a breakdown in relations with Beijing by giving Taiwan an unlimited defense guarantee would encourage Taipei to seize the opportunity for formal independence. Either of the latter two alternatives could become more possible if conditions change. Abandoning Taiwan could occur as a passive result of peaceful reunification if economic integration, social exchange, and shared material interests continue to grow and Taiwan succumbs to the PRC without a fight. Deciding to fight for Taiwan regardless of circumstances could come to be seen as logical if China as a full-grown superpower is overcome by hypernationalism and threatens aggression in the way that German, Japanese, and Soviet power did in the twentieth century. Neither of these alternatives is as likely as the current course, however, on which China will have no designs to conquer other countries—beyond re-establishing control of Taiwan—but will demand a leadership role as great or greater than that of the United States.

Conclusions

The new administration has every reason to promote the institutional model of improving regional order in Asia, even if the new president believes in the power politics model. The institutional approach will help in the economic dimension even though offering little in the military dimension. Washington can exploit the institutional approach for security matters in cases where it can get most countries to accept U.S. infringement of traditional sovereign prerogatives. For example, the Proliferation Security Initiative (PSI) asserts the right to interdict aircraft and ships suspected of transporting WMD.[27] The six-party talks on Korea and even the long-forgotten UN Command in Seoul can also be used to multilateralize and legitimize the security interests of the United States and its allies. Like NATO, such arrangements can use institutions for purposes of power politics. The only mistake would be in assuming that the institutional model is sufficient

---

[27] On the tension between the Proliferation Security Initiative and the international law of the sea, see Mark J. Valencia, *The Proliferation Security Initiative: Making Waves in Asia,* Adelphi Paper 376 (London: Routledge, 2005), 43–44.

as a comprehensive approach that subsumes security arrangements rather than assisting such arrangements at the margins.

The power politics model provides less consistent guidance. The main question this approach poses in theory is whether the United States should or can either organize its commitments and efforts to retain unprecedented primacy or work to manage a peaceful transition to multipolarity. In practice, it would be difficult for any president to get away with the second option forthrightly. Iraq deflates the most ambitious visions of primacy—the notion that dominant power should be used to overthrow bad governments and force countries to conform to U.S. notions of good order—but keeping the United States number one is popular across the political spectrum, from conservative hawks to Wilsonian liberals.

A shrewd president will promote primacy in rhetoric and prudence in action. How then to reverse the growth of Asian perceptions that the U.S. position in Asia is in decline?[28] The main line of advance on this problem lies at home in the changes in economic policy and performance needed to re-establish U.S. leadership in the region's international economic developments. The obstacles to decisive improvement in that respect are significant. Moreover, if China continues on the course traversed over the past few decades, the country will continue to make strides in regional diplomacy irrespective of whether the United States shapes up. Subjective effects aside, ascendancy and decline are matters of relative wealth and power. The threat of Japanese ascendancy perceived by so many in the 1980s evaporated; this could happen to China if its development derails. As long as the Chinese economy grows at close to twice the rate of the U.S. economy, however, and China continues to save and export at far greater rates, the PRC will be ascendant. By definition the United States will by some measure decline relatively, even if remaining superior for a long time. Unless these trends change, they will not cause dramatic shocks anytime soon but will over time whittle U.S. primacy away.

In the short term, the new president will find the safest choices on security policy in Asia to be keeping on the present course:

- stay ambiguous and flexible on defense of Taiwan

- press for a diplomatic deal with North Korea to account for and surrender nuclear weapons and materials with as many verification measures as possible

---

[28] For a hard-hitting argument that China is already surpassing the United States in influence in Asia, see Kishore Mahbubani, *The New Asian Hemisphere: The Irresistible Shift of Global Power to the East* (New York: PublicAffairs, 2008).

- modify the U.S. position in Korea via geographic relocation of U.S. forces but otherwise maintain the stance of the past 50 years
- affirm the traditional commitment to Japan but avoid twisting Tokyo's arm to contribute more militarily
- develop the strategic relationship with India as far as feasible
- prod Pakistan to help suppress al Qaeda and the Taliban
- keep up cooperative arrangements with friendly Southeast Asian countries and most especially Australia

To shape the future of the security equation in Asia in the right direction the U.S. president does not need to change everything. Many of the recent and traditional policies discussed are the optimal ones for as long as such policies can be sustained. To avoid decline by erosion and reactive policy, however, and to adjust efficiently to continuing and potential changes in power, influence, and politics within the countries of the region, the president may need to take some risks. For example, the administration might consider the sharper adjustments on Korea and Taiwan discussed above. Otherwise, the only way for the United States to sustain the unprecedented primacy enjoyed since the end of the Cold War will be to bank on either of two possible but unlikely developments: the collapse of China's economic success or an indefinite surge both in U.S. economic performance and in public tolerance for costly international exertion.

EXECUTIVE SUMMARY

This chapter evaluates the impact of China's rise on key areas of U.S. concern over the last eight years and suggests future policy options for the next administration.

MAIN ARGUMENT:
Though the U.S. and China have been cooperating to improve economic relations, combat terrorism, counter nuclear proliferation, and mitigate nontraditional security threats, the two states are also strongly involved in efforts to hedge against one another in ways that could lead to regional instability. Washington's ability to protect key areas of concern will require fashioning sophisticated policy approaches to Beijing that both enhance mutual incentives for positive-sum outcomes and avoid political manipulation by domestic groups in both countries.

POLICY IMPLICATIONS:
- The U.S. can neither afford nor will likely gain from a policy of sharp confrontation, public criticism, and high pressure designed to "compel" Beijing to cooperate more or to capitulate on issues.

- The U.S. would benefit from maintaining a steady focus on dialogue and negotiation with China, accompanied by persistent efforts to deter, dissuade, reassure, and enmesh.

- Also of benefit would be if the U.S. clarified its preferential type of security architecture in the Asia-Pacific and worked with China and other Asian powers to build such an architecture.

- Gaining support from domestic constituencies in the U.S. for a more constructive relationship with China would be more likely if the next administration were to explain more fully why such a relationship is in the interest of the U.S.

Managing China as a Strategic Challenge

Michael D. Swaine

During the past several decades, and particularly during the tenure of the George W. Bush administration, the dynamic economic growth, expanding capabilities, and deepening involvement of China (also known as the People's Republic of China, PRC) in a wide range of regional and global policy arenas have presented significant challenges and opportunities for Washington regarding many issues of critical national interest.

From a strategic perspective, China's growing presence and influence is particularly significant in three key areas. First and foremost, Beijing's rapidly expanding military, economic, and political presence in the western Pacific is altering the distribution of power in ways that could produce destabilizing security competition between China and other major powers nearby and aggravate sensitive regional hot spots such as Taiwan. More generally, China's presence could challenge the ability of the United States to continue playing its long-standing role as the dominant maritime security actor in the region. At the same time, the accelerating regional trend toward more extensive levels of multilateral security and economic relations presents opportunities for greater strategic cooperation among the major powers, with Beijing potentially playing an expanding role. Second, China's growing impact on bilateral and multilateral patterns of trade, technology, investment, and energy flows and supplies presents major implications, both positive and negative, not only for future economic stability and prosperity in Asia and beyond but also for the domestic U.S. economy.

Michael D. Swaine is Senior Associate with the China Program at the Carnegie Endowment for International Peace. He can be reached at <mswaine@carnegieendowment.org>.

The author would like to thank Stephanie Renzi, program manager at The National Bureau of Asian Research, and Wayne Chen, former junior fellow at the Carnegie Endowment for International Peace, for their contributions and assistance in the preparation of this chapter.

Such factors pose obvious security consequences for the United States and its allies. Third, China's overall willingness and ability to cooperate with the United States and other developed powers on WMD proliferation and nontraditional security threats, such as pandemics and environmental degradation, can vitally affect the evolution of international regimes in these two critical security-related areas.

In all three policy arenas China could become either an obstacle or an asset to the attainment of U.S. objectives and the protection of U.S. strategic interests, especially in Asia.[1] China's growing capabilities and influence serve not only to raise the stakes involved in Washington's strategic relations with Beijing and other powers but also to deepen and expand the types of interaction required to cope with and benefit from China's emergence.

In order to manage this highly dynamic strategic situation effectively, it may no longer be possible for Washington to focus primarily on intensifying engagement efforts with Beijing while also hedging against adverse developments by strengthening or expanding key long-standing alliances, deploying more military forces into the western Pacific, or enhancing key bilateral political relationships. Instead, U.S. policy toward China must proceed from a broader strategic approach toward Asia as a whole that reflects a deeper appreciation of larger regional trends involving both competition and cooperation, as well as a keener understanding of Chinese and U.S. objectives, the recent policy track record of Beijing and Washington, and the likely strengths and limitations of U.S. power and influence in the next decade.

This chapter addresses these factors as part of an overall assessment of U.S. strategic policy toward China. The first section identifies the fundamental interests and policy objectives of the United States and China that are of greatest relevance to the three strategic arenas outlined above. The second section describes and analyzes the evolution of Chinese policies and actions—as well as U.S. responses and initiatives—in each of these three areas during the Bush administration. The final section outlines the implications facing the United States that derive from the preceding analysis and provides a set of policy options for the next administration.

---

[1] This is less true for other issues of concern in U.S. relations with China such as human rights.

U.S. and Chinese Strategic Interests and Policy Objectives: Sources of Cooperation and Competition

The United States

The Asia-Pacific region is of vital importance to the United States, given the region's proximity to the U.S. homeland, economic dynamism, political diversity, geostrategic relationship to other vital regions, and inclusion of or shared borders with several major powers. Throughout the post–World War II era, the most critical U.S. security objective in the Asia-Pacific region has been the maintenance of predominant political and military influence across the vast reaches of maritime East Asia.[2] The United States has pursued this objective by maintaining the ability to project superior naval, air, and land power into or near any areas within this region. Washington has also sought to sustain close political and diplomatic relations as well as to establish explicit bilateral security alliances with key states, including Japan, South Korea, Australia, Thailand, and the Philippines.

The United States has viewed such a stance as essential in order to protect five key interests:

- preventing the emergence of a hostile power in the Asia-Pacific region that could limit or exclude U.S. access to the region

- preventing the emergence or intensification of regional disputes or rivalries that could disrupt overall peace and economic development

- ensuring freedom of commerce, market access, and strategic lines of communication throughout the region

- defending and encouraging democratic states and processes and discouraging the expansion of non-democratic movements or regimes hostile to the United States

- preventing the proliferation of dangerous weapons, technologies, and know-how across littoral Asia and coping with nontraditional security threats, in particular global and regional terrorism, pandemics, and environmental degradation

In addition, and closely related to such security objectives, U.S. policy in Asia also seeks to advance and protect global and regional norms and institutions via close political, diplomatic, economic, and social interactions

---

[2] This region stretches from the Aleutian and Hawaiian Islands to the Indian Ocean and includes many key strategic locations near the coast of the Eurasian land mass such as South Korea, Japan, Taiwan, the Philippines, Indonesia, Thailand, and Malaysia, as well as Australia and New Zealand in the South Pacific.

with a wide range of actors. The implications of these objectives for U.S. policy toward China in the three strategic arenas outlined in the introduction are quite clear.

Security. Regarding the Asian security environment, the United States has pursued a number of goals. First, Washington has sought to prevent the emergence of a full-blown strategic rivalry with Beijing centered on bilateral (or larger regional) arms races and a zero-sum approach to political and security relationships across the Asia-Pacific. Second, the United States has aimed to deter China's use of force against Taiwan while maximizing the conditions for a peaceful resolution of the Beijing-Taipei stand-off. Third, Washington has encouraged Chinese cooperation in preventing conflict on the Korean Peninsula, eliminating North Korea's nuclear weapons capability, and advancing the ultimate objective of peaceful reunification. Fourth, the United States has encouraged the peaceful resolution of outstanding territorial and resource disputes between China and other nearby states, especially Japan, India, and several countries belonging to the Association of Southeast Asian Nations (ASEAN). Fifth, the United States has at the same time tried to strengthen the U.S.-Japan alliance and advance Tokyo's willingness and ability to play a larger security role in Asia—in part to reduce the chances of a Sino-Japanese rivalry and also to counterbalance China's growing regional power. Sixth, with rising powers, such as India, the United States has sought to develop closer political, economic, and military relations, partly to increase strategic leverage against China. Washington has also tried to reassure smaller Asian nations that China's rise will not result in either a diminished U.S. presence in Asia or a new Cold War. Finally, the United States has encouraged the development of multilateral security-related forums and institutions that strengthen regional security cooperation without undermining U.S. bilateral security alliances or influence.

Economics. In the economic realm the United States has focused on achieving three key, interrelated objectives. First, on the broadest level, Washington has encouraged Beijing to contribute more actively and directly to the maintenance and evolution of the global economic order through the efficient operation of capitalist market systems and global free trade, especially in vital strategic commodities such as energy and natural resources. Second, the United States has tried to maximize the benefits, while minimizing the damage, that economic intercourse with China can produce for U.S. employment and corporate profits as well as for the overall health and safety of the U.S. consumer. Third, the United States has sought to contribute to the stability, openness, and productivity of the Chinese economy, especially as these factors relate to domestic social order and the broader impact of China on Asia and on U.S. allies.

Security-related international regimes. Regarding WMD counterproliferation, U.S. policies toward China have centered primarily on efforts to enhance China's nuclear safeguards and export controls. Additionally, the United States has sought to compel China's support for economic sanctions and other initiatives deemed necessary to curb Iran's alleged ambition to acquire nuclear weapons. The primary U.S. objectives in combating nontraditional security threats include the full integration of China into international regimes that address these issues and the expansion of bilateral and multilateral mechanisms for dialogue and information-sharing.[3]

Washington has potentially conflicting interests in each of these three arenas. On the one hand, the United States has a strong interest in vesting Beijing in the maintenance and protection of the regional and global order. On the other hand, however, the United States is served by deterring Beijing from engaging in actions or acquiring the level and type of power that could undermine stability and prosperity or directly threaten vital U.S. capabilities, particularly in Asia.

China

There is a significant level of congruence, or at the very least overlap, between U.S. and Chinese strategic interests and objectives. On the most fundamental level China's national objectives focus on the need to maintain and promote stability and prosperity in Asia in order to sustain high levels of undistracted domestic economic growth. Such growth is viewed as essential to meet China's three main goals. These goals are ensuring domestic order and development, which are critical to the preservation of the power and legitimacy of the Communist Party; defending China against foreign threats to both territory and sovereignty; and attaining high levels of international power and prestige.[4]

To achieve these goals, Beijing is pursuing a national strategy centered on four elements, all of which are largely compatible with U.S. interests. First, Beijing has adopted a highly pragmatic, market-led economic development program—albeit with significant administrative controls in certain areas. Second, China is pursuing an overall foreign policy of "peace and development." This policy is marked by the search for win-win outcomes,

---

[3] Banning Garrett, "U.S.-China Relations in the Era of Globalization and Terror: A Framework for Analysis," *Journal of Contemporary China* 15, no. 48 (August 2006): 389–415.

[4] Fei-Ling Wang states these goals as a "three-P incentive structure": the political preservation of the CCP (Chinese Communist Party) regime, China's economic prosperity, and Beijing's pursuit of power and prestige. See Fei-Ling Wang, "Preservation, Prosperity and Power: What Motivates China's Foreign Policy?" *Journal of Contemporary China* 14, no. 45 (November 2005): 669–94.

the maintenance of amicable political and security relations with virtually all nations, and the deepening of those types of interstate relationships that are most conducive to economic development. Third, Beijing is expanding its level of involvement in and support for international and multilateral regimes, institutions, forums, and dialogues in a wide variety of issue areas. Finally, China has exercised a general restraint in the use of force—whether toward the country's periphery or against other more distant powers. At the same time, China has increasingly worked to deter threats and increase Beijing's overall international influence by modernizing and streamlining the Chinese military.[5]

China's strategy relies enormously on the maintenance of stable—if not affable—relations with the United States. Hence, Beijing seeks to sustain cooperation with Washington and manage problems via dialogue and negotiation to the greatest extent possible. At the same time, Beijing remains highly suspicious of U.S. intentions and actions toward growing Chinese power and influence in many areas. As a result, China's leaders seek to deter, dissuade, or prevent certain shifts in U.S. policy toward China, which include an unambiguous position of opposition to or containment of China, strong sanctions or prohibitions on Chinese trade and investment policies, and constraints on China's global energy and trade policies. Chinese leaders further seek to prevent the United States from providing greater support for Taiwanese independence, undertaking destabilizing military and diplomatic actions on the Korean Peninsula, increasing greatly or making permanent the U.S. military presence in maritime Asia and South Asia, and intervening politically (and perhaps militarily) in disputes between China and other Asian powers, such as India and Japan.

In order to minimize the likelihood of such outcomes, Beijing has adopted two strategies: first, to reduce U.S. and international concerns over China's growing power and reach and, second, to hedge against the ability or willingness of the United States and other nations to create policies designed to frustrate the expansion of China's capabilities and influence.[6] The latter strategy includes the acquisition of military capabilities that would give China the ability to project power beyond its current territorial borders.

Overall, Beijing's strategic interests and objectives thus contain both cooperative and potentially conflicting strands. This basic tension in Beijing's strategy, evident in interactions with Washington over the past

---

[5] Avery Goldstein, *Rising to the Challenge: China's Grand Strategy and International Security* (Palo Alto: Stanford University Press, 2005), 17, 24; Wang Jisi, "Guanyu gouzhu Zhongguo guoji zhanlue de jidian kanfa" [Some Thoughts on Building a Chinese International Strategy], *Guoji Zhengzhi Yanjiu* (November 25, 2007): 1–5; and Evan S. Medeiros, "China's International Behavior: Activism, Opportunism, and Diversification," *Joint Forces Quarterly* 47 (4th Quarter 2007): 34–41.

[6] Goldstein, *Rising to the Challenge*, 29–30, 102–3.

eight years, stands at the center of the challenges and opportunities that China's rise presents to U.S. security policy.

Challenge and Response: Chinese and U.S. Policies during the Bush Administration

During the past eight years China has played an increasingly important and complex role in each of the three strategic arenas outlined above—China has been a U.S. collaborator, competitor, potential threat, facilitator, and source of continued U.S. growth. Reflecting this complexity, U.S. policies in each arena have sought to shape, encourage, support, deter, and in some cases oppose Chinese thought and actions, with varying levels of success. Moreover, during this period exogenous events have also emerged to shape, sometimes decisively, the evolution of the bilateral relationship and hence the direction and tenor of U.S. policies.[7]

Security in the Western Pacific: China's Emergence as a Strategic Player

The central strategic challenge presented by China during the past decade involves actions related to defense and foreign policy in the western Pacific and Central Asia. In particular, China's impact on the East Asian security environment since at least 2000 has resulted largely from the country's activities in four broad areas: (1) force modernization, including exercises and deployments, and military-to-military contacts; (2) policies toward Taiwan and North Korea; (3) economic and security relations with India, the ASEAN states, Japan, and Russia; and (4) China's involvement in multilateral security-related forums and institutions, including the Shanghai Cooperation Organization (SCO) in Central Asia.

Force modernization. Beijing's military modernization program is oriented largely toward strengthening China's capacity to augment its diplomatic and political leverage abroad and to protect expanding foreign economic assets and interests. At the same time, Beijing has sought to reduce the country's vulnerability to threats by other nations. Under this strategy the pace and scope of China's military modernization were originally intended to be gradual, incremental, and focused primarily on overcoming the general obsolescence of the People's Liberation Army (PLA). This approach reflected the Chinese leadership's view that a major war was

---

[7] Such events include the rise of India, North Korea's attempts to acquire nuclear weapons, and the emergence of pro-independence forces in Taiwan.

unlikely and that Chinese development required a primary emphasis on civilian over military growth.

During the past decade, however, the tempo of China's force modernization program has increased significantly and the program's focus has sharpened. Driving the modernization of the Chinese military are concerns over increasing U.S. military capabilities and growing tensions over the Taiwan issue. As a result, China has intensified efforts to acquire the military resources to deter and prevent Taiwanese attempts to attain *de jure* independence as well as U.S. efforts to assist Taiwan militarily in the event of a conflict. Such undertakings have included recent actions demonstrating the PLA's capacity to interdict U.S. satellite communications and to place submarines and surface warships in close proximity to U.S. aircraft carriers. Most recently, China's force modernization effort has also begun to place a greater emphasis on acquiring more ambitious power projection capabilities beyond Taiwan, apparently for the purpose of conducting area denial and extended presence missions along the littoral of the western Pacific. These acquisitions support China's larger efforts to deter potential aggressive actions, boost the country's image as a great power, and enhance its overall regional influence. In the strategic realm, Beijing has been steadily improving the survivability and potency of its small, retaliatory "counter-value" deterrent nuclear force by developing medium-, intermediate-, and intercontinental-range ballistic missiles that are more reliable, accurate, and mobile. Some of the latter are to be deployed on a new class of nuclear ballistic missile submarines.[8]

These improving PLA capabilities bear directly on the ability of the United States to maintain a strong deterrent capability in the Taiwan Strait and to preserve the country's position as the predominant maritime power in the western Pacific. China has already acquired advanced air, naval, missile, and electronic capabilities that begin to call into question the ability of U.S. Pacific forces to accurately detect, rapidly deploy against, and successfully interdict PLA forces in a fast-moving Taiwan crisis. Beijing is also steadily enhancing its ability to routinely deploy significant naval forces beyond China's immediate periphery. This trend has prompted some debate within U.S. defense circles over whether and to what degree China might be preparing to undertake a variety of future missions—for instance, maritime area control or sealines of communication (SLOC) defense and interdiction—that might alarm U.S. allies, such as Japan, and weaken

---

[8] See Michael D. Swaine, "China's Regional Military Posture," in *Power Shift: China and Asia's New Dynamics,* ed. David Shambaugh (Berkeley: University of California Press, 2005); and David Shambaugh, *Modernizing China's Military: Progress, Problems, and Prospects* (Berkeley: University of California Press, 2002).

regional perceptions of the United States as an unchallengeable security broker in the region.[9]

Taiwan and North Korea. Beyond such military advances, China's political, socio-economic, and diplomatic activities toward Taiwan and North Korea during the past eight years have also influenced the regional security environment in very significant ways. Beijing's stance toward Taiwan has evolved enormously during this period. This change in attitude has been marked by a number of Chinese actions, including the acquisition of increasingly potent instruments to deter independence, ever-greater levels of social contact and economic integration between Taiwan and mainland China, the establishment of constructive political contacts between Beijing and anti-independence elements on Taiwan, and the growing success of China's long-standing effort to limit Taiwan's international presence and influence.[10] In addition, the changing relationship has been influenced by the emergence of more credible (from Beijing's viewpoint) U.S. efforts to restrain the pro-independence activities of the Taiwan government and the recent overwhelming victory of more unification-oriented political forces in Taiwan's legislative and presidential elections.[11]

These developments have resulted in a level of cautious optimism in Beijing regarding at least the near-term future that bodes well for continued stability in relations with the United States on this issue. Nonetheless, Beijing continues to enhance its military capabilities vis-à-vis Taiwan and to assert China's right to employ "non-peaceful means" if necessary, as codified in the so-called Anti-Secession Law passed in March 2005. These actions, combined with the possibility that Taiwan's turbulent political system could shift again in the direction of independence, raise the prospect of future confrontation or even conflict with Washington. Such an outcome would most likely result from Beijing miscalculating that China's growing military prowess could be employed to deter movement toward de jure Taiwan independence or to resolve the issue of independence outright. On the positive side, the shift in domestic Taiwan politics toward greater

---

[9] This debate raises the question of whether Asian nations in fact regard the United States as performing such a role, a point discussed further below.

[10] China's confidence in the growing efficacy of its coercive capability vis-à-vis Taiwan is bolstered by Taipei's inability or unwillingness both to acquire major U.S. arms and to significantly increase Taiwan's level of defense spending. See Andrew N.D. Yang, "Taiwan's Defense Preparation Against the Chinese Military Threat," in *Assessing the Threat: The Chinese Military and Taiwan's Security,* ed. Michael D. Swaine et al. (Washington, D.C.: Carnegie Endowment for International Peace, 2007), 265–82.

[11] Yun-han Chu, "The Evolution of Beijing's Policy toward Taiwan during the Reform Era," in *China Rising: Power and Motivation in Chinese Foreign Policy,* ed. Yong Deng and Fei-ling Wang (Oxford: Rowman and Littlefield Publishers, 2005).

cross-Strait contacts presents a major opportunity for a long-term reduction in tensions.

Similarly, Beijing's political and diplomatic stance toward the Korean Peninsula has also evolved considerably in more positive directions during the past eight years. China now works quite closely with the United States to convince North Korea—by applying greater pressure and offering enticements—to cooperate and comply with agreements. At the same time, China has resisted applying extreme pressure to Pyongyang. For example, Beijing has rejected means such as cutting off or severely reducing long-standing and arguably vital supplies of food and oil to the impoverished regime. Beijing has also repeatedly stressed extreme opposition to any military solution.[12] Moreover, Beijing has not fully supported U.S.-led efforts to prevent Pyongyang from proliferating nuclear weapons materials—for example, through the Proliferation Security Initiative (PSI).[13] China's stance toward North Korea thus presents both considerable challenges and opportunities for U.S. efforts to contain, reduce, and eventually eliminate North Korea's nuclear weapons capability.

India, ASEAN, Japan, and Russia. China's activities with regard to India and the ASEAN states during the past eight years have also arguably contributed to general stability in the regional security environment while presenting a growing challenge to U.S. policies. The often tumultuous Sino-Indian relationship has improved enormously since at least 2000. Both sides have pledged that their long-simmering territorial dispute will not be allowed to undermine the positive development of bilateral relations.[14] Such positive changes clearly suggest that both countries wish to avoid a destabilizing security competition—a strategy that is obviously beneficial to the larger regional order. Beijing's concerted effort to improve its security relationship with New Delhi also remains subject to significant limitations, however. Complicating efforts to improve this relationship are

---

[12] See, for instance, Christopher P. Twomey, "China's Policy Towards North Korea and Its Implications for the United States: Balancing Competing Concerns," Center for Contemporary Conflict, Strategic Insights 5, no. 7, September 2006; Andrew Scobell, *China and North Korea: From Comrades-in-Arms to Allies at Arm's Length* (Carlisle: Strategic Studies Institute, 2004); and An Hongquan, "Cooperation and Dispute between China on N. Korea Nuclear Crisis" in *China-U.S. Relations: A Strategic Analysis,* ed. Bo Mengmei and Yuan Peng (Beijing: China Institutes of Contemporary International Relations, 2005), 215–35.

[13] The PSI embodies a set of principles and activities aimed at interdicting the transfer via air, land, or sea of WMD, their delivery systems, and related materials to and from nation-states and nonstate actors of proliferation concern. The initiative is agreed to by over 15 core nations (including the United States, Russia, Japan, France, Germany, and the United Kingdom) and is supported by over 60 other states. See "The Proliferation Security Initiative (PSI) At a Glance," Arms Control Today, October 2007, http://www.armscontrol.org/factsheets/PSI.asp.

[14] Jing-dong Yuan, "The Dragon and the Elephant: Chinese-Indian Relations in the 21st Century," *Washington Quarterly* 30, no. 3 (Summer 2007): 131–44.

mutual distrust and suspicion between the two rising powers, China's close strategic relationship with Pakistan, and the overall dynamics of the security dilemma.[15] In addition, China is watching carefully—and likely with some concern—India's improving ties with the United States.[16]

With regard to the ASEAN states, Beijing's security-oriented behavior in recent years also reflects an ongoing effort to enhance economic intercourse, deepen cooperative relations, and allay concerns over China's growing political, economic, and military power. In this effort China has focused primarily on bilateral and multilateral undertakings that emphasize confidence-building, mutual benefits, and non-interference in internal affairs. In addition to (and partly as a result of) such undertakings, Beijing has also worked energetically to facilitate the expansion of trade with and investment in Southeast Asian nations.[17] Yet the potential for strategic rivalry or confrontation over the region with India, Japan, and the United States doubtless remains. To some extent, China's intense focus on achieving common objectives with Southeast Asian nations may have "…allowed China to gain influence relative to the United States."[18]

Such Chinese actions present a complex set of challenges for U.S. policy. On the one hand, China's concerted efforts to enhance relations with both India and the ASEAN states are to some extent welcome as means of reducing distrust and enhancing stability and understanding. On the other hand, such improvements in relations are occurring in the face of growing strategic rivalry and potential tension between China and India involving competition in South and Southeast Asia. Additionally, there is a deepening impression in some parts of these regions that the United States is overly focused on counterterrorism and less attuned to local interests than it should be.

Relations with Japan over the past eight years may have constituted the most significant challenge to Beijing's efforts both to improve China's image and cooperation with other Asian states and to enhance its strategic leverage in the Asia-Pacific. During this period Sino-Japanese relations have encountered significant tensions, primarily over territorial disputes related to energy resources, historical issues associated with World War II, and China's growing nearby military presence and capabilities. The relationship

---

[15] The security dilemma describes a situation in which the efforts of states to enhance their own security can often decrease the security of other states, leading to an unintended, escalating spiral of political and military tension.

[16] Jing-dong Yuan, "The Geometry of Sino-Indian Ties," *Asia Times Online*, November 22, 2006; and Robert G. Sutter, *China's Rise: Implications for U.S. Leadership in Asia*, Policy Studies 21 (Washington, D.C.: East-West Center, 2006), 47–48.

[17] Medeiros, "China's International Behavior"; and Sutter, *China's Rise*.

[18] Sutter, *China's Rise*, 38.

has taken on many aspects of a strategic rivalry, despite rapidly expanding economic relations and concerted efforts to improve ties. Even with recent advances, China's relationship with Japan remains subject to the workings of the security dilemma, fed by growing military capabilities on both sides and the steady enhancement of Japan's role as a security actor in the Asia-Pacific.[19] Unresolved territorial disputes, continued volatility in Japan's domestic politics, and the persistence of strong negative emotions toward the other side, especially in China, have further aggravated Sino-Japanese relations.[20] Two issues present a major challenge to future U.S. efforts to maintain regional stability and avoid the emergence of a zero-sum approach to security interactions between China and Japan. The first is the inherent propensity for greater strategic rivalry and confrontation between Beijing and Tokyo over resources and other issues. The second is Japan's arguably increasing importance as a regional security actor and economic power and its status as the United States' primary security ally in Asia.

China's relationship with Russia during the past eight years has provided less ambiguous strategic benefits for Beijing and is probably subject to fewer sudden adverse shifts. This relationship nonetheless also confronts significant limitations. The most notable benefits have included the continuation of major arms sales and military-related technology transfers in areas that are highly relevant to China's deterrence efforts toward Taiwan and overall military modernization program. To a lesser extent, China has also benefited from the development of greater levels of security cooperation with Russia over the past several years, although the level of actual Sino-Russian cooperation has remained limited. Among the reasons for limited cooperation are the strong levels of mutual distrust between the two countries and the weak (albeit improving) strategic position of Russia in the Asia-Pacific and the Middle East. An additional reason is the potentially threatening nature of China's growing power, geopolitical presence, and economic dynamism (including for some Russians the "creeping colonization" of Russia's Far East). Cooperation is further limited by disputes over energy pipelines and prices and the fact that both Moscow and Beijing ultimately value the maintenance of a constructive relationship with the United States more than the development of a genuine anti-U.S. strategic alliance.[21] This situation suggests that on balance China's relations

---

[19] Japan's role has been enhanced largely as a result of the deepening U.S.-Japan security alliance and greater acceptance of such a role among the Japanese public.

[20] See, for instance, Mike M. Mochizuki, "Japan's Long Transition: The Politics of Recalibrating Grand Strategy," in *Strategic Asia 2007–08: Domestic Political Change and Grand Strategy*, ed. Ashley J. Tellis and Michael Wills (Seattle: The National Bureau of Asian Research, 2007), 105.

[21] See, for instance, Sergei Blagov, "Arms, Energy and Commerce in Sino-Russian Relations," China Brief 7, no. 16, August 8, 2007, 8–11.

with Russia have been and will likely remain for some time a largely marginal factor in the overall strategic landscape in Asia and beyond. Nonetheless, Russia's growing economic clout and great-power aspirations indicate that it is in the interest of Washington to improve relations with Moscow in order to maximize leverage in this strategic triangle.

Multilateral security institutions. Finally, in the strategic arena, observers have witnessed deeper levels and unprecedented types of Chinese involvement in bilateral and multilateral security-related activities in recent years. For example, China has participated in the development of new multilateral security-related organizations and meetings, such as the six-party talks, the SCO, ASEAN +3, and the East Asia Summit (EAS). China has been a vocal supporter of the EAS, has publicly endorsed ASEAN's dominant role within the summit, and has repeatedly disavowed any intention of seizing the summit's leadership. The EAS, however, has failed to establish itself as the primary mechanism or framework for East Asian community-building. Partly as a result, Beijing has increased support for the ASEAN +3 as the primary mechanism for the enhancement of a multifaceted Asian dialogue and the construction of a purely East Asian community.

China's promotion of cooperative security approaches was designed in part to present an alternative to the U.S.-led bilateral alliance structure in Asia. This undertaking, however, also increasingly reflects a recognition by Beijing that such multilateral initiatives can facilitate efforts to deal with common problems and opportunities (for example, domestic terrorist activities, nontraditional security concerns, and resource and territorial disputes). Beijing also understands that these initiatives can reassure many Asian (and particularly Southeast Asian) states that China's growing power and influence does not pose a threat to the interests of these states. Multilateral initiatives could establish China as a leading player in the effort to build an Asian community on economic and security issues, possibly without U.S. involvement.[22] These goals and activities present significant implications for U.S. policy and suggest the need for Washington to pay increasing attention to the role of multilateralism in Asian security affairs. There is little doubt that many Asian nations are focused on developing more inclusive, multifaceted security structures as part of an overall effort to dampen strategic rivalry among the major powers.

---

[22] Richard Giragosian, "The Strategic Central Asian Arena," *China and Eurasia Forum Quarterly* 4, no. 1 (2006): 133–53; and Medeiros, "China's International Behavior."

U.S. Policy

During the past eight years U.S. security policies toward China have attempted to address most if not all of the challenges and opportunities for U.S. interests presented by the PRC actions discussed above. In particular, in the military security arena Washington has sought to maintain deterrence stability in the Taiwan Strait and to reassure East Asian states that the United States remains engaged as the predominant maritime power in the region. Washington has also sought to strengthen the capacity of major Asian powers, especially key allies, to play a cooperative and constructive security role. Furthermore, the United States has tried to prevent or dissuade China from resorting to coercive diplomacy in the region while encouraging Beijing to become more transparent and reassuring in security affairs.

In the area of military deterrence, the United States has systematically and steadily enhanced its overall capabilities and influence by deploying additional naval and air weapons platforms to the region and engaging these forces in regular exercises and patrols. Washington has also diversified U.S. basing, strengthened military alliance or partnership cooperation, and deployed long-range strike capabilities. Beyond these largely region-wide efforts, the United States has focused on increasing its overall level of bilateral military assistance to Taiwan. In particular, Washington has assisted Taiwan through arms sales or offers to provide unprecedented weapons systems, such as submarines, as well as through greater levels of military consultation.[23] Moreover, the United States has also sought to coordinate the above military actions with political and diplomatic efforts designed to reassure other nations that Washington is not pursuing a containment policy toward Beijing or otherwise attempting to coerce China to alter its policies or behavior in ways that would threaten China's core interests (for example, those regarding Taiwan).[24]

While increasing U.S. military deterrence and reassurance capabilities in Asia, Washington has also sought to engage the Chinese government and military more directly. The United States has increased the scope and tempo of Sino-U.S. military-to-military contacts and published regular Department of Defense reports assessing PRC military capabilities, strategy, and doctrines. Washington has also repeatedly emphasized the need for greater transparency from Beijing regarding the pace, directions, and

---

[23] James J. Przystup, "The United States, Australia, and the Search for Order in East Asia and Beyond," in *The Other Special Relationship: The United States and Australia at the Start of the 21st Century*, ed. Jeffrey D. McCausland et al. (Carlisle: Strategic Studies Institute, February 2007): 261–78.

[24] Michael D. Swaine, "China: Exploiting a Strategic Opening," in *Strategic Asia 2004–05: Confronting Terrorism in the Pursuit of Power*, ed. Ashley J. Tellis and Michael Wills (Seattle: The National Bureau of Asian Research, 2004); and Przystup, "The United States, Australia, and the Search for Order."

ultimate purpose of China's military build-up. In addition, Washington has undertaken efforts to control or curtail specific types of advanced weapons, military technologies, and dual-use product sales and transfers to China both by U.S. and foreign corporations as well as by some foreign governments. In particular, U.S. efforts are focused on curtailing the sales of items that could significantly affect military stability across the Taiwan Strait. The latter effort has at times involved very intense pressure on military suppliers to China, such as the members of the European Union (EU) and—to a lesser extent and less successfully—the Russian government.[25]

To a significant degree U.S. efforts in the military arena have been effective in maintaining regional stability and increasing communication despite major increases in China's military capability. For example, efforts by the United States and other nations to encourage China to provide more information on its military strategy and force modernization program have arguably produced positive results. The PRC, for example, has published more detailed defense white papers and granted U.S. military personnel greater access to PLA facilities. Nevertheless, there is little doubt that China remains committed to reducing its vulnerability to potential U.S. threats and enhancing its overall strategic leverage. To achieve these goals, the PRC has strengthened its military capacity in ways that could increasingly aggravate the security dilemma between Washington and Beijing.

In the political and diplomatic arenas U.S. security strategy in Asia has attempted to complement military-related moves by working to strengthen overall defense cooperation with regional states and with key democratic allies in particular. This strategy has focused on facilitating Japan's emergence as a more active political-military partner—one that is capable of addressing a wide range of traditional and nontraditional security concerns within Asia and beyond. Such concerns include peacekeeping and involvement in the war in Iraq to the provision of extensive levels of support for U.S. military deployments in a possible future Taiwan crisis. Needless to say, such enhanced security cooperation with Japan has not all been connected with or directed against China. Such cooperation has, however, doubtless played an important part in U.S. efforts to maintain regional stability by counterbalancing growing Chinese political and military influence and discouraging outright Sino-Japanese strategic competition.[26]

---

[25] Shirley A. Kan, "U.S.-China Military Contacts: Issues for Congress," Congressional Research Service, CRS Report for Congress, RL32496, updated February 1, 2008; and Shirley A. Kan, "China and Proliferation of Weapons of Mass Destruction and Missiles: Policy Issues," Congressional Research Service, CRS Report for Congress, RL31555, updated February 8, 2006.

[26] Richard J. Samuels, *Securing Japan: Tokyo's Grand Strategy and the Future of East Asia* (Ithaca: Cornell University Press, 2007); and Przystup, "The United States, Australia, and the Search for Order."

In contrast to these efforts, Washington has by and large failed to strengthen its alliance and security coordination with South Korea, its other major ally in Northeast Asia. For many years the Bush administration alienated Seoul by openly criticizing its more accommodating approach to Pyongyang. This factor, as well as rapidly expanding economic trade between Beijing and Seoul, has caused South Korea to exhibit an increasing willingness to lean toward China during the past eight years, despite occasional Sino-Korean disputes over historical issues and Beijing's treatment of refugees from North Korea. Although this situation has improved in recent years, as a result of changes in U.S. policy toward North Korea and the emergence of a more pro-U.S. leadership in Seoul, there is little doubt that Washington has missed opportunities to improve its security relationship with Seoul in ways that might strengthen the U.S. posture vis-à-vis China.

Of more immediate and direct relevance to China's strategic position in Asia is U.S. policy toward Taiwan. Since at least the early 1980s, U.S. political and diplomatic policies toward the island generally have focused on preventing a confrontation with China in order to buy time for an eventual peaceful resolution to the dispute. On the one hand, Washington has reassured Beijing of the U.S. commitment to the "one China" policy. On the other hand, Washington has reassured Taipei that the United States will neither pressure Taiwan into negotiating a final resolution nor strike a deal with China at Taiwan's expense. At the same time, Washington has tried to deter both sides from undertaking unilateral actions that would greatly increase the chance of a major crisis or conflict. During the early years of the Bush administration, U.S. policy stressed the military deterrence side of this equation. This approach aimed to enhance the expression of U.S. resolve, to reduce the possibility of miscalculation, and to differentiate U.S. policy from what the Bush administration regarded as the overly accommodating stance the Clinton administration adopted toward Beijing. In more recent years, however—and especially after September 11 and the advent of the war in Iraq—Washington has sought to avoid confrontation with Beijing. The Bush administration addressed the political deterrence and reassurance side of the equation by actively rejecting attempts by the Taiwanese government to move significantly toward de jure independence and by repeatedly affirming the one-China policy in high-level talks with the Chinese leadership.[27]

This dual deterrence and reassurance approach has managed to sustain stability across the Taiwan Strait. As indicated above, the overwhelming

---

[27] Swaine, "China: Exploiting a Strategic Opening."

defeat of pro-independence political forces in Taiwan's legislative and presidential elections of early 2008 will most likely reinforce this stability and presents Washington with a major opportunity to reduce significantly the likelihood of a major confrontation with China during the next U.S. administration. Nonetheless, China's continued military build-up and strong distrust of Washington, Taiwan's failure thus far to strengthen its defensive capabilities in the manner and to the extent the United States desires, and the tumultuous, unpredictable, zero-sum features of Taiwan's political process will continue to require close attention and careful management.[28]

U.S. policy interactions with China regarding the North Korean nuclear crisis have shifted even more significantly in approach and emphasis than have interactions regarding the Taiwan issue. During the first term of the Bush administration, U.S. officials at times criticized Beijing for not using what the administration regarded as China's considerable economic and political leverage to pressure North Korea to comply with denuclearization objectives. Likewise, U.S. officials rejected Beijing's frequent calls for Washington to negotiate bilaterally with Pyongyang. Three factors, however—heightened tensions with Pyongyang; Washington's growing need, as the war in Iraq worsened, to avoid another foreign policy crisis; and Beijing's fear that the United States would take preemptive action or perform a "surgical strike" to bring about regime change in North Korea—eventually resulted in the emergence of a multilateral approach. This approach led to the creation of the six-party talks, along with frequent bilateral "sideline" discussions between Washington and Pyongyang. Most importantly, U.S. cooperation with China in efforts to denuclearize the Korean Peninsula has deepened over time, particularly following North Korea's ballistic missiles tests and nuclear detonations in July and October 2006, which created a heightened sense of crisis and left Beijing feeling betrayed. Washington now regards Beijing as a vital partner in this undertaking, despite continued mutual suspicion regarding each other's long-term goals on the peninsula and respective level of commitment to denuclearization.[29]

As suggested above, Washington's growing cooperation with New Delhi in several military-related areas has been part of a larger effort to encourage the evolution of a more friendly, cooperative, secure, and strong India via an array of unprecedented interactions. The ultimate objective of this

---

[28] Thomas J. Christensen, "U.S.-China Relations," testimony before the Subcommittee on Asia, the Pacific, and the Global Environment of the House Foreign Affairs Committee, Washington, D.C., March 27, 2007.

[29] Thomas J. Christensen, "Shaping China's Global Choices through Diplomacy," statement before the U.S.-China Economic and Security Review Commission, Washington, D.C., March 18, 2008; and Shen Dingli, "North Korea's Strategic Significance to China," *China Security* (Autumn 2006): 19–34.

undertaking has been to facilitate India's emergence as a new strategic actor in the Asia-Pacific. This approach has apparently been designed in part to improve Washington's ability to counterbalance growing Chinese power through a version of offshore balancing involving shifting relationships among other increasingly capable major Asian powers, including Japan and perhaps Russia. India's fierce independence, however, and the general complexities of any attempt to shape strategic interactions among major Asian powers suggest that such an undertaking could falter or fail if not properly managed.[30]

U.S. political and diplomatic policy during the past eight years has also responded to Chinese initiatives in Southeast Asia and elsewhere through a variety of bilateral interactions with smaller powers and via multilateral security venues. In recent years, however, U.S policy has arguably met with less success in this arena than in policies toward North Korea and Taiwan. In part, this is because such interactions between Washington and smaller powers have at times focused mainly on improving cooperation in combating terrorism rather than on political, economic, and social issues of interest to local nations. As noted, Beijing has in general been far more active than Washington in recent years in promoting and developing both bilateral and multilateral economic and security-related interactions, statements, and forums among states in Southeast Asia and elsewhere. As a result, the United States has a mixed record in dealing with the concerns of many Asian governments.[31] On the positive side, on several occasions Washington has been able to show smaller Asian powers that the United States possesses unrivalled capabilities in responding to large-scale, nontraditional security threats, such as the recent tsunami and earthquake disasters. After apparent hesitation, Washington also has shown support for some multilateral institutions (such as ASEAN and the six-party talks) and endorsed efforts to develop the current six-party talks on North Korea into a permanent security forum in Northeast Asia. The United States has generally failed, however, to identify priorities among proliferating multilateral initiatives or to assess how these initiatives relate to existing bilateral security relationships. Such interactions have by and large moved forward on separate tracks, with little apparent coordination.

Finally, the Bush administration has attempted to achieve greater levels of strategic understanding with Beijing and thereby advance

---

[30] Ashley J. Tellis, "What Should We Expect from India as a Strategic Partner?" in *Gauging U.S. Indian Strategic Cooperation*, ed. Henry Sokolski (Carlisle: Strategic Studies Institute, 2007), 231–58.

[31] Sutter, "China's Rise"; and Michael J. Green, "Organizing Asia: Politics, Trade, and the New Multilateralism," in *Global Forecast: the Top Security Challenges of 2008*, ed. Carola McGiffert and Craig Cohen (Washington, D.C.: Center for Strategic and International Studies, 2007), 25–26.

Washington's overall goals by supporting the creation and development of two security-related dialogues between senior officials: the U.S.-China Senior Dialogue and the nuclear strategy dialogue. The former is designed to provide a forum for the discussion of short-, medium-, and long-term U.S. and Chinese policies on political and security issues that bear on the functioning of the global system.[32] From the U.S. perspective this dialogue is intended to promote and advance China's role in the international system as a so-called responsible stakeholder.[33] The more recent nuclear strategy dialogue was initiated by the United States and announced by President Bush and President Hu in early 2006. The dialogue aims to increase understanding of each country's nuclear doctrines, "including the roles and capabilities of offensive and defensive systems and ways to avoid an arms race in space."[34] Unfortunately, this initiative has not shown much progress, largely due to apparent foot-dragging on the Chinese side. After considerable discussion the two sides finally agreed to a process for the dialogue in early 2008. Nonetheless, although still in their infancy, these two dialogues may promote mutual understanding and accommodation on immediate and long-term strategic issues that should become increasingly critical over time.

The Economic Dimension: Increasing Interdependence and Rising Stakes

Over the last decade China's policies in the foreign economic arena have taken on increasing strategic relevance for the United States. Four factors are behind this development: Beijing's sustained high levels of overall growth, growing dependence on foreign resources, deepening involvement in regional and global economic institutions, and expanding overseas trade, technology, and investment capabilities. These developments have greatly increased China's impact on the stability of U.S. and global economies, raised the relevance of economic and resource issues within the overall foreign security calculus, stimulated China's technology innovation,

---

[32] Such issues include energy security, terrorism, economic and trade-related issues, United Nations reform, and nuclear weapons proliferation with regard to Iran and North Korea.

[33] Robert B. Zoellick, "Whither China: From Membership to Responsibility?" (remarks to the National Committee on U.S.-China Relations, New York City, September 21, 2005), http://www.state.gov/s/d/former/zoellick/rem/53682.htm. The concept of the responsible stakeholder seeks to encourage Beijing to define its interests and role in the international system more clearly in dialogue with the United States in order to elicit China's more active participation in the maintenance and protection of that system. Unfortunately, in the past two years this dialogue has apparently been downgraded after the departure of its originator, Robert Zoellick, from his post as deputy secretary of state.

[34] Carla A. Hills and Dennis C. Blair with Frank Sampson Jannuzi, *U.S.-China Relations: An Affirmative Agenda, a Responsible Course* (New York: Council on Foreign Relations, 2007).

provided Beijing with the wherewithal to sustain high levels of defense spending, and given China a major voice in international forums.

As a result of its outward-oriented economic dynamism, Beijing has become an increasingly active participant in international economic organizations and forums, including the World Bank, International Monetary Fund (IMF), World Trade Organization (WTO), Asian Development Bank, and ASEAN +3. Beijing has also been promoting free-trade agreements in Asia and beyond. China's involvement in the foreign economic arena has greatly assisted the country's economy and has helped to build international confidence in Beijing's commitment to peaceful development and support for the basic norms of the international system. At the same time, Beijing's actions have also raised concerns over the PRC's growing leverage within international economic decisionmaking circles. Some observers are concerned that, as the PRC's financial and trade power increase, Beijing might seek to alter some of the largely Western-defined norms in this arena.

Of even greater importance, China's increasing reliance on foreign trade, investment, and expertise to maintain the country's rapid growth has posed direct consequences for the economies of other major powers, including many Asian and European nations as well as the United States. In particular, Beijing's intensive search for reliable, affordable, and efficient sources of energy has exerted a significant impact on its foreign policies in many regions and poses significant implications for defense. Some observers now conjecture that Beijing might increasingly focus its naval and air forces on securing greater access to energy markets and protecting transportation routes. In the past few years the search for more stable energy supplies has also led China to try to acquire oil and gas assets in Africa, Latin America, Central Asia, and the Middle East by strengthening political ties with energy-rich but often despotic regimes—thus raising human rights concerns among Western democracies. Additionally, this search for energy supplies has raised a larger fear that Beijing is pursuing mercantilist policies that could distort market forces and intensify national rivalries.[35]

In recent years China's trade performance has resulted in the accumulation of a very large current account surplus. Combined with high levels of inward FDI and large inflows of speculative capital, this factor has produced over one trillion dollars in foreign exchange reserves, twice the level in 2004. In theory China could significantly influence the value of the dollar if the country were to divest itself rapidly of a large amount of these reserves. Most analysts, however, believe that such an action is highly

---

[35] See, for instance, Erica Downs, "China," Brookings Institution, Brookings Foreign Policy Studies Energy Security Series, December 2006.

unlikely, given that the resulting rapid, major devaluation of the dollar would likely damage the Chinese economy significantly.[36]

The Sino-U.S. economic relationship is now critical to the economic health and vitality of both nations. On the one hand, as Thomas Christensen has noted, this relationship "has opened China's economy to quality U.S. products and services, has helped educate and inspire a generation of Chinese entrepreneurs, engineers, and officials, and has contributed to keeping inflation low in the U.S. by lowering prices on a wide range of consumer goods and inputs to U.S. production."[37] On the other hand, this expanding bilateral economic relationship has also generated significant problems. These problems include tensions over the safety of Chinese products and alleged violations of intellectual property rights, Chinese attempts to acquire U.S. companies in so-called strategic sectors of the U.S. economy (such as oil and natural gas companies, high technology products, and port facilities), U.S. concerns over China's record in implementing WTO commitments, and the alleged adverse impact on U.S. employment of the massive and growing U.S. trade deficit with China.[38]

In response to these developments, and to attain the three U.S. economic policy objectives described above, Washington has undertaken a wide variety of actions during the past decade, building on earlier moves.

First, the United States has actively supported China's admission to economic institutions and forums (especially the WTO), on terms that reinforce the major norms of these organizations, benefit the U.S. economy, and promote China's economic liberalization. U.S. officials recognized that China's entry into the WTO would be challenging, particularly in the areas of agriculture, services, intellectual property rights enforcement, and exchange rates. The United States nonetheless expected the benefits of economic liberalization to strengthen a trajectory of stable economic growth; to increase balance, efficiency, and openness in markets; and to have spillover effects in the areas of human rights and other basic freedoms. Accordingly, monitoring and enforcing China's implementation of its WTO obligations—especially those critical to U.S. domestic employment—have been a centerpiece of the Bush administration's

---

[36] "Issues of Importance to American Business in the U.S.-China Commercial Relationship," U.S. Chamber of Commerce, U.S. Chamber of Commerce Report, September 2007; and "China's Foreign Exchange Reserves," *Economist,* October 26, 2006.

[37] Thomas J. Christensen, "The State of U.S.-China Diplomacy," statement before the U.S.-China Economic and Security Review Commission, Washington, D.C., February 2, 2007, http://www.state.gov/p/eap/rls/rm/2007/79866.htm.

[38] See Nicholas R. Lardy, "The Transition to Consumption Driven Growth in China," in *China's Rise: Challenges and Opportunities,* ed. C. Fred Bergsten et al. (forthcoming, 2008).

economic policy toward China.[39] By Bush's second term of office, however, Washington was expressing a heightened sense of frustration with China's rate of progress on WTO compliance and other matters.[40] As a result, U.S. officials made increasingly forceful calls for the revaluation of the renminbi, the protection of intellectual property rights, and an end to mercantilist economic practices, particularly in China's increasingly intensive quest for energy. Washington also asserted that Beijing needed to make more progress in developing China's industrial policies, improving import and export restrictions, reversing discriminatory regulations and prohibited subsidies, protecting intellectual property rights, and limiting government intervention in the market.[41]

The U.S.-China Strategic Economic Dialogue (SED) emerged in part as a result of growing U.S. frustration and criticism in these and other areas. Led by the U.S. secretary of the treasury, the SED is an inter-agency effort designed to address a broad range of bilateral economic issues, including the impact of these issues on various domestic and international conditions (such as environment, health care, and education). The SED has made slow but steady progress in pressuring and encouraging China to address more comprehensive economic reforms, thereby likely reducing the incentives for provocative U.S. actions.[42] Moreover, although China has not fully complied with its WTO obligations and is unlikely to make rapid progress in this regard, it is fair to say that the Bush administration has succeeded in continuing to make this a priority for Beijing.

Nonetheless, as the U.S. economy has weakened and the American people have become less enthralled with globalization and more concerned over China's increasing power, public pressure in the United States has exerted a growing influence over the Sino-U.S. economic relationship. For instance, public pressure has influenced decisions to prevent or discourage Chinese investment in U.S. strategic sectors, such as ports, oil companies, and potential dual-use and high technology product areas. Partly as a result of such public sentiment, Congress has remained a vocal critic of China, labeling Beijing a "currency manipulator," blaming the PRC currency rate

---

[39] James A. Kelly, "The Future of U.S.-China Relations," testimony before the Senate Foreign Relations Committee, Subcommittee on East Asian and Pacific Affairs, Washington, D.C., May 1, 2001.

[40] See Thomas J. Christensen, "China's Role in the World: Is China a Responsible Stakeholder?" remarks before the U.S.-China Economic and Security Review Commission, Washington, D.C., August 3, 2006.

[41] Christopher R. Hill, "Emergence of China in the Asia-Pacific: Economic and Security Consequences for the U.S.," testimony before the Senate Foreign Relations Committee, Subcommittee on East Asian and Pacific Affairs, Washington, D.C., June 7, 2005, http://www.state.gov/p/eap/rls/rm/2005/47334.htm.

[42] Christensen, "The State of U.S.-China Diplomacy."

and trade practices for U.S. unemployment, and threatening to impose punitive tariffs on Chinese goods. The Bush administration, however, has generally discouraged such confrontational (and sometimes purely symbolic) actions—instead, favoring low-key, businesslike dialogue and negotiation.[43]

WMD Counterproliferation and Nontraditional Security Threats

Since at least the early 1990s China has become an increasingly important and supportive player in the international counterproliferation effort. During this time, Beijing has steadily enacted greater internal controls over activities related to WMD proliferation and stepped up support for international nonproliferation norms and procedures. Specifically, Beijing has signed or joined all major international nonproliferation agreements and regimes, significantly reduced its involvement in the transfer of WMD-related equipment and technologies (including delivery systems such as ballistic missiles), and formulated new domestic laws and regulations to govern the export and import of dual-use and WMD-related items. China has also joined the Nuclear Suppliers Group and has applied to join the Missile Technology Control Regime.[44] In addition to these activities, Beijing notably has supported international efforts to prevent Iran from acquiring nuclear weapons.[45] Beijing's support for international attempts to denuclearize the Korean Peninsula is even more significant.[46]

China's record on counterproliferation over the past eight years is by no means pristine, however. Supplies from PRC sources to Pakistan, Iran, and possibly other states have at times aggravated global WMD proliferation trends by providing "ambiguous technical aid, more indigenous capabilities, longer-range missiles, and secondary (retransferred) proliferation."[47] Most of this activity has involved dual-use or alleged weapons technologies, primarily applicable to missiles or chemical weapons. In many such instances Chinese suppliers were most likely profit-driven commercial firms acting independently of the PRC government. In addition, even though the PRC might share U.S. concerns over the proliferation of WMD,

---

[43] Elizabeth Price, Greg Hitt, and Andrew Batson, "U.S. Case Against China in WTO Shows New Mood, Bush Answers Calls for Tougher Actions, Risks Further Tension," *Wall Street Journal Asia,* February 5, 2007.

[44] Denny Roy, "Going Straight, But Somewhat Late: China and Nuclear Nonproliferation," Asia-Pacific Center for Strategic Studies, February 2006.

[45] Kan, "China and Proliferation."

[46] See Stephanie Kleine-Ahlbrandt and Andrew Small, "China's New Dictatorship Diplomacy: Is Beijing Parting with Pariahs?" *Foreign Affairs* 87, no. 1 (January/February 2008): 38–56.

[47] Kan, "China and Proliferation."

Beijing has often expressed reservations over the utility of sanctions and the credibility of some U.S. intelligence on states such as Iran, North Korea, and Pakistan. Such reservations strongly suggest that Beijing does not agree entirely with Washington's approach to counterproliferation; the two states even disagree over the definition of proliferation. Beijing is also concerned by Washington's supposedly unilateralist and interventionist attitude toward WMD and terrorist-related threats as well as by the development of new military doctrines in favor of preventive warfare.[48]

In this strategic arena the policies of the Bush administration have centered primarily on efforts both to enhance China's WMD safeguards and export controls and to compel PRC support for actions, such as economic sanctions, deemed necessary to curb Iran's alleged ambition to acquire nuclear weapons. Although China originally disregarded the Bush administration's allegations that Chinese exports to Iran were helping Tehran develop nuclear capabilities, the two countries have come to agree that Tehran's nuclear program presents dangers to the international nonproliferation regime. Despite original objections to economic sanctions, China has relaxed its stance and supported three rounds of UN sanctions resolutions on Iran. Beijing has not, however, scaled back economic ties with Tehran to the extent that the Bush administration would prefer. Although the United States and China thus do not see eye to eye on how best to address Iran's nuclear program, their ability to work together toward finding a resolution marks a positive development.

More broadly, the Bush administration has pressured China to become a more responsible nuclear weapons state. Washington has targeted China's weak export controls and imposed sanctions on more than 30 PRC "entities" for transfers related to missiles and chemical weapons. More ominously, U.S. officials have stated that some PRC entities are also involved with both missile and nuclear programs in Pakistan and Iran. Officials have even implied that the Chinese government possesses knowledge of at least some of these relationships.[49] Though denying such connections, Beijing has promulgated export controls on missiles, issued updated regulations on the export of dual-use chemical and biological agents, and promised to improve the government's enforcement of these controls and regulations.[50]

Since at least 2000 Beijing has been contributing to international efforts to cope with nontraditional security threats, including terrorism,

---

[48] "China Warns of Illegalities in U.S.-Backed Non-proliferation Plan," Agence France-Presse, December 4, 2003.

[49] Kan, "China and Proliferation."

[50] Paula A. DeSutter, "China's Record of Proliferation Activities," testimony before the U.S.-China Commission, Washington, D.C., July 24, 2003.

pandemics, piracy, illegal drug trafficking, environmental degradation, and financial and energy crises. Beijing increasingly recognizes the serious threats posed by failing states and the above security threats. Moreover, both China and the United States share the view that failing states—or, using the PRC term, "areas of instability"—exacerbate the potential for transnational threats. Beijing's growing concern and gradual willingness to actively address a range of nontraditional security threats mark a significant shift in its strategic interests and policies toward greater levels of cooperation, and even toward a willingness to exert leadership in these areas. At the same time, Beijing has in some cases—for example, during the SARS (severe acute respiratory syndrome) outbreak—inhibited international attempts to cope with such threats by stressing the need for internal controls rather than for transparency and communication.[51]

The Bush administration has adopted a wide variety of policies to deal with nontraditional security issues involving China. Participation on these issues includes multilateral organizations such as the Asia-Pacific Partnership on Clean Development and Climate (APP), the APEC Energy Working Group, and the International Partnership on Avian and Pandemic Influenza; ministerial meetings; and bilateral involvement in annual dialogues such as the U.S.-China Energy Policy Dialogue and the U.S.-China Global Issues Forum. Washington has also undertaken various issue-based missions to China, launched joint research programs, and exerted direct pressure on Beijing.[52] Although many of these initiatives remain in the early stages, the Bush administration has at least established channels for future dialogue and action.

Implications and Policy Choices

The successes and shortcomings of the Bush administration's stance toward China—combined with the underlying goals, trends, and assumptions noted at the beginning of this chapter—suggest that the United States can no longer afford, nor will likely gain from, a policy of sharp confrontation, public criticism, and high pressure designed to compel Beijing to cooperate more or to capitulate on fundamental strategic issues. The current U.S. approach of dialogue, negotiation, and management of most bilateral and related third-party strategic issues reflects an enduring underlying reality that has emerged over the past eight to ten years.

---

[51] Bates Gill, *Rising Star: China's New Security Diplomacy* (Washington, D.C.: Brookings Institution Press, 2007), 12–13; Shambaugh, "China Engages Asia"; and Susan L. Craig, *Chinese Perceptions of Traditional and Nontraditional Security Threats* (Carlisle: Strategic Studies Institute, 2007).

[52] Christensen, "U.S.-China Relations."

Simply put, the U.S. relationship with China has become too important, the interdependencies too extensive, the common problems requiring cooperation too many, and the consequences of hostile confrontation too damaging for Washington to employ a strategy centered on intense pressure and threats to achieve its objectives.

Equally important, the above analysis also suggests that no concrete, interest-based set of national imperatives—such as clashing territorial aspirations or fundamentally conflictual beliefs regarding regional and global norms—exists to drive Beijing and Washington toward strategic rivalry over at least the medium term. Perhaps the most significant source of such rivalry between Washington and Beijing stems from mutual suspicions regarding motives and intent. Each fears and hedges against possible attempts by the other to weaken, constrain, or undermine its position. Such fears derive more from broad assumptions, beliefs, and misunderstandings—along with changes in overall military capabilities and influence—than from unambiguous threats to the vital interests of either country. This is not to say that either country will never become a future threat to such interests. Rather, such potential threats are by no means inevitable, and if such threats emerge, their adverse effects could prove containable with skillful management.

Hence, the key strategic challenge for the next U.S. administration will be to strengthen and expand the incentives, opportunities, and means for maximizing cooperation with Beijing while minimizing those factors that could increase suspicion, misunderstanding, and overall security competition. This strategy would not preclude public and private criticism of China, the application of significant pressure or leverage, or even Washington's use of coercive diplomacy when necessary to achieve vital objectives. Nevertheless, the overall tone and message of U.S. policy toward China would do well to remain positive, affirmative, and businesslike. Moreover, negative or pressuring messages and actions would be tailored for effect as part of an overall coordinated strategy of carrots and sticks directed toward specific ends. Such an approach requires clear vision and a level of domestic political acceptance by U.S. leaders and ordinary citizens that is often lacking in U.S. policy toward China.

Therefore, the next administration's first order of business regarding China should be to set the right tone and provide a solid foundation for a productive Sino-U.S. relationship. Washington will need to explain clearly and persuasively to both the American people and the world why establishing and sustaining a "candid, constructive, and cooperative" relationship with China serves the best interest of the United States, despite the many tensions and problems that will doubtless continue to exist.[53] In order to realize such a relationship, the new administration will also need to explain why it is essential that U.S. policies and actions encourage a "responsible," "prosperous," and "open" China whose development is equitable, sustainable, and environmentally sound.[54]

Merely stating such objectives is not sufficient, however. It is important that the next administration also explain, via tangible examples, how this type of relationship would serve specific U.S. interests. Key here would be a two-pronged approach: not only referring to how persistent negotiation with a generally positive set of goals has led to success in the past but also warning of the specific dangers that could result from a hostile or confrontational relationship. In this context it is important to carry over the concept of "responsible stakeholder" and apply this concept to both China and the United States. The next administration will want to emphasize the critical importance of working with China, as well as with other major powers, to shape and sustain international regimes and to create a global community that serves U.S. and Chinese interests over the long term— rather than merely to stress the need to elicit the PRC's acceptance of the existing order.

In explaining the key overarching themes and objectives of the U.S. relationship with China, the next administration should also emphasize the importance of maintaining a strong and active military, political, and economic presence in the western Pacific. Such a posture remains essential for the maintenance of deterrence stability in the Taiwan Strait and elsewhere. To merely state this as an ongoing objective would be insufficient and perhaps even counter-productive. The next administration will also find it important to explain why the Asia-Pacific is so strategically significant to the United States and why a strong U.S. presence in the region promotes stability and serves the interests of the major regional powers, including China. Moreover, using as evidence the views of other powers in the region, Washington will need to explain the irreplaceable value of the U.S. military presence as a public good and not simply or primarily as a counterweight to rising Chinese power.

These themes and objectives imply an ambitious agenda of specific policy actions in the three strategic areas discussed above. Many of these policies will amount to a continuation of existing practices, albeit in some cases with a higher level of consistency and coordination than during the

[53] Christensen, "U.S.-China Relations."

[54] Many of the recommendations and new initiatives in this section are found in Hills, Blair, and Jannuzi, *U.S.-China Relations*.

Bush administration. At the same time, these policies should also include new initiatives.

Security

In the security arena it is important for the next administration to communicate more clearly the optimal type of security architecture that the United States should seek to establish and maintain in the western Pacific. U.S. officials and outside policy analysts often simply assert that Washington must sustain its current level of military predominance, which is centered on existing bilateral security alliances in the region, in order to maintain stability and counter or hedge against confrontational moves by other powers (usually China). On a number of issues, the United States has rarely, if ever, made an explicit effort to define internally the U.S. position and then explain this position to outside audiences: exactly how much U.S. military presence is sufficient to perform these and other functions in the context of a highly dynamic strategic environment, how the U.S. military power and alliance structure should relate to existing or emerging multilateral security structures, whether the U.S government is able to apply the level of resources required to sustain U.S. predominance, and why a U.S.-dominated power structure will remain superior to a more evenly balanced regional power structure.

The next administration should therefore re-examine the overall size, composition, and function of the U.S. military presence, as well as of the bilateral security alliances and bases upon which that presence depends. This process would be part of an overall effort to exert greater conceptual leadership over the evolving East Asian security structure. Such an examination cannot take place, however, without a more clear and detailed understanding both of the likely constraints that will exist on U.S. resources in the future and of the security-related ambitions, interests, fears, and capabilities of other major powers in the region, especially China. As some observers have pointed out, Washington is already experiencing a version of "imperial overreach" in Iraq, originally exacerbated by a poor understanding of the Middle Eastern strategic environment.[55] This danger could also emerge in Asia in the face of an increasingly capable China, a rising India, and a more diversified pattern of security interactions. One way in which the United States is apparently attempting to compensate for the prospect of its declining relative power in the region is by promoting Japan as a more capable and willing partner in regional security. Washington is also coping

---

[55] See J. Stapleton Roy, "The Rise of China and the Outlook for U.S.-China Relations" (remarks presented to the National Committee on U.S.-China Relations, Shanghai, February 28, 2005).

with this prospect by encouraging the emergence of India as a new regional power center, an effort that is part of a strategy of offshore balancing. The next administration will need to give greater thought to the combined impact of these undertakings on the East Asian strategic environment and the existing U.S.-led hub-and-spoke system of bilateral alliances.

This approach will require not only greater U.S. self-examination but also more security-oriented dialogues with other nations, including China. In other words, the United States needs to work with China and other states to develop a more inclusive Asian security dialogue and eventually a regional architecture that can relate more meaningfully to the U.S. structure of bilateral alliances. The notion of a permanent security forum in Northeast Asia based on the six-party talks is a possible starting point that could be supported by the next administration. The specific agenda and possible practical results of such an undertaking would need to be clearly discussed and agreed upon, however, by all parties early in the formation process. Moreover, the relationship of North Korea to such a forum would also need to be determined in advance. Other possible multilateral security-oriented dialogues worth considering in relation to China include: trilateral discussions among the United States, Japan, and China, especially regarding issues that relate to Sino-Japanese tensions (for example, Japan's security agenda and China's military strategy and modernization program); trilateral discussions among the United States, China, and South Korea regarding the future of the Korean Peninsula; and trilateral discussions among the United States, China, and India regarding opportunities and concerns that affect this newly emerging strategic triangle. These discussions could be subsumed within a larger regional security structure. In considering the value of such trilateral dialogues, however, Washington will need to assess the possible impact on key alliance partners, such as Japan and Australia, as well as the relationship of these discussions to broader dialogues.[56]

As part of this effort, and perhaps even more important for bilateral Sino-U.S. relations, Washington should strengthen and expand the Senior Dialogue with Beijing. Washington might include in the dialogue's agenda a more systematic discussion of medium- and long-term trends affecting the regional strategic environment and the resulting security requirements of both nations. In addition, the next administration would benefit from moving forward with the recently launched nuclear strategy dialogue with Beijing and considering a broader, high-level military strategic dialogue as well. Such dialogues can deepen mutual understanding and reduce mutual suspicion both by identifying potential areas of strategic tension over the

---

[56] For example, in the case of the first two trilateral discussions, Washington would need to consider the relationship of these discussions to the Northeast Asian security forum.

medium to long term and by exploring ways to reassure the other side regarding fears and assumptions.

Either as part of these dialogues or in a separate venue, Washington should also encourage a sustained discussion with Beijing on how to improve the ability of both sides to avoid and manage future potential politico-military crises (for example, over Taiwan or North Korea). The next administration should also deepen its military-to-military interactions with China and press Congress to jettison many of the rigid limitations on such contacts contained in the 2000 Defense Authorization Act. Despite the concerns mentioned above, such interactions, if properly designed and implemented, offer significant potential for bilateral relations.

The next administration will want to continue the long-standing U.S. policy of dual deterrence and reassurance regarding Taiwan. This policy would aim for maintaining stability across the Taiwan Strait and strengthening the prospects for improvement in Taipei-Beijing relations resulting from the 2008 Taiwanese elections. Such moves could include unambiguous and strong support for the resumption of official cross-Strait political contacts as well as the expansion of so-called functional ties in economic and social areas. The United States should not resist such contacts, which could contribute to a reduction in tensions and movement toward an eventual peaceful resolution of the Taiwan issue. At the same time, it is important that the next administration continue to strengthen the ability of the United States to detect and rapidly respond to a possible Chinese use of force. The administration's policy toward Taipei should deemphasize the provision of additional big-ticket weapons systems and focus on providing the essential infrastructure, logistics, ordnance, and other materials that will better operationalize Taiwan's existing defensive capacity. In addition, Washington would want to strongly oppose any attempt by Taipei to acquire an offensive deterrent of any kind. Overall, it is important that Washington consult closely with Taipei to develop a comprehensive strategy toward Beijing that involves political, economic, and military quid pro quo options designed to strengthen cooperation and reduce tensions while also maintaining the stability of deterrence across the Taiwan Strait. Finally, Washington should continue to discourage, or in some cases prevent, Beijing's acquisition of military capabilities or related technologies that could directly challenge U.S. military superiority in critical areas relevant to Taiwan.

The next U.S. administration must certainly continue to work closely with Beijing on the North Korean nuclear issue, despite some differences over tactics and emphasis. In this effort, Washington will need to convey clearly and convincingly to Beijing that the United States remains both committed to the denuclearization of the North Korean regime and opposed to the use of force against Pyongyang. The United States should continue to work with and through the United Nations; in addition Washington should coordinate its negotiating approach to Pyongyang with the other members of the six-party talks. In order to allay Chinese concerns and facilitate greater PRC cooperation with the United States, the next administration must work both bilaterally and through multilateral dialogue to develop greater understanding between Washington, Beijing, Seoul, and Tokyo regarding the future of the Korean Peninsula. In particular, greater understanding is needed on such issues as a permanent peace accord, the unification process, the future disposition of U.S. forces, and the presence of WMD. In order to facilitate this process, and to improve the ongoing negotiations with North Korea, the next administration will want to continue recently initiated efforts to improve ties with Seoul to the greatest extent possible, including efforts to enhance trilateral dialogue among Washington, Seoul, and Tokyo.

With regard to the U.S. bilateral relationship with Japan, to some extent Beijing has been encouraged to cooperate more closely with Asian nations and to become more integrated into the Asian system overall by the combination of a strengthening U.S.-Japan alliance and more robust U.S. efforts at deterrence and reassurance across the Asia-Pacific. Yet U.S. efforts to enhance Japan's security role and military capabilities in Asia and beyond could also prove counter-productive. In particular, such efforts could heighten anxieties in China—and perhaps elsewhere—in ways that fuel rather than dampen security competition while undermining incentives for cooperation and confidence-building. The next administration will need to provide a fuller and more convincing account of the ultimate scope and objectives that should guide the expansion of Japan's security posture both within and outside the U.S.-Japan alliance. In the absence of a more open and inclusive security architecture in the Asia-Pacific, sustained high levels of U.S. support for such expansion could contribute significantly to regional bipolarization. In general, the United States needs to couple any advances in military posture and relationships with regional states that have clear implications for China with reassuring political initiatives designed to improve security relations and build confidence among all major regional powers.

In order to avoid projecting an overly alarmist assessment of growing PLA capabilities to Japan and other countries, the next administration might also work to make the annual Department of Defense report to Congress on the Chinese military a more accurate, balanced, and comprehensive assessment of PLA force modernization and doctrinal development. Although providing much good information on these topics, the annual report at times has adopted what many outside PLA specialists regard as questionable, overly alarmist interpretations of Chinese motives and intentions. The report has also included inconsistent and incomplete data on some weapons systems and modernization programs. The result is a document that is sometimes as much a political statement as it is a serious specialist examination of the Chinese military. To some extent, this outcome is unavoidable, given the political dimensions of the inter-agency process involved in the drafting of the report, the classification issues that arise, and the intensely political nature of Congress, the report's primary sponsor. More can be done, however, to make the report a more reliable assessment of PLA modernization.[57] At the same time, Washington should continue to press China for more information on its military modernization program.

The next administration should also make every effort to facilitate and sustain improved relations between Tokyo and Beijing. It is clearly in Washington's interest to encourage greater cooperation and reconciliation between Japan and China over all areas of contention, including territorial disputes, economic rivalries, and historical issues. A confrontational Sino-Japanese relationship would obstruct U.S. efforts to work with Beijing in a wide variety of areas. Moreover, under some circumstances—for example, a conflict over resources in the East China Sea—such a relationship could even draw Washington into a military confrontation with Beijing. The next administration could therefore consider advancing its interests through the promotion of a U.S.-China-Japan forum and perhaps through an offer to provide Washington's good offices "to facilitate Sino-Japanese dialogue on areas of mutual interest, such as maritime security, energy security, counter-terrorism, and nonproliferation."[58]

Economics and Trade

In the critical area of economics and trade, the next administration can contribute significantly to the maintenance and improvement of Sino-U.S. relations by acting more decisively to address problems within the U.S. economy. This approach would include, for example, shrinking the size of the U.S. deficit, raising the savings rate, reducing consumption, strengthening the educational system, and investing more in technological innovation. Many of the problems that Americans lay at the doorstep of

---

[57] See Dennis J. Blasko, "The 2007 Report on the Chinese Military: The Top 10 List of Missing Topics," *Joint Forces Quarterly* 47 (Fourth Quarter 2007): 48–54.

[58] Hills, Blair, and Jannuzi, *U.S.-China Relations.*

Beijing are actually due—in part at least—to U.S. mismanagement of these and other economic and trade-related issues.[59]

Second, when addressing U.S. economic and trade concerns with Beijing, the next administration—and Congress in particular—should recognize that integrating China into the global economy and eliciting China's greater acceptance of international norms are multilateral challenges. Such challenges will require consultation and coordination with many nations in the international community. As suggested above, adopting a purely unilateral or protectionist approach to such issues is unlikely to produce many positive results. Moreover, such an approach could even prove counter-productive, given the regional and global nature of many economic problems.

Third, on specific bilateral economic and trade issues, the next administration should continue the approach of the Bush administration in emphasizing persistent, quiet dialogue and negotiation rather than applying public, confrontational pressure. Such an approach, if properly timed and gauged to appeal to specific interests within the Chinese bureaucracy and economy, usually produces more positive outcomes than do threats, finger-pointing, and cajoling. Given China's growing economic leverage and influence within the global economy and in the bilateral Sino-U.S. economic relationship, a confrontational approach is more likely to produce credible counter-threats from the Chinese side than compromise or accommodation.

Fourth, the next administration could utilize the WTO Dispute Settlement Body more systematically to achieve greater Chinese compliance with the country's obligations as a WTO member. Furthermore, the administration will want to eschew actions that would "punish China in a manner that would violate [U.S.] WTO obligations or would benefit a few litigious industries at the expense of broader economic interests."[60]

Fifth, it is important that the next administration continue the Strategic Economic Dialogue with China, which should remain focused on long-term, strategic issues (such as energy efficiency, climate change, and balanced economic development) rather than on short-term problems (such as China's currency revaluation and violations of intellectual property rights). More immediate issues should be handled through technical contacts between specialized ministries or through the WTO dispute-settlement process. A

---

[59] C. Fred Bergsten et al., *China: The Balance Sheet: What the World Needs to Know Now about the Emerging Superpower* (New York: PublicAffairs, 2006); and Hills, Blair, and Jannuzi, *U.S.-China Relations.*

[60] Robert E. Scott and Daniel J. Ikenson, "Should the Next U.S. President Adopt a Tougher Stance on Trade Policy with China?" Council on Foreign Relations, Online Debate, March 31–April 4, 2008, http://www.cfr.org/publication/15888.

focus on long-term, broad issues is necessary in order to overcome narrow, stove-pipe approaches, increase broad-based strategic thinking, and thereby facilitate greater cooperation between Washington and Beijing in handling common economic challenges.

Finally, the United States should continue to encourage Beijing to realize that the best way for China to pursue its interests in the energy sector is not by seeking preferential equity deals with unstable regimes, or by acquiring deepwater, long-range power projection capabilities, but rather by working through market mechanisms to help strengthen global markets overall. This effort has enjoyed only sporadic support in Washington and is at times undermined by actions taken by other branches of the U.S. government— such as when Congress strongly opposes the sale of U.S. oil companies to Chinese firms. Such moves short-circuit established procedures for vetting sensitive economic transactions and arguably weaken the attempt to encourage China to base its energy policies on market-based criteria. In addition, the next administration may want to facilitate China's eventual membership in the International Energy Agency.

WMD and Nontraditional Security

Regarding U.S. policy toward China in the area of WMD counterproliferation, Washington will need to intensify past efforts emphasizing the combination of dialogue, public and private pressure and inducements, coordination with other nations, support for international regimes, and targeted and low-key sanctions against specific violating Chinese entities. The next administration should also continue to assist China in the development of controls over the transfer of dual-use items by providing expanded technical assistance to Beijing in strengthening export control and border control programs and capabilities.[61] At the same time, it is important that Washington re-examine its entire approach to the control of the sale of advanced and dual-use products and technologies to China. The sheer number and complexity of U.S. regulations governing such exports have grown over the years, thus generating criticism among many businesses, experts, and foreign observers that regulations have become excessively complicated, inconsistent, and unwieldy.

Also critical will be prioritizing greater attention to working with China to address the increasingly important nontraditional security threat of global warming and environmental degradation. As Elizabeth Economy suggests, Washington needs to develop a limited and coherent set of

---

[61] "2007 Report to Congress," U.S.-China Economic and Security Review Commission, November 2007, http://www.uscc.gov/annual_report/2007/report_to_congress.pdf.

priorities in this area. One approach is to focus on strengthening the legal system with regard to environmental protection or the promotion of energy efficiency in China. Given the size of China and low capacity of the Chinese government to address this problem, the United States must first exhibit overall leadership in order to produce any genuine results.[62]

Finally, the effective formulation and implementation of the above policy options will require the strong support and involvement of the president of the United States. The next president must personally set the tone and direction of policy and vest unambiguous authority in his national security advisor to provide supervision and coordination to the entire policy process. Moreover, it is important that the president ensures that senior officials in key positions within the major agencies working on China policy (the Departments of State, Defense, Treasury, and Commerce and the U.S. Trade Representative Office) include as many individuals as possible with significant China-related expertise. Past experience has shown that without such direct presidential engagement, National Security Council oversight, and agency expertise, policy toward China can easily become uncoordinated, contradictory, and driven by competing personal and bureaucratic interests. The U.S. relationship with China has become too important to permit such dysfunctionality.

Clearly, the next administration faces very significant challenges in coping with an increasingly capable, influential, and rapidly changing China. The policy record on both sides and the larger environment within which both nations operate, however, suggest that this situation also presents the next administration with a historic opportunity to shape the course of a rising great power while also altering Washington's behavior in ways that could provide stability and prosperity for many years to come.

---

[62] Elizabeth C. Economy, "The Great Leap Backward?" *Foreign Affairs* 86, no. 5 (September/October 2007): 38–59.

EXECUTIVE SUMMARY

This chapter assesses the last eight years of Japanese security policy and U.S.-Japan relations and draws implications for the next U.S. administration.

MAIN ARGUMENT:
- Having historically relied on U.S. extended deterrence, Japan has also pursued "comprehensive security," integrating military concerns with attention to economic, food, and other nontraditional security arenas.
- During the era of the Bush and Koizumi administrations, Japan expanded the country's military capabilities as well as cooperation with the U.S.
- Japan's major military concerns are China and the DPRK.
- Domestic politics and Japan's comprehensive views of security continue to direct Japan away from rapid increases in security posture.

POLICY IMPLICATIONS:
- If the U.S. can ensure confirmed denuclearization of the DPRK while coordinating with Japan on abductees and missiles, Japan will be less likely to lose trust in the U.S. or move radically to enhance the country's military capabilities.
- If the U.S. maintains positive relations with both China and Japan, the temptation for either state to view the other as a threat will be reduced.
- If divided government continues in Japan, the country will be less likely to embrace enhanced military roles and missions, and even minor security issues will be politicized.
- If the U.S. and Japan can cooperate on security issues in a division of labor that includes non-military activities such as global warming, disaster relief, and pandemics, the two states will build greater harmony into the relationship. This harmony may also then benefit the military relationship.

Japan: Divided Government, Diminished Resources

T.J. Pempel

The relationship between Japan and the United States has given Washington its most important and dependable East Asian partner for over 50 years. Episodic disagreements and the inherent asymmetries in the relationship have not impeded a mutually beneficial security, economic, and diplomatic partnership. Although future cooperation and close ties remain a common goal of Tokyo and Washington, Japanese policymakers face new global and regional challenges at the very time when the domestic political and economic resources they need to confront these challenges have been weakened by economic sluggishness and a divided government. Numerous challenges now present themselves to the governments of both countries—and more will surely face the incoming U.S administration. In dealing with these challenges, the new administration will likely find Japan to be a less unified partner than Washington might want, particularly on military cooperation. Other areas such as global warming, disaster relief, and nontraditional security provide more favorable opportunities for future cooperation. How the new U.S. government chooses to see these challenges—as frustrations or as opportunities—will go a long way toward either improving or weakening the bilateral partnership.

This chapter assesses the last eight years of Japanese security policy and U.S.-Japan relations and draws policy implications for the next U.S. administration. After first providing an overview of Japanese grand strategy,

T.J. Pempel is Professor of Political Science at the University of California–Berkeley. He can be reached at <pempel@berkeley.edu>.

The author would like to thank Christopher W. Hughes, Peter J. Katzenstein, Ellis S. Krauss, Robert M. (Skipp) Orr, Richard Samuels, Steven Vogel, and two anonymous reviewers for helpful comments. Any remaining factual or judgmental errors remain the author's own.

the chapter examines bilateral military ties under the Bush and Koizumi administrations and analyzes Japan's two main security concerns, the Democratic People's Republic of Korea (DPRK) and China. The chapter then addresses the current ability of Japan to be responsive to any new security challenges, given a divided government and diminished resources. Finally, the chapter identifies the major issues in the bilateral relationship that will confront the next U.S. administration and examines the implications of these issues for U.S. policy.

Japanese Grand Strategy and Core National Objectives

For the past 60 years the template mapping Japanese grand strategy was the so-called Yoshida Doctrine.[1] This doctrine—engineered by Prime Minister Yoshida Shigeru soon after World War II and bearing conspicuous residues even today—anchored Japan's military security in a close bilateral relationship with the United States while keeping military expenditures religiously close to 1% of GNP and freeing public resources for enhanced economic development. Non-military routes provided the path to greater national autonomy. The beneficial consequences for Japan were military security and the world's second largest economy.

The large numbers of U.S. military forces permanently stationed on Japanese soil have been a reliable keystone in the U.S. arc of bases stretching from the Aleutians through Korea and Japan and further south through Australia and Diego Garcia. The robust U.S. military presence in Japan has fostered U.S. global strategy and, in combination with Japan's limited military expenditures, reduced fears across Asia of either a regional power vacuum or a potential Japanese military resurgence.

Japanese security policies have nevertheless been the subject of intense domestic political debate for most of the postwar years. Until the early 1990s a vigorous political left and a palpable public disposition toward pacifism as well as preponderant domestic norms helped Japan's conservative mainstream keep tight limits on military activities and expenditures despite periodic U.S. and domestic pressures to the contrary.[2] Meanwhile, local governments frequently impeded national initiatives, particularly on military and basing issues.

---

[1] Kenneth B. Pyle, *Japan Rising: The Resurgence of Japanese Power and Purpose* (New York: Public Affairs, 2007), chap. 8.

[2] Peter J. Katzenstein, *Cultural Norms and National Security: Police and Military in Postwar Japan* (Ithaca: Cornell University Press, 1996); and Peter J. Katzenstein, *Rethinking Japanese Security: Internal and External Dimensions* (Oxford: Routledge, 2008).

Facing the classic alliance dilemma of entanglement versus abandonment, Japan's ruling conservatives have shown more fear of abandonment than of unwanted enmeshment in U.S. military activities. Yet Tokyo has hedged against over-reliance on Japan's military links with the United States. Thus, while the United States has traditionally defined "security" primarily in military terms, Japan has self-consciously pursued "comprehensive security" (*sogo anzen hosho*). Resource poor and late to industrialize, Japan has continually confronted a gnawing dependency on foreign imports of raw materials and an inescapable vulnerability to economic shocks from abroad.[3] Formally articulated by Prime Minister Ohira Masayoshi in 1980, comprehensive security initially centered on Japan's need to cope not only with military threats but also with a range of economic, environmental, food, energy, pandemic, and illegal drug challenges. Japan's 1996 National Defense Program Outline (NDPO) furthered this theme.[4]

Geographic proximity is a vital first line in Japan's security planning. Japan's central concern has been warding off threats and improving ties to the rest of the Asian region; Tokyo's greatest asset in advancing this agenda has been the country's economic and technological prowess. From the 1950s into the early 1990s the combination of Japanese foreign aid, investment monies, and the regional production networks of private Japanese companies were the catalyst for the "East Asian economic miracle." Japan also pursued a multidimensional approach to security through cooperative, multilateral frameworks within Asia that included the Asia-Pacific Economic Cooperation forum (APEC), the ASEAN Regional Forum (ARF), ASEAN +3, and the East Asia Summit (EAS) as well as regionally focused cooperation in a host of nontraditional security areas such as global warming and human security. The result was a strategy of "bilateralism plus."[5]

In the process of establishing this multidimensional approach, Tokyo bolstered Japan's regional security and economic fortunes and enhanced the country's claim as putative regional leader. At the height of Japan's economic success, Tokyo believed Japan could "shape its strategic environment from a position of leadership within Asia without having to

---

[3] Kenneth B. Pyle and Eric Heginbotham, "Japan," in *Strategic Asia 2001–02: Power and Purpose*, ed. Richard J. Ellings and Aaron L. Friedberg (Seattle: The National Bureau of Asian Research, 2001), 77.

[4] Pyle and Heginbotham, "Japan," 71–126.

[5] Christopher W. Hughes and Akiko Fukushima, "U.S.-Japan Security Relations: Toward Bilateralism Plus?" in *Beyond Bilateralism: U.S.-Japan Relations in the New Asia-Pacific*, ed. Ellis S. Krauss and T.J. Pempel (Stanford: Stanford University Press, 2004), 61–63.

remilitarize."[6] In taking this preponderantly commercial focus with the promise of a "win-win" scenario, Tokyo avoided destabilizing the regional balance of power while buffering Japan against any military backlash from the country's immediate neighbors.

In the last decade or so Japan has also—as part of a general hedge against exclusively military approaches to security—taken on a larger global role in multiple arenas that fit with Tokyo's definition of comprehensive security. An initial supporter of the Kyoto Protocol, Japan continues to press for multilateral action on global warming. Japan also supported the International Criminal Court and signed an international agreement to ban anti-personnel landmines. In cooperation with a number of other countries, Japan advanced the concept of "human security" as a core doctrine of the United Nations. Japan also joined 147 other countries in adopting a new cultural diversity treaty negotiated within the framework of the UN Educational, Scientific and Cultural Organization (UNESCO), a move opposed only by the United States and Israel. Japan has cooperated with other countries on a range of nontraditional security issues such as drug trafficking, restrictions on biofoods, and piracy, among others. In short, though aspiring to be recognized as a great power, Japan has worked with many "middle powers" to create a more secure global environment without reliance on military means.[7] Such moves have often enjoyed widespread global support despite opposition from the United States.[8]

Unsurprisingly, Japan's differing conceptions of security have separated Tokyo from Washington on certain key issues. Even at the height of the Cold War, for example, Japan pursued far closer economic relations with China than did the United States. Seeking to ensure stable oil supplies from the Arab Middle East during the first oil shock of 1973, Japan broke definitively with U.S. support for Israel. More recently Japan provided tangible military support for U.S. actions in Afghanistan and Iraq even as Japanese diplomats simultaneously pursued a "dual hedge," downplaying the country's U.S. links so as to protect Japan's vital oil channels to Saudi Arabia and Iran.[9] Additionally, with more than 10% of Japan's oil imports coming from Iran,

---

[6] Michael J. Green, "Japan is Back: Why Tokyo's New Assertiveness is Good for Washington," *Foreign Affairs* 86, no. 2 (March/April 2007): 143.

[7] Yoshihide Soeya, *Nihon no "midoru pawaa" gaiko: Sengo Nihon no sentaku to koso* [Japan's "Middle Power" Diplomacy: Choices and Conceptions in Postwar Japan] (Tokyo: Chikuma Shinsho, 2003).

[8] Yves Tiberghien and Julian Dierkes, "Minerva's Moment: Japan, Canada and the EU in Global Institution-Building" (paper prepared for a conference at the University of British Columbia in Vancouver, Canada, August 21–22, 2006).

[9] Eric Heginbotham and Richard J. Samuels, "Japan's Dual Hedge," *Foreign Affairs* 81, no. 5 (September/October 2002): 114.

and with Japanese firms having won the preferential negotiating position for Iran's Azadegan oil field, Japan was slower than other U.S. allies to pressure Tehran on Iran's nuclear program.

No single event so challenged Japan's self-definition of its security policies or so transformed the country's grand thinking than did the 1990–91 Gulf War.[10] Reiterating a long-standing position that Article 9 of the Japanese constitution prohibited the sending of military forces abroad, Tokyo rejected Washington's requests for even a token military supplement to U.S. invasion forces. Under withering hectoring from U.S. Treasury Secretary James Baker, Japan eventually contributed a total of $13 billion to underwrite the war effort—by far the largest contribution from any single country—only to have this gesture disdained as "checkbook diplomacy." Indeed, one major newspaper advertisement by the Kuwaiti government thanking the countries that had helped Kuwait regain independence failed even to mention Japan. Made painfully aware that commercial success alone would not guarantee global power and influence, Japanese policymaking circles swirled in a paroxysm of resentment and reassessment over how best to supplement Japan's preponderant reliance on economic tools and to make a more "positive contribution" to international peace and stability. The result has been a steadily enhanced military capability, a greater willingness to utilize Japanese security personnel abroad, and closer military cooperation with the United States. Still, Japan has avoided any headlong plunge in those directions

Japan's self-defined strategic vision has also been gradually extended beyond the country's immediate neighborhood. In 2004 the Japan Defense Agency (upgraded to the Ministry of Defense in 2007) formulated the National Defense Program Guidelines (NDPG). The NDPG called for Japan to move beyond traditional "defensive defense" both to prevent threats from reaching Japan and to improve the international security environment.[11]

These efforts to redefine or supplement Japan's long-standing grand strategy have spurred vigorous debate among policymakers.[12] The closest Japan has come to agreement on any unifying strategic concept has been an effort to re-brand itself as a "normal" power.[13] Rarely, however, does

[10] Shinichi Kitaoka, Yamazaki Masakazu, and Watanabe Taizo, "Wangan Senso to wa nani datta ka: Nihon tenkanten o furikaeru" [What Do We Make of the Gulf War: Reflecting on Japan's Turning Point], *Gaiko Foramu*, no. 158 (September 2001): 28–37.

[11] Japanese Defense Agency, *Defense of Japan: 2006* (Tokyo: Boeicho, 2006), 103–4.

[12] Richard J. Samuels, *Securing Japan: Tokyo's Grand Strategy and the Future of East Asia* (Ithaca: Cornell University Press, 2007), chap. 5.

[13] The term "normal power" was first popularized by Ozawa Ichiro, *Nihon Kaizo Keikaku* (Tokyo: Kodansha, 1993), published in English as *Blueprint for a New Japan* (Tokyo: Kodansha, 1994).

the term "normal" generate comprehensive agreement on operational tangibility. Yet Japan's ongoing recalibration of its regional and global role provides a powerful opportunity for the United States to play an active part in that self-definition so as to maximize Japan's readjustments to U.S. self-interest.

Enhanced Military Cooperation under Bush and Koizumi

The eight years of the Bush administration overlapped heavily with five-and-a-half years of Koizumi Junichiro's prime ministership (April 2001–September 2006), and for much of that time the two leaders saw eye to eye on strengthening military cooperation between their two countries. The redefinition of Japan's military role during this period was not without problems; however, in the wake of Koizumi's departure and in the waning years of the Bush administration the two countries have faced substantially more difficulties in continuing that close military collaboration, largely because of changes in leadership and the fact that Japan now has a divided government.

Upon first taking office, the Bush administration committed to bolstering bilateral ties with Japan and reversing what it viewed as errant Clinton policies that treated China as a "strategic partner." The Bush strategy pivoted on the contradictory presumption that China would be the United States' next major "strategic competitor." Under this strategy, Japan would thus be showcased as the core U.S. ally in East Asia and the bilateral relationship would move from "burden-sharing" to "power-sharing." The outlines of this new policy were articulated in the October 2000 election-year report "The United States and Japan: Advancing Toward a Mature Partnership" penned by Richard Armitage along with a number of Japan specialists, many of whom joined the Bush administration.[14]

The events of September 11 catalyzed vast changes in U.S. strategic activities. The 2001 Quadrennial Defense Review, the June 2002 speech delivered at West Point by Bush, and the September 2002 and March 2006 publications of the National Security Strategy were the major articulations of the Bush administration's new approach. The invasions of Afghanistan and Iraq were their most concrete manifestations. A less visible but vital underpinning of the new strategy was a U.S. rebasing plan aimed at enhancing U.S. military flexibility. No longer would the United States focus

---

[14] Richard L. Armitage and Joseph Nye, "The United States and Japan: Advancing Toward a Mature Partnership," Institute for National Strategic Studies, Special Report, October 11, 2000.

on "bases in places" to deter attacks by neighboring states. Instead the United States would shift to a limited number of extensive bases in a few "bedrock" allied states (such as Japan and probably Australia) supplemented by smaller facilities holding pre-positioned equipment in a larger number of "lily pad" countries to which highly mobile U.S. forces could deploy quickly in response to changing contingencies. Turning the U.S. military into a more agile and globally flexible force for an altered global strategy meant weaving U.S. bilateral alliances into a more comprehensive fabric.[15]

Numerous policymakers in Japan, especially within the military and the ruling Liberal Democratic Party (LDP), welcomed the U.S. shift as the perfect incentive to invigorate Japan's military and bolster bilateral military ties in accord with long-shelved plans. The radical collapse of the Japanese Socialist Party, the country's main pacifist opposition, had conveniently diluted a major pro-pacifist impediment to these efforts. U.S. calls for a more activist and militarily involved Japan found an enthusiastic supporter in Koizumi.

Koizumi took office on April 24, 2001, when the ruling LDP was in deep electoral trouble. As prime minister, Koizumi promised to reform his party even if that meant destroying the party in the process. Exploiting changes begun earlier, Koizumi dramatically boosted the powers of the prime minister's office and the cabinet, weakened the powerful policymaking abilities of party factions and bureaucratic agencies, and combined his enhanced executive control with swashbuckling media savvy in the service of engineering reforms on two key policy fronts—economic deregulation and an enhanced Japanese military.[16]

In contrast to Japan's feckless behavior during the first Iraq war, Koizumi acted quickly and decisively in support of U.S. actions following September 11. Following a visit to the United States within two weeks of the attacks, Koizumi returned home and pushed through several new laws to amend the Self-Defense Forces (SDF) law, to combat terrorism, and to dispatch three convoy vessels to the Indian Ocean—all within six weeks of the U.S. invasion of Afghanistan. Japan also chaired the January

---

[15] Christopher W. Hughes, "Japanese Military Modernization: In Search of a 'Normal' Security Role," in *Strategic Asia 2005–06: Military Modernization in an Era of Uncertainty*, ed. Ashley J. Tellis and Michael Wills (Seattle: The National Bureau of Asian Research, 2005), 105–34.

[16] Ellis S. Krauss and Robert Pekkanen "Explaining Party Adaptation to Electoral Reform: The Discreet Charm of the LDP?" *Journal of Japanese Studies* 30, no. 1 (Winter 2004): 1–34; T.J. Pempel, "Japanese Strategy Under Koizumi," in *Japanese Strategic Thought toward Asia*, ed. Gilbert Rozman, Kazuhiko Togo, and Joseph P. Ferguson (New York: Palgrave, 2007), 109–33; Margarita Estevez-Abe, "Japan's Shift toward a Westminster System: A Structural Analysis of the 2005 Lower House Election and Its Aftermath," *Asian Survey* 46, no. 4 (August 2006): 632–51; and Samuels, *Securing Japan*, 72–77.

2002 meeting on Afghan reconstruction, taking the opportunity to play to Japanese strengths in nation-building.

On Iraq Koizumi distinguished himself as one of the industrial world's few vigorous supporters of U.S. actions, pushing ahead despite the lack of popular support.[17] Koizumi engineered a series of legal changes allowing Japan to send a contingent of non-combat ground troops to Iraq and pledged $1.5 billion in aid to Iraq along with $3.5 billion in loans to the Madrid donors' conference. Though primarily symbolic in military terms, this response was more militarily robust than anything Japan had done in the past half-century.[18] Japan proceeded even though "America consider[ed] itself a nation at war while Japan [did] not."[19]

Koizumi also bolstered Japan's own military capabilities and integrated SDF activities more closely with those of the United States. A round of military modernization that began in late 2001 included the addition of aerial tankers and helicopter-carrying destroyers. Japan's December 2004 NDPG outlined a host of new security directions. Previously Japan had been deliberately vague regarding potential sources of military challenge; the NDPG, however, explicitly identified the DPRK and China as Japan's most probable threats. No longer focusing exclusively on preventing conventional attacks on Japan's home islands, the country would instead prepare for threats both from ballistic missiles and from terrorists. The NDPG also gave enhanced attention to broader regional and global conditions that might imperil Japanese security. Peacekeeping operations would be integral to Japan's new security, as would the creation of a multifunctional military capability with a centralized SDF command and a rapid reaction force. Perhaps most importantly, the new NDPG also committed Japan to be the first foreign participant in the U.S. missile defense system and ended the prior ban on the export of military technologies for items developed in that project. Japan gave missile defense budgetary priority in the 2005–09 Midterm Defense Program and accepted deployment of the U.S. missile defense destroyer, USS *Shiloh*. Japan also made various moves to enhance U.S.-Japanese weapons systems interoperability. Japan's national spy satellite system in outer space was upgraded as was the status of the Japan Defense Agency, which achieved full ministerial status on January 9, 2007.

---

[17] The defeat of the Taliban regime in Afghanistan was relatively welcome in Japan (46% support); the invasion of Iraq much less so (71% opposed with only 16% supporting). Paul Midford, *Japanese Public Opinion and the War on Terrorism: Implications for Japan's Security Strategy*, Policy Studies, no. 27 (Washington, D.C.: East-West Center, 2006), 29–30.

[18] Heginbotham and Samuels, "Japan's Dual Hedge," 116.

[19] James L. Schoff, "Transformation of the U.S.-Japan Alliance," *Fletcher Forum of World Affairs* 31, no. 1 (Winter 2007): 85–101, http://fletcher.tufts.edu/forum/archives/pdfs/31-1pdfs/Schoff.pdf.

The two sides completed a formal dialogue on alliance transformation in May 2007, giving new emphasis to power projection, amphibious capabilities, force transformation, and improved command and control.[20] Tokyo established new areas of technological cooperation with Washington on cyberspace defense operations, surveillance and reconnaissance, integrated disaster relief planning and response, robust air and missile defense systems, and shared intelligence, among other areas.[21]

Of particular significance, the capabilities and activities of the Japan Coast Guard (JCG)—not officially part of Japan's Self-Defense Forces— were also expanded under Koizumi. The JCG's five hundred ships are slated for a major modernization at a cost of $450 million between 2006 and 2012. Japan's coast guard is also involved in numerous military-to-military cooperation activities with neighboring coast guards and has become the core of Japan's maritime security efforts in Southeast Asia. Coast guard vessels have even become part of Japanese aid packages with the transfer of JCG ships to Indonesia and the Philippines, a move that narrowly remains outside Japan's overt national ban on weapons transfers.[22]

Though Japan has no substantial Muslim population and views terrorism through a different optic, Koizumi ensured close anti-terrorism cooperation with the United States by freezing the assets of terrorist organizations and aligning Japan's anti-money-laundering provisions with new international conventions. Tokyo has ordered Japanese embassies and consulates to be more assiduous in screening visa applicants and has exchanged customs officials as part of the U.S. Container Security Initiative.[23] Japan joined the U.S.-initiated Proliferation Security Initiative (PSI) in 2003 and the following year hosted a PSI maritime interdiction exercise. In May 2006 the Defense Policy Review Initiative further strengthened the functions of the bilateral alliance for regional—and now global—security.

Japan also allowed the United States to deploy a Nimitz-class nuclear-powered aircraft carrier, the USS *George Washington,* to replace the conventionally powered USS *Kitty Hawk* at Yokosuka beginning in August 2008. In a shift that enhances Japan's role in the U.S. global military strategy and deepens ties between the U.S. military and the Japanese Ground SDF, Japan permitted the transfer of U.S. Army I Corps command functions from

[20] Hughes, "Japanese Military Modernization," 122.

[21] Thomas A. Drohan, *American-Japanese Security Agreements, Past and Present* (Jefferson: McFarland, 2007), 174–75.

[22] Richard J. Samuels, "'New Fighting Power!' Japan's Growing Maritime Capabilities and East Asian Security," *International Security* 32, no. 3 (Winter 2007/2008): 101–3.

[23] H. Richard Friman et al., "Immovable Object? Japan's Security Policy in East Asia," in *Beyond Japan: The Dynamics of East Asian Regionalism,* ed. Peter J. Katzenstein and Takashi Shiraishi (Ithaca: Cornell University Press, 2006), 106.

Fort Lewis, Washington, to Camp Zama in Kanagawa Prefecture. Japan proceeded with this transfer despite elite fears that this move represented both a substantive change in the geographical scope of the Japan-U.S. Security Treaty and a further shift in Japan's security policy from "collective defense" to the more sweeping principle of "collective security."[24]

Yet Japan continues to resist complete interoperability and has sought to protect national production of key weapons systems. Japanese policymakers have also resisted an explicit commitment to collective defense. They continue to limit SDF dispatch to non-combat functions, underscoring Japan's contention that such actions are predicated not on the bilateral alliance but on specific UN resolutions. In these ways, Japanese policymakers have retained legal safeguards that limit the country's participation in military operations that are not sanctioned by the UN and have avoided setting precedents that, under the bilateral security treaty, might commit Japan to specific actions in any future East Asian conflicts.[25]

Japan's enhanced military role and closer cooperation with the U.S. military dovetailed with Koizumi's renewed push for constitutional revision, particularly related to Article 9. Revisionist sentiment had been heavily promoted both by the *Yomiuri Shimbun* and by numerous conservative politicians who characterize Article 9 as a major barrier to international cooperation. Public support for revision increased during the Koizumi administration, and a national referendum law, detailing the electoral procedures under which such a revision would be carried out, was passed in May 2007 and has set the stage for holding such a referendum as early as 2010.

Important supplements to U.S.-Japan military cooperation have also gone forward since the turn of the century. Among these supplements are the initiation of the U.S.-Japan Joint Security Consultative Committee (JSC), also called the "two plus two" meeting because it involves each country's foreign and defense secretary or minister; the U.S.-Japan Strategic Development Alliance (SDA) to coordinate the two countries' development assistance; and the Trilateral Security Dialogue among the United States, Japan, and Australia. In short, major transformations of the alliance were carried out largely under the Koizumi administration. Equally important is that Japan's treatment of specific regional problems has largely dovetailed with U.S. approaches.

---

[24] See, for example, Hughes, "Japanese Military Modernization," 105–34; and Hughes and Fukushima, "U.S.-Japan Security Relations," 55–86.

[25] Hughes and Fukushima, "U.S.-Japan Security Relations," 75–76.

Having outlined the general dynamics of the U.S.-Japan military partnership, this chapter now will explore the two key regional players that most directly affect Japan's military security and the impact these concerns might have on the U.S.-Japan security relationship.

The DPRK: A "Dagger Still Pointed at the Heart of Japan"

No single country is presumed by Japanese policymakers to pose a more immediate military threat than the DPRK. In August 1998 the DPRK launched a long-range Taepodong-1 missile over northern Japan in "a brazen act that shook the Japanese out of their remaining complacency about North Korea the way *Sputnik* shook the United States in 1957."[26] By 2008 the DPRK had material for eight to ten nuclear weapons, a substantial contingent of long-range missiles, and a fleet of spy ships. The DPRK is the only country in Northeast Asia that has not signed the Chemical Weapons Convention. Furthermore, well over 100,000 pro–North Korean residents in Japan were, until recently, contributing as much as one billion yen a year to the DPRK, and DPRK transfers of illegal drugs (especially methamphetamines) to Japan create a serious domestic social problem.[27] On December 22–23, 2001, bilateral tensions turned into a shooting exchange when a vessel from the recently invigorated Coast Guard engaged in Japan's first hostile combat since World War II by firing on and sinking a DPRK spy ship that had penetrated Japanese waters. The Japanese government salvaged the wreck and put it on public display in downtown Tokyo well marked with signs underscoring the threats posed by the ship and the DPRK.

Despite the many problems between Japan and the DPRK—and despite the January 2002 "axis of evil" speech given by Bush—Tanaka Hitoshi, then director general of Asian and Oceania affairs at the Ministry of Foreign Affairs, persuaded Koizumi after extensive behind-the-scenes negotiations to travel to Pyongyang in September 2002 seeking the normalization of bilateral relations. Instead, the trip opened a Pandora's box surrounding Japanese citizens abducted by the DPRK decades earlier. Kim Jong-il personally admitted that the DPRK had carried out the abductions; however, what was intended as a goodwill gesture that would smooth relations instead inflamed Japanese public opinion—particularly when only five of the sixteen abductees identified by Japan were released. The DPRK claimed that three of those identified by Japan had never

26 Michael J. Green, *Japan's Reluctant Realism: Foreign Policy Challenges in an Era of Uncertain Power* (New York: Palgrave, 2001), 22.

27 Keiichi Tsunekawa, "Why So Many Maps There? Japan and Regional Cooperation," in *Remapping East Asia: The Construction of a Region*, ed. T.J. Pempel (Ithaca: Cornell University Press, 2005), 101–48.

been in the country and the other eight had died under mysterious circumstances. Japanese media and the domestic right wing exploded in an anti-DPRK frenzy demanding that the regime give a "full accounting" of all abductees and that Japan freeze efforts to normalize bilateral ties. Japan-DPRK relations remained frozen until the DPRK announced on June 16, 2008, that it would reinvestigate the previously "closed" abductees issue, providing a potential breakthrough in stalled bilateral ties, the outcome of which was still unclear as of this writing.

In October 2002, in the immediate aftermath of Koizumi's trip, the United States publicly accused the DPRK of secretly pursuing a program to produce highly enriched uranium. These accusations led to the major crisis over the DPRK's nuclear activity that has percolated ever since. Responding to U.S. charges, Pyongyang ended its adherence to the Treaty on the Non-Proliferation of Nuclear Weapons (NPT), declared that it was pursuing a nuclear weapons program, and reactivated its plutonium plant at Yongbyon. The DPRK subsequently carried out provocative missile tests in July 2006 and exploded a small nuclear device that October. These actions deepened pre-existing Japanese perceptions of the DPRK as a menacing neighbor. That the DPRK is planning specific military adventures toward Japan remains unlikely but, as Samuels has aptly noted, "The DPRK makes it very easy for threat inflators."[28]

The six-party talks that began in August 2003 took a multilateral approach to the DPRK's nuclear program. Cooperation between Japan and the United States was the watchword throughout the initial years of these talks, with both sides equally committed to the complete and verifiable denuclearization of the Korean Peninsula. Japan also worked with the United States on curtailing North Korean WMD and the smuggling of drugs and currency. The most visible evidence of these mutual efforts has been Japan's large-scale monitoring and inspection of DPRK ships entering Japanese ports and cooperation in the PSI.[29]

When the six-party talks stalled in late 2004, Koizumi relied on his personal ties with Bush to encourage a softening of the U.S. negotiating posture. Following the DPRK's missile testing in July 2006, however, Japan took an even tougher position. Imposing unilateral sanctions, Tokyo closed Japan's ports to DPRK ships, ended visits by North Koreans to Japan, and pressed for severe UN sanctions. A Japanese court has cracked down on Chosen Soren—the de facto DPRK embassy in Japan—ordering the payment of $550 million on overdue debts the DPRK owes the Japanese

---

[28] Samuels, *Securing Japan*, 149.

[29] Friman et al., "Immovable Object?" 44.

government. After Koizumi left office and Abe Shinzo succeeded him as prime minister, Japan's position toughened further even as the United States shifted to a softer negotiating stance following the DPRK nuclear test and the 2006 U.S. congressional elections. The United States and Japan moved further apart as Washington began to decouple the abductees issue from the DPRK's demand to be removed from the U.S. list of state sponsors of terrorism. Throughout the Abe administration, Japanese representatives remained the most hawkish of the six parties vis-á-vis the DPRK, including making clear Japan's unwillingness to provide any economic assistance to the DPRK (as laid out in the September 13, 2007 agreement) until the country had met Japanese demands on abductees—even at the expense of faster denuclearization. With events moving quickly in the six-party talks, multiple possibilities have now emerged for Japanese-DPRK relations, ranging from bilateral reconciliation to continued hostility with many combinations in between. Regardless, however, the DPRK is likely to remain for some time as at best an unfriendly neighbor and at worst an ongoing threat to Japan's military security.

A Rising China

China has presented Japan with a more ambiguous security situation. China's rise has been accompanied by double-digit growth in the country's annual military budget, the not always transparent bolstering of the Chinese missile program and blue water navy, and expansion of the country's space program and cyber capabilities as well as Beijing's aggressive search for guaranteed energy sources. Additionally, cross-strait relations have become increasingly worrisome for Japan—starting with Chinese missile tests over Taiwan in 1996 and Beijing's passage in 2005 of the so-called Anti-Secession Law claiming China's unilateral right to respond with military force should Taiwan move excessively toward independence. With Japanese shipping dependent on sea lane access in and around Taiwan, China's continued assertion of territorial rights both to the Senkaku Islands in the South China Sea and to Taiwan poses a potentially serious challenge to Japanese security. Furthermore, Japan and China disagree on their respective boundaries in the East China Sea, an issue that added to tensions when both sides began exploring for natural gas in the contested waters. Equally disconcerting to Japan, China has a permanent seat on the UN Security Council whereas Japan's efforts in 2005 to gain similar representation were successfully opposed by China and South Korea (the Republic of Korea, or ROK) as well as by much of Asia (with at best tepid support from the United States). Meanwhile, China's white-hot economic growth rates continue to enhance the country's regional and global leverage at a time when Japan's economy, though far more sophisticated, remains decidedly sluggish.

Yet for Japan, offsetting such worries is the reality that economic ties to China have deepened substantially since bilateral relations were normalized in 1972. Today China is a major target for Japanese FDI as well as Japan's most important trading partner. Japanese policymakers are thus divided as to whether to view China as a threat or as an opportunity—mirroring similar ambiguities within Washington.

The normalization of bilateral relations in 1972 ushered in 25 years of "smile diplomacy" between the two countries. Trade, FDI, and overseas development assistance (ODA) from Japan cascaded into China, and Japan was the first of the OECD (Organisation for Economic Co-operation and Development) countries to lift economic sanctions following the Tiananmen Square massacre. China's staggering growth rates, however, became a poignant contrast to Japan's withering economic vitality during this period. China—the prior foreign aid supplicant—was emerging as a potential regional and global challenger. In 2006, for example, China accounted for 29.4% of the world's total growth; Japan, in contrast, accounted for only 2.6%.[30]

China, initially a reluctant regionalist, also became an advocate of improved ties with Southeast Asia and the ROK as well as with Central Asia, showing increasing diplomatic deftness through its "charm offensive." China's ready accession to a code of conduct in the South China Sea and generally more forthcoming engagement in ARF along with Track I and Track II frameworks lessened prior tensions between China and Southeast Asia, as did China's proven ability to provide greater trade benefits to Southeast Asia than could Japan. China demonstrated this ability when Chinese prime minister Zhu Rongji at the China-ASEAN summit in 2001 proposed—and then China quickly signed—a comprehensive free-trade agreement (FTA) liberalizing trade in six hundred items with ASEAN, including promise of an "early harvest" that opened Chinese markets to agricultural exports from Southeast Asia. A stunned Koizumi appeared feckless in following up with a proposal only to explore the issue of creating a comprehensive economic partnership. With agricultural and fisheries exports so critical to the growth strategies of most countries in Southeast Asia, ASEAN trade with China jumped almost 60% in 2005 over 2004.[31] Meanwhile, the Japan-ASEAN

---

[30] "International Trade and Foreign Direct Investment," Japan External Trade Organization (JETRO), 2007, 20, http://www.jetro.go.jp/en/stats/white_paper/2007.pdf.

[31] Donald E. Weatherbee, "Strategic Dimensions of Economic Interdependence in Southeast Asia," in Strategic Asia 2006-07: Trade, Interdependence, and Security, ed. Ashley J. Tellis and Michael Wills (Seattle: The National Bureau of Asian Research, 2006), 275.

comprehensive economic partnership that materialized in 2007 not only was slow to develop but excluded any meaningful liberalization of Japan's primary sector.

China's normalization of relations with the ROK added to Japan's worries. In 1991 China accounted for less than 1% of ROK trade while the United States accounted for 26% and Japan followed in second place with approximately 20%. By 2006 China's share was 22% while that of the United States had dwindled to 15% and Japan had fallen to third place. Further, in a move that stunned both U.S. and Japanese policymakers, former ROK president Roh Moo-hyun proposed that South Korea serve as a "balancer" between China and Japan in Northeast Asia. Despite Japan's industrially sophisticated economy, the country's position at the unchallenged center of regional economic developments was no longer axiomatic.[32]

As Koizumi warmed to the United States, he also oversaw a chilling of relations between Japan and China (as well as with the ROK). Reacting to the shift in the economic dynamism of China and South Korea as well as to the painfully negative visit of Chinese president Jiang Zemin in the fall of 1998, Tokyo reduced and redirected Japan's ODA to China in October 2001, ending multi-year pledges and shifting the focus of ODA away from infrastructure and construction to emphasize environmental protection, increased living standards, education, institution-building, and technology transfers. China remained, however, the second largest recipient of Japanese aid (behind Iraq) in the latest year for which figures are available (2005–06).[33]

Public visits by Koizumi to the Yasukuni Shrine and right-wing nationalists' inflammatory rationalization of Japanese actions in World War II soured relations with China and the ROK. By the end of the Koizumi administration, summit meetings between Japan and its two Northeast Asian neighbors had ceased, and cross-national rhetoric was toxic.

Ironically it was the nationalistic Abe who improved the climate with fence-mending visits to both Seoul and Beijing almost immediately after taking office. A reciprocal visit by Chinese premier Wen Jiabao the following spring further thawed relations. Even more positive was President Hu Jintao's five-day visit in May 2008, the first visit to Japan by a Chinese president since the disastrous 1998 visit by Hu's predecessor, Jiang Zemin. "Kumbaya" rhetoric on friendship for generations in the joint communiqué issued during the meeting was bolstered by actual

---

[32] Andrew MacIntyre and Barry Naughton, "The Decline of a Japan-Led Model of the East Asian Economy," in Pempel, *Remapping East Asia*, 77–100.

[33] Organisation for Economic Co-operation and Development (OECD), *International Development Statistics*, (Paris: OECD, 2008), http://www.oecd.org/dataoecd/42/5/40039913.gif.

substance: Japan and China explicitly declared that they were not enemies and that recent developments in both countries should be viewed as peaceful. The two countries also pledged to cooperate on regional and global issues not of immediate commercial or strategic concern and laid the groundwork for resolving differences on exploration in the East China Sea. A political agreement for joint gas exploration was finally reached on June 18, 2008. Whether or not these exchanges will prove to be the starting point for a sustained reduction in the previously tense interactions during the Koizumi years remains to be seen. For the moment, however, Sino-Japanese relations show evidence of a rapid and undeniable warming supported by both sides, but with considerable emphasis in particular by Prime Minister Fukuda Yasuo.

Japan in 2008: Responding to Challenges with Diminished Resources

When Koizumi took office Japan was in the midst of a struggle to adjust the country's post-bubble economy to the advancing globalization of finance and a stall in world trade negotiations. Each presented challenges to Tokyo's strategic effort to expand Japan's economic influence globally and within Asia. The Asian financial crisis of 1997–98 and the harsh conditions the International Monetary Fund (IMF) imposed in the crisis' aftermath left deep financial and psychological scars across Asia.[34] Japan was particularly stung by the negative reactions to Japanese efforts to offer the affected economies rapid relief by creating an Asian Monetary Fund. The offer of assistance was summarily squashed by the combined pressures of the United States, the IMF, and China, each resisting any challenge to their respective influences or any enhancement of Japan's own.

The stalling of the World Trade Organization (WTO) Doha Round negotiations also diminished Japanese influence over the global trade regime. The unwillingness of Japan to accommodate the early voluntary sector liberalization (EVSL) plans pushed by APEC not only signaled Japan's inability to rely exclusively on global trade negotiations but also demonstrated to the rest of the world how disruptive Japan's lingering trade protection could be.

By the year 2008 it was an economically and politically enfeebled Japan that sought to cope with a widening set of security challenges. Years of

[34] Richard A. Higgott, "The Asian Economic Crisis: A Study in the Politics of Resentment," *New Political Economy* 3, no. 3 (November 1998): 333–56; and T.J. Pempel, ed., *The Politics of the Asian Economic Crisis* (Ithaca: Cornell University Press, 1999).

ineffective economic policy gyrations finally resulted in Japan's return to modest GNP growth rates of slightly over 2% per year from 2004 through 2007. Although many Japanese corporations underwent substantial transformations in their methods of operation, the country as a whole did not experience a return to full employment (particularly for recent college graduates), labor and capital productivity continued to lag behind most industrial economies, public sector debt remained at astronomical levels, and massive pockets of structural inefficiency continued to fester. A rapidly aging population generated higher demands for social spending and added to the stringent budgetary constraints. As a result, policymakers' economic flexibility was sharply constricted. Previously valuable tools such as ODA suffered major cutbacks, with Japanese ODA in 2007 at only 62% of the level a decade earlier.[35] Expanded military budgets were equally problematic. Defense budgets have been effectively flat since 1994, and in 2007 the defense budget was reduced for the fifth year in a row.[36]

Japan's political capabilities were no less profoundly hobbled. Koizumi's radical moves to enhance Japan's military posture were matched by his effort to break new ground in Japan's economic policies. Among other things, Koizumi reduced the country's non-performing loans and engineered a systematic cutback in politically generated pork while challenging a number of costly public corporations, a move that included his reform of the Japanese postal system.

In conjunction with postal reform, Koizumi engineered a masterful purge of two dozen of the most anti-reform members of his party in the September 2005 election. Turning the election into a mandate on "reform" versus "resistance," Koizumi led a landslide victory for the LDP, which gained over two-thirds of the seats in the lower house of parliament for the first time in postwar history. Koizumi's victory set the stage for a potentially permanent shift in the party's composition by emasculating the anti-growth, pork-barrel forces that had long impeded the country's economic dynamism and by enhancing Koizumi's pro-U.S., pro-military executive policymaking powers.

Yet Koizumi did little during his final year in office to capitalize on his electoral victory, and his successor, Abe, squandered a sterling opportunity to build on Koizumi's victory. Instead, Abe reversed course by welcoming back into the party all but one of the "anti-reformers" who had been purged in 2005. Although Abe did avoid Yasukuni and made important visits to

---

[35] Ministry of Foreign Affairs, *Japan's Overseas Development Assistance White Paper 2007: Japan's International Cooperation* (Tokyo, 2007), http://www.mofa.go.jp/policy/oda/white/2007/ODA2007/html/zuhyo/index.htm.

[36] Samuels, *Securing Japan*, 195; and Katzenstein, *Rethinking Japanese Security*, 19.

Korea and China, he embraced narrowly nationalistic and crony-driven incompetence at home while ignoring economic reform. Abe's effort to initiate a quadrilateral security dialogue among Japan, the United States, Australia, and India blended compatibly with Minister of Foreign Affairs Aso Taro's promotion of an "arc of freedom and prosperity."[37] Both sought to give new direction to Japan's foreign policy. China and Russia, however, perceived both efforts as veiled containment, and Abe's successor, Fukuda, has downplayed such efforts, working hard to improve Japan's relations across all of Asia, with particularly emphasis on China. Australian prime minister Kevin Rudd meanwhile unilaterally scrapped the quadrilateral talks in the spring of 2008.

Abe's ineptitude torpedoed the LDP's potential to consolidate its reform constituency, thus setting the party up for a devastating loss in the upper house election of 2007. As a result, Fukuda came into office facing a divided government with the upper house and its powerful veto ability being under the control of the opposition Democratic Party of Japan (DPJ). Issues that might once have escaped parliamentary battles are consequently now hostage to partisan infighting.

As ready examples, the DPJ held up reauthorization of the law allowing Japanese ships to support U.S. actions in Afghanistan, thus requiring that the ships leave their posts until the reauthorization was eventually pushed through the lower house by the LDP's two-thirds majority. In July 2008 the government was forced to give up its plan to create a National Security Council similar to that of the United States. The DPJ also exerted heavy pressure on Minister of Defense Ishiba Shigeru to resign over a possible cover-up following the collision of a maritime SDF Aegis ship and a Japanese fishing vessel. Basing issues, revisions to the status of forces agreement (SOFA), the military budget, appointments of senior officials, and the acquisition of new weapons systems such as the F-22 Raptor are but a few of the areas where similar controversies have already arisen or are likely to arise. Divided national government all but forecloses the probability of reaching the required two-thirds vote in both houses of parliament required for constitutional revision. To date, Fukuda has proven adept at limiting the opposition's capacity to block LDP efforts, despite the upper house voting a non-binding measure of censure against him on June 11, 2008. Much of Fukuda's success, however, is attributable to his being far more conciliatory on policy substance than his two immediate predecessors.

The next lower house election—which must be held by fall 2009—is likely to reduce the current government's two-thirds majority, thereby

---

[37] Taro Aso, "Toward an Arc of Freedom and Prosperity" (address delivered at the International House of Japan, Tokyo, March 12, 2007), http://www.mofa.go.jp/policy/pillar/address0703.html.

depriving the LDP of the power to override upper house vetoes. A DPJ majority, although electorally unlikely, would present even greater difficulties for alliance policies. Barring a party realignment or some form of working coalition between the government and the opposition, the probability is high that Japan will experience six to nine more years of fractured government and policy stasis. Security issues and U.S.-Japanese relations are likely to become politically expedient footballs, making it ever more difficult for Japanese policymakers either to consolidate Koizumi's reforms or to initiate even modestly new directions with the same single mindedness shown under Koizumi. It would thus be wise for U.S. policymakers not only to improve relations with opposition forces but also to be less ambitious regarding what they seek militarily from Japan. Even the most pro-U.S. Japanese government is likely to face high domestic political hurdles that will impede controversial initiatives.

Critical Issues for the Next U.S. Administration and Potential Changes in Policy

For the new U.S. administration, the most important foreign policy concern will likely be the recalibration of U.S. policies in the Middle East and Central Asia. The wars in Iraq and Afghanistan and threats from Muslim fundamentalists have become the monocular lens through which Washington views all parts of the world. The damage to U.S. global prestige—from the war in Iraq, Abu Ghraib, Guantanamo, CIA rendition policies, and a unilateral foreign policy—has been greater in most countries than in Japan.[38] Nevertheless, in a 2005 survey 52% of Japanese surveyed distrusted the United States, compared to only 37% who saw the U.S. as basically trustworthy.[39] The most recent Pew Survey of International Attitudes, however, showed that Japan, which had one of the survey's highest levels of trust in the United States in 2007 (61%), experienced one of the largest drops in trust of the United States in 2008 (falling to 50%).[40] Even the normally pro-U.S. Japanese public evinces growing doubt over U.S. policies. As one critic has described the situation, "…American universalism today, as in 1918, would be more attractive were it not so transparently self-serving."[41]

---

[38] "America's Image Slips, but Allies Share U.S. Concerns over Iran, Hamas," Pew Global Attitudes Project, June 13, 2006, http://pewglobal.org/reports/display.php?ReportID=252.

[39] Midford, *Japanese Public Opinion*, 47.

[40] Pew Global Attitudes Project, Washington, D.C., http://www.pewglobal.com.

[41] Samuels, *Securing Japan*, 186.

The heightened focus on the wars in Iraq and Afghanistan during the Bush administration has prevented top U.S. policymakers from devoting significant time or energy to Japan or Asia as a whole. Particularly damaging has been the failure of many high-level U.S. officials to attend important meetings in Asia. Such a gesture might have shown support for Asian regionalism and helped to convince Japan and other Asian countries of Washington's long-standing commitments.

An incoming administration will benefit from remembering the importance of classical geopolitical and strategic considerations as well as the value of multilateralism, diplomacy, and U.S. soft-power assets. The risks involved otherwise—of evaluating Japan's value to the United States primarily in terms of Tokyo's support for the war on terrorism—are likely to leave Japanese policymakers bewildered over the U.S. stance on the DPRK, Taiwan, and China, which are matters of far greater concern to Japan than the war on terrorism.[42]

Beyond such important atmospherics, a number of more concrete issues are likely to confront the new president. These issues can be divided into three sets: issues related to ongoing negotiations with the DPRK, issues related to China, and issues related to explicitly bilateral relations between Japan and the United States.

The Six-Party Talks

Since the agreement of September 2005, and even more so since the agreement of February 2007, Japanese policymakers have come increasingly to fear three things regarding the DPRK situation. First, they worry that the United States might decouple the abductees issue from the issue of denuclearization. Countless Japanese politicians and much of the national media have built careers by demanding a full accounting of the whereabouts of the abductees. During the first six months of 2006—after being ordered to focus on the abductees issue—NHK (Japan Broadcasting Corporation) ran over two thousand stories on the DPRK, seven hundred of which dealt with the abductees (an average of three stories per day).[43] The abductees issue furthermore rates twenty percentage points higher in opinion polls measuring Japanese concerns than does the issue of DPRK denuclearization.[44] Even though Bush gave assurances to former prime

---

[42] Kurt M. Campbell, "America's Asia Strategy during the Bush Administration," in *The Future of America's Alliances in Northeast Asia*, ed. Michael H. Armacost and Daniel I. Okimoto (Stanford: Asia-Pacific Research Center, 2004), 27.

[43] Robert Marquand, "In Japan, North Korea Abductees are National Obsession," *Christian Science Monitor*, November 15, 2006.

[44] The author thanks Ellis S. Krauss for sharing relevant opinion surveys.

minister Abe that the United States would consider Japan's position, Japanese policymakers show a growing fear that a final deal might be struck at the expense of the abductees issue. Fukuda has been quieter on this issue than was Abe, but the issue still simmers. Although many Japanese policymakers will admit that denuclearization must ultimately take priority over the abduction of fewer than a dozen Japanese citizens, the issue is not likely to play out this way in domestic politics.

Of equal concern to Japanese policymakers is the possibility that the United States will ultimately turn an occluded eye toward the retention of nuclear material by the DPRK. In this regard, developments on the U.S.-Indian nuclear pact energize both the DPRK and Japan. Pyongyang hopes India will become a precedent for the recognition of the DPRK as a nuclear power outside the NPT, while Japanese policymakers fear that Washington might allow the DPRK to retain some nuclear material— thereby risking regional nuclear proliferation, causing the collapse of the already weakened NPT, and lowering Japan's confidence in U.S. commitments. This scenario could even push Japan to begin exploring the county's own nuclear options.

Third, Japan is greatly worried by the DPRK's missile program, an issue that has received comparatively little overt attention in the six-party talks. This is yet another area in which the United States could work closely with Japan.

Japanese economic aid to the DPRK remains a vital ingredient in any resolution of the nuclear problem, as was clear in the September 2005 agreement. Though the economic integration of the DPRK into the region is an issue on which Japan can play a vital role, existing differences on key issues—in particular the issue of the abductees—threaten to drive a wedge between the United States and Japan. The resolution of difficulties between the United States and Vietnam on accounting for U.S. prisoners of war sets a valuable precedent for permitting joint Japanese-DPRK teams to investigate and resolve the questions surrounding the abductees.

In mid-June 2008 the DPRK and Japan reached a tentative breakthrough agreement that the DPRK will reinvestigate the abductees issue. As of this writing, however, Japan is awaiting the actual results of the investigation before removing any sanctions and is urging the United States to wait on removing the DPRK from the list of state-sponsors of terrorism until Japan is satisfied on the issue. Secretary of State Condoleezza Rice meanwhile declared on June 18, 2008, that the removal would be relatively automatic once the United States was satisfied with the accuracy and completeness of the DPRK's declaration of the country's nuclear programs.[45] Timing will surely be critical in determining whether U.S. and Japanese positions in the talks will again become close or whether the two countries will instead find themselves divided.

The U.S.-Japan-China Triangle

Japan's longer-term uncertainties concern China. Japanese policymakers are divided over whether, and how best, to maintain positive ties with China. In particular, many top leaders worry that warmer U.S.-Chinese ties might lead to "Japan passing." This concern expands as China continues to play a role both in the six-party talks and in the war on terrorism, and as U.S.-Chinese economic ties deepen. Japanese policymakers worry that the Bush administration's obsession with the Middle East has blinkered Washington's attention to changes in East Asia, particularly to China's increased influence in the region. As one critic has aptly described this situation:

> Although the United States by most measures dwarfs China's power, a funny thing happened while America went to war. China's influence in diplomatic situations, in boardrooms of corporate power, in military councils, and in multilateral settings has risen inexorably and exponentially. This is probably the most significant strategic development in Asia in over a decade, the importance of which cannot be [overestimated], but there is little real recognition in the United States of the ground moving under their feet in Asia.[46]

Japan's long-standing efforts to counterbalance China's rising regional strengths have concentrated on leveraging Tokyo's financial and technological assets. Japan has thus sought to keep Asian regional bodies focused primarily on finance and economics (areas in which Japan's capabilities outshine those of China)—hence Japan's support for the Chiang Mai Initiative (CMI) and the Asian Bond Market Initiative. Japan has also favored open regional bodies that would include the United States (such as APEC and ARF) and is involved in a variety of multilateral anti-pollution efforts. In addition, Japan's Ministry of Economy, Trade and Industry (METI) put forward a proposal in 2007 for the Economic Research Institute for ASEAN and East Asia, now headquartered within the ASEAN Secretariat and with regional operations elsewhere in Asia. Tokyo also pressed to expand the membership of the East Asia Summit to sixteen countries. Several new members—India, Australia, and New Zealand, for example—could act as counterweights to China's regional influence.

---

[45] Condoleezza Rice, "U.S. Policy Toward Asia" (address delivered at the Heritage Foundation, Washington, D.C., June 18, 2008), http://www.state.gov/secretary/rm/2008/06/106034.htm.

[46] Campbell, "America's Asia Strategy during the Bush Administration," 26.

The United States has, however, recently given short shrift to such Asian regional efforts and to economic policy as a strategic weapon more generally. Instead, Washington has sought to "securitize" economic policies by, for example, insisting on anti-terrorist statements from APEC and using FTAs as a tool of foreign policy.[47] Japan has also been seeking FTAs for political rather than economic ends, as Tokyo's pursuit of an FTA with Australia has made evident.[48] The 2007 Armitage-Nye report went so far as to suggest a U.S.-Japan FTA.[49] Surely this would be an economic and political boon to both countries and to the bilateral relationship at the macro level. Tokyo has, however, been balancing the U.S. alliance with Japanese regional involvement in Asia, while Washington has focused almost exclusively on the alliance. The United States will need to be prepared to recognize that bilateralism alone is no longer the sole channel pursued by many governments in Asia, including Japan. Additionally, the United States would benefit by viewing recommitment to involvement in Asian and Asia-Pacific regional institutions and economic interactions as an opportunity not only to bolster U.S.-Japanese ties but also to alleviate any residual Japanese fears that China will dominate the Asian region at Japan's expense.

At present Japan-China relations have been warming, as reflected in the exchange of visits in 2007–08 and the mutual agreement on gas exploration in the East China Sea. More startling was an agreement announced after the devastating earthquake in Sichuan in May 2008 that Japanese SDF personnel would be allowed to enter China to provide air transport for relief assistance—an astonishing alteration to the negativity in the bilateral relationship under Koizumi. Wide publicity of the alleged Chinese request was, however, followed two days later by an announcement that the deal was squashed—with the two governments giving competing explanations. Still, under Fukuda relations between Japan and China have unquestionably improved in a substantial manner.

The triangular relationship is difficult to manage. Depending on the extent to which any warming of U.S. ties with China threatens to leave Japan on the sidelines, Japanese policymakers may question the degree to which Japan can trust the United States. Washington can stress that the triangular relationship is not equilateral and that the Japan-U.S. leg is inherently stronger than either of the other two legs. Yet to the extent

[47] Richard A. Higgott, "US Foreign Policy and the 'Securitization' of Economic Globalization," *International Politics* 41, no. 2 (June 2004): 147–75.

[48] Ann Capling, "Preferential Trade Agreements as Instruments of Foreign Policy: An Australia-Japan Free Trade Agreement and Its Implications for the Asia-Pacific Region," *Pacific Review* 21, no. 1 (March 2008): 27–43.

[49] Richard L. Armitage and Joseph S. Nye, "The U.S.-Japan Alliance: Getting Asia Right through 2020," Center for Strategic and International Studies, CSIS Report, February 2007, 17.

that Beijing interprets U.S. ties with Japan as a threat to China's legitimate interests, China is likely to respond by acting in precisely the hostile manner that the United States wishes to avoid. The United States can thus also play an important role in reassuring China over Japan. Even as strategic preparations must proceed in planning for potentially dangerous contingencies, both the United States and Japan would benefit from working with China where possible in a condominium of powers aimed at reducing mutual suspicions. In the process China is likely to become socialized as the "responsible stakeholder" Robert Zoellick has advocated.[50]

With regard to Asian regionalism, the United States can and would do well to return to secretarial level participation in ARF, utilizing the group along with Track II processes and the Shangri-La Dialogue to more positively engage the new Asian multilateralism. Such actions also hold out the promise of regionally focused U.S.-Japan cooperation in areas such as global warming, pandemic diseases, disaster relief, and a host of other nontraditional security areas that draw on the respective national assets of both countries. Japanese domestic political cleavages are far less likely to impede such regionally beneficial and non-military areas of bilateral cooperation.

Explicitly Bilateral Issues

A host of largely technical but problematic issues—particularly within the military sphere—will confront the new administration. The stalled relocation of the Futenma Marine Corps Station has festered since 1996. Local political opposition both to various proposed new sites and to specific configurations of the aircraft runways continues with no end in sight that might satisfy both the U. S. Marine Corps and local residents.[51]

Japan also plans to upgrade the military's fighter jets, and the U.S. F-22A Raptor is a prime candidate for adoption. Meanwhile, the U.S. Air Force is anxious to sell the Raptor to trusted allies to boost overall sales. Rather than buy the Raptor "off the shelf" to more quickly gain any military edge in Asia, Japan wants to license production—thereby gaining access to top technologies while also supporting Japan's domestic defense industry.

In addition, Japanese opposition leaders have been pressing since March 2008 for revisions to SOFA. Proposed changes would include: requiring the roughly 22,000 SOFA personnel who live off base to register as resident

---

[50] Robert Zoellick, "Whither China: From Membership to Responsibility?" (remarks before the National Committee on U.S.-China Relations, New York, September 21, 2005), http://www.ncuscr.org/files/2005Gala_RobertZoellick_Whither_China1.pdf.

[51] Christopher W. Hughes and Ellis S. Krauss, "Japan's New Security Agenda," *Survival* 49, no. 2 (June 2007): 167.

aliens with local authorities, guaranteeing the immediate handover of SOFA personnel suspected of crimes, ensuring a full environmental clean-up of military facilities handed over to Japan, and requiring an evaluation of U.S. military facilities every eight years. Opposition politicians also want to renegotiate current host nation support payments.

Although processes are in place to resolve such issues, the United States will need to address Japan's multiple worries. The next administration will need to continue to offer reassurance that the bilateral alliance remains Japan's most credible defense against regional threats while at the same time allowing Japan sufficient flexibility to pursue its own, occasionally different, security goals.[52] Less guaranteed is how the two countries can manage disagreements in areas such as sanctions on Iraq, the six-party talks, and dealings with Asian regional bodies. Given their numerous insecurities, Japanese policymakers will require continual reassurances that the United States will not abandon the country on issues the Japanese view as vital.

Any U.S. expectations that Japan will become a full-fledged military partner in support of U.S. global strategy are sure to be frustrated, partly because Japan has never fully bought into such a role but also because Japan is even less likely to do so now, given the current domestic political stalemate and Japan's ongoing economic constraints. Identification of broad areas where the security policies of the two countries can be complementary and collaborative—but that are not simply camouflage for greater military cooperation—is fundamental to the bilateral relationship. Closer ties between Japan and the United States, as well as reassurances for Asia as a whole, are likely to be the result.

The incoming president can take various concrete steps. Among the most valuable would be for him to make a trip to Asia with Tokyo as the first stop—ideally even before taking office. Such a visit should be primarily a "listening trip" designed to acquaint the new president and key administration personnel with Japanese and other Asian perceptions on the broad range of concerns. What is critical is the ability of the incoming administration to hear the Japanese articulate how they think their country can work with the United States to deal with the multiple challenges Japan faces globally and bilaterally. In this context, two early presidential commitments would be valuable: one to turn invigorated attention to global warming (an ongoing issue of concern to Japan) and another to reinvigorate U.S. resources for public diplomacy and soft power, including an increased role for area expertise within the Department of State and other government agencies.

---

[52] Michael J. Green, "U.S.-Japanese Relations after Koizumi: Convergence or Cooling?" *Washington Quarterly* 29, no. 4 (Autumn 2006): 101–10.

The choice of the U.S. ambassador to Japan is also vital. Past presidents have often relied on former congressional heavyweights for the position since bilateral economic issues involving a high degree of congressional influence were often central to the U.S.-Japan relationship. Bush opted for someone whom he personally trusted. The new president would benefit from seriously considering appointing someone with a strong regional geopolitical vision who could bring to the job a capacity to anchor the Japanese relationship in the complex regional context. Additionally, given Japan's divided government, the U.S. embassy in Japan will need to maintain good ties not only with the LDP and government officials but also with the opposition.

Finally, the incoming president would be wise to take note of the symbolic potential of the years 2010–11. Japan will host APEC in 2010, whereas 2011 marks the 60th anniversary of the San Francisco Peace Treaty that ended the war between Japan and the United States. The U.S. president will be in Japan for APEC, and this visit would provide an excellent opportunity to reaffirm the importance of the bilateral relationship as well as to lay out future areas for cooperation.

In all of these situations, however, the United States must be prepared to acknowledge that a politically divided Japanese government will find it more difficult for to act quickly and with internal cohesion on many aspects of bilateral military and security cooperation. This will be the case no matter what the issue—be it settling multiple remaining technical issues on basing or SOFA, phasing in greater military cooperation, or reaching agreement on broad issues such as those under discussion in the six-party talks.

Japan relies heavily on U.S. guarantees and is continually concerned over the depth of the U.S. commitment and the circumstances that might diminish U.S. credibility. With a nuclear-armed DPRK testing intermediate-range ballistic missiles over Japan and sending spy ships to penetrate Japan's exclusive economic zone (EEZ), and with an economically powerful Chinese dragon breathing hot across the region, any doubts over U.S. willingness to protect Japan could provide encouragement to those limited but vocal voices calling for Tokyo to accelerate Japan's conventional build-up or even to develop nuclear deterrence. Were Japan to do so, it could launch an extensive conventional and or nuclear arms race across Asia that would clearly be against U.S. interests in the region.

Japan has begun to move from an introspective focus on "self-defense" to a more expansive conception of Japanese military security in conjunction with Japanese regional and global potential. With this shift having started, it would behoove the United States both to acknowledge the validity of Japan's long-standing concept of "comprehensive security" and to take advantage of Japan's non-military capabilities as part of a joint effort to advance global security along multiple tracks. By acknowledging that Japan can make a vital contribution regionally and globally through the country's economic, technological, and organizational capabilities, the United States could encourage Japan to embrace an expanded and activist role—a role that Japan finds harder to pursue when the primary focus of the bilateral relationship is simply the military component of security. Fukuda recently suggested that Japan has a powerful role to play as a "peace fostering nation."[53] It would be helpful for the United States to acknowledge that reality and to integrate the U.S. bilateral strategy with that broader Japanese perspective.

---

[53] "Policy Speech by Japanese Prime Minister Yasuo Fukuda to the 169th Session of the Diet," Press Release, January 22, 2008, http://www.us.emb-japan.go.jp/english/html/pressreleases/2008/0122.html.

EXECUTIVE SUMMARY

This chapter assesses U.S. strategy on Korea and proposes a policy agenda for the next administration.

MAIN ARGUMENT:
Three main issues will define future U.S. strategy on the Korean Peninsula: (1) changes in South Korean views of North Korea and their implications for U.S.-ROK relations, (2) North Korea's nuclear weapons development, systemic decline, and the consequences for nonproliferation strategy and regional diplomacy, and (3) South Korea's increasing economic and military capabilities, their effects on regional geopolitics, and U.S. perceptions of long-term U.S.-ROK defense relations.

POLICY IMPLICATIONS:
- The calls of South Korea's new government for closer relations with the U.S. enhance the prospects for effective policy management and redefinition of alliance goals. The U.S. cannot, however, assume automatic policy congruence with South Korea. Competing strains of Korean nationalism could also prove a limiting factor in bilateral relations.

- The risks posed by North Korea's nuclear weapons development and internal vulnerabilities remain palpable. The U.S. (in consultation with regional actors) would benefit from mitigating these risks, increasing access into North Korea, and managing the potential for disruptive change.

- U.S. policy toward North Korea will be most effective if it simultaneously addresses regional stability and nonproliferation; policy outcomes skewed to a single objective will be incomplete and quite possibly unworkable. It is important that the U.S. impart unequivocally to Pyongyang that full relations with the outside world will not be possible if North Korea seeks to retain its nuclear capabilities.

- The U.S. will want to give increased attention to a multilateral peace and security mechanism but only if non-adversarial relations among all states prove possible.

The Korean Peninsula in U.S. Strategy: Policy Issues for the Next President

Jonathan D. Pollack

This chapter addresses U.S. strategy on the Korean Peninsula and identifies a policy agenda for the next administration. The commitment of South Korea's new president, Lee Myung-bak, to closer relations with Washington enables the United States to weigh future policy options in more comprehensive terms. What are the risks and opportunities for U.S. interests? What would be the goals of a reconfigured alliance? Where might Korea—North as well as South—fit in U.S. conceptions of Northeast Asia in the longer run?

The existence of separate Korean states—each with starkly divergent histories, national identities, and development paths—has long defined U.S. policy. Past history, however, should not inhibit consideration of future strategic possibilities. The Republic of Korea (ROK) is a major ally of the United States and an increasingly consequential international actor, but there are major disagreements within South Korea on its longer-term political and strategic identity. The Democratic People's Republic of Korea (DPRK) continues to pose major risks to U.S., South Korean, and regional security interests. Although the DPRK asserts that it seeks a transformed relationship with the United States, it is both a nuclear-armed state and a system experiencing profound economic and societal decline. Addressing the DPRK's nuclear weapons capabilities will almost certainly be bequeathed to the next U.S. administration, as will the possibilities of the continued

Jonathan D. Pollack is Professor of Asian and Pacific Studies and Chairman of the Asia-Pacific Studies Group at the Naval War College. He can be reached at <jonathan.d.pollack@gmail.com>.

The judgments in this paper are the author's own and should not be attributed to the Naval War College, the Department of Defense, or the U.S. government.

erosion of the North Korean system and its consequences for regional stability. At the same time, the United States must weigh the peninsula's larger significance to U.S. strategic interests and policy objectives.

To assess U.S. policy options, this chapter will focus on four principal issues. First, the chapter will address how the two Koreas define and deliberate their respective strategic identities. The next section will assess the major policy developments of the past decade—concentrating on internal political change in South Korea and the effects of such change on the U.S.-ROK alliance, the second North Korean nuclear crisis, and major shifts in the U.S.-ROK defense relationship. Third, the chapter will analyze how South Korea and North Korea view the United States in their underlying strategic calculations. Fourth, the chapter will weigh policy options for the next U.S. administration, focusing on the nuclear weapons issue, the redefinition of the U.S.-ROK alliance, the management of potential instability in North Korea, and the role of the Korean Peninsula in long-term U.S. strategy.

The Grand Strategies of the Two Koreas

The two Koreas inhabit separate political and economic universes and confront widely divergent future prospects. Profound disparities in identity and power define their respective strategic horizons. The ROK is now a major factor in international politics and economics. Its citizens, though still exhibiting intense local and regional loyalties, are increasingly educated, prosperous, and articulate. South Korea is the world's thirteenth largest economy—with some estimates placing this rank higher, depending on exchange rates—and President Lee (at least for aspirational purposes) has stated that the ROK should strive to become the world's seventh largest economy within the next decade.[1] Seoul occupies a pivotal strategic position between continental and maritime Asia; South Korea's identification with globalization, though resisted by various domestic constituencies, is also beyond dispute. By every measure of national power save aggregate military capabilities, South Korea has outstripped North Korea by ever wider margins.[2]

In stark contrast, North Korea remains mired in militarization, exclusivity, and backwardness. Pyongyang is linked to the outside world

---

[1] Julia Cunico, "The Bulldozer Moves In: Lee Myung-bak Is Inaugurated as the Republic of Korea's President," *Korea Insight* 10, no. 3 (March 2008): 1; see also "South Korea's Election: What to Expect from President Lee," International Crisis Group, Asia Briefing no. 73, December 21, 2007, 4.

[2] For a detailed overview, see Jonathan D. Pollack, "The Strategic Futures and Military Capabilities of the Two Koreas," in *Strategic Asia 2005–06: Military Modernization in an Era of Uncertainty*, ed. Ashley J. Tellis and Michael Wills (Seattle: The National Bureau of Asian Research, 2005), 136–72.

primarily through limited trade and investment ties with China and South Korea and through international aid and humanitarian assistance. Beyond hortatory calls to become "a powerful and prosperous nation" by the centenary of Kim Il-sung's birth in 2012, and barring extraordinary international breakthroughs, the DPRK's options for addressing the state's profound internal problems are decidedly bleak. The succession to Kim Jong-il represents another looming uncertainty, with the possibilities only dimly understood by the outside world. North Korea's isolation has been reinforced by the heightened economic sanctions imposed following the October 2006 nuclear test, especially by Japan. Indeed, notwithstanding the enunciation of various market-oriented policies in 2002, recent policy statements, replete with renewed calls for economic autarky and reiteration of the primacy of *songun* (military-first) principles, have reverted to earlier state-centered concepts.[3] Amid acute deprivation, North Korea grimly persists, without definitive indications of where the country is headed or how Pyongyang proposes to get there.

South Korea's Strategic Alternatives

South Korea has three primary strategic alternatives. The ROK can pursue (1) a U.S.-centered strategy, (2) an autonomous strategy, or (3) a diversified or hedged strategy. None of these approaches is fully explicated, and all three entail potential tensions and contradictions.

A U.S.-centered strategy represents the preferred choice of Lee Myung-bak. The April 2008 National Assembly elections resulted in a slim majority for the ruling Grand National Party, though the party's narrow electoral advantage and intra-party factional rivalries as well as intense domestic opposition ensure that Lee's policy priorities will be contested throughout his term in office.[4] Although the ROK president retains significant discretionary authority over foreign policy, national security affairs, and inter-Korean relations, internal political challenges will nonetheless constrain the new government's pursuit of its preferred strategy.[5] President Lee seeks to build upon the alliance ties of the past five and a half decades, with Seoul assuming increased responsibility for South Korea's own defense. The threat from

[3] Rudiger Frank, "Socialist Neo-conservatism in North Korea? A Return to Old Principles in the 2008 New Year Joint Editorial," Nautilus Institute, Policy Forum Online, April 22, 2008, http://www.nautilus.org/fora/security/0832.Frank.html.

[4] The country's stark regional polarization remains a source of potential instability and inhibits policy consensus on critical domestic and international issues, including issues that will require constitutional revision. Peter M. Beck, "South Korea: Voting for Change," *Korea Herald*, April 16, 2008.

[5] See, in particular, "South Korea's Elections: A Shift to the Right," International Crisis Group, Asia Briefing no. 77, June 30, 2008.

North Korea, however, seems a far less credible rationale for the alliance in the 21st century; thus Seoul is focusing increasingly on longer-term regional geopolitics. Policymakers believe that a reaffirmed relationship with the United States will enable South Korea to pursue relations with Japan, China, and Russia with much greater confidence. The ROK is surrounded by major powers that in the past either had strategic designs on the peninsula or dominated the peninsula outright. Although South Korea is now a potent, highly developed state that is increasingly integrated with its more powerful neighbors, in terms of size and population the ROK remains a lesser power. Seoul therefore believes that a strengthened alliance with Washington remains essential to protecting ROK interests. South Korean policymakers also believe that an enhanced alliance with Washington is needed to ensure ROK interests in relation to North Korea.[6]

Leaders in Seoul recognize the need to demonstrate why a closer alliance relationship serves U.S. as well as South Korean interests. In the April 2008 U.S.-ROK summit George W. Bush and Lee Myung-bak pledged both countries to a "strategic alliance" that would move beyond long-standing terms of reference.[7] This aspiration posits deeper, more binding understandings with respect to security, trade, diplomacy, and various global issues. Future directions, however, remain unsettled. For example, the Korea-U.S. free-trade agreement—negotiated between the United States and the Roh Moo-hyun administration—would enable far greater market access and economic interdependence but the agreement remains unratified and has generated strong opposition on both sides of the Pacific.

Somewhat ironically, the United States has seldom posed the question of what it wants and expects from South Korea. Decades of U.S. political-military dominance on the peninsula help explain this phenomenon. For example, the United States has long pressured South Korea to enhance host nation support for U.S. forces and has urged that the ROK favor U.S. defense firms in major weapons purchases. In addition, Washington strongly endorsed the participation of ROK military units in Vietnam and Iraq. The ROK, however, is no longer a highly dependent state, and the country's interests and strategies are increasingly diversified. U.S. military

---

[6] As Lee Myung-bak observed in a pre-inaugural interview: "The country with which North Korea desires to normalize its relations most is the United States. If our relations with the United States were bad, there would be nothing we can do between the United States and North Korea. Only when our relations with the United States are good is it possible for us to play a role in normalizing relations between North Korea and the United States." Lee Myung-bak, joint interview with *Dong-a Ilbo, Asahi Shimbun,* and the *Wall Street Journal,* as reported by Ho Chin-sok, "ROK-U.S. Relations Were Clouded Over the Past 10 Years, So It Is Right to Use the Word 'Restoration,'" *Dong-a Ilbo,* February 2, 2008.

[7] See "Full Text of South Korea-U.S. Summit Statement," *Korea Times,* April 20, 2008, http://www.koreatimes.co.kr/www/news/nation/2008/04/116_22786.html.

force levels have been appreciably reduced, and despite the DPRK's nuclear weapon and missile capabilities, the United States is far less worried about the possibilities of renewed hostilities on the peninsula.[8] The ROK is also building highly capable defense industrial capabilities of its own, thereby diminishing the country's long-standing reliance on U.S. weapon systems and defense technologies.

With the election of an ROK president well-disposed toward the United States, Washington again regards the alliance with Seoul as among the core U.S. security partnerships in Asia. U.S. policymakers also value ROK contributions to international peacekeeping and humanitarian operations.[9] Neither Washington nor Seoul, however, has broached a strategic concept that moves appreciably beyond a bilateral framework. Though the United States clearly encourages the ROK to explore security cooperation with Tokyo and Washington, Seoul has yet to demonstrate serious interest in this possibility. The ROK instead remains focused on a reinvigorated bilateral alliance with the United States. A renewed partnership with Washington would reduce South Korea's potential vulnerabilities and diminish long-standing fears of alliance decoupling from the United States. Yet the ROK also recognizes that China could construe enhanced bilateral or trilateral security relations as inhibiting future accommodation with Beijing or as an attempt to counter Chinese power and influence.

Lee Myung-bak calculates that a U.S.-centered approach will heighten the ROK's pride of place in future U.S. strategy. In Lee's thinking, closer relations with Washington will increase U.S. attentiveness to South Korean policy interests. Lee, however, is also mindful of the domestic forces arrayed against him. South Korea's long-standing dependence on U.S. power and the ROK's past subordination to U.S. interests have largely ended, but the pervasive involvement of the United States in South Korea's internal evolution of the past six decades continues to reverberate within the ROK body politic. Even with the ascendance of a conservative majority in the ROK, the political opposition will challenge efforts by Lee to align fully with the United States. Closer ties with the United States will therefore depend on future U.S. strategy, the congruence of this strategy with ROK

---

[8] In recommending that all U.S. military personnel assigned to the peninsula be eligible for family-accompanied tours, Secretary of Defense Robert Gates asserted, "I don't think anybody considers the Republic of Korea today a combat zone." Yochi J. Dreazen, "North Korea Has Confined Nuclear Help, Gates Says," *Wall Street Journal,* June 4, 2008.

[9] For an initial effort to explore these possibilities in a report prepared by a U.S.-ROK expert panel, see "The Search for a Common Strategic Vision: Charting the Future of the US-ROK Security Partnership," co-directed by G. John Ikenberry, Chung-in Moon, and Mitchell Reiss, East Asia Foundation, February 2008, available at the Nautilus Institute website, http://www.nautilus.org/fora/security/08018USROKForum.pdf.

interests (as perceived within South Korea), and Lee's ability to fashion a viable consensus within ROK domestic politics.

An autonomous strategy constitutes a second policy option, with distinct variants from the Right and the Left.[10] The fullest example of the right-wing variant dates from the Park Chung-hee era (1961–79). Despite his reliance on the United States, President Park retained ample wariness about long-term U.S. intentions and sought to strengthen South Korea's indigenous economic, technological, and military capabilities. This process included the pursuit of a covert nuclear weapons program during the 1970s, through which Park believed the ROK could avoid dependence on the United States and achieve strategic dominance over North Korea. Though U.S. pressure compelled Park to forgo his nuclear ambitions, the commitment to longer-term autonomy—including military autonomy— remains a potent factor in ROK national aspirations.[11]

The left-wing variant of autonomy posits a pan-Korean identity. This approach envisions both Koreas sharing a common strategic destiny, premised on economic integration and political reconciliation as well as on a reduced U.S. peninsular and regional role. This approach also extends to a more self-reliant defense strategy that would be independent of all major powers, including the United States. Enhanced indigenous defense capabilities would proceed in tandem with development of a cooperative multilateral security order. This vision was pursued most fully under former president Roh Moo-hyun, to the ample consternation of the Bush administration. Roh sought to move beyond South Korea's long dependence on the United States; he was also not prepared to follow the U.S. lead on policies toward North Korea and China.

A more diversified or hedged approach represents a third South Korean strategic option. Though close relations with the United States would continue, these relations would not preclude policy initiatives toward North Korea and other Northeast Asian states. This approach was evident under Kim Dae-jung and to a lesser extent under Roh Moo-hyun. Both presidents sought to move away from the ROK's authoritarian past (including the national security legislation of earlier decades) and to engage with former adversaries, especially North Korea. Kim and Roh believed that

---

[10] For an insightful depiction of competing strains of ROK strategic thought, see Jongryn Mo, "What Does South Korea Want?" *Policy Review*, no. 142 (April/May 2007), http://www.hoover.org/publications/policyreview/6848122.html.

[11] For an extended exploration, see Jonathan D. Pollack and Mitchell B. Reiss, "South Korea: The Tyranny of Geography and the Vexations of History," in *The Nuclear Tipping Point: Why States Reconsider Their Nuclear Choices*, ed. Kurt M. Campbell, Robert J. Einhorn, and Mitchell B. Reiss (Washington, D.C.: Brookings Institution Press, 2004), 254–92. Jongryn Mo characterizes Park as a "realist nationalist," as distinct from the "pro-American nationalist" position that he associates with the Grand National Party. Mo, "What Does South Korea Want?"

the transformation of inter-Korean relations was essential to reconfiguring regional political and security relationships. Reconciliation and threat reduction with neighboring states and the development of a cooperative regional security regime would free the ROK from residual Cold War entanglements. Defense modernization would provide South Korea with additional freedom of action. The return of wartime operational control of ROK military forces to Korean sovereignty in 2012 could bear directly on this strategy.

North Korea's Strategic Alternatives

North Korean pronouncements suggest an unwavering commitment to strategic autonomy. Past pledges to *juche* (self-reliance), long associated with Kim Il-sung, have been abetted by the songun policy espoused by Kim Jong-il. Though some analysts believe that this slogan is devoid of operational meaning, the songun policy is clearly designed to justify a broad range of policies, including the nuclear weapons program and a state-centered economic strategy. The military-first policy also ratifies and reinforces Kim Jong-il's claims to unquestioned leadership.[12] The DPRK, however, does not perceive a contradiction between Pyongyang's pursuit of political and strategic autonomy and the solicitation of economic and humanitarian assistance. North Korean strategy also allows for concessions and policy adjustments with external powers, without which diplomacy would be devoid of purpose.[13]

Pyongyang's involvement in diplomatic negotiations, especially with the United States, nevertheless begs the issue of the DPRK's underlying strategic objectives. Three prospective paths can be inferred from North Korean policy statements. The subtext for all such deliberations is how the DPRK hopes to advance the prospects for North Korea's longer-term survival. The military-first strategy posits the retention of national defense capabilities—including nuclear capabilities—unless and until

---

[12] There are innumerable references to the songun policy in North Korean editorials and policy pronouncements. Though length and intensity of expression do not necessarily constitute conviction or unambiguous internal support for the policy, Kim Jong-il is closely associated with the military-first policy and its extensive propagation, and presumably believes his legitimacy is tied directly to the policy. See, for example, the joint New Year's day editorial in *Rodong Sinmun, Choson Inmingun,* and *Chongnyon Chonwi,* Pyongyang Korean Central Broadcasting Station in Korean, January 1, 2008, http://www.korea-np.co.jp. For a detailed exposition of the policy's purposes and functions within North Korea's internal politics, see Han S. Park, "Military-First Politics (Songun): Understanding Kim Jong-il's North Korea," Korea Economic Institute, Academic Paper Series, February 21, 2008, 118–30, http://www.keia.org/Publications/OnKorea/2008/08Park.pdf.

[13] For a detailed exploration, see Robert Carlin and John W. Lewis, *Policy in Context: Negotiating with North Korea: 1992–2007,* Center for International Security and Cooperation, Report, January 2008, http://iis-db.stanford.edu/pubs/22128/Negotiating_with_North_Korea_1992-2007.pdf.

the DPRK receives unambiguous commitments in three areas: validation and legitimacy as an independent state, security assurances of various kinds, and major economic and political compensation for definitively forgoing its nuclear program. All are associated with the stated goal of full diplomatic relations with the United States, provided that Washington ends what North Korean officials characterize as the U.S. "hostile policy" toward the DPRK.

The elasticity and ambiguity of this label, however, is almost boundless.[14] Barring an extraordinary policy reassessment in Pyongyang, the DPRK deems relinquishment of its nuclear capabilities, including fissile material and any fabricated weapons, the last step in a very protracted process. By North Korea's logic this step would require the United States to fundamentally alter its defense strategies in Northeast Asia, including security collaboration with the ROK. Periodic hints from North Korean officials that the DPRK would not object to the continued presence of U.S. forces on the peninsula verge on the fanciful: these officials assume that U.S. regional military planning would no longer focus on North Korea and imply that the United States would be prepared to enter into strategic understandings with the DPRK to constrain the growth of Chinese power and influence. In the absence of a major strategic breakthrough with the United States, Pyongyang therefore deems nuclear weapons central to its security calculations. The leadership believes that these capabilities ensure that the DPRK will remain on the U.S. diplomatic radar screen, that the country will not be subject to coercion or outright attack, and that Pyongyang will maintain crucial bargaining leverage with all outside powers. For added measure, North Korea believes that its nuclear capabilities level the playing field with major powers (including the United States) while relegating non-nuclear states (i.e., South Korea and Japan) to lesser status.

There are, however, two imaginable alternatives to current North Korean strategy. One alternative posits a "development first" approach, which assumes that economic needs—including a readiness to undertake fundamental internal change—will ultimately trump possession of nuclear weapons. This approach presumes movement toward denuclearization and increased normalcy in the DPRK's relations with the outside world, especially with the United States. Although there are scattered indications of internal debate over longer-term development priorities, there is no persuasive evidence that the senior leadership is willing to break definitively with past policies and even less evidence that military prerogatives will

---

[14] Author's discussions with DPRK diplomatic and military officials, Pyongyang, April 10–11, 2008.

be subordinated to economic requirements.[15] Indeed, the leadership in Pyongyang may well believe that the DPRK can achieve at least partial economic recovery without definitively yielding its nuclear capabilities. North Korea also calculates that the country can address its most acute economic shortcomings through collaboration with NGOs and relief agencies or through selective trade and investment ties with the outside world, especially in resource exploitation. These deliberations seem largely independent of specific trade-offs with respect to the nuclear issue.[16]

A third prospective path presumes a "muddling through" strategy, suggesting indecision or division at the top of the system, or an incapacity or unwillingness of the leadership to make definitive strategic choices regarding North Korea's future. This course of action does not preclude selective concessions to other states. Indeed, North Korea describes an "action for action" principle as Pyongyang's preferred negotiating objective. This approach, however, leaves future measures contingent on as yet unspecified steps in the six-party talks that the United States and other interlocutors might be prepared to undertake. Thus, the path ahead remains strewn with unknowns and uncertainties. This situation underscores the singular importance of nuclear capabilities to North Korea's survival strategy, even if outside powers explicitly reject the DPRK's efforts to legitimate these capabilities.

Assessing the Policy Record

Weighing future U.S. strategy options requires an assessment of the legacy of the past decade. The intent in this section is not, however, to revisit specific decisions and actions in copious detail. First, the section will highlight how differing perceptions and policy calculations contributed to upheaval and at times major stress in U.S.-Korea relations. Second, the section will examine the continuing effects of these policy disputes. Attention will focus on three issues: changes in South Korean attitudes and strategies toward North Korea and the implications of these changes for U.S.-ROK relations, the renewed North Korean nuclear crisis and the

---

[15] For a suggestive if overstated analysis of North Korean internal debate over economic priorities, see Robert L. Carlin and Joel S. Wit, *North Korean Reform: Politics, Economics, and Security*, Adelphi Paper 382 (London: Routledge, 2006).

[16] For two suggestive examples of relevant possibilities, see Bradley O. Babson, "Visualizing a North Korean 'Bold Switchover': International Financial Institutions and Economic Development in the DPRK," *Asia Policy*, no. 2 (July 2006): 11–24; and Stephan Haggard and Marcus Noland, "A Security and Peace Mechanism for Northeast Asia: The Economic Dimension," Stanley Foundation, Policy Analysis Brief, April 2008.

consequences both for nonproliferation strategy and for U.S. regional diplomacy, and changes in U.S.-ROK defense relations.

South Korea's Internal Transition

South Korea has undergone repeated internal political realignment over the past decade. Four broad trends have shaped these changes and their consequences for relations with the United States: accelerated development, the democratization of politics, the demilitarization of politics, and a major demographic transition. The election of Kim Dae-jung in 1997 presaged major change in the U.S.-ROK alliance, but the latent tensions in bilateral relations remained largely submerged until the Kim-Bush summit in early 2001 and the election of Roh Moo-hyun in late 2002. Roh appealed to very different political and class interests in Korea. Younger generations of Koreans sought to displace more traditional business, governmental, and military elites from their accustomed role, and Roh explicitly devalued relations with the United States.[17] Lee Myung-bak's election constituted an explicit rejection of Roh's record. Lee's ascent to the presidency thus portends a return to normalcy in bilateral relations. The turbulence and uncertainty of recent years, however, still warrant review.

Roh's presidency was dominated by repeated upheaval and political drama. Though elected as a minority candidate and by a very thin margin, Roh viewed his victory as a mandate for large-scale change in policies toward the United States. His electoral triumph occurred in the aftermath of the accidental deaths of two Korean school girls during a June 2002 U.S. military training exercise. This horrific incident sparked widespread public protests that undermined support within the ROK for the alliance and for the large-scale presence of U.S. forces. Roh had little identification with the prior history of the alliance. His determination to shed long-standing policies led to heightened tensions with the Bush administration and with senior U.S. military officers in South Korea. Mounting animosities between the two governments over the North Korean nuclear issue exacerbated these tensions. Highly public differences helped validate the arguments of U.S. officials—most notably then secretary of defense Donald Rumsfeld—who were increasingly skeptical of the value both of the alliance and of the in-country deployment of major U.S. military forces. Nonetheless, Roh selectively accommodated U.S. policy needs, especially by deploying South Korean forces to the Middle East where for a time the ROK contingent

[17] For a searing critique of the Roh administration and the resulting consequences for Korea's domestic order and international relationships, see Byung-kook Kim, "The Politics of National Identity: The Rebirth of Ideology and Drifting Foreign Policy in South Korea," in *Korea: The East Asian Pivot*, ed. Jonathan D. Pollack (Newport: Naval War College Press, 2006), 79–120.

constituted the third largest force serving in Iraq. In addition, during the final year of his presidency, and perhaps sensing the consequences of the growing estrangement in bilateral ties, Roh pushed vigorously for the Korea-U.S. free-trade agreement, a point conceded even by some of his fiercest critics.

Though Roh did not bear exclusive responsibility for the deterioration in bilateral relations, his behavior elicited barely concealed contempt from senior U.S. officials, including George W. Bush. Roh's efforts at reconciliation with the DPRK—culminating in an October 2007 visit to Pyongyang in the waning months of his presidency—were largely independent of the nuclear issue. Roh's efforts to shift toward a "balancer" position in East Asia—including his disassociation from the U.S.-Japan alliance and his explicit divergence from U.S. efforts to incorporate South Korea in regional contingency planning—reflected the pursuit of a security strategy detached from the United States. Roh sought to exploit nationalist sentiment within the ROK, especially among younger Koreans. Despite the free-trade agreement and improved diplomatic coordination in the aftermath of the North Korean nuclear test, the two countries were operating largely on separate pages. Roh's resounding repudiation in the December 2007 presidential election halted the slide in bilateral relations, and the rebuilding of alliance relations is now underway, although Lee continues to face major challenges to his leadership and core policy priorities, including major initiatives with the United States. The large-scale protests of May–June 2008, triggered by Lee Myung-bak's decision to resume imports of U.S. beef, abruptly diminished confidence in Lee's leadership, which seems likely to inhibit his ability to pursue a closer partnership with Washington. Without a sense of shared purpose in the alliance and without the requisite domestic support for closer bilateral ties, U.S.-ROK relations could again be subject to political manipulation and uncertainty.

The Return of the Nuclear Issue

The North Korean nuclear saga is too complex for detailed reconstruction in this chapter.[18] It is necessary, however, to contrast the Bush administration's shifting policies between the president's first and second terms and the consequences of these shifts both for nonproliferation

---

[18] For the author's own views, see Jonathan D. Pollack, "The United States, North Korea, and the End of the Agreed Framework," *Naval War College Review* LVI, no. 3 (Summer 2003): 11–49. For an exhaustive account of the negotiations through the summer of 2006, see Yoichi Funabashi, *The Peninsula Question: A Chronicle of the Second Korean Nuclear Crisis* (Washington, D.C.: Brookings Institution Press, 2007).

strategy and for bilateral relations. Beginning in the summer of 2002, when U.S. intelligence first concluded that North Korea was exploring uranium enrichment as an alternative means to produce fissile material, sharply antagonistic policy approaches bedeviled the Bush administration. Echoes of these differences persist. In his first term, Bush, convinced that there was no realistic possibility of North Korea forgoing its weapons program by inducement or reassurance, favored a compellent approach. Predominant efforts focused on stigmatizing and isolating the DPRK and on foreclosing options for bilateral engagement. The administration quickly ended U.S. obligations under the Agreed Framework, without any evident consideration either of what would supplant this agreement or of how Pyongyang might react to the shifts in U.S. policy. North Korea responded by rapidly reactivating its long-dormant plutonium program, which had been held in check since 1994. The reactivation of this program culminated in North Korea's first nuclear detonation in October 2006.

Although the Bush administration claimed that Washington favored a "diplomatic approach," the multilateral discussions undertaken in Beijing following the collapse of the Agreed Framework were ritualized and unproductive. The United States sought an unequivocal commitment from North Korea to dismantle the country's entire nuclear weapons infrastructure and fully disclose all nuclear activities before the United States would broach possible compensation. This policy stance reflected the administration's profound antipathies toward Pyongyang and an aversion to the step-by-step approach pursued under President Clinton. Indeed, the word "negotiations" was not even employed in the earliest rounds of talks in Beijing.

Despite the presumed danger of nuclear weapons proliferation—officially promulgated in the White House's National Security Strategy of November 2002—policymakers displayed little urgency during the protracted nuclear stand-off. First, the United States was unwilling to offer inducements to North Korea or to engage in meaningful bilateral discussions. Second, Washington lacked even remotely feasible military options to eliminate North Korea's nuclear weapons potential without grievous risk to the interests of the United States and the region. Third, there were no indications that the DPRK would either relent or collapse. The Bush administration, therefore, seemed increasingly bereft of meaningful policy options. It was only following North Korea's claim in early 2005 that the country had manufactured a nuclear device and the DPRK's steady accumulation of weapons-grade plutonium that administration officials began to re-examine their approach to policy. With various interruptions and major tensions along the way—including North

Korea's testing of a nuclear device—the diplomatic process ultimately achieved headway, resulting in a shuttering of the reactor complex at Yongbyon, subsequent steps to disable those facilities, and Pyongyang's provision of data on the operation of its reactor and estimated fissile material inventory. The nuclear test also galvanized the participants in the six-party talks, especially the United States and China. As of June 2008, however, the initial denuclearization milestones are not yet completed to the satisfaction of all parties.[19]

If the United States sought to inhibit North Korea from pursuing development of nuclear weapons, the policy failed. Notwithstanding acute international pressure and grievous internal difficulties, Pyongyang grimly persevered in its nuclear activities. The DPRK was not dissuaded by warnings from Washington and other parties and was unmoved by the importuning of principal benefactors in Beijing and Seoul. North Korea became the first state to withdraw from the Treaty on the Non-Proliferation of Nuclear Weapons (NPT) and reactivated the long-dormant nuclear facilities at Yongbyon in early 2003. As a consequence, North Korea at present likely possesses sufficient separated plutonium to manufacture four to ten weapons. This plutonium inventory derives almost entirely from two sources: spent fuel rods canned and monitored for eight years under the Agreed Framework and additional spent fuel amassed following resumption of operations at the Yongbyon reactor. Uncertainties and unknowns also persist regarding North Korean reprocessing undertaken in the late 1980s and early 1990s prior to the negotiation of the Agreed Framework.[20]

The Bush administration's second-term strategy has been far more sober and realistic. The United States and other participants in the six-party talks have not wavered from insisting on verifiable denuclearization as the ultimate goal. All of Pyongyang's interlocutors remain unprepared

---

[19] The relevant documents include "Joint Statement of the Fourth Round of the Six-Party Talks Beijing, September 19, 2005," U.S. Department of State, September 19, 2005, http://www.state.gov/r/pa/prs/ps/2005/53490.htm; "North Korea-Denuclearization Action Plan," U.S. Department of State, February 13, 2007, http://www.state.gov/r/pa/prs/ps/2007/february/80479.htm; and "Six Party Talks—Second-Phase Actions for the Implementation of the September 2005 Joint Statement," U.S. Department of State, October 3, 2007, http://www.state.gov/r/pa/prs/ps/2007/oct/93217.htm.

[20] For authoritative estimates, see David Albright and Paul Brannan, "The North Korean Plutonium Stock, February 2007," Institute for Science and International Security, ISIS Report, February 20, 2007, http://www.isis-online.org/publications/dprk/DPRKplutoniumFEB.pdf; David Albright, Paul Brannan, and Jacqueline Shire, "North Korea's Plutonium Declaration: A Starting Point for an Initial Verification Process," Institute for Science and International Security, ISIS Issue Brief, January 10, 2008, http://www.isis-online.org/publications/dprk/NorthKoreaDeclaration10Jan2008.pdf; and Siegfried S. Hecker, "Report of Visit to the Democratic People's Republic of North Korea (DPRK). Pyongyang and the Nuclear Center at Yongbyon, February 12–16, 2008," Center for International Security and Cooperation, Report, March 14, 2008, http://iis-db.stanford.edu/pubs/22146/HeckerDPRKreport.pdf.

to accept or acknowledge the DPRK's nuclear capabilities. Progress in denuclearization has been halting but cumulative, with North Korea beginning to provide information essential to fulfilling the agreed-upon steps in the six-party talks. These steps include the May 2008 provision of more than 18,000 pages of operating records from the Yongbyon nuclear complex and the June 2008 declaration of its plutonium inventory, thus enabling far fuller efforts to verify the DPRK's fissile material holdings and weapons potential.[21] In return for the latter step, the Bush administration immediately announced that it would remove long standing trade restrictions imposed on North Korea under the Trading with the Enemy Act and also notified the Congress of the administration's intention to rescind North Korea's designation as a state sponsor of terrorism.[22] The immediate task in the six-party talks is completion of specific technical steps that would prevent the DPRK from continuing to augment the country's weapons potential—that is, capping if not ending the nuclear program. The disablement process also requires agreement on a verification protocol and the subsequent evaluation of Pyongyang's submitted documentation on its nuclear history that this protocol would permit. The June data, moreover, does not explicitly address U.S. allegations of North Korean exploration of uranium enrichment or Pyongyang's reported involvement in building a graphite-moderated reactor in Syria that was destroyed in an Israeli air attack during September 2007. Should major uncertainties linger on either issue, the prospects for completion of all reciprocal steps specified in the six-party accords remain problematic. At the same time, the documentation Pyongyang provided does not include any information on the number of nuclear weapons that North Korea claims to possess.

Even presuming satisfactory resolution of these issues, the future denuclearization agenda is exceedingly daunting. This agenda includes the dismantlement of the Yongbyon facility (technical estimates for completing this process range as long as a decade), likely North Korean demands to revisit the now-cancelled light-water reactor project negotiated under the Agreed Framework, and the ultimate disposition of DPRK weapons-related materials and technology, fissile material, and fabricated weapons.[23]

[21] Fact Sheet, Office of the Spokesman, U.S. Department of State, Washington, D.C., May 10, 2008; Helene Cooper, "In Disclosure, North Korea Contradicts U.S. Intelligence on Its Plutonium Program," New York Times, May 31, 2008; and Evan Ramstad, "North Korea Discloses Its Nuclear-Weapons Efforts," Wall Street Journal, June 27, 2008.

[22] Fact Sheet, Office of the Spokesman, U.S. Department of State, Washington, D.C., June 26, 2008.

[23] For a sobering assessment of the technical and environmental issues entailed in decommissioning the reactor complex, see Jooho Whang and George T. Baldwin, "Dismantlement and Radioactive Waste Management of DPRK Nuclear Facilities," Sandia National Laboratories, Cooperative Monitoring Center Occasional Paper, April 2005.

All these issues will entail protracted negotiation and substantial political and economic compensation, and success is far from assured. Indeed, it is doubtful that there is sufficient time or internal agreement within the Bush administration or sufficient concurrence by Congress to negotiate, let alone implement, all such steps. Pyongyang's readiness to forgo extant weapons capabilities in any plausible near- to medium-term scenario is even more questionable. The DRPK leadership—apparently having concluded that the Yongbyon facility is a dwindling asset—has in all likelihood decided to forgo further plutonium production. Though Pyongyang is now intent on determining the presumed worth of closure and ultimate dismantlement of this facility to the United States and the other participants at the six-party talks, this would be far from the end of the nuclear program.[24]

Barring major negotiating breakthroughs in the final months of the Bush administration, North Korea in early 2009 will retain a weapons potential and presumed inventory of completed weapons well in excess of what the country possessed at the outset of the Bush administration. Even assuming that Pyongyang is ultimately prepared to forgo its nuclear capabilities, the price tag for yielding the country's fissile material and fabricated weapons will be much higher than in the negotiations of the 1990s. Though some of the damage to U.S. interests has been ameliorated, the consequences of the administration's first-term policy persist and will need to be addressed fully by the next U.S. president.

Transforming the U.S.-South Korean Defense Relationship

The U.S.-South Korean security relationship has undergone profound change over the past half-decade. Notwithstanding the nuclear crisis, U.S. forces on the peninsula have been reduced appreciably, and major changes in U.S. deployment patterns continue. These developments, though partly triggered by ample U.S. pique at Roh's distancing South Korea from the United States, also reflect the overturning of decades-long policy inertia as well as competing U.S. force requirements. Relevant considerations included the Department of Defense's belief that U.S. military strategy, and in particular the trip-wire function of U.S. forces, had long outlived its utility; the urgent need for additional U.S. forces in Iraq; increased local sensitivities over the U.S. military "footprint"; the Department of Defense's determination to elevate South Korean forces to a lead role in peninsular defense; and the Pentagon's parallel effort to shift the U.S. peninsular focus to a power projection mission. Following multiple rounds of negotiations and various unilateral decisions, Washington decided to withdraw a third

---

[24] Hecker, "Report of the Visit to the DPRK," 1.

of U.S. combat units from the peninsula and to redeploy many of the remaining units to air and sea hubs far south of Seoul. For added measure, Roh in 2006 argued that South Korea should regain wartime operational control of all ROK forces. Then secretary of defense Donald Rumsfeld leapt at the opportunity—arguing that the process should be completed as early as 2009. Following his appointment as secretary of defense, Robert Gates agreed to a revised target date of April 2012. Regardless of the modifications in timetable, these changes constitute a genuine transformation in the role of U.S. forces and mark the largest alterations in force levels and functions in decades.[25] The changes will also require the ROK to develop new defense capabilities and competencies to supplant those long performed by U.S. forces. This process not only will entail major expense but also will raise major question marks about the military effectiveness of the changes.

Viewed in terms of South Korea's longer-term autonomy, there is an undoubted logic to the recalibration of U.S.-ROK defense relations. The primary impulse for Roh's actions and U.S. responses, however, were political, not military. At the same time that U.S.-ROK relations had entered uncharted waters, the Bush administration was vigorously pursuing a more integrated alliance with Japan. Over major objections voiced by numerous senior retired officers, Roh continued to push for major changes in defense policy, and some of these steps generated appreciable support within the ROK armed forces. These included articulation of a "cooperative self-reliant defense strategy" and the Defense Reform 2020 plan, which envisioned major reductions in South Korean ground forces and a shift to a much more technology-intensive force.[26] Defense Reform 2020 posited highly ambitious modernization plans geared toward enhanced flexibility and jointness, with some of the planned weapons acquisitions (especially in maritime power) more appropriate for regional rather than peninsular missions.

The goals outlined in Defense Reform 2020, however, including the budgetary assumptions underlying such plans, were unrealistic. Diminished economic growth estimates seem likely to curtail some of the ROK's ambitious modernization plans, and Lee has personally cautioned

---

[25] For additional details, see Jonathan D. Pollack, "U.S. Strategies in Northeast Asia: A Revisionist Hegemon," in *Power and Security in Northeast Asia: Shifting Strategies,* ed. Byung-kook Kim and Anthony Jones (Boulder: Lynne Rienner Publishers, 2007), 72–76; and Terence Roehrig, "Restructuring the U.S. Military Presence in Korea: Implications for Korean Security and the U.S.-ROK Alliance," *Academic Paper Series on Korea* 1 (2008): 132–49, http://www.keia.org/Publications/OnKorea/2008/08Roehrig.pdf.

[26] Taik-young Hamm, "The Self-Reliant National Defense of South Korea and the Future of the U.S.-ROK Alliance," Nautilus Institute, Policy Forum Online, June 20, 2006, http://www.nautilus.org/fora/security/0649Hamm.html; and Yong-sup Han, "Implementing the Republic of Korea's Defense Reform 2020," *Quarterly U-Security Review* 1 (March 31, 2007).

against excessive expectations in military modernization.[27] The new defense leadership seems likely to slow some of these programs, though the plans for indigenous weapons development and purchase of maritime, air, cruise missile, missile defense, and information capabilities all continue. Notwithstanding the logic of longer-term military self-sufficiency, South Korea seems all but certain to remain among the global leaders in purchases of U.S. weaponry in the years to come.[28] At the same time, despite the openly expressed desire of the ROK to rebuild the alliance relationship, senior South Korean officials continue to voice caution in aligning with U.S. regional defense priorities. U.S. officials, for example, anticipated increased ROK interest in ballistic missile defense and in the Proliferation Security Initiative (PSI) under Lee, but the new leadership has maintained an arm's length approach to any prospective involvement in integrated U.S. missile defense and counterproliferation strategies.[29]

Though operational military collaboration was largely undisturbed during the Roh presidency, the reapportionment of roles and responsibilities in the alliance touches on matters of enormous sensitivity within South Korea. These changes will extend to major shifts in decades of inherited U.S. policy, including command relationships between the Pacific Command and United States Forces Korea (USFK) as well as adjustments between United States Forces Japan (USFJ) and USFK. During the ROK presidential campaign, defense advisors to Lee raised the possibility of revisiting the decisions on return of wartime operational control. Senior U.S. military officials are openly opposed to any major reconsideration of these policy changes, and the new government in Seoul has not tabled any such requests. Numerous issues, however, remain unaddressed in U.S.-ROK defense consultations. The complexities in a bifurcated command arrangement and the equitable allocation of roles and responsibilities are daunting. What will be the primary strategic purposes of a more autonomous ROK military? What are the implications of a redefined command relationship for the full range of prospective contingencies and war plans? What will be the balance between peninsular and regional capabilities? Despite the impending return of operational control of all military forces to South Korean sovereignty, does the ROK still envision a highly integrated alliance, or is there a longer-term indigenous defense

[27] Kim Yon-se, "Growth Required to Reinforce Military," *Korea Times*, March 12, 2008.

[28] Foreign military sales to the ROK in 2007 surpassed $3.7 billion, making the ROK the third largest customer globally, behind only Saudi Arabia and Taiwan. Alexander A. Arvizu, "A New Beginning for the U.S.-South Korea Strategic Alliance," statement before the House Foreign Affairs Committee, Subcommittee on Asia, the Pacific, and the Global Environment, April 23, 2008.

[29] See, for example, the comments of Minister of Foreign Affairs Yu Myung-hwan, as cited in Jung Sung-ki, "Seoul Urges Pyongyang to Act by August," *Korea Times*, March 28, 2008.

concept that South Korea hopes to pursue? Is there essential congruence between the United States and the ROK on the future role of U.S. forces on the peninsula? Is South Korea willing to explore extra-peninsular missions in conjunction with U.S. military forces, or does the prospect of intense domestic opposition negate any such possibilities? All such issues await clarification and serious discussion.

South Korean and North Korean Policy Perspectives

The next U.S. administration would do well to assess how the respective expectations of Seoul and Pyongyang toward the United States can best serve U.S. policy goals. There is an ironic, somewhat paradoxical symmetry in the importance that South Korea and North Korea each attach to relations with the United States. Both assert that relations with Washington are fundamental to their respective national strategies. Both prefer to deal with one another, if at all, through their separate ties with the United States. Even though relations with Seoul will remain incomparably more important to U.S. policymakers than relations with Pyongyang, there is a need to clarify, and, to the extent possible, mesh U.S. and ROK policy agendas toward the DPRK. In the absence of close consultation between the United States and South Korea, significant unintended consequences could result from U.S. policies toward either or both Koreas. To elucidate future policy choices, it is necessary to examine how Seoul and Pyongyang envision their crucial policy priorities—including relations with Washington—and where inter-Korean relations fit in this context.

South Korea's Shift to the Right

During his campaign for the presidency Lee Myung-bak pledged to undertake major shifts in policy, and he moved quickly to carry out these pledges. In his February 2008 inaugural address Lee unambiguously declared that he would put significant distance between his strategies and those of his immediate predecessors.[30] He emphasized that politics needed to move from "the age of ideology" to "the age of pragmatism," with South Korea's "economic revival…our most urgent task."[31] Lee indicated that these underpinnings would also govern his approach to inter-Korean relations. In addition, he reiterated an earlier pledge to assist in North Korea's economic rehabilitation and to raise the per capita income there to $3,000 within

[30] "Full Text of Lee's Inaugural Speech," *Yonhap,* February 25, 2008.
[31] Ibid.

ten years, premised on "North Korea abandon[ing] its nuclear program and choos[ing] the path to openness."[32] Although Lee had already made a commitment in principle to support an international development fund for North Korea totaling $40 billion, these pledges were notional and not serious policy commitments. Lee's enunciated policies toward the DPRK are condition-based rather than inducement-based. Moreover, in his inaugural address Lee made no mention of the South-North summit declarations of June 2000 and October 2007 signed by Kim Jong-il and Kim Dae-jung and by Kim Jong-il and Roh Moo-hyun. These accords were premised on greatly enhanced economic collaboration and the quasi-normalization of South-North relations. Lee's pointed omission of both agreements may constitute an effort to shelve, slow, or even negate these accords.

Compared to South Korea's economic advancement and rejuvenation of the U.S.-ROK alliance, accommodation with the DPRK is a decidedly lesser priority for Lee.[33] In sharp contrast, Kim and Roh believed that reconciliation with North Korea was essential to their larger strategies. Lee contends that he will pursue enhanced inter-Korean relations only if Pyongyang takes unambiguous steps in denuclearization and in opening to the outside world, and it seems doubtful that Lee expects much of a response from Pyongyang. Lee also claims that humanitarian assistance to North Korea remains unconditional. Senior officials, however, assert that human rights and lingering controversies related to Korean War POWs and abductees are now on the government's policy agenda.[34] Though Lee also proposed the establishment of liaison offices in both capitals, North Korea summarily rejected this policy initiative.[35] There is as yet little evidence of an alternative ROK strategy toward South Korea's desperately poor but nuclear-armed neighbor, and it is possible that Lee does not envision the need for such an alternative. Indeed, after months of silence following Lee's election, Pyongyang in late March resumed a confrontational political stance toward South Korea—excoriating the new president with political invective not directed at an ROK leader for more than a decade.[36] Characterizations of Lee as "pro-U.S." and "anti-unification" highlight the renewed political

---

[32] Ibid.

[33] For a discerning early assessment, see Yong Seung Dong, "The North Korea Policy of the Lee Administration," *East Asian Review* 20, no. 1 (Spring 2008): 3–22.

[34] See the remarks of the Korean minister of unification, Kim Ha-joong, in *Chosun Ilbo*, March 11, 2008; and Choe Sang-hun, "South Korea Adds Terms for Its Aid to the North," *New York Times*, March 27, 2008.

[35] Glenn Kessler, "South Korean Leader Plans New Outreach To the North," *Washington Post*, April 18, 2008.

[36] "Self-destruction Is the Only Thing That the South Korean Authorities Will Gain through Their Anti-North Confrontation," *Rodong Sinmun*, March 31, 2008.

chasm that has opened between North and South, and this chasm seems unlikely to close anytime soon.

The Bush administration is understandably heartened by the election of a South Korean president who seeks to expand relations with the United States. Though encompassing trade, security relations, and regional diplomacy, these ties benefit U.S. interests primarily in an ROK-only context. At the same time, although Lee is giving ample emphasis to the economic dimension of U.S.-ROK relations, there is a glaring asymmetry between the preponderant weight of ROK economic relations with China, Japan, and the European Union—now South Korea's three leading trade partners—and Seoul's continued reliance on the United States as its primary security guarantor.[37]

To test future possibilities, the next U.S. administration will want to work vigorously with South Korea on at least two levels. First, both governments will find it important to develop a coordinated policy toward Pyongyang that protects U.S. and ROK interests and denies Pyongyang any opportunity to insert itself between Washington and Seoul. This policy would benefit from candid discussions between the United States and South Korea on whether leadership succession in Pyongyang affords possibilities for opening a larger window into the North Korean system. Second, there is a parallel need for Washington to initiate a discussion with Seoul on Northeast Asia in the longer term, including South Korean priorities in economic, political, and security relations with Japan and China and how these priorities correspond to U.S. regional strategic goals. This discussion would also extend to consideration of future multilateral political and security arrangements among all affected parties—even though discussions in the latter area are at best provisional and depend critically on the development of non-adversarial relations among all involved states. North Korea remains the strategic outlier in this process. Pyongyang may well sustain efforts to open doors to the United States, but Washington will want to ensure that any steps toward more normal relations between the DPRK and the outside world do not exclude or marginalize South Korea and Japan.

North Korea's Survival Strategy

The DPRK is a damaged society and a degraded system. The decline within North Korea's economy was fully revealed in the famine of the

---

[37] For relevant data, see Sung-hwan Lee, "Korea's Recent Economic Performance with the U.S. and the Region" (unpublished paper, July 2007).

mid-1990s, with the evidence of dysfunction apparent at multiple levels.[38] The scale of North Korea's needs defies imagination, and even though short-term infusions of food and humanitarian assistance could prove essential to avoiding another acute internal crisis, few of the challenges confronting the DPRK admit to an easy fix.[39] Though there is evidence of informal marketization in the countryside and in some cities, these changes were generated largely from the bottom up, and the leadership eyes these developments very warily. Senior officials seem incapacitated by the depth and intractability of the country's problems and remain unable or unwilling to acknowledge the scale of deprivation and crisis.

Yet the system endures. Despite pervasive internal liabilities, the DPRK does not seem on the edge of collapse or breakdown. This durability may help explain why the nuclear issue is likely to persist for many years to come: the issue is the primary asset with which the leadership can expect to bargain with the outside world. There is a close connection between the system's capacity for survival and North Korea's retention of nuclear capabilities. The DPRK's only other meaningful source of leverage with external powers concerns the potential consequences of an acute internal crisis that could spread beyond North Korea's borders; the country's prospects as a trade and investment partner remain very limited.

The DPRK is Washington's longest running adversary in the international system. Leaders in Pyongyang assert that full diplomatic relations with the United States would ultimately enable North Korea to forgo the entirety of the country's nuclear capabilities. At least in a conceptual sense, North Korea has stated that it is prepared to place many of its eggs in the U.S. basket. The reasons for this policy stance seem fairly straightforward. Inter-Korean relations have again entered a deep freeze, and—though a certain level of economic engagement with South Korea seems likely to persist—unconditional aid from the ROK has ceased. Relations with Japan have experienced an even deeper decline: trade with Japan is now virtually non-existent, and Pyongyang asserts that North Korea will refuse to deal fully with the Japanese leadership as long as Japanese economic sanctions against the DPRK remain in force. Although China is North Korea's largest trading partner and primary provider of oil and food, the DPRK remains wary of Chinese economic dominance and

---

[38] For an especially gripping analysis, see Hazel Smith, *Hungry for Peace: International Security, Humanitarian Assistance, and Social Change in North Korea* (Washington, D.C.: United States Institute of Peace Press, 2005).

[39] The UN World Food Program has warned repeatedly of the possibility of a major humanitarian crisis in 2008, focused primarily on highly worrisome projections of food supply. Blaine Harden, "Global Changes Skew Calculus of Food Aid for N. Korea," *Washington Post*, March 15, 2008; and Blaine Harden, "Huge Gap Predicted in Supply of Food," *Washington Post*, April 17, 2008.

very likely retains longer-term concerns over Chinese political influence as well. Russia, though a potential partner both in energy development and in infrastructural projects, remains mindful of North Korean's massive unresolved debt obligations dating from the Soviet era and is thus extremely unlikely to commit major financial resources to the DPRK.

By default and perhaps by design, North Korea views the United States as the DPRK's partner of choice. Pyongyang may well believe that a strategic breakthrough with the United States will open the requisite doors to increased international assistance, commerce, and investment. North Korea's leaders also suggest that a "bold switchover" in U.S. policy would compel South Korea and Japan to follow Washington's lead. In Pyongyang's prevailing frame of reference, the United States is the posited linchpin to major changes in North Korea's strategic position. The United States, however, does not want U.S.–DPRK relations and inter-Korean relations to proceed on very different trajectories, nor does Washington want changes in relations with North Korea to undermine U.S.-ROK relations. In this regard, the next administration needs to weigh any prospective U.S. assistance to the DPRK against the risks that such assistance could provide Pyongyang the equivalent of an "end run" around Seoul, thereby reducing the South's potential leverage with the North. These risks underscore the necessity of ongoing consultations with the ROK, especially to address the potential for divergence in policy priorities toward the DPRK.

For the United States the core issue is not the realism or credibility of North Korean policy assumptions. Rather, Washington must determine whether the DPRK's acute internal needs and the desire for U.S. affirmation could convince leaders in Pyongyang to undertake unprecedented and almost unimaginable political concessions, including concessions on nuclear weapons and in relations with South Korea and Japan. Where does the United States maintain policy leverage with North Korea, and how might a future administration test these possibilities? Are there potential opportunities for increased access into the North Korean system, especially with the Korean People's Army, and how fully should the United States pursue such opportunities? Will such steps also serve South Korean interests? The possibilities need to be evaluated and tested.

The United States faces an unavoidable engagement dilemma with the DPRK. If Washington is prepared to negotiate indefinitely with a nuclear-armed North Korea, do leaders in Pyongyang increasingly presume ownership and legitimacy to their weapon capabilities and that the United States accepts these circumstances as well? Does an indeterminate nuclear outcome thereby undermine the confidence of Seoul and Tokyo in security guarantees from the United States? The United States recognizes that the devastation and pathology of a deeply wounded system and the nuclear issue are interconnected. Washington will need to be attentive to the opportunity to open windows if not doors into North Korea, though with full awareness of the interests of U.S. allies and regional partners. At the same time, the United States does not want South or North Korea to avoid dealing with one another by maintaining separate, exclusive relations with Washington. The challenge for the next administration will be to devise a "two legs" strategy that engages with both Seoul and Pyongyang while facilitating meaningful relations between south and north. If the ROK and DPRK both believe that closer relations with the United States are essential to their long-term interests, then it will benefit Washington to exploit these possibilities. It is equally essential, however, that the United States impart to Pyongyang that any effort by North Korea to retain its nuclear capabilities will foreclose opportunities for normal relations with Washington and deny Pyongyang other potential political and economic benefits that it seeks from the outside world.

Implications for the Incoming Administration

The Korean Peninsula simultaneously presents major opportunities and risks for the United States. The defining imperatives for the next administration will be to sustain a U.S. role on the peninsula that reduces the risks of instability, avoids heightened confrontation between Seoul and Pyongyang, does not trigger major power rivalry in Northeast Asia, does not enable North Korea to retain or enhance its nuclear capabilities, and allows the United States to fully explore a sustainable regional order in collaboration with all U.S. partners in Northeast Asia. This is a tall order, but this agenda underscores the singular importance of the Korean Peninsula to long-term U.S. interests. South Korea is an emergent power of genuine consequence. North Korea, however, is both dangerous and endangered, and U.S. policymakers cannot assume that internal conditions in the DPRK will remain indefinitely static. It is therefore necessary for the United States and the DPRK's immediate neighbors to do more than play for time, and for Washington to weigh steps to move beyond the inherited legacies of the Cold War with both South and North Korea.

Revisiting Nuclear Diplomacy

The largest near-term uncertainties concern the nuclear issue. The Bush administration is seeking to complete the milestones in the October 2007 six-party agreement, which mandates the definitive disabling of the

Yongbyon nuclear complex and the verified disclosure of North Korea's nuclear history In hindsight, fulfilling these tasks by the target date of December 2007 was far too optimistic. Realization of these goals by the end of Bush's second term would represent the most significant accomplishment in a quarter century of efforts to inhibit North Korea's nuclear weapons development, though such an accomplishment would still leave Pyongyang in full possession of its extant weapons inventory and plutonium stockpile. North Korea's plutonium production capabilities, however, would be capped, with no realistic possibility of Pyongyang reversing these constraints. Equally important, satisfactory resolution of long-festering controversies over North Korea's prior nuclear activities would create a meaningful floor for subsequent negotiations. Such an outcome, however, is far from assured.

As is often observed by policymakers, the perfect is the enemy of the good. At times the Bush administration has argued for verification procedures that presume a degree of disclosure by Pyongyang that seems almost unimaginable.[40] At this writing, it is not possible to determine whether there is sufficient congruence in U.S. and North Korean interests to achieve a mutually acceptable outcome in the Bush administration's remaining months in office. Pyongyang might opt to play for time and await the next administration, which would make any full implementation of the six-party accords of 2007 impossible. Even an incomplete outcome, however, is better than none at all. The next administration would then need to determine how to build on this record, rather than disparage or even disown its predecessor's accomplishments. This bears in particular on the larger commonality of interests achieved between the United States and its diplomatic partners during the Bush administration's second term. It will not be advisable if the next president begins his term in office by revisiting the fundamentals of nuclear diplomacy, especially given the quiet success of the six-party process in building relationships and enhancing communication with the other participants in the talks, particularly China. Any renewed fissures between the United States and its diplomatic partners would also enable Pyongyang to exploit these differences and impede future steps in the denuclearization process. The United States may well remain Pyongyang's preferred interlocutor, but it is important that the next administration impart that U.S. dealings with North Korea are integrally tied to a multilateral process.

The next administration, however, may want to reassess future policy arrangements in nuclear diplomacy. There is a clear need to vest the

[40] See, in particular, Condoleezza Rice, "U.S. Policy toward Asia" (address given at the Heritage Foundation, Washington, D.C., June 18, 2008).

principal U.S. negotiator with full decisionmaking authority. The internecine bureaucratic warfare during the Bush administration ill served U.S. interests and made the negotiating challenges far more intractable. Despite the inevitable policy differences and divergent bureaucratic responsibilities, the next administration will find it necessary to speak and act with a coherent voice on the nuclear issue. This process could begin with an explicit mandate from the new president. It is not advisable that the incoming assistant secretary of state for the Bureau of East Asian and Pacific Affairs again serve as the lead nuclear negotiator. The negotiations during the second Bush term required a disproportionate commitment of Assistant Secretary Christopher Hill's time and energy, as distinct from the larger array of responsibilities entailed in this position. A division of labor that does not diminish the stature of either appointment is very much needed.

In this context Northeast Asia could be the lead negotiator's primary operating domain. The U.S. representative might be designated as special negotiator for the Korean Peninsula and be based in the region, most plausibly in Seoul. Though violating many of the established verities of Washington bureaucratic politics, this approach would far more fully attune U.S. policymakers to the core concerns and strategic equities of all regional actors while also offering a more cost-effective approach to policy management. At present the United States suffers from an inherent geographic disadvantage in interactions with regional partners. Washington should no longer be a visiting fireman. Basing a senior U.S. official in Northeast Asia would enable the United States to address and shape multiple possibilities. This move would also place the relevant capitals (with the exception of Moscow) within several hours flying time. Both symbolically and operationally, this policy change would attest to the next administration's determination to achieve core goals both in regional security and in nonproliferation that encompass full collaboration with U.S. regional partners.

Although it is not possible to determine whether all the disablement and declaration goals will be fulfilled before the end of the Bush administration, it seems increasingly implausible that Pyongyang will seek to reconstitute its plutonium production capabilities. Should all involved parties prove unable to reach a satisfactory diplomatic outcome, North Korea might signal its intention to resume nuclear weapons and missile development or undertake observable actions toward these ends. The new administration would then need to weigh appropriate responses in deterrence, defense, and crisis management. If the United States concludes that the DPRK will not enter into binding constraints on the country's nuclear weapons activities, the next administration—in conjunction with regional allies and in full consultation with China and Russia—would need to quickly mitigate acute consequences for nonproliferation and regional security. Possible North Korean actions could include additional nuclear tests or preparations for another test, potential efforts to deploy its extant capabilities, or the transfer of nuclear expertise, materials, and technology. Any of these steps would constitute profound challenges to the United States and to global and regional security.

Without a determined U.S. response to such possibilities, the damage to U.S. regional interests and to the nonproliferation regime would be acute. Worrisome scenarios could include efforts by Japan or South Korea to pursue independent policy options, including a more active strategic hedge by one or both states. Such hedging could extend to how each country characterizes its nuclear energy future and longer-term weapons potential. In all likelihood, developments in one state would be quickly followed by developments in the other. This outcome would be a devastating setback for U.S. strategic interests. A new administration will want to do everything possible to limit the risks of such a setback by making the long-term security of Seoul and Tokyo an unambiguous U.S. policy commitment.

A decision by Pyongyang to augment its extant nuclear capabilities would reinforce North Korea's self-imposed isolation. There would be a continued need, however, to maintain communication with the DPRK, especially in the event of further defiance of nonproliferation norms and endangerment of regional security. Closer consultations among all affected parties—focused on imposing additional constraints and costs on North Korean behavior without triggering an acute crisis or war—would also be essential. To be sure, this worrisome scenario presumes North Korea's definitive rejection of additional nuclear diplomacy. Yet even if Pyongyang sustains the negotiating process, there will be no easy or cost-free resolution of the nuclear question. The next administration will want to fully revisit these issues, which concern the long-term future of Northeast Asian security as much as nuclear proliferation.

A Reconfigured Alliance Bargain

The election of Lee Myung-bak provides a clear opportunity to review future directions in the U.S.-ROK alliance. The goal must be to ensure that both governments and both militaries possess a full understanding of the steps entailed in the return of wartime operational control of ROK military forces to South Korea in April 2012. The adjustments announced during the Bush-Lee summit—i.e., that U.S. forces would be retained at the level of 28,500 rather than 25,000 military personnel, as enunciated in the earlier agreements—suggest that both sides do not see these accords as carved in stone.

It would be a serious error, however, if this adjustment presages a major policy reassessment. Despite South Korean concerns over North Korea's nuclear program, it is time for the ROK to undertake full responsibilities as a sovereign state. Though the tasks and costs of this transition will be substantial and long-term, deferring or revisiting these decisions is not warranted. Such a move would delay South Korea's emergence as a mature regional power and could well inject needless tension and difficulty in U.S.-ROK security relations. At the same time, return of operational control to ROK commanders will deflate long-standing North Korean arguments that South Korea operates exclusively at the behest of the United States and is therefore not a worthy interlocutor. The argument is fraudulent on its face; for added measure, these presumed differences did not prevent greatly increased contact between the two militaries over the past half-decade—though this contact occurred under a presidential administration in Seoul that was almost preternaturally committed to reconciliation.

Two larger, unaddressed issues concern the implications of the alliance for the future role of U.S. forces on the peninsula and the role of ROK forces in U.S. regional strategy. It would be important for both governments to clarify how each envisions the larger purposes and longer-term directions of the alliance and how these visions (assuming there are such visions) mesh with one another. Both countries are seeking to ensure ROK security as the United States bequeaths primary responsibility to Seoul for roles and missions previously fulfilled by U.S. forces. This plan, however, pertains almost exclusively to peninsular security. The next administration might therefore examine the ROK's prospective regional role, especially given the enhancement of South Korea's maritime, air, information, and intelligence capabilities. Many of these emergent capabilities presume military competencies that could extend beyond the peninsula. A long overdue task is to envision the larger purposes of these forces and their relationship to future U.S. strategy, including the implications both for the U.S.-Japan alliance and for the ROK's long-term relationship with China. Though planning against North Korea will necessarily remain the major focus in the alliance, it is not too soon to ask how an increasingly capable ROK military sees its longer-term role, and what this vision implies for future security cooperation with U.S. forces.

Planning for Acute Contingencies

The subtext of virtually all deliberations on strategy toward North Korea—including the nuclear negotiations—concerns the longer-term viability of the DPRK as an independent state. Can North Korea survive in the absence of major internal change? Or could internal change trigger destabilization or even the end of the regime? Does North Korea's seeming stability mask internal brittleness and vulnerability that could directly undermine the current leadership's hold on absolute power? What steps might stimulate disruptive change, and what would be the potential consequences of such change for North Korea's neighbors? These questions have animated analysts ever since the end of the Cold War. The determined persistence of the DPRK—abetted by the state's exceptionalist norms, a highly centralized power structure, and a compliant citizenry—should caution against expectations of abrupt, unexpected change. Not unlike Dylan Thomas's memorable poem, North Korea refuses to "go gentle into that good night." Yet can the DPRK indefinitely defy the laws of economic and political gravity? Might another poet, T.S. Eliot, prove more prescient, and North Korea ultimately end "not with a bang, but a whimper"?

A strategy of constriction and isolation imposed undoubted costs on North Korea but has not resulted in the end of the regime. If anything, this strategy reinforced the leadership's hold on power. It thus seems appropriate that the United States pursue two simultaneous steps: enhance access into North Korea and (in conjunction with Seoul and other regional states) prepare more fully in the event that leaders in Pyongyang are not able to retain full control over events. To be sure, there has long been U.S. and ROK contingency planning for disruptive outcomes in the DPRK. Though necessary for operational military policy, these plans do not capture the totality of possibilities, especially given a nuclear-armed North Korea. The political succession process in the DPRK looms as an additional uncertainty. All regional states clearly prefer a more measured economic and political transition but none can preclude the possibility of more abrupt internal change. Beijing in particular can be expected to prepare quietly for instability in the DPRK. Seoul faces the added challenge of weighing these possibilities as the ROK assumes increased responsibilities in the U.S.-ROK alliance.

At present there is minimal discussion among the directly affected states concerning potential instability in North Korea and the implications of such instability for national-level responses. For example, if the United States and China were to activate contingency plans in the absence of close communication, there is a non-trivial possibility of a much larger international crisis, caused more by inadvertence than by design. There is a long overdue need for frank, though discreet, intergovernmental consultations. These exchanges would best be undertaken before a disruptive scenario unfolds, not after one has begun. It seems possible that any such discussions could build on the increased candor and comfort levels achieved among interlocutors in the six-party talks. Addressing this task is potentially as challenging and consequential as the nuclear issue itself.

The United States and Korea in the Longer Term

For 60 years a divided peninsula has been a fixture in regional geopolitics. There is no assurance that unification will occur over the coming decade, and the policies of all surrounding powers as well as North Korea's grim resilience continue to work against unification. A ten-year time horizon, however, should not posit only modest extrapolations from the status quo. Economic integration on the peninsula, should it transpire, could prompt developments equal to or more profound than the peninsula's division following Japan's surrender, including the possibility of unification. Indeed, the large-scale consequences of such potential change help explain the risk-averse strategies of North Korea's immediate neighbors. This issue also pertains to the unfinished character of Northeast Asian security. The six-party talks have sought to explore a future regional peace and security mechanism but these discussions have been preliminary and largely conceptual. Credible institutional arrangements presuppose normal, non-adversarial relations among all six states, and such relations remain a remote prospect. A benign outcome, moreover, cannot be assumed.

Even in the absence of unification the ROK's emergence as a major international actor is indisputable. Though not a great power, South Korea—as characterized by Lee Myung-bak in his February 2008 inaugural address—is an "advanced country" that can now "stand shoulder to shoulder with the most advanced countries."[41] The new government is seeking to focus on the ROK's strategic horizons and future standing in the global system. The scope of the country's assets and capabilities—its strategic location, industrial and technological capacities, prominence in international trade, highly educated populace, and longer-term political and military aspirations—already makes South Korea a state of ample consequence. The door has opened to a fuller, long-term relationship with the ROK, and the next president will need to decide if the United States should walk through it.

The next administration will also want to envision the Korean Peninsula in the longer term. This process must begin, however, with the reality of two Korean states, not one. It is necessary that the United States pursue

[41] "Full Text of Lee's Inaugural Speech."

simultaneous, mutually reinforcing outcomes with both South and North Korea fully aligned with longer-term U.S. regional and nonproliferation objectives. Simultaneity has eluded U.S. policymaking on the peninsula, but the stakes are too high not to try again. Washington has long sought strategic convergence with South Korea, although this will require navigating the shoals of Korean nationalism. Different challenges loom with North Korea. The DPRK is a wounded state that has yet to make a definitive choice on the country's future directions, especially on its readiness to forgo nuclear weapons development. Washington has conveyed to the DPRK that a normal relationship with the outside world is possible, but it is equally important that the United States impart to Pyongyang the consequences if North Korea is unprepared to choose this path.

The Korean Peninsula is at the epicenter of strategic change in Northeast Asia, and the next administration needs to ensure that the United States is a central participant in this process. U.S. policymakers, however, can neither pursue goals in exclusive or proprietary fashion nor expect to control all forces at work on the peninsula or in the region. The United States, however, does not want to be overtaken by events or captured by policy agendas set by others. It remains for the next president to develop a Korea strategy commensurate with Northeast Asia's centrality to long-term U.S. political, economic, and security interests and to work with all regional partners in order to fulfill this strategy.

EXECUTIVE SUMMARY

This chapter reviews Russia's assertive return to the international arena and Moscow's strategy to build an international coalition to balance the U.S.

MAIN ARGUMENT:
Russia's ambitions are out of line with the country's diminished capabilities. Russia faces numerous challenges domestically—including a demographic crisis, decrepit infrastructure, and an obsolete industrial base—that unless dealt with will impede the country's growth. Russia's economic recovery is fragile and reliance on raw materials exports leaves the country vulnerable to fluctuations of the global marketplace. Moscow's ability to maintain stability will hinge on economic conditions, which could require potentially destabilizing reforms. Though Russian military capabilities have improved, many problems inherited from the 1990s remain.

POLICY IMPLICATIONS:
- For the U.S., Russia remains a key country—a force in Eurasian geopolitics, an energy exporter, a balancer of China, and a presence in international financial markets. The U.S. would benefit from a policy toward Russia that recognizes the country's significance for Eurasia and the world more broadly. This would require a thorough assessment of the country's strengths and weaknesses, flexibility and commitment to core U.S. principles, careful prioritization, and an understanding that improving relations will require a long-term perspective and difficult trade-offs.

- The bilateral relationship is capable of delivering considerably more, but no foreign policy vision can guarantee that the two countries will be able to cooperate beyond their core interests. Any new political effort toward Russia would thus benefit from proceeding slowly and cautiously with managed expectations.

Mind the Gap: Russian Ambitions vs. Russian Reality

Eugene B. Rumer

Russia's return to the ranks of major powers after nearly two decades of international retreat and domestic turmoil has been one of the key developments in the international arena in recent years. Outsiders have speculated about a return of the Cold War or the emergence of a multipolar world framed by new economic powers, among which Russia might play the pivotal role in opposing U.S. hegemony. Russian elites, long tired of their country's seemingly interminable decline and confusion, have found the resurgence a source of considerable pride and political consolidation. Building on newfound prosperity and long-standing ambitions, Russian leaders have demanded that their country be treated with the respect and deference fitting a great power that enjoys a special sphere of interests and a special place in the world. These claims have caught many—perhaps most—outside of Russia as much by surprise as did the breakup of the Soviet Union nearly two decades ago. The Russian turnaround appears nearly as surprising as Russia's decline was devastating.

This chapter argues that notwithstanding Russia's impressive achievements and progress in recent years, the country still faces a number of obstacles. Russia's domestic politics are far from reaching sustainable equilibrium, the nation's economic outlook remains precariously tied to its mineral wealth, and the military, although recovered from the shock of the 1990s, has by no means regained its strength. To secure a place alongside other major powers, Russia will need to overcome many obstacles—mainly

Eugene B. Rumer is a Senior Fellow at the Institute for National Strategic Studies at the National Defense University. He can be reached at <rumere@ndu.edu>.

The views expressed here are those of the author and do not reflect the official policy or position of the National Defense University, the Department of Defense, or the U.S. government.

in the domestic arena where present circumstances do not adequately support Moscow's ambitions in the international arena.

Moreover, Russia's foreign policy posture has produced disappointing results. Russian interests (as defined by Moscow) are increasingly challenged along the nation's western, southern, and even eastern borders. This chapter will argue that Russia's ambitions do not match its capabilities, which owing to several key structural factors will constrain Russian foreign policy options in the future. Moscow's foreign policy vision exceeds the country's capabilities and is due for a correction. This correction, however, may not happen for some time, as near- and medium-term factors favor continued Russian growth.

The first part of this chapter provides an overview of the grand strategy that emerged in the final years of the Putin presidency. An assessment of Russia's economic conditions, domestic political situation, and military capabilities follows. The chapter then presents a brief overview of Russian foreign policy accomplishments and concludes with recommendations for U.S. policymakers for managing the relationship with Russia, in all its complexity, in the coming years.

Russian Grand Strategy: Back to the Future

Throughout Vladimir Putin's presidency the principal objective of Russian foreign policy was to re-establish Russia as a major player in world affairs and prove Russia worthy of the full membership in the pantheon of great powers that the Soviet Union once had. That goal was perceptible in virtually every speech Putin delivered and in every appearance with foreign dignitaries and before domestic audiences—on television, during marathon press conferences, in live call-in shows and online sessions, and in meetings with average citizens in various parts of the country.

Russia spans eleven time zones on two continents, possesses a nuclear arsenal second to none, and occupies a permanent seat on the UN Security Council. It might seem surprising then that the leader of a country with Russia's stature would feel compelled to demonstrate his country's greatness with the urgency Putin attached to the task. That urgency, however, comes as no surprise to those who witnessed Russia's decline at home and retreat abroad during the 1990s, and especially not to the Russian people, who experienced that decline first hand.

A Realist Grand Strategy

R-e-s-p-e-c-t. Putin's international strategy involved, above all, speaking loudly on behalf of Russia and projecting an image of strength, confidence, and competence. These actions had the effect—presumably intended—of underscoring the difference between Putin and his predecessor, Boris Yeltsin, whose erratic performance in the 1990s had served as an embodiment of Russia's diminished circumstances. By his confident posture, Putin conveyed the message that his country was no longer the diminished Russia of yesteryear, relegated to geopolitical insignificance.

Another far more consequential aspect of this strategy involved steps by which Putin intended to capitalize on increased domestic prosperity and stability, as well as on the underlying factors that generated that prosperity and in turn led to stability. Key among these factors are Russia's oil and gas wealth and its unmatched abundance and variety of other mineral resources. This unparalleled endowment is coupled with a unique geographic position. The fortuitous timing of global economic trends allowed Russia to exploit its natural advantages as the leading world economies developed an appetite for energy and raw materials.[1]

The Kremlin has sought to establish Russia as the critical supplier of oil and gas, if not globally, then certainly in Eurasia. Economic muscle gives Russia increased political prominence in Europe and Asia. Energy and mineral wealth therefore provide the material foundation for Moscow's newly confident voice in the international arena. Russia seeks to become an "energy superpower"—a country whose superpower status rests on energy resources. Its strategy is thus to "speak loudly and hold a big pipe."

A sphere to call its own. As a corollary to this strategy, Russia has pursued several objectives, the most important of which is the re-establishment of an exclusive sphere of influence throughout the territories of the former Soviet Union. Russian foreign policy analysts articulated a Russian version of the Monroe Doctrine soon after the breakup of the Soviet Union. The intent of this doctrine was to assert Russia's special interests in the former Soviet countries and the right to protect those interests.[2] The doctrine gives Moscow not only special access to these neighboring countries, including right of oversight over their foreign and security policy decisions, but also the ability to deny access to others.

---

[1] Though Russia's resource wealth is undoubtedly a critical factor in the state's recovery, this chapter argues that this wealth constitutes Russia's Achilles' heel: a weakness that keeps the Kremlin from implementing much-needed reforms in a variety of sectors—reforms that would reduce Russia's vulnerability to the uncertainties of the global marketplace.

[2] Lesley H. Gelb, "Foreign Affairs; Yeltsin as Monroe," *New York Times,* March 7, 1993, http://query.nytimes.com/gst/fullpage.html?res=9F0CEED91430F934A35750C0A965958260.

Russia's economic recovery has made it possible for the country's policymakers to act on these long-standing ambitions. Policymakers have relied on a range of instruments—for example, trade, Russian-language propaganda, and favorable visa regimes—to reassert the country's pre-eminence in the former Soviet space. Chief among these instruments has been energy trade. In essence, Russian pursuit of control over the former Soviet lands has taken the form of squeezing nations for political gain by raising prices on Russian oil and gas deliveries.[3]

Multipolarity vs. U.S. hegemony. A lack of appreciation for "soft power" permeates Russian foreign policy and reflects Russian policymakers' penchant for a balance of power approach to international relations. Such an approach is pursued at the expense of the values-based approaches that have gained prominence in Europe and the United States in the post–Cold War era. Speaking at the security conference in Munich in 2007, Putin criticized U.S. attempts to impose Washington's ideological preferences on other countries.[4] According to Putin, no single power's values and interests should be allowed to dominate the international system; a world of one superpower is inherently unstable. Stability can be ensured only by achieving balance of power and interests among key actors in a multipolar world. The combined GDP of India, China, Brazil, and Russia is greater than the GDPs of the United States and the European Union (EU), Putin noted, adding that this redistribution of economic weight should produce changes in political influence and lead to multipolarity.[5]

Putin's approach to international relations evidently is shared by his successor, the new Russian president Dmitry Medvedev. On a visit to Berlin in early June 2008, Medvedev delivered the first major foreign policy address of his presidency. In this speech, Medvedev invited other European nations to design a new European security system based on "'naked' national interests, undistorted by any ideological motives."[6]

Although the Kremlin recognizes several major powers important to the international system, one power occupies a special place in Russia's strategy—the United States. The Kremlin perceives Washington as the

---

[3] "Russia-Belarus Oil Blockade Ends," *BBC News,* January 11, 2007, http://news.bbc.co.uk/2/hi/business/6248251.stm; Rupert Wingfield-Hayes, "Oil Row Highlights Changing Ties," *BBC News,* January 8, 2007; and Marianna Grigoryan, "Armenia: Gas Price Hike Stirs Discontent," *EurasiaNet,* March 22, 2006, http://www.eurasianet.org/departments/business/articles/eav032206a.shtml.

[4] Vladimir V. Putin (speech at the 43rd Munich Conference on Security and Policy, Munich, February 10, 2007), http://www.securityconference.de/konferenzen/rede.php?sprache=en&id=179.

[5] Ibid.

[6] Dmitry Medvedev, "Vystupleniye na vstreche s predstavitelyami politicheskikh, parlamnetskilh i obshchestvennykh krugov Germanii" [Speech at the Meeting with Representatives of Political, Parliamentary and Public Circles of Germany] (speech given at a meeting in Berlin, June 5, 2008), http://kremlin.ru/appears/2008/06/05/1923_type63374type63376type63377_202133.shtml.

principal challenge to global security: the sole remaining hegemonic power eager to construct a unipolar world dominated by one ideology— an ideology that serves only to conceal U.S. interests.[7] According to this view, U.S. desire for hegemony has been the chief source of instability throughout the former Soviet countries. Washington's attempts to spread democracy in these countries have led to greater regional turmoil, harmed Russian interests, and endangered the stability and security of the Russian Federation itself.

Russian foreign policy has thus sought to protect the country's interests in the former Soviet lands as well as in Europe and Asia. Principal goals include mobilizing opposition to the sole remaining global hegemon and promoting the idea of multipolarity as a model of stability. This alternative to U.S. hegemony is envisioned as a system where critical decisions are made by a constellation of major powers—Russia, India, China, and key European nations—that together would provide counterweight to the United States in the international arena.

Russia lacks the requisite capabilities to recreate the bipolar world of the second half of the twentieth century. Instead, Russian policymakers strive to create an arrangement that resembles the balance of power system of the nineteenth century, where Europe and by extension the world were managed by a constellation of key powers.

Realist, but Realistic?

What may have worked well in the nineteenth century is not guaranteed to work equally well in the twenty-first century. The international system of the nineteenth century, based on a handful of European empires with governments ranging from autocratic to partly democratic, makes a poor prototype for today's globalized world.

It is even questionable whether Moscow could take advantage of a nineteenth-century-style balance of power system, considering Russia's unenviable position vis-à-vis other major powers in Europe, Asia, and elsewhere. There is an economic, military, and demographic gap between today's Russia and the other major actors in Eurasian geopolitics (specifically, the EU, the United States, and China). This gap is much greater than that which existed between the Russian empire and major European powers a century and a half ago. The impact of this gap has been compounded by the effects of globalization, whose rapid pace has left Russia little room to maneuver and adapt. The proverbial correlation of forces is hardly in

---

[7] Putin (speech at the 43rd Munich Conference).

Russia's favor; the current resurgence rests on questionable foundations, and the long-term outlook for Russia remains uncertain.

The gap between Russian rhetoric and capabilities is evidently not lost on the more reformist members of the country's elite. Some have expressed concerns over the impact of an assertive foreign policy on the country's economic development.[8] This appears, however, to be a minority opinion among the country's elite.

For the short-term future, a resurgent, assertive, and somewhat antagonistic Russia—resentful of the U.S. military presence in Central Asia, opposed to further enlargement of the North Atlantic Treaty Organization (NATO), and critical of U.S. plans for missile defenses in Europe—is likely to be a fixture on the foreign policy agenda of the next U.S. administration. U.S. policymakers may have to contend with and find ways to counter this resurgent Russia without compounding the many challenges already facing the United States abroad.

The State of Russia

By most accounts, the first decade of the 21st century has been good to Russia. The country's rapid transition from near ruin to unparalleled prosperity has shattered virtually all long-held notions concerning Russia's present condition and future course.

Russia's Economic Recovery

The financial crisis of 1998, during which the ruble collapsed and Russia defaulted on obligations to creditors at home and abroad, marked the nadir in the country's post-Soviet transformation. Russia's currency was worthless, and the economy was turning out goods that nobody wanted to buy, which only detracted value from the production inputs.[9]

The 1998 crisis unfolded in the wake of painful reforms that left millions of Russians struggling to survive. The hope that the pain and social dislocation those reforms produced would be quickly followed by recovery and stabilization was not realized. The crisis of 1998 seemed to underscore that there was no hope for Russia whatsoever.

---

[8] Neil Buckley and Catherine Belton, "Moscow Warned Hard Line Endangers Economy," *Financial Times*, January 30, 2008, http://www.ft.com/cms/s/0/01288834-cf71-11dc-854a-0000779fd2ac,dwp_uuid=70662e7c-3027-11da-ba9f-00000e2511c8.html.

[9] Clifford G. Gaddy and Barry W. Ickes, "Russia's Virtual Economy," *Foreign Affairs* 77, no. 5 (September/October 1998): 53–67.

The country's political paralysis seemed to compound the pain of economic and social dislocation. Led by an aging and erratic president, with a parliament dominated by the opposition, and still suffering from the physical and psychological wounds inflicted in the course of the humiliating military campaign in Chechnya, Russia appeared to have reached a dead end. In an address to the gloomy nation at the close of 1999, Putin—still acting as Yeltsin's prime minister—warned his fellow countrymen that hard work would be required on the difficult road ahead and that Russia's destination could not be taken for granted.[10]

Less than a decade after that 1999 address, Putin projected an entirely different image when speaking at the St. Petersburg International Economic Forum in June 2007. Brimming with confidence, Putin called for a new global financial architecture to give a more prominent role to Russia and other rising economies outside the established group of seven (G-7) framework.[11]

Putin's confidence appeared well justified. The state coffers, nearly empty at the time of the 1998 collapse, were bursting with revenue. Russian gold and hard currency reserves stood near the half trillion dollar-mark and were rising, whereas in 1999 the reserves amounted to $12 billion.[12] Russian GDP stood at approximately $200 billion in 1999; in 2007 the GDP was $1.2 trillion.[13] Per capita GDP grew from $2,000 in 1998 to $9,000 in 2007.[14]

The glowing macro-indicators describing the Russian economy, however, tell only half the story. These indicators fail to convey the full extent of the country's situation at the end of a spectacular decade.

Russia owes its good fortune above all to the surging price of natural oil, gas, and mineral resources in the world markets during much of the current decade. In 1999 oil and gas accounted for less than 13% of Russian GDP; in 2007 they accounted for nearly 32%.[15] Additionally, in 2006 oil, fuels, and gas accounted for nearly two-thirds of all Russian exports.[16]

---

[10] Vladimir V. Putin, "Rossiya na rubezhe tysyachiletiy" [Russia on the Threshold of the Millennia], *Nezavisimaya Gazeta,* December 30, 1999, http://www.ng.ru/politics/1999-12-30/4_millenium.html.

[11] Vladimir V. Putin (speech at the 11th St. Petersburg International Economic Forum, St. Petersburg, June 10, 2007), http://www.russiancourier.com/en/info/kremlin/73781.

[12] Central Intelligence Agency, *The World Factbook* (Washington, D.C.: Central Intelligence Agency, 2008), https://www.cia.gov/library/publications/the-world-factbook/geos/rs.html#Econ.

[13] Anders Aslund, "The Russian Economy Facing 2017," in *Alternative Futures for Russia to 2017,* ed. Andrew C. Kuchins (Washington, D.C.: Center for Strategic and International Studies, 2007), 27, http://www.csis.org/media/csis/pubs/071214-russia_2017-web.pdf.

[14] "Smoke and Mirrors," *Economist,* March 1–7, 2008, 27.

[15] Ibid., 29.

[16] Economist Intelligence Unit, "Country Briefings: Russia," *Economist,* http://www.economist.com/countries/Russia/profile.cfm?folder=Profile-FactSheet.

Despite the obvious benefits of higher energy prices, the natural advantage that Russian oil and gas represent for the country's development is also a source of serious problems. Russia's hydrocarbon wealth is a double-edged sword. Though fueling the country's recovery, hydrocarbon resources also have raised the prospect of excessive resource dependency. "Dutch disease" is likely to take a particularly acute form in Russia—so much so that Russian experts have even proposed rebranding the effect the "Russian syndrome."[17]

Moreover, some observers argue that Russian dependence on oil and gas revenues has exceeded the definition of resource dependence and turned into an addiction. In other words, this dependence has reached systemic proportions, with the consequences penetrating many other sectors of the country's economy. As a result, much-needed reforms have been thwarted by the requirement to sustain the addiction.[18]

The situation in which Russia finds itself at the end of the first decade following the post-Soviet recovery is not easy. In the words of prominent Russian economist, business lobbyist, and former senior government official Aleksandr Shokhin, "the high rate of growth so far has been achieved thanks to the sectors that are protected from competition from imports: retail, finance, services, construction."[19] According to Shokhin, "in the long run, the threat is that it could lead to deindustrialization."[20] One striking example of this phenomenon is a Russian power-generating company's recent order for generating equipment placed with China—an order that Russian industry is unable to fulfill.[21]

Russian oil, gas, and other mineral wealth have long been expected to fuel the redevelopment of the Russian economy—not just in the natural resource sector but across the board—and lead to the country's resurgence as an industrial power. Yet this scenario has not come to pass. Scenarios for Russian economic modernization are still the stuff of forecasts and proposals for the future rather than reports and analyses of accomplishments.[22]

---

[17] "'Russian Syndrome': Worse than 'Dutch Disease,'" *Expert*, April 16, 2007, http://eng.expert.ru/printissues/expert/2007/15/ekonomika_rublya_editorial/.

[18] Barry W. Ickes, "Putin, Coase, and Khodorkovsky," presentation, October 2007, http://econ.la.psu.edu/~bickes/coasepres.pdf.

[19] "Shokhin: Rossii grozit deindustrializatsiya" [Shokhin: Russia Is Threatened with Deindustrialization], *RU Today*, April 18, 2006.

[20] Ibid.

[21] Simon Shuster and Jacqueline Cowhig, "Chinese Playing Big Role in Russian Power Expansion," *International Herald Tribune*, May 5, 2008, http://www.iht.com/articles/2008/05/05/business/energy.php.

[22] Natalya Alyakrinskaya, "Upast ili podnyatsya" [To Fall or to Rise], *Moscow News*, June 1, 2007, http://www.mn.ru/issue.php?2007-21-17.

Besides oil and gas, which account for nearly two-thirds of Russian exports, metals make up nearly 14% and machinery and equipment almost 6% of Russian exports.[23] Such heavy economic dependence on oil cannot but serve as a reminder that the 1998 financial crisis took place shortly after the price of oil in the world market descended to near the $10 per barrel (bbl) mark.

As noted in preceding paragraphs, Russian economists and government officials are sensitive to this vulnerability. Putin himself has lamented the energy dependence aspect of Russian economic development. Speaking at the February 2008 meeting of the State Council, Putin noted that the country has not been able to

> escape the inertia of development based on energy and raw materials…we have addressed the task of modernizing the economy only on a fragmentary basis. This inevitably leads to Russia's dependence on imports of [manufactured] goods and technologies, to our being locked into the position of a raw materials appendage to the world economy. [24]

Putin proposed and sought funding for several high-priority "national projects" in areas deemed essential to correct these shortcomings and improve the country's long-term economic outlook—including health, demographics, education, and nanotechnology.[25] Russian policymakers have singled out nanotechnology for special treatment as a particularly important and promising field in which to achieve a competitive economic advantage in the future.

The effects that nanotechnology and other national projects will have on Russian economic development appear uncertain—notwithstanding generous government funding and widespread publicity—as is quite frequently the case with big, high-priority projects initiated and sponsored by the government. The uncertainty stems from several important factors that suggest the path ahead for the Russian economy may be far more difficult than macro-economic indicators alone would lead one to believe.

Although globalization overall and the rise of new markets for Russian exports have benefited Russian economic interests by fueling global appetite for the country's raw material exports, the rise of new industrial economies

---

[23] "Country Briefings: Russia."

[24] Vladimir V. Putin, "Vystupleniye na rasshirennom zasedanii Gosudarstvennogo Soveta 'O strategii Rossii do 2020 goda'" [Speech at the Expanded Session of the State Council on "Russian Development Strategy to the Year 2020"] (speech to the State Council, Moscow, February 8, 2008), http://kremlin.ru/text/appears/2008/02/159528.shtml.

[25] Vladimir Putin, "Beginning of the Meeting on Developing Nanotechnology" (speech delivered at the Russian Research Centre, Kurchatov Institute, Moscow, April 18, 2007), http://www.kremlin.ru/eng/sdocs/speeches.shtml?month=04&day=18&year=2007&prefix=&value_from=&value_to=&date=&stype=&dayRequired=no&day_enable=true&Submit.x=4&Submit.y=8.

in China, India, Latin America, and elsewhere has increased competitive pressures on Russia's manufacturing sector. So far, Russia has not well met the competitive challenge from abroad.

World Bank data indicates that in 2006 more than one-third of all FDI in Russia was allocated to extractive industries. The manufacturing sector received 19%, yet half of that was apparently directed to metals and food.[26] In 2007 the situation was worse: extractive industries received 50% of FDI while manufacturing received only 15%.[27] There is no indication in Russian statistics on FDI that the country's economic revival and attendant investment boom will spark reindustrialization and recapitalization of new sectors of the economy. In fact, recent data suggests that outside the energy sector FDI has fallen from 1.6% of GDP in 1999 to 0.65% in 2007.[28]

Overall Russian investment figures are consistent with the picture that emerges from FDI figures. In 2007 resource industries increased their share in total investment from 15.2% in 2005 to 17.3%. Manufacturing industries' share in total investment, however, declined from 17.6% in 2005 to 15.7% in 2007.[29]

Yet even if Russia were to settle for the role of raw materials supplier— an appendage to the industrialized world, and a very important one at that—the outlook for the country's critical oil and gas sector is less than bright. On its present path of development, Russia faces a key challenge in having to deal with the impact of the widely anticipated decline in gas field production. Bringing new fields online, in order to sustain and expand gas exports to Europe, is a massive undertaking. Russia is experiencing a shortfall in domestic gas output of some 60 billion cubic meters (cm) of gas. Of the 710 billion cm of gas Russia must produce, 400 billion is slated for domestic consumption, 257 billion for export, and 53 billion to address Gazprom's own needs. Gazprom produced 550 billion cm of gas in 2006 (the same amount as in 2005). Independent Russian companies produced 95 billion cm more. The 65 billion cm shortfall was made up by imports of gas from Central Asia. Russian forecasts show this deficit of natural gas will continue for the foreseeable future.[30]

---

[26] "Russian Economic Report #14," World Bank, June 2007, http://web.worldbank.org/WBSITE/ EXTERNAL/COUNTRIES/ECAEXT/RUSSIANFEDERATIONEXTN/0,,contentMDK:21362587 ~menuPK:305605~pagePK:2865066~piPK:2865079~theSitePK:305600,00.html.

[27] "Russian Economic Report #16," World Bank, June 2008, http://siteresources.worldbank.org/ INTRUSSIANFEDERATION/Resources/rer16_Eng.pdf.

[28] "Smoke and Mirrors," 29.

[29] "Russian Economic Report #16," 5.

[30] Sergei Dubinin, "Epokha Defitistov" [The Epoch of Deficits], Gazeta.ru, June 19, 2007, http:// www.gazeta.ru/comments/2007/06/19_a_1823690.shtml?print.

The challenge for Russia is to develop new fields. Yet new fields will be very expensive to develop. According to Sergey Dubinin, former chairman of Russian Central Bank and former deputy chairman of the board of Gazprom, that task is simply beyond Gazprom's ability unless the company can secure outside investment—foreign and domestic. In Dubinin's words, "the epoch of cheap gas in Russia has ended."[31]

Instead of aggressively courting foreign investors, however, the Russian government has increased control over the energy sector while marginalizing the role of foreign companies in projects in which they had previously played a leading role. Shell had to yield its controlling interest in the Sakhalin-2 gas project to Gazprom. BP, under pressure from the Russian government, sold to Gazprom a stake in the Kovykta gas field held through the TNK-BP venture. In 2006 Gazprom announced plans to develop the Shtokman field by itself, using foreign companies as subcontractors rather than shareholders in the project. Foreign companies had hoped for as much as a 49% equity stake as shareholders. Recent reports on the restructuring of the Shtokman deal indicate that the French company Total has been invited to take a 25% stake in the operating company. Although details of the arrangement remain unclear, and it thus would be premature to draw conclusions about a major policy shift, the invitation to Total would indicate a change in the Russian government's stance toward foreign investors.[32]

Moscow's record of apparent indifference to long-term indicators suggests an uncertain future for Russia's aspirations to exert influence in the international arena as an "energy superpower." There are widespread doubts in the expert community about the outlook for Russian oil and gas production.[33] In addition, outside Europe and former Soviet regions, where Russia enjoys a geographic advantage, Moscow has not succeeded in securing a prominent place as price-maker on a global scale. Russia remains a price-taker in a market dominated by the Organization of the Petroleum Exporting Countries (OPEC), which Russia has been reluctant to join. Moscow shows occasional outbursts of enthusiasm for proposals to switch the flow of Russian oil and gas to Asia (from Europe) and thus achieve flexibility with respect to choice of markets. Given the costs associated

[31] Dubinin, "Epokha Defitistov."

[32] Judy Clark and Nina Rach, "Gazprom to Develop Shtokman Alone, Pipe Gas to Europe," *Oil & Gas Journal* 104, no. 39 (October 16, 2006), http://www.energybulletin.net/21287.html; "Russia Welcomes Total back to Shtokman Field," *Russia Today*, July 13, 2007, http://russiatoday.ru/business/news/10765; and Andrew E. Kramer, "Gazprom and Total Strike a Deal for Offshore Gas Field," *International Herald Tribune*, July 12, 2007, http://www.iht.com/articles/2007/07/12/business/gazprom.php.

[33] Greg Walters, "Russian Oil Output May Fall for First Time in Decade in 2008," Bloomberg, March 27, 2008, http://www.bloomberg.com/apps/news?pid=20601072&sid=arXTpOY4omL4&refer=energy.

with such schemes—likely to reach into tens of billions of dollars—these proposals appear to be no more than pipedreams.[34]

Russia's economic recovery, therefore, appears less strong than Russian leaders are prone to describe. The situation is further aggravated by a number of long-term structural factors that will affect Russian economic performance and position in the international arena in the years to come:

- a severe demographic crisis due to ongoing population decline, which will have a number of ramifications including shortages both of labor for the economy at large and of manpower for the largely conscript-based Russian army[35]

- a crumbling infrastructure, which will require government investments of as much as $1 trillion by the year 2020[36]

- an obsolete and obsolescent defense industrial base, which undermines Russia's ability to sustain arms exports, a key source of revenue[37]

- pervasive corruption, which stifles economic activity

Russia's economic recovery thus rests on a fragile foundation. In the years to come Russian leaders will have to proceed with caution in order to protect economic achievements and further engender conditions beneficial to long-term, sustainable development and growth. Their actions in domestic and international arenas in the next four years will likely be telling with regard to the country's long-term direction at home and abroad.

---

[34] Nadejda M. Victor, "Russian Geopolitical Geometry through a Gas Prism," in *Russia Watch: Essays in Honor of George Kolt,* ed. Eugene B. Rumer and Celeste A. Wallander (Washington, D.C.: Center for Strategic and International Studies, 2007).

[35] The Russian population declined from approximately 150 million at the time of the Soviet breakup in 1991 to 142 million in 2007. This trend may continue well into the future, with Russia's population projected to decrease to 134 million by 2015. See "Russian Population in Steep Decline," *BBC News,* October 24, 2000, http://news.bbc.co.uk/1/hi/world/europe/988723.stm. Although the Russian media has reported recent improvements in birth rates, the overwhelming opinion of demographers, both Russian and foreign, is that the country's demographic outlook remains very bleak. See Anatoliy Vishnevskiy, "Rossiya v mirovom demograficheskom kontekste" [Russia in the Global Demographic Context], February 7, 2008, http://www.polit.ru/lectures/2008/02/07/vyshnevsky_print.html; and Nicholas Eberstadt and Hans Groth, "Dying Russia," *Wall Street Journal Europe,* April 25, 2008, http://www.aei.org/include/pub_print.asp?pubID=27870.

[36] This is Putin's own estimate. See Gleb Bryanski, "Update 4—Russia to Spend $1 Trillion on Infrastructure," Reuters UK, September 21, 2007, http://uk.reuters.com/article/oilRpt/idUKL2121712020070921.

[37] This includes arms exports to such important markets as China and India. See "80% of Russia's Defense Industry Is Obsolete," Rosbalt, August 18, 2004, available at the CDI Russia Weekly website, http://www.cdi.org/russia/270-14.cfm; "Russia Spends $1.1 Bln Annually on Defense Industry—Gov't," Ria Novosti, March 15, 2007; and Stephen J. Blank, *Rosoboroneksport: Arms Sales and the Structure of Russian Defense Industry* (Carlisle: Strategic Studies Institute, 2007), http://www.strategicstudiesinstitute.army.mil/pdffiles/PUB749.pdf.

The Domestic Political Setting: Peace for Now

Russia's economic recovery has coincided with a remarkable turnaround in the country's domestic political fortunes during the first decade of the new century. Putin's legacy to his successor, Dmitry Medvedev, is a country that appears to be at peace with itself. Putin's long-standing high approval rating has been miraculously transferred to his successor. Public opinion experts suggest that even if the parliamentary and presidential elections were not fair and were conducted in ways that benefited the Kremlin's political interests, the results are still broadly representative of the public mood. Putin's chosen successor would have been elected no matter what. In fact, for the much of 2007 the most popular candidate to succeed Putin as president was Putin himself.

There are, however, clouds on the horizon in Russian domestic politics. Though showing high approval ratings for Russian leaders, polling data also reveals significant fault-lines in the political landscape—underscoring the possibility for future tensions and conflicts.

Opinion polls conducted in Russia have revealed a gap between Putin's popularity and voter disapproval of the policies of Putin's government. In a November 2006 poll Putin had an approval rating of 77%, whereas the approval rating of Prime Minister Mikhail Fradkov stood at 44%, and that of the government as a whole at 40%. Furthermore, 44% of respondents thought the country was on the wrong path, compared to 38% who thought the country was on the right path. Likewise, 65% of respondents were dissatisfied with the state of affairs in the country, 63% disapproved of the government's economic policy, and 81% disapproved of the moral climate in the country.[38]

Russian citizens have many complaints against their government. The government is unable to deal with unemployment, inflation, lack of social benefits, or social inequality. Police, prosecutors, and security services are interested only in their own well-being and do nothing in the interest of the common folk. Russians have lost trust in police, courts, and local government. Voter dissatisfaction with the country's domestic condition runs deep and stands in stark contrast with the highly favorable opinion Russians seem to have of Putin and Medvedev personally.

Income inequality in particular appears to be a serious problem, with many Russians still struggling to make ends meet. One-third of respondents

---

[38] "Sotsialno-politicheskaya situatsiya v strane v Octyabre 2006 goda" [Socio-political Situation in the Country in October 2006], Levada Center, Press Release, November 2, 2006, http://www.levada.ru/press/2006110202.print.html.

in a 2006 poll described their economic situation as "bad" or "very bad."[39] More than half described the situation in the region where they lived as "tense" or "explosive." Fewer than 15% of those polled were willing to let stand the results of the privatization conducted in Russia in the 1990s, and nearly 80% wanted to change those results in one way or another.[40]

Globalization is a wild card that will affect Russian politics in ways not easy to predict. Russian voters are more and better connected to the outside world than at any other time in the history of the country. Unlike people in China, Russians have unimpeded access to the Internet. According to a public opinion poll conducted at the end of 2006, 22% of Russian households reported having a personal computer, 35% of respondents reported using a computer at least once a week, and 28% reported accessing the Internet (other than using e-mail) at least once a week.[41] In September 2006 there were well over one million Russian-language blogs.[42]

Russians are free to travel abroad as tourists, and millions do. More foreigners are traveling to Russia as well. Russians are thus connected to the world and enjoy opportunities to learn about the outside world and to form their own opinions about their country. In other words, the Russian populace is not easy to control and manipulate, and its behavior is far more difficult to predict today than a generation ago. It is therefore easier to understand the strong response of Russian political elite to U.S. and European support for democratic movements in the former Soviet states as well as in Russia proper. This response has included not only restrictions on opposition parties and movements and on access to mass media but also,

---

[39] "Osenneye nastroyeniye Rossiyan" [The Mood of Russians in the Autumn], Levada Center, Press Release, October 11, 2006, http://www.levada.ru/press/2006101105.html. The Gini index for Russia in 2007 was 41.3. For comparison, Denmark has a high degree of income distribution equality and a Gini index of 24; Bolivia, with a high degree of income distribution inequality, has a Gini index of 59.2. See Index Mundi, http://www.indexmundi.com.

[40] Aronov, "Vse li my v odnoy lodke? Chto derzhit na plavu kapitanov Rossiyskogo biznesa" [Are We All in the Same Boat? What is Keeping Afloat the Captains of Russian Business], *Izvestiya,* June 26, 2007, http://www.izvestia.ru/economic/article3105510/; "Sotsialno-politicheskaya situatsiya v strane v Avguste 2006 goda" [Socio-political Situation in the Country in August 2006], Levada Center, Press Release, September 13, 2006, http://www.levada.ru/press/2006091302.print.html; and "Sotsialno-politicheskaya situatsiya v strane v Sentyabre 2006 goda" [Socio-political Situation in the Country in September 2006], Levada Center, Press Release, October 3, 2006, http://www.levada.ru/press/2006100301.print.html.

[41] "Uroven osnashchennosti telefonnoy svyazyu i internetom" [The Level of Telephone and Internet Penetration], Levada Center, Press Release, October 5, 2006, http://www.levada.ru/press/2006100502.print.html.

[42] "Yandex issledoval Russkoyazychnuyu blogospheru" [Yandex Has Studied the Russian-Language Blogosphere], Yandex, Press Release, September 26, 2006, http://company.yandex.ru/news/2006/0926/index.xml.

on occasion, physical confinement and intimidation.[43] Russia's political elite have viewed the Rose, Orange, and Tulip revolutions—which led to the overthrow of entrenched, long-serving governments in Georgia, Ukraine, and Kyrgyzstan in 2003, 2004, and 2005 respectively—as more than mere disturbances on the country's doorstep.

Public opinion data suggests that average as well as elite Russian voters hold a rather negative view of the color revolutions in neighboring countries. A series of polls conducted during and shortly after the Orange Revolution in Ukraine revealed that a plurality of Russians (48%) endorsed Putin's actions during the crisis. A majority (51%) favored the pro-Moscow candidate supported by the Kremlin. Russians by a five-to-one margin thought that Victor Yushchenko's victory in the Ukrainian presidential election would be less favorable for Russia than Yanukovich's.[44]

Russian leaders may still be concerned over the state's ability to control grass-roots Russian domestic politics. The notion that Russia has reverted to Soviet-style authoritarianism does not adequately reflect modern-day Russians' expanding use of the Internet, cell phones, and opportunities for foreign travel.[45] Rather, Russians appear content for the time being to give up a measure of personal freedom in exchange for economic prosperity and political stability—especially while memories of the previous decade are very much alive. Russia does not consider the status quo a happy state of affairs, however. The Kremlin's ability to sustain the economic status quo appears critical to the population's willingness to go along with the current arrangement. Should the current arrangement prove unsustainable, fault-lines in the country's political landscape are likely to become more pronounced.

The political transition from Putin to Medvedev triggered a political crisis inside the Kremlin, as different factions fought for advantage in a perceived temporary vacuum of power. The rest of the country, however, seemed little affected by the struggle inside the Kremlin walls. Yet if the fragile equilibrium between Russian economics and politics is disrupted and those inside the Kremlin avoid making the difficult decisions that will be needed to move Russia forward, the rest of the country could set the agenda

---

[43] Clifford J. Levy, "Kremlin Rules—It Isn't Magic: Putin's Opponents Vanish from TV," *New York Times,* June 3, 2008, http://www.nytimes.com/2008/06/03/world/europe/03russia.html?_r=1&scp =1&sq=delyagin&st=nyt&oref=slogin; and "Kasparov Gets 5 Days in Jail for Marching," *New York Times,* November 25, 2007, http://www.nytimes.com/2007/11/25/world/europe/25russia.html.

[44] Levada Center, Public Opinion Survey Press Release, January 28, 2008, http://www.levada.ru/ press/2005012802.html; Levada Center, Public Opinion Survey Press Release, February 28, 2008, http://www.levada.ru/press/2005022801.html; and Levada Center, Public Opinion Survey Press Release, December 16, 2004, http://www.levada.ru/press/2004121601.html.

[45] "Abonentov sotovoy svyazi v RF stalo bolshe chem zhiteley" [There Are More Cell Phone Users than Residents], *Nezavisimaya Gazeta,* June 18, 2006, http://www.ng.ru/economics/2007-06-18/4_cell.html.

for the nation in the coming years. This outcome is entirely possible, and even likely, given the country's vastness and regional and ethnic diversity, the complex economic and political interests of regional elites, and the impact of globalization.

The Military: Better, but Better than What?

Russia's ability to flex its military muscle has been one of the most widely noted aspects of the turnaround in recent years. Russia's actions in the military arena have included resumption of long-range bomber patrols and naval deployment to the Mediterranean. Moscow has also threatened to target Prague and Warsaw with nuclear missiles should the Czech Republic and Poland accept components of U.S. ballistic missile defenses on their territories.

A closer look, however, suggests that the Russian military remains a mere shadow of its former self. The undeniable improvements in the military's capabilities have to be put in the context of the conditions that prevailed in virtually every sphere of Russian life—economic, political, and military—during the previous decade.

In the 1990s the Russian military was reeling and appeared at times on the verge of collapse. Officers and their families, left homeless, were not paid for months during the vast redeployment of forces from Eastern Europe and former Soviet states. The military campaign in Chechnya cost thousands of lives and resulted in a humiliating truce between Moscow and rebel commanders—a low point for the Russian military, which was still reeling from events in Afghanistan. Ships rusted in ports, planes did not fly, tanks had no fuel, and soldiers did not train. The once mighty and proud military machine had ground to a standstill.

In 2008 the Russian military projects a different image. The war in Chechnya has been won. There is more and better housing for military personnel, and reports of salaries not paid or not paid on time have long been forgotten. Defense expenditures are rising to as high as $70 billion.[46] In addition, the transition to a partially volunteer or contract force is underway. Major cuts in the size of the military establishment are reportedly over as well. With its authorized strength now set at approximately one million soldiers, the military has entered a new phase—one of modernization.[47]

The armed forces consist of three services—the army (360,000), the navy (142,000), and the air force (160,000)—and three separate branches—

---

[46] International Institute for Strategic Studies, *The Military Balance 2008* (London: Routledge, 2008), 211.

[47] Ministry of Defense of the Russian Federation, "Struktura vooruzhennykh sil" [Structure of the Armed Forces], webpage, http://www.mil.ru/848/1045/index.shtml.

the Strategic Rocket Forces (40,000), the space troops (40,000), and the airborne troops (35,000).

Russia maintains a robust force to serve as the ultimate deterrent against potential aggression and to guarantee the country's sovereignty. Nearly 500 land-based, silo-based, and mobile missiles can deliver nearly 1,800 warheads. The twelve ballistic missile submarines carry more than 600 nuclear warheads. Finally, Russia's nearly 80 bombers can carry nearly 900 long-range, nuclear-armed cruise missiles.[48]

Although representing only a fraction of the Soviet Union's Cold War arsenal, these numbers amount to more than adequate deterrent capabilities. Some analysts have suggested that Russian nuclear capabilities are in decline and that this trend, along with U.S. missile defense deployments, could disrupt the U.S.-Russian strategic nuclear balance. This notion, however, appears to be far-fetched.[49]

Comparisons of Russia's current nuclear arsenal to that of the Soviet Union and applications of Cold War–era concepts of nuclear stability to the current situation are simply misleading. Russia's current nuclear arsenal serves a fundamentally different purpose. Russia and the United States are no longer locked in a nuclear stand-off. Russia appears to have put aside the notion that it needs counterforce-targeting capabilities against the United States. Russia instead appears to rely on nuclear forces as a deterrent against both nuclear and conventional threats, as well as a guarantee of its strategic sovereignty. This nuclear strategy in effect adopts a posture of minimal deterrence. Although Russia maintains a relatively small nuclear arsenal, this arsenal is sufficiently robust to deter potential attackers from either carrying out a disarming strike against Russia or threatening Russia or its interests with conventional weapons.

Russian plans provide for significant changes in land-based ballistic missiles. Silo-based SS-18, SS-19, and SS-25 ICBMs are to be withdrawn from service by 2015. By 2015 the Strategic Rocket Forces are expected to have 34 mobile and 66 silo-based SS-27 ICBMs. The Strategic Arms Reduction Treaty (START I), including the ban on multiple independent re-entry vehicles (MIRV), expires on January 1, 2009. Moscow plans to arm new missiles with MIRV warheads that will provide sufficient hedge against U.S. ballistic missile defense capabilities. Strategic Rocket Forces expect to have some 500 land-based warheads; the overall number of warheads,

---

[48] This information is derived from an independent Russian web-based database available at the Russia Strategic Nuclear Forces website, http://russianforces.org/current/.

[49] Keir Lieber and Daryl Press, "The Rise of U.S. Nuclear Primacy," *Foreign Affairs* 85, no. 2 (March/ April 2006), http://www.foreignaffairs.org/20060301faessay85204/keir-a-lieber-daryl-g-press/the-rise-of-u-s-nuclear-primacy.html.

including sea- and land-based systems, will be approximately 1,500—well below the 2,200 limit of the Moscow Treaty.[50]

The Russian ballistic missile submarine (SSBN) fleet is in the process of downsizing. The current thirteen boats include six Delta III submarines assigned to the Pacific Fleet, six Delta IVs assigned to the Northern Fleet, and one Typhoon submarine also assigned to the Northern Fleet.[51] Moscow plans to withdraw the entire Delta III class of submarines from service over the next few years.[52]

Despite widespread domestic criticism of Russian strategic weapons programs, there can be little doubt that Russia has the means to maintain a credible deterrent, at sea as well as on land and in the air. This position is in keeping with Moscow's apparent posture of minimal deterrence. The fact that a relatively small number of weapons is required for that purpose should speak for itself.

Russian conventional capabilities are often criticized in the Russian press as well. Considering the inherent differences between the two sides of Russian defense, the ill effects of the previous decade are bound to linger longer in the conventional sphere. Years of underfunding and delayed modernization, large-scale reductions in the size of the armed forces, and attempts at military reform have taken their toll on the Russian army.

The demographic situation imposes a major constraint on the size of Russia's armed forces. The military relies largely on conscripts to fill its ranks. Russia is already faced with a situation in which the pool of available manpower fails to meet the military's requirements, both in terms of size and in terms of quality of recruits: poor health renders many young Russian men unfit for service, chronic discipline problems are aggravated by the brutal hazing of recruits, and military pay and living conditions are poor.[53]

The Russian military has long tried to implement at least a partial shift from an all-conscript army to a volunteer and contract army. The funding to implement this shift, however, has not been available. The Russian economic recovery has resulted in new problems: due to the country's declining population and labor pool, the military now competes with the civilian economy for quality personnel. Moreover, military branches and specialties requiring technical skills as well as elite units, such as airborne

---

[50] Aleksey Nikolskiy, "Mutatsiya 'Topolya,'" [Topol's Mutation], *Vedomosti*, May 5, 2007, http://www.vedomosti.ru/newspaper/article.shtml?2007/05/08/125470.

[51] Data for the Russian ballistic missile submarine (SSBN) fleet is available at the Russia Strategic Nuclear Forces website.

[52] See the Russia Strategic Nuclear Forces website.

[53] Keir Giles, "Where Have All the Soldiers Gone? Russia's Military Plans versus Demographic Reality," Conflict Studies Research Centre, Russian Series, October 2006, http://www.defac.ac.uk/colleges/csrc/document-listings/caucasus-publications.

troops, have a strong demand for contract soldiers. This demand further cuts into the supply of manpower available to the regular army.[54]

The Russian military's modernization prospects look even bleaker, given the state of the defense industry and tight procurement budgets. Procurement budgets have been notoriously low, leaving the defense-industrial complex to rely on foreign buyers.[55] With rising defense budgets, procurement funds increased to $11.6 billion in 2007—a 28% increase from 2006.[56] These are still modest numbers, however, considering the size of the Russian military and the lean diet the defense industry had been on for more than a decade. In the opinion of Russian experts, the industry is by no means guaranteed to overcome the lingering effects of that decade.[57]

Although by Cold War standards the state of Russian defense is not enviable, Russian security is no longer measured with Cold War yardsticks. Russia lacks the sophisticated weaponry fielded by some NATO countries, and Russian military planners still insist on worst-case scenarios and the importance of sheer military capabilities and their destructive potential. Yet circumstances in which this capabilities gap would become relevant are hard to imagine.

Despite many problems, the Russian military remains the biggest and arguably the only credible military force in the former Soviet Union. The military is acquiring more capabilities likely to be relevant to the challenges Russia and its neighbors could face in that giant region in the foreseeable future.

---

[54] Keir Giles, "Military Service in Russia: No New Model Army," Conflict Studies Research Centre, Defense Academy of the United Kingdom, Russian Series, May 2007, http://www.defac.ac.uk/colleges/csrc/document-listings/russian; Pavel Felgenhauer, "Russian Military: After Ivanov," Institute for the Study of Conflict, Ideology, and Policy at Boston University, May 21, 2007, http://www.bu.edu/phpbin/news-cms/news/?dept=732&id=45147; and Anatoliy Tsyganok, "Budet li v Rossiyskoy armii professionalnyy serzhant?" [Will There Be Professional Sergeant in the Russian Army?], *Polit.ru*, June 4, 2007.

[55] Anatoliy Tsyganok, "Razgovory o perevooruzhenii Rossiyskoy armii—mif" [Talk about Professional Army Is a Myth], *Independent Expert Opinion*, June 30, 2006; and "Gosoboronoilluziya podmenila gosoboronpokaz" [State Defense Illusion Has Replaced State Defense Orders], *Polit.ru*, November 11, 2005.

[56] Andrey Frolov, "Russian Defense Procurement in 2007," Centre for Analysis of Strategies and Technologies, Moscow Defense Brief 2, no. 8, http://www.mdb.cast.ru/mdb/2-2007/item1/item2/.

[57] Nikolay Kirillov, "Akhillesova pyata oboronosposobnosti strany" [The Achilles Heel of the Defense Capabilities of the Country], *Nezavisimoye Voyennoye Obozreniye*, November 10, 2006, http://nvo.ng.ru/armament/2006-11-10/6_opk.html; Viktor Myasnikov, "Voyenprom yeshchyo likhoradit" [The Defense Industries Are Still Feverish], *Nezavisimoye Voyennoye Obozreniye*, December 23, 2005; Igor Plugataryov, "Novyye 'mi' i 'ka' letyat v proshloye" [New "Mi" and "Ka" Are Flying into the Past], *Nezavisimoye Voyennoye Obozreniye*, May 25, 2007, http://nvo.ng.ru/printed/7332; Mikhail Lukanin, "Oboronka zadirayet tseny" [The Defense Industry Is Raising Prices], *Nezavisimoye Voyennoye Obozreniye*, April 6, 2007, http://nvo.ng.ru/printed/7251; and Aleksandr Karpovich and Oleg Bulatov, "'Bereg blizhnego deystviya" [The Shore of Near Action], *Nezavisimoye Voyennoye Obozreniye*, June 8, 2007, http://nvo.ng.ru/printed/7359.

The fact that Russia "missed" the revolution in military affairs is likely to be largely irrelevant to Moscow's ability both to project power in support of political objectives and to intervene in crises around the country's periphery. Russia's nuclear capabilities are adequate for deterring the "big war," and its conventional capabilities, though relatively low tech by the standard of the 21st century, appear adequate to the tasks at hand. Those tasks include counter-insurgency in the North Caucasus, stability operations and crisis interventions in neighboring countries, and peacekeeping and "showing the flag," most likely in neighboring countries or in UN-mandated contingencies.

The one million–strong army that exists on paper provides a psychological hedge and mobilizational framework for a major contingency. For a country of Russia's size and military tradition, no amount of rationalization can overcome the legacy of a large military establishment. The real-time deployable capabilities of the Russian military are likely to be concentrated in the military's elite components: airborne troops, select ground troop units, and Special Forces units, including units that belong to agencies other than the Ministry of Defense.

The Russian military is neither a spent force (as during the 1990s) nor the mighty military machine that the numbers on paper would lead one to believe. The truth is likely to be somewhere in the middle. In areas where key Russian interests are concentrated, the Russian military has re-emerged as a presence to be reckoned with.

Russian Foreign Policy

Russian foreign policy has been the subject of growing attention. The country's leaders have spoken confidently about the country's renewed aspirations and have sought to secure Russia's position as a major power in the international arena. The hallmarks of the Russian diplomatic effort are opposition to U.S. missile defense deployments in Europe and desire for an exclusive sphere of influence in the former Soviet space. These hallmarks are well known, as is Russian pursuit of a multipolar international system that would balance U.S. influence.

The results of these policies, however, so far are mixed at best, and some foreign policy challenges continue to loom large on Russia's international agenda. One of the key objectives of Russian foreign policy is to establish a zone of special interests in the former Soviet lands. This goal of a secure belt of friendly regimes around Russia is proving elusive, despite Moscow's vociferous opposition to Ukrainian and Georgian membership in NATO and use of energy trade for political advantage. Moreover, power plays in

Ukraine, Georgia, and even Armenia—long considered one of Moscow's closest allies among the former Soviet states—appear to have backfired. Russia's actions have only encouraged these states to seek closer ties to the West. Virtually all of Russia's neighbors are pursuing relationships with NATO and the EU. The United States and several European countries are actively promoting energy transportation projects in the Caspian region, thus bypassing Russia. The activity of out-of-region partners and interlocutors in the former Soviet lands has reached unprecedented levels, and if Ukraine and Georgia are successful in their pursuit of NATO membership, a new political, psychological, and security barrier could be overcome in the next few years.

Russia's hold on political and security affairs in Central Asia looked relatively safe after both the U.S. expulsion from Uzbekistan in 2005 and the apparent success of diplomatic efforts in the Shanghai Cooperation Organization (SCO). Yet even in this region results are not encouraging from the standpoint of Russia's interests. Moscow undeniably has attempted to use the SCO as a vehicle for balancing the United States and has enlisted China in this effort to dominate Central Asia.[58] Beijing, however, appears to have used the SCO for its own purposes—as a vehicle for expanding China's economic and political presence in the region. Beijing does not seem to be interested in turning the SCO into an anti-U.S. alliance.[59]

Indeed, the principal long-term challenge to Russian influence in Central Asia appears to come not from the United States but from China. China's presence and economic ties in the region have been steadily expanding—most significantly in the area of energy but in other areas as well.[60] Thus, although the SCO has so far performed a useful function for Russia, the organization arguably has been an even more useful instrument for Chinese policy by increasing China's presence and influence in Central Asia. This influence represents a major challenge for Russian economic, political, and strategic interests—a challenge that the country's policymakers

---

[58] Fred Weir, "Russia, China, Looking to Form NATO of the East?" *Christian Science Monitor,* October 26, 2005, http://www.csmonitor.com/2005/1026/p04s01-woeu.html.

[59] Author's personal conversation with a Chinese colleague, Washington, D.C., August, 2005.

[60] Stephen Blank, "China's Emerging Energy Nexus with Central Asia," Jamestown Foundation, China Brief 6, no. 15, July 19, 2006, http://www.jamestown.org/publications_details.php?volume_id=415&issue_id=3805&article_id=2371291; and Sebastien Peyrouse, *Economic Aspects of the Chinese-Central Asia Rapprochement,* Silk Road Paper, September 2007 (Washington, D.C.: Central Asia-Caucasus Institute and Silk Road Studies Program, 2007), http://www.silkroadstudies.org/new/docs/Silkroadpapers/2007/0709China-Central_Asia.pdf.

have yet to address, but of which they are becoming increasingly aware.[61] The notion that the SCO represents a Russian-Chinese condominium in Central Asia—which ignores the divergent interests of both countries in the region—is unlikely to endure, considering the stakes for Moscow, as well as its long-standing concerns over the economic, strategic, and demographic imbalances in Russia's vast provinces bordering China.[62]

Russian pursuits in Europe have similarly produced mixed results at best. Europe's confidence in Russia as a supplier has been undermined by Moscow's "energy diplomacy" on the continent and by its asserted intent to use energy for political recognition to regain superpower status. This approach has given new urgency to European discussions regarding a common energy policy and diversification away from heavy reliance on Russian supplies.

Russian threats to target Poland and the Czech Republic with nuclear missiles—in retribution for their agreement to deploy U.S. missile defense components—have stirred up fears of a new Cold War while doing little to disrupt U.S. deployment plans. Moreover, Russian anti-ABM rhetoric arguably has been one of the key factors mobilizing Eastern European support for Ukrainian and Georgian membership in NATO as a hedge against further Russian expansion, a development that does not serve Russian interests.

Moscow's attempts to play the pivotal role vis-à-vis Iran with regard to taming Iran's nuclear ambitions likewise have been unsuccessful, with Russia having failed to gain respect and recognition either in the Middle East or in Europe. Iranian authorities have repeatedly snubbed Russian proposals to establish joint reprocessing facilities, yet Moscow has displayed little apparent adverse reaction.[63] Iran appears to be in the driver's seat in the relationship. Despite numerous slights, Moscow has been reluctant to risk aggravating Tehran.

Thus on issue after issue, and especially on those designated by Moscow as priorities, Russian foreign policy has proven to be of limited utility and

---

[61] "Kitayskiy faktor v novoy strukture mezhdunarodnykh otnosheniy i strategiya Rossii" [The Chinese Factor in the New Structure of International Relations and Russian Strategy], Nikitsky Club, transcript of a discussion of leading Russian foreign policy and China experts, September 22, 2004, http://www.nikitskyclub.ru/article.php?idpublication=4&idissue=32.

[62] Peter Brookes, "America's Peril in the Orient," RealClearPolitics, April 22, 2008, http://www.realclearpolitics.com/articles/2008/04/americas_perils_in_the_orient.html; and "Kitayskiy faktor v novoy strukture mezhdunarodnykh otnosheniy i strategiya Rossii."

[63] Steven Lee Myers, "Iran Welcomes Russia's Offer to Enrich Uranium Jointly; Details Remain," *New York Times*, January 26, 2006, http://www.nytimes.com/2006/01/26/international/middleeast/26iran.html; Radio Free Europe/Radio Liberty (RFE/RL), "Iran: Is Russia's Offer Just a Diplomatic Device?" interview with Mark Fitzpatrick, February 13, 2006, http://www.rferl.org/featuresarticle/2006/02/10B0A4F8-5260-4E98-8A90-588F1D75F9AB.html.

even counter-productive. Admittedly, Moscow's ambitious declarations and moves have attracted the attention of foreign policymakers and the general public alike, with the result that Russia is now more feared, especially in neighboring countries. Nonetheless, Russian foreign policy has not achieved the intended results of stopping U.S. missile defenses and NATO enlargement, securing a ring of satellite nations, and reaffirming Russia's position as a great power. Most importantly, Moscow's posture does not address the biggest question facing Russia in the international arena: how to deal with the looming challenge of China at a time when the long-term outlook for Russia is clouded by major structural factors that constrain Russia's options both domestically and internationally.

Implications for the United States

Despite many differences and mutual frustrations, the United States does not have the luxury of ignoring Russia and freezing the relationship until better times. The realities of the globalized world, combined with U.S. interests in and around Russia, leave Washington no alternative but to pursue a cooperative relationship with Moscow—regardless of whether this relationship is based on shared values or common interests. In pursuing such a relationship, the United States will need to combine patience with firmness. The long-term trends do not favor Russia, which is contending with a multitude of domestic and foreign challenges. In addition, closer cooperation with the West offers Moscow the best chance for meeting these challenges—a realization that Russian political elites can be expected to come to and act upon over time. Despite the numerous challenges it faces abroad and at home, the United States still enjoys a number of significant advantages in the security, political, and economic spheres.

Notwithstanding all the uncertainty surrounding future U.S.-Russian relations, Russia promises to remain one of the key countries on the U.S. foreign policy agenda. As outlined above, Russia's situation is a product of geopolitics and economic trends as well as of its nuclear arsenal and regional impact throughout Eurasia. Broadly speaking, U.S. interests in Russia can be described as follows:

- the security of Russia's vast nuclear arsenal and technologies
- Russian restraint with respect to conventional weapons trade
- the stability and sustainability of Russia's energy supply
- Russia's constructive participation in Eurasian geopolitics
- Russia's constructive participation in global financial markets

- the evolution of Russian domestic politics toward a more stable, inclusive, and sustainable system

To advance these interests, U.S. policymakers will be well-advised to explore several initiatives, both new and old.

Arms Control and Nonproliferation

Arms control. As part of their national security agendas, both major U.S. political parties have already embraced the return to an arms control agenda with Russia that would be more robust than in recent years. Although both the United States and Russia have long declared the Cold War nuclear rivalry to be over, both sides still maintain nuclear arsenals that can be justified only in the Cold War terms of mutually assured destruction. Moscow has always been reluctant to embrace the Bush administration's proposal to abandon formal arms control treaties in favor of greatly simplified treaties and unilateral reductions. The 2002 Moscow Treaty—which Russian policymakers and analysts viewed as inadequate—had been made possible only by the prospect the treaty raised for better overall relations with the United States. With that prospect substantially diminished, Moscow's appetite for a formal strategic nuclear arms control treaty has increased. This shift is likely due to several factors:

- an overall preference for traditional diplomacy and formal treaties
- concerns over the unconstrained nature of U.S. defensive and offensive strategic programs and the long-term impact of these programs on the U.S.-Russian strategic balance
- a desire for a unique relationship with the sole remaining global superpower

A return to a more robust arms control agenda could produce several benefits for the United States:

- a more positive overall relationship with Russia
- improved transparency (through verification) of the Russian nuclear complex
- strengthening of continuing Cooperative Threat Reduction (CTR) efforts in Russia
- a stronger global nonproliferation regime

A more robust U.S.-Russian arms control agenda could signal to Russia that the United States is not seeking a unilateral advantage but is committed to maintaining strategic balance with Russia indefinitely. The benefits of such a move for the United States would be hard to overestimate; combined with other measures, this move could, for example, lead to a more cooperative Russian stance on Iran.

Furthermore, the return to a more active arms control agenda could reduce U.S. and Russian nuclear arsenals. Such an outcome would strengthen U.S. political and moral arguments for a more robust global nonproliferation regime, thus enhancing Washington's ability to mobilize international support for nonproliferation objectives.

In light of these significant benefits to U.S. nuclear nonproliferation interests, the costs of a more robust arms control agenda with Russia appear to be negligible. These costs would derive mostly from the implementation of an arms control agreement.

Iran's WMD. Given the serious challenge that Iran's nuclear program poses to U.S. national security, the United States should continue to involve Russia in multilateral efforts to address this threat. New strategic arms control initiatives with Moscow could encourage or leverage a more cooperative Russian stance with respect to Iran. The experience of the past decade, however, suggests that Russia is unable to "deliver" Iran. Moscow's support thus may prove to be necessary but insufficient for resolving the issue of Iran's nuclear ambitions. The fate of those ambitions appears to be determined in Tehran. Thus, keeping Russia engaged and supportive of international efforts in this area remains a desirable but nonetheless secondary aspect of U.S. policy.

Conventional arms sales. Few U.S. policy initiatives are likely to have a major impact on Russian conventional arms sales. Given that domestic orders are limited by the Russian army's meager procurement budgets, arms sales represent a major commercial opportunity for manufacturers in Russia. A traditional, binding nuclear arms control treaty, however, could have a positive impact on overall U.S.-Russian relations by providing U.S. policymakers with a better climate in which to pursue Russian restraint in conventional arms sales, especially in relation to problem states such as Iran. U.S. arguments will be further enhanced if the United States focuses on the sales of most importance to U.S. interests rather than on pursuing blanket constraints on Russian arms sales.

Stability and Sustainability of Energy Supply

Energy plays a special role in Russian foreign and domestic policies, and Russia has increasingly regarded sole control over its energy resources to be a matter of sovereign right. U.S. leverage on energy issues is thus likely to be limited. U.S. interests might be better served by not pursuing some of the recently proposed U.S. initiatives in this area, including a vague but highly publicized proposal for an energy version of NATO. An energy NATO offers alliance members few tangible benefits, short of raising the specter that the alliance might use force to counter Moscow's attempts to leverage energy trade for political gain. Moreover, in pursuing this proposal the United States would run the risk both of reinforcing Russian views that energy trade can be wielded as a weapon and of strengthening Russian reluctance to engage in serious dialogue on energy security.

The United States should continue its efforts to engage Russia in a constructive dialogue on energy security. Although unproductive so far, the idea of such a dialogue is premised on the expectation that Moscow's willingness to engage in serious dialogue on energy security will hinge on the outlook for Russia's oil and gas sectors. Most industry experts predict that the ability of Russian producers to sustain and expand current production levels will require a new and aggressive effort on the part of the Russian government to attract new investment. Such a dialogue should focus on creating opportunities for U.S. energy companies to invest in Russia's energy sector that are not limited to oil and gas.

Eurasian Geopolitics and the Future of NATO

Russia will remain a critical player in Eurasia. If one lesson stands out from the entire post–Cold War era, it is that one ignores Russia at one's own peril. Geography alone guarantees that no global power—no matter how technologically advanced, economically endowed, and militarily capable— can enjoy unrestricted and unfettered access to Eurasia without Russia's consent.

NATO enlargement has produced spectacular results, expanding the zone of stability, security, and prosperity in Europe. Prospects for future enlargement, however, warrant reassessment. This is not to suggest that NATO's "open door" policy should be reversed, but rather that now may be a time to re-evaluate the priority assigned by U.S. policy to the NATO enlargement project.

The prospect of Georgia and Ukraine joining NATO has raised questions concerning the heretofore geopolitically cost-free nature of the alliance's eastward expansion. Although NATO's expansion has contributed immeasurably to the concept of a Europe whole, free, and at peace, given Moscow's goal to create a geopolitical sphere of influence around Russia's periphery, Georgia and Ukraine appear to fall within Moscow's proverbial red lines. How will Moscow respond to the push by NATO and the United

States to include Tbilisi and Kiev in the alliance? Although no one can answer this question with certainty, such a move appears to carry substantial risks. For example, the issue of NATO expansion threatens to distract Russia, Europe, and the United States from other major bilateral and international issues, such as nuclear proliferation, the rise of China, and energy security. To mitigate these risks a re-prioritization of the NATO expansion project on the U.S.-European agenda may be called for. The argument in favor of doing so is further bolstered by widespread recognition that neither Georgia nor Ukraine is ready for membership in the alliance.

To handle the issue of NATO expansion—perhaps the most important issue on the U.S.-Russian agenda—the United States and NATO will have to combine firmness and determination with flexibility and patience. In addition to reaffirming commitments to continue security and political cooperation with Georgia and Ukraine, the United States should support the domestic transformation of both countries. At the same time, Washington would do well to make clear to Moscow that Washington could never agree to relegate Georgia and Ukraine to Russia's exclusive sphere of influence. U.S. support for Georgia and Ukraine could emphasize their aspirations for closer European integration and EU membership with a focus on internal transformations that over time would make these two countries not only eager but also desirable candidates for EU membership. Furthermore, the United States and its allies should reaffirm NATO's strong commitment to the "open door" policy.

At the same time, the United States and its allies should not establish or yield to pressure for politically driven deadlines. Instead, the progress of Georgia and Ukraine toward NATO membership should be based on the continued success of their domestic transformation. This standard is consistent with NATO membership criteria that were developed in the 1990s and adapted to the specific needs and circumstances of each country. Accordingly, for Ukraine, the focus should be on further progress in security sector reform as well as, above all, normalization of the country's turbulent domestic politics—in which NATO membership itself remains one of the more divisive issues. For Georgia, NATO membership should be conditioned first and foremost on a new approach to restoration of sovereignty and territorial integrity that would place greater emphasis on negotiations than on use of force.

In addition, the United States could explore new approaches to resolving some of the "frozen" conflicts in the Caucasus instead of adhering to approaches that have been tried without success for nearly two decades. For example, the United States and its European allies could attempt to expand their engagement with Abkhazia as a means to broaden discussions with key actors in regional security matters. Moreover, instead of rejecting the Kosovo settlement as a precedent for settling regional or "frozen" conflicts, the United States and its allies could explore how the lessons of the settlement might be applied to other frozen conflicts.

In pursuing this course toward Ukraine, Georgia, or breakaway territories in the former Soviet space, U.S. policymakers should keep in mind that Moscow's assertive diplomacy has made Russia highly unpopular with its neighbors. Most of these countries welcome sustained, constructive engagement from the West.

Beyond the specifics of Ukraine's and Georgia's membership prospects, the United States and its European allies will need to revisit the question of whether a bigger NATO is necessarily better able to serve the cause of European security and stability. The premise underlying NATO expansion—a new Europe and Russia united by the bond of shared values—has not come to pass. Yet modern-day Russia is hardly the threat to Europe that the Soviet Union once was. Neither friend nor foe, Russia has re-emerged as an indispensable part of European security. Russia defies traditional models of partnership and competition, yet needs to be made part of the continent's security architecture. Thus, the challenge before the United States and its allies is to craft a new model of relations with Russia— one that takes into account Russia's interests, yet protects and advances the shared values of the United States and Europe.

Notwithstanding the many other challenges facing the United States, U.S. leadership in efforts to devise a new, sustainable balance in Eurasian geopolitics is indispensable and remains an important priority in U.S. foreign policy. Europe, though having taken a more active interest in its eastern neighbors, remains reluctant to extend the vision of a Europe "whole and free" to include Ukraine, Georgia, or Moldova. Without U.S. leadership, efforts in this area could stall and succumb to the EU's enlargement fatigue.

A Rising China

Russia will clearly also play a major role on the Asian continent. In the years to come even more than in previous decades, the United States will be confronted with the challenge of rising China. Russia will be an important factor in this context.

The United States and Russia share the same challenge, if not the same goals, with respect to China: how to deal with the rising power while avoiding conflict and protecting national interests. Russian concerns over growing Chinese influence from Central Asia to the Far East are becoming increasingly pronounced. Russian policymakers are likely no less preoccupied with the challenge of rising China than are policymakers in the United States. The nature of the challenge China poses to Russia, however, presents Moscow with a series of difficult choices. Many of these choices are domestic in origin—how to secure and develop Russia's Far Eastern provinces, how to protect Russian sovereignty while taking advantage of economic cooperation with China in the Far East, and how to develop access to Chinese markets without becoming hostage to Chinese economic dynamism.

Deteriorating Russian-Chinese relations, let alone outright competition between the two powers, are not in the interest of the United States. U.S. interests would be well served, however, by a cooperative Russia as a constructive counterweight to China's influence in Asia.

Although in recent years Russian resurgence has generally been viewed in the United States as detrimental to U.S. interests, a further weakening of Russia would also hurt U.S. interests. A weaker Russia would be far less suited to the role of geopolitically balancing China and would risk becoming Beijing's junior partner. Such a turn of events could lead to a range of adverse consequences for the United States—from a Russo-Sino anti-U.S. condominium in Central Asia to geopolitical destabilization in the Far East and a China-Russia bloc in the UN Security Council. These and other unintended consequences of a deteriorating U.S.-Russian relationship are poorly understood but potentially far-reaching. Such consequences should be taken into account when considering U.S. policies in Eurasia in general and toward Russia in particular.

Promoting a Responsible International Posture and Positive Domestic Change

U.S. policymakers are likely to have relatively few levers for affecting Russian behavior abroad and especially at home. Perhaps the most promising general approach to Russia—whether in the sphere of international finance or domestic politics—builds on the foundation laid by former deputy secretary of state Robert Zoellick in a 2005 speech on U.S.-China policy. Zoellick advocated dealing with a rising China as a "responsible stakeholder," a country that has achieved a major stake in the international system, with all its complexities.[64] China now has both the interest and the responsibility to protect that stake.

---

[64] Robert A. Zoellick, "Whither China: From Membership to Responsibility?" (remarks before the National Committee on U.S.-China Relations, New York City, September 21, 2005), http://www.state.gov/s/d/former/zoellick/rem/53682.htm.

U.S. policy that is good for dealing with a rising China is also good policy for dealing with a declining Russia. As a declining power, Russia ought to have an even greater stake in the existing system of international relations than does China. China's rise is arguably among the key reasons for Russia's relative decline, and Russia may slide even further if current trends persist. In other words, Russia should have even more of an incentive to protect and strengthen the existing international system than China does because the decline of this system and the alternative arrangements likely to replace it would probably be less favorable to Russian interests than the status quo.

Though the task of elaborating a specific approach to Russia based on the "responsible stakeholder" model is outside the scope of this chapter, as a general framework the model holds out the possibility of a constructive dialogue with Moscow. Such a dialogue would target Russia's international posture as well as its domestic development in a wide range of areas, from rule of law and anticorruption measures to nuclear security and counterterrorism. This model would also enable the United States to emphasize Russia's responsibility to uphold the norms of the international system at a level commensurate with Moscow's declared stake in this system.

In conclusion it should be noted that neither an approach based on the responsible stakeholder model nor any other approach outlined elsewhere in this chapter would guarantee improvement in U.S.-Russian relations—or even a more cooperative Russian posture toward U.S. interests in Russia or elsewhere in Eurasia. These approaches, however, offer a framework, on the one hand, for capitalizing on the progress made in the difficult and complicated relationship between the two countries and, on the other hand, for avoiding some of the most obvious mistakes of the past.

EXECUTIVE SUMMARY

This chapter examines India's expanded power and international role and draws implications for U.S. policy.

MAIN ARGUMENT:
With a booming economy, an increasingly trade-driven foreign policy, an expanding footprint both in Asia and on the global scene, and strong relations with the great powers, India's strategic horizon is generally positive. The U.S. is India's most important outside friend, and the new relationship between the two countries is based on important common interests, especially in Asia and in Indian Ocean security. Yet at the same time India's foreign policy outlook rests on a strong political commitment to "strategic autonomy"—avoiding even the appearance of undue outside, and especially U.S., influence on its policy. U.S. experience with partnerships, however, involves mainly working with junior partners. This disconnect complicates the task of developing the U.S.-India partnership.

POLICY IMPLICATIONS:
- The partnership between India and the U.S. will be most effective if they develop a new model for selective cooperation, one based on their common interest in the security and prosperity of the region extending from the Persian Gulf to the Pacific Ocean. The two states have developed strong bilateral ties. They can now begin to develop a common view of the world, or at least of the areas where their interests are close.

- For the U.S., India is a key element in the emerging balance of forces in Asia. A larger Indian role in Asian regional integration and global governance would suit both countries' interests.

- The biggest danger to U.S.-India cooperation in advancing Asian security would come from U.S. military action in Iran.

Partnering with India:
Regional Power, Global Hopes

Teresita C. Schaffer

The end of the Cold War and a two-decade surge in India's economic growth marked a turning point in India's strategic approach to the world and relationship with the United States. A similar transformation characterizes the U.S. approach to India. Beginning in the late 1990s the United States cultivated a new relationship with India based on the premise that India's rise favors U.S. interests. The question this approach poses for the new administration is whether and how this promising beginning can become a truly strategic partnership. This chapter argues that such a partnership can develop on a foundation of shared interest in the security and prosperity of the region extending from the Persian Gulf to the Pacific Ocean. Under such a foundation the United States and India would need to discuss more candidly what kind of global cooperation will advance their shared interest. The two countries would also need to develop a new partnership model, more selective in its foreign policy ramifications than existing U.S. alliances and more in tune with India's concept of sovereignty.

To illuminate the possibilities and the pitfalls of the U.S.-India relationship, the chapter begins with a look at India's strategic outlook. India has been strategically in good shape in this first decade of the new millennium. India has a booming economy, an increasingly trade-driven foreign policy, an expanding footprint in Asia and on the global scene, and strong relations with the great powers. Yet there are also dark spots: the slow infusion of prosperity into India's countryside, the unsettled and sometimes violent state of India's neighborhood, and India's dependence on expensive energy imports from a volatile Middle East and other politically

Teresita C. Schaffer is Director of the South Asia Program at the Center for Strategic and International Studies (CSIS). She can be reached at <tschaffer@csis.org>.

controversial regions. The United States is India's most important external connection—the country that can best facilitate India's emergence as a serious global player. The broad lines of India's approach to the world converge with U.S. interests more than at any time since India gained independence.

India's foreign policy includes a strong commitment to strategic autonomy, which in Indian usage entails not aligning foreign policy with that of another country. Some U.S.-India policy differences (such as differences over Iran) have therefore become symbols of Indian sovereignty. The notion of strategic autonomy is the greatest challenge that India and the United States face in managing their new partnership.

The chapter next examines where India fits into the U.S. strategic outlook and how the United States has developed the partnership with India thus far. India's strategic importance to the United States derives both from a common commitment to preventing Asia's domination by a single power and from a common dependence on the smooth functioning of energy markets and maritime security in the Indian Ocean. The democratic bond—often cited as the basis for U.S.-India relations—is now amplified by more tangible common interests.

The United States and India have made tremendous strides in strengthening bilateral ties. Active defense links, expanding trade, and a raft of working groups that create real relationships among counterpart officials while tackling sometimes prosaic problems have changed the way the two governments relate to one another. India and the United States have done little, however, to explore the extent to which they share a common vision of the world. In some areas common interests are apparent; in other areas, such as issues related to Burma and Iran, there are important disagreements.

A new administration will want to develop a more global partnership with India and to have a strong India as a player in the de facto balance of power in Asia. The policy most likely to advance this goal centers on integrating India more fully into the Asian scene and into global institutions. Such an approach would also provide the best framework for dealing with the next century's policy minefield of issues, including some on which Indian and U.S. views diverge such as climate change. Paradoxically this approach might even provide political space for India and Pakistan to manage better their stubborn dispute. Success is not guaranteed, however. A serious economic slowdown or post-election political deadlock in India would certainly inhibit the kind of partnership that would benefit both countries. U.S. military action in Iran could seriously disrupt U.S.-India relations, at least temporarily. Yet the odds for such a partnership look favorable. The current partnership has been built by both major parties in each country; the new leaders elected in the coming year in India and the United States should therefore have a solid political base on which to build.

India's Strategic Objectives

India's policymakers are generally reluctant to articulate a grand strategy as the basis of policy. There is a strong consensus, however, that India should recover the major place in world politics India regards as its birthright. India's most important international goals, as outlined below, have remained quite stable through the years; what has changed is the country's capacity to achieve these goals and the means of doing so.

When it gained independence in 1948, India was a poor country whose international desires reached far beyond its actual power. A decade into the new century, India's owes its rising strength to the acquisition of nuclear arms, nearly ten years of rapidly growing defense expenditures, and an economy that is one of the fastest growing in the world. The expanding economy has led the world to see India as an important global actor, while the acquisition of nuclear weapons and investment in military power projection capability have given India's policymakers a new assertiveness and confidence. Both factors reduce the gap between goals and capabilities.

India's security objectives form four concentric circles. The first circle is the home front: India wants to contain internal insurgencies and to prevent neighboring states from inciting future unrest. Besides violence in Kashmir, India faces unrest in the northeast and opposition from Naxalite insurgents in the central part of the country. These problems are aggravated by porous borders—especially with Nepal and Bangladesh, where insurgents have found sanctuaries.[1]

The second circle is South Asia, encompassing neighbors across India's land borders (excluding China) and Sri Lanka. Aiming to protect the country's standing as the preeminent regional power, New Delhi seeks safety and stability in these border areas and the regions just beyond them. Although Indian strategists identify China as the primary security challenge and Pakistan as a secondary threat, Pakistan remains the neighbor with whom India has the most acute dispute. A four-year ceasefire has reduced the near-term risk of conflict, but the India-Pakistan problem is still susceptible to sudden spikes in violence. With both countries possessing

---

[1] The importance of sanctuaries in Nepal and Bangladesh is a common theme in discussions with Indian security officials and analysts; for one fairly typical example, see Wilson John, "The Roots of Extremism in Bangladesh," Jamestown Foundation, Terrorism Monitor 3, no. 1, January 13, 2005, http://www.jamestown.org/terrorism/news/article.php?articleid=2369092.

nuclear weapons, this situation is potentially the most dangerous one in the region.

Moving outward, the third circle is India's "expanded neighborhood" extending from the Persian Gulf and Central Asia in the west to Southeast Asia and China in the east. Indian officials and strategists speak of the region to the east as an area of opportunity; the west, which includes Afghanistan, Central Asia, and the Middle East, is fraught with potential danger.[2] India has pursued four major objectives in its expanded neighborhood: to protect sea lanes in the Persian Gulf and Indian Ocean (through which 70% of India's oil supplies must travel), to keep the rivalry with China under control while cultivating opportunities for cooperation, to enhance India's role in Asia, and to mitigate the threat of Islamic extremism.

Fourth, on the global scene India seeks to be, in the words of one observer, a "member of the board of the world." The recent election of a senior Indian diplomat as secretary general of the commonwealth plays a part in this effort, as do attempts both to reposition India as a country capable of giving as well as receiving economic assistance and to expand ties in Africa.[3] The most sought-after prize in this quest is a permanent seat for India on the UN Security Council.

Greater economic growth has pushed India toward a more economically driven foreign policy. It is hard to find a formal Indian speech on foreign policy that does not start with the premise that India's goal is to sustain and increase economic growth by expanding exports, diversifying energy sources, and encouraging investment.[4] Given that oil represents nearly one-third of India's import bill, the foreign policy importance of economic factors will remain high.

India's approach to the world's most powerful countries has also evolved. For at least the last decade, the relationship most important to India has been that with the United States. By contrast, the economic footprint of Russia, which remains a major military supplier to India, has all but disappeared because Russian energy resources lack a transportation route to the Indian market. China on the one hand is India's largest partner for trade

---

[2] This theme recurred in multiple interviews conducted by the author in New Delhi in February 2008. Formal public statements are generally more circumspect. See Shivshankar Menon, "India and International Security" (address to the International Institute for Strategic Studies, London, May 3, 2007), available at http://www.meaindia.nic.in/speech/2007/05/04ss01.htm.

[3] The commonwealth is the worldwide association of Britain and its former dependents.

[4] See, for example, Menon, "India and International Security"; and Shri Pranab Mukherjee, "Indian Foreign Policy: A Road Map for the Decade Ahead" (speech delivered at the 46th National Defence College Course, New Delhi, November 11, 2006).

in goods and on the other presents the greatest security challenge.[5] The tension arising from the need to balance between rivalry and cooperation will be a constant in India's relationship with China. Although India also has important economic ties with Europe and oil-producing countries, primarily in the Middle East, the political and strategic content of these ties is thin.

India's growing relationship with the United States, intensifying ties with East Asia, and focus on economics all suggest a much more pragmatic approach to grand strategy and foreign policy than was the case during the Cold War. At the same time, one core idea underpinning India's traditional foreign policy remains firmly in place: the principle of strategic autonomy—the commitment to maintaining India's national freedom of action without becoming beholden to any major power. In practice, this principle has come to mean that however close its partnership with the United States, India wants to avoid any suggestion that Washington is dictating India's actions. This policy of strategic autonomy resonates not only with India's elites but across the whole political spectrum.[6]

The idea of strategic autonomy also provides an important bridge between India's democracy and foreign policy. Although, as in most democracies, elections in India are rarely won or lost on foreign policy, the Indian government is accountable to a parliament for which strategic autonomy is an article of faith. Foreign policy issues—such as the proposed nuclear deal with the United States—have thus figured in parliamentary and coalition politics. As India and the United States cultivate a new partnership, democracy will be both a bond and a complication.

India Emerging as of 2008

Eight years into the new millennium India remains by far the most powerful country in South Asia and is becoming a significant power in the expanded neighborhood beyond this region. New Delhi's global role, however, is still emerging—a gleam in the country's collective eye. Though governments led by both major parties have been implementing a new foreign policy for fifteen years, India's political system and foreign policy

---

[5] Data available from the Ministry of Commerce and Industry, Government of India, Export Import Data Bank, http://commerce.nic.in/eidb/icntq.asp and http://commerce.nic.in/eidb/ecntq.asp.

[6] One of the best discussions of the idea of strategic autonomy occurred in an oral presentation by Pramit Pal Chaudhuri (East-West Center, Washington, D.C., January 17, 2008), which is summarized at http://www.eastwestcenter.org/ewc-in-washington/events/previous-events-2008/jan-17-2008-pramit-pal-chaudhuri/.

instincts are still occasionally caught between old habits and new, less familiar goals.

The Home Front

India's strategic approach rests on a strong democratic foundation with stable institutions. Since 1989 India has been governed by coalitions, with the larger national parties having alternated in the leadership of government. As these parties' collective share of the vote has fallen, regional parties, often represented only in one state, have gained.

Democracies tend to be slow and tentative in implementing new economic policies that will make the country prosperous. The cost to India of this "democracy tax" has been especially steep since 2004, when the governing coalition's majority in parliament could only be maintained with the support of a group of left-wing parties—the one constituency that has real reservations over India's changed foreign policy. Yet India has also reaped a "democracy dividend": the democratic system has improved the long-term viability of economic policy changes once these changes have gained parliamentary approval.

India's domestic economic transformation continues, with GDP growth topping 9% in 2005–07. Between 2001 and 2007 per capita GDP increased 86%, and India can reasonably expect to sustain growth of 7–10% for the next decade. During this same period exports rose 17.6% per year and the share of trade in India's economy nearly doubled, increasing from 23% to 37%. India's famed IT industry now employs 1.6 million people, with a share of the GDP that grew from 1.2% to 5.4% between 1998 and 2007 (see **Figure 1**). IT exports are now worth over 25% of total goods exports. The launch in January 2008 of the Tata Nano car, which will sell for the equivalent of $2,500, is a timely reminder that India's industrial sector is now growing as well.[7]

India's ability to continue expanding its role in the global economy will depend, however, on continuing economic reform. Economic growth has been uneven across the country. The economies of a few states, especially in the south and west, have surged ahead, while economic growth in the heavily populated north Indian heartland has barely kept pace with population growth (see **Figure 2**). Likewise, the disparity among states in terms of per capita income has increased since 1970. Thirty years ago the residents of India's richest state, Punjab, earned 3.4 times the per capita

---

[7] Percentages computed from data from the Ministry of Finance, Government of India, *Economic Survey 2007–2008*, A-3, A-80–81, http://indiabudget.nic.in/es2007-08/esmain.htm; and "Strategic Review 2008," NASSCOM, February 2008, http://www.nasscom.in/upload/5216/Strategic_Review_Feb2008.doc.

FIGURE 1   India's IT industry over the last ten years

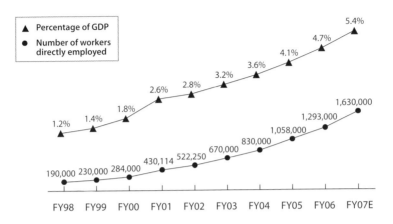

SOURCE: This figure is adapted from NASSCOM, "Indian IT Industry: NASSCOM Analysis," August 2007, http://www.nasscom.in/upload/5216/Latest_IT_Industry_Factsheet_Aug_07.pdf.

GDP of residents of Bihar. In the period from 2000–04 Punjabis earned 4.5 times more than Biharis.[8]

Economic growth has also been uneven across industries. India's most dynamic economic sectors, including IT, are major beneficiaries of globalization, with the services industry and a few successful industries having maintained double-digit growth. Successful industries include iron and steel, textile fibers, scientific equipment, and automotive parts. By contrast, agriculture—which sustains 60% of India's population—has grown an average of only 2.6% a year in the past decade.[9] The sectors left out of India's success will be a drag on the economy and a source of political pressure in coalition governments.

India's dilapidated infrastructure is another potential speed bump for economic growth. The telecommunications infrastructure has seen remarkable progress, with India having achieved teledensity of 26% after crossing the 300 million mark in telephone subscribers in March 2008.[10] India's roads, railways, airports, and energy infrastructure, however, are

---

[8] Catriona Purfield, "Mind the Gap—Is Economic Growth in India Leaving Some States Behind?" International Monetary Fund, IMF Working Paper, WP/06/103, April 2006, 4, http://www.imf.org/external/pubs/ft/wp/2006/wp06103.pdf.

[9] Computed from data from the *Economic Survey 2007–2008*, A-5, http://indiabudget.nic.in/es2007-08/chapt2008/tab13a.pdf.

[10] Telecom Regulatory Authority of India, Press Release, no. 43, April 25, 2008.

FIGURE 2   Map of Indian states coded by economic growth rates

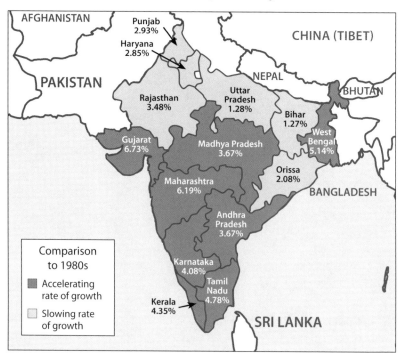

SOURCE: Data from Montek S. Ahluwalia, "State Level Performance under Economic Reforms in India" (paper presented at the Centre for Research on Economic Development and Policy Reform Conference on Indian Economic Prospects: Advancing Policy Reform, Stanford University, May 2000), table 2.

NOTE: Figure shows annual rates of growth of per capita gross state domestic product (% per year) from 1991–92 to 1998–99. States are shown as they existed in 1999.

lagging. Industry estimates of the needed infrastructure investment cluster around $100–150 billion per year. This figure represents approximately 10% of India's GDP and double the percentage of GDP that India has invested in infrastructure in recent years.[11] To improve the country's infrastructure it is critical that New Delhi expand and improve access to higher and technical

---

[11] There are at least half a dozen infrastructure financing conferences planned for the second half of 2008. The estimates of the needed investment in infrastructure on which they are based are all in the same range. See the documents announcing the 2nd Global Infrastructure Leadership Forum, scheduled to be held in Washington, D.C., in December 2008, http://www.asiatradehub.com/India/intro.asp.

education as well as mobilize capital by developing new ways of linking the public and private sectors.[12]

Despite substantial opening to the global market, India remains a relatively inward-looking economy. Although in IT—India's globalization champion—two-thirds of production is exported,[13] across the economy the percentage of trade and foreign investment in the Indian economy is still well below the equivalent percentage in China and other high-growth countries. Though it has benefited from international market opportunities, India has also become vulnerable to slowdowns in the global economy and spiking international prices for energy and food.

India will need considerable energy to fuel further economic growth. The International Energy Agency (IEA) estimates that India's energy requirements will increase by 3.6% per year over the next 25 years, and that India will overtake Japan as the world's third largest oil importer by 2030.[14] As a result, India has made diversification of energy supply sources a major foreign policy priority. New Delhi's pursuit of energy relationships with Iran, Burma, and Sudan is a source of friction in India-U.S. relations.

The Key Partner: The United States

Shifting the stance of relations between India and the United States from indifference and suspicion to partnership constitutes a major success for India's post–Cold War foreign policy. The economic relationship flowered first. The United States, by far India's largest export market, bought 15% of India's goods exports and 61% of its IT-related exports in 2007. The United States is also the principal source of foreign investment.[15] Active security relations have become part of this relationship as well, especially in the current decade. Owing to the changing global environment and closer bilateral relations, India and the United States have become more aligned on

---

[12] Author interviews with senior Indian economic officials, February 2008.

[13] "Key Highlights of the IT-BPO Sector Performance in FY 2007–08," NASSCOM, February 2008, http://www.nasscom.in/upload/5216/Strategic_Review_Feb2008.doc.

[14] International Energy Agency, *World Energy Outlook 2007: China and India Insights* (Paris: Organisation for Economic Co-operation and Development, 2007), 165–69; see also the "Executive Summary" from the *World Energy Outlook 2007,* 8, http://www.iea.org/Textbase/npsum/WEO2007SUM.pdf.

[15] "Indian IT-BPO Sector Performance in 2006," NASSCOM; Ministry of Commerce and Industry, Government of India, Export Import Data Bank; and "Foreign Direct Investment in India: A Snapshot," Confederation of Indian Industry (CII), Briefing Paper, http://www.indiaat60.in/backgrounders/Foreign-direct-investment-in-india.pdf. According to the CII brief, Mauritius accounts for 57% of FDI, owing to an investment treaty that provides significant advantages to investors who route their capital through Mauritius. The United States is the second largest source of FDI in India and is probably the ultimate source of much of the Mauritius investment, though the source of this FDI is impossible to document.

security issues in South Asia. This alignment in turn has led India to view the U.S. presence in the region—militarily in the Indian Ocean region and politically in the smaller South Asian states—as a relatively benign factor.

Nonetheless, four main disagreements over security policy still color the larger U.S.-India relationship. The first concerns Pakistan, which the United States regards as a vital if troubled ally in the war on terrorism but which India sees as a source of terrorism. India's conventional military superiority over Pakistan is secure, and New Delhi's other goal—avoiding domestic chaos in Pakistan that would undermine India's security—is well aligned with U.S. interests. In Indian eyes, however, the U.S.-India and U.S.-Pakistan relationships remain competitive despite considerable U.S. efforts to "dehyphenate" the two countries.

The second disagreement concerns trade. Expanded trade often generates new trade problems despite good political relations. Although the United States looms large in India's foreign trade, the reverse is not true. Whereas U.S. trade strategy has stressed market-opening measures, India's strategy has been to slow the pace of those reforms that carry a high political price tag. The fact that so many trade issues are dealt with multilaterally gives these issues a public profile that complicates the process of working out pragmatic solutions.

Third, India has not yet escaped the nuclear isolation that has for 35 years troubled relations with the United States. Although the proposed U.S.-India agreement on civil nuclear cooperation was to have transformed the relationship and brought India close to the nuclear mainstream, the agreement has been controversial in both countries. The agreement will be discussed in greater depth below, but the important point to note here is that this controversy has injected the United States into India's domestic political debate. The nuclear cooperation agreement has been largely opposed in India by the Left, the only political group with fundamental objections to New Delhi's underlying partnership with Washington.

This controversy in turn raises the fourth and most fundamental issue complicating U.S.-India relations: the interaction between U.S.-India ties and strategic autonomy. India has viewed differences with the United States on Iran (and to a lesser extent Myanmar) as U.S. challenges to India's right to determine its own foreign policy. This disagreement reflects different expectations of what impact, if any, a U.S.-India partnership should have on issues on which the two countries have different interests and policies.

The Inner Circles: Domestic Insurgencies and the South Asian Neighborhood

India's dominant position in its immediate neighborhood is not threatened, but trouble within and around India is more widespread than a decade ago. India has achieved limited success in taming domestic insurgencies. In the past few years northeast India and parts of central India affected by the Naxalite insurgency have been the scene of regular violence at a level that, although not very high, has nonetheless been sufficient to cause great concern to the government. Indian press reports estimate the number of Naxalite insurgents to be as high as twenty thousand. Recent incidents include an attack on a district headquarters in February 2008 that resulted in twenty police fatalities and a haul of one thousand rifles. The victory of the Maoists in the April 2008 constituent assembly election in Nepal is an ominous sign that the Naxalites may soon have a friendly government in place across India's porous northern border. Violence and militancy have also increased on the other side of India's borders—in Bangladesh, Sri Lanka, and, most recently, Tibet.

In Kashmir violence has declined from the high levels of the late 1990s. Nonetheless, a breakthrough in resolving the Kashmir dispute still seems far away, as dialogue with separatists has achieved little. On the India-Pakistan front, a ceasefire has held quite well since November 2003, and a complex dialogue process in place since January 2004 has been supplemented by reasonably productive back-channel talks. Neither government possesses the political strength to sell a Kashmir agreement that goes beyond the established Indian and Pakistani positions, however, and Pakistan is not prepared to deal with other India-Pakistan issues before resolving the Kashmir dispute.

India wants Pakistan to remain peaceful and stable. Although the Indian government avoided publicly commenting on Pakistan's February 2008 elections, officials privately described the elections as an expression of popular will and a welcome rejection of the Islamic religious parties. The Indian government is still uneasy, however, over the emerging post-election picture, with unclear lines of authority and a divided successor government possibly unable or unwilling to continue Musharraf's relatively forward-looking policies toward India. New Delhi also looks with deep disquiet on the unsettled situation in Afghanistan. Though making significant financial and technical contributions to the reconstruction of Afghanistan, India has been limited to a very modest security role.[16]

---

[16] Multiple author interviews with senior Indian officials, February 2008; and Menon, "India and International Security."

The Outer Circles: The Indian Ocean, Asia, and the Middle East

India has good reason to be pleased with its strategic position in the Indian Ocean region and East Asia. Although its footprint in these regions is still substantially smaller than China's, India has made itself a player in the emerging balance of power. New Delhi's overtures have been well received by countries in the region who do not want China to be the only major regional power taking an interest. Expanding relations with the United States, especially on security issues, have facilitated India's bid for a larger role in Asia.[17] Indian policy, however, has still not addressed the question of what type of U.S. role India would like to see in Asian institutions.

India's "look east" policy has intensified both political and economic relations throughout the region from Southeast Asia through Japan. Exports to the Association of Southeast Asian Nations (ASEAN) countries grew six-fold, increasing from 6% to 10% of India's total exports between 2001 and 2007.[18] India's dialogue partnership with ASEAN and membership in the East Asia Summit speak to a stronger political relationship with Southeast Asia. Further east, military exercises with Japan and Australia are part of India's increasing security interest in East Asia—though New Delhi is careful to situate these exercises in the context of a multidirectional set of security relations in the region.

India's relationship with China is more ambiguous. Since early this decade, the two countries have emphasized cooperation. Trade between India and China has increased more than five-fold,[19] and both countries have engaged in a more substantive political dialogue—including regular but not terribly productive talks on border issues—and in periodic low-level military exercises. Nevertheless, China remains India's principal long-term security challenge. China's military modernization, development of military access and facilities around the Indian Ocean, and strong attachment to Pakistan are all causes for Indian concern.

To the west, India not only possesses a major economic and strategic stake in the Persian Gulf but also enjoys an important strategic relationship with Israel, now India's second largest external military supplier. New Delhi has thus far succeeded in pursuing both sets of interests without being challenged either by its Arab and Iranian friends or by Israel. The Persian Gulf supplies 64% of India's oil imports.[20] Gulf countries provide 25% of

---

[17] Author interviews with Indian officials, February 2008.

[18] Ministry of Commerce and Industry, Government of India, Export Import Data Bank.

[19] Ibid.

[20] "Integrated Energy Policy: Report of the Expert Committee," Planning Commission, Government of India, August 2006, 59, http://planningcommission.nic.in/reports/genrep/rep_intengy.pdf.

India's remittance income and employ 4–5 million expatriates.[21] Iran also provides land access to Afghanistan and Central Asia. The future of the Gulf region, however, will be determined by forces over which India exercises little control: the outcome of the U.S. war in Iraq, negotiations between Israel and the Palestinians, and India's growing demand for evermore expensive oil.

India's Global Persona

India's quest to shape world governance has progressed more modestly than the Indian government would prefer. India is a regular guest at meetings of the group of eight (G-8), and one of the country's senior diplomats has just been elected secretary general of the commonwealth. Though New Delhi's effort to secure a permanent seat on the UN Security Council seems unlikely to garner the support of the current Security Council leadership anytime soon, Indian officials are campaigning hard for a non-permanent Security Council seat opening in 2011. Achieving the global status India seeks, however, will have a cost: this status will oblige India to take public positions on controversial issues, a prospect not all Indian officials welcome.

For the United States, Defining a New Partnership

The importance U.S. policymakers now attach to India represents a major change in U.S. priorities since the Cold War. For half a century U.S. policy toward India and Pakistan was usually a package deal. Pakistan was an intermittent and sometimes controversial ally, with periods of intense collaboration in the heyday of U.S. alliance-building in the 1950s and during the campaign to remove the Soviet army from Afghanistan in the 1980s. The primary U.S. political interest in India was preventing conflict between India and Pakistan, a task which gained urgency when both countries joined the nuclear club implicitly around 1990 and explicitly in 1998. Today India and Pakistan both seem committed to managing relations peacefully, affording the United States the luxury of de-emphasizing India-Pakistan diplomacy—although a renewed risk of conflict would catapult this issue back to the top of the U.S. agenda.

The broader U.S. approach to Asia historically rested on two foundations. One has been alliances with Japan and other Asian countries that have served to undergird the U.S. military and economic presence in

---

[21] "Invisibles in India's Balance of Payments," Reserve Bank of India, Bulletin, November 2006, http:// rbidocs.rbi.org.in/rdocs/Bulletin/PDFs/74250.pdf.

the western Pacific. The second, especially since the 1970s, has been the U.S. military presence in the Persian Gulf, which derived from that region's dominant role in international energy markets. Bureaucratically and strategically, India figured little in the larger Asian context.

The U.S. evolution from this rather aloof posture to one of real partnership with India reflects major changes in the global strategic environment. With the end of the Cold War, Asia is increasingly important for U.S. strategic interests. Although Russia's role in the region is still not entirely clear, the United States, China, and Japan have always played major roles in Asia. Economic growth and expanding political ties to the east have made India a more significant player in Asia than the country was in the past—and a player with which the United States wants to work.

U.S. officials tend to describe the partnership with India as a long-overdue discovery by both countries of their shared bond as democracies. Yet this democratic bond existed throughout the Cold War—a period of difficult and substantively thin U.S.-India relations during which India relied mainly on the Soviet Union. What has made a U.S.-India partnership more valuable now are the tangible interests the two countries share. Both the United States and India would like Asia to remain a multipolar environment, neither dominated by nor hostile to China. Both countries want to engage with China and to anchor China in a peaceful region. The United States also wants to work with India on promoting peace and security in the Indian Ocean region, through which much of the world's vital energy trade passes. Trade and investment have always been central to U.S. ties with East Asia and have become important for India as well. In addition, the United States is comfortable with India's dominance of its immediate South Asian neighborhood, especially now that New Delhi no longer regards U.S. military presence in the Indian Ocean region with suspicion.

Building the Bilateral Infrastructure

Although the rationale for the new U.S.-India partnership is largely regional and global, the process of building it has been mainly bilateral. Under governments led by both major parties in both countries, the United States and India have significantly increased the quantity and sophistication of contacts between the top and middle levels of their governments. This process has been not just an "alphabet soup" of meetings and working groups but also a much greater mutual understanding between Indian and U.S. officials.

The most striking change is in security ties. During the Cold War suspicions on both sides made a serious security dialogue almost impossible. Whereas India looked on the United States as "Pakistan's friend," the United States viewed India as a country that was first and foremost connected with the Soviet Union. Since the end of the Cold War the security relationship has become the most dynamic element in the government-to-government dialogue.

U.S. goals in the security relationship are both political and military. Politically, the U.S. seeks to develop (and hopefully expand) the arena for cooperation; militarily, the goal is to create interoperability so cooperation can actually take place. The United States has advanced the concept of a global maritime partnership: a loose network of navies that share certain broad goals and are capable of working together on an issue-by-issue basis as the need arises.[22] This is a fairly unstructured arrangement within which India can work without challenging the country's commitment to strategic autonomy.

Since 1991 three documents have set forth road maps for military cooperation between India and the United States. Each document has established a more ambitious framework than the last.[23] India and the United States have also worked together in two real military operations. In 2002 India escorted a number of U.S. high-value cargoes through the Strait of Malacca, and in late 2004 and early 2005 the two countries collaborated on relief efforts after a tsunami devastated the Indian Ocean region. Joint exercises have increased in size and sophistication over the past decade. Though the navies are the most enthusiastic partners, other services have completed joint exercises as well. Additionally, in 2007 India and the United States participated in joint exercises with Japan and Australia as a first step toward establishing a loose cooperative relationship among all four major Asia-Pacific democracies. Such exercises and operations have moved India and the United States closer to interoperability—a key U.S. goal and a requirement for closer cooperation in the future.

This operational link has facilitated an enhanced strategic dialogue between the United States and India involving cabinet ministers, senior military officers, and other officials further down the chain of command. The main instrument for this dialogue is the Defense Policy Group, a consultative mechanism chaired by the U.S. under secretary of defense for

---

[22] John Morgan Jr. and Charles Martoglio, "Global Maritime Network," *Defense News,* November 30, 2005, http://www.military.com/forums/0,15240,81652,00.html; and Michael G. Mullen, testimony before the Senate Armed Services Committee, March 29, 2007.

[23] Steven B. Sboto, "U.S. Army, India and U.S. Military Cooperation and Collaboration: Problems, Prospects and Implications" (thesis submitted to National Defense College, 2001), 7–9; "New Framework for the U.S.-India Defense Relationship," Embassy of India, Press Release, June 28, 2005; and "U.S.-India Defense Relationship," U.S. Department of Defense, March 2006, http://www.defenselink.mil/news/Mar2006/d20060302us-indiadefenserelationship.pdf.

policy and the Indian defense secretary. This group has been a useful but rather formal channel. Though this dialogue should logically rest on shared strategic interests, in practice both countries have been somewhat inhibited in discussions of China and the Middle East, the two natural focal points.[24]

The third and thus far least developed aspect of security relations is defense trade. Military sales have always played a central role for the United States in achieving interoperability and strategic communication with other militaries. Though India's military is interested in purchasing state-of-the-art U.S. weapons systems, Indians have bitter memories of the U.S. government's cancellation of the fuel-supply contract for the Tarapur nuclear power plant in 1978. Indian defense officials thus worry about future disruptions. With the United States already having lifted most export restrictions on sensitive or dual-use technologies, the U.S. bureaucratic system has lagged behind policymakers on defense trade issues and created frustration in India.

On balance, bilateral security relations between the United States and India have been successful. The issue of terrorism has produced more mixed results, however. Though India's concern over terrorism, and specifically over Islamic extremist terrorism, is at least equal to that of the United States, each country has been trying to mobilize the other as an active participant in its own agenda. Whereas India initially hoped that the United States would brand Pakistan as a supporter of terrorism, the United States wanted to work with Pakistan as an ally. Likewise, whereas the United States saw India as a useful participant in global anti-terrorism efforts, India preferred to maintain a bilateral dialogue with the United States on terrorism. In the end the Joint Terrorism Working Group, which both countries set up, has proven a fairly effective way of coordinating modest, practical steps to address the problem of terrorism. The working group has not served, however, as a vehicle for larger strategic alignment.[25]

Unlike U.S.-India relations with respect to security and terrorism, the economic relationship between the two countries is overwhelmingly private. Although trade between India and the United States increased 79% between 2000 and 2007, India still accounts for just over 1% of U.S. trade—a large enough share to make the country a significant trading partner for U.S. corporations and the U.S. government but not large enough to put India in

---

[24] Author interviews with participants from both the United States and India, September 2006–February 2008.

[25] The press release following the February 2007 meeting of the group gives a good sense of the scope of discussions. See "Joint Statement on Indo-U.S. Counter-Terrorism, Joint Working Group Meeting," U.S. Embassy, New Delhi, Press Release, February 28, 2007, http://newdelhi.usembassy. gov/pr022807.html.

the top tier.[26] Similarly, though an important destination for U.S. investors, India is not at the top level.

The two governments have engaged in a number of high-level economic dialogues involving senior officials and private business and scientific personalities. The dialogues have focused on issues of concern to India, such as energy, agricultural research, infrastructure financing, and space cooperation. Beyond these designated issues each dialogue has sought to deepen the interaction between the two governments while exploring solutions to trade and investment problems so that the private economic relationship can prosper. In the same vein, private partners are exploring—and the U.S. government is encouraging—the development of new linkages between Indian and U.S. educational institutions in the hope that U.S. universities can help meet the urgent demand for more and better higher education that will support the workforce driving India's dynamic economic growth.[27] The actual work of building this economic relationship, however, has been accomplished largely by private participants.

Within this largely private economic relationship, the most exciting element is the IT industry. The U.S. and Indian IT industries are tightly interlinked. Both industries developed largely beyond the reach, or even the view, of the governments and represent a major source of growth and innovation in their respective countries. These industries have shared labor, integrated their production processes, traded software in both directions, and exchanged investments. Note also that the United States buys 61% of India's IT-related exports.

The centerpiece of U.S. efforts to build a bilateral relationship is the agreement on civil nuclear cooperation on which the United States and India have been working since July 2005. More than anything else that the two countries have done, this agreement represents a turning point in U.S.-India relations. As one of only three countries that never signed the Treaty on the Non-proliferation of Nuclear Weapons (NPT), India for thirty years had been a major target of U.S. nonproliferation policy. New Delhi's maintenance of a nuclear program outside the NPT framework and detonation of a military nuclear device in 1998 put India squarely outside the boundaries of a NPT-based policy.

From the start, the terms for the proposed agreement were an uneasy compromise. The United States was prepared to make significant changes

---

[26] See the foreign trade statistics for "U.S. Trade in Goods" from the U.S. Census Bureau, http://www.censusbureau.biz/foreign-trade/balance/index.html#I.

[27] See, for example, Karen P. Hughes, "Higher Education: A Keystone in U.S.-India Relations," *Times of India,* March 24, 2007, available at the Embassy of the United States, New Delhi, India website, http://newdelhi.usembassy.gov/pr032607.html.

in its domestic nonproliferation laws, and was also prepared to seek liberalization of the rules of the Nuclear Suppliers Group that the United States had helped set up some years earlier. The laws that the United States was prepared to change imposed tighter restrictions than the NPT. Washington wanted to remain in compliance with the NPT itself, by facilitating only civilian, not military, nuclear development in India. New Delhi, by contrast, wanted full freedom to develop both the civilian and the military sides of India's nuclear program.

The agreement became a magnet for controversy in both countries and a case study in the difficulty of getting the political systems of two countries to work in sync. In the United States the supporters of traditional nonproliferation policy in both parties opposed the agreement. In India there were initially three sources of disagreement. The opposition party did not support the agreement but likely would have if their party had held power. India's nuclear scientists, who had suffered from U.S.-sponsored sanctions for decades, objected out of fear that the agreement would be a Trojan horse aimed at imposing restrictions on the nuclear program. The third source of disagreement was the government's leftist political allies, whose real objection was not to nuclear trade but to a close relationship with the United States.

The first major hurdle the agreement faced was passing U.S. legislation to legalize civilian nuclear cooperation with India. After a long and stormy debate, the Hyde Act passed the U.S. Congress with large majorities in both houses and parties and was signed by President Bush on December 18, 2006. The legislation, however, included a provision requiring nuclear trade to be cut off in the event of another Indian nuclear test and hortatory language on India's Iran policy. Opponents in India immediately lambasted these provisions as intrusions on India's sovereignty.

As the next step in this process, the 123 Agreement—a bilateral cooperation agreement between India and the United States—was finalized in July 2007 following long and difficult negotiations. Though largely neutralizing the objections of Indian nuclear scientists, the agreement only indirectly addressed both countries' political goals, including those related to the issue of testing.

The announcement of the 123 Agreement brought the objections of leftist parties in India to a fever pitch. Threatened with the loss of its parliamentary majority, the Indian government grew nervous over moving ahead with the agreement. Three steps remained: securing a safeguards agreement between India and the International Atomic Energy Agency (IAEA), securing the agreement by consensus of the Nuclear Suppliers Group to civil nuclear trade with India, and passing final legislation in the

United States. India eventually resumed negotiations with the IAEA and established a high-level consultative group between the government and its leftist allies to try to find a formula for moving ahead with the nuclear deal with the leftists' acquiescence. The leftists' threat to bring down the government intimidated the government into freezing negotiations with the IAEA. Once momentum had slowed, work on the deal never regained the pace necessary to reach an agreement before the U. S. and Indian elections set for late 2008 and early 2009. It thus appears that this issue will be left for successor governments to resolve—under much more difficult circumstances.

Owing to these factors, the impact of the proposed civil nuclear cooperation agreement on the emerging India-U.S. partnership is mixed. The United States has been willing and able to make major changes in policy and law on India's behalf. The Indian government and the Congress Party leadership, on the other hand, proved to be indecisive and hesitant at a critical moment despite evidence that public opinion supported close relations with the United States and despite the lack of serious opposition to the deal.[28] With the political compulsions and sensitivities of the two countries consistently working against each other, democracy turned out to be more a complication than a bond.

The Weak Link: Looking at the World Together

Despite the controversy churned up by the nuclear agreement, the United States can claim considerable success in putting in place the structure of a strong bilateral relationship. Washington and New Delhi have been less successful, however, in creating a truly global partnership. The United States and India have far more common interests on the global scene than they once did, and this has deepened the roots of their partnership. Although an expanded dialogue on their respective global visions will become more important as India's power and global footprint grow, the tension between these common interests and the politics of India's strategic autonomy has inhibited the ability of both countries to pursue a common cause on the world stage.

Washington and New Delhi have consulted closely and often on India's immediate neighborhood. New Delhi's traditional distaste for U.S. diplomatic initiatives aimed at Indian relations with Pakistan or Kashmir has mellowed, and India even welcomed U.S. crisis management efforts in

---

[28] The most comprehensive polling on these issues was conducted by the Center for the Advanced Study of India at the University of Pennsylvania. See Devesh Kapur, "India-U.S. Relations. What Does the Indian Public Think?" Center for the Advanced Study of India, http://casi.ssc.upenn.edu/india/iit_Devesh2.html.

2002 and 2003. As long as the India-Pakistan peace dialogue continues, the United States is happy to refrain from assuming a direct role in India's affairs and India is equally pleased with this relatively detached posture. Renewed violence in India or across the Line of Control leading to a fresh India-Pakistan crisis would strain U.S. relations with India.

On other issues in the region the United States and India agree more often than not. For example, the two countries are in agreement on the fragile political process in Nepal, the problems of interrupted democracy in Bangladesh, and the resumption of war between the Tamil Tigers and the Sri Lankan government. On Afghanistan—where India is anxious to maintain a visible role even though the United States has given priority to managing Pakistan's sensitivities—both countries agree on the need to sustain a viable and moderate Afghan government.

Although Indian and U.S. interests are closely aligned on Asian security issues, this agreement has not led to much common or coordinated action. India's views on China largely parallel those of the United States. Without using the term, both New Delhi and Washington want and expect to see a de facto balance of power emerge in Asia. At the same time, not wanting to feed Chinese concerns over encirclement, New Delhi is wary of explicit consultations with the United States on China. India's expanding relations with Japan and Australia are also in line with U.S. interests. Likewise, in the Middle East the United States and India are both strongly committed to the security of the Persian Gulf region, and India is a tacit beneficiary of whatever stabilizing impact the U.S. military presence may have. Both countries additionally have important economic interests in the Gulf region—for example, India has a major military supply relationship with Israel.

Yet disagreements have impeded any serious official discussion of Middle East issues. The most serious disagreement is over Iran. In Washington's view, Iran is a rogue state, the premier state sponsor of terrorism whose nuclear ambitions are uniquely dangerous and which the United States thus must seek to contain and isolate. India does not wish to see Iran acquire nuclear weapons but disagrees with the rest of the U.S. agenda. India's reasons for cultivating a relationship with Iran include geography (Iran provides India land access to Afghanistan and Central Asia), economics (Iran supplies approximately 10% of India's oil imports), and domestic politics. Partly because of the perceived sensitivity of Indian Muslims to ties with Iran and partly because of the high-profile U.S. effort to line up India behind the isolation campaign, Iran has become the preeminent symbol of strategic autonomy for India's left-leaning politicians. Political opponents pilloried the government for its IAEA votes against Iran.

On other Iran-related disagreements, however, the Indian government has held its ground. A case in point is the unsuccessful U.S. effort to dissuade India from participating in a proposed gas pipeline from Iran through Pakistan to India. Although the project is moving fitfully and India has strategic concerns over importing gas through Pakistan, New Delhi will not withdraw from the enterprise on account of U.S. policy toward Iran.

Global Governance and the Multilateral Arena

As India tries to expand its role in the world, New Delhi wants a greater voice in global governance. U.S. and Indian priorities, however, are out of step. The United States encourages a larger Indian role in principle. A 2005 White House briefing, for example, expressed the U.S. intention to "help India become a major power in the 21st Century."[29] Yet the United States has been either cool or indifferent to most of India's concrete ambitions for participation in global leadership and has shown little interest in encouraging Indian membership in Asian regional institutions.[30]

Regular participation as a guest in meetings of the G-8 has become India's major vehicle for high-level involvement in global governance. From the U.S. perspective, the G-8 provides an ideal forum. The forum includes a small number of major countries, and because the deliberations are private India does not need to take a public position on politically controversial issues.

Decades-old habits make it hard, however, for India to side with the United States in multilateral organizations. In 2007 India voted with the United States on UN votes 14% of the time, slightly below the world average of 18%.[31] India's track record undoubtedly contributes to Washington's reluctance to expand the membership of the UN Security Council. The United States has tried to find common ground in global trade negotiations, as evidenced by the frequent meetings between Minister of Commerce Kamal Nath and U.S. Trade Representative Susan Schwab. Though their

---

[29] "Background Briefing by Administration Officials on U.S.-South Asia Relations," U.S. Department of State, Office of the Spokesman, March 25, 2005, http://www.state.gov/r/pa/prs/ps/2005/43853.htm.

[30] "Bush, Rice Skip ASEAN Summit Meetings," *Manila Mail*, August 14, 2007, http://www2.manilamaildc.net/article2483.html; and "West Worried India Would Tip APEC Balance: Official," Agence France-Presse, September 6, 2007, http://afp.google.com/article/ALeqM5hZoirSNiHlYD3ZRa5JhKVsPbnKrA.

[31] "Voting Practices in the United Nations, 2007," Bureau of International Organization Affairs, U.S. Department of State, May 5, 2007, 89–98, 224, http://www.state.gov/p/io/rls/rpt/c25867.htm.

public press releases speak of "greater convergence," the practical results seem fairly meager.[32]

India is not a participant in the International Energy Agency (IEA), founded in the 1970s as a forum for energy consumers to work together toward energy security. IEA rules require that all members first join the Organisation for Economic Co-operation and Development (OECD); this excludes the world's two most rapidly growing energy markets, China and India. Although the United States recognizes that India's presence in the IEA would clearly benefit both India and the international community, lifting the institutional obstacles to membership would require more effort than the United States has been willing to devote.

Partnership and Strategic Autonomy

The two countries hold different views of what it means to be partners. The United States expects and assumes a greater effort at foreign policy convergence than India does. This outlook grows out of a half-century of dealing primarily with allies who start with a formal linkage to U.S. policy goals and who also are substantially weaker than the United States. The U.S. tendency to refer to all friendly countries as "allies"—a propensity of members of Congress and commentators—reinforces this presumption. The habits that this outlook spawns are likely to persist in some degree even under a new administration less inclined toward unilateral action than the Bush administration.

India, by contrast, starts from the concept of strategic autonomy and resists any presumption that its policies will align with the foreign policy positions of other countries, especially those of the United States. The controversy over the U.S.-India nuclear deal in 2007–08 and the political storms provoked by India's votes against Iran in the IAEA both illustrate the political hold of the idea of strategic autonomy. India's previous foreign policy experience was with non-alignment rather than with alliances. In the Cold War relationship with the Soviet Union, India rarely if ever was pushed to leave the comfort of a non-aligned consensus position.

In both India and the United States, Iran as well as Burma have become symbols of this larger conceptual difference. Differences over these countries tend to be aired publicly, with considerable emotion, generating resentment and misunderstanding. The creation of a new model of partnership capable of dealing with these different expectations is the most basic task that

---

[32] Author interviews with U.S. officials, October 2007. For a representative example of the outcome of bilateral discussions on global trade, see Suman Guha Mozumder, "Kamal Nath Meets US Envoy over Agri Subsidies," Rediff News, May 9, 2008, http://in.rediff.com/money/2008/may/09nath.htm.

Indian and U.S. officials will need to undertake if they wish to make their relationship truly strategic.

Issues on the Horizon

Rising food and energy prices are already putting pressure on India's balance of payments and trade policy, thus causing potential problems with the United States and with India's Asian neighbors. The price of oil topped $126 per barrel in early 2008. With prices at half that level in 2006, oil accounted for one-third of India's imports, and India's net oil import bill (after subtracting substantial exports of petroleum products) came to $42.9 billion, equivalent to one-third of the country's merchandise exports. This gap will increase if current oil prices continue.[33] The fallout from this situation will roil domestic politics and complicate the effort to rationalize energy policy. As discussed earlier, India's emphasis on diversifying energy supplies already is a source of political tension with the United States. Likewise, rising food prices have already led to export restrictions, with troublesome consequences for India's customers, and could easily provoke a political crisis.

The second looming issue is climate change. Whereas the Bush administration has adopted a minimalist position on this issue, the Indian government has argued that reducing carbon emissions is an urgent priority and that the industrialized world must take responsibility. If a future U.S. administration decides to take climate change seriously, the Indian government's reluctance to accept any commitments could go over badly in Washington, setting off a highly emotive argument in both the bilateral and multilateral arenas.[34]

Potential Strategies

Current U.S. strategy gives primacy to the bilateral relationship. Both countries are working hard to build up security relations, boost trade and investment, improve the flow of high tech trade, and develop closer links inside and outside of government in such fields as energy, education, health, and scientific research. The current U.S. approach puts less emphasis on

---

[33] Data from the Ministry of Commerce and Industry, Government of India, Export Import Data Bank.

[34] Kapil Sibal (address at the 13th Conference of Parties of the United Nations Framework Convention on Climate Change, Bali, December 12, 2007), http://www.meaindia.nic.in/speech/2007/12/12ss01.htm; Shyam Saran, "Climate Change—From Back Room to Board Room—What Indian Business Needs to Know about India's Approach to Multilateral Negotiations on Climate Change" (speech delivered in Mumbai, April 21, 2008), http://www.meaindia.nic.in/speech/2008/04/23ss01.htm.

finding feasible areas of cooperation outside the bilateral context and de-emphasizes India-Pakistan diplomacy. The nuclear agreement has become a kind of gatekeeper for the bilateral relationship: other major decisions have slowed down, waiting for the outcome of the nuclear discussions. Though the partnership will continue even if the nuclear agreement is not implemented in 2008, the fate of the nuclear deal will influence options for developing this partnership.

Four Alternative Strategies

South Asia first. A "South Asia first" strategy would be most pertinent if a new India-Pakistan confrontation were to plunge the region into crisis. This approach assumes that the consequences of an India-Pakistan war would be so catastrophic that a long-term solution to the dispute would become the top priority. Though this scenario seems unlikely in the short term, there is a history of sudden and severe crises erupting between India and Pakistan—sometimes provoked by parties not fully controlled by either government.

Under this first scenario the United States would push for an India-Pakistan settlement as a precursor to working more intimately with both India and Pakistan. Washington would use its strong relations with both countries to help their governments resolve the decades-old dispute. Success would unquestionably benefit U.S. interests and contribute to world peace. This strategy, however, would require an enormous commitment of time and political engagement from senior U.S. leaders, probably spanning several administrations. Moreover, even in a post-crisis situation, India would be uncomfortable with a major U.S. initiative and, given that the United States is unlikely to endorse Pakistan's position in the dispute with India, Pakistan would have strong reservations as well. Because neither the Indian nor the Pakistani government at present is strong enough to sustain a breakthrough in settlement discussions, a U.S. initiative would have to aim at laying the groundwork for a future day when both governments can draw on a more solid domestic base.

Security first. A "security first" strategy would give priority to security issues and to ties with the Indian military. Though expanding trade and investment provide an essential foundation for a security first policy, their growth will largely be determined by the decisions of private companies and by India's economic policies. Security relations, on the other hand, can only be developed by governments. This approach would engage India in a serious strategic dialogue on the Middle East, maritime security in the Indian Ocean, and East Asia, while expanding the present program of military-to-military relations. To be sustainable on the U.S. side, this strategy would require a breakthrough on defense trade. Although this approach has the advantage of building on common interests that are easy to identify, and the Indian military is eager to proceed, a security first strategy would require an understanding at the political level of how the Indian government will characterize the U.S. partnership. A relationship dominated by security ties would be a significant departure from the status quo, and one that politicians in India would need to get used to.

Going global. A global strategy would focus on developing Asian and global cooperation. The underlying premise of this approach is that India, which in any case is becoming more active in global deliberations, will be a constructive participant in world politics only if the country is treated as a serious player. Under this approach the United States would use its support for India's membership in Asian regional institutions and global leadership groups to leverage a serious dialogue on the goals of global and regional governance in which the two countries would try to move beyond their current difficulty in working together in a multilateral setting. The United States would work to bring India into the major international and Asian regional organizations to which New Delhi aspires—starting with the G-8, continuing with Asian regional institutions, and working up to more difficult settings, such as the UN Security Council.

This approach would recognize the broader interests of both countries as well as India's global ambitions. Yet perhaps the biggest advantage of such a strategy would be the creation of a setting for addressing emerging issues that need a worldwide approach, such as climate change and a possible energy shortage. Even though bringing India into the IEA's discussions on energy security, for example, would not be a panacea, this step would surely help the international response to record-high energy prices. The disadvantage of a global strategy is that in the early stages India would not be an easy partner with which to work. Laying the groundwork for international cooperation thus would require an enormous commitment of time in bilateral consultations.

A strategic pause. U.S.-India economic ties will continue to expand in the next decade, likely regardless of what the two governments do. There is little to recommend an approach that would relegate India to the foreign policy periphery. The "strategic pause" option, rather, involves continued work on the economic relationship but a slowdown in the development of non-economic areas of the partnership. Not only has India experienced trouble moving ahead with a nuclear agreement that the United States considers very favorable, but New Delhi still has difficulty publicly siding with Washington in multilateral forums. Under these circumstances a strategic pause strategy could consolidate the bilateral gains of the past decade and continue to remove obstacles to trade and investment without creating expectations of great transformations in the next couple of years. This result is easily achievable and involves little downside risk. The disadvantage is that this approach will almost certainly involve missed opportunities at a time when shifts in global economics and politics make a more sophisticated relationship with India increasingly beneficial.

Four Wild Cards

These four alternative strategies are based on the trends outlined in the above analysis of U.S.-India relations. It is worth reflecting on four "wild cards" that could affect the environment in the next decade. The first two wild cards could push India and the United States into an unwanted strategic pause, the third could create the circumstances for a serious estrangement, and the last would reignite familiar U.S. concerns over South Asia as an international flashpoint. Though this fourth situation might tilt policy toward the "India-Pakistan first" option, such an outcome would not fundamentally change the U.S.-India relationship.

A major economic slowdown in India. Today's more open Indian economy is more vulnerable to international economic downturns than in the past. Partly due to the slowdown of the U.S. economy, India's growth is likely to slow by one or two percentage points in 2008. If international developments were to worsen, India's export markets shrink, and the vibrant outsourcing market contract, India would face large-scale discontent extending beyond the already troubled rural population. This situation would paradoxically make it more difficult to continue market-based economic reforms and would create irresistible pressure for budget-busting subsidies on energy and foodstuffs—which in turn could further depress economic growth. Though not signaling sudden death, such a result would certainly depress India-U.S. relations. Without the spur of expanding economic relations, India-U.S. relations would also be more vulnerable to political upsets.

Post-election political deadlock in India. After over a decade of coalition governments India has plenty of experience with putting together a multi-party government. Yet if the parliamentary elections in 2009 or in a subsequent election produce a truly unmanageable result, the country could face a period of uncertainty. A major increase in the profile of single-state parties could further complicate this situation, especially if the parties representing the large backward states in northern India emerged as key members of a coalition. This could lead to stasis in decisionmaking on the political and economic issues at the heart of the partnership with the United States.

U.S. military attack on Iran. U.S. military action against Iran's nuclear installations would cause a crisis in U.S.-India relations. Such a decision would trigger outbursts in India from both friends and foes of the U.S.-India partnership, revive Cold War–era suspicions of U.S. intentions in the world, and seriously disrupt India's energy supplies and hence its economic development. These disruptions would of course coincide with a spasm of outrage in the Middle East. Such fury would take considerable time to die down, damaging the standing of the United States in India and the region. Thus a U.S. invasion of Iran would leave U.S.-India relations far worse than they are today and could lead to a significant realignment of political sympathies in the larger Asian region.

India-Pakistan war. A fresh India-Pakistan crisis would cause serious anxiety in Washington and lead to an intense burst of U.S. crisis management diplomacy. Yet barring a major Indian assault on the Pakistani heartland or other efforts to disable Pakistan's government or military, an India-Pakistan war would not alter the basic shape of the U.S.-India relationship. Although a major Indian attack on Pakistan appears unlikely in a nuclear environment, the most serious danger is miscalculation by either India or Pakistan of the other's red lines.

Toward a Selective Global Partnership

The new U.S. relationship with India has been built on both countries' hopes that a stronger India in a more powerful Asia can be a force for peace and prosperity in the world. U.S. administrations of both major parties have spent a decade and a half building the bilateral infrastructure for a new partnership. The party that takes over in January 2009, Democrat or Republican, should build on this foundation. The future of the nuclear deal will have a powerful impact on how India and the United States work together in the future. At the same time, the partnership risks turning into a laundry list unless the two countries start to develop at least some elements of a global vision. The most promising way for the new administration to do this would be to build its policy around the "going global" option sketched out above. This policy will be most productive if the next administration also works with India to develop a new model for partnership that is compatible with the global U.S. role and with India's prickly sense of national sovereignty.

Going Global and Regional Integration

Under this type of policy, the administration would build on the existing bilateral relationship but add a global dimension. The most public manifestation of this policy would be U.S. support for India's membership in Asian regional organizations and in global leadership institutions. In light of the difficulty that the United States and India have experienced while working together in multilateral settings, however, this U.S. offer of support should be preceded by a dramatically intensified dialogue between the two countries on global issues. Indian elections will take place only three or four months after the new administration assumes power in Washington, so there may be new governments in both countries. This would be an ideal time for taking a fresh look at regional and global goals.

This *tour d'horizon* would cover the regions of greatest mutual interest (namely the Middle East and East Asia) as well as India's immediate neighborhood. Some of the issues involved, such as security in the Indian Ocean and Southeast Asia, are relatively easy to discuss, provided the two countries field the right teams. Other issues involve political sensitivities (for example, China) or policy disagreements (for example, policy toward Iran, Pakistan, and Afghanistan). The objective of this global dialogue would be for each side to better understand the other's assessment of and policies in areas of mutual interest. Armed with that understanding, Washington and New Delhi would then look for areas where coordinated action is feasible. In particular, discussions would do well to focus on regional institutions in Asia and on ways for the United States and India to support each other through these institutions.

The global dialogue also needs to cover issues demanding global governance, such as energy and food security, climate change, and international health. Although India and the United States will have some differences in these areas—especially on climate change—both recognize the need for a global approach that fully engages both countries. The international trade agenda would be an important part of this dialogue. Multilateral trade issues are often contentious between India and the United States; major policy differences and the politics of trade in both countries will keep this controversy alive. Yet it should be possible to identify one or two significant trade issues that both countries can support.

In carrying out this global dialogue, the United States would make clear its intention to lay the groundwork for a larger Indian institutional role in global and regional governance, one based on a better understanding by both countries of their global goals. U.S. support for Indian membership would logically begin with the institutions where U.S. and Indian goals are reasonably well aligned. The formal expansion of the G-8 would provide the best starting point. The structure of the G-8 and the discretion that usually surrounds its discussions are ideal for avoiding the sterile debate that has occurred at the WTO and in the UN. Although the issue of IEA membership for India is technically complicated, the benefits of folding the world's second fastest-growing energy market into the premier energy consumers' organization are clear, and achieving these benefits is worth substantial effort. A logical next step would be greater Indian integration into Asian regional organizations: to support India's entrance into APEC and perhaps to quietly encourage ASEAN to invite India into the organization's more restrictive dialogue groups. India will be looking for U.S. support for permanent membership in the UN Security Council; assuming that some level of common understanding emerges, such support would come later in the process.

India's membership in these organizations would bring its share of frustrations as differences of interests and style surface. The United States and India would need to discuss with some candor how to deal with one another in regional and global settings to give both countries realistic expectations regarding the prospects for cooperation in these organizations. In the medium and longer term, however, this posture would encourage the pragmatists in the Indian government and build the experience of common action between senior Indian and U.S. officials. If the global and especially the Asian regional scene is moving toward a rough balance of power, the United States will want India not only to be recognized as an important global player but also to realize that the United States helped it gain this recognition.

Redefining Partnership

In order to succeed, however, this effort will need to be complemented by a new understanding of what it means for the United States and India to be partners and how their partnership can be compatible with India's commitment to strategic autonomy. The models with which the United States has worked in the past are inadequate for such an understanding. India has no interest in becoming an ally (and indeed the United States does not have much appetite for taking on new alliance obligations).

A new model for partnership would begin with two qualities: selectivity and predictability. India and the United States would need to identify in general terms the international issues on which the two countries can work together without too much strain. Both countries would want to avoid unpleasant surprises in the multilateral arena. On some issues the partners would expect to support each other publicly; on others support might be offered behind the scenes. On still other issues neither country would expect much support. If taking a global approach is successful, the list of international issues on which New Delhi and Washington cooperate would expand over time, and their cooperation itself might become more public.

In the past India-Pakistan diplomacy has often been the lead element in U.S. relations with India. Barring an acute crisis it should not be the lead issue now. All the factors that make a settlement hard to imagine today will still be in place in early 2009. On the other hand, the new administration dare not ignore the potential dangers in this stubborn dispute. If the new Pakistani government stabilizes, and when India has a new government, the United States may wish to quietly encourage India and Pakistan to intensify peace efforts. Even though this will not make the United States popular in India, the dispute is still the most serious danger hanging over the larger region. If a diplomatic window opens, the United States and other international powers would do well to take advantage of it.

EXECUTIVE SUMMARY

This chapter examines how Australia's strategic objectives have been affected by security challenges from 2000 to 2008, how Australian and U.S. responses to these challenges have interacted, and how the alliance is adjusting.

MAIN ARGUMENT:
Although the U.S. and Australia have strengthened the alliance since 2000, especially on the military and intelligence fronts, the limits are starting to show: Australia is less concerned by China's rising power than the U.S., the Australian public has mixed feelings over aspects of the alliance, and a new Labor government in Canberra, though committed to the alliance, wants to present a relatively independent face. Leadership transitions in both countries amount to an opportunity for alliance consolidation and renewal.

POLICY IMPLICATIONS:
- The new U.S. administration would benefit from close attention to the alliance and seeking to renew it in tandem with a multi-dimensional and balanced set of policies in Asia, including maintaining a strategic presence, sustaining an emphasis on engagement with China, pursuing greater participation in regional institutions, and ensuring that policy toward Asia is not overshadowed by terrorism and the Middle East.

- A demonstrable willingness to hear Australian advice, especially on Asian issues, will help remind Australia that the alliance is working.

- Realistic expectations on Australia as an ally would flow from a recognition of the limits of the country's defense capabilities and the multiplicity of Australia's regional security challenges.

- Prolonged inattention to Australia would risk turning the alliance's limits—such as differing views of China—into vulnerabilities for U.S. positions in Asia and globally.

Australia: Allied in Transition

Rory Medcalf

Americans looking at Australia tend to see so much that is familiar that they can underestimate the differences. For example, most Australians do not consider democracy promotion an important goal of foreign policy.[1] The next U.S. administration will inherit a U.S.-Australia alliance that appears in good health, based on many convergent interests, common values, a history of shared sacrifice, and bipartisan support in both countries. It will thus be doubly important to consider how Australia's strategic outlook might be altering and to contemplate what Washington can do to keep the alliance current and resilient in a changing Asia. One hundred years after the Great White Fleet visited the Antipodes, raising Australia's earliest hopes of the United States as a great and powerful friend, it is timely to take stock of the alliance.[2]

One immediate reason for such an appraisal is the November 2007 election in Australia of a Labor government under Kevin Rudd. This election ended eleven years of conservative government under John Howard and prompted debate in Australia over whether Labor's emphasis would be on continuity or change in external policies. Some initial signs suggested the latter. Prime Minister Rudd's government soon distanced Australia from several important Bush administration positions, for example by ratifying the Kyoto Protocol on climate change and by withdrawing Australia's combat battalion from Iraq. There were also hints that Australia would diverge with

Rory Medcalf is Director of the International Security Program at the Lowy Institute for International Policy in Australia. He can be reached at <rmedcalf@lowyinstitute.org>.

[1] Only 29% of Australians surveyed see "promoting democracy in other countries" as "very important." Allan Gyngell, "The Lowy Institute Poll 2007: Australia and the World: Public Opinion and Foreign Policy," Lowy Institute for International Policy, 2007, 19.

[2] Peter Edwards, *Permanent Friends? Historical Reflections on the Australian-American Alliance* (Sydney: Lowy Institute for International Policy, 2005), 5–6.

the United States over the importance of cultivating partnerships with Japan and India. These hints notably included an early prime ministerial visit to Beijing, not Tokyo or New Delhi; a confrontation with Japan over whaling; a reversal of Howard's decision to sell uranium to India; and the rejection of a quadrilateral dialogue among the democracies. Rudd's fascination with China added to claims of an alleged pro-China tilt.

Yet Kevin Rudd is no radical. He sees the U.S. presence as essential to strategic stability in Asia and has emphasized his credentials as a friend of the United States in the tradition of 1980s prime minister Bob Hawke and his World War II Labor predecessor John Curtin, who famously looked to the United States for help against Japan.[3] By the time of his first prime ministerial visit to Washington in March–April 2008, it was clear Rudd wanted overall continuity in the alliance. His declaration that he saw the United States as a "force for good"[4] struck a chord in Republican and Democratic camps alike.[5] On Japan, Rudd moved to repair misunderstandings with a mid-year visit, while his foreign and trade ministers took pains to reassure New Delhi that India was not forgotten.

The Rudd ascendancy is not the only reason to survey the alliance. The 2008 presidential election raises related questions over the directions the alliance might take under new leadership in both countries after eight years of an exceptionally close and personalized Bush-Howard partnership and in light of changes in the strategic environment. Given the rise of China, other trends in Asian geopolitics, the broad currents of U.S. foreign policy, and Australia's sense of its place in the world, there remain some long-term uncertainties over the depth and consistency of Canberra-Washington strategic ties. It is all the more pertinent, therefore, that the overlap of transitions in Washington and Canberra presents an opportunity for consolidation and renewal of the alliance in adapting to the challenges of the Asian century.

This chapter is divided into five sections. The first overviews Australia's grand strategy. The second section examines how Australia has responded to challenges to its strategic policies from 2000 to 2008, followed by a third section on how Australia's decisions have been influenced by U.S. interests, objectives, and actions, as well as how the alliance has evolved during this time period. The chapter then explores options for the United States to

---

[3] Kevin Rudd, "ANZUS and the 21st Century," *Australian Journal of International Affairs* 55, no. 2 (July 2001): 307–10, 313–14.

[4] Kevin Rudd, "The Australia-US Alliance and Emerging Challenges in the Asia-Pacific Region" (speech at the Brookings Institution, Washington, D.C., March 31, 2008), http://www.pm.gov.au/media/Speech/2008/speech_0157.cfm.

[5] "Kevin Rudd Gets a Glowing Review from US Conservatives," *Australian*, April 3, 2008, http://www.theaustralian.news.com.au/story/0,25197,23473724-20261,00.html.

adjust its expectations of and approaches to the alliance, which cannot be considered in isolation from wider regional and global policies. A conclusion presents ways in which the United States might sustain, strengthen, or make better use of the alliance in service of U.S. and Australian interests.

Australia's Four-Element Strategy

To understand the Australia-U.S. alliance, it is necessary to have a sense of the perennial issues in Australia's strategic orientation. Australia has many attributes that mark the nation as secure—an island continent with massive resources, high levels of wealth and development, a stable democratic system, and an advanced military. Yet Australia's strategic culture involves feelings of insecurity and isolation. These stem from nineteenth century exposure to the great-power rivals of the British Empire and from concerns for much of the twentieth century over vulnerability in the face of expanding Asian powers and populations (heightened by Japan's aggression in World War II). Contemporary worries over terrorism, the proliferation of weapons of mass destruction, the fragility of neighboring states, and the changing power dynamics of Asia reinforce these feelings. Australia, with the world's eleventh largest defense budget, suffers from an unusual strategic anxiety for a country that faces no foreseeable conventional military threat to its territory.

Australia's security has long had four key elements: defense self-reliance (in an alliance context), the U.S. alliance, bilateral ties in Asia, and support for regional and global institutions and norms. The ANZUS treaty with the United States (and New Zealand) was signed in 1951, within recent memory of war with Japan. Australia's diplomacy in Asia and engagement with the United Nations emerged quickly in the second half of the 1940s. The shift to defense self-reliance intensified with the British withdrawal from Asia and the Guam Doctrine, which circumscribed the U.S. military role in the region.[6] By the mid-1970s all four elements were in evidence, and by the 1980s these elements had consolidated into coherent and mutually reinforcing policy fundamentals.

Australia is bipartisan on the broad shape of this four-part security policy; differences are in degrees of emphasis. Conservatives have tended to focus on the alliance and key bilateral relationships, including those in Asia. Labor has traditionally emphasized defense self-reliance, the UN, and engagement with Asia, both bilateral and multilateral. Thus, the Rudd

6 Hugh White, "Australian Strategic Policy," in *Strategic Asia 2005–06: Military Modernization in an Era of Uncertainty,* ed. Ashley J. Tellis and Michael Wills (Seattle: The National Bureau of Asian Research, 2005), 306.

government claims to have a foreign policy based on three pillars—the U.S. alliance, UN membership, and engagement with Asia—and the anticipated white paper in late 2008 reviewing Australian defense policy is unlikely to jettison the pursuit of self-reliance in combat.

From a U.S. perspective, one salient characteristic of Australian grand strategy, in all its variants, is a multilayered (if not strictly hedging) aspect: for all the confidence and effort Canberra invests in the alliance, by no means is the alliance counted on as the only source of Australian security.

The First Element: The Alliance

Australia derives multiple benefits from the alliance with the United States. At the deepest level, there is understood to be a security guarantee, such as provided for in the ANZUS Treaty:

> (Article III) The Parties will consult together whenever in the opinion of any of them the territorial integrity, political independence or security of any of the Parties is threatened in the Pacific. (Article IV, paragraph one) Each Party recognizes that an armed attack in the Pacific Area on any of the Parties would be dangerous to its own peace and safety and declares that it would act to meet the common danger in accordance with its constitutional processes.[7]

In practice, both countries have come to accept that their mutual alliance obligations transcend in depth and breadth the formal language of the treaty. The willingness of the United States to assist Australia in the event of a major military threat has been understood by Australian governments to include the extension of the U.S. nuclear deterrent. Canberra also sees the alliance as delivering many other advantages: exceptional access to and potential influence on U.S. policymakers, privileged access to U.S. intelligence, preferential access to U.S. defense-related technology, and potential economic gains from access to the U.S. market under a 2004 free-trade agreement (FTA), augmented by a liberal business visa arrangement.[8] The government also perceives the alliance as a diplomatic multiplier, giving Australia extra influence.[9]

In return for these advantages, Australia provides a range of regional and global benefits to the United States, including direct military support: Australia is the only country to have fought alongside the United States in every major war since and including World War I. Although the Australian

---

[7] The text of the Australia-New Zealand-United States Security (ANZUS) Treaty is available at http://australianpolitics.com/foreign/anzus/anzus-treaty.shtml.

[8] Edwards, *Permanent Friends?* 2–3.

[9] Paul Dibb, "Australia-United States," in *Australia as an Asia-Pacific Regional Power: Friendships in Flux?* ed. Brendan Taylor (London: Routledge, 2007), 33.

contribution to U.S.-led operations is modest in terms of firepower, the Australian Defence Force (ADF) is of high quality and, largely owing to the alliance, is also technologically advanced as well as relatively interoperable with U.S. forces at a high level. The force is small, however, with fewer than 57,000 full-time personnel, and has difficulty sustaining more than a few thousand troops on distant deployments. Still, Australian military support is disproportionately valuable because of the presentational advantages of having such a willing, respected, and capable coalition partner. In addition, the United States gains from Australian diplomatic and intelligence backing on many issues, including nonproliferation and counterterrorism. Australia hosts a critical joint facility for intelligence at Pine Gap near Alice Springs in the Northern Territory. Furthermore, the United States generally benefits from independent Australian actions to manage challenges in the local region, the "arc of instability" encompassing East Timor and the southwestern Pacific. The caricature of this role as being that of a "deputy sheriff," along with other accounts suggesting Australia has a subservient position in the alliance, overlooks the imperatives of independence and self-interest that drive Australian policy. Canberra is animated by a greater spirit of realpolitik than is sometimes appreciated in Washington.

Other Elements: Self-reliance, Bilateralism, and Institutions

The confidence Canberra places in the alliance does not equate to blind faith. Since the 1970s self-reliance has been a staple of Australia's defense policy. Though defined in Australia's 2000 defense white paper as the ability "to defend Australia without relying on the combat forces of other countries," implicit in this policy of self-reliance is an expectation of and allowance for assistance from the United States.[10] The "defense of Australia" imperative is for Australia to be able to protect itself against foreseeable conventional threats (often considered to be code for possible Indonesian adventurism) with an emphasis on possessing superior air and naval capabilities, especially submarine capabilities, in Australia's northern approaches.[11] In addition, however, self-reliance has come to include a requirement to be able to take a lead in stabilizing fragile states in the neighborhood.[12] The realization that Australia would not want to count on the support of U.S. combat forces in

---

[10] Department of Defence of the Commonwealth of Australia, *Defence 2000: Our Future Defence Force 2000* (Canberra, 2000), xi.

[11] On Indonesia as a potential conventional threat to Australia, see Paul Dibb and Richard Brabin-Smith, "Indonesia in Australian Defence Planning," *Security Challenges* 3, no. 4 (November 2007), 82–85.

[12] Department of Defence of the Commonwealth of Australia, *Australia's National Security: A Defence Update 2007* (Canberra, 2007), 26.

regional stabilization operations played a role in the 1999 East Timor crisis, in which Australia led a military intervention under circumstances that could have led to hostilities with Indonesia.[13]

Beyond defense self-reliance and the U.S. alliance, Australian security policy is embedded in the pursuit of strong and stable bilateral relationships in Asia, especially with Indonesia, China, and Japan. Australia's relations with all three countries have evolved well. The democratization of Indonesia has occurred more comprehensively and with less turmoil than Australia could have hoped; the tragedies of the Jemaah Islamiyah terrorist bombings in Bali and Jakarta have led to counterterrorism collaboration that has brought the two countries' security establishments closer together. A new era of cooperation between Australia and Indonesia, following the 1999 rupture over East Timor, is underpinned by a security treaty signed in 2006.[14] China's dramatic rise to become Australia's largest trade partner has been accompanied by intensified political relations and official dialogues, marked by President Hu Jintao and President Bush addressing the Australian Parliament in the same week in 2003. Japan remains Australia's largest export market, and defense ties between these two U.S. allies have consolidated with a 2007 security declaration that allows for deepening cooperation in military exercises and intelligence sharing as well as annual "two plus two" joint meetings of Australian and Japanese defense and foreign ministers.[15] Meanwhile, Australia has begun to cultivate India as another key Asian power.

Australia also sees security benefits in promoting institutions for regional and global order. In addition to long-standing support of the UN and global regimes against WMD proliferation, Australia has been active in the creation and development of regional frameworks, notably the Asia-Pacific Economic Cooperation (APEC) process, the ASEAN Regional Forum (ARF), and the East Asia Summit (EAS). Yet Canberra is well aware of the weakness of Asian regionalism, especially in managing the risks of armed conflict between states, and shows no sign of departing from the long-held view that the U.S. strategic presence in and commitment to Asia remains of much more fundamental importance.

---

[13] The United States did provide logistical and intelligence support to the 1999 East Timor operation, as well as a degree of over-the-horizon reassurance. Indonesian forces could never have been sure that, if attacked, the Australians would not have received combat support from U.S. forces. Author's conversation with Andrew Shearer, former foreign policy advisor to Prime Minister John Howard, Sydney, May 2008.

[14] "Lombok Treaty," available at the Australian Treaties Database of the Department of Foreign Affairs and Trade, http://www.info.dfat.gov.au/treaties/.

[15] "Japan-Australia Joint Declaration on Security Cooperation," available at the Ministry of Foreign Affairs of Japan website, http://www.mofa.go.jp/region/asia-paci/australia/joint0703.html.

Navigating a Sea of Troubles:
Australia's Strategic Policy Challenges, 2000–08

In the era of the George W. Bush administration, these Australian strategic settings have been both borne out and adjusted as Australia has responded to multiple global and regional challenges—notably the war on terrorism and changing power relations in Asia—and, just as critically, to U.S. reactions. An audit of Australian security policy in 2008 must also account for policy continuities and potential discontinuities arising from two coincidences of Australian and U.S. electoral tides: first, Australia possessed the same government for all but the final year of the George W. Bush period; second, the next U.S. administration will encounter a relatively new Australian government under Rudd that for domestic political reasons portrays itself as distant from Howard-era policies. These coincidences are important because a defining quality of Howard's approach was his extraordinary closeness to the Bush administration in world-view, policy decisions, and personal rapport.[16] Rudd's Australia may feel compelled to exaggerate differences with Bush-era policies and personalities but will also see the change of U.S. administration—no matter who wins—as a politically cost-free opportunity to renew and consolidate an alliance that the country does not want to weaken.

Terrorism, Afghanistan, and Iraq

Australia's support for the U.S.-led fight against jihadist terrorism has been intensive at a political level, even if more modest operationally. Howard was in Washington on September 11 and immediately invoked ANZUS for the first time in the treaty's history. Australian forces have been in Afghanistan, on and off, from the start of Operation Enduring Freedom. Australia is one of the few U.S. allies to accept combat roles in that country and in 2008 had approximately one thousand personnel in the dangerous Oruzgun Province. Rudd has declared at least as much support for NATO operations in Afghanistan as Howard did, sustaining Australia's deployment and helping Bush lobby Europe to contribute more troops.[17] This support may be intended in part to offset any negative alliance-management consequences for the withdrawal of Australian combat forces from Iraq. Yet

---

[16] Greg Sheridan, *The Partnership: The Inside Story of the US-Australian Alliance under Howard and Bush* (Sydney: University of New South Wales Press, 2006).

[17] Kevin Rudd and Joel Fitzgibbon, "Joint Press Conference with Minister for Defence," press conference, Canberra, March 19, 2008, http://www.pm.gov.au/media/Interview/2008/interview_0141.cfm.

even so, Afghanistan could be a serious test in the years ahead: if casualties rise and a convincing strategy for Western success remains elusive, the Rudd government could face public pressure to withdraw. A mid-2007 poll showed the Australian public evenly divided on whether to keep troops in Afghanistan.[18]

Canberra has also been a substantial U.S. partner in other aspects of the war on terrorism, contributing assets for maritime security in the Persian Gulf and the Arabian Sea, cooperating in intelligence and policing, proscribing terrorist groups, and thwarting terrorist financing. For Australia, terrorism has also been a regional challenge. The October 2002 Bali bombing, in which 88 Australians died, was followed by attacks in Jakarta (including one on the Australian embassy in 2004) and another in Bali in 2005. Australian police, intelligence, diplomatic, and capacity-building contributions have played an influential role against terrorism in Southeast Asia. Although having focused primarily on Indonesia, Canberra has also extended cooperation to Manila and Washington in the southern Philippines, where terrorists have sought sanctuary.

On Iraq, Australia was one of the few countries to contribute troops to the U.S.-led invasion in early 2003, including air power and Special Forces. The Howard government stood by the United States on Iraq through the WMD intelligence scandal and the errors, travails, and carnage of occupation and insurgency. Howard's standing in Washington even survived revelations that Australia's wheat export authority had breached UN sanctions by trading with Saddam Hussein's regime. The Rudd government, however, is determined to set itself apart from Howard's positions on Iraq. This is in step with long-standing Labor views and Australian majority sentiment: a poll of Australian public opinion by the Sydney-based Lowy Institute in 2007 showed that 57% of respondents wanted the country to end military involvement in Iraq, with only 37% remaining in favor.[19] Accordingly, in June 2008 the Rudd government fulfilled an election commitment to withdraw the single Australian combat battalion its predecessor had retained in Iraq. Nonetheless, Australia continues to support security and reconstruction efforts in Iraq with a small presence of non-combat military personnel, an aid program, and training for the Iraqi police. Australia is also sustaining a naval presence in the Persian Gulf.

[18] Gyngell, "Lowy Institute Poll 2007," 10.

[19] Ibid.

Riding the Waves: Power Shifts in Asia

In the Asia-Pacific region, Canberra has had to adapt to shifting major power dynamics, notably the rise of China and India as well as assertiveness by Japan in the face of decline.

It is not always fully grasped in Washington that Australia is less troubled by the rise of China than is the United States or indeed much of the Western world. The 2007 Lowy opinion poll suggested only a small degree of difference between how warmly Australians regarded the United States and China; the same poll showed that only 19% of respondents considered themselves "very worried" by China's growing power.[20] Greenhouse emissions aside, China's economic growth has been an unmitigated benefit for Australia's welfare; it has fuelled a resources boom, especially in iron ore, that has been critical to Australia's sustained strong economic performance. Benefits have come in job creation, rising incomes, tax revenues, and—critically for a nation of shareholders—corporate profits. In the year preceding March 2007, China overtook Japan to become Australia's largest trading partner.[21] For the first time in history Australia's trade flows were out of step with its strategic allegiances.[22]

In tandem with close economic ties has come intensified diplomatic engagement, with the emphasis on pragmatism, convergent interests, cooperation in building Asian stability and prosperity, and a downplaying of security mistrust. Rudd is keen to build on Howard-era achievements in Australia-China relations, and he has quickly proceeded to hold the first round of a foreign ministers' strategic dialogue bequeathed by Howard. Rudd makes no secret of his deep interest in China: he served in Beijing as a diplomat, was a student of Chinese history and culture, and has the singular attribute of being the first Mandarin-speaking leader of a Western country. More important, however, are the structural trends, likely to deepen, of Australia's economic enmeshment with China and the imperative to try to minimize U.S.-China strategic competition.

Warming bilateral relations do not mean that Australia will automatically shy away from affronting China when there is a clash of interests or values. Efforts by Chinese sovereign wealth funds to buy into major Australian companies are of rising concern in Canberra; the Rudd

---

[20] Gyngell, "Lowy Institute Poll 2007," 6, 9, 18.

[21] David Uren, "China Emerges as Our Biggest Trade Partner," *Australian,* May 5, 2007, http://www.theaustralian.news.com.au/story/0,20867,21674786-2702,00.html.

[22] Allan Gyngell and Michael Wesley, "Regional Diplomacy Has New Impetus," *Australian Financial Review,* April 3, 2008, 79.

government has swiftly moved to limit such investments.[23] It is also striking that Rudd used his first prime ministerial visit to China to speak out more publicly on human rights in Tibet than Howard had, including in a speech in Chinese.[24] Rudd would seem to harbor no illusions regarding China.[25]

Alongside engagement with Beijing, Australia under Howard and now Rudd is quietly hedging against the possibility that China's rise may become destabilizing. This possibility has been a factor in Canberra's efforts to enhance and update Australia's defense capabilities and tighten the already-close U.S. alliance. Despite the politeness of official Australian expressions of defense policy, which dwell more on the dynamics of power relations in Asia than on China's military modernization, it would be reasonable to speculate that China is the major power Australian planners have in mind when setting capability requirements.[26] Under Howard, Australia also made a point of advancing security cooperation with powers seen in Washington as potential balancers of Chinese military might—Japan, India, and Indonesia—including, in the first two cases, through "minilateral" subgroups. The Rudd government seems uncomfortable with this, however. Though sustaining support for the Trilateral Strategic Dialogue with the United States and Japan, the government is unlikely to seek to deepen that process rapidly and has rejected a nascent quadrilateral forum involving India.

In whichever ways Canberra recalibrates relations with Beijing, ultimately the Rudd government is likely to harbor fears of a scenario that also presumably troubled Howard: that Australia would need to choose between the United States and China in a security crisis. This question gained in piquancy as the alliance and the Australia-China trade relationship simultaneously strengthened, beginning with Richard Armitage's 1999 ultimatum warning that Washington would expect Australian forces to fight alongside the United States for Taiwan.[27] The significance of this question

[23] "Principles Guiding Consideration of Foreign Government Related Investment in Australia," available at http://www.treasurer.gov.au/DisplayDocs.aspx?doc=pressreleases/2008/009.htm&pageID=003&min=wms&Year=&DocType.

[24] Michelle Grattan and Mary-Anne Toy, "Rudd Confronts China on Human Rights," *Age,* April 10, 2008, http://www.theage.com.au/articles/2008/04/09/1207420486421.html.

[25] In an essay early in his parliamentary career, Rudd noted that China "was not a status quo power" and had "pursued a regional foreign policy offensive primarily aimed at undermining the credibility of the principal U.S. alliances." Rudd, "ANZUS in the 21st Century," 307.

[26] Department of Defence, *Defence Update 2007,* 19–20; and Department of Defence, *Defence 2000,* 17–19.

[27] Richard Armitage, then an advisor to the Bush presidential campaign, told the Australian American Leadership Dialogue in August 1999 that the United States would expect Australia to provide meaningful military support to the United States in a Taiwan crisis. Allan Behm, *Submission to JSCFADT Inquiry into the Economic, Social and Strategic Trends in Australia's Region and the Consequences for Defence Requirements* (Canberra: Parliament of Australia, 2006), 18.

intensified in 2004 when then foreign minister Alexander Downer made an ambiguous statement over whether ANZUS would automatically be invoked in a Taiwan conflict, and again when Howard sidestepped by saying that there was nothing inevitable about strategic competition between the United States and China.[28] Howard's remark was more a matter of tactfully selective analysis and wishful thinking than a statement of policy. The remark served him well, however, and Rudd will likely maintain a similar public position.

One area where Rudd could depart substantially from Howard's approach is in attempting to position Australia as a conduit and messenger, if not necessarily a mediator, between the United States and China. Rudd appears interested in flirting with such a role. He has spoken of Australia's potential as a diplomatic bridge between the developed and developing world (including China and India) in climate change negotiations. While in the Opposition he spoke positively of a proposal for Australia to urge the United States and China to reduce competition in their nuclear weapons postures and programs.[29] Nonetheless, Rudd and his government are likely well aware of the practical limits for Australia in mediating between big powers confident in their abilities to manage relations themselves.

It remains difficult to imagine Australia rejecting a U.S. request for military assistance in a confrontation with China. The judgment is widely held among Australian strategic analysts that this situation would be an alliance breaker.[30] In any case, an argument can be made that the idea that Australia would need to make a fateful choice between its Chinese economic partner and its U.S. ally is based on the false assumption that an option for a business-as-usual trading relationship with China would somehow continue. In reality, the global economic damage from a U.S.-China clash or prolonged cold war would be such that Australia's commercial gains from the relationship with China would suffer greatly regardless of whether Canberra took sides or not.[31] This reality, along with the fact that

[28] In response to a question at a press conference in Beijing in 2004 regarding how Australia's alliance obligations might play out in a Taiwan confrontation, Downer said: " …the ANZUS Treaty is invoked in the event of one of our two countries…being attacked. So some other military activity elsewhere…does not automatically invoke the ANZUS Treaty." Hamish McDonald and Tom Allard, "ANZUS Loyalties Fall Under China's Shadow," *Sydney Morning Herald,* August 18, 2004, http://www.smh.com.au/articles/2004/08/17/1092508475915.html#.

[29] For further details on Australia's potential as a diplomatic bridge on climate change, see "Warming Up for Bali," *Australian,* December 10, 2007, http://www.theaustralian.news.com.au/story/0,25197,22895691-16382,00.html. For further details on Rudd's interest in addressing U.S.-China nuclear competition, see Peter Hartcher, "Rudd Looks to Alliance in Asia-Pacific," *Sydney Morning Herald,* August 24, 2007, http://www.smh.com.au/news/opinion/peter-hartcher/2007/08/23/1187462436353.html.

[30] Dibb, "Australia-United States," 44; and Behm, *Submission to JSCFADT Inquiry.*

[31] Sheridan, *The Partnership,* 196.

the Australian-U.S. intelligence relationship would immediately involve Australia in support of the U.S. war effort, reinforces the conclusion that it remains nigh on inevitable that Australia would, however reluctantly, side actively with its ally in the unlikely event of U.S.-China hostilities.

Under Howard, Australia also built stronger security relations with Japan through efforts including the Trilateral Security Dialogue, a 2007 joint declaration on security cooperation, cooperation in Iraq (where Australian troops protected the Japanese contingent), and relief operations following the 2004 tsunami. Australia's motives were not narrowly based on concern over Chinese power but involved a wish to normalize Japan's security posture in ways that would reassure the region and help provide public goods in responding to transnational security challenges. The Rudd government will sustain these directions, although probably with diminished enthusiasm; there remains potential for bilateral differences, such as over disagreements on whaling and Japanese suspicions of a tilt toward China, to affect the wider relationship.

Looking northwest, after decades of indifference, false starts, and nuclear differences, Australia's relations with India have greatly improved in the past decade. This has been driven by booming trade ties (India is Australia's fastest growing export market at a rate of 30% per year), convergent interests in counterterrorism and maritime security, and the dramatic transformation in U.S.-India relations. In 2007 the Howard government announced a policy revolution to introduce a civil uranium supply arrangement, contingent on the U.S.-India nuclear deal and bilateral safeguards. The Rudd government's reversal of this decision on the basis that Australia should not sell uranium to states that are not party to the Treaty on the Non-proliferation of Nuclear Weapons (NPT) underlines the Labor government's conundrum: how to reconcile Labor's crusading self-image on arms control with the wish to intensify ties with one of the key powers of the new century. Canberra and New Delhi are near the brink of strategic partnership, but the uranium issue and their differing comfort levels with China's rise could yet seriously complicate the endeavor.[32]

Resource demand from major economies in Asia, especially China, India, Japan, and South Korea, is helping Australia weather the more unsettling aspects of economic and financial globalization. Australia's unusual circumstances as a liberalized economy reliant on exports of commodities and services make the country well placed to benefit from Asian growth, especially as Asia's rising economies move up the

---

[32] Rory Medcalf, "Australia-India Relations: Hesitating on the Brink of Partnership," East-West Center, Asia Pacific Bulletin, no. 13, April 3, 2008, http://www.eastwestcenter.org/fileadmin/stored/pdfs/apb013.pdf.

value-added production chain. These strengths of Australia's economic situation make it likely that the Rudd government will cope with current domestic political and economic challenges, including uncertainties in international financial markets and high interest rates at a time when Australians are struggling with overpriced housing and record household debt. Given Labor's traditional vulnerability to accusations of fiscal irresponsibility, the Rudd government is restraining spending. A tension is emerging, however, between this fiscal rectitude and the demands of the strategic environment: there is not only a need to sustain spending increases for modernizing the nation's defense capabilities but also a need to resource overstretched diplomatic capacities to meet Labor aspirations for "creative middle power diplomacy," not least now that Rudd has indicated that Australia will campaign for a nonpermanent seat on the UN Security Council for 2013–14.

Australia's Crowded Security Horizons

Certainly Australian defense planners are aware that the distribution of military power is changing in the region and that, without increased and prudently directed spending, Australia risks losing its regional edge in combat capability. Several elements are likely to feed into Canberra's thinking, including Chinese military modernization and blue water naval aspirations; Russian sales of advanced platforms to China, India, Indonesia, Malaysia, and Vietnam; and potential Chinese and Russo-Indian missile sales to Southeast Asian states. The actual and potential introduction into Southeast Asia of modern submarines, Sukhoi combat aircraft, cruise missiles, and beyond visual range air-to-air missiles are points of concern, even as Australia's diplomatic relations with the countries of the Association of Southeast Asian Nations (ASEAN) and those countries' relations with one another reach increased levels of mutual confidence.

The Australian public, however, is more concerned by the dangers of WMD proliferation and use than by conventional military threats.[33] Just as public fears for much of the past decade focused on WMD acquisition and use by terrorists and rogue states, Australia's actions under Howard centered on functional cooperation targeted at the hard proliferation cases of Iran and North Korea as well as on preemptive action against Iraq. In light of the Iraq experience, however, it is unlikely that the Australian public would support the use of force against Iran. The Lowy Institute's 2007 opinion poll found that, although 62% of Australians surveyed believed Iran was trying to develop nuclear weapons, only 9% favored military action to thwart these

---

[33] Gyngell, "Lowy Institute Poll 2007," 10.

ambitions.[34] Under Labor, Australia is also likely to shift to putting a greater emphasis on multilateral, treaty-based arms control efforts, including the pursuit of nuclear disarmament.

As if Australia's security horizons were not crowded enough, Canberra has become increasingly concerned over the instability of its South Pacific neighborhood. Many motives have combined to prompt repeated security interventions by Australia in this region over the past decade, most notably in East Timor and the Solomon Islands. These reasons include state fragility and the prospect of state failure, the risk of Australia being affected by outflows of refugees and transnational crime, humanitarian impulses, Australia's sense of responsibility for a neighborhood in which the country is the largest power, and a determination to forestall external powers from establishing strategic bases in the region. Although Rudd has declared preference in principle for moving away from Howard's "military first" approach to the South Pacific's chronic governance problems, the dispatch of troops in early 2008 to manage a fresh East Timor crisis suggests Australia faces rolling deployments in the arc of instability. Fiji is another troubled country on Australia's watch. Finally, the possibility of a collapse of the rule of law in Papua New Guinea remains a scenario that would stretch Australian capabilities beyond their limits.

Australian security planners thus consider it fortunate that their country's largest neighbor, Indonesia, has successfully managed a transition to democracy. Several positive developments have made Indonesia "the dog that didn't bark" in the story of Canberra's regional security, including the maintenance of Indonesian territorial integrity (through both the Aceh peace process and the prevention of a fresh crisis in West Papua), Indonesia's return to strong rates of economic growth, the decline in communal conflict, the failure of jihadist ideology to make irreversible inroads in the syncretic mainstream of Indonesian Islam, and the friendly pragmatism of foreign policy under President Yudhoyono. The Howard government's efforts to consolidate these developments (for instance through a massive aid program after the 2004 tsunami) were important in Indonesia's transition as well. Massive internal instability, powerful separatist insurgencies, an upsurge in extreme nationalist or jihadist sentiment, or a confrontational external orientation by a militarily strong Jakarta would mark a sharp deterioration in Australia's strategic environment.

Instead, the potential threat from the outside world that most concerns Australians is the impact of climate change: the 2007 Lowy poll showed

[34] Gyngell, "Lowy Institute Poll 2007," 10–11.

that 55% of Australians surveyed were "very worried" by this threat.[35] Climate change and associated issues of energy efficiency and food and water security have dramatically risen in the priorities of the Australian public and governments, both state and federal, in recent years. Australia has only recently begun, however, to look for serious policy responses, and the country faces energy and external policy tensions that will be hard to resolve. Australia, for instance, has the world's largest uranium reserves yet possesses no nuclear power reactors as a consequence of public attitudes and an abundance of cheap coal. Though uranium exports are increasing, including to China and Russia, the Rudd government forbids such sales to India, despite urging India to manage its emissions. The nexus of climate change, nuclear energy, and nuclear proliferation will pose one of the most difficult policy dilemmas for Australian governments in the decades ahead.

Adjusting the Alliance: U.S.-Australia Relations, 2000–08

During the eight years of the Bush administration, the United States has faced multiple security challenges, including September 11, the invasions of Afghanistan and Iraq, the rise of China, the resurgence of Russia, and nuclear proliferation concerns centered on Iran, North Korea, and the A.Q. Khan network. Added to these have been transnational threats to global order, security, and development. These threats have not only included jihadist terrorism but also state fragility and failure, the potential emergence and spread of new pandemics, energy insecurity, and environmental challenges relating to climate change and overuse of resources such as growing stresses on food and water supply. In dealing with these myriad problems, the United States has needed to manage a mix of great expectations, great disappointments, and emerging challenges regarding Washington's role as a leader in the international system.

Australia's experience in handling multiple and simultaneous security problems has been on balance of large benefit to the United States. Australia has been a particularly valuable ally because Canberra has acutely perceived so many of the security threats facing the United States as global challenges that Australia also has a national interest in helping address.

Yet Canberra's responses to Australia's own troubles and opportunities have sometimes also had mixed and complicating impacts both on the alliance and on the ways in which Washington has responded to security challenges. These impacts have been most apparent in two ways. The first relates to Australia's imperative to handle stability and governance challenges

---

[35] Gyngell, "Lowy Institute Poll 2007," 9.

in its own region. On the positive side for Washington, the consequences of this Australian imperative have been less of the world for the United States to worry over and the setting of examples both of leadership in mustering regional coalitions and of innovatively combining military and civilian efforts to address state fragility. On the negative side, however, Australia's neighborhood commitments reduce the efforts the county can afford to devote to supporting U.S.-led coalitions further afield. As the second Nye-Armitage report described in 2007:

> Within the alliance, major problems stem from differences in perspective, with the United States placing a greater emphasis on the global context, while Australia seeks to balance its regional and global interests.[36]

The other and potentially more profound way in which Australia's crowded and complex security outlook has mixed effects on the alliance and for Washington is in Canberra's differing perspectives on Asian power dynamics, in particular Canberra's focus on China as an opportunity.

Success Stories…

In managing the alliance during these past eight years, Washington has generally succeeded in taking advantage of, facilitating, and rewarding the positive aspects, especially Australian support in the war on terrorism. The United States has had reasonable success in keeping and consolidating Australia's position as its closest ally in Asia, despite simultaneously strengthening the U.S.-Japan alliance and building a strategic partnership with India. Washington's achievements in alliance management with Australia were, however, in large part responses to Canberra's actions, including Australian activism in quickly joining both the war on terrorism and the Iraq coalition as well as the subsequent and parallel Australian activism in seeking privileges in its relationship with the United States. Contrary to some perceptions within Australia, the Bush administration went to considerable lengths to accommodate the Howard government's pressures for special treatment, notably on four fronts: intelligence sharing, defense technology access, an FTA, and a business visa program.[37] The administration gave diplomatic support to Australian security interventions in its neighborhood and eventually acceded to Canberra's pressure to allow

---

[36] Richard L. Armitage and Joseph S. Nye, "The U.S.-Japan Alliance: Getting Asia Right through 2020," Center for Strategic and International Studies, CSIS Report, February 2007, 10, http://www.csis.org/component/option,com_csis_pubs/task,view/id,3729/type,1/.

[37] Author's conversation with Andrew Shearer.

an Australian detainee at Guantanamo Bay to complete his sentence in his home country.

A key to strengthening the alliance has been in intelligence sharing. In 2004 Bush issued a directive instructing U.S. agencies to amend the national disclosure policy to allow much greater Australian access to U.S. intelligence and systems, particularly in relation to joint military operations and terrorism.[38] This was the fruit of tenacity on Australia's part, including efforts at the highest level.

In reviewing and expanding military capabilities, Australia has focused on securing access to advanced U.S. defense technology and maximizing interoperability with U.S. forces. This has meant the prominent inclusion of U.S. platforms and systems in the country's defense shopping lists, with items such as the Aegis combat system for Australia's new surface combatant vessels, Abrams tanks, C-17 Globemaster heavy-lift aircraft, the F-35 Joint Strike Fighter (on which Canberra's final approval was still pending in late 2008), and the F/A-18E/F Super Hornet aircraft. Australia has become anxious to streamline and lock in preferential access to U.S. technology and information. Such efforts culminated in the signing in September 2007 of the U.S.-Australia Defense Trade Cooperation Treaty. Once ratified by the U.S. Senate, this agreement will put Australia on a par only with the United Kingdom in ease of access to U.S. defense technology, allowing the license-free trade of defense goods and services between the two governments and U.S. and Australian companies that meet security requirements.[39] The deepening defense technology relationship comes in the context of progress on Australia-U.S. military interoperability made during the Bush years. Only Britain now has greater levels of interoperability with U.S. forces or integration of personnel into U.S. operational decisionmaking structures. In the U.S.-Australia context this integration has required much give and take. For instance, Australian military support for Operation Iraqi Freedom came with conditions, notably Australian veto powers on coalition targeting decisions.[40] Australia now has high levels of interoperability and familiarity with U.S. CENTCOM in addition to traditional closeness to PACOM.

Although opinion is divided over the value for Australia of the Australia-U.S. FTA, the agreement was clearly the most intense trade negotiation Canberra had ever concluded, and the FTA's success could not have been envisaged "in the absence of the close relationship between John

---

[38] Sheridan, *The Partnership*, 97.

[39] "Fact Sheet: U.S.-Australia Defense Trade Cooperation Treaty," *U.S. Fed News*, September 6, 2007.

[40] Sheridan, *The Partnership*, 70–72.

Howard and George W. Bush" that followed September 11 and Australian support for the Iraq war.[41] Though the FTA was not a simple reward for backing the United States in Iraq, it is important to take into account the context of intimate security partnership that was essential in generating the political will in Washington needed to overcome elements of domestic U.S. resistance to aspects of the agreement. A similar case can be made regarding the Howard government's achievement in securing for Australia a separate visa category specifically for thousands of businesspeople and professionals to live and work temporarily in the United States.[42]

Beyond accepting the four institutional foundations (intelligence, defense technology, free trade, and visas) of the Howard government's strategy to enhance relations with the United States, the Bush administration has proved reasonably responsive to Australian perspectives and ideas on how to manage the alliance and the alliance system in Asia. Foreign Minister Downer's efforts to shape the trilateral dialogue with Japan were welcomed by Washington, and his alerting the Bush administration to the importance of changes in Asia's diplomatic architecture drew close attention, if not a fundamental change, in U.S. thinking.

…and Misgivings

In the past eight years Canberra has also seen at times a fitfulness in the way the United States relates to East Asia, and has grown uneasy whenever Washington has appeared to place either the war on terrorism or concerns over Chinese military modernization front and center of U.S. diplomacy toward Asia. Australia's participation in Asian regional forums and determination to improve ties with Asian powers independently of the U.S. alliance system can be seen partly as insurance against the possibility of a declining U.S. strategic commitment to Asia, even though Australia will keep striving hard for, and is broadly expecting, that commitment to remain.

The United States has been far from universally successful in cementing Australian support for its policies in Asia or globally. The Australian public and the foreign and security policy communities have been divided on almost every aspect of U.S. external policy under Bush, including the administration's actions in confronting many of the challenges outlined earlier: terrorism, WMD proliferation, Iraq, climate change, energy security, China, and the changing power and institutional character of Asia.

---

[41] Allan Gyngell and Michael Wesley, *Making Australian Foreign Policy,* 2nd ed. (Melbourne: Cambridge University Press, 2007), 271.

[42] "New Visa for Australians Opens Up Major Business Opportunities in the United States," Australian Minister for Trade website, Press Release, May 11, 2005, http://www.trademinister.gov. au/releases/2005/mvt036_05.html.

Many U.S. positions on these issues have diminished the Australian public's comfort levels with the alliance and have added to pressures for change in external policy directions under the new Labor government. The Lowy Institute's opinion polls on Australian attitudes toward foreign policy have tracked a decline in how important the Australian public considers the ANZUS alliance for their country's security. In 2005 45% of respondents deemed the alliance very important, but this figure fell to 42% in 2006 and to 36% in 2007.[43] Of the 39% of respondents to the 2007 opinion poll who stated they had a somewhat unfavorable or very unfavorable opinion of the United States, 69% cited Bush and 63% cited U.S. foreign policies as among their reasons.[44] Rudd will need to constantly manage these perceptions, which are strong in the Left of his party, when considering additional areas of Australian support for U.S. positions.

Options for the New Administration

What, then, might be options for the United States to consolidate the gains of the past eight years in the alliance, guard against slippage, and potentially renew the alliance so that it is ready for a changing Asia?

In considering alternative policy options for the United States, it is meaningless to speak purely of an "Australia policy"; as is logical for an alliance, almost every aspect of U.S.-Australia relations is related to each country's perspectives on and actions regarding third parties and external issues. It would be an artificial exercise to spell out a neatly bounded set of alternative Australia policies isolated from regional and global security challenges. The following discussion, therefore, elucidates some options in U.S. policies toward selected Asia-Pacific and global security issues with a focus both on the implications for helping or hindering the U.S.-Australia alliance and on how the alliance might in turn help or hinder U.S. options.

Of course, one option might appear to be benign inattention. Neglect, however, has never been a serious option for managing this relationship. The less an Australian government can perceive or demonstrate the alliance's value in addressing national concerns—such as Asian stability and prosperity as China rises or handling a crowded security horizon—the less scope there will be for the United States to make fresh or sustained demands on the alliance when necessary. Moreover, the limits of the alliance would start to look like vulnerabilities in U.S. positions more widely, and could

---

[43] Gyngell, "Lowy Institute Poll 2007," 9.

[44] Ibid., 25.

become weaknesses, especially were Australia to opt out of some future military coalition.

Australia and the Long Struggle

In combating terrorism and jihadist ideology, the United States is more likely to enlist and sustain deep Australian support to the extent that Washington can maintain its shift away from the paradigm of the war on terrorism and toward a long struggle involving a number of strategies. These include an emphasis on national resilience, a maximum level of international cooperation, a sophisticated and well-resourced engagement in the battle of ideas, an emphasis on intelligence and policing cooperation, and the judicious use of military force.

In Afghanistan the United States will want to watch Australia's position carefully, including the country's stated commitment to stay for the long haul. This undertaking comes with conditions: Rudd and Minister of Defense Joel Fitzgibbon have repeatedly warned that they can justify risking Australian lives only if confident that there is a NATO strategy for success, including integration of civilian and military efforts and sufficient European force contributions. Rudd has implied that he considered these conditions satisfied by the outcome of NATO's April 2008 Bucharest summit. Many factors, however, will likely conspire to make his government reconsider its position before long. These include the near certainty of further disappointments in NATO processes and contributions, the prospect of further Australian casualties, the likelihood of other contingencies straining Australia's defense force closer to home, and the reasonable possibility that the white paper review of defense policy underway in 2008 could re-emphasize the need to operate in Australia's neighborhood. Given all this, Washington could choose to let Australia quietly draw down its troops in Afghanistan, accepting that this ally had already done enough. Yet, from a U.S. perspective, this could well be a mistake because of the example that would be set for other partners and the fact that, without a substantial Afghanistan role, it would be hard to explain how Australia was sharing risks with its ally in active hard security terms. A hypothetical Australian pullout from Afghanistan would add both to the withdrawal of Australian combat forces from Iraq and to the question marks over Australian involvement in any future fronts in the Middle East in raising questions over Australia's global commitment to the alliance.

Australia in Asia

Turning to Southeast Asia, though Australia benefits from U.S. actions in supporting regional counterterrorism efforts, Canberra would be uncomfortable if the United States were to change course by allowing the fight against terrorism to dominate its regional diplomacy, unlikely though such a change might be. In particular, Canberra would disapprove of the United States putting emphasis back on a military-led counterterrorism strategy, the use of military force against suspected terrorist targets, the exaggeration of the maritime terrorist threat, or any policy approach that conflated the region's various insurgencies and radical movements into one danger. This is partly due to Australian sensitivity to ASEAN sovereignty concerns and the country's need to live with these neighbors come what may. More broadly, Australia would be concerned to see a return to U.S. policies toward Southeast Asia from the period shortly after September 11, which by focusing so much on terrorism helped allow China to build influence in the region.[45]

Australia would also be troubled, however, were the United States to define policy toward Southeast Asia primarily as a contest with China. Australia has no intrinsic problem with efforts by the United States or others in seeking to limit the extent of Chinese sway over external affairs decisionmaking in ASEAN capitals; indeed, some ASEAN countries, notably Indonesia, Singapore, and Vietnam, seem keen to engage other powers, including Australia, in soft balancing against China. Canberra, however, would prefer a sophisticated and multi-layered style of U.S. engagement with Southeast Asia, including expanding and sustaining recent efforts at diplomacy with ASEAN and ASEAN-centered institutions. Canberra will not see its interests, or those of Washington, well served if the United States allows challenges in other parts of the world, notably the Middle East, to distract from attention to an increasingly prosperous, powerful, and diplomatically confusing East Asia.

In considering options toward Asia, a new administration will want to be mindful not only of Australian interests but also of the ways in which Australian perspectives could inform and refine U.S. policy. In this context, the watchwords from an Australian point of view would be balance (in two senses of the word), engagement, inclusiveness, and attention. Though Australia, especially the country's security establishment, will appreciate a degree of soft balancing of Chinese power, Canberra will also encourage

---

[45] As recently as the September 2007 APEC summit, Bush focused a speech to regional business leaders on the war on terrorism, while Hu Jintao spoke of business opportunities. See Charles Hutzler, "Hu's Up, Bush Down at Pacific Rim Summit," Associated Press, September 7, 2007, http://www.washingtonpost.com/wp-dyn/content/article/2007/09/07/AR2007090701568.html.

Washington to consolidate recent progress in emphasizing engagement in an "engage and hedge" strategy toward Beijing. The Rudd government will be more sure than the Howard government was regarding the scope for and value of including China as a regional and global stakeholder, not only in diplomatic processes such as the six-party talks on North Korea but also in using the People's Liberation Army to provide international public goods such as maritime security, disaster relief, and peacekeeping. Australia's preference for inclusiveness will also extend to pursuing involvement in regional processes in which it has large interests: hence Canberra's effort to transcend geography and seek a place in any permanent security mechanism that might emerge from the six-party talks.[46]

On China specifically, Australia can be expected to be intent on minimizing prospects for U.S.-China strategic competition as well as on attempting to help forestall any movement toward major tensions in China's relations with other powers, notably Japan and India. If the United States becomes increasingly concerned about China as a security competitor, Washington could find itself needing to work harder to convince Australia—more so than Japan or India—that these concerns are well-founded and relevant to Australian interests.

Within the alliance, as well as within trilateral policy coordination involving Japan, a disconnect could emerge between Australian public opinion and broad foreign policy on one hand (in support of engaging China) and the capability preferences of the defense establishment on the other. Australia's involvement in missile defense research, a Howard-era legacy on which the Rudd government by mid-2008 still had not declared a final position, could become diplomatically hard to handle partly because of this tension. This is the case even though the limited, ship-based capabilities that interest Australia are neither being designed nor pursued with China primarily in mind.

Checklist for a Contemporary Alliance

Although the U.S.-Australia alliance is not in peril, a new administration in Washington cannot consistently assume a convergence of national interests or automatic Australian support for U.S. foreign and security policies, and would be ill-served by complacency or fitful attention toward Australia. Australia will continue to seek from the United States a

---

[46] "Australia Calls for Northeast Asia Security Structure," *ABC Radio Australia,* April 2, 2008, http://www.abc.net.au/ra/programguide/stories/200804/s2205827.htm.

sophisticated and multidimensional balance and depth in the integration of the alliance and Asia policies.

Accordingly, and taking into account the breadth of security and foreign policy challenges facing Australia, this chapter concludes with some general guidelines and specific prescriptions for the next administration to consider in handling the alliance.

Lock in the Howard-Bush Legacy

The administration will greatly benefit from striving to honor U.S. obligations under the agreements on free trade, intelligence sharing, and defense trade forged between Bush and Howard. Prioritizing the ratification of the U.S.-Australia Defense Trade Cooperation Treaty would help ensure continued progress toward interoperability of U.S. and Australian forces, help equip the Australian military for multiple roles in a wide range of contingencies that would serve U.S. interests in world order, and generally reassure Australia about the benefits accruing from ANZUS. While locking in this legacy, the United States would benefit from respecting the Labor style of being an independent-minded ally. Australia's Labor government will be at pains to emphasize its independence of thought and action. The government will seek to deliver, and to be seen to deliver, wise and forthright counsel to Washington with the candor of a friend who is not afraid to speak unpalatable truths. This is not entirely unlike the challenging definition of friendship (*zhengyou*) Rudd has offered to China.[47] Such an approach is likely at times to involve substantive criticism of aspects of U.S. policy and official analysis regarding Asia, China, nonproliferation, climate change, the conduct of the war on terrorism, and, potentially, the pros and cons of possible future U.S.-led military actions. The new administration would be well advised to accommodate a measure of such criticism, especially when offered in conjunction with policy alternatives consistent with U.S. interests. Given that Australia is sensitized to and possesses much expertise on East Asian affairs, such advice will more likely be useful to the United States in regard to this region than on most other issues. This is not to overlook the larger body of Asia expertise within the U.S. system but rather to observe the analytical benefits of testing such expertise against and synthesizing it with the alternative assessments and discreet advice Australia can offer.[48]

---

[47] Kevin Rudd, "A Conversation with China's Youth on the Future" (speech at Peking University, Beijing, April 9, 2008), http://www.pm.gov.au/media/Speech/2008/speech_0176.cfm.

[48] Rudd has made a similar point. See Rudd, "ANZUS in the 21st Century," 310.

Highlight Mutual Interests

The new administration may find it helpful to assist Rudd in convincing his party's Left that the alliance can serve the Left's definition of Australia's interests. In conjunction with the previous suggestion, the administration would do well to make some effort to adjust policy and rhetoric in ways that can help repair the damage to the U.S. image in Australia sustained over the past eight years. This will be easier on some issues than on others. Broad reaffirmations of support for the UN would help. One area where progress is possible is nuclear arms control. The prospect that renewed efforts at nuclear disarmament could be priorities under a new administration would enthuse an Australian Labor government: such an effort would be consistent with Australian policy and would help manage domestic constituencies. Such an eventuality would be not unlike the dynamic that prevailed in the 1980s, when the Hawke government was able to demonstrate to a worried Australian public that U.S.-Australia joint facilities helped maintain stable deterrence. The influence of the Kissinger, Schultz, Perry, and Nunn quartet in supporting a disarmament movement of "realistic idealists," the embrace of aspects of this agenda by the presidential candidates, and the disarmament language in the communiqué of the 2008 meeting of the Australian defense and foreign ministers and the U.S. secretary of defense and deputy secretary of state may be signs of things to come in this aspect of Australia-U.S. relations.[49] The Rudd government is convening a panel of international experts to chart a way forward in nuclear disarmament and in shoring up the NPT, and would welcome U.S. approval of this initiative.[50] Other Australian priorities would include encouraging U.S. ratification of the Comprehensive Test Ban Treaty, pursuit of a verifiable Fissile Material Cut-off Treaty, further U.S.-Russia arms reductions, and nuclear arms control in Asia.

Respect Differences

Not all of Canberra's and Washington's defense objectives or interests will align, notably those regarding Indonesia. Australia will be keen to encourage deeper U.S. security engagement with Indonesia, including arms sales, but only to a point. Even if Indonesia's consolidation of democracy and reasonably pro-Western foreign policy continue,

---

[49] For the communiqué, see "Australia-United States Ministerial Consultations: 2008 Joint Communiqué," Australian Department of Foreign Affairs and Trade website, http://www.dfat.gov.au/GEO/us/ausmin/ausmin08_joint_communique.html.

[50] Kevin Rudd, "Building a Better World Together" (speech at Kyoto University, Kyoto, June 9, 2008), http://www.pm.gov.au/media/Speech/2009/speech_0294.cfm.

Indonesia will be a country against which Australian defense planners will keep striving to preserve a capability edge. At the same time, it could well be in U.S. interests to influence Australian views and reduce lingering threat perceptions some Canberra officials hold concerning this large and successful Muslim democracy.

Recognize Australia's Defense Resource Limitations

The quality of the Australian military and Howard's frequent use of the ADF risk making Australia a victim of its own success, raising expectations unduly over how much the military can do. The United States will need to temper demands for Australian military support—bearing in mind that at any given time Australian forces are likely to be deployed in or are being held aside for a wide range of theaters (especially in Australia's neighborhood) on missions ranging from combat to stabilization to disaster relief. Disappointment with some European commitments to Afghanistan should not translate automatically into pressure on Canberra to do more. With the foregoing in mind, when the United States considers that an Australian force contribution would be diplomatically or militarily irreplaceable, Washington may find it beneficial to study Australia's circumstances closely, including any rationale given for opting out. There will be times when Australia's defense resources and public support for deployments are under heavy strain. There may also be times when other commitments serve more as an excuse than a reason for Canberra to say no.

Support Policy Consistency on Nuclear Challenges

Australia faces painful dilemmas in reconciling its policies on nuclear nonproliferation and disarmament, the role of nuclear energy in combating climate change, and uranium exports. Renewed U.S. engagement on nuclear disarmament would positively change the context in which the United States and others might seek Australia's involvement in efforts toward international oversight and management of the nuclear fuel cycle, thus potentially furthering nonproliferation, energy security, and emission reductions. Moreover, such a changed context, especially were both the United States and Australia to help draw India into a more constructive role in nuclear arms control, could also in time help the Rudd government revisit the question of uranium exports to consolidate Australia-India relations. Otherwise, continued stagnation and pessimism regarding international nuclear arms control could deepen the Australian public's concern and confusion over nuclear energy and nuclear weapons proliferation. This concern could increase the chances of Australia's isolating itself from global nuclear energy cooperation and from U.S.-led attempts to bring India into the nonproliferation mainstream.

Retain a Powerful Strategic Presence in Asia

For all of Australia's concern that Washington might put too much emphasis on the military side of U.S. diplomacy toward Asia, Australia does not want to see U.S. military disengagement from the region. Canberra continues to recognize that the U.S. military presence and alliance system underwrites Asia's peace and prosperity. This presence cannot be measured by a narrow calculus of troop numbers; Australia is comfortable with the lower U.S. profile involved in rebasing away from parts of South Korea and Japan. Strong U.S. strike and defensive capabilities, along with a visible maritime presence, remain very much in Australia's interests, and Australia is likely to remain broadly supportive of and reassured by a powerful concentration of U.S. forces on Guam. Canberra, however, would additionally like to see consistent patterns of engagement and diplomacy in the way these and other U.S. assets are shown to fit into wider U.S. objectives supporting regional stability, such as through implementing the new cooperation-based maritime strategy.

Avoid One-Dimensional Security Policy in Asia

A set of Asia policies defined narrowly through a lens of either counterterrorism or concerns over Chinese power will not resonate with Australia or Australians, and Australian proposals to embed such priorities in broader engagement with a changing Asia will warrant a hearing.[51] Terrorism and Chinese power are of concern to Canberra, but Australia wants to be confident that the United States will emphasize the preservation of regional stability and prosperity in cooperation with many regional partners and in the face of transnational challenges, changing major-power dynamics, and nascent regional structures.

Advance Regional Multilateral Forums in Asia

Rudd has signaled that Australia wants to consolidate and strengthen regional diplomatic architecture, perhaps through coordinating existing forums or seeking a new and overarching arrangement.[52] The APEC process

---

[51] Dibb, "Australia-United States," 46–47.

[52] Kevin Rudd, "Address to the Asia Society Australasia Centre, Sydney: It's Time to Build an Asia-Pacific Community" (speech to the Asia Society Australasia Centre, Sydney, June 4, 2008), http://www.pm.gov.au/media/Speech/2001/speech_0286.cfm.

is likely to decline as a strategic forum: membership in the organization, which includes Latin American countries, is motley, and China opposes expanding the security agenda of the organization due to Taiwan's participation. Meanwhile Asia-centric alternatives will likely become stronger. Australia might thus encourage the United States either to join the EAS or to help or take the lead in establishing a new forum.

The United States would be well advised to consider reviving the EAS membership option, which was rejected by the Bush administration. The EAS footprint is a coherent map of an economically enmeshed region (the ten ASEAN states, China, Japan, South Korea, India, Australia, and New Zealand) and also is largely comprised of countries that want and need an Asian order based on a workable accommodation between a strategically engaged United States and a powerful but not destabilizingly dominant China. If at the same time the United States sees scope for the six-party talks (perhaps minus North Korea) to be the kernel of a new regional security architecture, then Washington may want to seek a way to include Australia, as a member or an associate, given Australia's core economic equities in North Asia.

Another way in which the United States could easily strengthen its diplomatic capital in East Asia, and thus satisfy Australia and other allies regarding the U.S. commitment to the region, would be to engage more consistently with ASEAN and ARF, the region's only formal multilateral process devoted to a wide range of security issues. In recent years the U.S. secretary of state has skipped ARF foreign ministerial meetings as often as not. Another way for the United States to improve engagement with ASEAN states would be to move beyond Washington's on-again, off-again initiative for a summit with ASEAN leaders and make such a summit a firm annual institution.

Engage Australia in Engaging China

The Australia-U.S. alliance will be easier to handle in the years and decades ahead if the United States continues to consolidate its relationship with China as one in which engagement takes primacy over balancing. In thus "shaping China's global choices through diplomacy," to quote Deputy Assistant Secretary of State Thomas Christensen, Washington may see increasing benefit in enlisting Australia both as an interpreter of China and Chinese perspectives and as a regional voice in support of U.S. messages.[53] In

---

[53] Thomas J. Christensen, "Shaping China's Global Choices through Diplomacy," statement before the U.S.-China Economic and Security Review Commission, Washington, D.C., March 18, 2008, http://www.state.gov/p/eap/rls/rm/2008/03/102327.htm.

addition, the United States could implement its new cooperative maritime strategy by seeking opportunities to engage China, among other regional powers, in the provision of international public goods such as disaster relief. The United States would find Australia, with strong links in regional naval diplomacy, a useful player in any plurilateral efforts at security cooperation involving China.

Remember Australia while Deepening Security Ties with Japan and India

The Rudd government seems less convinced than was Howard's that there is overriding good in Washington strengthening defense ties with Japan and India. To the extent that the next administration continues in this direction, especially toward a perceived or actual balancing of Chinese power, Washington will likely have to make an extra effort to convince Canberra that such developments can contribute to a stable regional order and thus to Australian interests. One way that the United States might be able to persuade Australia (and perhaps even to some small extent China) that plurilateral security arrangements, such as the Trilateral Strategic Dialogue or even a quadrilateral dialogue that included India, could have stabilizing effects would be to allow partners the transparent use of such forums to seek to influence and moderate U.S. perspectives on security challenges.[54]

Be Clear Regarding Expectations

Finally—especially when there are differences with China, small, large, or critical—the United States would want to be mindful not to force Australia to choose when there is no pressing need to do so but also not to allow Australia to imagine or pretend there is no need to choose if there actually is. In particular, developing and sustaining a set of highly confidential discussions between the new U.S. administration and the Australian government would help clarify expectations on both sides in the event of key conceivable regional security crises, including regime collapse in North Korea, tensions between China and Japan, or a China-U.S. military confrontation.

---

[54] Rory Medcalf, "The Changing Asia-Pacific Security Web," *Age,* March 16, 2007, 15, available at http://www.lowyinstitute.org/Program_IntSecurity.asp.

STRATEGIC ASIA 2008–09

REGIONAL STUDIES

EXECUTIVE SUMMARY

This chapter considers U.S. policy toward Southeast Asia.

MAIN ARGUMENT:
The strategically pragmatic Southeast Asian states prefer that the U.S. maintains a strong presence in the region because they see the U.S. as playing a critical role in ensuring regional stability, an imperative that has increased with the rise of China. Key countries in the region are increasingly asserting their own interests, however, leveraging both the "second front in the war on terrorism" card and the China card in relations with the U.S.

POLICY IMPLICATIONS:
- In order to win reciprocal support for U.S. global strategic priorities, the new administration will find it helpful to pursue policy options that support Southeast Asian autonomy and regional strategic preoccupations.

- Given the centrality of economic development in Southeast Asia's strategic world-view and because the primary threats and opportunities resulting from China's rise are economic, it is important that the new administration build sustained economic relationships with all Southeast Asian countries.

- Limits to U.S. bilateral defense cooperation in the region will push the new administration to focus on a relatively independent U.S. military role that acts more as a deterrent to China than as outright containment of the country.

- Rather than intervene directly to support moderate factions of political Islam in the region—which might render moderate Muslim political and religious groups less credible at home—the new administration would instead benefit from focusing on policies to boost the governance, accountability, development, and conflict resolution capacities of Southeast Asian states that face problems with terrorism.

Southeast Asia: Strategic Diversification in the "Asian Century"

Evelyn Goh

In what has been widely touted as the "Asian century," the fortunes of Southeast Asia, a relatively less significant subregion of Asia, have improved but remain uncertain. Over the last eight years the strategic landscape in Southeast Asia has been marked by a sense of great uncertainty but also by unparalleled opportunity.

The uncertainty has been engendered by doubts concerning the continued strategic commitment of the United States to the region, by dissatisfaction over the U.S.-led war on terrorism, and by worries over the impact of that war on regional stability and domestic political security. Contributing to this uncertainty are continuing concerns with regard both to China's strategic intentions and to the at times difficult relations between China and other major powers (especially the United States and Japan). Southeast Asia has also, however, enjoyed a renaissance of opportunity arising both from the George W. Bush administration's explicit recognition of the region as a strategically important front in the global campaign against terrorism and from expanding relations with a rising China that by association have granted economic, political, and strategic significance to the region. By raising the region's strategic significance in military, political, and economic dimensions and by beginning to institutionalize important aspects of these higher-profile relationships with individual countries and with the Association of Southeast Asian Nations (ASEAN) as a whole, the

Evelyn Goh is Reader in International Relations at Royal Holloway, University of London. She can be reached at <evelyn.goh@rhul.ac.uk>.

This essay is based on Evelyn Goh, "Southeast Asian Reactions to America's New Strategic Imperatives," in *Asia Eyes America: Regional Perspectives on U.S. Asia-Pacific Strategy in the 21st Century*, ed. Jonathan D. Pollack (Newport: Naval War College, 2007).

Bush administration provided a critical post–Cold War turning-point for Southeast Asia. This level of increased significance has, in turn, provided crucial reassurance and opportunities for Southeast Asia—a region with a driving imperative for strategic diversification in order to avoid being dominated by any one power.

The following analysis departs from much of the prevailing literature that suggests that power in the region is shifting away from the United States toward China, criticizes the Bush administration for its inattention to the region, and makes the claim that U.S. unilateralism has alienated Southeast Asian states.[1] This chapter argues that the strategically pragmatic Southeast Asian states prefer to have a strong U.S. presence in the region because they see the United States as playing a critical role in ensuring regional stability. This imperative has increased rather than decreased with the rise of China. As such, the Bush administration's renewed focus on the region has been fundamentally welcomed at the larger strategic level, even as the administration's policies have created problems at the domestic political level and U.S. unilateralism has engendered widespread criticism. Any conclusion that U.S. policy and interests in Southeast Asia are in jeopardy reflects a failure to understand the strategic world-view, preferences, and dynamics of the region.

Thus, the incoming U.S. administration should approach Southeast Asia with the assurance that strategic partners and shared interests are to be found in this region, which welcomes U.S. attention, involvement, and preponderance. The new administration should be cognizant, however, that key countries in the region are not pushovers. These countries possess increasing bargaining leverage in dealing with the United States because they are the second front in the war on terrorism and they hold the China card. Based on an understanding of the regional imperative to diversify dependencies, the new administration will want to focus on developing policies that both support Southeast Asian autonomy and gain regional cooperation for U.S. strategic priorities. In this regard, the incoming administration will want to focus on two core challenges: China's regional influence and the war on terrorism.

As regards the first challenge, U.S. strategic competition with China has special resonance in Asia. In considering how to deal with a rising China, the new administration will need to decide under what conditions it might accept China as an Asian great power. In judging Beijing's long-term

[1] See, for instance, David Shambaugh, *Power Shift: China and Asia's New Dynamics* (Berkeley: University of California Press, 2005); Ellen Frost, *Asia's New Regionalism* (Boulder: Lynne Rienner, 2008); and Joshua Kurlantzick, *Charm Offensive: How China's Soft Power Is Transforming the World* (New Haven: Yale University Press, 2007). One exception is Robert Sutter, *China's Rise in Asia: Promises and Perils* (Lanham: Rowman and Littlefield, 2005), chap. 7.

intentions, the administration will want to pay attention to how China treats the smaller Southeast Asian states in a neighborhood that contains critical sealines of communication but no strong indigenous balancer. Though Southeast Asia has experienced encouraging results by enmeshing China in multilateral institutions and engaging the country in conflict management since the mid-1990s, tougher challenges lie ahead in such areas as delivery on trade agreements and the growing negative socio-environmental impacts of China's development, especially in the weaker Southeast Asian states in Mekong region.[2] These concerns help explain why the Southeast Asian states remain wary of China and continue to place importance on the U.S. strategic role in the region.

Second, Southeast Asia's importance to the United States in the war on terrorism will necessitate that the new administration pay more attention to managing the politics of alliances and strategic partnerships in the region. Intractable linkages exist between Washington's global strategic priorities and the balance of power politics within Southeast Asia. Linkages with domestic politics and ideologies may be, however, a more critical factor in determining the effectiveness of the new administration's approach to counterterrorism in the region. As demonstrated vividly over the last eight years in the issues of terrorism, religious politics, and human rights, the ideational and political agendas of strategic partners can constrain and even seriously undermine U.S. strategic imperatives in the region. The new administration will be well served by prioritizing clearly its strategic objectives in Southeast Asia and by developing more effective means—especially through recognizing and supporting local strategic preoccupations—to persuade critical countries in the region to support its agenda. This chapter suggests that the new administration prioritize the building of sustained and serious economic relationships with all Southeast Asian countries. Regarding military relations, Washington should continue to maintain a strong U.S. presence and indirect strategic support for partners in the region. The most sensitive policies, however, lie in the political dimension, where this chapter recommends that the new administration adopt more selective and indirect approaches to regional institutions and provide pragmatic ways to strengthen governance, education, and capacity-building throughout the region. It is difficult but not impossible to generalize regarding the ten countries that make up ASEAN. This chapter draws on broad areas of agreement among the

---

[2] See Evelyn Goh, *Developing the Mekong: Regionalism and Regional Security in China-Southeast Asian Relations,* Adelphi Paper 387 (London: Routledge, 2006).

states but identifies important ways in which their views, priorities, and expectations diverge regarding the United States.[3]

This chapter consists of four main sections. The first section describes in greater detail the strategic imperatives of Southeast Asian countries and introduces the shared constraints and principles that shape the region's policies toward the United States. The second section assesses Southeast Asia in the wake of the Bush presidency in terms of the critical strategic and security issues that preoccupy the region's leaders. The third and key section identifies the core regional strategic issues that pertain to the United States, discusses how the United States has responded to these challenges in light of its own strategic priorities, and evaluates the successes and limitations of the U.S. approach in the context of Southeast Asian constraints and differences. The chapter concludes by highlighting three outstanding "big picture" strategy questions that need to be addressed in U.S. relations with Southeast Asia and suggests changes in U.S. approaches to the region that will help secure mutual core strategic goals.

The Strategic Objectives of Southeast Asian States

As a collection of small- and medium-sized states that mostly gained independence after World War II, Southeast Asia suffers from some key external and internal strategic insecurities. The constraints under which Southeast Asian states both perceive themselves and formulate policies, and the key principles that these states have developed to cope with such limitations, warrant critical attention from the new U.S. administration.

Southeast Asian states essentially wish to maximize the limited autonomy that small states can expect to possess in the international system. Historically, the bitter post-independence dispute between Indonesia and

---

[3] The theoretical construct of this analysis—Southeast Asia's strategic diversification—is a further elaboration of "omni-enmeshment," a concept the author has developed in-depth in Evelyn Goh, "Great Powers and Hierarchical Order in Southeast Asia: Analyzing Regional Security Strategies," *International Security* 32, no. 3 (Winter 2007/08): 113–57. For definitional purposes, omni-enmeshment is engaging with a state to draw it into deep involvement in international and regional society, enveloping the state in a web of sustained exchanges and relationships, with the long-term aim of integration. In the process, the target state's interests are redefined, and its identity possibly altered, so as to take into greater account the integrity and order of the system. Building on this notion, "strategic diversification" in this chapter refers to a state's implementation of omni-enmeshment on a range of pivotal issues that advance that state's strategic interests and leverage vis-à-vis the target state. This chapter will explain the key drivers, variables, and conditions underpinning Southeast Asia's strategic diversification approaches on issues germane to U.S. policies in the region. For reference, the catalogue of issues identified in this chapter is analogous to Evelyn Goh, "Southeast Asian Reactions to America's New Strategic Imperatives," in *Asia Eyes America: Regional Perspectives on U.S. Asia-Pacific Strategy in the 21st Century*, ed. Jonathan D. Pollack (Newport: Naval War College, 2007). To elucidate the challenges and choices on Southeast Asia facing the next U.S. administration, this chapter provides further granularity on these strategic issues.

Malaysia for bilateral and regional leadership ensured that the original core regional security principle of ASEAN was the prevention of intramural hegemony.[4] This renunciation of indigenous dominance has also been transposed as preventing regional hegemony by any one external power. Thus, anti-hegemony is a central theme in the regional strategic discourse.

Regional strategic policies are motivated by two intervening drivers—uncertainty and diversification. An important driver and instrument of strategy for ASEAN states, uncertainty is the principle by which these relatively small and diverse states manifest their deep collective sense of vulnerability vis-à-vis bigger actors. The Southeast Asian states' apprehension over the growing might of China and sensitivity to the crucial role of the United States in regional security underscore their need to manage uncertainty. Indeed, the issue of U.S. interest and commitment is a constant theme in the management of regional uncertainty, most notably in the wake of the U.S. withdrawal from Vietnam in 1978 and following the end of the Cold War in 1989. After the terrorist attacks of September 11 Southeast Asian states worried that Washington's attention would be focused on the Middle East and at home to the exclusion of other parts of the world. In Southeast Asia, both regional security strategies involving military relationships with major powers and regional security institutions are derived to manage these uncertainties.[5]

To cope with their inevitable dependence on the vagaries of great-power preferences, policies, and actions, Southeast Asian states have adopted strategic diversification, the second driver. It is important to understand that although all the major Southeast Asian states—Indonesia, Malaysia, the Philippines, Singapore, Thailand, and Vietnam—openly acknowledge that they cannot avoid being within the ambit of the great powers these states nonetheless share the vigorous desire not to fall into the exclusive sphere of influence of any one great power.[6] Therefore, a critical strategy for these states is the diversification of dependence—in economic and strategic terms—on the United States, Japan, China, and, increasingly, India.[7] To this end, the Southeast Asian states regard the United States as a guarantee

[4] Michael Leifer, *ASEAN and the Security of South-East Asia* (London: Routledge, 1989); and Ralf Emmers, *Cooperative Security and the Balance of Power in ASEAN and the ARF* (London: RoutledgeCurzon, 2003).

[5] Yuen Foong Khong, "Coping with Strategic Uncertainty: The Role of Institutions and Soft Balancing in Southeast Asia's Post–Cold War Strategy," in *Rethinking Security in East Asia: Identity, Power, and Efficiency*, ed. J.J. Suh, Peter J. Katzenstein, and Allen Carlson (Stanford: Stanford University Press, 2004), 172–208.

[6] See Evelyn Goh, ed., *Betwixt and Between: Southeast Asian Strategic Relations with the U.S. and China*, IDSS Monograph no. 7 (Singapore: Institute of Defence and Strategic Studies, 2005).

[7] Alice Ba, "Southeast Asia and China," in Goh, *Betwixt and Between*, 103.

in two ways. Geographical distance mutes U.S. domination, and the non-imperial history of the United States suggests the benignity of U.S. power; additionally, U.S. strategic dominance provides a very real bulwark that deters potential dominance by any other Asian great power. In other words, Southeast Asian states derive hope from the expectation that a rising power such as China will always be balanced out in the regional strategic landscape by the dominance of the United States—and that together the United States, China, and other powers will offer smaller states multiple opportunities in the strategic realm.[8] For Washington, understanding that Southeast Asian policymakers prefer maintaining U.S. strategic primacy in the region expands the strategic space to maximize options. Even as Southeast Asian states work to incorporate and socialize China as a regional great power, they concurrently help buttress the U.S. presence in the region and desire an even greater economic, if not military, role for the United States in order to maintain the clear gap in capabilities between the two big powers.[9]

Despite their strategic preference for underlying U.S. dominance, the Southeast Asian states experience recurring tensions between the strong desire for autonomy and the pragmatic recognition of inevitable dependency. These tensions lead to somewhat schizophrenic Southeast Asian strategic relations with Washington that are often accompanied by strong rhetoric, vociferous advocacy within the region and in the United States as well as sophisticated political manipulation.[10] Fundamentally, there is pragmatic recognition of the United States as a superpower and the inevitability of the U.S. footprint on the region. Beyond that, however, there is a continuum of opinion ranging from deep appreciation of the United States as a benign superpower and essential stabilizing force in the region (Singapore's perspective)[11] to the grudging acknowledgement of the United States as the power capable of deterring and balancing other

[8] Goh, "Southeast Asian Reactions," 202–3.

[9] For an explicit analysis of the Southeast Asian strategy of facilitating a U.S.-led regional hierarchy, see Goh, "Great Powers and Hierarchical Order in Southeast Asia."

[10] See, for instance, Kishore Mahbubani, *Beyond the Age of Innocence: Rebuilding the Trust between America and the World* (New York: PublicAffairs, 2005); and Kishore Mahbubani, *The New Asian Hemisphere: The Irresistible Shift of Global Power to the East* (New York: PublicAffairs, 2008).

[11] According to the former prime minister of Singapore, Goh Chok Tong, the United States is a "reassuring and stabilising force" in Southeast Asia and the U.S. presence a "determining reason for the peace and stability Asia enjoys today." See Goh Chok Tong, "ASEAN-US Relations: Challenges" (speech delivered to the Asia Society, New York, September 7, 2000), http://www.asiasociety.org/speeches/tong.html.

regional powers, even if Washington's specific policies are unattractive (the perspective held by Malaysia and Vietnam).[12]

The Current Southeast Asian Security Landscape

Although counterterrorism will likely continue to be the major U.S. strategic preoccupation, it is critical for the new administration to understand that terrorism has not been a central strategic issue for Southeast Asian states, either before or since September 11. Rather, the chief features of the regional strategic landscape—the key challenges that regional leaders currently face—are twofold. The overarching strategic challenge is how to manage great-power involvement in the region as the balance of power shifts with the rise of China and the continued preponderance of the United States. The second challenge is the constant and sometimes overwhelming imperative of domestic resilience and nation-building for states that are still struggling to manage religious and ethnic diversity, transitions to democratic governance, economic reforms, and development in the face of unprecedented economic competition.

Managing the Balance of External Powers

The management of great-power relations is not an abstract grand strategic enterprise; for the Southeast Asian states, managing these relations constitutes national and regional security in vital ways. Structurally, the main challenge is how to incorporate China into international society, or more specifically how to make room for China without getting subsumed into the country's sphere of influence and without alienating other major powers, especially the United States. Though the Southeast Asian states agree on the need to maintain the diversity of great-power involvement in the region, the preferences of individual states run a spectrum, depending on their ability to create strategic options. At a collective level the ASEAN grouping has tried hard to institutionalize multiple great-power interests in the region, most prominently through the ASEAN Regional Forum (ARF). The Southeast Asian states established ARF at the end of the Cold War as a

---

[12] For analyses of Malaysia's strategic outlook and facilitation of U.S. military presence in the region, see Amitav Acharya, "Containment, Engagement, or Counter-dominance? Malaysia's Response to the Rise of China," in *Engaging China: The Management of an Emerging Power*, ed. Alastair Iain Johnston and Robert S. Ross (London: Routledge, 1999), 139–40; and "US and Malaysia Extend Defence Pact by 10 Years," *Straits Times*, May 10, 2005. On Vietnam's growing relations with the United States in the context of constraints posed by China, see Evelyn Goh, *Meeting the China Challenge: The U.S. in Southeast Asian Regional Security Strategies*, Policy Studies 16 (Washington, D.C.: East-West Center Washington, 2005); and Le Linh Lan, "Vietnam," in Goh, *Betwixt and Between*, 73–82.

way of keeping the United States involved in the region, socializing China in peaceful regional norms, and enmeshing both powers in regional security dialogue with the aim of facilitating peaceful adjustment to the changing distribution of power in the region.[13] ARF continued to develop during the Bush administration, despite disagreements among ASEAN states over the speed of institutional progress.

The regional rhetoric in Southeast Asia overtly promotes a "balance" of power among the major players.[14] Operationally, however, what is meant by this rhetoric is unclear: though in common usage "balance of power" implies an equilibrium in the distribution of power among the major powers, many Southeast Asian policymakers favor the continued preponderance of what they perceive as benign U.S. power in the region. This preference is evident in the various ways in which key countries support the U.S. military and political presence in Southeast Asia. Apart from the Philippines and Thailand, which are formal U.S. allies, Singapore has the strongest defense links with the United States. Singapore hosts a U.S. naval logistics command center and built a naval base to berth U.S. aircraft carriers. Despite domestic political constraints, Indonesia and Malaysia also maintain military ties with the United States, including port call arrangements, ship repair facilities, and discreet joint exercises. These alliances and strategic partnerships were all boosted during the Bush administration's war on terrorism. At the end of 2001, U.S. troops returned to the ground in the Philippines to help Manila in its fight against Abu Sayyaf separatists in Mindanao. By 2003 the Philippines and Thailand had been elevated to major non-NATO ally status, and in 2005 Singapore increased bilateral security cooperation with the United States under a new framework agreement that covered counterterrorism, counterproliferation of WMD, joint military exercises and training, and defense technology.[15] The Bush administration also restored bilateral military relations with Indonesia in 2005, ending a boycott that had been

---

[13] Evelyn Goh and Amitav Acharya, "The ASEAN Regional Forum: Comparing Chinese and American Positions," in *Advancing East Asian Regionalism,* ed. Melissa Curley and Nicholas Thomas (London: Routledge, 2007), 96–115; Alastair Iain Johnston, "Socialization in International Institutions: The ASEAN Way and International Relations Theory," in *International Relations Theory and the Asia-Pacific,* ed. G. John Ikenberry and Michael Mastanduno (New York: Columbia University Press, 2003), 107–62; and Khong, "Coping with Strategic Uncertainty," 202.

[14] See, for instance, recent statements to this effect by Juwono Sudarsono, Indonesian minister of defense, in "Jakarta Minister Warns Washington to Redefine Its Role in the Region," *Straits Times,* June 5, 2006. See also statements by Fidel Ramosin, former president of the Philippines, in Ralph A. Cossa, "Pax Asia Pacifica?" Center for Strategic and International Studies, PacNet, no. 30, June 28, 2006, http://www.csis.org/media/csis/pubs/pac0630.pdf.

[15] Major non-NATO ally status makes Thailand and the Philippines eligible for priority delivery of defense materiel and the purchase of certain controlled items such as depleted-uranium tank rounds. These two states are allowed to stockpile U.S. military hardware, participate in defense R&D programs, and benefit from a U.S. government loan guarantee program for arms exports.

in place since Indonesia's controversial military intervention in East Timor in 1991. These Southeast Asian states have been eager to support the U.S. strategic imperative of counterterrorism primarily as a means to anchor U.S. interest in the region. At the same time, these states have opportunistically logrolled their own long-standing counter-insurgency battles under the counterterrorism rubric, thereby gaining impetus and political support for these old problems in the new atmosphere post–September 11. Thus, these states do not regard the fact that U.S. troops have fought part of the war on terrorism on Southeast Asian soil (in the Philippines) as a problem, given that this U.S. action coincides with the interests and needs of Manila and neighboring states such as Malaysia, which have suffered spillover effects from the insurgency in Mindanao. As discussed further in the next section, however, the limits of this mutuality of interest have been tested. The war in Iraq, specifically, has created problems. For instance, domestic opposition forced Thailand to surreptitiously provide overflight and basing facilities for U.S. operations, and President Arroyo withdrew Philippine troops from Iraq in exchange for a Filipino worker kidnapped in 2005.[16] These are examples of the need to bind the superpower to the region giving way to a state's domestic political constraints.

Against the background of general agreement among ASEAN states that a forward U.S. military presence is essential to regional stability, however, there is still a spectrum of positions in Southeast Asia vis-à-vis the relative roles of the United States and China. At one end of the spectrum are countries that engage with China but place greater faith in strategic relations with the United States. The Philippines and Singapore are at this end. The Philippines is motivated by its alliance with the United States and by territorial disputes with China in the South China Sea, whereas Singapore has, for political and ideological reasons, deepened strategic identification with Washington since September 11. In the middle of the spectrum are countries that seem to be steering a course between the two powers, due to their geographical distance from China and to domestic political constraints on their pursuit of closer overt strategic ties with Washington. Indonesia and Malaysia fall under this category. Although supporting U.S. presence in the region, policymakers in both these countries evince sufficient concern over the unilateralism and apparent anti-Islamism of U.S. foreign policy to suggest the need to carefully balance out U.S. influence with Chinese influence. At the opposite end of the spectrum are countries whose security

16 On support from Thailand, see N. Ganesan, "Thaksin and the Politics of Domestic and Regional Consolidation in Thailand," *Contemporary Southeast Asia* 26, no. 1 (April 2004): 26–44; and Chookiat Panaspornprasit, "Thailand: Political Thaksinization," in *Southeast Asian Affairs 2004*, ed. K. Kesavapany (Singapore: Institute of Southeast Asian Studies, 2004): 264–65.

strategies are more closely dominated by the central role of China. These are the continental Southeast Asian countries: Myanmar, Thailand, and the Indochinese states (Vietnam, Cambodia, and Laos)—all of which are constrained strategically by China for different reasons. Thailand views China as a status quo power and places great emphasis on the economic opportunities China provides. Thus, Thailand attempts to maximize its hedging strategy by maintaining close ties with both powers but, despite an alliance with the United States, prefers a relationship that is "not too close."[17] In comparison, between 2003 and 2005 Vietnam accepted the first port call by a U.S. frigate since the Vietnam War, participated in the joint Cobra Gold military exercises, and started sending military officers to training in the United States. Even though Vietnam has a more recent history of conflict with the United States, the real constraint that limits the extent of Vietnam's strategic relations with the United States is Hanoi's desire not to alienate and antagonize China. The historical animosity between Vietnam and China is long and bitter, and they still have unresolved territorial disputes in the South China Sea, but Hanoi's current priority is to avoid conflict with China and concentrate on economic and national development. The strategic options available to Cambodia, Laos, and Myanmar are even more limited given their underdevelopment and location, and, in the case of Myanmar, diplomatic isolation.[18] Whether and how this spectrum of preferences and constraints affects Southeast Asia-U.S. strategic ties depends upon the extent and depth to which the two sides may wish to push current arrangements. Current divergences in the strategic positions of Southeast Asian states primarily follow the maritime-continental divide and secondarily the divide between Muslim and non-Muslim states. Any attempt by Washington either to develop forward basing or close defense relations in the continental hinterland of Southeast Asia or to push for more overt defense cooperation with Thailand, Indonesia, or Malaysia will likely encounter serious limitations.

External great powers are also critical to economic development in Southeast Asia, where economic security cannot be separated from national and regional security. Government leaders in the region see economic growth and development as the basic facilitator of socio-political progress, regime stability, and peaceful state-society and inter-state relations.[19] In this regard, the United States also plays a critical role as the largest market for Southeast Asia and one of the top investors in the region. All Southeast Asian

---

[17] Author interviews with Thai policy advisers, Bangkok, August 2004 and April 2007.

[18] The foregoing summary derives from Evelyn Goh, "Introduction," in Goh, *Betwixt and Between*, 1–8.

[19] Leifer, *ASEAN and the Security of South-East Asia,* chap. 1.

states are currently preoccupied with managing growing competition—from China, in particular, but also from India—and coping with the restructuring of the regional production networks around China; in this context, the roles of the United States and Japan as the traditional economic powerhouses in the region have in fact become even more important.

Although the net outcome of China's economic growth on Southeast Asia is still debated, it appears that China and many Southeast Asian countries are more competitive than complementary in their economic goals. The widespread concern regarding Chinese competition for foreign investments in the region is symptomatic: while ASEAN currently secures 20% of FDI in Asia (excluding Japan), China has been attracting 50–70%. Some analysts argue that the drop in the level of FDI flowing to ASEAN is more the result of fallout from the 1997 financial crisis than of direct competition from China, but the figures still pose questions over Southeast Asia's long-term ability to attract FDI. Southeast Asian manufacturing faces stiff Chinese competition as rapid growth and foreign investment make China the world's preeminent low-cost manufacturer, not only of traditional labor-intensive goods like textiles but increasingly of IT, hardware, and electronics. Vietnam, Indonesia, and Thailand are especially worried about intensifying Chinese competition for U.S. and European Union (EU) textile quotas, and the rapid expansion of China's nontraditional exports such as machinery and electronics is having the most disruptive impact on Indonesia, Thailand, Malaysia, and the Philippines.[20] China's export-led economic growth over the last two decades has led to the reconfiguration of the vertical production chain across East Asia, with component manufacturing retained in more technologically advanced or better-skilled locations—such as Taiwan, Singapore, and Thailand—and final assembly taking place in China.[21]

Thus, Southeast Asian states now have the urgent imperative not to get pulled into a Sinocentric regional economic order. In this context, the need to diversify economic dependencies by maintaining and deepening ties with the United States, Japan, and other economic powers becomes

---

[20] "China Boom Will Boost Region's Prosperity," *Straits Times,* April 25, 2002; "Turning a Rising China into Positive Force for Asia," *Straits Times,* September 26, 2001; and Friedrich Wu et al., "Foreign Direct Investments to China and ASEAN: Has ASEAN Been Losing Out?" *Economic Survey of Singapore* (Third Quarter 2002): 96–115, http://app.mti.gov.sg/data/article/355/doc/ESS_2002Q3_FDI.pdf.

[21] In other words, "the balance of power over what is produced in East Asia has not dramatically shifted...what we see instead is China acting as the manufacturing conduit through which the regional deficit is processes, with China running deficits with 'supplier' states in East Asia, and surpluses with 'demand' states in Europe and North America." Shaun Breslin, "Power and Production: Rethinking China's Global Economic Role," *Review of International Studies* 31, no. 4 (October 2005): 743.

especially important. A prominent example of this diversification strategy is the regional drive toward trade agreements with major powers. Shortly after the United States and Singapore announced talks for a free-trade agreement (FTA) in 2000, China decided to open negotiations for an FTA with ASEAN, which was endorsed in June 2001 with a target date of completion in 2010.[22] Japan followed suit by signing its first regional FTA with Singapore in January 2002 and by proposing to launch talks for an FTA with ASEAN, also with a target date of 2010.[23] South Korea has agreed to implement an FTA with ASEAN by 2016. Furthermore, Australia signed an FTA with Singapore in July 2003 and announced in November 2004 that Canberra would begin negotiations for an ASEAN-wide FTA. Following agreements with Singapore and Thailand in 2004–05, India is currently negotiating an FTA with ASEAN as a whole. Among the institutional links Southeast Asian states are building with Middle East countries are the Thai-initiated Asian Cooperation Dialogue and the Singapore-initiated Asia-Middle East Dialogue (AMED).[24]

Managing Intra-regional and Domestic Challenges

Coping with structural competition, adjustment, and reform in the economic realm is one key aspect of the intractable domestic political challenges and security concerns that consume a significant proportion of the attention of key Southeast Asian governments. Regime security and governance concerns confronted by these governments range from democratic transition and national reconstruction in post-Suharto Indonesia to political instability and civil-military tensions in Thailand and the Philippines. Both governments face constant high-level pressures from a variety of domestic political exigencies, including unruly coalitions and opposition parties playing on ethnic or religious sentiment, military coups, and elections. These same states also face domestic insurgency and separatism—in Aceh, Mindanao, and the south of Thailand—all of which are long-running conflicts arising from dissatisfaction with political representation and socio-economic distribution. These domestic political issues often relate to broader regional or international security issues, including Washington's global counterterrorism campaign, but the Southeast Asian governments involved often make policy decisions with

---

[22] The Singapore-U.S. FTA was signed in 2004. Talks for a bilateral Singapore-China FTA are in progress.

[23] Kwan Weng Jin, "Japan Moots Regional Free Trade Pact by 2010," *Straits Times,* April 5, 2006.

[24] For details of the Asia-Middle East Dialogue (AMED), see the organization's website http://app.amed.sg/internet/amed/homepage.asp.

their domestic considerations firmly at the forefront of their agendas. As discussed in the next section, this leads to a disjuncture between U.S. policy priorities and deeper domestic expectations and concerns within Southeast Asia.

In addition to domestic political considerations, key intra-regional conflicts and suspicions are crucial drivers of foreign policy. These intra-regional conflicts include the historical conflict (*confrontasi*) between Indonesia and Malaysia; Singapore-Malaysia tensions over issues ranging from ethnic conflict to communication links to water supplies; Malaysian territorial disputes with Singapore, the Philippines, and Indonesia; Thai-Vietnamese tensions over borders, migration, and leadership in continental Southeast Asia; and competing claims to islands in the South China Sea involving the Philippines, Vietnam, and Malaysia. Disagreements over how to approach the problems associated with the isolationist junta government of Myanmar, which is contentious within as well as outside the region, increasingly also pose a conflict.

Finally, as a region defined by a multiplicity of fluid land and maritime borders and overlapping sealines of communication, Southeast Asia is often preoccupied with so-called nontraditional security issues that are transboundary and non-military in nature. These issues include infectious diseases such as SARS, avian flu, and AIDS; piracy; the trafficking of drugs, arms, and people; money laundering; and terrorism. These issues form the core of regional security cooperation in Southeast Asia. This is important to note because such issues lend themselves to a distinctive set of coping mechanisms that emphasize cooperation through high-level political commitment trickling downward to agreements for joint monitoring, information sharing, policing, legislative development, and other non-military activities. In turn, this approach has influenced how Southeast Asian states prefer to deal with the newer threat of transnational terrorism linked to the international networks that target the United States. Thus, there is an inherent tension between the highly militarized U.S. approach to counterterrorism and a more diversified set of regional concerns that are removed from the classic national security paradigm.[25]

The United States and Southeast Asia

The task of relating the strategic challenges Southeast Asian states face to U.S. strategic interests is made difficult by the asymmetry of power

---

[25] See Jonathan Stevenson, "Demilitarising the 'War on Terror,'" Survival 48, no. 2 (Summer 2006): 37–54.

and influence. Although the United States looms large in Southeast Asian regional security calculations, the region, by contrast, is relatively peripheral to leaders in Washington, whose focus is on managing worldwide strategic interests and crises. The Bush administration's approach to the region has been characterized by continuation of three elements: a relatively low priority on the region in U.S. foreign policy, a focus on bilateral relations with key countries (rather than a collective regional focus), and a view of the region firmly through lenses of broader, global imperatives.

U.S. strategic interests are directly affected by a number of the key strategic preoccupations of Southeast Asian states, including the impact of China's rise, various violent insurgency movements, democratic transition, and regional transnational security issues. U.S. responses to these challenges have been framed in terms of U.S. national security objectives (particularly counterterrorism and counterproliferation) and filtered through existing bilateral security relations with specific states. Washington has developed these responses in the context of affirming U.S. intent to remain the leading power in the Asia-Pacific. The following analyzes the four main challenges that the Bush administration has focused on in its approach toward Southeast Asia: counterterrorism, maritime security, economic growth, and maintaining U.S. leadership.

Counterterrorism

Southeast Asia is an important front in the U.S.-led war on terrorism. As discussed in the previous section, the Bush administration intensified security relations—including military, intelligence, and policing—with Southeast Asian allies and friends and reintroduced troops into the Philippines.

Because Washington has identified extremist Islamic terrorism as the primary threat to U.S. security, Southeast Asia, with its sizable and mainly moderate Muslim populations, has taken on particular and exemplary significance in the current administration's longer-term battle for "hearts and minds." Notably, the Bush administration has tried to cultivate Malaysia as the model of a modern, moderate Muslim state, despite former prime minister Mahathir Mohamad's voluble anti-Western rhetoric and Kuala Lumpur's sometimes critical stance on U.S. policy in the Middle East. Thus, Prime Minister Abdullah Badawi's *Islam Hadhari* ("civilizational Islam," a mode of Islamic governance distinct from other, more radical brands of Islam) concept has been praised by U.S. officials as a tolerant and modern version of the religion, and Washington has held up Malaysia's inter-ethnic power-sharing structure as an example for the government in Iraq.[26] Underlying Washington's policies in particular has been a conviction that the Southeast Asian brand of Islam is more moderate, and that in this region there is a rising Muslim middle class consisting of devout Muslim professionals who are pragmatic and receptive to certain Western ideas and values. The Bush administration has therefore tried to boost proponents of moderate Islam in Southeast Asia as a countervailing force against radical Islam.

At the same time, Washington has also tried to support the democratically elected government in Indonesia, the largest Muslim country in the world. After the devastating tsunami in December 2004, the rapid relief efforts of U.S. forces helped to boost favorable public perceptions of the United States in Indonesia, but more important to Jakarta was the restoration in 2005 of International Military Education and Training (IMET) and Foreign Military Financing (FMF). Visits to Jakarta by Secretary of Defense Donald Rumsfeld (in 2005) and his successor Robert Gates (in 2008) underscored the changes in U.S. policy toward Indonesia. Limits remain, however, on the pace and extent to which full bilateral military relations can be resumed.[27]

Fighting terrorism has also entailed the promotion of democracy and human rights in Southeast Asia. The linkage between democracy, human rights, and ethnic harmony in forestalling terrorism and ensuring national security was clear in Bush's State of the Union address in January 2006:

> On September the 11th, 2001, we found that problems originating in a failed and oppressive state 7,000 miles away could bring murder and destruction to our country. Dictatorships shelter terrorists, and feed resentment and radicalism, and seek weapons of mass destruction. Democracies replace resentment with hope, respect the rights of their citizens and their neighbors, and join the fight against terror. Every step toward freedom in the world makes our country safer.[28]

Democracy promotion has thus become an important pillar of U.S. policies toward Southeast Asia, and especially toward Indonesia, regarded by the Bush administration as the hotbed of extremist Islamic terrorist threats in the region. Though few Southeast Asian leaders have publicly criticized the administration's aspirational statements, ASEAN states have serious reservations about the administration's blanket goal of democracy promotion, as discussed below. These reservations arise from common

---

[26] "Iraq Can Learn from BN Formula," *New Straits Times*, October 25, 2005.

[27] "U.S. Wants Military Cooperation Boosted," *Jakarta Post*, June 7, 2005; and Bruce Gale, "Ties with US Far from Cosy," *Straits Times*, March 21, 2008.

[28] George W. Bush, "State of the Union Address by the President" (speech given at the U.S. Capitol, Washington, D.C., January 31, 2006), http://www.whitehouse.gov/stateoftheunion/2006/.

regional sensitivity about external interference in domestic affairs and from the troubled nature of democracy in many of these states.

Maritime Security

Historically, Southeast Asia's strategic value derives from its geographical position as a critical maritime thoroughfare between the Persian Gulf and Indian Ocean and the Pacific Ocean. Many of the world's trade and energy shipments, as well as significant levels of U.S. assistance to friends and allies, flow through this route. In the new strategic climate, therefore, Southeast Asian sea routes have come under special scrutiny in relation to new terrorist threats to container security and the transport and proliferation of WMD.

At the global level, Southeast Asia is an evitable focus of U.S. initiatives to secure maritime trade against terrorism. These initiatives include the Container Security Initiative (CSI), of which Thailand and Singapore are members, and the Proliferation Security Initiative (PSI), which promotes international cooperation for the interdiction of WMD at sea. The first Southeast Asian PSI exercise was conducted in the South China Sea in August 2005, with participation from Singapore, Japan, Australia, and New Zealand.

Regionally, U.S. leadership in maritime security initiatives has been more problematic. In 2004 then commander-in-chief of the U.S. Pacific Command, Admiral Thomas Fargo, proposed a Regional Maritime Security Initiative (RMSI) in which U.S. naval forces would cooperate with littoral states to provide security in the Strait of Malacca. This suggestion was met with opposition from Malaysia and Indonesia, both of which objected to U.S. patrols in their territorial waters. Subsequently, the three littoral states—Singapore, Malaysia and Indonesia—agreed on coordinated trilateral naval patrols. In July 2005 these three states requested equipment, training, and intelligence assistance from other countries, including the United States, Japan, and Australia. Later that year these states and Thailand added joint anti-piracy aerial patrols (the Eyes in the Sky program) and indicated that the United States and Australia might be invited to participate at a later stage.[29]

Obstacles to a prominent role for the United States in regional maritime security stem in part from differences in priorities among the Southeast Asian littoral states, the United States, and other user states. The

---

[29] That said, at the 2006 Shangri-La Dialogue Secretary of Defense Donald Rumsfeld stated that the United States is "satisfied" with the efforts of the littoral states to secure the straits and would play a role only if these states wanted it to do so. See "US Not Looking to Increase Presence in Region," *Straits Times,* June 5, 2006.

latter grouping, along with Singapore, is most concerned over piracy and the threat of maritime terrorism. Malaysia and Indonesia, however, place priority on other issues, including territorial and maritime sovereignty, the difficulties of policing a traditionally mobile transborder maritime population, combating arms trafficking to and by separatist rebels, piracy threats to fishermen, and environmental pollution.[30]

Economic Growth

In general, the Southeast Asian states perceive economic growth and development as beneficial to regional stability because it increases interdependence and cooperation and raises the costs of armed conflict. Southeast Asia is the fourth-largest U.S. trading partner, with two-way trade of over $183 billion in 2007 and U.S. direct investment of over $90 billion in 2006. One notable development in economic policy under the Bush administration has been the Enterprise for ASEAN Initiative (EAI), which provides a dialogue framework for countries that are ready to negotiate bilateral free-trade agreements with the United States. Though ASEAN countries remain subject to the same conditions as before EAI, and no government expects negotiations to be easy, the initiative is a sign of Washington's recognition of the economic imperatives of the region.

Southeast Asian bilateral trade with the United States increased during the Bush administration, though not as dramatically as did trade with China (see **Figure 1**). ASEAN exports to the United States, which amounted to $80,550 million in 2000, had increased to $109,322 million by 2007. Although still below the level of exports to the United States, ASEAN exports to China also increased between 2000 and 2007. Having surpassed the level of exports to Japan in 2007, the region's exports to China are poised to surpass the level of those to the United States in the near future.

ASEAN's imports from the United States increased during the Bush administration as well (see **Figure 2**). From a starting point of $51,609 million in 2000, imports from the United States increased to $74,014 million in 2007. Southeast Asian imports from China have surged from $18,652 million in 2000 to $104,435 million in 2007, surpassing in 2006 the level of imports from Japan. Increasing trade volume between ASEAN and each of these states suggests that the region is building stronger economic ties with all three major powers.

---

[30] Sam Bateman, "Burden Sharing in the Straits: Not So Straightforward," Institute of Defence and Strategic Studies, IDSS Commentaries, no. 17, March 20, 2006, 1–3, http://www.ntu.edu.sg/rsis/publications/Perspective/IDSS0172006.pdf; and Sheldon Simon, "U.S.-Southeast Asia Relations," *Comparative Connections* 6, no. 4 (January 2005): 68.

FIGURE 1   Southeast Asian exports, 2000–07

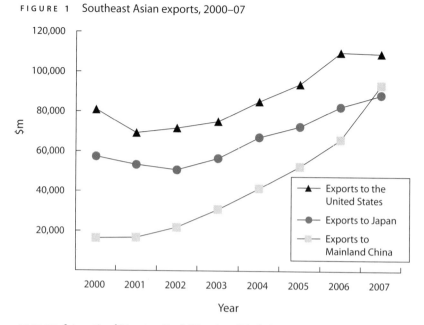

SOURCE: International Monetary Fund, Direction of Trade Statistics Database, 2008.

Singapore was the first Southeast Asian country to sign an FTA with the United States in January 2004, and a Thai-U.S. FTA is currently being negotiated. The Philippines and Malaysia have trade and investment framework agreements (TIFA) with the United States, and Kuala Lumpur began FTA negotiations with Washington in 2006. Some regard these developments as political rewards for cooperation in the war against terrorism, but Southeast Asian states generally value economic agreements and believe that FTAs will have beneficial consequences that outlast the campaign against terrorists.

After four years of lamenting that Southeast Asia had been reduced to a front in the war on terrorism—at the expense of all else—regional leaders and policymakers greeted the May 2005 tour of the region by Robert Zoellick, then deputy secretary of state, as a symbolic turning point. Zoellick very effectively conveyed the impression that Washington would not ignore issues of concern to the region, chief among which was the maintenance and extension of economic ties with the United States.[31]

---

[31] Evelyn Goh, "Southeast Asia Bright on US Radar Screen," *Asia Times,* May 28, 2005.

FIGURE 2 Southeast Asian imports, 2000–07

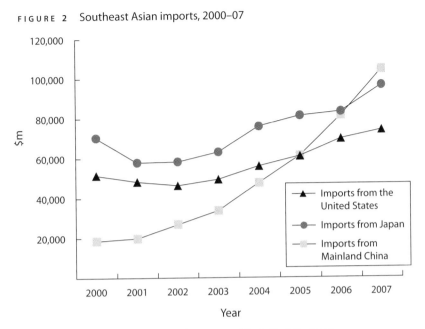

SOURCE: International Monetary Fund, Direction of Trade Statistics Database.

Furthermore, given the traditionally bilateral approach toward Southeast Asia, U.S. Trade Representative Susan Schwab's August 2006 signing of a U.S.-ASEAN TIFA establishing a regular and formal multilateral dialogue on trade and investment with the region as a whole was a significant move. In a related vein, in July 2006 Secretary of State Condoleezza Rice signed an Enhanced Partnership Plan of Action with ASEAN foreign ministers that placed economic cooperation at the top of the agenda.

U.S. Leadership

No Southeast Asian state disputes that the United States plays a predominant role in regional security and stability, even in the context of China's rising influence in the region. The Bush administration envisaged an extension of U.S. dominance in the world, especially in regions like Southeast Asia that have critical bearing on the threats of terrorism and proliferation. Yet, many questions remain regarding both the character of U.S. leadership and questions of how the United States can maintain regional dominance without conflicting with the other major regional powers.

The Bush administration has suggested a range of policy alternatives for the Asia-Pacific region. At the minimalist end is the official line reiterating that the United States "is and always will be a Pacific nation" that "will stay engaged in this part of the world" and intends to remain a major force in East Asia.[32] The maximalist line was indicated indirectly by the 2002 National Security Strategy, which unabashedly declared the Bush administration's intention to strengthen U.S. primacy in the post–Cold War world by maintaining armed forces "strong enough to dissuade potential adversaries from pursuing a military build-up in hopes of surpassing, or equaling, the power of the United States."[33] This was widely viewed as a warning to China and other rising powers not to challenge the U.S. preponderance of power. This belligerent stance, however, was not repeated in the 2006 National Security Strategy, which instead included a section on "cooperative action with other centers of global power."[34] In 2005 and 2006 a more moderate official line on U.S. leadership in the region emerged. As noted above, during his Southeast Asia tour in mid-2005, Zoellick assured the region that Washington would remain engaged while not competing antagonistically against Chinese influence.[35] This was reassuring in Southeast Asia but also led to questions over the degree and type of engagement regional states might expect from Washington and what the implications would be for China's growing influence.

For instance, the 2006 National Security Strategy stated that "our strategy seeks to encourage China to make the right strategic choices for its people, while we hedge against other possibilities."[36] This leads to several questions. Against what specific kind of negative Chinese behavior is Washington hedging? What does hedging entail, and what does this mean for countries in the region?[37] ASEAN states worry that Washington is merely recasting containment policies under the "hedging" rhetoric and

---

[32] "Rumsfeld Pledges that US Will Stay Engaged in the Region," *Straits Times*, June 4, 2006.

[33] National Security Council, *The National Security Strategy of the United States of America*, September 2002, 30, http://www.whitehouse.gov/nsc/nss.html.

[34] National Security Council, *The National Security Strategy of the United States of America*, March 2006, section 8, http://www.whitehouse.gov/nsc/nss/2006/.

[35] See "US Diplomat: Foolish to Limit China," *Straits Times*, May 11, 2005. Zoellick went on to call on China to become a "responsible stakeholder" in the international system, a term that has since become a touchstone of U.S. China policy. See Robert Zoellick, "Whither China: From Membership to Responsibility?" (remarks before the National Committee on U.S.-China Relations, New York, September 21, 2005), http://www.ncuscr.org/files/2005Gala_RobertZoellick_Whither_China1.pdf.

[36] National Security Council, *The National Security Strategy*, March 2006, 42.

[37] For discussions of hedging in the Asia-Pacific, see Evan S. Medeiros, "Strategic Hedging and the Future of Asia-Pacific Stability," *Washington Quarterly* 29, no. 1 (Winter 2005/6): 145–67, http://www.twq.com/06winter/docs/06winter_medeiros.pdf; and Evelyn Goh, "Understanding 'Hedging' in Asia-Pacific Security," Center for Strategic and International Studies, PacNet 43, August 31, 2006, http://www.csis.org/media/csis/pubs/pac0643.pdf.

that Washington's strategic competition with Beijing will eventually force Southeast Asia to choose overtly between the United States and China. Given their desire to avoid regional hegemony, and the imperative to focus on diversifying dependence on external powers, such an outcome is to be avoided at all costs. Toward the end of the Bush presidency, the State Department adopted a much more positive and constructive tone toward China, asserting that "the United States is not attempting to contain or counter China's growing influence, but rather to shape the choices that Chinese leaders make about how to use their growing power."[38] According to Deputy Assistant Secretary of State for East Asian and Pacific Affairs Thomas Christensen, the United States was "actively encouraging China to play a greater role in international diplomacy and in the international economic architecture…for purposes that buttress international development and stability and, therefore, coincide with the overall interests of both the United States and…China."[39]

An Assessment of the U.S. Approach to Southeast Asia

There have been mixed responses in Southeast Asia to the shifts in U.S. defense strategy and foreign policy under the Bush administration. On the one hand, the region has welcomed Washington's renewed focus on cultivating deeper economic ties and the administration's apparent recognition that a blunt policy to contain China would be counterproductive. On the other hand, Southeast Asian leaders remain uncomfortable with the central focus on counterterrorism and democracy promotion within the U.S. national security strategy, a worry that is rooted in the dilemma between their desire to retain benign U.S. dominance in the region and their need to deal with the self-centered style of Washington's leadership. Washington's preoccupation with U.S. national security interest, although undoubtedly frustrating for Southeast Asian policymakers, allows regional leaders to more easily assess U.S. strategic priorities and to translate those priorities into the regional context without worry that Washington might unexpectedly adopt strategic preferences specific to the region that diverge from global U.S. strategic aims.

In contrast to its approach for major Asian powers like China or Japan, the United States has no independent regional strategy for Southeast Asia. As a result, the assessment in this section refers only to the success

---

[38] Thomas J. Christensen, "Shaping China's Global Choices through Diplomacy," statement before the U.S.-China Economic and Security Review Commission, Washington, D.C., March 18, 2008, http://www.state.gov/p/eap/rls/rm/2008/03/102327.htm.

[39] Ibid.

and limitations of U.S. approaches to clusters of policy issues. In terms of responses to strategic challenges in Southeast Asia, U.S. efforts on counterterrorism have met with qualified success, whereas results related to democracy promotion have been limited and somewhat contradictory. The United States has experienced increasing success in the economic realm but has left serious questions outstanding on the issues of military transformation and regional engagement.

Counterterrorism. Regional leaders recognize that over the long term Southeast Asia might well remain the second front in the global counterterrorism campaign because of its sizeable Muslim population and strategic location. The invasion and occupation of Iraq, however, has posed a significant stumbling block to a closer Southeast Asian alignment with the United States. For Washington, the Iraq war is an extension of the war on terrorism, but Southeast Asian states (like many other nations) see the conflict in Iraq as a separate war that detracts from and undermines the war on terrorism. Indonesian and Malaysian leaders have found it particularly hard to lend high-profile support to U.S. counterterrorism policies because more radical Islamic political parties have been able to exploit the strong public opposition in Malaysia to the Iraq war. Given the growing prominence of political Islam in the region, there is a tendency for public perception that any political or religious group might be supported by the United States to cause suspicions over the group's credentials. As a result, mainstream secular political parties like United Malays National Organization (UMNO) in Malaysia find themselves having to adopt more religious stances so as to "out-Islamize" religious parties such as the Pan-Malaysia Islamic Party (Parti Islam Se-Malaysia, or PAS).

There are major differences between the U.S. and Southeast Asian campaigns against terrorism. In contrast to the Bush administration's portrayal of terrorism as a global, extremist, anti-Western conspiracy, variants of terrorism in Southeast Asia are intimately related to domestic politics, the underdevelopment of ethnic minority areas, and long-standing separatist movements. Though some of these groups have recently forged links with larger international funding and ideological networks, these linkages do not dislodge these groups from the domestic political contexts within which they operate or the political aims that they pursue. Thus, for instance, both the Thaksin and subsequent military governments in Thailand have turned down offers of U.S. assistance for the counterinsurgency campaign in the south of the country. Although collaboration with the United States on domestic counterterrorism might boost their intelligence capabilities, regional governments are less interested in short-term military capacity than in longer-term, non-military instruments of subregional development, socio-economic integration, and religious education reform—all of which would help sustain national integrity and sovereignty. In some of these aims, high-profile U.S. aid could prove more of a hindrance than a help because there is a widespread perception, especially given the war in Iraq, that the United States is anti-Islam, unilateralist, and interventionist.[40]

These pronounced differences between regional and U.S. policy agendas lead to practical limits in cooperation on counterterrorism and affect regional responses to some U.S. initiatives. Indonesia and Malaysia's reluctance toward the RMSI suggestion, as described above, stemmed as much from sovereignty concerns as from worries that a clear U.S. presence would attract maritime terrorist attacks.[41] The same logic drives regional discomfort with Singapore's overt tightening of security relations with the United States in recent years. Jakarta's reticence toward signing the PSI, amid the flurry of a restoration of bilateral military ties with Washington in 2005, is a further example. The Indonesian government cited public opposition to overt military cooperation with the United States as the reason for taking more time to consider the issue.[42]

Democracy promotion. Democratic processes, human rights, and freedom of expression and association are difficult issues in U.S.-Southeast Asia relations. Though recent assessments from Washington are more upbeat about elections and democratic transitions in the region, the elevation of democracy promotion in the Bush administration's national security strategy has met with skepticism and concern in Southeast Asian policy circles. Southeast Asian policymakers regard this emphasis on democracy promotion as awkward at minimum, if not meaningless and obstructionist—especially because of the region's share of troubled democracies in recent years. These include the attempted coup and impeachment hearings against President Gloria Macapacal Arroyo of the Philippines in 2005 and the corruption charges that led to the 2006 military coup against Thai prime minister Thaksin Shinawatra. Furthermore, moderate opinion-leaders in Indonesia and Malaysia are not helped by having their countries hailed by Washington as model Muslim democracies. A strident pro-freedom stance also limits Washington's influence in Southeast Asia in other ways. For instance, the military regime in Myanmar is a common problem, but

40 Goh, "Southeast Asian Reactions," 213.

41 Indeed, the newly elected Kevin Rudd government in Australia pulled troops out of Iraq for a similar reason, based on the belief that Australia's vulnerability to terrorist attack would diminish as a result of withdrawal from Iraq.

42 "Issues behind Indonesia Joining the PSI," *Jakarta Post,* June 14, 2006; and "PKS Urges Govt to Reject US Invitations to Join PSI," Antara News, June 7, 2006.

ASEAN has chosen to seek assistance and influence from Beijing and New Delhi rather than turning to Washington or the European Union.[43]

At the same time, democracy and freedom criteria are at times inconsistently applied in U.S. policy. For instance, despite having previously criticized Malaysia and Singapore for internal security acts that allow individuals suspected of threatening national security to be detained without charge, Washington adopted similar legislation. When the United States lifted its military embargo on Indonesia in 2006, human rights campaigners protested on the basis that Indonesian security forces had not sufficiently changed their human rights protection procedures to merit the action. Yet, human rights issues continue to feature prominently in U.S. relations with the region—especially relating to (although not limited to) Myanmar. The Bush administration, nearing its close, made both U.S.-ASEAN FTA negotiations and additional U.S. economic and military aid to the Philippines contingent on human rights performance. Washington also has criticized both Kuala Lumpur and Bangkok for domestic human rights violations.[44]

Economics. The area that shows the most encouraging signs of increasing convergence is economic cooperation between Southeast Asia and the United States. The Bush administration's advancement of the EAI is appreciated in the region, as is the administration's undertaking to help prepare Vietnam for World Trade Organization (WTO) membership. Washington's adoption of a more active multilateral approach to economic and political cooperation with ASEAN since 2006 has boosted relations greatly. Even though substantive development of trade agreements will require time and effort, economics will definitely remain at the top of the Southeast Asian agenda as the region remains preoccupied with economic adjustment and development strategies. The incoming administration should not only build on the momentum gained in the Bush administration's second term but also consider widening economic ties. At the bilateral level, for example, the new administration should take steps to normalize economic relations with Laos. At the multilateral and institutional levels, Washington will need to support regional financial and monetary reforms.

Military transformation. The new administration should consider two issues in Southeast Asia-U.S. relations that remain in question. The first issue concerns the implications of ongoing military transformation for U.S. military strategy and deployment in the Asia-Pacific. The

[43] "ASEAN Seeks Chinese, Indian Help on Myanmar," *Straits Times,* March 31, 2006.

[44] See Sheldon W. Simon, "U.S.-Southeast Asia Relations: The New ASEAN Charter Bedeviled by Burma's Impunity," *Comparative Connections* 9, no. 4 (January 2008): 55–63, http://www.csis.org/media/csis/pubs/0704qus_seasia.pdf.

revolution in IT and communications, including military applications in pre-positioned logistics and weapons platforms, will likely reduce the need for troops on the ground. The decision of the Bush administration to redeploy forces stationed in South Korea will bring troop levels in the region below the 100,000 mark. Though a smaller U.S. presence may not affect the capability of U.S. forces, the psychological implications must be carefully managed given that potential adversaries may misinterpret a reduction in numbers, thus reducing the deterrence effect of the U.S. military. An associated worry surrounds the ability of regional allies to take on an increased strategic burden with the reduction of the U.S. military presence. At the same time, the extent to which U.S. military transformation will make U.S. forces more able to deal with security challenges such as insurgencies—which involve lengthy, drawn-out campaigns that are manpower-intensive—remains unclear.[45]

Regional engagement. The second major question in Southeast Asian responses to the U.S. regional policies over the last eight years relates to Washington's approach to leadership and engagement in the region. In engaging Southeast Asia, will Washington continue to rely upon the traditional hub-and-spoke approach centered on bilateral alliances, or will it show innovation, particularly taking into account China's rising influence? The Bush administration has sent two signals related to this question. First, the 2006 National Security Strategy omitted the usual section on strengthening U.S. alliances, focusing instead on "coalitions of the willing" and on U.S. relations with various major powers. Although a reflection of the overriding U.S. focus on the Iraq war, this shift pointed to the possibility of a more general reorientation toward issue- or ideology-based informal security partnerships on Washington's part. Second, the United States, Japan, and Australia conducted their first ministerial-level Trilateral Security Dialogue in 2006. Some observers interpret this as a U.S. attempt to coordinate the two most important alliance relationships in the region into a multilateral framework aimed at containing China.[46] In contrast, at the regional level the United States was excluded from the East Asia Summit (EAS) inaugurated in December 2005. Washington has subsequently sent mixed signals on U.S. interest in joining this new dialogue process, but the

[45] "Defense Department Background Briefing on Global Posture Review," U.S. Department of Defense News Transcript, August 16, 2004, http://www.defense.gov/home/features/global_posture/gp20040924pm1.html; Bernard Loo, "U.S. Military Transformation and Implications for Asian Security," Institute of Defence and Strategic Studies, IDSS Commentaries, no. 39, July 1, 2005, 1–3; and Bernard Loo, "The 2006 Quadrennial Defence Review: Implications for Asian Security," Institute of Defence and Strategic Studies, IDSS Commentaries, no. 47, June 7, 2006, 1–3, http://www.ntu.edu.sg/rsis/publications/Perspective/IDSS0472006.pdf.

[46] For good analyses on this point, see William T. Tow et al., eds., *Asia-Pacific Security: U.S., Australia, Japan and the New Security Triangle* (New York: Routledge, 2007).

exclusion of the United States was widely regarded as marking a turning-point toward the development of Asia-only regional security institutions.[47]

These developments are neither conclusive nor coherent, but the attention paid to them in the region indicates the clear tension between the desire of Southeast Asian governments to have the United States remain a regional leader and worries over how Washington will maintain this role. Though Southeast Asian states have differing preferences on the exact mixture of the two elements, their hope is that Washington will strike an appropriate balance between credible deterrence (through partnerships and alliances) and constructive engagement in bilateral dialogues and regional institutions. The question of how the United States maintains leadership in Southeast Asia is critical because of the apparent contradiction between the region's imperative of avoiding hegemony and its preference for buttressing benign U.S. dominance in the region. This tension has been sustainable so far because the preference for U.S. leadership importantly turns on Southeast Asian perceptions of the benignity of U.S. power. Thus, regional leaders' growing concerns regarding the style and approach of U.S. leadership under the Bush administration are not merely petty political complaints; these concerns reflect a potentially crucial shift in perceptions of U.S. identity that could affect the extent and depth of strategic support for U.S. regional dominance. Current regional preferences for U.S. leadership are based on a combination of wariness over Chinese intentions and the pragmatic desire to diversify dependence. If the perception of U.S. benignity thus continues to be undermined, Southeast Asian reasons to support a continued U.S. role in the region will be limited to pragmatic power politics and will therefore necessarily be less enthusiastic and less comprehensive than otherwise.

In sum, the shared strategic world-view in this relatively peripheral and diverse region revolves around the principles of avoidance of hegemony and diversification of dependence, which shape and constrain strategic options for all Southeast Asian states. For these reasons, though states may differ in their ability to court one great power or another, and in the degree to which they are constrained by any such power, all Southeast Asian states share the desire to retain serious U.S. involvement in the region.[48] Fundamentally,

---

[47] Christopher Hill, assistant secretary of state for East Asian and Pacific affairs, stated in a press conference in Manila in March 2006 that he was consulting with various ASEAN states on a U.S. role in the East Asia Summit, but he stated in Singapore two months later that the Asia-Pacific Economic Cooperation (APEC) organization and the ASEAN Regional Forum (ARF) are key for the United States. See Catharin Dalpino, "U.S.-Southeast Asian Relations: U.S. Ratchets Up Regionalism and Boosts Ties with Muslim States," *Comparative Connections* 8, no.1 (April 2006): 65–73, http://www.csis.org/images/stories/pacfor/0601qus_asean.pdf; and Christopher Hill (remarks at the Lee Kuan Yew School of Public Policy, Singapore, May 22, 2006), http://singapore.usembassy.gov/hill.html.

[48] This discussion excludes Myanmar.

the new administration can expect that—far from alienating Washington—these states will want to maximize economic and technological gains from relations with the United States. None of the Southeast Asian states currently enjoying military strategic ties with the United States will want to diminish or downgrade these ties, and states that do not have such ties wish to develop them to some degree. Basically, no Southeast Asian state would choose to place all its eggs in the Chinese basket if possible; those states that seem to do so—Laos and Cambodia—are in de facto positions of holding very little strategic attraction for the United States and thus have no alternative to China.[49]

These shared constraints, preferences, and strategies work together to ensure that Southeast Asian states are not likely to opt for radically different relationships with Washington in the foreseeable future. Instead, the new administration will find that Southeast Asian states want strategic relations with the United States to strengthen along the critical tracks of day-to-day political-economic exchanges and gradual negotiations of military and economic policies, both to bring the two sides closer and to make relations more predictable. The imperative for strategic diversification will ensure that Southeast Asian states will work to keep the United States playing an important role in the region; the scope and depth of such support for continued U.S. dominance, however, will depend on perceptions of U.S. benignity and the degree of perceived tensions between U.S. commitments to the region and U.S. global strategic priorities.

Policy Options

The foregoing analysis has assessed the successes and limitations of U.S. policies in Southeast Asia, taking into account the strategic imperatives and preferences of regional countries. Though indicating that the incoming administration should expect continued support from key Southeast Asian states for U.S. leadership in the world and preponderance in East Asia, this analysis suggests that an understanding of the region's imperative for strategic diversification will be critical to effective policymaking toward the region. Fundamentally, the new administration will want to pursue policy options that will support Southeast Asian autonomy (principally vis-à-vis China but also with regard to avoiding overdependence on other great powers, including the United States) while gaining these states' cooperation for U.S. strategic priorities. The incoming administration will want to pay special attention to six regional priorities: (1) protecting

---

[49] Goh, "Southeast Asian Reactions," 216.

sealines of communication, (2) maintaining economic growth, (3) containing and preventing terrorism, (4) promoting democratization for stability, (5) turning China into a responsible stakeholder in the regional and international realms, and (6) protecting key allies (particularly Japan, Taiwan, and South Korea) and interests, such as maintaining the status quo in the Taiwan Strait and managing nuclear proliferation on the Korean Peninsula. As is evident from the foregoing discussion, strategic priorities cannot be contained within the Southeast Asian subregion alone; U.S. policy toward Southeast Asia is necessarily derived in part from broader East Asian security issues as well as global security concerns.

Southeast Asian states' "wish list" for the new administration's broad strategic priorities is likely to include the hopes of one regional leader that Washington:

> uphold America's commitment to globalization, free trade, and international rules; pursue constructive relations with China and other major powers; actively cultivate America's diverse interests in the Asia-Pacific, especially Southeast Asia; remain steadfast in the fight against terrorism; and take a long-term approach towards Iraq and Afghanistan.[50]

As this wish list demonstrates, there is no fundamental conflict between U.S. priorities in East Asia and the strategic interests of key Southeast Asian states. In the region there is firm appreciation for—and a desire to sustain—the U.S. role in maintaining international economic and strategic order and security as well as support for U.S. strategic priorities. Any tensions that exist or might arise result from suboptimal policies. Thus, instead of considering alternative policy choices, the new administration should ponder how to make most effective the two intractable core aims of any U.S. regional strategy: responding to China's rise and counterterrorism.

Regarding China, the new administration will want, first, to retain sufficient support in Southeast Asia in order to avoid a loss of U.S. influence to the extent that Chinese dominance in the region would be allowed to grow and, second, to manage regional conflicts so as to avoid armed conflict with China in East Asia. Vis-à-vis the continued war on terrorism, the new administration will have two priorities in Southeast Asia: (1) facilitating strategic partners such as Singapore and the Philippines in deepening and strengthening existing cooperation and (2) persuading countries in the region that are critical or reticent to support the U.S. counterterrorism agenda. It is clear that U.S. priorities on these two issues overlap: for instance, the degree to which support for a U.S. strategic role in the

[50] Lee Hsien Loong, "Keynote Address" (address to the Seventh International Institute of Strategic Studies Asia Security Summit Shangri-La Dialogue, Singapore, May 30, 2008).

region can be retained will depend on Washington's success in persuading unwilling countries of the necessity to cooperate in counterterrorism. In large part, the new administration will need to develop more effective means to demonstrate recognition of and support for regional strategic preoccupations so as to win reciprocal support for its own strategic priorities. The remainder of this chapter suggests how the new administration might harness the economic, military, and political elements of its Southeast Asian strategy more effectively toward its global security strategy.

Economic. Given that economic development is central to Southeast Asia's strategic world-view, and that the primary threats and opportunities resulting from China's rise are economic, the new administration should place priority on building sustained and serious economic relationships with all Southeast Asian countries. As discussed previously, when the Bush administration turned, albeit belatedly, to an economic focus in relations with Southeast Asia, regional leaders clearly and appreciatively read this as a signal that Washington cared about an issue of fundamental importance to their region. Over the last decade Washington has revived interest in using trade policy as a tool of statecraft and has been negotiating FTAs with important strategic countries and regions around the world.[51] During its second term the Bush administration clearly began to superimpose preferential trade agreements on top of security partnerships in Southeast Asia. The new administration must similarly recognize that a very significant element of the indirect security guarantee the United States provides to the region is economic. Southeast Asia's main worry vis-à-vis China is economic-related: particularly because of both the fear of losing FDI to China and the need to recover from the financial crisis, Southeast Asia requires U.S. support for the regional imperative to diversify economic relationships. Many of these states will therefore try to liberalize their domestic economies and financial regulations to become more attractive targets for U.S. investment. It is in Washington's interest to ensure that China's growing economic power does not, in the first instance, draw trade and investment away from Southeast Asia and, in the long term, completely dominate Southeast Asia. Washington should consider exploring the coincidence of interest with regional leaders who see maintaining and developing close economic relations with the United States as crucial. Together with Japan, the United States remains the region's most important economic partner in terms of investment, trade, communications, and technology. Southeast Asian states look to the United States for critical

---

[51] Richard E. Feinberg, "The Political Economy of the United States' Free Trade Arrangements," *World Economy* 26, no.7 (July 2003): 1019–40; and Michael Mastanduno, "Economics and Security in Statecraft and Scholarship," *International Organization* 52, no.4 (Spring 1998): 825–54.

assistance in building economic capacity against the China challenge. As China's share of the market grows in the coming years, governments in the region want to retain the United States and Japan as their dominant economic partners in order to ensure the diversity of their economic portfolios.

This translates into a diversity of expectations. At one end of the spectrum is Malaysia, whose prime minister complained in 2005 that "ASEAN expects the United States to be an important strategic economic and development partner as much as it is an important diplomatic partner," but Washington "gives a higher priority to ASEAN as a strategic partner for political and regional security purposes."[52] Responding to this assertion that a firmer focus on economic ties will help to facilitate cooperation on other fronts such as counterterrorism, Washington launched FTA negotiations with Kuala Lumpur in March 2006. At the other end of the spectrum is Vietnam, which copes with the rise of China mainly by building up national economic strength. Given the tight constraints on Hanoi's pursuit of significant strategic relations with Washington, the greatest contribution the United States can make toward Vietnam's security concerns, as the Vietnamese economy gradually opens and develops, is "helping nationalistic Vietnam to protect its independence by promoting economic growth through reform, trade, investment and technology."[53]

Military. The U.S. security guarantee to Southeast Asia and the protection of U.S. interests are undergirded by military deployment and commitments in the region. The new administration should continue to maintain a strong U.S. presence and indirect strategic support for partners in Southeast Asia. Washington also needs to consider, however, how the U.S. role in regional security relates to the regional strategic balance, particularly in response to China's growing influence. Here, the only overtly military element of U.S. bilateral relations with regional security partners is the Southeast Asian states' hopes for military ties and access to U.S. military technology to boost internal balancing capabilities (not only against China but also against neighboring states). Yet there are serious limits to bilateral defense cooperation—the relatively more modern Singapore armed forces are the only military force in Southeast Asia that can interact meaningfully with U.S. armed forces. The new administration will therefore want to focus more on a relatively independent military role in terms of a committed long-term forward presence in the region;

[52] Abdullah Ahmad Badawi, "Creating a Better Understanding of ASEAN-United States Relations" (speech delivered to the Asia Society, New York, September 15, 2005), http://www.asiasociety.org/speeches/badawi05.html.

[53] Nayan Chanda, "U.S.-Vietnam: A Balancing Act by Hanoi," *International Herald Tribune*, November 11, 2003, http://www.iht.com/articles/2003/11/11/ednayan_ed3_.php.

however, it will be critical that this presence serve mainly as a deterrent rather than for the outright containment of China.

In sum, the new administration will want to consider how to balance growing Chinese power peacefully in a way that provides a strong deterrence message while minimizing the security dilemma. First, peaceful balancing behavior by the United States stems primarily from the critical U.S. military presence and alliances in Northeast Asia, especially from Washington's successful deterrence posture in the Taiwan Strait and management of the North Korean problem. More generally, the United States needs to act not as a counterweight—a response that would assume the United States and China to be at power parity, which they are not—but as a large anchor that would, by continuing predominance, prevent dominance and deter adventurism by China. In this regard, the new administration may wish to reconsider the Bush administration's move toward forming an "alliance of democracies" in Asia. Such an alliance could take the form of a trilateral or quadrilateral security dialogue—the former involving the United States, Japan, and Australia, and the latter to also include India. Alternatively, an alliance might consist of institutionalized military exercises such as the multilateral Malabar exercises conducted in September 2007, which involved the navies of the United States, India, Japan, Australia, and Singapore. Apart from Singapore, other Southeast Asian states (and even Japan) have retreated from the Bush administration's moves, taking the view that these types of alliances are unnecessarily antagonistic and fuel an ideological zero-sum game. The problem lies in the ideological, "democratic" (that is, anti-authoritarian or anti-communist) character of such military groupings rather than in their multilateral or institutional nature.

Political. The most sensitive policies that the new administration has to consider lie in the political dimension, where the administration will be best advised to adopt more selective and indirect approaches. Two issues stand out: U.S. approaches to regional security institutions and to supporting moderate religious and political groups in particular countries as part of a "hearts and minds" campaign against terrorism.

With regard to the U.S. role in the regional strategic balance, one important set of considerations for the incoming administration relates to U.S. participation in regional institutions. Over the last decade regional institutions have flourished, even though the Southeast and East Asian version of multilateral cooperation—emphasizing decisionmaking based on consensus and informal diplomacy—does not quite accord with the U.S. model, which is more legalistic and formal. Indeed, though such institutions feature prominently in Southeast Asian and Chinese regional strategies, they are not the focus of U.S. regional policy. The United States, Australia, and

Canada have been frustrated by the slow pace of institutionalization and the "talk shop" nature of regional institutions, and the Bush administration has been criticized for ignoring these institutions. The new administration should note that the United States does not need to participate in all regional institutions. Such institutions are instrumentally useful, however, for Washington in sending signals and boosting policy effectiveness in the region. For a start, U.S. participation in regional institutions clearly signals U.S. membership in the Asian region. Although there is clearly disagreement among various ASEAN states on this issue, as evident in the row in 2005–06 over participation in the first EAS, no state has gone so far as to argue that the United States should be excluded from all or any of the key existing regional institutions. Still, this contentious issue is made more thorny by Washington's frequently lukewarm attitude toward ASEAN-led regionalism. Leaders in Singapore and Indonesia want Washington to participate more actively and constructively in regional institutions, if only to make clear that the region cannot afford to leave the United States out on important economic and security matters.

The new administration would benefit from being participatory but not reactive on this issue. For example, Washington should not worry over the EAS, which is not likely to evolve into the premier regional forum given that the key actors appear to lack sufficient interest. China and Malaysia are less enthusiastic about the EAS because of Australia's and New Zealand's participation, while Singapore, Japan, and Indonesia are cautious regarding the EAS because of potential Chinese dominance. Participation in the EAS would require signing on to ASEAN's Treaty of Amity and Cooperation (TAC), which could be another avenue for Washington to directly shape regional structures and maintain stability in the region.[54] Furthermore, Washington possesses a wider range of security and economic institutional channels and relationships with Southeast Asia than the other major powers. The United States combines formal military alliances with defense partnerships, various types of joint military exercises, intelligence cooperation, and the auspices of APEC and WTO, as well as a range of bilateral economic agreements and a dizzying array of cultural and educational exchanges and interactions. Thus, the new administration can afford to be selective in its choice of multilateral instruments and concentrate on a few mechanisms upon which Southeast Asian states place particular value. One good such mechanism to build on is the 2005 agreement to expand relations through the U.S.-ASEAN Enhanced Partnership—an agreement that emphasized trade, investment,

---

[54] "New Power Dynamics in Southeast Asia: Changing Security Cooperation and Competition," Stanley Foundation, Policy Dialogue Brief, October 2007, 1–4.

and closer cooperation against illegal drug-trafficking and on maritime and border security, thus moving beyond issues of counterterrorism and counterproliferation. The Bush administration has not so far (as of June 2008) fulfilled the initiative proposed in 2006 to hold an annual U.S.-ASEAN Summit; this is an important gesture that the new president might also pursue as a venue through which to cultivate U.S. participation in Southeast Asian affairs. Other possibilities include developing APEC mechanisms to support an Asian Bond Market and cooperating with like-minded Southeast Asian states to push ARF toward preventive diplomacy. Washington could also use the U.S.-ASEAN TIFA to broaden U.S. economic influence and investment in the region. The appointment of a special U.S. envoy to ASEAN from May 2008 has been well-received in the region. The new administration will want to consider these initiatives partly to counter Beijing's intensification of strategic relations with Southeast Asia within the ASEAN +3 framework, including the proposal for an East Asia FTA, implementation of the Chiang Mai Initiative for a regional currency swapping system, work toward a regional foreign exchange reserve pool, and military cooperation.[55] There is no need for the United States to be a member of every institution and dialogue forum that arises in the region. The main aim of selective participation would be to provide opportunities for strategic diversification in institutions that will yield mutual benefit for Southeast Asian states and the United States.

More pressing for the new administration is the regional political dimension of the war against terrorism. Worldwide, there are various degrees of dissatisfaction and discomfort with U.S. prosecution of the war in Iraq, and the new administration should address this problem at least insofar as it affects U.S. ability to effectively conduct the global counterterrorism campaign. Washington requires Southeast Asia's support not only in tackling root causes of Islamic radicalism in the region and important nodes of regional organizational and financial networks that promote terrorism but also as a demonstration of international political involvement and multilateral support for U.S. strategy. In order to build more substantive sustained political support among key Southeast Asian countries, the new administration will need greater sensitivity to the nexus between domestic politics and the security agenda that confronts leaders of these states. At the most immediate level, this sensitivity concerns the practical difficulties governments with large Islamic populations face in expressing explicit support for U.S. policies. Combined with leadership

---

[55] Robert Sutter and Chin-Hao Huang, "China-Southeast Asia Relations: Singapore Summits, Harmony, and Challenges," *Comparative Connections* 9, no. 4 (January 2008): 65–74, http://www.csis.org/media/csis/pubs/0704qchina_seasia.pdf.

transition, weak coalition governments, and the domestic politics of religion, popular opposition imposes significant political constraints on the degree to which regional governments can identify with U.S. policies.

For instance, the Indonesian defense minister publicly advised his U.S. counterpart in 2006 that "[i]n the application of security, including anti-terrorist laws, it's best that you leave the main responsibility of anti-terrorist measures to the local government in question." In addition to this reminder that U.S. security interests cannot subsume national sovereignty, he also bluntly cautioned that U.S. preponderance was threatening to Islamic communities:

> As the world's largest Muslim country, we are very aware of the perception, or misperception, that the United States is overbearing and overpresent and overwhelming in every sector of life in many nations and cultures...your powerful economy and your powerful military does lead to...a sense of threat by many groups right across the world.[56]

Such statements reflect the domestic political problems faced by secular or moderate governments of countries with large Muslim populations. For those on the outside, the growing role of political Islam in countries such as Indonesia and Malaysia appears to offer opportunities to intervene in support of moderate factions against radical factions, much the same way as a series of U.S. administrations agonized over how to support the moderate elements of communist leaderships against the revolutionaries during the Cold War. Yet the Bush administration's attempts to support moderate Muslim leaders in Malaysia have created domestic political problems and might even be counter-productive in that this support opens moderate Muslim political and religious groups to the charge that they are western lackeys, thus decreasing their popularity. Though Southeast Asian variants of Islam have traditionally been different from those of other regions, a degree of radicalization has in recent decades spread from movements in the Middle East, and the dynamics of transformation in political Islam are more complex than simple models of intervention lead one to believe. As such, religion will be, at best, an extremely blunt political instrument for U.S. strategic purposes. Focusing on vocational training, educational exchanges, and development aid will help boost Southeast Asian states' governance, accountability, development goals, and conflict resolution capacities, possibly stemming the growth of radicalism and terrorism. Southeast Asian governments will ultimately support U.S. counterterrorism efforts, given that U.S. resources can help to boost the region's ability to deal with the associated security challenges of domestic counter-insurgency, piracy,

---

[56] "Rumsfeld Gets Advice on Indonesia Visit," *International Herald Tribune*, June 7, 2006.

money-laundering, and other crimes. States in the region clearly prefer such cooperation to be conducted discreetly at functional levels, however, rather than with high-level publicity or overt aims of promoting religious factions. Even Singapore's leaders, who have been firm supporters of the war in Iraq, have counseled Washington that terrorism and radicalism must be fought with ideas, education, and trade, rather than by military force or imposing democracy.[57]

To sum up, the new administration will find that Southeast Asia is a more important region for the United States today than eight years ago. Southeast Asia is a vital strategic area that contains crucial partners for two of the most significant security challenges that the United States faces: the rise of China and international terrorism. In both of these areas, the twin roles of the United States as a regional bulwark or deterrent and as the world's and region's premier economic powerhouse are absolutely critical to the region. Southeast Asian states want to strengthen ties with both the United States and China, establish strategic relations where feasible, and work at deepening multilateral security dialogues. The new administration should collaborate in the pursuit of these goals and work with states in the region to persuade Beijing to build on the progress China has made in the last decade. With the multilateral and diplomatic support of ASEAN, U.S. management and peaceful socialization of a rising China may have a better chance of success. As for counterterrorism, though not all agree with the way in which the Bush administration has conducted the war on terrorism, states in the region are willing to support the enterprise if such support helps to ensure and sustain U.S. interest and involvement in the region. The new administration can overcome the limits of cooperation that stem from such instrumental logic, however, by adjusting the means of counterterrorism engagement in the region toward channels that pose fewer political problems for governments at home. In managing these two paramount challenges, the new administration will find that continued U.S. involvement in East Asia that helps to secure the strategic diversification the Southeast Asian states so deeply desire will greatly enhance the chances of a peaceful Asian century ahead.

---

[57] Goh Chok Tong, "Beyond Madrid: Winning against Terrorism" (speech delivered to the Council on Foreign Relations, Washington, D.C., May 6, 2004), http://www.cfr.org/publication.html?id=7004, reprinted in "Fight Terror with Ideas, Not Just Armies," *Straits Times,* May 7, 2004; and "Why America Bothers to Listen to Singapore," *Straits Times,* May 8, 2004.

EXECUTIVE SUMMARY

This chapter assesses how Pakistan's and Bangladesh's grand strategies and domestic dynamics are affecting U.S. counterterrorism, stability, and democracy goals in South Asia.

MAIN ARGUMENT:

- Pakistan's grand strategy, with an emphasis on balancing against Afghanistan and India, will continue to limit cooperation in the war on terrorism, regardless of whether elected civilian leaders retain power or the military intervenes again. The repercussions of Islamabad's clandestine regional policies are adding to internal challenges to the weak Pakistani state, which include an ethnic Pashtun insurgency on the border with Afghanistan.

- Bangladesh's internal development goals remain the basis of national consensus and legitimacy. Despite fears that partisan violence and Islamist extremism will make Bangladesh as unstable as Pakistan, the greater risk would be if military leaders retain power to press administrative reforms at the expense of political participation and economic growth.

POLICY IMPLICATIONS:

- Though many officials see the war on terrorism as the main U.S. equity in Pakistan, growing internal instability poses the greater challenge to U.S. interests and warrants consideration as Washington's top policy priority there. To gain legitimacy, solutions for many internal problems, including the future status of tribal areas, will need to be home-grown, but acknowledging the validity of Pakistan's domestic preoccupations could improve bilateral ties.

- Dhaka's role as a cooperative moderate Islamic ally warrants cabinet-level diplomacy. Along with other aid donors, Washington may be able to induce the military to agree on a timetable for re-democratization.

The Impact of Pakistan's and Bangladesh's National Strategies on U.S. Interests

Polly Nayak

Seven years into Pakistan's shaky role as the key front-line state in the war on terrorism in Afghanistan, growing tumult inside Pakistan is forcing U.S. attention to the country's internal dynamics and their implications for U.S. goals. Clear sources of concern for U.S. policymakers include the half-hearted counterterrorism cooperation by the Pakistani military; a widening, ethnically based Islamist insurgency in the northwest part of the country for which many Pakistanis blame the United States; and growing urban terrorism.

A closer look at the troubles affecting U.S. plans for Pakistan regarding the war on terrorism reveals that these problems are linked to the country's traditional grand strategy and national goals, which continue to shape its regional policies and internal dynamics. The first section of this chapter lays out, as the baseline for what is happening in Pakistan, these core goals and strategies and how they have shaped the de facto system there, the effects of which include perennial tensions with Afghanistan and India and efforts to undercut "unfriendly" governments in these countries. The second section examines the perverse effects of the country's dominant strategies and systems on the domestic situation and how the war on terrorism has unintentionally exacerbated these effects, resulting in challenges to Pakistan's internal stability and therefore to U.S. counterterrorism objectives. At issue is not only whether and how Pakistan's military and newly elected civilian leaders might manage these domestic problems but also whether there is any impetus to revise the "national narrative." A *sine qua non* for turning

Polly Nayak retired from government in 2002 and is an independent consultant. She can be reached at <poginski@aol.com>.

Pakistan around will be the ability and will of its leaders to win public legitimacy for new goals. An uncomfortable reality for the United States is that President Pervez Musharraf lost public support as much for acceding to the U.S.-led war on terrorism as for flouting the constitution to extend his stay in office yet again. The third section of this chapter examines how these trends might influence U.S. policy choices on Pakistan.

The chapter then looks at neighboring Bangladesh. Similarities between political dynamics in Pakistan and Bangladesh—including what some see as a triangle of democracy, Islamism, and the military—have raised concerns that Bangladesh is on the way to becoming another Pakistan. From a U.S. perspective two issues are at stake: whether Bangladesh will become more unstable and whether the country might become a hotbed of Islamist extremism. Accordingly, the fourth section discusses Bangladesh's core goals and strategies relative to those of Pakistan, the fifth compares political trends in the two countries, and the final section draws policy implications for Washington.

Regarding Pakistan, this chapter contends that, whereas many U.S. officials see the war on terrorism as the main U.S. equity in the country, growing instability actually poses the greater challenge to overall U.S. interests and warrants consideration as Washington's top policy priority there. The importance of Pakistan for U.S. counterterrorism is at least equal to that of Afghanistan. Pakistan's unity and tranquility are thus vital to effective counterterrorism as well as to regional stability and the continued security of the country's nuclear weapons. The immediate issues—tussles between Washington and Islamabad over how to manage the war on terrorism and over periodic support by Pakistan's security services and armed forces for militants—pale compared to the potential impact of an increasingly disorganized and weak Pakistani state. The decline of the state is epitomized more by a progressive loss of control and declining governance in some so-called settled areas of the country than by the state's inability or unwillingness to extend control to semi-autonomous tribal hinterlands in support of counterterrorism operations in Afghanistan. Although external variables such as militant activities by Afghan Taliban affect Pakistan's internal situation, Islamabad's diminished control of former proxy militant groups risks these groups instigating conflict with India on their own, among other possibilities of concern to Washington.

Even a partial shift in U.S. policy emphasis from pushing the war on terrorism to discreetly supporting Pakistani leaders' focus on national problems might improve relations and ultimately reduce anti-Americanism. To gain legitimacy, solutions to most of Pakistan's internal difficulties will need to be home-grown and politically negotiated. These internal problems include a weak and widely distrusted justice system, the reform of which could bolster counterterrorism efforts as well as system legitimacy. Paradoxically, U.S. aid to Pakistan's armed forces might help bolster civilian rule against military intervention. In time a greater focus on internal problems also might shift Pakistan away from aggressive regional policies linked to the country's traditional grand strategy and thereby advance the U.S. interest in regional peace.

This chapter argues that internal stability and system legitimacy are the premier U.S. interests in Bangladesh as well. Despite important similarities with Pakistan—including tensions between autocratically run political parties and the military and an Islamist political strand fostered but not fully co-opted by the army—Bangladesh's unique ethnic make-up, national identity, goals, and strategic interests have yielded distinct regional roles and different problems and opportunities for the United States. Islamism in Bangladesh is strongest in rural areas—an outgrowth of loyalties to local *imams* (Islamic leaders). Though opinion is divided on whether Bangladesh is at risk of becoming a staging ground for terrorist activities, U.S. policymakers would do well to consider pressing for a carefully negotiated return to civilian rule, lest disenchantment with the military's lack of legitimacy become a recruiting tool for currently fringe militant Islamist groups. More generally, Bangladesh warrants high-level U.S. attention to bolster the country's role as a moderate Muslim majority state with extensive international aid relationships and a promising civil society—in order to stem countervailing forces of instability and radical Islam.

Pakistan: An "Outside In" System Built to Counter Regional Threats

Understanding Pakistan's grand strategy and core national goals requires a review of its post-independence history. Soon after Pakistan's partition from India in 1947, the perception that Pakistan was encircled by two hostile neighbors—India on the east and Afghanistan on the west—emerged as a key ingredient in the country's national identity, unity, and internal and external policies. Iran, initially seen as a natural partner for the new state of Pakistan, became an intermittent competitor for regional influence after the Islamic Revolution. Contributing to Pakistan's early sense of encirclement was the fact that all five Pakistani provinces—four after the secession of East Bengal—bordered other countries. The strategies and structures created by the country's early leaders based on this vision of the world have proved very durable.

For many Pakistanis, proximity to a hostile India has remained the single irreducible national fact—highlighted by three full-blown wars and numerous close calls. Successive Pakistani governments have disdained India's system of secular government that claims to represent citizens of all religions, including Islam, as well as New Delhi's perceived drive for regional hegemony. In Islamabad's view, the latter is exemplified by Hindu India's underhanded grab for Muslim-majority Kashmir at the time of partition. Many in Pakistan still blame India for abetting the secession of East Bengal in 1971 and the birth of Bangladesh. Yet many Pakistanis also envy India's burgeoning economic and military power and the presumed advantages conferred by India's deepening ties to the United States, despite the largely negative view many take regarding U.S.-Pakistan cooperation on counterterrorism since September 11. Anxiety over Indian influence extends into the economic realm. The expansion of bilateral trade over the past several years—to Pakistan's economic benefit—has been constrained by fears that Pakistani industries will drown in a wave of Indian imports.

To Pakistan, Afghanistan appears to pose a different combination of threats: the danger that irredentist ethnic nationalism (in this case, Pashtun) would further splinter Pakistan, constant instability along Pakistan's western frontier, and a contested border, the Durand Line. Instability in Afghanistan also attracted meddling by Iran, the Soviet Union and some of its successor states, and, most alarmingly, India. Pakistan has answered these threats by attempting to manipulate groups and events in Afghanistan to its advantage while profiting from Central Asian trade that found its way across unruly international boundaries.[1]

Under civilian and military rule alike, Islamabad has engaged in balancing strategies, diplomatic and security-related, to neutralize India and Afghanistan. In earlier years Pakistan reached outside the region for protection and arms. Drawn to Pakistan by shared antipathy to India, for decades Beijing served as Islamabad's primary arms supplier and source of diplomatic support against New Delhi. Pakistan also joined successive U.S.-led Cold War defense pacts in the 1950s in the quest for counterweights to regional threats and for military resources. Islamabad later mobilized Afghan *mujahideen* (nationalist guerrilla fighters) against Soviet invaders at Washington's behest in the 1980s.

Pakistan also has practiced several types of non-conventional regional balancing against India and Afghanistan. Pakistan's nuclear weapons, like its relatively small but well-trained conventional military, have been designed

---

[1] Marvin G. Weinbaum, "Afghanistan and Its Neighbors: An Ever Dangerous Neighborhood," United States Institute of Peace, Special Report, no. 162, June 2006, http://wwwusip.org/pubs/specialreports/sr162_afghanistan.html.

with an eye to India. Developed with China's assistance, this nuclear arsenal is intended to offset India's larger conventional forces, deter India from conventional strikes (despite India's insistence that limited conventional war is possible between nuclear powers), and enhance Pakistan's international prestige and leverage.[2]

Islamabad also has clandestinely relied on militant groups to keep India and Afghanistan off balance; these militants were recruited, trained, and managed by the Pakistan Army and security services.[3] In Kashmir, Pakistan has used both local and Pakistan-based Islamist extremist groups, bolstered by so-called Afghan Arabs, as force multipliers against Indian troops. In Afghanistan, Islamabad has sponsored a string of pro-Pakistani local groups over the decades, many of them ethnic Pashtun militias, to gain "strategic depth" against India. Kingmaking by Pakistan's security services gave advantage to hard-line Islamist factions in the mujahideen fight against the Soviet occupiers in the 1980s. After the Soviet withdrawal from Afghanistan, Islamabad backed the rising Taliban in the mid-1990s as its next Afghan client group. This choice made Pakistan the focus of U.S. pressure to help eliminate al Qaeda even before September 11.[4] These militant groups have proved unexpectedly hard for Pakistan to control at home as well as in the target countries. Until recently, however, Pakistan did not worry over the possibility of significant domestic repercussions such as are facing the country now.

Pakistan's balancing act has required avoiding simultaneous trouble on more than one front. Although still very tentative, the current peace with India—maintained by the process of talking as much as by progress on the issues—has allowed Pakistan to focus on the western frontier since September 11. Pakistani officials nevertheless oppose the revival of India's energetic diplomatic and commercial presence in Afghanistan and fear that it is a cover for more sinister activities on Pakistan's doorstep. Allegations that Pakistan's security services helped plan car bomb attacks outside the Indian embassy in Kabul in July 2008 have increased tensions with both India and Afghanistan.

The rise of India and China—though predictably dwarfing Pakistan's modest gains over the past several years—has altered Islamabad's regional security calculus surprisingly little so far. India's rapid military

---

[2] See John H. Gill, "India and Pakistan: A Shift in the Military Calculus?" in *Strategic Asia 2005–06: Military Modernization in an Era of Uncertainty*, ed. Ashley J. Tellis and Michael Wills (Seattle: The National Bureau of Asian Research, 2005), 237–67.

[3] Carlotta Gall and David Rohde, "Militant Groups Slip from Pakistan's Control," *International Herald Tribune*, January 15, 2008.

[4] See Steve Coll, *Ghost Wars: The Secret History of the CIA, Afghanistan, and Bin Laden, from the Soviet Invasion to September 10, 2001* (New York: Penguin Press, 2004).

modernization has increased the importance to Pakistan of possessing
a nuclear deterrent. Also increasing the importance of such a deterrent
has been China's gradual relaxing of once-close ties to Pakistan in favor
of a more neutral stance, one favoring neither Islamabad nor New Delhi.
This shift in China's policy resulted from two main factors. The first is
the "push factor" of Beijing's growing concern over the long-term effects
of Islamabad's support for Muslim extremists against Pakistan's enemies.
Beijing was alarmed by the Pakistani military's training of ethnic Uighurs
from Xinjiang to fight the Soviets in Afghanistan; Islamabad's support for
the Taliban, which began in the mid-1990s, further raised the specter of
a region-wide Islamist victory that could destabilize China.[5] During the
1999 military confrontation between India and Pakistan in Kargil, China
famously remained silent rather than taking Pakistan's part for crossing the
Line of Control to seize territory on the Indian side.[6] It is unclear whether
Pakistan's security establishment has grown more attuned to China's
concerns over Islamism. Revelations about the "rogue" role of Pakistani
scientist A.Q. Khan in proliferating nuclear weapons technology for profit
have also reinforced China's reluctance to associate closely with Pakistan.[7]

The "pull factor" in Beijing's distancing from Islamabad has been the
opportunity to broaden China's ties to its fellow Asian giant, India, through
trade and joint investment. Even so, energy competition with India and a
desire to ensure access to vital sea lanes have spurred China in recent years
to invest in the construction of strategic port facilities in Pakistan—for
example, the Port of Gwadar in Baluchistan—as well as in Bangladesh
and Myanmar.[8] Once more, Pakistan's location has ensured its continued
importance to China as well as to other major global powers.

Pakistan's concerns over hostile neighbors have had three far-reaching
domestic effects. First, these concerns reinforced a preference among
successive leaders for a strong centrist political system designed to ensure
national unity under a common Islamic banner and to subsume the
nation's strong ethnolinguistic nationalities—Bengali, Punjabi, Pashtun,
Sindhi, Muhajir, and Baluch. These regionally based ethnicities were seen
as security vulnerabilities in part because the Baluch and Pashtun groups

[5] Willem van Kemenade, "China and Pakistan: New Friends Can't Compare," YaleGlobal Online, March 12, 2008, http://yaleglobal.yale.edu/display.article?id=10490.

[6] See Celia W. Dugger with Barry Bearak, "Kashmir Thwarts India-Pakistan Attempt at Trust," *New York Times*, July 4, 1999; and Ziad Haider, "Clearing Clouds over the Karakoram Pass," YaleGlobal Online, March 29, 2004, http://yaleglobal.yale.edu/display.article?id=3603&page=1.

[7] Van Kemenade, "China and Pakistan."

[8] Lisa Curtis, "China's Expanding Global Influence: Foreign Policy Goals, Practices, and Tools," testimony before U.S.-China Economic and Security Review Commission, Washington, D.C., March 18, 2008, http://www.heritage.org/Research/AsiaandthePacific/tst032008.cfm#.

overlap the borders with Iran and Afghanistan, respectively, and the Bengali and the Muhajir (immigrants from India who settled in Sindh) had ties to India. Pakistan's elite feared that unfriendly neighbors would exploit ethnic sentiments to pull Pakistan apart. In fact, the virtual denial of ethnic and regional impulses by successive governments, combined with de facto Punjabi dominance in the military and government, proved highly destabilizing as evidenced both by the secession of East Bengal in 1971 and by a variety of rebellions that turned on demands for greater regional autonomy. The semi-autonomous Federally Administered Tribal Areas (FATA) in western Pakistan were (and continue to be) exempted from strong central control. Missing from Pakistan was Muslim-majority Kashmir, which many Pakistanis thought was illicitly annexed by India and must be reclaimed.

Second, the obsession with regional threats, coupled with fundamental disagreements among civilian politicians over the new country's constitution and governing structure during Pakistan's first decade, helped justify the military's seizure and retention of political power as the self-proclaimed guardian of the state. Some have argued that nervousness over the potential for a "one man, one vote" policy to challenge Punjabi dominance contributed to the eclipse of democracy. The military's political rise was clinched by General Ayub Khan's coup in 1958. His olympian nation-building efforts reinforced the myth that the army is uniquely competent to modernize and govern as well as to protect. The external threat environment justified the military's large budgets and control of foreign policy as well as defense policy. When the military's policies failed and it ran out of political options, Pakistan returned to civilian governance under one or the other of the two large competing political parties—the center-right Pakistan Muslim League (PML) or the center-left Pakistan Peoples Party (PPP). The constant thread in successive governments was an oligarchy of landed "feudals," elite bureaucrats and military officers, and some business leaders.[9] Intolerant of perceived stumbles by civilian officials, the army toppled numerous elected governments, usually with the help of the president. Together, the army and the president outweigh the power of any parliamentary government headed by a prime minister.[10]

Third, the perception of a different type of threat to Pakistan's stability, demonstrations in response to the Islamic Revolution in Iran, spurred

---

[9] Stephen Philip Cohen, *The Idea of Pakistan* (Washington, D.C.: Brookings Institution, 2004).

[10] Three coups were mounted with no legal or constitutional basis by generals Ayub Khan in 1958, Zia ul-Haq in 1977, and Pervez Musharraf in 1999. Alan Kronstadt, "Pakistan's Scheduled 2008 Election: Background," Congressional Research Service, CRS Report for Congress, RL34335, January 24, 2008.

and shaped General Zia ul-Haq's nascent effort to Islamicize Pakistan in the late 1970s and early 1980s. Motivated by piety as well as by a quest for more power and legitimacy for the army, as head of state Zia had already begun transforming the legal system and building alliances with domestic Islamist groups that had been hitherto at loggerheads with the armed forces.[11] Uneasy over the intense though short-lived spike in Shia activism inspired by events in Iran, Zia began to systematically give advantage to Sunni institutions at the expense of Shia counterparts. The rapid spread of government-sponsored *madaris*, or Islamic religious schools (madaris is the plural of *madrasah*), became a way to counter both Iranian and domestic Shia influence, particularly along the border with Iran. After the Soviet invasion of Afghanistan, Saudi funding via the Pakistan military supported both jihadis in Afghanistan and militant Sunni groups in Pakistan—in each case, at the expense of Iranian influence.[12] Members of these groups were trained in camps run by the Pakistani military on the Afghan border, effectively ensuring crossover from the Afghan jihad.

Thus, Pakistan's political culture and structure as well as security policies have been rationalized by and shaped around a constant set of perceived regional threats that seemed to be best addressed by the military—a system fundamentally at odds with the U.S. stake in regional stability. For decades many Pakistani leaders have taken the system so defined for granted. The obvious question is what new circumstances might arise and challenge the premises of this system—and with what consequences, internal and external.

Pakistan on the Eve of a New U.S. Administration

It is hard to overstate the impact on Pakistan of siding with the United States in the war on terrorism. The counterterrorism cooperation U.S. officials demanded after September 11 conflicted directly with Pakistan's regionally focused goals and strategies. President Musharraf's decision to accede to U.S. pressure, abandon the Taliban, and fight Taliban allies in Pakistani territory triggered a domestic backlash that not only scuttled Musharraf's credibility but also called into question the capacity and legitimacy of the state, including the army. Musharraf's frenetic efforts to extend his stay in power and to manipulate the parliamentary election due

---

[11] Vali Nasr, "Military Rule, Islamism and Democracy in Pakistan," *Middle East Journal* 58, no. 2 (Spring 2004): 195.

[12] Vali Nasr, "Islam, the State, and the Rise of Sectarian Militancy in Pakistan," in *Pakistan: Nationalism Without a Nation?* ed. Christophe Jaffrelot (London and New York: Zed Books, Ltd., 2002), 90–95.

in late 2007 infuriated the public and contributed to the electoral victory of mainline civilian parties when the contest was finally held in February 2008. Cumulatively, these events have begun refocusing Pakistan's military and civilian elites on internal problems, a focus at odds both with the agenda of the war on terrorism and with the state of Pakistan's guiding vision.

Key Effects of the War on Terrorism

The bargain struck by Musharraf and supported by his corps commanders appeared simple. Musharraf forswore support to the Taliban and proffered logistic support to counterterrorism operations in Afghanistan, access to Pakistani airfields and military facilities, and assistance in sealing the border and apprehending fleeing Taliban and al Qaeda operatives. In return, U.S. policymakers reclassified Islamabad from near-rogue status to indispensable partner in Operation Enduring Freedom. Diplomatic and military relations were restored overnight, sanctions were lifted, and billions of dollars in military and economic aid flowed to Pakistan as a reward, initially with no strings attached. The post–September 11 deal, however, created great bilateral tension for two principal reasons: first, the resultant efforts at cooperation revealed a growing divergence between Islamabad's and Washington's strategic interests; second, these efforts exposed cleavages among Pakistan's political elites and fault-lines in domestic politics.

Growing strategic divergence. The first main source of tension between the two countries is that, despite Islamabad's reluctant acquiescence to the war on terrorism, the gaps between Pakistani and U.S. national priorities and goals in South Asia have limited Pakistan's will to cooperate.[13] These differences have been evident on a number of issues. The first issue is Pakistan's antipathy to President Hamid Karzai's U.S.-backed government in Afghanistan, which is dominated by former adversaries of both Pakistan and the Taliban. That Washington has encouraged India to participate in reconstructing Afghanistan has only deepened Pakistani discomfort with U.S. policy.

Second, to the outrage of U.S. officials, Pakistani army and paramilitary personnel generally have turned a blind eye to (and in some cases even facilitated) border crossings by Afghan Taliban. This failure of security forces to see a threat in the flow of Afghan Taliban into the country reflects a lingering perception of the Taliban as an instrument of Pakistan's regional policy. Although army leaders have cited a reluctance to interfere

[13] Polly Nayak, "U.S. Security Policy on South Asia Since 9/11—Challenges and Implications for the Future," Asia-Pacific Center for Security Studies, Occasional Paper Series, February 2005, 5–8, http://www.apcss.org/Publications/Ocasional%20Papers/U.S.Security3.pdf.

in the FATA in breach of long-time government agreements regarding jurisdiction, not surprisingly some officials simply seem disposed to retain the "Taliban option."[14] Above all, the army is loath to stir anger among Pakistani Pashtuns, including those in the armed forces, by rounding up co-ethnic Pashtuns. It has become evident in recent months that the public shares this unwillingness to confront tribal Pashtuns.

A third issue on which U.S. and Pakistani strategic interests have diverged is Kashmir. U.S. pressure on Islamabad to curb militant infiltrations of Kashmir helped end the 2001–02 military stand-off with India (which Washington perceived as a significant obstacle to the war on terrorism) and restart talks between India and Pakistan. Yet this also demonstrated that, despite denials, Pakistan could control at least some of the "Kashmir" militants. The post–September 11 addition—under Indian pressure—of the main Pakistan-based Kashmir militant groups to the State Department's list of terrorist groups signaled new U.S. intolerance for the "second track" of Pakistan's policy toward India. The surge in attacks across the Line of Control on Kashmir by Pakistani militants in July 2008 have raised anew old questions about the complicity of some Pakistani officials.

The fourth issue involving conflicting national goals is that U.S. security assistance given to Pakistan after September 11 has been used mainly to bolster Pakistani conventional military capabilities against India, not for counterterrorism or counter-insurgency equipment and training. This pattern recently has become a point of contention with U.S. officials.[15]

Fifth, Musharraf—seen by U.S. officials as a bulwark against a feared militant takeover—continued to strengthen and use Islamist parties as a counterweight to the two mainline non-religious parties, despite adverse impacts on the war on terrorism. By banning these parties—Benazir Bhutto's PPP and Nawaz Sharif's PML(N)—from participating in the 2002 parliamentary election, Musharraf allowed an Islamist coalition that opposed the war on terrorism to win political control of the North-West Frontier Province (NWFP) and Baluchistan, thereby tripping up counterterrorism operations by coalition forces on the border with Afghanistan.

Finally, the war on terrorism—termed "the American war"—has been deeply unpopular in Pakistan, where the perception of this war as

---

[14] Carlotta Gall, "At Border, Signs of Pakistani Role in Taliban Surge," *New York Times*, January 21, 2007, A1.

[15] K. Alan Kronstadt, "Pakistan and Terrorism: A Summary," Congressional Research Service, CRS Report for Congress, RS22632, March 27, 2007, http://assets.opencrs.com/rpts/RS22632_20070327.pdf.

anti-Islamic has been fed by the conflict in Iraq.[16] Many blame Musharraf for doing the bidding of the United States. The notion that Washington is dictating policy inside Pakistan has sparked an anti-U.S. reaction, even among moderates.[17] Many see this as another single-issue alliance with the United States and doubt Washington's will to stay engaged with Pakistan. Others have opposed the U.S.-led war on terrorism because it cemented the Bush administration's reliance on Musharraf and thus undercut U.S. support for a swift return of democracy to Pakistan. Until the Bush administration finally forced Musharraf's hand by decrying his state of emergency and pressing for free elections shortly before the February 2008 contest, many in Pakistan saw Washington as having given Musharraf a "pass" on democracy.

In sum, whereas U.S. officials have viewed Pakistan's lackluster efforts against the Taliban and the remnants of Islamabad's two-track policy toward Afghanistan and India as perfidious, Pakistan's security establishment has seen this approach as protecting core national objectives and strategies. Public objections to the war on terrorism have made a virtue of hedging on cooperation with the United States.

Domestic political fault-lines. The second major reason for continuing tension between the United States and Pakistan is that the war on terrorism has unintentionally widened long-standing but largely hidden fault-lines in Pakistani society, politics, and government, thereby reducing Islamabad's capacity and latitude to cooperate effectively. U.S. operations in Afghanistan drove Taliban militants across the border into the FATA and the NWFP. As a result, the war spread into Pakistan. By all accounts, the intensification of Pakistani operations in South Waziristan (an agency in the FATA), which began in 2004 at the urging of U.S. officials, helped turn Pashtun resistance into a full-blown insurgency. Outraged by what they see as Islamabad's betrayal of the Taliban in alliance with Washington, these self-styled "Pakistani Taliban" groups under the loose leadership of Baitullah Mehsud have targeted government security forces, even though the latter had typically ignored Taliban in favor of al Qaeda and other so-called foreign targets in the border areas.[18] The insurgency subsequently spread beyond

---

[16] In a 2007 opinion poll, 74% of Pakistani respondents opposed U.S. military action against al Qaeda and the Taliban inside Pakistan. "Pakistanis Reject U.S. Military Action against Al Qaeda; More Support bin Laden than President Musharraf: Results of a New Nationwide Public Opinion Survey of Pakistan," Terror Free Tomorrow, August 2007, http://www.terrorfreetomorrow.org/upimagestft/Pakistan%20Poll%20Report.pdf.

[17] Dexter Filkins, "Pressure on Musharraf: Anti-West Forces Brew," *New York Times*, June 15, 2002, A6.

[18] Carlotta Gall, "Aftereffects: Islamic Militants; In Pakistan Border Towns, Taliban Has a Resurgence," *New York Times*, May 6, 2003.

the FATA into settled areas of the NWFP that had long been viewed as secure. Many in Pakistan blame Musharraf, the Bush administration, and the army for what is seen as the use of excessive force against fellow citizens, and some worry that parts of the NWFP will secede permanently.

Thus, Pakistani security forces have found themselves in an unpopular internal conflict that they neither anticipated nor wanted, were slow to comprehend, and are ill prepared and ill equipped to fight. The army underestimated how its leverage had diminished as a result of three developments: Musharraf's new stance on the Taliban, the assassinations of many *maliks* (traditional tribal leaders), and the generational changes in the leadership, organization, and agenda of militant groups in Pakistan's northwest.[19]

Pakistan's militant strategy has backfired on the eastern front as well. The Kashmir conflict had long provided a sort of safety valve for the energies of militant groups that had been launched by Pakistan's security services and based in Pakistan. With this "vent" partially closed by Islamabad since 2003 in response to U.S. pressure and Indian demands, disaffected Pakistani militants—belonging to groups such as the Lashkar-e-Taiba, Jaish-e-Muhammad, and their smaller brethren—have declared war on the government and have been linked to several assassination attempts against Musharraf. Islamabad's recent quiet efforts to buy out and to settle these militants reportedly have worked only with the smaller groups.[20]

The war on terrorism has both highlighted and exacerbated the overall weakness of Pakistan's internal security capabilities. The inability of poorly trained and corrupt police to handle local security problems has required paramilitary forces to fill the void; in turn, the paramilitary's shortcomings have forced the army to fill the breach on counterterrorism and counter-insurgency in border areas, to the detriment of morale in all these security forces.[21] The spread of urban bombing attacks is straining Pakistan's embryonic investigative and forensic capabilities, the limits of which drew international concern after PPP leader and parliamentary candidate Benazir Bhutto's assassination in December 2007.

These trends have divided Pakistan's traditionally cohesive army. U.S. pressure for more vigorous Pakistani operations in border areas allegedly has sparked arguments among military leaders on whether to refocus

---

[19] John Lancaster and Kamran Khan, "Pakistan Losing Grip on Extremists: Attacks on Officials Linked to Al Qaeda," *Washington Post,* August 29, 2004, A1.

[20] Owen Bennett-Jones, "U.S. Policy Options Toward Pakistan: A Principled and Realistic Approach," Stanley Foundation, Policy Analysis Brief, February 2008, 6–7, http://www.stanleyfoundation.org/publications/pab/JonesPAB208.pdf.

[21] Non-attributable private observation by a Pakistani scholar at the Partnership for Global Security Conference in Washington, D.C., February 22, 2008.

the army on the growing insurgency problem along the western border or to continue arming and strategizing against India as a central threat.[22] Military operations in ethnic Pashtun areas have demonstrated the potential for ethnic loyalties to divide the ranks—as exemplified by the surrenders to Pashtun militants of both Pakistani Pashtun regulars and members of the local Frontier Corps, who are raised from surrounding communities by levy.[23]

Over time these internal troubles, assuming that they persist, likely will help to alter Pakistan's regionally driven goals and strategies, which do not address the new domestic threats. Efforts by security forces to grapple with these threats may reorder security priorities and strategies, despite the army's reluctance to depart from core military doctrine.[24] Public opinion may drive such a reappraisal, particularly if terrorism increases in urban areas, where most of the population now lives. Some Pakistanis are starting to see an unstable Afghanistan as threatening rather than buttressing stability at home, even though many distrust the current Afghan government. The risks of backing so-called Kashmir militants against India were underscored in December 2001 when an attack on India's parliament by one such group nearly sparked a full-blown war in the course of the following year.[25] Whatever the Pakistan Army's calculations in agreeing to restart talks with India in 2002, the talks have calmed tensions. Although 67% of Pakistani respondents polled in 2006 still expressed an unfavorable view of India, many in Pakistan have embraced "cricket diplomacy."[26] Barring another rupture of bilateral ties—such as could occur if a major terrorist attack on Indian interests were linked to Pakistani officials—peace with India may eventually build on itself, buttressed by public conflict fatigue and middle class economic aspirations. Alternatively, new threats—such as an unfriendly, nuclear-armed Iran—could prompt Pakistan to reassess the costs and benefits of traditional regional relationships, although even in this context Saudi Arabia would appear a more likely ally than India.

---

[22] Carlotta Gall and David Rohde, "Militant Groups Slip from Pakistan's Control," *International Herald Tribune*, January 15, 2008, http://www.iht.com/bin/printfriendly.php?id=9217373.

[23] Bennett-Jones, "U.S. Policy Options Toward Pakistan," 5.

[24] Eric Schmitt and Thom Shanker, "Pakistani Discord Undercuts Vow to U.S. to Fight Militants," *New York Times*, March 16, 2008.

[25] Polly Nayak and Michael Krepon, "US Crisis Management in South Asia's Twin Peaks Crisis," Henry L. Stimson Center Paper, no. 57, September 2006, http://www.stimson.org/southasia/pdf/USCrisisManagementFull.pdf.

[26] "China's Neighbors Worry About Its Growing Military Strength: Publics of Asian Powers Hold Negative Views of One Another," Pew Global Attitudes Survey, September 21, 2006, 2, http://pewglobal.org/reports/pdf/255.pdf; and Tunku Varadarajan, "Cricket Diplomacy: India and Pakistan Celebrate Their Weapons of Mass Destruction," *Wall Street Journal*, March 25, 2004.

Key Domestic Changes

The February 2008 parliamentary election gave the PPP and PML(N) a combined majority of seats over Musharraf's King's party. Even though the contest did not end Musharraf's term as president, the election was widely described as a referendum on his eight years as de facto head of government, ruling through the King's party. After retiring in November 2007 as army chief, Musharraf initially balked at subjecting himself to an open, transparent election. Many in Pakistan credited Washington with insisting, albeit at the last minute, on such a process. Chief of Army Staff Kayani's decision to desist from meddling in the election on behalf of Musharraf was also essential. Pre-election opinion polls made it clear that the public blamed Musharraf for militant violence at home and the use of excessive force against Pakistanis, as well as for breaking even the permissive rules he had forged—for example, by illegally declaring a state of emergency—in an effort to remain in power.[27] Thus, the election confirmed Musharraf's loss of legitimacy based both on his performance in office and on his violation of system norms. Relatively high voter turnout, despite threats of violence, confirmed the public's stake in participating in a meaningful contest. The election promised to revive the deliberative functions of the parliament, which had evaporated under Musharraf's rule.

The February contest also highlighted some conflicts among U.S. policy goals for Pakistan. For example, as an exercise in democracy, the election was a triumph. Moreover, as a practical matter, the United States required politically legitimate partners in Pakistan, and Musharraf had run out of legitimacy. The election results, however, also legitimated Pakistani push-back against U.S. counterterrorism objectives in the tribal areas. Whereas many in Pakistan were unenthusiastic about Pakistani military operations in the tribal areas, they actively opposed U.S. operations in Pakistan, particularly if these operations were unilateral. Defeating al Qaeda, the Taliban, and other militant groups ranked low among citizen concerns.[28] Partly in response to the widespread perception that the Musharraf government's strategy had failed, both PPP and PML(N) leaders campaigned on their support for negotiations with militant groups even though the

---

[27] "Pakistani Support for Al Qaeda, Bin Laden Plunges; Moderate Parties Surge; 70 Percent Want President Musharraf to Resign: Results of a New Nationwide Public Opinion Survey of Pakistan before the February 18th Elections," Terror Free Tomorrow, January 2008, 2, http://www.terrorfreetomorrow.org/upimagestft/TFT%20Pakistan%20Poll%20Report.pdf.

[28] "IRI Index: Pakistan Public Opinion Survey, January 19–29, 2008," International Republican Institute, http://www.iri.org/mena/pakistan/pdfs/2008%20February%2011%20Survey%20of%20Pakistan%20Public%20Opinion,%20January%2019-29,%202008.pdf.

military's previous efforts to negotiate with militant and tribal leaders in the FATA had failed to stop the fighting or dilute militant control.[29]

It will be unclear for several years whether Pakistan's leaders and elites will have made use of this election as a first step to repair and reorient the political system or whether more tactical concerns will prevail. At issue is how to fix a political system whose dysfunctions are exemplified by the virtual absence of power at the provincial level of government. Such problems are the product of reforms enacted several years ago to strengthen the president's hand by eliminating political checks and balances and competing centers of power.[30]

In early 2008 PPP and PML(N) leaders engaged in a bitter battle over which supreme court judges who had been fired by Musharraf should be reseated. The dispute served as a reminder of the difficulties of building consensus for complex tasks, let alone governing in coalition, given the decades of animosity between autocratic party leaders. Without effective cooperation, the winning parties risk replaying the political deadlock of the late 1980s when one party ruled at the national level while its rival ruled powerful Punjab Province. Inter-party squabbling also could allow the Islamist parties to become kingmakers by default. At the very least, the PPP and PML(N) will need to live down the fact that some of the most pressing problems facing Pakistan, including the erosion of services and of policing, grew on their watches.

It is also important to specify what the parliamentary election did not accomplish. First, the election did not assure a satisfactory civil-military relationship. Kayani stepped back from Musharraf and from the electoral process in part to protect the army's institutional interests from further damage by association with Musharraf's actual missteps or with civilian politicians' prospective ones. Given the military's de facto dominance and veto power, any civilian government must reach understandings with the military—a reality that created opportunities in the past for the army and security services to divide and rule civilian politicians. Averting military intervention thus will pose a challenge for the governing coalition. To keep the army happy and unified, civilian leaders will need to govern tolerably well and respect military "perks." Budgetary reductions will need to be

---

[29] Jane Perlez, "Pakistan to Talk with Militants, New Leaders Say," *New York Times*, March 22, 2008, A1, A5.

[30] Musharraf's reforms, like those of earlier military governments, deliberately empowered local leaders at the expense of provincial government. Ali Cheema, Asim Ijaz Khwaja, and Adnan Qadir, "Decentralization in Pakistan: Context, Content and Causes," John F. Kennedy School of Government Faculty Research Working Paper Series, Working Paper, no. RWP05-034, April 2005, http://ssrn.com/abstract=739712.

approached with care, and any effort to reorganize government security functions will risk triggering a military coup.

Second, the election did not take away from the army its monopoly on decisionmaking concerning war, counterterrorism, or counter-insurgency. This fact alone ensures that the Pakistani military will remain a key U.S. interlocutor as long as terrorism and insurgencies in South Asia are top priorities for Washington. By letting newly elected civilian officials issue the call for a ceasefire and talks with militant groups, the army gained political cover and legitimacy for its reported desire to negotiate a respite for security forces from the fight against militants in the tribal areas and the NWFP. It cannot be assumed, however, that the military will allow civilian leaders to play a role in reappraising Pakistan's regional security policies and stance. These policies have been a jealous preserve of Pakistani military and security services.[31]

Third, the election provided no particular impetus or mandate for either civilian or military leaders to undertake the relegitimization of the state's internal security function. This process is necessary for the government both to counter domestic terrorism and to re-establish its writ over the growing number of settled (not tribal) areas that have been quietly left to their own devices as state power diminished. Winning voluntary citizen compliance with laws, court rulings, and policies would require a strategic political commitment to the rule of law, a commitment supported by civil service reform to professionalize law enforcement once again.

Fourth, the election did not signify a reduced role for Islamist political parties, as some U.S. observers had hoped. Most of Pakistan's Islamist parties are ensconced in and committed to electoral politics. Even though mainstream Islamist parties all retain links to groups that engage in provocative illegal tactics—relationships that bear careful watching—those party members who have run in elections are not typically extremists aiming to topple the state of Pakistan.[32] Most Islamist parties in Pakistan, for example, pragmatically accepted the defeat of the Taliban, which they associated with army interests and not with their own goals. This pragmatism was supported in pre-election polls revealing that most respondents saw Islamist extremism as a serious problem for Pakistan but favored moderate Muslim civilian leaders.[33]

---

[31] Frédéric Grare, "Pakistan: The Myth of an Islamist Peril," Carnegie Endowment for International Peace, Policy Brief, no. 45, February 2006, http://www.carnegieendowment.org/files/45.grare.final.pdf.

[32] Anatol Lieven, "Pakistan: Real and Imaginary Risks," World Today, February 1, 2008.

[33] Note that how these polls defined "moderate" is unclear.

The electoral defeat of the Islamist Muttahida Majlis-e-Amal (MMA) alliance in the NWFP in some respects attested to the integration of Islamist parties into democratic processes in Pakistan. Reasons for the decline in these parties' vote share compared with 2002 included not only an anti-Musharraf boycott of the election by one of the parties and competition from the larger mainstream PPP and PML(N) but also local voter dissatisfaction with the alliance's record in office over the past five years—specifically with the alliance's failure to improve services and its alleged corruption. Thus, voters judged these parties on their performance, not their religious platforms. Some Islamist party leaders sided on contentious issues with the government, in this case Musharraf's, albeit for tactical political reasons. The leader of the Jamiat Ulema-e-Islam, for example, criticized militants in their stand-off in summer 2007 with security forces at the Red Mosque in Islamabad and came under threat from harder-line Islamists as a result.[34] These examples bolster evidence that participating in electoral politics may help temper the agendas and conduct of Islamist parties, as occurred with the Jamaat-i-Islami.[35]

In other circumstances, if both democratic processes and military unity were to unravel, Islamist parties might well assume a far less benign role from a U.S. perspective. These parties might try to systematically enforce more rigid interpretations of *sharia* (Islamic law), as Islamic vigilantes have done in various parts of Pakistan at times. Such a trend might grow if Pakistan drew closer to Saudi Arabia. Saudi Arabia's special relationship with Pakistan—which is built on their common Islamic, specifically Sunni, identity—is now bounded to an extent by U.S. ties to both Saudi Arabia and Pakistan. Should this change, a fresh upsurge might occur in Saudi NGO funding for hard-line Pakistani madaris and political organizations and in Sunni-Shia violence, as has occurred in the past. Such a trend could run counter to U.S. hopes for Pakistan's future as a moderate regional player.

The U.S. Response

Evaluating the U.S. Approach So Far

Since September 11, U.S. relations with Pakistan have been shaped by immediate security problems requiring short-term solutions, which have been mainly military, tactical, and focused on the border with Afghanistan.

---

[34] Carlotta Gall, "In Tribal Pakistan, Religious Parties Are Foundering," *New York Times,* February 14, 2008.

[35] Vali Nasr, *Vanguard of the Islamic Revolution: the Jama'at-i Islami of Pakistan* (Berkeley: University of California Press, 1994).

Even U.S. diplomacy aimed at ending the 2001–02 military confrontation between India and Pakistan was impelled by the need for a quick resolution that would enable Pakistani troops to return to the border with Afghanistan in support of U.S. counterterrorism operations there.

Three sets of initiatives exemplify how closely tied the U.S. agenda in Pakistan has been to the war on terrorism. First, concerned that Pakistan was replacing Afghanistan as a source of international terrorist attacks, the U.S. counterterrorism community tried to identify means to interrupt terrorist indoctrination and recruitment in addition to communications and financial networks. Soon after September 11, for example, U.S. officials pressed Islamabad to revise curricula and control the activities of Pakistan's madaris, which were found to be preaching—and in a few cases, conducting—violence against the United States.[36] U.S. aid also went toward reviving Pakistan's teetering public school system, whose decline helped increase madrasah "market share." Recent research on madaris indicates that their influence on militant recruitment has been overstated, and that many already have modern academic programs. At the same time, this research also suggests that reforming the most radical religious schools will be even more difficult than earlier assumed.[37] Moreover, Islamabad has been unenthusiastic about U.S. efforts to influence religious institutions.

Second, U.S. concerns over the security of Pakistan's nuclear stockpile from terrorists or rogue military elements prompted offers of U.S. technical equipment and advice to Pakistan's army.[38] This assistance emphasizes physical measures and personnel vetting in the military. Pakistani pride and distrust of U.S. motives will probably continue to preclude discussions of internal threats that might result from cleavages in Pakistan's security forces or from another A.Q. Khan trying to sell Pakistani nuclear technology.

Third, U.S. military planners recently have begun focusing counter-insurgency planning on the FATA in order to protect operations in Afghanistan and thus prevent more terrorist attacks against Western forces and areas loyal to President Karzai. Admiral Michael Mullen, chairman of the Joint Chiefs of Staff, stated "If I were going to pick the next attack to hit the United States, it would come out of the FATA."[39] Thus, the United States envisions large-scale development assistance to the FATA—some $750

---

[36] Brent Hurd, "Analysts Say Many Pakistani Madrassas Teach Worldview of Intolerance," *Voice of America*, July 20, 2005, http://www.voanews.com/english/archive/2005-07/Many-Pakistani-Madrassas-Teach-World-View-of-Intolerance.cfm?renderforprint=1&pageid=158309.

[37] Peter Bergen and Swati Pandey, "The Madrassa Scapegoat," *Washington Quarterly* 29, no. 2 (Spring 2006): 117–25; and C. Christine Fair, "Militant Recruitment in Pakistan: A New Look at the Militancy-Madrasah Connection," *Asia Policy*, no. 4 (July 2007): 107–34.

[38] Joby Warrick, "Pakistan Nuclear Security Questioned," *Washington Post*, November 11, 2007, A1.

[39] Schmitt and Shanker, "Pakistani Discord."

million over five years—as means to undercut local support for al Qaeda, the Taliban, and other militants in the border areas.

Although seen as a part of the war on terrorism, the proposed FATA assistance program also reflects a larger shift in U.S. thinking since early 2007, when critics of the security-driven aid program for Pakistan suggested that expanding non-military aid could help the country address critical economic and social deficits.[40] Though recognizing the importance of delivering promised aid to Pakistan's military, the U.S. Congress has taken the lead on increasing the economic share of aid and on seeking a "democracy dividend" to support the new civilian-led government. For fiscal year 2008, the estimated level of U.S. economic-related aid is expected nearly to equal security-related assistance, with an estimated $467 million and $478 million in aid, respectively.[41]

How successful has this approach been so far? Measured against the U.S. yardstick for short-term policy goals, U.S. officials can count several successes in Pakistan. First, despite bilateral disagreements over the war on terrorism, Pakistan has continued to provide valuable access and support for the resupply of coalition operations in Afghanistan. Second, cooperation from Pakistani troops along the border has been of great assistance at times. Third, Pakistan reportedly has tightened security around its nuclear arsenal.

On the negative side, the increasing preoccupation of Pakistan's elites with internal problems is at odds with the agenda of the war on terrorism; Pakistan's opposition to an official U.S. presence in the FATA has limited the utility of U.S. thinking about counter-insurgency strategies for the tribal areas. Unilateral U.S. operations from Afghanistan against targets in Pakistan remain particularly contentious. Moreover, implementation of U.S. plans for development assistance for the FATA has been delayed by difficulties in finding means to deliver and monitor U.S. aid in a region where the Pakistani government has no authority, local tribal leaders have been killed or forced to flee, and Western officials have no presence.[42] U.S. aid officials worry that resources will end up in Taliban hands or that any foreign fingerprints on aid will cause it to be rejected in this region where anti-Americanism runs high. Militant threats and violence against Pakistani NGOs in Swat Valley of the NWFP make it clear that such worries over

---

[40] Craig Cohen and Derek Chollet, "When $10 Billion Is Not Enough: Rethinking U.S. Strategy toward Pakistan," *Washington Quarterly* 30, no. 2 (Spring 2007): 7.

[41] K. Alan Kronstadt, "Direct U.S. Assistance and Military Reimbursement to Pakistan, FY2001–FY2008," Congressional Research Service, June 9, 2008.

[42] See Jane Perlez, "Aid to Pakistan in Tribal Areas Raises Concerns," *New York Times,* July 16, 2007.

implementing the program are justified.[43] These difficulties in devising ways to deliver aid to the FATA highlight a broader issue that affects non-military U.S. assistance for Pakistan. Apart from some well-received emergency aid following a major earthquake in Pakistan in 2005, U.S. assistance has received little publicity, reflecting U.S. efforts to tread softly in an anti-American environment.[44]

U.S. officials who are frustrated by the many obstacles to even short-term U.S. counterterrorism goals doubtless have considered adopting more direct approaches, but each of these has major downsides. For example, mounting unilateral attacks against militants on Pakistani soil over the objections of local security forces would risk bringing U.S. forces into direct conflict with Pakistan's army. The perceived affront to Pakistani sovereignty would surely deepen anti-U.S. public sentiment as well. Similarly, any outside effort to encourage Pakistan's elected officials to assert civilian control over the military and security services may founder both because of national pride and because of the gap between a prime minister's nominal powers and the de facto supremacy of the armed forces. The most likely scenario for a change to this line-up would be if some perceived failure of Pakistan's security policies mobilized citizens to demand transparency and genuine democratic oversight of such issues. Such a shift in public opinion could presage a major and positive change in the country's traditional national strategy and goals.

What Alternative U.S. Strategy for the FATA Can Be Envisaged?

When weighing implementation of FATA aid proposals already on the table, U.S. policymakers will need to stay attuned to the related debate in Pakistan over whether and how to change the status of the semi-autonomous tribal areas. This debate is partly a response to the spread of strife into settled areas of the NWFP after Pakistani forces initiated operations in the FATA. Two distinct proposals have surfaced based on different assumptions regarding the FATA's current social structure, the nature of support for the Taliban, and the capabilities of the Pakistani government. Both sides agree that the Frontier Crimes Regulation (FCR) that subjects entire tribes to punishment for the crimes of individual members is outdated and inhumane and that economic aid for the FATA is desirable. Opinions vary,

[43] Zofeen Ebrahim, "Pakistan: Cleric Turns Heat on NGOs," Inter Press Service, May 22, 2007, http://ipsnews.net/news.asp?idnews=37832.

[44] Teresita C. Schaffer, "South Asia," Center for Strategic and International Studies, Commission on Smart Power, Working Paper, July 2007, http://www.csissmartpower.org/scholarpapers/SchafferSouthAsia.pdf.

however, on whether changes in the FATA's status would have any impact on Taliban activity in Afghanistan.

Extend direct national or provincial governance to the FATA. Proponents, including the mainly Pashtun Awami National Party (ANP), see this plan as simultaneously promoting counter-insurgency, economic development, and human rights. The ANP believes the plan would resolve conflict over the Durand Line. According to this view, "Talibanism" caught on in the FATA because locals are unhappy with colonial-era administrative and judicial mechanisms, such as the political agent, that are "unsuited to modern governance."[45] The International Crisis Group argues that government appeasement allowed militants to establish a parallel policing and court system in the FATA and in settled areas of the NWFP; only retaking the area will reverse this trend. Respected Pakistani analyst Ahmed Rashid has similarly asserted the need to extend government authority into the FATA. Rashid has advocated giving FATA citizens a choice of forming their own province or joining the NWFP as the ANP favors.[46] This approach envisages providing economic development, jobs, and services to poor FATA residents to decrease the appeal of the militancy.

Underpinning this direct governance argument are six assumptions. The first is that FATA citizens prefer modern, top-down institutions. The second is that traditional tribal social structures are now largely irrelevant, in part because a new generation grew up without these structures. The third and fourth assumptions are that pro-Taliban tribals are in a minority and that the national government has the capacity to keep Taliban influences out of the FATA. The fifth is that the government is capable both of providing administrative and judiciary services in a region noted for scattered settlements, difficult terrain, and bad roads and of protecting government officials there. The final assumption is that economic aid will reduce incentives for locals to support pro-Taliban militants.

The "bridge-too-far" argument. Skeptics contend that the factors that make counter-insurgency efforts in the FATA so challenging would also impede extension of formal government to the region. Some skeptics believe that elements of traditional segmented tribal networks persist in the FATA. According to this view, allegiance to militant groups is determined by kinship networks, traditional obligations, and alignment with those who

---

[45] "Pakistan's Tribal Areas: Appeasing the Militants," International Crisis Group, *Asia Report*, no. 125 (December 11, 2006): 11–12. Under a system dating from British rule, each tribal agency had a political agent, or senior administrator, who was the appointed senior representative of the national authority. Political agents reported to the provincial governor. The system has frayed in recent years as militants killed off traditional tribal leaders, or maliks, on whom political agents relied to muster support for policies handed down from above.

[46] Ahmed Rashid, "Taking Back the Frontier," *Washington Post*, May 4, 2008, B7.

appear strong and thus is impervious to appeals to the hearts and minds of locals.[47] Other skeptics emphasize that reducing the influence of the Taliban in such areas would require discreetly providing local leaders with patronage and assistance in gaining territorial control, as well as exploiting remaining tribal ties.[48] This is slow, painstaking work, as former political agent Akbar Ahmed attested in the 1980s.[49] In this view, support from the Pashtun but largely urban-based ANP for mainstreaming the FATA does not equate to support from most tribal members living in the region or from those who have settled in other parts of Pakistan. Efforts to govern the FATA in the same way as settled areas risk uniting locals against an "occupying" national government.[50] In fact, some FATA tribal members want the FCR amended to permit governance by tribal *jirga* (council of elders) rather than direct government from outside.[51]

Some proponents of each view doubt that the national government will have the capacity to extend its rule into the FATA in the next several years. Pakistan lacks political mechanisms to connect provinces effectively to local government, let alone to aggregate the interests of scattered tribes. Pakistan's legal system—a patchwork of three types of law—is stretched to the breaking point and the current constitution is contested.[52]

Reconsidering the Big Picture

The framework for bilateral relations in coming years will depend in part on how civil-military relations play out in Pakistan and on the coherence, competence, and staying power of the civilian government. Nonetheless, the growing recognition in Washington that Pakistan itself is in jeopardy warrants a fresh look at U.S. policy through the lens of long-term U.S. interests in a secure Pakistan. U.S. counterterrorism stakes in Pakistan are at least equal to those in Afghanistan. An expansion of ungovernable areas into "settled" areas of Pakistan would risk attracting more illegal activities (for

---

[47] Thomas H. Johnson and M. Chris Mason, "No Sign until the Burst of Fire: Understanding the Pakistan-Afghanistan Frontier," *International Security* 32, no. 4 (Spring 2008): 41–77.

[48] William S. McCallister, "Strategic Design Considerations for Operations in Pakistan's Tribal Areas," Small Wars Journal web log, January 31, 2008, http://smallwarsjournal.com/blog/2008/01/operations-in-pakistans-tribal/.

[49] Akbar S. Ahmed, *Resistance and Control in Pakistan,* rev. ed. (London: Routledge, 2004).

[50] McCallister, "Strategic Design Considerations," 15–16.

[51] "Gillani's Announcement of Repeal of FCR Statement Elicits Mixed Reaction in FATA," *Daily Times,* March 30, 2008, http://www.dailytimes.com.pk/default.asp?page=2008%5C03%5C30%5Cstory_30-3-2008_pg7_29.

[52] See Faiz Ahmed, "Shari'a, Custom, and Statutory Law: Comparing State Approaches to Islamic Jurisprudence, Tribal Autonomy, and Legal Development in Afghanistan and Pakistan," *Global Juris* 7, no. 1 (March 2007).

example, increased drug trafficking) and displacing more fearful civilians internally or even across international borders. Additionally, further growth of urban terrorism in Pakistan would affect the country's economy and government operations.

The U.S. government has few levers with which to try to influence events, let alone trends, in Pakistan. The current relationship is premised mainly on aid. The temptation in Washington will be simply to condition and reformulate aid rather than reframing the policy. Although recent polling data suggests that aid can increase Pakistani goodwill toward the United States, it might be argued that U.S. aid for the longer term has been over-promised and that policymakers need to discuss time lines for assistance with Pakistani counterparts.[53] The U.S. experience with Bangladesh suggests that the constancy of close bilateral engagement builds the greatest goodwill.

Reframing U.S. policy on Pakistan more broadly would entail a holistic appreciation of factors affecting the country's future that are not related to terrorism—including, for example, the effects of Baluch unrest on Pakistan's energy prospects and on relations with Iran. It would also require a greater appreciation of the importance of national political authority and leadership to Pakistan's future. Despite U.S. equity in Islamabad's controlling the FATA region, the debate is at center a political one that should be resolved by Pakistanis, who will live with the outcome. Policy legitimacy—a clear basis in popular preferences, with sensitivity to local differences—will accord a higher value to "good local fit" than to "best practices," in the words of the World Bank's Christine Wallich.[54] Major changes in Pakistan's system—including its approach to regional ties—will have to grow from within, albeit with quiet encouragement from the United States and other major stakeholders in the region.

Continued stress on political legitimacy as a criterion for U.S. interlocutors would help further reduce Pakistan's suspicions that U.S. policy toward the country is purely expedient. In the months immediately after the early 2008 election, U.S. policymakers quietly moved in this direction, reaching out evenhandedly to a variety of civilian politicians. In that regard, U.S. military aid paradoxically may help mitigate budget friction between civilian and military leaders during this transition period. An important

---

[53] For polling data, see "Unprecedented Terror Free Tomorrow Polls: World's Largest Muslim Countries Welcome U.S. Navy: New Results from Indonesia and Bangladesh," Terror Free Tomorrow, 2006, http://www.terrorfreetomorrow.org/upimagestft/Final%20Mercy%20Poll%20Report.pdf.

[54] Christine Wallich (comments made at Practitioners in Development Seminar Series: Perspectives from Former Country Directors, Washington, D.C., October 6, 2004), http://info.worldbank.org/etools/docs/voddocs/328/1316/hi.htm#.

decision for U.S. policy will concern how much help to provide for internal security in Pakistan as distinct from border operations supporting coalition efforts in Afghanistan—particularly if violence in the NWFP prompts the U.S. military to shift resupply operations for Afghanistan from Pakistan to Russia or Central Asia.

Washington also will need to monitor opportunities to stabilize the region around Pakistan, preferably in consultation with key U.S. allies and with regional powers such as China and Russia. U.S. support for new trade or energy arrangements for Central Asia might boost Pakistan's opportunities. Buoying the dialogue between India and Pakistan will also remain a priority, given that renewed conflict between the two countries could undermine U.S. progress on many fronts and add new pressures on Pakistan's economy and internal stability.

Other policy shifts in Washington, of course, also could affect bilateral relations. For example, a return to the U.S. policy of pressing Pakistan to cap or accept restrictions on its nuclear weapons program might trigger a nationalist reaction against perceived U.S. meddling, just as U.S. pressure for action against the Taliban did.

Finally, U.S. policymakers will need to continue planning for several possible contingencies—including spoiler attacks by Pakistani "Kashmir" militants on high-value Indian targets with the intention of disrupting India-Pakistan detente, or attacks on Indian interests in Kashmir encouraged by Pakistani security officials in an effort to influence New Delhi's policies on Kashmir or Afghanistan. High-impact "wild cards" include the potential emergence of factions in the Pakistan Army, the de facto loss of the government's control over all border areas, an attempt by Sindh Province to secede, a major escalation of Baluch nationalism, or a return by the military to power against civilian wishes. An even higher impact wild card would be an attempt by dissidents in the military to seize control of nuclear weapons. By adopting a combination of the policies outlined above, Washington might avoid ever having to ask who lost Pakistan.

Bangladesh: An "Inside Out" Development State

Born of successive post-colonial splinterings of British India, Bangladesh is similar to Pakistan in many respects. Both are Muslim majority states with populations of approximately 130 million people. Each, though nominally a democracy, has been under military rule for long periods. In the name of national preservation, these military-led governments have manipulated, divided, weakened, or suspended political parties. In each case, starting in the late 1970s military leaders promoted Islamism as a successor to leftist ideologies, a source of political legitimacy, and a means of shoring up sagging national unity. Although the two countries are culturally and socio-economically dissimilar—a factor contributing to Bangladesh's secession from Pakistan in 1971—both have experienced growing polarization between an urban and Westernized (though generally not secular) middle class and socially conservative citizens. Many of the latter are adherents of fundamentalist versions of Islam and were educated in traditional madaris. The most obvious difference between Pakistan and Bangladesh has been the way in which successive governments in each country have framed their respective national identities, goals, and strategies, which is the topic of the rest of this section.

In addition, Bangladesh, unlike Pakistan, began with an uncontested, unifying ethnolinguistic identity whose denial by Pakistan's leadership justified the bitter fight for independence. Bangladesh's first constitution committed the government to parliamentary democracy. Within the first five years, Bangladesh's government, by then under military leadership, redefined the citizens of Bangladesh, previously known as "Bangalees," as "Bangladeshis" and later defined the country as Islamic to distinguish it from its sister "Hindu" state of West Bengal next door. Bangladesh's only rebellious minority, the population of the Chittagong Hill Tracts, was eventually accorded special autonomy after years of negotiations.

Whereas Pakistan's leaders found national purpose and unity in countering regional threats to their country's security, Bangladesh's leaders focused on creating a neutral development state. In contrast to Pakistan, whose need for economic support has consistently taken a back seat to the quest for security assistance, Bangladesh has openly pursued international development aid. This approach has earned the government a reputation with multilateral and bilateral donors as a model recipient in many respects. Bangladesh is a politically moderate majority Muslim state eager to improve the welfare of its mostly rural people, with a well-developed network of local NGOs that can competently deliver project assistance, bypassing corrupt or ineffectual government administrators. Although Bangladesh is now technically aid-independent, relationships with bilateral donors, such as Japan and the United States, and with multilateral organizations still loom large in its foreign policy.

As a weak state surrounded by hostile nuclear-armed dyads—namely, India-Pakistan and India-China—Bangladesh has sought to avoid regional security entanglements by looking outside the region for assistance and protection. The country's proximate regional challenges include Myanmar, Pakistan, and, most prominently, India. The first is a smaller and poorer neighbor, the second an unfriendly parent state, and the third a militarily and economically dominant state, seen by Bangladesh as a bully. This image of India as a bully was crystallized for Bangladesh when, immediately after East Bengal Province broke away from Pakistan with India's help, Indian troops confiscated all the heavy military equipment left behind by defeated Pakistani forces, leaving the new nation with neither external defense nor internal security resources.[55] This traumatic evidence from Bangladesh's birth of its inability to protect itself underpins the government's active support for the international mechanisms and institutions that protect small countries, including the United Nations and the South Asian Association for Regional Cooperation (SAARC). Even though the Bangladesh Army's role at home is confined to border security, Bangladesh has distinguished itself as an important source of troops for international peacekeeping.

India's "bullying" and economic dominance remain major domestic political issues in Bangladesh. India's rapid economic growth has drawn streams of illegal immigrants from Bangladesh. Conversely, New Delhi sees Bangladesh both as a willing sanctuary for Indian insurgents, including the United Liberation Front of Asom (ULFA), and as a transit route for Pakistan-sponsored militants. Indian officials have recently charged that extremists from Bangladesh are mounting attacks in India. New Delhi has responded to these perceived threats by building a wall, as it has along parts of the Line of Control with Pakistan in Kashmir, in order to seal the porous frontier. In turn, unhappiness with these developments is said to have buttressed Dhaka's resistance to investments by Indian industrialists, such as the Tata family, in Bangladeshi infrastructure and energy. Dhaka demanded numerous trade concessions when New Delhi sought to negotiate transit across Bangladesh for a natural gas pipeline from Myanmar. As a result, since 2007 India has threatened to pursue a more costly pipeline circumventing Bangladesh if the interim government in Dhaka does not soften its demands.[56] Bangladesh may decide to emulate Myanmar and increase efforts to play China off against India. Dhaka may calculate that China's investment in port construction in Bangladesh will dispose India to be more flexible in future bilateral dealings. Bangladesh's quest for assistance with nuclear power from China and Russia is likely to stir Indian concerns over the country's ability to ensure plant safety and the security of

---

[55] Talukder Maniruzzaman, "Bangladesh in 1976: Struggle for Survival as an Independent State," Asian Survey 17, no. 2 (February 1977): 191–200.

[56] Srinjoy Bose, "Energy Politics: India-Bangladesh-Myanmar Relations," Institute of Peace and Conflict Studies, Special Report, no. 45, July 2007, 1–3, http://www.ipcs.org/IPCS-Special-Report-45.pdf.

nuclear materials—or perhaps even over Dhaka's potential nuclear weapons aspirations.[57]

Although the identity, core goals, and national strategies Bangladesh initially chose reflected a focus on internal development and a commitment to democracy, this agenda did not translate into the formation of consensus for strong institutions as fruits of nation-building. What is dysfunctional in Bangladesh is its governance, not its external relations or internal discourse. Despite an optimistic political culture and public fondness for elections, successive governments have ruled by dividing, not uniting, and by mobilizing supporters into the streets to counter those of the opposition. The weak responses of incumbent administrations—both military and civilian—to repeated natural disasters such as cyclones, floods, and famines have revealed shortcomings in government organizational capabilities and have sparked protests and revolts. The loss of "performance legitimacy" has been the frequent cause of government turnover. Thus, the stability suggested by fifteen consecutive years of army rule followed by sixteen years of civilian government before control of the government returned to the military in early 2007 is largely illusory.

Such problems caused the collapse in 1975 of the country's first government, led by founding father Sheikh Mujibur Rahman and his leftist Awami League (AL). The urban, elite-based AL had secured broad support for the independence movement from peasants with promises of land reform. The party's increasingly autocratic conduct and the failure of both its economic policies and its response to widespread famine and floods sparked a public revolt that brought the military into power, ending Bangladesh's brief first attempt at parliamentary democracy.

The two military regimes that successively ran the country for the next decade and a half used political control mechanisms similar to those of their Pakistani counterparts—though for purely tactical domestic ends and with largely local consequences. In Bangladesh, unlike in Pakistan, the military was riven with political factions, resulting in several intra-army coup attempts. After defeating the leftist factions, military strongman Ziaur Rahman ("Zia") sought to bolster his legitimacy and support by Islamicizing the constitution and allying with the country's Islamists, specifically the Jamaat-i-Islami (JI), whose leaders had been exiled in disgrace for siding with Pakistan against Bangladesh's independence in 1971.[58] As in Pakistan,

---

[57] Anand Kumar, "Bangladesh's Quest for Nuclear Energy," Institute for Defence Studies and Analyses, IDSA Strategic Comments, October 17, 2007, http://www.idsa.in/publications/stratcomments/AnandKumar171007.htm.

[58] On the rise of Bangladesh's Jamaat-i-Islami party, see Bhuian Md. Monoar Kabir, *Politics and Development of the Jamaat-e-Islami, Bangladesh* (Delhi: Asian Publishers, 2006), 207.

the army-Islamist alliance brought moderate Islamist parties into the political mainstream and pulled national politics to the Right. Bangladesh's Islamist parties, however, were quick to distance themselves from the military and establish political autonomy. Like Pakistan's army, Bangladesh's armed forces under Zia's successor, General Hussain Muhammad Ershad, packaged their rule as democracy. Military leaders altered the constitution to create a strong presidential system, established a "King's party," held a referendum, and allowed anti-AL elements to form the right-of-center Bangladesh Nationalist Party (BNP). The army's efforts to manipulate an election, however, sparked a boycott by the opposition and broad protests. The collapse of the second military regime opened the way for the return of a parliamentary system in 1990.

Dominated by the BNP under Khaleda Zia and the AL under Sheikh Hasina and marked by their fractious alternation in power, parliamentary government from 1991–2006 restored the machinery of democracy but further weakened key institutions of government. Competition between the two parties for patronage further politicized the bureaucracy and deepened corruption while the new institution of the caretaker government politicized the judiciary.[59] The original distinctions between the BNP—with its urban middle-class business base and pro-Pakistani, pro-Islamic tilt—and the rural-centered pro-Indian AL gave way to competing personality cults between Khaleda and Hasina. Pluralism, however, flourished. Bangladesh's small leftist parties persevered. Although eclipsed by the two large parties, new and diverse Islamist parties mushroomed in Bangladesh in the 1990s. These groups, though small in size, had appeal because they appeared cleaner and more earnest than the BNP and AL and because the values these groups set forth seemed to rise above the partisan fray.[60]

Moreover, despite partisan strife and political disorder, the country's economic and social indicators—including life expectancy, unemployment, health, and education—steadily improved, in part because economic development remained a consensus goal. Key to the so-called Bangladesh paradox, wherein the country maintained steady economic growth, poverty reduction, and social progress despite weak governance, were the roles of NGOs and private investment as well as targeted government efforts.[61]

---

[59] Ali Riaz, *Islamist Militancy in Bangladesh: A Complex Web* (London and New York: Routledge, 2008), 6–28.

[60] "Bangladesh Today," International Crisis Group, Asia Report, no. 121, October 23, 2006, 11–12.

[61] World Bank, *Bangladesh: Strategy for Sustained Growth,* Bangladesh Development Series 18, July 2007, xv and xxiv, http://siteresources.worldbank.org/SOUTHASIAEXT/Resources/Publications/448813-1185396961095/4030558-1185396985915/fullreport.pdf.

Bangladesh's vibrant civil society also has been credited with helping to maintain this paradox.

Nevertheless, over the past six years, spiraling partisan violence and deteriorating public security have raised concerns that improvements in Bangladesh's social and economic indicators might be at risk. Largely unchallenged vigilante attacks by Islamists began damaging the country's reputation for tolerance and blurred the boundary with terrorism. As in Pakistan, these trends have raised a number of questions, specifically whether basic political dynamics in Bangladesh have changed, whether the established national narrative of the development state has been affected, and what impact the military's de facto takeover in early 2007 might have.

Bangladesh on the Eve of a New U.S. Administration

Bangladesh's recent return to military rule and Pakistan's recent emergence from such rule seem like opposite halves of the same cycle. Yet the domestic instability and partisan political violence that preceded the de facto coup in Bangladesh differed markedly in genesis, scope, and impact from the instability that preceded the 1999 coup in Pakistan. Likewise, the stakes and opportunities for U.S. policy are significantly different in the two countries. Most importantly, in sharp contrast to Pakistan, Bangladesh has been peripheral to the U.S.-led war on terrorism.

The trigger for the abrogation of democratic processes and the de facto return of the military in Bangladesh was tactical and political: the AL and the BNP refused to negotiate an end to a stalemate on procedures for elections that were scheduled for late 2006. This political confrontation set off violent demonstrations and work stoppages, causing the political system to grind to a halt.

The military's intervention to prolong caretaker rule in order to restore order and repair the electoral system initially was greeted with some relief at home as well as abroad. Although convinced of the legitimacy of the political process and somewhat inured to political violence, many Bangladeshis had grown uneasy over the increasing lethality of partisan attacks in the cities. Thus, the postponement of elections seemed desirable to protect the national goal of economic development as well as the international donor objective of improving internal stability. The pause in electoral democracy promised to improve the integrity of the process, which was a U.S. priority. The stated reform agenda reassuringly focused on restoring credibility to institutions damaged by partisan manipulation of the electoral process—for example, by reconstituting the election commission and judiciary, which had been stacked by the outgoing BNP-led coalition, and by redressing blatant corruption.[62]

It soon became apparent, however, that the military intended to remain in power. Military officials cracked down harshly on all political activity, arrested senior leaders of the AL and the BNP, and rounded up local and national officials and prominent businessmen on corruption charges. Moreover, the military announced plans for broader, longer-term reforms that implied the continuation of military rule beyond the end of 2008, the point at which officials had promised to hold a parliamentary election to return the country to civilian rule. Many of the reforms were technocratic in nature and designed to expunge rather than channel political negotiations and organizations. Military loyalists replaced dismissed administrators.[63]

As in Pakistan after 1999, initial relief over the military's return to power—with its promise of probity and competence—gave way to unease over the vulnerability of the new order to old problems, such as corruption.[64] Of greatest concern in Bangladesh was the growing damage to investor confidence and economic growth in the year after the military takeover. Relying increasingly on performance legitimacy to justify their takeover, the generals now risk a public backlash if they stay in office.

Another key factor in Bangladesh—even without the regional perturbations affecting Pakistan—is Islamist extremism. Like their counterparts in Pakistan, Bangladesh's leaders have been slow to acknowledge the growth of a problem with domestic militancy.[65] One reason may be that some of the main Bangladeshi extremist groups publicly declared themselves only in 2005. Although it is now clear that extremist activity grew before September 11, U.S. concerns with respect to Bangladesh at the time centered on the possibility for opportunistic international terrorist activities in a turbulent country with weak and corrupt law-and-order functions and a history of domestic Islamist political activism. September 11 brought more U.S. attention to Bangladesh and spurred bilateral counterterrorism consultations and technical U.S. assistance.

Despite warnings that Bangladesh could be the site of the next Islamist revolution, the problem there is much smaller than that in Pakistan and so far has involved no challenge to government control of territory. Unlike

---

[62] "Restoring Democracy in Bangladesh," International Crisis Group, Asia Report no. 151, April 28, 2008, 6.

[63] Ibid., 16–20.

[64] "Bangladesh Clamps Down," *Economist,* February 10, 2000; and "The Clean-up: Bangladesh," *Economist,* November 10, 2007. The latter reports that the intelligence services were accumulating shares in private media companies as the price of releasing these companies' owners from detention.

[65] Alex Perry, "Reining in the Radicals," *Time,* February 28, 2005.

the extremist militant groups that now threaten Pakistan's internal stability, those in Bangladesh are not the product of years of official sponsorship. Moreover, notwithstanding unconfirmed reports after September 11 that al Qaeda and Taliban fighters transited the port of Chittagong and some less central areas of the country, there is little evidence that Bangladesh's militant groups take direction from outside the country—although they surely draw inspiration from extremist actions elsewhere.[66]

Views vary on how much this home-based extremism may threaten Bangladesh's stability in the medium term, in part because information is spotty and contradictory. Some analysts point out that extremist activity has been occurring in Bangladesh for some time. From this perspective the trend line looks less alarming, especially considering the high concurrent levels of partisan violence and crime.[67] Trend analysis on extremist activity is further complicated by the fact that what is now being described as terrorism had been called "targeted political violence" or "vigilantism."[68] Most observers agree that, although tolerant brands of Islam are generally still embraced in Bangladesh, support for Islamist goals and pressure tactics is increasing, particularly in rural areas. Some see this trend as a local outgrowth of separate "little traditions."[69] In contrast, other analysts see a systematic effort by hard-line *mullahs* (Islamic clerics) to capture and impose their values on local institutions, including the judicial system, thereby creating Islamist enclaves. Some of these mullahs reportedly have succeeded in closing down local development projects by issuing a *fatwa* (religious decree that invokes Islamic law) against NGOs, much like their counterparts in Pakistan's Swat area.[70]

There is consensus that Islamist militant groups in Bangladesh have grown by exploiting lawlessness and ineffective governance. As in Pakistan, some militant groups are linked to Islamist parties that were initially fostered by the military. Their religious identity provided these groups a cloak of legitimacy, which made authorities reluctant to put them out of business. Bangladesh's tumultuous political scene also helped obscure

---

[66] On fighters allegedly transiting the port of Chittagong and other areas, see "Bangladesh Today," 1–3. Bangladesh's first suicide bombing occurred in December 2005. See David Montero, "Islamic Extremism Strikes Bangladesh," Frontline/World web log, January 31, 2006, http://www.pbs.org/frontlineworld/blog/2006/01/bangladesh_what_1.html.

[67] "Bangladesh Today."

[68] Ali Riaz, *God Willing: The Politics of Islamism in Bangladesh* (Lanham: Rowman and Littlefield Publishers, 2004).

[69] Taj I. Hashmi, "Islamic Resurgence in Bangladesh: Genesis, Dynamics and Implications," in *Religious Radicalism and Security in South Asia*, ed. Satu Limaye, Robert Wirsing, and Mohan Malik (Honolulu: Asia-Pacific Center for Security Studies, 2004), 35–72.

[70] Ali Riaz, "Traditional Institutions as Tools of Political Islam in Bangladesh," *Journal of Asian and African Studies* 40, no. 3 (2005): 171–96.

militant activities. Some believe that the inclusion of two Islamist parties—
one of them the venerable JI—in the BNP coalition of 2001–06 helped create
a permissive environment for extremists.[71] Others cite the opportunities
provided by Bangladesh's transit role in the international black market for
small arms.[72] Until 2005, when donors threatened to suspend aid if the
government did not take steps to reduce violence and Islamic militancy,
senior officials publicly denied knowledge of groups such as the Jagrata
Muslim Janata Bangladesh (JMJB), a lead element for several years in
religious and militant attacks in the north.[73]

It seems unlikely that the suspension of democracy will improve
Bangladesh's ability to cope with such difficulties as are described above;
to the contrary, the absence of alternatives might even increase the appeal
to young Bangladeshis of Islamist organizations that continue operations
even when the formal political system has been suspended. Nevertheless,
in a move interpreted by some as a sop to U.S. counterterrorism concerns,
the military-backed interim government arrested and executed the leaders
of the most violent militant groups in 2007—an approach whose long-
term impact remains to be seen.[74] By one account, the crackdown merely
dispersed the remaining militants.

The U.S. Response

Evaluating the U.S. Approach So Far

In dealing with recent and prospective difficulties in Bangladesh, U.S.
officials begin with an important advantage: decades of mostly cordial
bilateral engagement and policies premised on a long-term view of
Bangladesh's problems and needs. Since inception, Bangladesh has been
a top recipient of U.S. aid, largely targeted to economic development or
social capital. The fiscal year 2006 congressional budget justification of the
U.S. Agency for International Development succinctly summarized U.S.
hopes for Bangladesh. The United States hopes for a "better functioning
democracy" capable of delivering better governance and human rights;
"continued economic prosperity to provide stability and hope for all

---

[71] "Bangladesh Today," International Crisis Group, 11.

[72] Riaz, *Islamist Militancy in Bangladesh.*

[73] Perry, "Reining in the Radicals."

[74] See Bibhu Prasad Routray, "Home-grown Islamist 'Neutralised' but Shadowy Masterminds
Survives," *Weekly Dur Desh,* March 25, 2007, http://www.durdesh.net/news/Article499.html.

Bangladeshis to stem the potential growth of extremism"; and improved bilateral relations.[75]

U.S. support for Bangladesh's top priority, economic development, has paid rich dividends in goodwill toward the United States, despite growing public opposition to the U.S.-led war on terrorism. Many Bangladeshis assume incorrectly that the United States is their leading bilateral donor, which is in fact Japan.[76] In partnership with other donor countries and organizations, Washington has periodically exerted pressure on Dhaka on domestic issues, often to good effect—as in the February 2005 démarche where donors demanded that Dhaka either clamp down on security problems and address growing corruption and declining governance or risk suspension of aid.[77]

What Alternative U.S. Strategies Can Be Envisaged?

U.S. policy opportunities and constraints will depend partly on events in Bangladesh and the surrounding region. As in Pakistan, political legitimacy will be key both to successful counterterrorism efforts and to internal stability. Washington has not yet pulled out the stops on the democracy issue. U.S. policymakers could join with other donors to press Bangladesh's "transitional" military government for a timetable for re-democratization. The recent example of Musharraf's Pakistan is a reminder that constraining party participation and depoliticizing governance in favor of technocratic solutions will place new stresses on the system, particularly in Bangladesh's participatory political culture. U.S. advocacy for a return to democracy in Bangladesh would help dispel concerns among Westernized elites over a double standard on democracy. Returning the country to the chaotic *status quo ante* would not, however, advance U.S. interests. Critical to avoiding the problems of the recent past would be a negotiated consensus with political parties, including the BNP and the AL, on boundaries for political demonstrations. The value placed by Dhaka on protecting Bangladesh's international image improves the chances that international pressure would succeed. For instance, concerted interventions by foreign donors reportedly

---

[75] See the U.S. Agency for International Development (USAID), "Budget Justification to the Congress, Fiscal Year 2006," http://www.usaid.gov/policy/budget/cbj2006/ane/bd.html.

[76] According to Terror Free Tomorrow, four-fifths of Bangladeshis opposed U.S.-led efforts to fight terrorism. This number is comparable to the percentage of Pakistanis and Indonesians who opposed U.S. counterterrorism efforts. The high overall favorable level of opinion for the United States in Bangladesh was attributable to U.S. aid. See "Unprecedented Terror Free Tomorrow Polls," 4.

[77] Perry, "Reining in the Radicals."

induced the government to crack down on human trafficking in 2005 and on Islamist militant groups in 2006.[78]

Security worries will continue to limit U.S. cultural diplomacy efforts on the ground in Bangladesh. As a result, future soft-power efforts may need to rely more on media and educational materials. Although U.S.-backed programs focused on stimulating job creation would address a leading concern in Bangladesh, costly new initiatives will face stiff competition from competing U.S. commitments elsewhere in the region, especially if the U.S. budget is cut.

Uncertainties over trends in Bangladesh warrant close monitoring for the emergence of wild card scenarios. Some of these scenarios turn on a potential increase in terrorism. Bangladeshi Islamist extremists might adopt insurgent tactics against government forces (as counterparts have done in Pakistan), target Americans in Bangladesh, or export terrorism to expatriate communities in Asia or in Europe. A different type of wild card would be the rise of Maoist extremism in Bangladesh, as has occurred in parts of India and in Nepal. U.S. contingency planning for Bangladesh also will need to encompass possibilities unrelated to terrorism, such as continuous economic setbacks—which would threaten a linchpin of national consensus—or outside military aggression—for example, from Myanmar.

U.S. policy options for responding to increased terrorism in Bangladesh differ little from those for Pakistan: more training of local security forces in counterterrorism and counter-insurgency, more cooperation with Bangladesh's neighbors on counterterrorism and intelligence, and a more direct U.S. role in tracking or apprehending militants. If terrorism were to surge in Bangladesh, U.S. policymakers might consider the merits of "backseat driving" rather than trying to directly steer Dhaka's response in order to avoid stirring nationalist rejection. Multilateralizing counterterrorism advice and training also might help defuse Bangladeshi resistance to being treated like a "second Pakistan."

Considering the Big Picture

Cementing the goodwill of Bangladesh's elite may yield valuable dividends for Washington in the future. As in Pakistan, the best insurance policy for U.S. entrée and influence in Bangladesh in times of crisis is high-level engagement by Washington policymakers during quiet times. Apart from U.S. equities in Bangladesh's own stability, cooperation from Dhaka may be key to future U.S. options in multilateral forums or on issues relating to Pakistan, Myanmar, or even China. As a result, the next

---

[78] "Bangladesh Today," 5.

administration should renew cabinet-level U.S. visits to Bangladesh when security conditions permit.

Putting Bangladesh—a long-time "poster child" for Islamic democracy—back on Washington's senior policy agenda would pave the way for raising Bangladesh's visibility on the agenda of cooperative diplomacy with U.S. allies and international organizations. Finally, given Bangladesh's ambivalence toward India, tact would dictate minimizing communications to Dhaka through New Delhi. Ultimately, U.S. aid, as in Pakistan, also will remain important to U.S. influence in Bangladesh.

EXECUTIVE SUMMARY

This chapter considers U.S. policy toward Central Asia/Afghanistan.

MAIN ARGUMENT:
The challenge for the U.S. in this region is to strengthen weak sovereignties; promote effective, secular governance based on consent; eliminate poverty; and build middle classes receptive to modern education and values. This will render the region secure, self-governing, well-disposed toward the West, and an attractive model for Muslin societies elsewhere. The opening of continental trade bridging Europe, China, the Indian subcontinent, Russia, and the Middle East is a critical tool for achieving this.

POLICY IMPLICATIONS:
- Success in Afghanistan is a prerequisite for achieving these goals. The U.S. must help Kabul significantly expand its army and police and help it deliver effective governance. The U.S. should also work to broaden security options in the region beyond existing Russian and Chinese-dominated structures.

- A successful U.S. strategy will acknowledge that the strategies of Central Asian states are based on the development of balanced relations with external powers. This requires a regional approach based on sustained relationships. These will offer a balancing alternative to the region's growing dependence on Russia and China.

- The 1992 trade and investment framework agreement between the U.S. and regional states could become a useful forum. Engaging Central Asian firms in Afghanistan reconstruction could also encourage regional interaction. The U.S. should welcome present and future initiatives to create purely regional consultative organs.

- Steady engagement will advance human rights and democratization more effectively than punitive measures. "Democracy promotion" might be expanded beyond elections to include the development of parliamentary rights and institutions, and good governance generally.

A Regional Approach to Afghanistan and Its Neighbors

S. Frederick Starr

Afghanistan absorbs more money and costs more American lives than any foreign concern except Iraq. Much has been achieved there; much has not. This chapter seeks to answer the question, how can the United States "get it right" in Afghanistan?

One must ask at the outset if the subject is Afghanistan alone, or the broader Central Asian region of which Afghanistan is a part. Since these two have constituted a single cultural zone for 3,000 years, the chapter assumes that they offer related challenges and possibilities today. It is convenient to view both the five former Soviet states and Afghanistan as part of a broader zone, "Greater Central Asia." The immediate U.S. concern there is to thwart terrorism, but the region presents broader challenges: to strengthen weak sovereignties, promote effective governance, eliminate poverty, and build a middle class that is open to modern values.

These are all Muslim societies whose traditions favor moderation and openness, notwithstanding recent manifestations of radicalization. Because of this, the United States has a stake in their success. How to meet this challenge must lie at the heart of any effective strategy for the region.

An effective strategy would heed the interests and activities of other powers in the region and at the same time flow from an understanding of how the regional states themselves (including Afghanistan) perceive the many pressures to which they are subject. The chapter therefore reviews the strategies of Russia and China in Central Asia as well as those of Japan, India, Europe, and the United States.

S. Frederick Starr is Founding Chairman of the Central Asia-Caucasus Institute at the School of Advanced International Studies (SAIS), Johns Hopkins University. He can be reached at <sfstarr@jhu.edu>.

It is now clear that a one-sided emphasis on Afghanistan after September 11 has eroded what were successful U.S. policies in the former Soviet states of Central Asia. This has created geopolitical space that Russia and China have rushed to fill. Convinced that the U.S. focus is elsewhere, regional countries have had no choice but to fall into line. The United States has yet to solve the Rubik's Cube of Afghanistan, but its inaction elsewhere in the region has undermined the security of other states in Central Asia.

The Central Asian states seek to advance their own agendas amidst this welter of pressures by promoting "balance" among their principal partners. These states have added a positive new twist to this old concept: instead of balancing enemies, they seek to balance friends. This enables regional states to maintain cordial relations with all their external neighbors and to use each relationship to balance the others. A successful U.S. strategy in the region will acknowledge this principle and work with it.

How can the United States position itself in the region as a balance to China and Russia? Success in Afghanistan is a prerequisite, and to this end the United States should help the Afghans expand their army to 150,000 and help Kabul deliver good governance to the population. Many related aspects of reconstruction can be effectively advanced by engaging firms from the rest of Central Asia rather than from further abroad.

The United States is the only country in a position to broker an understanding between Afghanistan and Pakistan. The chapter considers how this might be done and proposes specific rewards to Pakistan following an agreement, including support for Pakistan's various trans-Afghan transport projects that are now languishing. Since these benefit the rest of Central Asia as much as Pakistan or Afghanistan, they can become the key to a new region-wide strategy.

To date, the United States has proposed no serious response to the Shanghai Cooperative Organization (SCO), which has now even approached Afghanistan. A first response by the United States might be to greatly expand the trade and investment framework agreements (TIFA) that it has signed with regional states. The chapter suggests that the countries themselves, mindful of their need for balance, will welcome this.

U.S. officials will surely ask about the cost of what is proposed here. Bluntly, the total cost for Afghanistan since 2001 is far less than what the United States spent in the 1950s and 1960s to transform South Korea or

Taiwan.[1] Moreover, U.S. expenditures on Central Asian countries are surpassed by expenditures on dozens of countries of far less geopolitical significance.[2] Between 1998 and 2006 the average annual expenditure on each of the former Soviet republics of Central Asia was only $54 million, as compared to $97 million for each of six Balkan countries. One must also compare these costs with the price the United States would pay for strategic failure in the region.

Starting with a review of Russian and Chinese policy toward what might be called Greater Central Asia, the following presentation discusses the policies of other relevant countries and of the United States. The next section then considers how Central Asian states and Afghanistan respond to the realities confronting them, and the extent of their recent progress. Following this, the chapter proposes principles for a new, positive phase of U.S. policy toward the region, and suggests how they might be implemented. The chapter concludes by listing immediate actions to be taken.

The Environment of Greater Central Asia

Between the collapse of the USSR and September 11, U.S. policy assumed that "Central Asia" consisted only of five former Soviet republics, i.e., Kazakhstan, the Kyrgyz Republic, Tajikistan, Turkmenistan, and Uzbekistan. Following the defeat of the Taliban government, U.S. policy acknowledged that through the millennia Afghanistan, too, has been an integral part of Central Asia. The establishment in 2006 of a new Bureau of Central and South Asian Affairs in the Department of State reflected this understanding. In a cultural sense, one might also suggest that the Chinese autonomous region of Xinjiang, with its large Turkic and Muslim population, and the northwestern part of Pakistan should also be borne in mind when considering any future U.S. policy for the region. The case *pro et contra* for including Iran is discussed below.

All these diverse states and regions interact with one another in important ways. They also interact significantly with countries beyond the region, including the United States. This leads to the obvious conclusion

---

[1] The only person to have attempted this important budgetary comparison is Sam Brannen of the Center for Strategic and International Studies, Washington, D.C. While the Afghan expenditure is, of course, ongoing, Brandon's evidence indicated clearly the vastly greater sum spent by the United States to bring about transformation in South Korea and Taiwan. See Sam Brannen, "Comparison in Real and Nominal Dollar Terms of the U.S. Foreign Assistance to Taiwan and South Korea," (unpublished manuscript, 2004).

[2] See United States Agency for International Development, "U.S. Overseas Loans and Grants [Greenbook]," 2007, http://qesdb.usaid.gov/cgi-bin/broker.exe?_program=gbkprogs.country_list. sas&_service=default&unit=R.

that any successful policy toward Afghanistan or toward Central Asia should be regional in scope. While recognizing the profound differences within the region, it must address the realities of what might be called "Greater Central Asia."

What features are common to the countries comprising this region? First, they are Muslim. Acutely conscious of their defining contributions to the early history of Islam, these countries consider that they have as much claim as the Arab countries to being the heartland of the faith. The Hanafi tradition that predominates across the region is notable for its moderation and openness to the world. Second, the former Soviet countries have high levels of education. Afghanistan's literacy rate remains very low but is rising fast. Third, they are new states, having emerged from colonial control by Russia or Britain. Afghanistan may have been formed two centuries ago but it, too, has an entirely new government. This means these states are struggling not only to formulate new laws, set up parliaments, and so forth, but to assure their very sovereignty. Finally, with the exception of Pakistan, all are emerging from socialism and the habits it engendered. It is no exaggeration to say that all the values that the United States seeks to advance in the region were alien to its governments and populations a mere fifteen years ago.

It is not surprising that the leaders of these new states are profoundly conscious of their weakness in the face of internal and external threats. Americans might usefully recall the conditions that prevailed in their own country during the early Republic. This said, the geopolitical realities of Central Asia are far more threatening than what the United States faced two centuries ago. Central Asia is alone among world regions in being ringed by dominant world economies. No other world region has four nuclear states on its borders, two of which, Russia and China, have their own grand strategies that embrace Central Asia and have created integrative mechanisms for achieving them.

Protective of their sovereignties, Central Asian states view all projects for "integration" with caution, even when they are unavoidable. Their approach is to favor projects that focus on economics, counterterrorism, or drug trafficking, rather than geopolitical goals. The same concerns have hindered their own efforts at intraregional cooperation, which is needed to assure regular supplies of water and energy and to open potentially lucrative channels of continental trade. The only issue on which all five former Soviet states have agreed has been the creation of a nuclear free zone in Central Asia.[3]

China, Russia, and Greater Central Asia

The grand strategies of the states of Central Asia arise from their perceptions of the threats facing them. Theirs is a world of geopolitical dangers inherent in Central Asia's location at the heart of the Eurasian land mass. Any effective U.S. policy should therefore be two-sided, addressing their concerns as well as those of the United States. To this end, it is important to understand both the opportunities and dangers presented by each of the major external powers relevant to the region including, of course, the United States itself. Fragile young states cannot pursue benefits by ignoring associated threats. From a Central Asian perspective, all policy must first be defensive.

Russia is linked to the region through an institutional network created during more than a century of colonial rule. Productive relations with this neighbor are essential but in the short run are hostage to the "imperial hangover" that currently prevails in official Russia. The Putin government pandered to this mood, creating or exploiting such reintegrative instruments as Eurasian Security Organization (Eurasec), the Eurasian Economic Space, and the SCO. These, along with the state energy monopoly, Gazprom, are the tools by which Russia seeks to advance its geopolitical control.[4]

The history of the now defunct Central Asia Union is instructive. Founded in the mid-1990s, this was a purely Central Asian entity until Russia demanded to join as an observer and then as a member. Once accepted, Russia dissolved the purely regional organization and merged it into a new Russian-dominated entity. Earlier, the United States had hoped that the entire region, as well as Russia, would join the World Trade Organization (WTO), obviating the need for a more localized trade zone. But while Kyrgyzstan succeeded in joining the WTO[5] and Kazakhstan is on the threshold of doing so, the other countries are far from meeting WTO

---

[3] On this project, see "Statement by Ministers of Foreign Affairs of the Republic of Kazakhstan, the Kyrgyz Republic, the Republic of Tajikistan, Turkmenistan and the Republic of Uzbekistan," Press Release, September 8, 2006, http://cns.miis.edu/pubs/week/pdf_support/060908_ministers_statement.pdf; and Scott Parrish and William Potter, "Central Asian States Establish Nuclear-Weapon-Free-Zone Despite U.S. Opposition," James Martin Center for Nonproliferation Studies, CNS Research Story, September 5, 2006, http://cns.miis.edu/pubs/week/060905.htm.

[4] On Gazprom and Central Asia, see Stephen Blank, "Russia and Central Asian Gas: Recent Trends and Their Implications," Central Asia-Caucasus Institute, Central Asia-Caucasus Institute Analyst, March 19, 2008, http://www.cacianalyst.org/?q=node/4817.

[5] John Quigley, "Kyrgyzstan's Accession to the WTO," European Institute for Asian Studies, EurAsia Bulletin 8, no. 1 and 2, January–February, 2004, 16–24.

requirements. This has left ample space for Russia's politicized version of an "economic community."

Similarly, Eurasec initially comprised only three Central Asian states, but Russia rushed to enroll Uzbekistan after the latter's feud with the United States in 2005–06. Eurasec is now moving swiftly to integrate military and intelligence functions. By doing so, Eurasec threatens to marginalize NATO, which during the 1990s engaged in constructive work across the region (excepting Turkmenistan) through its Partnership for Peace program but today is focused overwhelmingly on Afghanistan alone.[6]

The SCO was initially a Chinese initiative designed to neutralize Kazakhstan, Kyrgyzstan, and Tajikistan as bases for secessionist propaganda launched against its Turkic region of Xinjiang. China invited Russia to be a co-founder. President Putin had other ideas, however.[7] Having unsuccessfully opposed the readiness of Central Asian states to cooperate with Washington after September 11, Putin tried to use the SCO to marginalize the U.S. presence. It was Putin who proposed in 2005 that the SCO go on record against U.S. military presence in the region.[8] Under pressure from Moscow, the SCO now assumes a more closed character and has adopted a tougher stance with respect to the United States, thus limiting the security choices of the Central Asian states. Recent demarches by SCO to Afghanistan, taken without consultation with the United States or NATO, indicate clearly the likely future directions of this organization.

By promoting the SCO's expansion, China seeks to create a region-wide consultative group that will legitimize China's voice in economic and security affairs. Unlike Putin, China seeks to avoid conflict with the United States and is in fact cooperating de facto with Washington on regional transport.[9]

China offers all Central Asian states, including Afghanistan, welcome investments in extractive projects (gold, copper, zinc, diamonds, molybdenum, and uranium) and also broke Gazprom's monopoly over energy exports from the region. But China poses a threat to all Central

---

[6] "Partnership for Peace: Framework Document," January 10–11, 1994, available on the North Atlantic Treaty Organization (NATO) website, http://www.nato.int/docu/comm/49-95/c940110b.htm.

[7] On the Shanghai Cooperation Organization (SCO), see Vladimir Portyakov, "The Shanghai Cooperation Organization: Achievements, Problems, Prospects," *Far Eastern Affairs: A Russian Journal on China, Japan and Asia-Pacific* 35, no. 4 (2007): 1–9.

[8] Even though the SCO's actual resolution on foreign military in Central Asia did not mention the United States, and could be interpreted as applying equally to Russia, Putin convinced the press that Central Asian states themselves had voted to eject the United States from the region. Author's personal interviews with the participants.

[9] As exemplified by China's new road across the Pamirs to Tajikistan, which connects eventually to the new U.S. bridge over the Panzh River (Amu Darya) to Afghanistan.

Asian states. Chinese manufactures already dominate the Central Asian economies. Uzbekistan openly fears that this will lead to deindustrialization, and has therefore reinforced its protectionist regimen to withstand the Chinese danger.

A similar threat is posed by the possible large-scale inflow of Chinese workers. The Central Asian states watched this process unfold in China's Xinjiang province, which has moved from being 99% Turkic and Muslim in 1949 to having almost a Han Chinese majority today. They fear that Chinese immigration will leave Central Asia with large Chinese trading colonies in the major cities and the local population relegated to secondary centers and agriculture.

Such prospects make the Central Asian states more receptive to alternative visions of economic cooperation. But to date, the only alternative has been offered by Russia and, as described above, it involves political integration. There are many other multilateral organizations to which the Central Asian states belong.[10] All can help Central Asian states pursue their goals, but none aspires to offer any kind of serious counterweight to the entities promoted by Russia and by China.

Other Powers and Greater Central Asia

This does not mean, however, that other countries are not immediately relevant to the concerns of the Central Asian states. Among these, Japan, Korea, India, and the European Union (EU) are particularly significant. Japan's involvement entails institutional reform, economic development and humanitarian assistance, and other issues. While carefully avoiding frontal competition with China and Russia in the region, Japan has adroitly positioned itself as a powerful friend and patient champion of market economics and democracy, backing its support with timely investments. All of these ties are crystallized in Japan's distinctive "Japan Plus Central Asia" initiative, in which all Central Asian states participate and which will doubtless soon include Afghanistan as well.[11] This structure provides for annual meetings at the presidential level supported by a web of ministerial ties, all of them focusing on specific projects that are beneficial to both parties. Central Asian governments welcome this relationship, not least because it arouses none of the fears of hegemony to which both Russian and

---

[10] The Economic Cooperation Organization (along with Turkey, Pakistan, Afghanistan, and Iran) has never aspired to do more than coordinate some transport infrastructure projects and set up a joint development bank in Istanbul. The 56-member Organization of Islamic Conference embraces all Central Asian states.

[11] Takeshi Yagi, "'Central Asia Plus Japan' Dialogue and Japan's Policy toward Central Asia," *Asia Europe Journal* 5, no. 1 (March 2007): 13–16.

Chinese ties give rise. Japan has initiated this institutional approach on its own, without involving the United States or any other third party. Thus, the relationship with Japan offers all the Central Asian states and Afghanistan an "anchor to windward" that elicits no corresponding security fears.[12]

Much the same can be said of relations with Korea. Koreans have shown themselves to be venturesome investors in the region and steady partners in other respects. But in spite of its interest in the large Korean minorities in Uzbekistan and Kazakhstan, Korea has shied away from broader geopolitical issues in its dealings with Central Asia, showing no interest in developing a more institutionalized relationship.[13]

In terms of undeveloped potential, India's relationship to Central Asia dwarfs its relationship to all other Asian states.[14] India's economic might alone commands attention, as does its proximity—New Delhi is less than three hours by plane from all the Central Asian capitals, as compared to about six hours for either Beijing or Moscow.[15] Nor is India suspected of harboring geopolitical pretensions in Central Asia, although its competition with China is obvious to all. An exception is India's close link with Afghanistan, which since September 11 has become a new front in India's ongoing confrontation with Pakistan.

Only in the past two years has India begun to awaken to its potential in Central Asia. India's refurbishing in 2007 of a small airbase at Aini in Tajikistan marked the first instance of India projecting its military power abroad. Russia initially welcomed this move but then objected vehemently, realizing that the airbase could dilute its own military aspirations in the region.[16] It remains unclear whether India will follow this up with other initiatives in the economic and political spheres. Japan would doubtless welcome such steps, for they would reinforce its own approach to the region. The chief impediment is India's lack of easy access to the region by land. Any easing of tensions between India and Pakistan will open the possibility

---

[12] Christopher Len, "Japan's Central Asian Diplomacy: Motivations, Implications and Prospects for the Region," *China and Eurasia Forum Quarterly* 3, no. 3 (November 2005): 127–49, http://www.silkroadstudies.org/new/docs/CEF/CEF_Quarterly_November_2005.pdf.

[13] For an optimistic view of Korea's relations with Central Asia, see the editorial by Vice Minister of Foreign Affairs and Trade Cho Jung-pyo, "Korea, Central Asia Coming Closer," *Korea Times,* November 18, 2007, http://www.koreatimes.co.kr/www/news/opinon/opi_view.asp?newsIdx=13914&categoryCode=198.

[14] On India's relations with Central Asia, see Scott Moore, "Peril and Promise: A Survey of India's Strategic Relationship with Central Asia," *Central Asian Survey* 26, no. 2 (June 2007): 279–91.

[15] New Delhi is 1,631 kilometers (or 1,014 miles) from Almaty, as compared with 3,280 kilometers (or 2,038 miles) for Beijing and 3,108 kilometers (or 1,931 miles) for Moscow.

[16] Stephen J. Blank, *Natural Allies? Regional Security in Asia and Prospects for Indo-American Strategic Cooperation* (Carlisle: Strategic Studies Institute, 2005), http://www.strategicstudiesinstitute.army.mil/pubs/display.cfm?pubID=626.

of overland trade and hence greatly expanded relations with Central Asia. However, even a strengthening of India's diplomatic presence will be of significance, given Russia's and China's ambitions.

Meanwhile, the growing presence of Indian traders and entrepreneurs across the region and the deepening interest of Indian strategists in Central Asia suggest that a shift has already begun. The fact that over 2,500 years India has never invaded Central Asia beyond Afghanistan but has been repeatedly invaded from those territories sets India in stark contrast to both Russia and China—a fact that is not lost on Central Asian policymakers.

By contrast, the threats arising from closer ties with Pakistan outweigh potential benefits.[17] Notwithstanding the size of its economy and its large and competent middle class, Pakistan is seen throughout Central Asia, as well as in Afghanistan, as a source of instability. This perception is reinforced by outdated but persistent Soviet-era stereotypes of Pakistan as a land of backwardness and ignorance. The presence there of Islamic fighters from Uzbekistan only deepens the prevailing suspicions.

This said, an expanded Pakistani presence in Central Asia is not excluded. General Musharraf's multiple visits to the region after September 11 suggest that broader rapprochement is possible. Tajikistan aspires to export electricity to Pakistan and Turkmenistan—hoping to build a pipeline across Afghanistan to Pakistan and possibly India—and has maintained cordial relations with Islamabad since gaining independence.[18] Of more immediate importance is Pakistan's new port at Gwadar. Once secure access to Afghanistan's Ring Road is established, this facility can become the gateway for all of Central Asia to the Indian subcontinent and Southeast Asia.[19] The fact that Pakistan sponsored the entry of Afghanistan into the Central Asian Regional Economic Cooperation (CAREC) is especially promising in this regard. Initiated by the Asian Development Bank, CAREC is the best hope for linking Central Asia and Afghanistan with the large economies to the south.[20] It is relevant that the late Benazir Bhutto, during her presidency, instituted a far-sighted planning process

[17] For a competent review of Pakistan's relations with Central Asia, see Meena Singh Roy, "Pakistan's Strategies in Central Asia," *Strategic Analysis* 30, no. 4 (October–December 2006): 798–833, http://www.idsa.in/publications/strategic-analysis/2006/oct dec06/Meena%20Singh%20Roy.pdf.

[18] "Islamic Republic of Afghanistan: Preparing the Natural Gas Development Project," Asian Development Bank, Technical Assistance Consultant's Report, December 2007, http://www.adb.org/Documents/Reports/Consultant/37085-AFG/37085-TACR-AFG.pdf.

[19] On this port, see Tarique Niazi, "Gwadar: China's Naval Outpost on the Indian Ocean," Jamestown Foundation, February 16, 2005, http://www.jamestown.org/news_details.php?news_id=93#.

[20] "Central Asia Regional Economic Cooperation: Comprehensive Action Plan," October 18–20, 2006, available on the Asian Development Bank website, http://www.adb.org/Documents/Events/2006/Fifth-Ministerial-Conference/Comprehensive-Action-Plan.pdf.

for opening such land routes to Central Asia.[21] With her party now once more ascendant, these old plans might be revived. In other words, it is not excluded that a post-Musharraf Pakistan will be less threatening to both Afghanistan and Afghanistan's Central Asian neighbors.

Many factors might lead one to conclude that Iran is even better placed than Pakistan to become an important presence in Central Asia. With close variants of Farsi being the official language of Tajikistan and Afghanistan and widely spoken in Uzbekistan as well, Tehran would appear to be a natural partner to the region. But post-Khomeini Shia Iran is treated with caution across Sunni Central Asia. Accepting this reality, Iran today focuses on economic ties, which are limited but mutually beneficial. Iran, with help from Russia and India, is now constructing a new port at Chabahar on the Persian Gulf with the intention of making it the chief southern gateway for the region.[22] This project, which has the explicit goal of neutralizing Pakistan's Gwadar, is viewed with favor in the region. But Chabahar, to the extent it succeeds, will not only enhance Iran's role in the Afghan economy but, more important, will undermine Pakistan's commitment to the smooth flow of trade across Afghanistan.

From the standpoint of U.S. interests, it is more important that Gwadar succeeds than that Chabahar fails. Indeed, since the further evolution of Iran is not known, it is important to keep open the possibility of fully integrating Iran into the policies proposed here. The geographic and economic logic of this is clear, as is the historical/cultural basis, notwithstanding the religious differences. The conditions for future inclusion would be the termination of Iran's sponsorship of terrorism and signs of progress toward a more secular constitution. If these conditions are met, then the United States might broaden its Greater Central Asia strategy to include Iran and make the concomitant organizational changes.

The Gulf states present an entirely different set of opportunities and concerns. On the one hand, they are astute investors whose projects in Kazakhstan and elsewhere are helping build whole sectors, including tourism. Several Central Asian countries, led by Kazakhstan, are doing some Islamic investing. On the other hand, groups in these same countries have provided not always welcome support to fundamentalist Muslim entities within Central Asia, and Saudi Arabia actively proselytizes there its austere and, to Central Asians, heterodox, form of Islam. Thus, while trade between

---

[21] Tahir Amin, "Pakistan, Afghanistan and the Central Asian States," in *The New Geopolitics of Central Asia and Its Borderlands,* ed. Ali Banuazizi and Myron Weiner (Bloomington: Indiana University Press, 1994), chap. 8.

[22] On Chabahar, see "Developing Eastern Transit Axis," *Iran Daily,* September 4, 2005, http://www.iran-daily.com/1384/2367/html/focus.htm.

the Gulf and Central Asia is booming and Dubai has become the gateway to Kabul, the Central Asian countries have exercised restraint in handling their political and security relations with the Gulf.

Following 1991, Turkey developed great enthusiasm for ties with its long-lost "cousins" to the East, but this did not survive the Turkish economic slump of the mid-1990s. Ties renewed thereafter as Turkish businessmen became active in every country of the region, and some 150 secondary schools and a half-dozen universities were set up and funded by the Turkish government or Muslim philanthropic groups.[23] But if Central Asian leaders participate in Ankara's "Turkic summits,"[24] they are by no means convinced of Prime Minister Erdogan's commitment to secularism.

EU members are together the second-largest outside investors in Central Asia, mainly due to energy investments but increasingly extending to other sectors as well. However, the European countries, with respect to Central Asia, have chosen to focus on issues of importance to themselves, while ignoring others that are of urgent importance to the regional governments, notably security.[25] True, European countries participated in NATO's successful Partnership for Peace program in the region, but they have otherwise hung back, leaving such matters to the United States. Worse, the EU and Germany in particular have shown themselves something of a spoiler with respect to the efforts of the United States and other democratic countries in the region. Thus, the EU refused the Asia Development Bank's proposal to expand its CAREC program to include the United States, the EU, and Japan, even in the face of Japanese and U.S. support for the measure. This negative approach extends even to drug trafficking across the region from Afghanistan, even though Europe is the sole consumer of more than 90% of Afghan opiates. Brussels remains utterly deaf to the suggestion that this might impose on Europe some moral duty to assist the impoverished farmers who grow the raw product, as the U.S. government has done in Colombia under both Democratic and Republican administrations.

Soaring energy prices and Russia's growing role as a source of EU energy have recently prompted Europe to set up regular regional consultations with Central Asian countries at the presidential and ministerial levels. Yet

---

[23] For an excellent review of the school movement, see Bayram Balci, *Missionnaires de l'Islam en Asie centrale: Les écoles turques de Fethullah Gülen* [Islamic Missionaries in Central Asia: the Turkish Schools of Fetulah Gulen] (Istanbul: Institut Français d'Etudes Anatoliennes, 2003).

[24] Igor Torbakov, "Strengthening the 'Eastern Vector': Ankara Hosts Turkic Summit," Jamestown Foundation, Eurasia Daily Monitor 3, no. 214, November 17, 2006, http://www.jamestown.org/edm/article.php?article_id=2371657.

[25] On EU relations with Central Asia, see "European Union and Central Asia: Strategy for a New Partnership," Council of the European Union, October 2007, http://consilium.eu.int/uedocs/cmsUpload/EU_CtrlAsia_EN-RU.pdf.

as of now the EU promotes its own agenda of energy and investment but holds aloof from addressing the Central Asian states' overriding security concerns. This is notably true for Afghanistan. Not only have the large Western European countries been reluctant participants in the NATO mission, but the EU has refused to recast its TRASECA program to include transport across Afghanistan to India as well as directly to China. Thus, while the Europeans are not viewed as a threat (unless they renew their enthusiasm for immediate democratic reform), neither are they yet viewed as a serious geopolitical presence.

The United States, Afghanistan, and the Former Soviet Republics of Central Asia

U.S. activity in the region began with the United States' immediate diplomatic recognition of the new states in 1992 and led to a broad program of support throughout the 1990s. Thanks both to the usefulness of many of these programs and to the eagerness of the new Central Asian states for contact with the heretofore demonized North American power, U.S. presence was widely appreciated. This positive phase culminated in 1998 when Congress passed a Silk Road Strategy Act championed by Senator Brownback of Kansas.

Yet down to 2001 the United States did nothing to address the Central Asian states' (and Russia's) chief security concern, namely Afghanistan. With respect to Afghanistan, Washington preferred to focus on containing the Afghan pathology rather than identifying and addressing its root causes.[26] Several governments in the region tried to warn the United States of the danger of Afghan-based terrorism, but to no avail.[27] On February 16, 1999, a series of explosions rocked Tashkent.[28] The perpetrators were radical Islamists linked to like-minded groups in Afghanistan and Pakistan. Further attacks in Kyrgyzstan in 1998 and 1999 brought only perfunctory responses from Washington. Many in Central Asia asked if Washington was interested

---

[26] See speech by Madeleine K. Albright (presented in Tashkent, Uzbekistan, April 17, 2000), available at Civil Society International's website, http://www.civilsoc.org/resource/albright.htm.

[27] For example, forum meetings at the Central Asia-Caucasus Institute in Washington included March 3, 1999, when the Uzbek ambassador, Sadyk Safaev, and Nancy Lubin discussed "Terrorism Comes to Uzbekistan," and December 1, 1999, when Abdurashid Kory Bakhromov, mufti of Uzbekistan, Sherzod Abdullayev of the Embassy of Uzbekistan, John Shoeberlein of Harvard University, and Glen Howard of Science Applications International Corporation addressed the topic "Political Islam and Terrorism in Central Asia." Unpublished summaries are available from the Central Asia-Caucasus Institute.

[28] Gulnoza Saidazimova, "Uzbekistan: Effect of Tashkent Explosions Still Felt Two Years Later," Radio Free Europe/Radio Liberty, March 27, 2006, http://www.rferl.org/featuresarticle/2006/03/db00d0e9-c2e7-4be7-89c7-5ca39ec49f3d.html.

in promoting their security or only that of the United States. In short, did Washington respect the goals of the Central Asian states themselves?

For a brief moment after September 11 a new age of U.S.-Central Asian cooperation seemed to be dawning, but this did not happen. Instead, U.S. policy in Greater Central Asia withered after September 11 as attention focused almost entirely on Afghanistan. Russia and China moved deliberately and successfully to take advantage of U.S. inattention.

Several factors account for the rapid and steady erosion of U.S. presence in formerly Soviet parts of Central Asia. First, even though President Bush, speaking in 2002, called emphatically for a regional approach to Afghanistan, no such program was forthcoming.[29] Second, Secretary of State Colin Powell, eager to assuage President Putin, repeatedly assured the world that the United States would not extend its presence in the region beyond the conclusion of the Afghan campaign. This prompted China and Russia to redouble their efforts through the SCO. Third, the budgetary claims of Iraq and Afghanistan overwhelmed all other concerns, including Central Asia. Such funding cut-backs continue today. Whereas the total non-military assistance budget for all former Soviet states in 2008 was $396 million, for 2009 it will be a mere $346 million, a 12.6% reduction from a very low base.[30]

When they sensed that the United States was retrenching in Central Asia, the Central Asian states began reassessing how they viewed the United States. In the process, many came to view the United States not just as a friend whose attention had been drawn elsewhere, but as a threat. This perception was greatly strengthened from the U.S. campaigns for democracy and human rights.

The U.S. concern for democratic institutions and human rights was nothing new in 2001. Ever since the Helsinki Agreement of 1975 it had been one of the three pillars of U.S. foreign policy, the other two being support for market economies and international security. During the 1990s this commitment found expression in government-funded programs carried out largely by NGOs.

Down to 2001 nearly all of these programs carried on with little outright conflict with host governments. Progress in some countries was slow and in at least one, Turkmenistan, non-existent. But Central Asian states viewed this part of the U.S. agenda as inevitable, at times beneficial,

[29] Speech delivered by George W. Bush at the Virginia Military Institute in Lexington, Virginia, April 17, 2002, published as "Remarks at the Virginia Military Institute in Lexington," *Weekly Compilation of Presidential Documents* 38, no. 16 (April 22, 2002): 642–46.

[30] Joshua Kucera, "US Aid Budget to Eurasia: A Monument to 'Interagency Pettiness,'" EurasiaNet February 12, 2008, www.eurasianet.org/departments/insight/articles/eav021208a_pr.shtml.

and under any circumstances worth cooperating with as part of a larger range of interactions.

After 2001 the United States raised the tempo. Programs that had previously been expected to bear fruit over years or even decades were now told to achieve immediate results. Some of this pressure arose from governmental patrons, particularly from the State Department's Bureau of Democracy, Human, Rights, and Labor, and some rose from the NGO community itself. Meanwhile, U.S. approaches to the promotion of democracy had stagnated. Developed for Eastern Europe in the late 1980s, these approaches remained unchanged in Central Asia nearly a generation later. Rather than asking how they could be improved, the proponents of an active policy of democratization demanded they be implemented unchanged and on an abbreviated timetable.

The successful Rose Revolution in Georgia in November 2003, and then the Orange Revolution in Ukraine in January 2005, left governments in Central Asia fearing a U.S.-sponsored "domino effect" in their own region. Precisely this seemed to be occurring when the Kyrgyz government fell in the Tulip Revolution of March 2005. This was more an abdication than a revolution, but regional governments were convinced it was Washington's work. The charge was false, but triumphalist statements by the U.S. Embassy in Bishkek and some NGOs seemed to support it. A mere five months later some 180 Uzbeks died when an armed band attacked a prison in Andijan and were in turn fired upon by Uzbek security forces. The U.S. and EU were quick to censure the Uzbek government and slow to acknowledge that the attackers had themselves been heavily armed and were associated with a radical Islamist group, as Tashkent claimed.[31]

These moves, coming on the heels of cut-backs in U.S. programs in the region and statements from Washington that the United States would eventually be withdrawing, told regional governments that they should not look to Washington. The fact that no U.S. president had ever visited Central Asia, and that the only frequent high-ranking visitor there had been the secretary of defense, seemed to confirm that Washington's horizons did not extend to Central Asia, and that when they did they presented more of a threat than an opportunity.

---

[31] Time has proven Akiner's early assessment to be valid in most essentials. See Shirin Akiner, *Violence in Andijan, 13 May 2005: An Independent Assessment,* Silk Road Paper (Washington, D.C.: Central Asia-Caucasus Institute and Silk Road Studies Program, 2005), http://www.silkroadstudies.org/new/inside/publications/0507Akiner.pdf.

How States of Greater Central Asia Respond to Their Complex Environment

It was noted above that Central Asian governments have struggled to establish basic institutions and deliver services to populations accustomed to receiving everything from the state. Of equal urgency is their need to reckon with the threatening geopolitical environment in which they live. As noted above, Central Asian countries and Afghanistan look out on a ring of great and middling powers, many of them nuclear and most posing serious challenges to their political, economic, or cultural identities.

Is there any wonder that these new states constantly dodge and parry in response to one international threat after another? They all operate in the keen awareness that their first priority must be to consolidate sovereignty, steering a course among the greater powers—initially Russia and China, then the United States, and now also Japan, India, and the EU—to accomplish this. Hence, domestic policy in Central Asia mixes with foreign policy, especially the quest for sovereignty and stability. Under these circumstances, the only way a U.S. proposal regarding the Central Asian states' domestic policies can make headway is if it is accompanied by credible proposals regarding their sovereignty and security.

In their relation to the major powers, the states of Central Asia experimented unsuccessfully with two solutions before embracing a third strategy. The first, championed by Uzbekistan down to 2005, was to replace the one-sided subordination to Russia with a one-sided dependence on the United States. Uzbekistan after independence was subjected to massive overt and covert pressure from Moscow. Tashkent's solution was to place itself under a U.S. security umbrella.

For years, no country in the United Nations voted more consistently with the United States than Uzbekistan. Following September 11 the Uzbek government proposed and received a strategic partnership with Washington. (In spite of the rupture in 2005 and Uzbekistan's subsequent détente with both Moscow and Beijing, it remains in effect today.) This was a bold move but in the end proved unsustainable because powerful forces in Washington opposed it and because the United States was unwilling to respond adequately to pressures on Tashkent from Moscow and Beijing. Down to 2003 Tajikistan did much the same, embracing Moscow to neutralize threats from Uzbekistan and Afghanistan. With no alternative, the new government in Afghanistan follows the same path, by means of a strategic partnership with Washington. But in recent years Tajikistan has moved away from a one-vectored alignment with Moscow, while

Afghanistan has discovered that the U.S. link does not obviate the need for ties with other power centers.

Beginning in 1992, Turkmenistan followed a second and radically different strategy based on non-alignment.[32] Thanks to the centuries in which the Turkmen tribes maneuvered between Saffavid Persia and Shabanid Bukhara, this policy comes naturally to Turkmenistan, but it ill suits other regional states.

The third solution was pioneered by Kazakhstan beginning in 1997, when it turned to China in order to "balance" Russia. Three years later it turned to the United States to balance both Russia and China. The key to what became known as Kazakhstan's "multi-vectored" approach is to build strategic partnerships with all three powers.[33] Today this policy has eroded under pressure from Russia's Eurasec, Gazprom, and the SCO, but it nonetheless remains in place. Kazakhstan's successful campaign to gain the Organisation for Security Co-operation in Europe (OSCE) presidency is evidence of a more recent effort to engage Europeans as a fourth element in the balance.[34]

Hoping to gain similar space for maneuvering, Uzbekistan, Tajikistan, the Kyrgyz Republic, and Afghanistan have all sought to diversify and balance their links with major powers. The case of Tajikistan is particularly striking, as it has expanded its relations with the United States, China, and India to balance pressures from Moscow and Tashkent, while Uzbekistan has expanded relations with China and the EU and renewed ties with the United States for the same purpose of achieving balance.[35]

The problem with this "balanced" approach is that it assumes that the external powers are willing to live within the limits that "balance" implies.[36] President Putin's tendency to view the world in "zero-sum" terms is incompatible with such a policy, but the presence of China and the United States among Kazakhstan's key partners leaves Russia with little choice. This approach also leaves regional states with little room for maneuver when

[32] For a skeptical view on Turkmenistan's unaligned foreign policy, see Barbara Kiepenheuer-Drechsler, "Trapped in Permanent Neutrality: Looking Behind the Symbolic Production of the Turkmen Nation," *Central Asian Survey* 25, no. 1–2 (March–June 2006): 129–41.

[33] On this policy, see S. Frederick Starr, "Kazakhstan's Security Strategy: A Model for Central Asia?" *Central Asia Affairs* 1, no. 3 (January 2007): 16–21.

[34] Thomas H. Knox, "The OSCE Chairman-in-Office and the Republic of Kazakhstan," *Helsinki Monitor* 18, no. 2 (April 2007): 106–18.

[35] Erkin Akhmadov, "A Thaw in Relations Between West and Uzbekistan," Central Asia-Caucasus Institute, Central Asia-Caucasus Analyst 10, no. 6, March 19, 2008, 18–19, http://www.cacianalyst.org/files/080319Analyst.pdf.

[36] The beginnings of a discussion of this issue can be found in Emilian Kavalski, "Partnership or Rivalry between the EU, China and India in Central Asia: The Normative Power of Regional Actors with Global Aspirations," *European Law Journal* 13, no. 6 (November 2007): 839–56.

two of their major external partners collude, as do China and Russia in the SCO. The only ways out of this dilemma are either to add additional partners or to create or join some other multilateral entity to balance the one put forward by the colluding partners. Finally, it must be stressed that this focus on relations with major powers leaves regional states disinclined to build cooperative ties with one another. Yet intraregional issues remain, and several of them could suddenly become urgent.

The Progress of Regional States since Independence

Accounts in the international press and reports by Western advocacy groups offer a largely negative portrayal of the regional states. Judged only by such sources, these states are ruled by authoritarian and corrupt "presidents for life" who prevent free and fair elections and hamper the work of parties and parliaments. Those not enriched by oil and gas exports are mired in poverty and dependent on remittances sent from Russia by migrant laborers. As to Afghanistan, it is said to be rapidly slipping backwards into chaos.

If accurate, such a picture would make it hard to justify the United States devoting significant attention or resources to Afghanistan or Central Asia as a whole. Undeniably, corruption has been endemic there. But is this surprising when there are thousands of underpaid administrators and police, and when legal systems are still in the throes of change? And should we wonder at the lack of presidential succession when these societies for a millennium expected their khans to serve for life, when the Soviet system never once achieved change at the top without the old leader first dying, and when seniority alone empowers village "white beards" (*aksakals*) across the region to decide local issues?

More than balancing these negative developments is the good news from Central Asia that goes largely unreported. Bitter civil wars in Tajikistan and Afghanistan are now in the past, and the new states are intact. No one is proposing to redraw national borders, no group proposes to separate from Afghanistan, and ethnic clashes have largely died out elsewhere. Western predictions of religious strife have not materialized beyond localized outbursts, and secularism reigns everywhere, even in the nominally "Islamic" Republic of Afghanistan. With the advance of privatization, Kyrgyzstan joined the WTO a decade ago, Kazakhstan is on the lip of membership, and both Tajikistan and Afghanistan have accession as their goals.

The long-term direction of change in Central Asia is most evident in education. Uzbekistan and Kazakhstan have sent thousands of students abroad for study, focusing them in the United States, Europe, and other market-based democracies.[37] Tajiks, Kyrgyz, and Afghans also take advantage of opportunities to study abroad, with the result that across the region there exists a growing middle class with a modern outlook on how states should treat their citizens. Four thousand new schools have opened in Afghanistan, with 43% of the students female; adult literacy classes are oversubscribed; and tens of thousands of students are studying through correspondence courses. No wonder that the Taliban have targeted these schools, and that parents defy the Taliban to enable their children to study at them. Even Turkmenistan, where education long stagnated, is now showing signs of renewal.

The charge that Central Asian countries are dragging their feet on democratization also requires some clarification because it ignores the variety of the region's political cultures. Thus, countries built around irrigated oases (Uzbekistan, Tajikistan, and northern Afghanistan) are far more hierarchical and less given to collective decisionmaking than the formerly nomadic peoples like the Kazakhs and Kyrgyz, with their more "horizontal" traditions. But impatient champions of democratic reform choose to ignore such difference, taking instead a "one size fits all" approach that would not even fit all Western European countries. The only approach that works is an organic one. Any sound U.S. policy should begin with the recognition that the promotion of democracy is more akin to gardening than to engineering.

Absent from the list of achievements is any serious sign of regional thinking in Central Asia. In part this is a manifestation of the inevitable nationalism of new states everywhere. Such attitudes hamper their taking advantage of possible new trade routes to the south, which would benefit them economically and strengthen their sovereignty. Another shortcoming is the slow pace of institution-building across the region. For all their differences, all six countries have in common their large, ill-trained, dispirited, and corrupt civil services. This pervasive flaw leaves them with important governmental institutions that are unsuited to free societies and market economies.

This same failure accounts, in part at least, for the state of affairs that causes observers to judge these governments as overweening and hostile to the rights of citizens. This charge is not unjustified, but the situation is due more to grossly incompetent administrators than to sinister design. Leaders and bureaucrats know they cannot implement decisions through normal processes and hence resort to top-down commands that brutalize

---

[37] On Kazakhstan's Bolashak program, see Rafis Abazov, "Kazakhstan's Bolashak Program: Short-term Fix or Long-term Program?" Central Asia-Caucasus Institute, Central Asia-Caucasus Analyst 8, no. 19, October 4, 2006, 5–7, http://www.cacianalyst.org/files/20061004Analyst.pdf.

and corrupt civil society. Until civil services are reformed, and adequately trained and paid, it is hard to imagine this situation changing.[38] The only effective way to meet this challenge is for the United States to work with, rather than on, the governments in question.

The Paradox of Progress in Afghanistan

After the collapse of the USSR, Washington conceived Central Asia as part of the "former Soviet Union" and not as something in its own right. It was therefore natural for U.S. policy there to be conducted by former Soviet hands operating out of the same European Bureau in the State Department that had earlier managed relations with the USSR. Inevitably, this turned the region into a peripheral zone, the center being the new Russia that emerged under Yeltsin. In order to avoid the appearance of waging a new "Great Game" against the new, free, and democratic Russia, Washington deferred to Russia's declared interests there.

Functionally, U.S. policy was parceled out among three agencies, with free markets handled by USAID, security by the Pentagon and CIA, and the democracy account by the State Department. In keeping with the prevailing view of the day, it was assumed that groups outside of government could advance democracy and free markets more effectively than could governmental programs. Accordingly, USAID and the State Department contracted out much of their work to big U.S. firms, contractors, and U.S.-based NGOs. In the former Soviet republics the Pentagon meanwhile worked largely through NATO and its Partnership for Peace program.

The attacks on the World Trade Center elevated Afghanistan from the status of neglected backwater to the prime focus of U.S. foreign policy. But the rest of Central Asia was reduced to a minor supporting role for the Afghan mission. With respect to Afghanistan itself, Washington's strategic goals were entirely negative, namely, to bring down the Taliban government in Kandahar and to destroy al Qaeda. These goals, broadened slightly to embrace a general war on terrorism, were then extended de facto to the region as a whole. As this happened, Central Asia ceased to be a peripheral zone for Washington's Russia policy and became instead a peripheral zone for its policy in Afghanistan. The only sphere in which the State Department continued to show vigor in the rest of Central Asia was in "democracy promotion," which it pursued zealously but without any coordination with agencies advancing security and economic development there.

[38] Talaibek Koichumanov, Joomart Otorbayev, and S. Frederick Starr, *Kyrgyzstan: The Path Forward*, Silk Road Paper (Washington, D.C.: Central Asia-Caucasus Institute and Silk Road Studies Program, 2005), http://www.silkroadstudies.org/new/inside/publications/0511Kyrgyz_E.pdf.

Meanwhile, unanticipated and extremely important consequences of the U.S. engagement in Afghanistan were emerging. By destroying Taliban rule, the United States had created the possibility, for the first time since the USSR closed its southern border in 1937, of opening direct transport links between Central Asia, the Indian subcontinent, and Southeast Asia. This in turn presented the grand prospect of reopening the continental land routes across Eurasia that had been closed for centuries.

U.S. officials realized that it was in the U.S. interest to pursue this goal. Their decision in 2005 to reorganize the Department of State so as to leave former Soviet countries of Central Asia and Afghanistan under the same bureau and to link them both with Pakistan and India directly facilitated this strategy.

All the while, the stated objectives of the Afghan mission remained as they had always been. Repeated statements from the secretary of state that the U.S. presence in the region would cease once Afghanistan was stabilized were taken as evidence of the United States' flagging will. Why align one's country with the United States when Moscow and Beijing were clearly committed for the longer-term?

The truth is that the U.S./NATO mission in Afghanistan has long since outstripped its original negative goals, even though neither of those goals has been fully achieved. Meanwhile, U.S. strategy across Central Asia has yet to identify and embrace the positive goals that have become attainable thanks solely to U.S. actions there. Until this happens, the United States will be struggling uphill. But as soon as the United States embraces a new, positive strategy it will be met with support from its friends in the region and from countries elsewhere who discover their own interest in a positive outcome.

Principles of a Comprehensive U.S. Strategy for Afghanistan and the Region

What, then, should be the U.S. strategic goals with respect to Afghanistan and Central Asia? Clearly, defeating the Taliban and destroying al Qaeda should remain a priority. But these goals are best pursued in the context of a broader and more positive regional purpose.[39] This would be true even if the rise of the SCO and Russia's Eurasec did not call for a strategic response from the United States.

---

[39] Some of the positive goals set forth here were proposed by S. Frederick Starr in *A "Greater Central Asia Partnership" for Afghanistan and Its Neighbors,* Silk Road Paper (Washington, D.C.: Central Asia-Caucasus Institute and Silk Road Studies Program, 2005), http://www.isdp.eu/files/publications/srp/05/fs05greatercentral.pdf.

The core of U.S. strategy should be the development in all these Muslim societies of secular systems of government that treat their people as citizens rather than subjects, promote market-based prosperity, protect citizen's rights to participate in a free society, and provide access to modern knowledge through education and information. Such states will be pro-Western and pro-American while being at the same time fully part of the Muslim world and Asia, and also good neighbors and partners to nearby major powers. By so doing, they will establish Greater Central Asia as a hub of continental trade that will render the region economically viable. It is appropriate that these states will enter into close and even strategic arrangements with other powers. However, U.S. security interests demand that these states not become fully absorbed into the security system of any other power or powers, that they maintain sovereignty and the ability to shape their own fate, that they develop over time as democratic societies with market economies and secular governments, and that the region of which they are a part provides that degree of cooperation that enables the United States to project power globally. That they be self-determining subjects in their own right, rather than the mere objects of plans by others, fully accords with the interests of these states themselves.

The incoming U.S. administration should find an early opportunity to reaffirm that, as noted in the 2006 Silk Road Strategy Act II, U.S. interests in Afghanistan and Central Asia are serious and long term.[40] This is necessary, given what regional states and neighboring powers (e.g., Russia and China) see as the ambiguities in current U.S. policy. Such a statement, along with the outlines of programs to implement it, should come from Congress as well as from the administration. This could be accomplished through a bipartisan commission of members of the U.S. Senate and other leading citizens, akin to the Baker-Hamilton Commission on Iraq. Such statements by the administration and Congress should also clearly indicate to Russia and China that U.S. strategy for the region is not directed against anyone and is, in fact, compatible with active roles for other powers, so long as they respect the sovereignty of regional states and seek to build security from within the region rather than impose it from without.

Implementation and Tactics

The United States' own actions confirm that its original security goals in Afghanistan cannot be achieved without broadening them to include economic development and the building of free institutions. Moreover,

---

[40] *Silk Road Strategy Act of 2006*, S 2749, 109th Cong., 2nd sess., available at http://www.govtrack.us/congress/billtext.xpd?bill=s109-2749.

the United States has already begun to recast its strategy in regional terms, sensibly basing it on the three traditional pillars of security, economic development, and democratic institutions. Most of the elements of a broader regional approach to Afghanistan already exist. What is needed is for the United States to embrace them in a manner that makes them mutually reinforcing and to present them as the blueprint for a longer-term commitment.

Security. Henceforth, the United States will need to learn from its mistakes and approach security in Greater Central Asia as a single process, without playing parties off against each other. This in turn requires a number of strategic moves.

The first precondition for long-term security in the region is a viable Afghan army and effective police. Present goals for the Afghan National Army should be raised at once to at least 150,000, while Europeans must actively re-engage in police training. The creation of such army and police forces must be a prime NATO priority.

Closely related to this is the need to bring Pakistan and Afghanistan into a constructive relationship with each other. The best means of achieving this is for the United States to mediate at the highest level after preparatory work carried out by the existing tripartite commission. Such mediation must address Pakistan's concerns over a possible future Pashtunistan, as well as Afghanistan's concerns regarding the border. As it approaches these sensitive issues, Pakistan must know that the potential benefits of cooperation will be greater than what it receives from its present policy.

What should the United States offer Pakistan? If Islamabad ceases all support for Taliban forces and al Qaeda and opens its border to continental trade, the United States should respond with a "peace dividend." The United States could assure funding for all trans-Afghan transport links from Pakistan, including roads, electric grids, telecom, and the Turkmenistan-Afghanistan-Pakistan-India (TAPI) pipeline. The United States should use its ties with India to help resolve outstanding issues between Pakistan and that country. This would transform Pakistan's economy and also its security, while doing more than anything else to enhance the security and economic viability of the region as a whole.

In the area of security, the United States should immediately reopen a dialogue with NATO concerning its longer-term objectives in the region. At the least, this means giving all regional states an alternative to what has become, since September 11, the near-total domination of Russian and Chinese security structures. To provide some kind of balance, NATO and the United States do not need to mimic the "closed shop" approach of Russia's Eurasian security initiative. Instead, they can offer a kind of á la carte menu that includes practical measures for improving border security, expanding train-and-equip programs, improving interoperability, anti-drug enforcement, and engaging Central Asian countries in appropriate non-fighting support roles in Afghanistan.

If constraints in Europe cause NATO to balk at such a region-wide commitment, the United States should immediately begin hedging in the direction of creating a new security architecture for this region, one that includes India, Turkey, and, eventually, Iran. If the United States delays in developing this option it may well find that the SCO and Eurasec have effectively closed the region to other powers, creating a serious geopolitical imbalance that is equally damaging to the sovereignty of regional states and to the interests of external powers other than China and Russia.

Parallel to this, the United States should enter into five-year military-to-military agreements with each country similar to what it has recently renewed with Kazakhstan. At the same time, the United States might apply for observer status in the SCO. Prior to doing this, the United States should consult directly with Central Asian governments and seek their support for such a step.

Such measures will strengthen the ability of NATO and the United States to achieve their goals in Afghanistan, while leaving regional countries more receptive to a continued and even expanded Western presence in the broader region. By such means, the United States will prevent the SCO and CSTO from limiting the choices of Central Asian states regarding their own security and development.

Economic development. Regarding economic development, the United States should move immediately to reduce tariffs on key Afghanistan products and should prevail on EU countries to do likewise. The latter step should be promoted as a means for the EU to finally shoulder responsibility for the damage that its citizens' addictions inflict on the Afghan and Central Asian economies and societies.

The United States should also move more actively to set up a region-wide forum for airing trade and investment issues of mutual interest. Such a forum would, of course, include Afghanistan. A useful building block for such a forum exists in the TIFA that the United States and Central Asian states entered into beginning in 1992.[41] Unfortunately, preoccupation with the Afghan mission caused the United States to neglect its own initiative, and recent efforts to revive the TIFA have been desultory, in spite of the Central Asian states' keen interest in energizing it. To revive the TIFA the United States should take a more proactive role in developing long-term

[41] For the text of this agreement, see Office of the United States Trade Representative, http://www.ustr.gov/assets/Trade_Agreements/TIFA/asset_upload_file683_7722.pdf.

agendas, introduce regular ministerial meetings working groups and technical-level meetings, draw the private sector into TIFA activity, welcome representatives of the World Bank and other financial bodies to meetings, and desist from hectoring members on the value of WTO accession. The TIFA, thus reconfigured, could play a role in the development of export routes for Central Asian gas westward across the Caspian Sea and for Central Asian hydroelectric power to Afghanistan and Pakistan, both with private involvement. It could also be a forum for considering trade-related issues like the sanctity of contracts.

To indicate that this will be a permanent institution for regional cooperation in the economic, cultural, and humanitarian areas, a qualified TIFA office should be established in the region, possibly on a rotating basis. In short, the United States should either adopt an active strategic plan for developing the TIFA as a response to the SCO or withdraw from the economic field.

A further essential step, possibly within the framework of a renewed TIFA, is to give enterprises from Afghanistan's Central Asian neighbors a share of the contracts for rehabilitating infrastructure in Afghanistan. This should have been done before now, in spite of U.S. claims to being interested in opening Central Asia's door to the south. Immediate progress in this area will also help build the middle class in Central Asia, a goal that is scarcely advanced when, as recently occurred, a major contract for developing Afghan copper goes to China rather than to bidders from Kazakhstan or Uzbekistan.

Beyond this, the new strategy should no longer conceive Afghanistan and the region of which it is a part as a peripheral area but as a potential center or hub in its own right. The Office of the Special Advisor on Central Asian Trade should be strengthened and charged with working with regional governments to develop a strategic plan for joint activity in the sphere of transport development. This should be done jointly with Japan, European partners, India, and the Asian Development Bank's CAREC program. Once these links are working, they could be extended to Russia and China. The United States will play a significant role in this process simply by being the persistent convener, which it has so far failed to do. By no means do all the steps needed to open continental trade involve costly infrastructure, and many of the most productive ones entail merely removing bureaucratic impediments at the borders. The United States should immediately redouble its efforts to accomplish this.

"Good governance" and democratization. U.S. efforts at building democracy in Central Asia now suffer badly from inertia and the absence of strategic thinking. Beyond this, at both the symbolic and practical levels

Washington has failed to convince regional states that it understands and supports their own aspirations. Without this, it is impossible to raise political issues effectively. Any workable program in the area of good governance, rights, and democratization must rely on soft power rather than punitive threats and coercion. This means engaging official persons as well as opposition groups, and it means working with the governments rather than on them. The United States has learned how to do this in Afghanistan. It should now start doing so in the rest of the region.

A necessary step in this direction is to broaden the definition of "democracy promotion" beyond elections to include the evolution of parliamentary rights and institutions, and especially the steady reform of those institutions of state (including ministries of internal affairs) that have done so much to thwart citizens' rights and the development of normal market economies. Accountability, responsiveness, transparency, and good governance generally are as essential to democracy as elections. Moreover, they contribute directly to social stability. The Central Asian states will welcome cooperation in this area as soon as they see it as contributing to stability rather than undermining it. Only in this way can the United States find cooperative partners for its democracy agenda.

Afghanistan's need for programs promoting good governance is acute. This, rather than democratization per se, should be the immediate priority there. A first step would be to engage the Karzai government in an evaluation of the entire civil administration. Helping Kabul to build on strengths and address areas of weakness will strengthen public confidence in the new government.

Along the way, the United States will need to remove impediments and disincentives of its own making. Among these is the Jackson-Vanik Amendment. Originally intended as a tool for promoting Jewish emigration from the USSR, this has now evolved into a general but notably counter-productive weapon for use against recalcitrant governments in the struggle for democracy. A primitive impediment to trade and technology transfer, it has already been suspended in the case of Armenia, Ukraine, and Georgia and should immediately be suspended without conditions across Central Asia and Afghanistan.

A further step that will facilitate the United States' constructive engagement in the area of democracy building is to remove existing uncertainties with respect to likely U.S. action in the case of popular uprisings and so-called color revolutions. By no means does this mean renouncing the right to support democratic movements, but it does mean making absolutely clear that the United States seeks change through democratic processes rather than through outpourings on the streets. It also means explaining beforehand what the United States will and will not do when confronted with regional clashes between state and society.

Above all, this calls for investment in educational exchanges, particularly at the undergraduate level. Only by training a new generation of citizens with first-hand knowledge of democratic life will enduring change occur. No country in the region except Kazakhstan can afford to fund these exchanges on its own. Investments in this area will pay off handsomely and will promote their needs as well as ours. Failure to act will hand over the emerging leadership class to be trained in less open and democratic countries.

Three Keys to Implementing the Proposed Strategy

To succeed, such a program will require changes within Washington itself. First, the above objectives should be pursued simultaneously and in a mutually reinforcing manner. This is in sharp contrast to what has existed to now. In Afghanistan, security has been pursued with a single-mindedness that sometimes thwarts not only economic, institutional, and democratic development but security itself. In the rest of Central Asia democratization has sometimes become a test that states must pass in order to reap benefits in the other two areas. This has not worked and won't work. An approach that advances all three together will make U.S. policy a single whole and will be accepted as serious in every country.

This calls for improved coordination within the U.S. government. Urgently needed is a serious inter-agency planning effort. Only such a systematic inter-agency planning process can focus and energize inter-agency meetings. For Afghanistan, this actually occurred between 2003 and 2006, due to the fact that a presidential envoy was named to assure such coordination. Without such a joint planning effort, the tendency of the various departments to work independently of each other will continue to vitiate the overall program.

The creation of the Bureau of Central and South Asian Affairs was a positive but insufficient step. To assure the necessary attention to Afghanistan and Central Asia, either a presidential envoy or other high-level official should be named to lead inter-agency activity in this area or, failing that, the Bureau of Central and South Asia should be broken into two parts. Experience proves that nothing short of these steps will assure the necessary level of high-level attention that the region requires and reap the synergies that integrated and mutually reinforcing programs can bring.

Second, unlike the immediate post–September 11 strategy, this one should be vetted with the states of the region themselves, and also with such key partners as Japan, India, and Britain even before it is adopted. Thereafter such consultation and coordination should be detailed and regular. The United States can easily seek the views of Afghanistan and the regional states on the issues covered by such a new policy, and can keep them better informed thereafter.

Regarding major international partners, NATO should be engaged from the outset. To date, NATO's Afghan mission has proven divisive, leading to doubts as to whether it is the appropriate instrument for this mission. A more diversified engagement with Central Asia as a whole could reduce that divisiveness and create a more constructive climate for NATO's Afghan project. As to Afghanistan, NATO's engagement there should be made more robust, but through the present á la carte system. The United States' NATO partners need to recognize that NATO's failure there will do irreparable damage to its credibility everywhere.

Moreover, activities in the economic and political areas should be coordinated closely with Japan and its "Japan Plus Central Asia" program, and with India, which is poised to become far more active in the region than formerly. The EU's refusal to play an active part with the United States in CAREC suggests that lower expectations from that quarter may be necessary. But before drawing such a conclusion, the United States should re-engage with European countries and with the EU on the new, regional strategy in the hope of finding common ground and a basis for collaborative actions.

Neither Russia nor China should be allowed a veto over the proposed strategy, any more than the United States has been offered a veto over Russian or Chinese strategies in the region. But since the policies advanced here do not contradict the legitimate security interests of either Russia or China, it is reasonable to keep both countries informed and to offer to engage them on issues of common concern. However, this can never be allowed to become a process of negotiation over the heads of the regional states themselves.

Third, while tactics may vary over time, these objectives should remain in place long enough for them to assure real and sustainable progress. Since this requires a series of constructive relationships that scarcely exist today, this will take time. Many question whether the U.S. political system permits the steady pursuit of truly strategic objectives such as those set forth here. Fortunately, there exist many instances, such as the construction of the Baku-Ceyhan pipeline over a period of fourteen years, which prove that the United States can muster the necessary tenacity and patience when needed.

Costs and Downside Risks

Even if the necessary tenacity and patience exist, can the United States afford the financial cost of what is proposed here? This question is all the more pertinent as the country goes into economic recession.

In addressing this, compare the cost of the present Afghan mission with earlier U.S. projects to create security, economic development, and open political systems in Taiwan and South Korea. As noted earlier, the costs of those missions were dramatically higher than is Afghanistan today;[42] moreover, current expenditures in all the rest of Central Asia are less than what the United States spends in many countries where the stakes are far lower.

Beyond this, if the mission in Afghanistan and Central Asia is reconceived along the lines proposed here, the new balance of potential risks and gains should elicit the engagement of, and investments from, other states friendly to the United States. The challenge is to turn what now appears largely as a U.S. concern to defeat al Qaeda and drive back the Taliban into a larger concern to bring stability and development to a region that was until recently a seedbed of extremism and terrorism.

Any fair evaluation of the financial burden required by the strategy proposed here should also be weighed against the costs if the current approach were to fail, as is entirely possible. Bluntly, the alternative to success is ominous, imposing costs in many areas besides the purely financial. Among these costs are the following:

- The revival of Afghanistan as a haven for terrorist groups, including those from the Middle East, with associated dangers to the United States, Europe, and Asia.

- The renewal of Taliban rule and externally-sponsored radicalism in Afghanistan and the possible extension of Taliban rule to Pakistan and even to formerly Soviet parts of Central Asia.

- The destruction of NATO's credibility, forcing the United States to bear an additional burden for defense.

- The closing of Central Asian trade to the south, sealing Russian and Chinese hegemony over the region.

- The creation of an opening for Iranian/Russian influence over a future Afghanistan.

---

[42] Brannen, "Comparison in Real and Nominal Dollar Terms," (unpublished manuscript, 2004). See footnote 1 for more details.

- The renewal of Pakistan's old program of "strategic depth," which would destabilize Afghanistan, sharpen the India-Pakistan conflict, and extend Russian-Chinese geopolitical competition to the Afghanistan-Pakistan region.

What Decisions Must Be Made Now?

In conclusion, let us review some of the decisions and actions that should be taken immediately:

- To redefine U.S. strategic goals in Afghanistan in regional rather than national terms, in the process embracing the positive opportunities that have arisen since the destruction of Taliban rule. This should be done in bipartisan terms through a Congressional commission, as well as through actions by the new administration.

- To reaffirm that U.S. interests in all Central Asia, as in Afghanistan, are serious and enduring.

- To enter into frank discussion with NATO allies and other friends (Japan, India, etc.) to enlist their support for the new strategy and, even with a clear commitment from NATO, to engage other relevant countries in the proposed strategy of regional development.

- To increase NATO support for the Afghan National Army to enable it to expand to at least 150,000 troops, and for the Afghan police.

- To engage the governments of Afghanistan and other Central Asian partners in discussion of the new strategy before it is finalized and implemented.

- As a means of stimulating the non-opium economy of Afghanistan and neighboring Central Asian states, to take steps to reduce U.S. tariff barriers for Afghan agricultural produce; and, in the same vein, to urge European opium-consuming countries to recognize their moral responsibilities toward the impoverished producers of the raw material through significantly increased aid programs.

- To activate the TIFA along the lines proposed above and include Afghanistan.

- To initiate a review of Jackson-Vanik for the purpose of reducing or eliminating its negative impact on the states of the region.

- To open possibilities for firms from other states of Central Asia to participate in Afghan development projects.

- To mediate a comprehensive agreement between Pakistan and Afghanistan that would match Pakistan's non-interference in Afghanistan with U.S. support for major trans-Afghan transport projects benefiting both countries, including road access to Gwadar Port, the TAPI pipeline, and Tajik hydroelectric transmission lines.

- To indicate to all regional states the U.S. support for a purely regional organization (without participation by external major powers) that would promote cooperation and coordination but not necessarily "integration."

- To indicate clearly to Russia and China that the new strategy is not directed against them and could, in fact, heighten their security, opening the way to longer-term collaborations.

- To make the necessary organizational changes in Washington and in the field so as to coordinate U.S. actions in the spheres of security, economic development, and democracy building, and to render them mutually reinforcing.

STRATEGIC ASIA 2008–09

SPECIAL STUDIES

EXECUTIVE SUMMARY

This chapter evaluates the water resource challenges confronting the developing countries of Asia and their implications for broader regional and global security concerns.

MAIN ARGUMENT:

Water security throughout the developing countries of Asia is poor and under growing threat. This insecurity poses risks for public health, political stability, and continued economic growth both within Asia and abroad.

- Within many Asian states, conflicts are flaring over competing demands for water and growing public health challenges. Weak state capacity compounds the challenge of addressing gaps in water security.

- Asia must also contend with the potentially devastating impacts of global climate change: rising sea levels, increasing pestilence and disease, extreme flooding and droughts, and declining agricultural productivity.

- India and China, the two most populous developing Asian economies, sit at the headwaters of several of Asia's most important rivers. As these states increasingly tap into shared water resources, they are shaping the water security opportunities and challenges for the rest of the region.

POLICY IMPLICATIONS:

The U.S. can assist Asia in addressing serious water security issues.

- Of particular use would be for the U.S. to extend integrated policy and technology assistance on water resource management to Asia's water resource, environment, and public health agencies.

- Washington could extend its mediation efforts in the Mekong Basin to other critical emerging conflicts to enhance the leverage of weaker states.

- Of benefit would be U.S. leadership on global climate change to help mitigate or counteract the anticipated significant downsides of climate change for Asia's water resources.

Asia's Water Security Crisis: China, India, and the United States

Elizabeth Economy

Water security has become one of the great global challenges of the 21st century. In just over half a century, world population has soared from 2.5 billion in 1950 to 6.5 billion in 2007. This population increase has contributed to a doubling of irrigated areas and a tripling of water withdrawals across the globe.[1] As a result, tensions within and among countries over access to water are rising, public health is increasingly endangered, and long-term global economic growth is more and more at risk.

Conceptions of what constitutes water security differ, but at the most basic level water security connotes access to safe drinking-water and sanitation.[2] Water security can be threatened both by economic water scarcity and by physical water scarcity—conditions that the International Water Management Institute (IWMI) suggests affect one-third of the world population.[3] As the IWMI has described, economic water scarcity occurs when "water resources are abundant relative to water use, with less than 25% of water from rivers withdrawn for human purposes, but malnutrition

Elizabeth Economy is C.V. Starr Senior Fellow and Director of Asia Studies at the Council on Foreign Relations. She can be reached at <eeconomy@cfr.org>.

The author wishes to thank Jaeah Lee, research associate at the Council on Foreign Relations, for her excellent research assistance in the preparation of this chapter.

[1] International Water Management Institute, *Water for Food, Water for Life: A Comprehensive Assessment of Water Management in Agriculture* (London: Earthscan, 2007).

[2] Some analysts define water security as the equitable access to safe drinking water and sanitation, while others consider water security to be sustainable access to adequate quantities of water, of acceptable quality for human and environmental uses, on a watershed basis.

[3] "Map Details Global Water Stress," *BBC News,* August 21, 2006, http://www.news.bbc.co.uk/2/hi/science/nature/5269296.stm.

exists...human and financial capacity are limiting."[4] Physical water scarcity, in contrast, emerges when "more than 75% of river flows are allocated to agriculture, industries or domestic purposes."[5]

Water, of course, is part of the essence of life. Malin Falkenmark of the Stockholm International Water Institute offers an elegant understanding of why water security matters:

> [Water] acts as a silent messenger and a unique solvent continuously on the move through the landscape, in incessant contact with ecosystems; it is a key component of land productivity and plant production; it has many different functions for societal human life: for health; for food production; for industrial production and the generation of income; for energy production; for navigation; and so on.[6]

Many other scholars and policy analysts, including Thomas Homer-Dixon, Robert Kaplan, and Shlomi Dinar, consider water scarcity to be a potentially key contributing factor to intrastate and interstate political or even armed conflict. As Dinar has noted, "environmental change and resource scarcities can lead to economic decline, social turmoil, disputes or forced migration, which may in turn lead to instability, violence, and even armed conflict."[7] Homer-Dixon has argued further that poor countries are likely to be more susceptible to environment-related conflict than are rich countries. Poor countries generally lack not only the material and intellectual resources of wealthier states but also strong social and political institutions. All these factors enable states to respond more effectively to environmental challenges.[8]

Not surprisingly, many nations and international organizations now list water security at or near the top of the agenda. Water security has been enshrined in UN human rights resolutions and is a cornerstone of the UN's Millennium Development Goals.[9] In many parts of the advanced industrialized world, such as Europe and Canada, officials and NGO activists are now working together to develop rigorous legislation to protect

---

[4] International Water Management Institute, *Water for Food, Water for Life*, 8.

[5] "Map Details Global Water Stress."

[6] Malin Falkenmark, "The Greatest Water Problem: The Inability to Link Environmental Security, Water Security and Food Security," *Water Resources Development* 17, no. 4 (2001): 541.

[7] Shlomi Dinar, "Water, Security, Conflict, and Cooperation," *SAIS Review* 22, no. 2 (Summer–Fall 2002): 232.

[8] Thomas F. Homer-Dixon, "On the Threshold," *International Security* 16, no. 2 (Fall 1991): 888.

[9] See "Asia Water Watch 2015: Are Countries in Asia on Track to Meet Target 10 of the Millennium Development Goals?" Asian Development Bank, December 2005, http://www.adb.org/Documents/Books/Asia-Water-Watch/asia-water-watch.pdf.

national water resources and help ensure broader security interests.[10] Yet throughout much of the developing world, including large swaths of Asia, efforts to manage a growing water security challenge are in a nascent stage, with the dimensions of the challenge seeming to far exceed the institutional capacity of individual states to address it.

This chapter explores the various dimensions of Asia's water security challenge. What range of pressures on water supplies does the region currently confront and need to address in the coming decades? What are some of the impacts on economic growth, public health, and social stability in key states within the region? What are the likely flashpoints for interstate conflict? The chapter focuses particular attention on China and India, which are perhaps the region's most important actors with regard to future water security issues. Both states confront serious domestic challenges regarding their abilities to meet water needs for large populations and growing economies, and both states occupy strategic positions in determining overall water security for the region. The chapter concludes by examining how the United States might engage on issues of water security in Asia to enhance the region's efforts to secure future water security and to further U.S. interests.

The Nature and Scope of the Challenge

As the world collectively looks forward, the developing countries of Asia will be at the center of the greatest opportunities and challenges for enhancing global water security. By 2050 an additional 2.7 billion people—almost two-thirds of whom will be in Asia—will need access to clean water and all the related necessities such as food and energy.[11] Already as many as 635 million people in Asia lack access to safe water, and 1.9 billion people lack access to effective sanitation.[12] A 2006 UN report evaluated Asia's current challenge in unsparing terms: Asia's per capita availability of freshwater—3,920 cubic meters—is less than that of any other continent outside of Antarctica.[13]

---

[10] Karen Bakker, "New Land Use Restrictions to Protect Water Security," University of British Columbia, UBC Reports 53, no. 1, January 4, 2007, http://www.publicaffairs.ubc.ca/ubcreports/2007/07jan04/water.html.

[11] United Nations Development Programme (UNDP), *Human Development Report 2006* (New York: Palgrave Macmillan, 2006), http://hdr.undp.org/en/media/hdr06-complete.pdf.

[12] Ibid., 33.

[13] Brahma Chellaney, "Climate Change and Security in Southern Asia: Understanding the National Security Implications," RUSI Journal 152, no. 2 (April 2007): 63.

At the same time, developing Asian economies are experiencing some of the most rapid economic growth in the world. Led by China and India, hundreds of millions of people throughout Asia have been and are being lifted out of poverty. The consequences for water security, however, have been serious. Household and industrial demand for water is skyrocketing, as are levels of water pollution. All of the fourteen major river systems in India are seriously polluted; in Delhi alone 200 million liters of raw sewage and 20 million liters of waste are dumped into the Yamuna River daily.[14] In China over a quarter of the water that flows through the country's seven major river systems is considered unfit even for agriculture or industry.

This section examines four aspects of Asia's water dilemma. First, demand is rapidly outpacing supply for a number of reasons, including shifting agricultural priorities, increasing use of energy, and widespread urbanization. Second, water insecurity is exacerbating public health challenges and domestic conflict in Asia and may provoke international disputes. Third, domestic policy responses to this dilemma, though substantial, have been insufficient. Fourth, future climate change is likely to exacerbate Asia's water problems.

Demand Outstrips Supply

Agriculture. At the present time agriculture is by far the major user of water in Asia. In some Asian countries water for agriculture accounts for nearly 90% of total water use. Overall, irrigated agriculture accounts for nearly 79% of water use, industry accounts for 13%, and households account for 8%.[15] Water policy experts have identified a strong correlation between regions heavily dependent on irrigated agriculture and high overall overuse of water.[16] Farmers who use groundwater, for example, often do not pay for the actual volume of groundwater used for irrigation, and the energy costs for pumping are heavily subsidized. This combination of factors produces a devastating cycle of overpumping, subsidence, and need for more energy to pump water from deeper in the ground. In Asia this cycle is most evident in the Indo-Gangetic Plain in South Asia and in the North China Plain, where water use exceeds minimum recharge levels.[17] In some parts of India, farmers have dug wells as deep as 1,500 feet in attempting to access water for crops. The transportation process—simply moving agricultural produce

---

[14] UNDP, *Human Development Report 2006*, 142–43.

[15] United Nations Economic and Social Commission for Asia and the Pacific (ESCAP), *Statistical Yearbook for Asia and the Pacific 2007* (New York: United Nations, 2007), 57–61.

[16] See International Water Management Institute, *Water for Food, Water for Life.*

[17] Ibid.

from farms to warehouses or urban centers—also engenders significant water loss. In many Asian countries between 25% and 50% of crops, fruits, and vegetables produced are lost through production, transportation, distribution, and storage.[18]

Agriculture's relative share of water demand is decreasing as industry and household demand grow. Yet in absolute terms, the agricultural demand for water is increasing and is unlikely to diminish in the foreseeable future.[19] As Asia continues to make economic progress, Asians are becoming more affluent and are choosing to eat more protein, such as meat. One consequence will be heightened water demand: animal husbandry requires more water than does crop production.[20]

The polluted water emanating from Asia's growing aquaculture industry poses a particular and growing threat to the health of people in and outside the region. Waste from aquaculture ponds and pens, such as fertilizer and biological waste, is often released into surrounding bodies of water. Such waste destroys mangrove forests, "which are crucial for filtering nutrients, cleansing water, and protecting ecosystems from floods and storms."[21] Moreover, farmed fish that enter into the wild may change the ecosystem by threatening native species through "acting as predators, competing for food and habitat, or interbreeding and changing the genetic pools of wild organisms."[22]

China's aquaculture industry in particular has been a source of both domestic and international concern. China produces 70% of the world's farmed fish. The country's pell-mell growth and poor environmental controls, however, have led Chinese fisheries to use water that is highly contaminated by sewage, agricultural waste, and agricultural run-off such as pesticides. These fish farms in turn discharge wastewater that further pollutes the water supply. Guangdong has experienced public health problems from fish contaminated with DDT. The European Union, Japan, and the United States have over the past few years repeatedly blocked shipments of contaminated seafood from China.[23]

Thailand has also encountered domestic challenges from its aquaculture industry. Food and Water Watch estimates that the approximately

---

[18] Asian Development Bank, *Asian Water Development Outlook 2007* (Manila: Asian Development Bank, 2007), 3, http://www.adb.org/Documents/Books/AWDO/2007/AWDO.pdf.

[19] Ibid., 3.

[20] Ibid., 2.

[21] International Food Policy Research Institute, *The Future of Fish: Issues and Trends to 2020* (Penang: World Fish Center, 2003), 5, http://www.ifpri.org/pubs/ib/ib15.pdf.

[22] Ibid., 5.

[23] David Barboza, "In China, Farming Fish in Toxic Waters," *New York Times,* December 15, 2007.

four hundred square miles of shrimp ponds in Thailand produce more phosphorous waste than do three million people.[24] In Trang, a southwestern province in Thailand bordering the Andaman Sea, shrimp farmers have released polluted pond water into the sea. As the number of farms increased, polluted water migrated back to the ponds, contaminating future harvests as well as mangroves. *Earth Island Journal* has estimated that half of Thailand's mangroves on the eastern and southern coasts have been destroyed, costing thousands of local fishermen their jobs.[25]

Energy. Energy is also an increasingly important driver of Asia's water landscape. Large-scale generation of electricity invariably requires water. Asia's demand for electricity is growing at a rate of 5% to 8% annually, and in some cases, such as in China, even faster.[26] Moreover, traditional energy sources such as large-scale hydropower (which affects water flow) and coal are being joined by new and often water-intensive energy sources such as biofuels. India and China, for example, have both set ambitious goals for biofuel production to limit their growing fossil fuel imports. China wants to increase national biofuel production 400% by 2020 to meet approximately 9% of the country's projected gasoline demand.[27] To meet this biofuel target, an IWMI report concludes that China would need to produce 26% more maize. The same report notes that India's biofuel targets would require 16% more sugar cane than the country currently produces. To produce one liter of maize-based ethanol in China requires 6 times more irrigation water than in the United States and over 25 times more than in Brazil. Irrigation requirements are even higher in India, where ethanol production is dependent on highly irrigated sugar cane. As the Asian Development Bank (ADB) has noted, an important gap in our understanding of future water security in Asia is precisely how the region's growing energy demand and projected energy mix over the next twenty years will translate into water demand.

Urbanization. Urbanization will likely compound the challenge of rising demand and increasing pollution. Asia's population is expected to

---

[24] "Suspicious Shrimp: The Health Risks of Industrialized Shrimp Production," Food and Water Watch, December 2006, http://www.foodandwaterwatch.org/fish/publications/reports/suspicious-shrimp. Phosphorous contributes to algae blooms, which can lead to eutrophication, essentially producing a biologically dead body of water.

[25] Ioannis Gatsiounis, "In Thailand, Pollution from Shrimp Farms Threatens a Fragile Environment," *International Herald Tribune,* March 20, 2008.

[26] For information on Asia's demand for electricity, see Asian Development Bank, *Asian Water Development Outlook 2007,* 9.

[27] "Study Warns That China and India's Planned Biofuel Boost Could Worsen Water Scarcity, Compete with Food Production," Consultative Group on International Agricultural Research, Press Release, October 11, 2007, http://www.iwmi.cgiar.org/News_Room/Press_Releases/releases/2007/IWMI_Biofuels_%20Release.pdf.

grow by nearly 500 million within the next ten years, and virtually all of this growth is expected to be in urban areas.[28] By 2025 the urban population is likely to increase by 60%, with much of this growth in China. Unless countries adopt significant new policy and technology approaches, this massive urbanization process will significantly heighten water insecurity in both Asia's mega- and smaller cities.

As the ADB reported in a recent study on water issues, "the rates and extent of urbanization in developing Asia have generally far exceeded the capacities of the national and local governments to plan and manage the demographic transition process soundly, in terms of providing clean water and wastewater management services efficiently, equitably, and sustainably."[29] Asia's largest cities, such as Dhaka, Jakarta, Chongqing, and Karachi, have grown so rapidly over the past few decades that they have not managed to keep up with collecting, treating, and safely disposing of wastewater. With more such megacities planned throughout the region, issues of waste and wastewater treatment will become paramount. Currently waste treatment is minimal, and even when collected, wastewater is often discharged directly to nearby rivers, lakes, or oceans. The result is that water in and around many urban centers in developing Asian countries is now heavily contaminated. Water wastage is also a significant problem in many of these cities: more than 50% of water that enters the system never reaches consumers due to leaks and poor management.[30] In virtually all of these developing megacities, local political capacity is weak, and there is an absence of long-term planning, inadequate management of technical and administrative capabilities, a lack of investment funds, and high levels of corruption.[31]

Even the smaller satellite cities—those with populations of up to one million people or so—will confront growing water insecurity. These smaller centers, which will be home to more than one-fourth of Asia's urban residents, do not have adequate financial and political power or technical management capacities to handle higher urbanization rates. The ADB argues that without much more aggressive action, these centers will be the major water and wastewater "black holes" of the future.[32]

The growing middle class in Asian cities has also created new forms of household demand for water. In China, for example, wealthy urban

---

[28] Asian Development Bank, *Asian Water Development Outlook 2007.*

[29] Ibid., 16.

[30] Ibid., 26.

[31] Ibid., 17.

[32] Ibid., 14.

residents are beginning to purchase second homes with lawns that need to be watered and enjoy water-intensive sports such as golf. In India, Coca-Cola factories that produce bottled water and other drinks for India's middle class have sparked serious conflict: the factories' water usage has provoked a series of protests among farmers in a number of localities throughout the country who blame the company for draining aquifers and destroying farmers' livelihoods.[33]

The Impact of Water Insecurity

The failure of states to provide water security in parts of Asia has resulted in several types of emerging security challenges: public health concerns, social unrest, and even violent conflict. Lack of access to safe water and sanitation contributes to a number of public health problems. According to the World Health Organization (WHO), more than 9% of the global disease burden could be prevented by better management of water (drinking-water and water for sanitation and hygiene).[34] Most of the 1.8 million child deaths from diarrhea each year arise from dirty water and poor sanitation.[35] In China diarrhea is the leading cause of death in children under the age of five, and in India an estimated 1.5 million children die of diarrhea annually.[36] In China alone the Ministry of Water Resources estimates that 190 million people fall ill each year due to contaminated drinking-water. Dengue fever, a critical water-related health challenge, led to tens of thousands of people falling ill and hundreds of deaths throughout Southeast Asia in 2007. The disease is transmitted by a particular type of mosquito that breeds in water storage containers or in standing water sites amid poorly disposed solid waste. The disease easily crosses national boundaries through unknowingly infected travelers.

Competing demands for water also fuel domestic unrest, and weak state capacity compounds the challenge of addressing gaps in water security. Protests rooted in lack of access to clean water are commonplace. In Pakistan in April 2002, for example, approximately 50 people resorted

---

[33] Nandlal Master, Lok Samiti, and Amit Srivastava, "India: Major Protest Demands Coca-Cola Shut Down Plant," Centre for Research on Globalization, Global Research, April 8, 2008, http://www.globalresearch.ca/index.php?context=viewArticle&code=MAS20080408&articleId=8591.

[34] Jamie Bartram, "Flowing Away: Water and Health Opportunities," World Health Organization, Bulletin of the World Health Organization 86, no. 1, January 2008, http://www.who.int/water_sanitation_health/publications/editorial/en/index.html.

[35] UNDP, Human Development Report 2006, 42.

[36] Keya Acharya, "Environment–India: Water Aplenty, Nor a Drop to Drink," Inter-Press Service News Agency, April 18, 2008.

to a road blockade at Bhareri village in protest against water shortages.[37] In December 2006 residents in South Delhi marched to protest the government's failure to fulfill promises to provide around-the-clock water supply.[38] In July 2007 more than one thousand Chinese villagers in Sichuan Province stormed a brewery, claiming that the brewery was dumping wastewater without treatment and contaminating crops and underground well water.[39] In August 2007 hundreds of people in Khanyar, Kashmir, staged demonstrations that blocked the road for hours, protesting the failure of the Public Health Engineering Department to provide adequate water.[40]

Conflict has been particularly intense in China, where disputes over water reportedly rose from 16,747 cases in 1986 to 94,405 in 2004.[41] Some disputes involved tens of thousands of people. In Zhejiang Province in 2005, for example, more than twenty thousand people stormed thirteen chemical plants that were polluting local water and spoiling crops. Villagers believed these plants were also contributing to higher rates of miscarriage than the norm.

Conflict between traditional agricultural users and new urban centers and industry is also common. Agricultural producers in the Mae Teng irrigation area of Thailand have protested the transfer of water to Chiang Mai, where municipal authorities struggle to cope with the rising demand of urban and industrial users. There have also been conflicts between rice farmers in Thailand, who use freshwater for their rice fields, and shrimp farmers, who use brackish water. Pesticides from the rice fields kill shrimp; brackish water damages rice.[42]

At the most dangerous level, water insecurity coupled with a sense of political impotence can produce a deadly form of water-based conflict. In the Karrum region of Pakistan in June 2006, fourteen people were killed during village disputes over irrigation channels following a decline in water availability. In China violent protests followed the announcement of a plan to divert reservoir water in Shandong Province from agriculture to industry.[43]

---

[37] Chander Shekhar Sharma, "Water Scarcity Brings Villagers to Streets," *Tribune* (India), April 20, 2002, http://www.tribuneindia.com/2002/20020421/himachal.htm#1.

[38] "Residents March in Protest against Water Crisis," *Hindu*, December 12, 2006, http://www.thehindu.com/2006/12/12/stories/2006121210480400.htm.

[39] Chris Buckley, "China Farmers' Protest Hits Brewery," Reuters, July 29, 2007, http://www.alertnet.org/thenews/newsdesk/PEK262806.htm.

[40] "Water Scarcity Triggers Protest," *Greater Kashmir*, August 3, 2007, http://www.greaterkashmir.com/Full_Story.asp?date=3_8_2007&Cat=1&ItemID=32.

[41] "China Company: Coca-Cola's New Formula," *EIU Views Wire Select*, April 2, 2008.

[42] Prangtip Daorueng, "Thailand: Pollution Sparks Conflicts along Bang Pakong River," Inter Press Service News Agency, November 16, 2007.

[43] UNDP, *Human Development Report 2006*, 178.

The Vidarbha region of India has become widely known for the thousands of debt-ridden farmers who have committed suicide. A neighboring region, Marathwada, has also begun to see a rash of such suicides. After years of draining groundwater, some villages in Marathwada obtain drinking-water twice per week. The number of factories in one 50-kilometer radius has dropped from fifteen to half that over the past several years.[44]

Water scarcity can also heighten tensions in an ongoing conflict. In the southern Philippines, for example, local government plans to dig a deep irrigation canal provoked a fire-fight between the Moro Islamic Liberation Front (MILF) and the Civilian Volunteers Organization in Shariff Aguak. The MILF believed the irrigation canal would affect thousands of hectares of farmland. One commander argued, "If we cannot do anything, then it is better to die fighting than to die in hunger."[45]

In Nepal as well, both the lack of access to water and the restrictions on land ownership and access to forest resources have together provided a natural breeding ground for the Maoist insurgency. A U.S. Agency for International Development report describes this situation:

> Village water sources are often located on private property, and the owner is free to restrict access to the water, creating conflict with other members of the community. Streams that are used for drinking water are sometimes partially diverted for irrigation, leaving little drinking water in the dry season, and creating conflict with downstream users. Sometimes when piped drinking water systems are developed by the government or donors, the placement of the taps inadvertently disadvantages some segments of the community, causing lasting low-level conflict. [46]

International conflict is also a possibility. As countries in Asia work to address water insecurity issues, they also often introduce new political and economic challenges for themselves and their neighbors when tapping into shared water resources to meet growing domestic demand. The damming, diverting, and polluting of international rivers by upstream users exacerbate the water-based insecurities downstream countries must negotiate. In Asia the challenge is magnified by the political and economic inequality between nations that naturally control water resources, such as China and India, and the much smaller and weaker Southeast, South, and Central Asian states downstream.

---

[44] Anupama Katakam, "Marathwada's Turn," *Frontline,* August 26–September 8, 2006, http://www.hinduonnet.com/fline/fl2317/stories/20060908004101400.htm.

[45] "Truce Monitors Defuse Water Dispute in South Philippines," *BBC News,* April 11, 2007.

[46] "Conflict over Natural Resources at the Community Level in Nepal Including Its Relationship to Armed Conflict," United States Agency for International Development, May 2006, available at http://www.forestconflict.com/documents/Nepal%20NatResConflictReport.pdf.

According to the UN Development Program, "international water basins—catchments or watersheds, including lakes and shallow groundwater, shared by more than one country—cover almost half of the earth's land surface. Two in every five people in the world today live in these basins, which also account for 60% of global river flows." [47] For 800 million of these people living in river basins, over half their water comes from another country.[48] Bangladesh represents an extreme case; Bangladesh depends on flows from India for over 90% of the country's water. The manner in which upstream countries manage infrastructure development (particularly dams, hydropower plants, and fisheries), water usage, and pollution therefore has significant consequences for water security. These consequences affect not only people in upstream states but also millions of others downstream from these states. A 2003 study by the UN and Oregon State University determined that as many as 57 river basins in Asia lack a workable framework for cooperation and are potential flashpoints for conflict.[49]

Violence between Asian nations over water resources takes place only rarely. Since 1948 virtually all of the world's 37 water-based conflicts that turned violent occurred between Israel and one of its neighbors. In South, Southeast, and East Asia, the Oregon State University-UN study identified well over 600 international disputes during this same time period, but these disputes were overwhelmingly confined to "political outbursts."[50] Nonetheless, water security has become a significant factor in broader political and security battles among states in Asia and, given the looming threat of global climate change, is likely only to increase in importance.

Domestic Policy Responses

The real challenge for Asia, however, is not simply to manage these small-scale localized protests but rather to get ahead of broader trends in development and water usage that threaten to undermine long-term economic growth, public health, and social stability. Asia's water landscape is not static. The significant changes anticipated in population, diet, energy use, and levels of urbanization will engender a potentially dramatic increase in levels of water demand and pollution.

---

[47] "State of the World 2005 Trends and Facts—Water Conflict and Security Cooperation," Worldwatch Institute, http://www.worldwatch.org/node/69.

[48] UNDP, *Human Development Report 2006*, 210.

[49] UN Department for Economic and Social Affairs, "International Rivers and Lakes," Newsletter, no. 39, June 2003, 6–7, http://www.un.org/esa/sustdev/sdissues/water/rivers_lakes_news39.pdf.

[50] Ibid., 8.

Asia's leaders are well aware of the challenge they face in meeting current and future water security needs. Throughout the region, experiments in water governance are underway. Since 2001 Indonesia has elected representatives to serve on local water management bodies to improve the transparency and accountability of financial administration of irrigation facilities.[51] China's leaders have set impressive targets for wastewater treatment, pollution reduction, and water conservation. The government has also passed new laws to increase public access to environmental information. In many parts of the country cities are undertaking water pricing trials or implementing advanced technologies to help mitigate problems. The water-scarce province of Tianjin, for example, is adopting advanced water membrane technology to help address a serious water pollution and shortage problem. The World Bank and the international NGO National Resources Defense Council (NRDC) have joined forces with Jiangsu Province in a pilot program to publicly score factories' water conservation and treatment programs. Chinese NGOs are similarly energized to tackle the issue of water security. Greenpeace Beijing and the Institute of Public and Environmental Affairs are seeking to ensure that multinational corporations adopt international standards in water conservation and wastewater treatment efforts on the ground in China. A broad coalition of more than twenty environmental NGOs in China also called on consumers to boycott the products of businesses listed as violators of pollution discharge standards.[52]

India is similarly concerned about water security. The country has pledged to the UN Millennium Development Goals to halve the number of Indians without access to safe drinking-water by 2015.[53] In Hyderabad the local government is utilizing a U.S.-based biological treatment technology to address a staggering water pollution problem.[54] Additionally, many Indian environmental NGOs are engaged on water security issues, often helping to bring to light traditional water management techniques, such as rainwater harvesting. NGOs also work to empower poorer communities in India, typically the most disadvantaged in meeting water security needs. Environmental activists in India are concerned over the government's propensity for large-scale dams and other water projects as well as over the privatization of water systems. Activists believe these strategies are

---

[51] UNDP, *Human Development Report 2006*, 192.

[52] Jun Ma and Xiaoyi Liao, "China's Clean Choice," *OECD Observer*, no. 261 (May 2007), http://www. oecdobserver.org/news/fullstory.php/aid/2238/China%92_clean_choice_.html.

[53] Acharya, "Environment–India."

[54] Jim Hight and Garth Ferrier, "Building Capacity to Monitor Water Quality: A First Step to Clean Water in Developing Countries," Organisation for Economic Co-operation and Development (OECD), OECD Trade and Environment Working Paper, no. 2006-03, 2006.

poor substitutes for smaller-scale technical efforts toward recycling, reuse of gray water, and minimization of losses in the transmission and distribution of water.[55]

Yet water security in the developing countries of Asia overall remains a distant goal. The political economies of most developing countries in Asia do not support the rapid deployment and utilization of best practices and technologies. In China, for example, there is both significant corruption and an authoritarian but highly decentralized political economy, which means that directives are issued but often not followed. China also suffers from poor enforcement capacity, weak price signals to encourage conservation and wastewater treatment, and a lack of transparency—although this is slowly changing—concerning large water-related infrastructure projects, such as river diversions and dams. This policy environment poses a challenge not only for the Chinese themselves but also for the many countries that share water resources with China. India and Indonesia also are plagued by corruption, negative incentives to conserve and treat water, and a decentralized system in which central directives often stall at the local level. To some extent, however, effective policy in these two countries, particularly India, may be challenged more often by the plethora of actors engaged in the policymaking process than by the lack of transparency.[56] Thus, for all these countries, meeting the water security challenge in Asia will mean fundamental institutional innovation.

At the same time, the rapidly expanding knowledge base and rising wealth in Asia bring new opportunities to resolve many of these water-based conflicts and potential security threats. In many instances the challenge is one of water management rather than of absolute scarcity. This suggests that there is significant opportunity for the United States and others to help address many of the security-related water challenges. Such challenges include enhancing the capacity of states—at the local and central level— both to adopt and implement new approaches and technologies as well as to resolve or prevent conflict.

Global Climate Change: The New Reality for Asia's Water Resources

Attempting to achieve and ensure national water security, Asia's leaders know the region is in a race against time. Climate change threatens to heighten dramatically the uncertainty and threat of serious water-related

---

[55] Dipak Roy, "UNDP-UNICEF Join Hands to Promote Water Prudent Society," UNICEF India, http://www.unicef.org/india/wes_1698.htm.

[56] Alan Richards and Nirvikar Singh, "Inter-state Water Disputes in India: Institutions and Policies," *International Journal of Water Resources Development* 18, no. 4 (2002): 611–12.

problems for the region. Climate change is likely to increase the scope and scale of natural disasters, contribute to rising sea levels, radically shift agricultural patterns, introduce new opportunities for the spread of disease, and heighten water insecurity.

Already the Himalayan glaciers that support Asia's most critical rivers are melting at an increasing rate. According to a 2007 survey conducted by the China Aero Geophysical Survey and Remote Sensing Center for Land and Resources, at the current rate the Himalayan glaciers could be reduced by nearly a third by 2050 and by up to half by 2090.[57]

As these glaciers melt, China's Yellow and Yangtze rivers, which support the richest agricultural regions of the country and derive much of their water from the glaciers, will experience floods initially, then drought. As a result, the Chinese government predicts up to a 37% decline in the country's wheat, rice, and corn yields in the second half of the century. The rise in sea level may submerge an area the size of Portugal along China's eastern seaboard—an area home to more than half the country's population and 60% of the country's economic output.[58]

The situation is similarly dire for South Asia. Indian security expert Brahma Chellaney outlines it thus:

> Melting glaciers will produce extensive flooding in India and Bangladesh, followed by a reduction in river flows. In southern Asia, climate changes are likely to bring about important shifts in temperature and rainfall patterns, a rise in sea levels, and a rise in the frequency and intensity of anomalous weather events, such as cyclones, flooding and droughts. These trends, cumulatively, would play havoc with agriculture and impact hydropower generation and conservation strategies. The weaker the economic and social base and higher the reliance on natural resources, the more a community will be adversely affected by climate change. In other words, the poorer parts of southern Asia, including Bangladesh, Nepal and Indian states like Assam and Bihar, are likely to bear the brunt.[59]

The socio-economic impacts could be severe: disruption of safe drinking-water sources, large-scale migration into South Asia's already heavily burdened cities, and serious public health challenges.[60] For both South and Southeast Asia, climate change also portends greater uncertainty in the monsoons. Monsoons plague the region but also are critical to ensuring a water supply throughout dry periods in the rest of the year. Indonesia in particular is concerned that climate change,

---

[57] Chellaney, "Climate Change and Security," 65.

[58] Elizabeth Economy, "China vs. Earth," *Nation*, May 7, 2007.

[59] Chellaney, "Climate Change and Security," 65.

[60] Ibid., 67.

characterized by warmer temperatures and more rainfall in tropical regions, will accelerate the spread of dengue fever by creating conditions that mosquitoes thrive in.[61]

China and India at the Headwaters

Within Asia there are numerous long-standing conflicts over water resources; indeed, among many countries there are multiple conflicts, such as those in Central Asia over the Aral Sea and the Syr Darya and the Amu Darya rivers. By virtue of the fact that several of Asia's longest and most important rivers begin in the Himalayas and the Tibetan Plateau, however, China and India are central players in many of the key controversies surrounding shared water resources in Central, South, and Southeast Asia. The efforts by these two countries to resolve—or not resolve—such conflicts bear special attention.

India and China are particularly important actors in the region: both countries are strategically located at the headwaters of many of the continent's most important rivers. By shifting their water usage practices, these two states are dramatically affecting the water security of countries in Southeast, Central, and South Asia. The need to negotiate over water resources shared among states, already a challenge throughout much of the region, promises only to intensify. In many cases water conflicts play into centuries-old security concerns among states with little shared history of cooperation.

Several of the conflicts that engage China and India, such as those centered on the water resources of the Mekong, Irtysh, and Brahmaputra rivers, are raising regional tensions. China and India are developing plans for upstream reserves that will have dramatic impacts on the lower reaches. Though there are negotiating mechanisms in place for most of these shared resources, the power dynamic—both in terms of which state controls the resources and the size and relative power of that country—means that satisfactory resolution continues to elude the downstream countries. China in particular asserts its right to control the resources within the country's borders. Within the UN, China is one of only three nations to reject fundamentally the idea of national integrity, which asserts that states have the right not to be adversely affected in their development potential

---

[61] Eliza Barclay, "Climate Change Spurring Dengue Fever Rise, Experts Say," *National Geographic News,* September 21, 2007, http://news.nationalgeographic.com/news/2007/09/070921-dengue-warming.html.

by the activities of upstream riparian countries. Instead, Beijing asserts sovereignty: the right to harness the potential of national resources.[62]

Looking across several current transboundary water conflicts in Asia that engage China, India, or both states, there is unsurprisingly little indication that either country is willing to cede significant water rights to downstream states. Yet in several cases new actors and forums are emerging that may help constrain unilateral action. China's actions on the Mekong, Irtysh, and Brahmaputra rivers may be affected by emerging alliances among domestic and international actors who desire a say in shaping policy outcomes. Moreover, recent intervention in these water conflicts by other large powers, such as Russia and the United States, may give the otherwise weaker downstream states added negotiating leverage. India has traditionally been more forthcoming than China in engaging downstream countries, such as Bangladesh and Pakistan, in negotiations over water use rights. Yet Bangladesh finds India's current moves to link major rivers flowing from the Himalayas, such as the Ganges and Brahmaputra, a source of serious concern. Bangladesh appears relatively powerless to affect India's plans. Issues such as growing radicalism and social instability on India's borders, however, as well as the potential for large-scale migration, offer a strong incentive for India to consider the water security interests of Bangladesh.

China: The Mekong, Irtysh, and Brahmaputra Rivers

China's efforts to exploit the resources of the rivers that emanate from the Himalayas and the Tibetan Plateau are part of a broader strategy to develop the country's western provinces and autonomous regions. The "go west" campaign, launched in 1998 by former president Jiang Zemin, is moving tens of millions of Han Chinese into China's west, a region traditionally populated by ethnic minorities. The campaign is designed to exploit the rich mineral, water, and oil and gas reserves of the area and to ensure the political stability of the region. Control over the Mekong, Irtysh, and Brahmaputra rivers, therefore, is likely an integral aspect of a much larger move to secure the country's borders and future economic growth.

The Mekong River, the twelfth longest river in the world (4,350 kilometers), begins in China in the Tibetan Plateau and crosses six countries before reaching the Mekong Delta. More than a third of the population of Cambodia, Laos, Thailand, and Vietnam (approximately 60 million people) lives in the lower Mekong Basin, and the river is essential for drinking-

---

[62] Timo Menniken, "China's Performance in International Resource Politics: Lessons from the Mekong," *Contemporary Southeast Asia: A Journal of International and Strategic Affairs* 29, no.1 (April 2007): 97–120.

water, food, irrigation, hydropower, transportation, and commerce. Nearly "2% of the total world catch and 20% of all fish caught from inland waters of the world" are produced in the lower Mekong fisheries.[63] Nearly half of Cambodia's people rely on the Mekong River, and the delta supports more than half of Vietnam's rice production and one-third of Vietnam's GDP.[64]

The resources of the river are overseen broadly by the Mekong River Commission (MRC), which is a forum for sharing data and managing disputes. China participates as an observer but has rejected all entreaties to join as a full member, fearing infringement of national sovereignty. As a result, China has been able to slowly but steadily encroach on the river's resources. China's overriding interest in the water resources of the Mekong has been power generation. China currently possesses two large hydroelectric dams on the Lancang (the upper reaches of the Mekong within China's territory) and has begun construction of a third, which will be the second-largest dam in the country after the Three Gorges. China is also planning at least five more dams. In addition, Chinese firms are planning to build and operate large-scale dams in other countries along the Mekong as part of broad agreements on infrastructure and power development. China has also begun to transport oil along the Mekong from a port in Thailand's northernmost province, Chang Rai. The governments of Thailand, Laos, and Burma signed the oil transport deal without consulting environmental groups or Cambodia or Vietnam.[65]

The dams have provoked concern among environmental activists and businesses throughout the region. Chinese NGOs are worried over issues such as forcible resettlement of villagers and loss of biodiversity. Downstream countries allege that the dams already have disrupted the flow of the river and adversely affected fisheries, and that further damming will devastate business. Thai and Burmese activists have called on Chinese firms to be more transparent regarding dealings in planned hydropower projects but have met with little success.[66] Activists, along with the agricultural and fisheries industries, are concerned over pollution by oil tankers as well as the potential for an oil spill. Thai business leaders have complained that Beijing controls the dams on the Mekong to China's advantage: releasing

---

[63] "China Turns Mekong River into Oil-Shipping Route," *Vancouver Sun,* January 8, 2007.

[64] UNDP, *Human Development Report 2006, 208.*

[65] "China Starts Shipping Oil via Mekong River," Xinhua News Agency, December 28, 2006, http://english.people.com.cn/200612/28/eng20061228_336639.html.

[66] Joshua Kurlantzick and Devin Stewart, "Hu's on First," *National Interest Online,* November 1, 2007, http://www.nationalinterest.org/article.aspx?id=16026.

water when Chinese ships are scheduled to travel downstream and closing water gates when Thai boats are due to sail to upstream ports.[67]

The complaints and concerns of nonstate actors and downstream countries have largely gone unheeded. Indeed the chief obstacle to resolution is simply getting China to the table. Some analysts have suggested that China might move from observer status to full-fledged member of the MRC, thereby perhaps giving the MRC the opportunity to cooperate with China to meet basin-wide needs such as redesigning China's dams on the Mekong.[68] There is no evidence, however, that China is interested in taking advantage of such an opportunity.

Other analysts have suggested broadening the scope of the Greater Mekong Subregion project to include water resource management. This project, which the ADB has advanced for more than a decade, aims to integrate the Mekong region through power, transport, and communications linkages. From the perspective of the water security interests of the downstream countries, however, the prospects that such a move would achieve the desired result are dim. Much of the ADB's work has focused on linking the economies of the region through large-scale hydropower—an effort for which outside experts and the UN have criticized the ADB on environmental grounds.[69]

A third option also has emerged. The U.S. Agency for International Development has initiated a program with the MRC to work on joint planning and sustainable management of the water resources of the lower Mekong River Basin. One of the explicit goals of the project is facilitating strategic engagement with Beijing on planned development activities in China that would have significant potential downstream impacts.[70] Both a united front among the downstream countries and the ability to link the Mekong River issue to the U.S.-China relationship could give the weaker actors greater leverage in efforts to bring China to the negotiating table.

China has proved similarly reluctant to engage in serious cooperative water resource management efforts with another downstream neighbor: Kazakhstan. The two countries share some twenty transboundary rivers. Serious conflict has been brewing over the resources of one of the rivers most significant to Kazakhstan's water security—the Irtysh. According to

---

[67] Evelyn Goh, *Developing the Mekong: Regionalism and Regional Security in China–Southeast Asian Relations Asian Studies,* Adelphi Paper 387 (London: Routledge, 2007), 47.

[68] Michael Klare, "Wars for Water?" *Newsweek,* April 16, 2007.

[69] Marwaan Macan-Markar, "UNEP Faults Asian Development Bank Project," Inter Press Service News Agency, July 17, 2007, http://ipsnews.net/news.asp?idnews=38568.

[70] "MRC and USAID Support Transboundary Cooperation," Mekong River Commission, Press Release, April 23, 2007, http://www.mrcmekong.org/MRC_news/press07/23-apr-07.htm.

the Kazakh government, more than one-quarter of the country's citizens depend on the Irtysh as their main source of water. The government argues that rice production has already suffered as a result of a drop in the river's water levels. Lack of water has led Kazakhstan to avoid developing close to fifteen thousand square kilometers of arable land for cotton production.[71]

China began diverting water from the Irtysh in the 1990s. The country has re-routed 500 million cubic meters of water from the river annually through a canal to irrigate Chinese agriculture and to supply water to the Karamai oil fields. By 2020 China plans to double the annual volume of water diverted to one billion cubic meters. Local officials are pushing aggressively to develop water-intensive industries such as cotton and petroleum production as well as to increase agricultural production in wheat.[72] Moreover, Chinese authorities claim that Xinjiang, which borders Kazakhstan, will be home to as many as 40 million new Chinese. At least one Chinese official has asserted that China anticipates utilizing as much as 40% of the Irtysh's effluence.[73]

Kazakhstan is concerned not only by a growing shortfall in the river's water resources but also by rising pollution. The river carries nitrates, petroleum products, and heavy metals, the concentration of which would increase if flows diminished.

Kazakhstan has had somewhat greater success than the MRC in bringing China to the negotiating table. In 1998 the Kazakh press published several heated articles on China's water usage and construction of a canal that diverted water from the Irtysh. The publication of these articles threatened to upset the broader political, economic, and security relations between the two countries. As a result, China negotiated a framework agreement that was signed in 2001. The agreement failed, however, to produce a common understanding and approach concerning utilization of the river's resources, and Beijing has refused to take the more formal step of creating a joint authority to oversee the Irtysh. Although a Sino-Kazakh consultative commission did draft an agreement in 2006 to share information on water quality, the commission does not appear to have the capacity to discuss water extraction issues.[74]

---

[71] Sebastien Peyrouse, "Flowing Downstream: The Sino-Kazakh Water Dispute," Jamestown Foundation, China Brief 7, no. 10, May 16, 2007, 7, http://www.jamestown.org/terrorism/news/uploads/cb_007_010.pdf.

[72] UNDP, *Human Development Report 2006*, 210.

[73] Jeremy Allouche, "The Governance of Central Asian Waters: National Interests Versus Regional Cooperation," in "Central Asia at the Crossroads," *Disarmament Forum*, no. 4 (2007), 52, available at http://www.unidir.org/bdd/fiche-periodique.php?ref_periodique=1020-7287-2007-4-en.

[74] Peyrouse, "Flowing Downstream," 9.

Like members of the MRC, Kazakhstan may benefit in the future from the engagement of a larger power. Russia, which is also affected to an extent by China's practices on the Irtysh, has indicated interest in addressing the water security issue. In fall 2007 then president Putin noted that Russia and Kazakhstan have good prospects for cooperation over the Irtysh, but that common approaches needed to be developed among Russia, Kazakhstan, and China.[75] The introduction of water resource management into a broader regional framework may also provide a boon to Kazakh interests. At its 2007 summit, the Shanghai Cooperation Organization, of which China, Russia, Kazakhstan, and the other Central Asian states are members, raised water usage and water rights over international rivers as a topic for continued discussion.[76]

China also faces an emerging conflict with the country's most populous Asian neighbor, India. Both India and Bangladesh have become concerned over China's apparent plans to dam the Brahmaputra (known in China as the Yarlung Tsangpo) and divert part of the river to the Yellow River. Chinese officials first seriously explored the idea in 2003, when Chinese scientists did a feasibility study on the potential for a major hydropower project on the Brahmaputra that would divert 200 billion cubic meters annually to the Yellow River. The plan received a significant boost within China in 2006 with the publication of a book, *Tibet's Waters Will Save China*. Penned by several former Chinese officials, the book was quite popular and reportedly was positively received by both Premier Wen Jiabao and President Hu Jintao. During the 2007 National People's Congress, a bill was proposed to move forward on the project, receiving support from 118 generals and more than 700 specialists.[77]

Not surprisingly, experts in India and Bangladesh have voiced significant opposition, arguing that the impact on both countries would be devastating and that as much as 60% of the total water flow would fall drastically.[78] Maminul Haque Sarker from the Centre for Environmental and Geographic Information Services in Bangladesh argues that fifteen to

[75] "Conservation Primary Task of Russia-Kazakhstan-China Cooperation," Central Asia General Newswire, October 4, 2007.

[76] Bruce Pannier, "Central Asia: SCO Leaders Focus on Energy, Security, Cooperation," *Radio Free Europe/Radio Liberty*, August 16, 2007.

[77] Lixiong Wang, "Xizang zhi shui jiu Zhongguo, shei lai jiu Xizang?" [Tibet's Water Rescues China: Who Will Save Tibet?] Boxun, April 24, 2007, http://www.peacehall.com/news/gb/china/2007/04/200704240006.shtml.

[78] Ryan Hodum, "Conflict over the Brahmaputra River between China and India," American University, Inventory of Conflict and Environment Case Studies, no. 205, May 2007, http://www.american.edu/ted/ice/brahmaputra.htm.

twenty small and medium rivers dependent on the Brahmaputra will die if China's plan succeeds. Chellaney further describes the situation:

> Having extensively contaminated its own major rivers through unbridled industrialization, China now threatens the ecological viability of river systems tied to South and Southeast Asia in its bid to meet its thirst for water and energy....The mega-rerouting would constitute the declaration of a water war on lower-riparian India and Bangladesh.[79]

Even some Chinese scholars have voiced disapproval. Tibet expert Wang Lixiong published a dissenting view, asking "Who will save Tibet?" Lixiong argued that the Tibetans should be consulted on any plan involving water resources on their land.[80]

Although Bangladesh reportedly has not taken any diplomatic initiative to discuss the issue with China, India has tried to move quickly. New Delhi has already formally requested a joint working group to discuss the issue, supposedly even approaching Hu Jintao directly in 2007. More than a year later, however, no meeting has been reported.

India: The Brahmaputra, the Ganges, and the Indus Rivers

Like China, India seeks to harness the resources of rivers within the nation's boundaries to meet internal water security needs. New Delhi has planned a grand-scale project to build a network of dams as part of a river-linking project. The project would divert water both from the Ganges and from part of the Brahmaputra in the north of the country to the drought-prone southern and eastern states. The plan is estimated to involve construction of more than 965 kilometers of canals, cost as much as 200 billion dollars, and take fourteen years to complete.[81]

India and Bangladesh have already negotiated a series of treaties over the past several decades to help protect Bangladesh's access to a stable volume of water flow. Since the most recent treaty signed in 1996, however, Bangladesh is reportedly losing a large volume of water every year. Unlike the earlier 1977 treaty, the 1996 agreement makes no provision to augment water flow through regional cooperation.[82] The treaty also does not address the pollution of river water, and Bangladesh now faces threats to agriculture

---

[79] Brahma Chellaney, "China Aims for Bigger Share of South Asia's Water Lifeline," *Japan Times*, June 26, 2007, available at http://www.globalpolicy.org/security/natres/water/2007/0626chinawater.htm.

[80] Wang, "Xizang zhi shui jiu Zhongguo, shei lai jiu Xizang?"

[81] John Vidal, "India's Dream, Bangladesh's Disaster," *Guardian*, July 24, 2003, available at http://www.countercurrents.org/en-vidal240703.htm.

[82] Sumita Sen, "The Indo-Bangladesh Water Conflict: Sharing the Ganga," in *Water Conflicts in India: A Million Revolts in the Making*, ed. K.J. Joy, Biksham Gujja, Suhas Paranjpye, Vinod Goud, and Shruti Vispute (New Delhi: Routledge, 2007).

and fisheries from heavy concentrations of toxic chemicals and heavy metals in the water. Furthermore, the 1996 treaty does not provide for any arbitration or dispute settlement.

For Bangladesh the river-linking project portends an even greater water security challenge. Bangladeshi government scientists believe the plan would be disastrous for agriculture and would dry out significant areas for much of the year.[83] Many environmental activists and former government officials in India also oppose the river-linking project, calling the project little more than a giant politically motivated gift to key voter constituencies.[84] One prominent environmental activist, Medha Patkar, has argued that the project "would destroy the river valley civilizations by displacing hundreds of thousands from their habitats."[85] Patkar has called upon the Indian government to raise the issue within the context of the South Asian Association for Regional Cooperation.

Unlike China, however, India continues to discuss the river-linking project with downstream neighbor Bangladesh. In part, the Indian government is concerned over the potential for a more Islamized and radicalized Bangladesh, which could undermine social stability in India through growing refugee flows. Chellaney argues that India could well determine that the trade-off between greater water resource access, on the one hand, and social stability, on the other, is a trade-off the nation cannot afford:

> India cannot shape developments within Bangladesh, but it can try to be a positive influence. India has to deal with the situation in Bangladesh in strategic terms, with a long-term approach. If Bangladesh's radicalization and political turmoil were to continue, India's security will be very seriously undermined by hostile elements operating out of Bangladesh. A Bangladesh that sinks deeper in extremism and fundamentalism will be a serious geopolitical headache for India. But a Bangladesh from where the refugee flows become a torrent will be a geopolitical nightmare for India.[86]

There have even been some reports that local Indian officials oppose the river-linking plan and that it may not move forward.

A water rights treaty brokered between India and Pakistan offers one of the more hopeful signs that effective cooperation can occur in water basin management among Asia's developing countries. Pakistan depends on rivers flowing from Indian-administered Jammu and Kashmir. The 1960 Indus Waters Treaty reserves 56% of the catchment flow for Pakistan, with India

---

[83] Vidal, "India's Dream."

[84] "Indian Environmentalist Warns against River Link Project with Bangladesh," *Daily Star*, December 20, 2004.

[85] "Indian Environmentalist Warns against River Link Project."

[86] Chellaney, "Climate Change and Security," 67.

receiving the remainder. At the same time the treaty gives India the right to build hydroelectric plants on the three rivers reserved for Pakistan so long as the plants do not change the water flow downstream into Pakistan.[87] The treaty was initially brokered by the president of the World Bank. Since that time the Permanent Indus Commission, which oversees the treaty, has survived and functioned during two major wars between India and Pakistan.

The potential for water resource control to become a weapon in a broader political or security battle between the two countries still remains. In 2002, for example, shortly after five Pakistani terrorists attacked the Indian parliament, the former Indian high commissioner to Pakistan, Gopalapuram Parthasarathy, voiced the view that New Delhi should abrogate the Indus Waters Treaty, noting that India "should make it clear to Pakistan that if it can bleed us in Jammu and Kashmir," India has "the capability to starve them."[88] Although India maintained treaty commitments, Parthasarathy's threat carried widespread support among hard-liners.

Policy Implications for the United States

Asia's current state of water insecurity raises several significant challenges for the United States. Tainted food products, particularly fish, are an increasingly common export from Asia and pose a public health concern for the American people. Diseases such as dengue and SARS (severe acute respiratory syndrome) are enabled by unsanitary conditions, and globalization has made spread of such diseases a concern far beyond any host nation's borders.[89] In addition, a sustained crisis in the provision of safe water and sanitation can provide fertile ground for political radicalism that can translate into support for violent and destabilizing politics, as has occurred in Nepal and Pakistan. Moreover, Asia's economic dynamism and integration into the global economy has made the region an essential element of continued U.S. economic well-being. Significant water-induced constraints on growth in Asia would raise the price of many consumer goods and agricultural products and have a profound impact on the U.S. economy.

The United States therefore has a direct and significant interest in working actively to help Asia address water security needs. As a first step,

---

[87] Chellaney, "Climate Change and Security," 66.

[88] James Kraska, "Sustainable Development Is Security: The Role of Transboundary River Agreements as a Confidence Building Measure (CBM) in South Asia," *Yale Journal of International Law* 28, no. 2 (Summer 2003): 493.

[89] "Inadequate Plumbing Systems Likely Contributed to SARS Transmission," World Health Organization Media Centre, September 26, 2003, http://www.who.int/mediacentre/news/releases/2003/pr70/en/.

the United States could articulate a vision of water security akin to that put forward in the UN Human Development Report:

> Water sharing is not a zero sum game…. Two overarching challenges define transboundary water governance strategies at the start of the 21st century. The first is to move beyond inward-looking national strategies and unilateral action to shared strategies for multilateral cooperation. …The second is to put human development at the centre of transboundary cooperation and governance.[90]

The United States has a related opportunity to help forge a new consensus to combat climate change. Though the nations of Asia may be particularly at risk from the threat of climate change, they have proved reluctant to take aggressive action toward the global challenge. In fact, the danger remains that climate change will act as a spur for China and India to concern themselves even less with the water security needs of neighboring states downstream. Neither China nor India has stepped up to adopt significant measures designed to limit contributions to the problem. Rather, both states have focused on the responsibility of the developed world, as the major historic contributor to climate change, to adopt stringent measures to limit emissions. This posture is neither surprising nor without justification. In the face of the water security challenges these nations already confront, however, a more aggressive plan of action seems warranted. There is a logic to Washington taking action to reduce U.S. greenhouse gas emissions and to put in place adaptive measures that of course goes beyond the potential impact on Asia's water resources. Nonetheless, emissions reduction is one critical representative area that highlights the likely urgent nature of the challenge and need for response.

At the regional level, the United States could find it helpful to seek opportunities to work with actors committed to a long-term, sustainable water policy. An optimal policy would ensure the broadest possible protection of water security interests and avoid highly asymmetrical outcomes that significantly disadvantage one or more parties. The 2003 Oregon State University-UN study found that few treaties had adequate reference to "water quality management, monitoring and evaluation, conflict resolution, public participation and flexible allocation methods."[91] These treaties therefore typically fall short in promoting long-term water management. U.S. engagement in the MRC is a potentially positive example of forging broad consensus around a comprehensive water resource usage strategy. The United States in this case is attempting to provide additional leverage to the weaker actors in the negotiations—the downstream

---

[90] *Human Development Report 2006*, 204.

[91] UN Department for Economic and Social Affairs, "International Rivers and Lakes."

Southeast Asian countries. This case is also an opening for the United States to engage China directly in bilateral talks by becoming an active participant in the multilateral Mekong Basin effort. The United States might play a similar role in the emergent conflict among India, China, and Bangladesh over China's planned diversion of the Brahmaputra.

The most important level at which the United States can engage in the water security of Asia, however, is working with domestic actors within a given country both to strengthen the policy environment and to increase opportunities to utilize technologies.[92] The extent to which individual countries in Asia are able to meet future water security needs and avoid continuing the current trajectory will depend to a significant degree on evolution in the policy environment of each country. There are a number of actions that the United States could take to further this end.

Internationally, the United States could raise the profile of water security within the ongoing environmental discussion in the Strategic Economic Dialogues that the Department of the Treasury holds with China and India. The focus on energy issues in these dialogues misses the integral importance of water to any future development potential in Asia.

Opportunities also exist to initiate experiments in environmental zones in the larger developing Asian countries. The decentralized nature of the political system in India, China, and Indonesia, among other countries, is suited to regional experimentation. These experiments would help ensure the adoption of best practices in efficiency of water use, water pricing, wastewater treatment, and adoption of appropriate technologies. An integrated approach to experimentation that engages the energy, public health, urban planning, and other sectors will ensure the most effective and coordinated adoption of innovative policy efforts and new technologies.

The United States could also engage the corporate and NGO sectors. Multinational corporations have an important role to play in water security. With U.S. retailers and manufacturers sourcing from hundreds of thousands of factories throughout Asia, these companies are well positioned to ensure that such factories meet if not exceed Asian countries' environmental laws and regulations. A regular consultative framework that included U.S. NGOs and multinational corporations could feed ideas and opportunities for cooperation with Asian countries on water security into ongoing bilateral and multilateral forums.

---

[92] The options for action that follow were adapted from an unpublished policy brief prepared by the author for an Asia Foundation working group session, "America's Role in Asia," chaired by J. Stapleton Roy and Michael Armacost, Washington, D.C., on May 20, 2008.

EXECUTIVE SUMMARY

This chapter examines the military power projection capabilities and policies of four major states in the Asia-Pacific region—the U.S., China, Japan, and India—and draws implications for the U.S.

MAIN ARGUMENT:

Despite the military modernization programs underway in the region, the power projection capabilities of China, Japan, and India will remain limited and their policies restrained. The U.S., which possesses the dominant force projection capabilities in Asia, is modernizing its forces and seems committed to continue using them in a restrained manner, often in support of the common good. Long-standing Asian flashpoints are contained, and future contentious issues do not seem susceptible to settlement by military force. Thus, rather than initiating a scramble for power and influence in the region, the major nations in Asia seem more likely to use their power projection capabilities for symbolic purposes, and there are encouraging signs that these countries are considering more multilateral cooperative operations.

POLICY IMPLICATIONS:

- China, India, and Japan will not match the power projection capability of the U.S. These countries are, however, all developing the ability to deploy forces with the military capacity to threaten U.S. power projection task groups. In the event of crises in which their interests differed from those of the U.S., these countries could demand to play a role.

- A scramble for power and influence among major Asian powers would be likely if a drawdown of the U.S. forward-deployed military presence occurs in Asia.

- Encouraging Asian governments to concentrate on the positive and cooperative uses of power projection capabilities for the common good will help counter internal advocates who call for more aggressive and nationalist policies. Such encouragement would promote habits of cooperation that support peaceful development.

Military Power Projection in Asia

Dennis C. Blair

Major power war in Asia is a mercifully remote possibility today. The two flashpoints remaining from prior wars—the Korean Peninsula and the Taiwan Strait—are contained by a stable structure of mutually understood policy declarations and deterrent military forces. Despite border incursions and clashes, the Kashmir dispute between Pakistan and India is similarly stable, and the development of nuclear weapons by both these countries has further reduced the likelihood of full-scale war between them. There remain land border disputes, notably those between China and India, and conflicting economic claims in the South and East China seas, but these disputes have not generated protracted tensions and sustained arms races among the claimants. The instincts of Asian governments tend increasingly toward peaceful resolution of differences.

Growing military power projection capabilities and the potential for more assertive policies by China, Japan, and India darken this bright picture. These countries have neither had expansive ambitions to extend their territories and influence far from their shores nor possessed substantial military forces that could assert influence at a distance. The United States—the only country with such a capability—has, since the end of the Vietnam War, used military power in a restrained manner. Other countries in the region have generally recognized the common good this U.S. policy provides, and the sheer size of the U.S. dominance in power projection capability in Asia has discouraged competition.

In recent years, however, China, India, and Japan have all begun to consider developing increased military capability to influence more distant events. Military programs are under development in each of these countries that could, in time, provide deployable task forces for overseas operations.

Dennis C. Blair holds the John M. Shalikashvili Chair in National Security Studies at The National Bureau of Asian Research. He can be reached at <blair@nbr.org>.

Developments in China are of special concern. China's recent increases in military spending have been the largest in the region, and the country's even more rapidly increasing economic power has caused widespread concern over China's ambitions for influence beyond its borders.

Should the major countries of Asia develop power projection forces and pursue more active unilateral military diplomacy in Asia, such a shift would change the peaceful nature of the region and cause greater suspicion, political competition, and even conflict. Though not inevitably leading to major conflict, such increased diplomacy would certainly increase tension in the region, raising mistrust and worst-case fears. Disputes that are now deferred or handled by negotiation could become catalysts for military confrontation. The nations of Asia would look to their own defenses and seek to line up friends and allies to form offsetting formal or informal alliances, increasing the chances of a cold war in Asia and a more dangerous environment for confrontations, clashes, or conflicts.

Most damaging to the peaceful Asian security landscape would be an aggressive, sustained power projection policy by a major nation—China, India, or Japan. Any nation on this track would routinely deploy military task forces to crisis areas and insist on solutions and settlements to its liking; such a country would stir up dormant disputes and then use the threat or application of military force for more advantageous arrangements. Such a nation would be seeking to become a more dominant power in the region, one that could not be crossed without penalty and one enforcing deference across the range of issues in its interest.

There is an alternative future for Asia, even if major nations develop military forces more capable of power projection. If these powers were to use these more capable forces in multilateral military cooperation for the common good under widely beneficial and widely accepted policies, the peaceful nature of the region would be strengthened as a result.

This chapter begins with a discussion of the definition, purposes, and history of power projection operations in Asia. The next section surveys the current and future potential capabilities of the major countries. A final section discusses the future power projection policies of these countries.

The conclusion of this survey of power projection developments in Asia is generally positive. U.S. power projection capabilities and strategy seem relatively stable and will continue to be the most powerful in Asia. China, India, and Japan are increasing their capabilities, and there are vocal advocates of more aggressive policies in each of these countries. Official ambitions are cautious and restrained, however, and there is no sign in any of the three countries of a national decision to pursue a broad-based and substantial power projection capability. In addition, there are encouraging trends toward multilateral military cooperation throughout the region that could accommodate increased power projection capability by major nations without raising regional tensions.

Power Projection Definition and History

Definition

Power projection is political influence exerted at a distance through the use or threat of military force. It is useful to think of power projection operations according to their underlying political purposes. Nine types of power projection operations are described below. The first five, being generally unilateral and aggressive, can contribute to regional tension. The last four, which are more often multilateral and reactive, often contribute to easing regional tensions.

- *Economic/Territorial Aggression*: Occupation by force of disputed territory or sustained armed patrol of disputed maritime economic development regions.

- *Punitive Attack*: Military action to punish another country for a policy or a specific action.

- *Coercive Threat*: Threatened military action to prevent another country from pursuing a policy or taking a specific action.

- *Political Intervention*: Threatened or actual military action to support a political faction within another country.

- *Symbolic Show of Force*: Deployment of forces to signal interest and involvement with no intention of engaging in combat.

- *Peace Operations*: Deployment of forces, generally in a coalition, to establish or enforce peace within a country where there is ongoing or potential violence.

- *Protection of Trade*: Escort of merchant shipping to protect against attack by other nations or pirates.

- *Humanitarian Response*: Deployment of forces to provide relief to the victims of natural or man-made disasters.

- *Rescue Operations*: Military action to rescue citizens in danger or being forcibly held in another country.

U.S. Power Projection in Asia

The three decades since the end of the post-colonial wars in Southeast Asia have seen virtually all these nine types of power projection operations. During that period only the United States has maintained the capability to project serious military force throughout the region, and U.S. power projection operations have been the most common. U.S. power projection operations in East and South Asia have generally been restrained, however, and have been usually accepted and often welcomed in the region. As the following examples illustrate, these operations have most often contributed to the common good in such areas as humanitarian relief, protection of trade, and peace operations.

- *Political Intervention*: In 1989, when Colonel Gringo Honasan attempted a military coup against the Aquino government in the Philippines, the United States flew military jets over Manila, signaling opposition to the coup.

- *Symbolic Show of Force*: The United States sent a carrier battle group into the Indian Ocean during the 1971 Indo-Pakistan War and deployed two carrier battle groups to the vicinity of Taiwan following Chinese missile firings in 1996. In neither case did the United States intend to undertake combat operations with these forces.

- *Peace Operations*: The United States has participated in peacekeeping operations in Asia but has not played the leading role. Examples include the United Nations peacekeeping operation in Cambodia from 1991–93 and the 2002 Australian-led peacekeeping deployments to East Timor, which continue today.

- *Protection of Trade*: In the late 1980s both parties in the Iran-Iraq War conducted attacks on ships in the Persian Gulf. Kuwait supported Iraq, which led the country's shipping to be threatened by Iran. The United States protected Kuwait's oil exports against Iranian attacks by reflagging and escorting Kuwaiti ships.[1]

- *Humanitarian Response*: The United States led international military relief operations in Bangladesh in 1991 and tsunami relief operations in Indonesia and Sri Lanka in 2004–05.

---

[1] For more detail on U.S. activities in the Persian Gulf during the Iran-Iraq War, see David B. Crist, "Joint Special Operations in Support of Earnest Will," *Joint Force Quarterly*, no. 29 (Autumn/Winter 2001/02): 15–22, http://www.dtic.mil/doctrine/jel/jfq_pubs/0629.pdf.

- *Rescue Operations*: U.S. ships and a small force of marines attacked Koh Tang Island off Cambodia in 1975 in an unsuccessful attempt to rescue the captured crew of the U.S. merchant ship *Mayaguez*.[2]

In addition, the United States conducts a massive military exercise program throughout Asia, including annual major exercises in Thailand (Cobra Gold), Guam (Valiant Usher), and Korea (Foal Eagle, previously Team Spirit), as well as hundreds of smaller exercises.[3] U.S. military forces are ubiquitous in the region and thus are part of its geopolitical fabric.

Power Projection by Asian Countries

No Asian country has conducted power projection operations as substantial or as often as the United States has. Other countries have, however, used or threatened to use military force to assert political influence beyond their borders. Apart from the United States, China has been the most active user of power projection capability. As the following examples show, Chinese power projection operations have been conducted close to home and have mostly been unilateral and aggressive in nature.

- *Economic/Territorial Aggression*: China has occupied islands in Southeast Asia by force, notably in 1974 when a Chinese naval task force fought off attacks by the South Vietnamese navy in the Paracel Islands. China and Vietnam also fought in 1988 over the occupation by the People's Liberation Army Navy (PLAN) of Fiery Cross Reef in the Spratly Islands. This battle resulted in the sinking of three Vietnamese ships and the loss of over 70 Vietnamese sailors. China further expanded its position into Mischief Reef in 1995, although this expansion occurred without violence.[4]

- *Punitive Attack*: In 1979 China sought to teach Vietnam a lesson in a one-month invasion by division-sized forces. The reasons for military action were complicated and included clashes between Vietnam and

---

[2] For more on this incident, see Peter Huchthausen, *America's Splendid Little Wars: A Short History of U.S. Military Engagements from the Fall of Saigon to Baghdad* (New York: Penguin, 2003), 1–2.

[3] For more information on U.S. military exercises, see the U.S. Pacific Command website at http://www.pacom.mil/about/pacom.shtml.

[4] For further information on the history and current claims on the Spratly Islands by several Asian states, see Soh Guan Huat, "Unwarranted Despair or Unfulfilled Hopes: An Examination of the Possibility of Armed Conflict and the Prospects for Peace over the Spratly Islands," report, 1997, available at GlobalSecurity.org, http://www.globalsecurity.org/military/library/report/1997/Soh.htm.

China over control of Cambodia, maritime claims in the Spratlys, and the treatment of ethnic Chinese in Vietnam. Although the tactical results of the incursion were in Vietnam's favor, Beijing served notice that China would exact a price if Vietnam did not take into account Chinese interests in Southeast Asia.[5]

- *Coercive Threat*: Since the late 1990s China has built an ever-growing arsenal of ballistic missiles ranging (i.e., capable of striking) Taiwan and in 1995 and 1996 fired missiles into the waters around Taiwan. The purpose of the missile build-up and firings has been coercion with the intent to prevent Taiwan from moving toward independence.

- *Peacekeeping Operations*: In contrast to the previous examples, China's participation in UN peacekeeping activities has increased in recent years. The country provides 566 of the 12,754 troops in UNMIL in Liberia, 444 of the 8,718 troops in UNMIS in Sudan, and 343 of the 12,532 troops in UNIFIL in Lebanon.[6]

- *Humanitarian Response*: The People's Liberation Army (PLA) has worked hard to increase the military's domestic humanitarian response capability. PLA flood relief operations in 1998 and earthquake response in May 2008 received wide praise domestically. Because of shortcomings in long-range transportation and logistics capabilities, PLA overseas humanitarian response operations have been limited. For example, the military's contribution to the 2004 tsunami relief operations was slower coming and less than that of smaller countries.

Other countries' power projection operations in Asia have been occasional and usually small-scale. They include the following examples.

- *Economic/Territorial Aggression*: In 1973 a large Indonesian amphibious task force invaded East Timor, then known as Portuguese Timor. Vietnam, Malaysia, and the Philippines have occupied disputed islands in the South China Sea, although without major military engagements.

---

[5] "Chinese Invasion of Vietnam, February 1979," GlobalSecurity.org, http://www.globalsecurity.org/military/world/war/prc-vietnam.htm.

[6] The numbers given for troops are as of February 2008. For the number of Chinese troops committed to UN peacekeeping operations, see "UN Missions Summary Detailed by Country," UN Department of Peacekeeping Operations, February 29, 2008, http://www.un.org/Depts/dpko/dpko/contributors/2008/feb08_3.pdf. For the total number of UN troops by mission, see "UN Missions Summary of Military and Police," UN Department of Peacekeeping Operations, February 29, 2008, http://www.un.org/Depts/dpko/dpko/contributors/2008/feb08_4.pdf.

- *Coercive Threat*: North Korea (also known as the Democratic People's Republic of Korea, or DPRK) routinely rattles its rusting saber, threatening dire military consequences to South Korea, the United States, and Japan should these countries conduct certain actions against DPRK interests.

- *Political Intervention*: India has maintained a modest power projection capability, and—beyond wars with Pakistan—has used this capability sparingly. For example, India unsuccessfully attempted to end the civil war in Sri Lanka and in 1988 restored the government to power in the Maldives.

- *Symbolic Show of Force*: New Zealand deployed two frigates to Muroroa Atoll in French Polynesia in 1973, where France was conducting nuclear tests. The French navy had been aggressively clearing the testing area of protest boats but did not attempt to drive the New Zealand frigates away. Not long afterward France suspended nuclear testing there.

- *Peacekeeping Operations*: Many Asian countries participated both in the UN peacekeeping operations in Cambodia from 1991 to 1993 and in the Australian-led peace enforcement operation in East Timor beginning in 2002. Many Asian nations have long and proud traditions of peacekeeping that have involved sending troops around the world. India, Pakistan, Bangladesh, Nepal, Malaysia, Indonesia, Australia, New Zealand, South Korea, and Fiji are stalwarts of UN peace operations. Japan's participation in peacekeeping operations, however, has been controversial and sporadic.

- *Humanitarian Response*: Most Asian countries send military forces to assist their neighbors when natural disasters strike. The most recent prominent example is the multilateral military response to the tsunami that devastated a number of Asian countries in 2004. An interesting and little-known operation was the response of Singaporean helicopters to Hurricane Katrina. Based in Texas, three Singaporean CH-47 Chinooks deployed to Louisiana and rescued many New Orleans citizens stranded by the floodwaters.[7]

---

[7] "RSAF Deployment to Assist in Hurricane Katrina Relief Operations," Singapore Ministry of Defence, Press Release, September 2, 2005, http://www.mindef.gov.sg/imindef/news_and_events/nr/2005/sep/02sep05_nr.html.

Power Projection Capability: The Military Tools

These brief accounts of the types and history of power projection operations in Asia show that the countries of the region are familiar with the concepts and practice of political influence through the use of military force at a distance. This chapter will now look more closely at the tools of power projection: the military forces themselves. Virtually all nations in Asia maintain maritime, ground, air, and missile forces for the defense of national territory. Some of these defensive forces have inherent power projection capability, especially in nearby areas. For example, the Indonesian forces used for the amphibious occupation of East Timor in 1973 were the same forces that were used to address rebel insurgencies in prior years. The Chinese forces that invaded Vietnam in 1979 were drawn from nearby military districts. What distinguishes power projection forces from defensive forces is the ability to operate in substantial numbers at longer distances for sustained periods. The development of unique power projection capabilities causes unease in the region over the intentions of the country that develops them. Maritime, ground, air, and missile forces have their own power projection characteristics, and all require support beyond what is needed for the same forces at their home bases.

Maritime Power Projection

The core of maritime power projection capability is naval task groups that can project power ashore: aircraft carrier battle groups and amphibious landing ship task groups. To be effective beyond a symbolic show of force, these task groups must be able to sustain and defend themselves from both maritime and shore-based attack. A combination of destroyers and cruisers with advanced surface-to-air missile systems, antisubmarine frigates with embarked helicopters, and submarines and maritime patrol aircraft comprise a task group that can protect itself. Without these balanced defense capabilities, task groups operating off hostile coasts are vulnerable to diesel-electric submarines as well as to antiship missiles delivered by shore-based aircraft, patrol boats, and shore-based batteries. Supply ships provide deployed battle groups with fuel, food, and ammunition, while air deliveries from nearby shore bases supply smaller, high-priority spare parts and personnel.

Both aircraft carrier task groups and amphibious landing task groups vary in size and capability, with the U.S. Navy possessing the most capable by far. These groups can be based either on nuclear-powered aircraft carriers operating fixed-wing, fourth-generation aircraft or on advanced, large amphibious landing ships operating vertical or short take-off and landing

(VSTOL) aircraft, rotary-wing helicopters, and air-cushion landing craft. Highly capable cruisers, destroyers, maritime patrol aircraft, and nuclear submarines provide defensive capabilities.

By contrast, the navies of other countries field less capable maritime power projection groups. A good example is the British task force assembled for the Falklands War in 1982. Britain deployed two aircraft carriers with vertical or short take-off and landing aircraft embarked and loaded troops and equipment into converted merchant ships. Short take-off and landing aircraft, missile destroyers, frigates, and nuclear submarines provided defense, and a combination of naval and civilian vessels provided resupply. This force had severe limitations, however. Attacks by antiquated Argentine aircraft and equipment wear and tear caused almost enough damage to force the British to return home before launching an amphibious assault. Littoral nations in East and South Asia all have the similar capability to threaten naval task groups approaching their coasts—at least those groups that do not include advanced antiaircraft and antisubmarine escort ships.

Ground Forces Power Projection

Serious sustained ground force projection operations are based on amphibious and air assault capabilities. Forced military entry into another country requires specially trained amphibious or air assault troops, fire support to suppress opposition during the assault, and the logistics capability to reinforce and sustain the initial assault. For large-scale operations, naval forces are needed to provide initial fire support and resupply by sea in order to sustain combat operations and continued occupation. Because of the inherent advantages of defense, an attacker will generally need a large margin of superiority to ensure success. Many countries have learned that, although smaller forces can make successful landings in lightly defended areas or against weak opposition, a successful initial assault is not the end of an operation. Often the more difficult task once ashore is maintaining control against irregular insurgent forces.

A special case of ground force power projection is the long-range raid. The forces employed in making these raids can range in size from commando squads to airborne battalions. Notable historical examples include the successful Israeli commando raid on the Entebbe airport in Uganda in 1976 and the unsuccessful U.S. attempt to rescue hostages in Tehran in 1979. Being much shorter in duration, these raids do not have the extensive logistics requirements of sustained power projection operations.

Ground forces make up the bulk of most peace operations. These operations can be large-scale, involving tens of thousands of troops, with peace enforcement missions under Chapter VII of the UN Charter sometimes even involving serious combat. Peace operations are less demanding than power projection operations, however, because they do not involve forced entry. Peace operation forces enter the area of operations without opposition and generally have safe areas of support nearby. Intelligence, communications, and logistics support are much easier for peacekeeping than for opposed power projection operations: because there is less threat of attack, commercial transportation and contract services are available, and coalition partners often provide support. Extensive peacekeeping experience does not, therefore, translate into strong power projection capability. Bangladesh, Nepal, the Scandinavian countries, Malaysia, and Indonesia have long peacekeeping traditions and extensive experience, yet none of these states has the ability to project and sustain ground forces into hostile environments at a distance.

Air and Missile Strikes

Air and surface-to-surface missile strikes are a specialized form of power projection with unique capabilities, limitations, and political implications. The primary power projection purposes of states are punitive attack and coercive threat. Though virtually every country in Asia possesses aircraft that can bomb the country's neighbors, this capability is limited by aircraft range, which is several hundred miles unless accompanied by tankers. Several countries maintain non-nuclear missile arsenals. There are no defenses in Asia against ballistic missiles (although India is working on such a system), but the threat of these missiles is limited because they are not reusable weapons. Aircraft, in contrast, can make multiple strikes, but may be shot down by aircraft or air defense missiles while traveling to and from targets. Furthermore, pilots can be captured and used for political leverage.

The United States has used both aircraft and Tomahawk land-attack cruise missiles for power projection purposes. Many of these strikes have been punitive—responding to another country's actions in order to discourage more of the same. The 1986 air attacks on Libya are one such example. Other strikes have been designed to destroy targets the United States considered dangerous, such as the Tomahawk strikes on WMD facilities and command posts in Sudan and Iraq.

Ballistic missile attacks have been used or threatened in fewer cases. The notable exception has been North Korea, which has often conducted ballistic missile tests for symbolic purposes, seeking to demonstrate that the DPRK could strike Japan or South Korea if Pyongyang chose to do so. By also cultivating an image of unpredictability and unreasonableness, North Korea has successfully used missile capabilities to cause neighboring countries to tread very lightly on DPRK interests, real or asserted. Beijing has used China's large and growing ballistic missile inventory primarily to coerce Taiwan, making very clear that China is prepared to punish Taiwanese movements toward independence.

Missile strikes and air strikes can be an effective power projection force in support of punitive political objectives to pose the threat of damage to an adversary that takes or continues hostile actions. Strikes have effect, however, only if the political context is appropriate. North Korea's missiles range China and China's range Russia, but these missiles do not provide political influence in either relationship. Finally, missile and air strikes lose effectiveness if used repeatedly in a limited fashion.

Command, Control, Communications, Intelligence, Surveillance, and Reconnaissance (C3ISR) for Power Projection

Accurate, up-to-date intelligence information and real-time communications between headquarters and power projection units are essential for the success of a power projection operation, unless an operation is merely a symbolic deployment. Power projection operations have high political significance and are generally conducted within a context of political negotiations. In addition, worldwide media and the Internet will generate a great deal of information regarding any military operation. For these reasons, the military and political leaders of the country conducting the operations need up-to-date knowledge of the situation on the ground.

The explosive growth of worldwide commercial communications has made high-bandwidth, highly reliable communications available in virtually any country in the world. Using international commercial communications, a military task force anywhere in the world can be in close touch with its headquarters. Commercial sources, however, do not provide adequate worldwide intelligence, surveillance, and reconnaissance capabilities to conduct power projection operations. Commercial satellite imagery is now available with one-meter resolution but is not timely enough for sustained military operations. For this reason, task forces can include fixed-wing aircraft, helicopters, or unmanned aerial vehicles (UAVs) for reconnaissance in permissive environments. These same aircraft can collect signals intelligence able to be interpreted by intelligence centers in the task force headquarters. In order for task force commanders and military and political leaders in the deploying country to obtain a real-time, reliable picture of an objective area, several conditions must be met. The deploying country must possess imagery and signals intelligence satellite systems linked to forward reconnaissance systems, have intelligence analysis capabilities in the task force, and have larger specialized intelligence staffs in rear bases.

Logistic Support for Power Projection

Virtually any advanced country can employ missiles or bombs to conduct a simple air strike up to several thousand kilometers from one of its bases. To bring military power to bear in a protracted crisis or to operate at greater distances, however, a country needs to use staging bases and access to meet its objective. This requirement is true for maritime task forces as well as for air task forces. A country that plans to develop an extended power projection capability needs to develop overseas bases from which to refuel, resupply, and repair ships and aircraft.

Base and access agreements between countries are generally restricted to specific purposes, and, when a country plans a power projection operation during peacetime, negotiations must be held country-by-country for landing, transit, and support for that operation. The permission of even a long-time ally cannot be assumed. When the United States conducted air strikes against Libya in 1986, many NATO partners refused not only to allow U.S. basing but also to grant even overflight permission. F-111 bombers were required to fly along a lengthy route from the United Kingdom through international airspace in the Atlantic and over the Gibraltar Strait rather than take the shorter route across France or Spain.

Power Projection Capabilities and Purposes

Table 1 shows the types of military forces applicable to different purposes of power projection operations. Maritime task forces are clearly the most versatile form of power projection. Most major Asian countries are located on islands or peninsulas or have long coastlines where major cities are located, and important trade routes cross the seas and straits in the region. As a result, any country aspiring to greater power projection capability in Asia must develop its naval task forces. Ground forces can project power in peaceful conditions and—if part of large coalitions—do not need to be balanced, militarily sustainable formations. Missile and air strikes serve important but limited functions. For all forms of power projection, C3ISR and logistics support capabilities are essential if the operation is to last longer than a few days.

TABLE 1   Types of power projection and related military functions

Purpose \ Type of power projection	Air and missile strikes	Maritime	Ground forces	C3ISR	Logistics
Economic/ territorial		✓	✓	✓	✓
Punitive attack	✓	✓	✓	✓	✓
Coercive threat	✓	✓		✓	
Political intervention	✓	✓	✓	✓	
Symbolic show of force		✓		✓	
Peace operations		✓	✓	✓	✓
Protection of trade		✓		✓	✓
Humanitarian response		✓	✓	✓	✓
Rescue operations		✓	✓	✓	

Future National Power Projection Capabilities in Asia

United States

U.S. maritime, air, and deployable ground forces are larger by far than those of any country in the region, and the United States has the flexible C3ISR capabilities and logistic support arrangements to sustain projection operations for weeks and months. Current U.S. plans are to maintain and modernize these power projection capabilities in Asia.

Maritime. In the summer of 2008 the USS *George Washington* replaced the USS *Kitty Hawk* as the U.S. aircraft carrier homeported in Japan. The *George Washington* is nuclear-powered and so can steam indefinitely at top speed, covering more than 750 nautical miles per day. In addition, the *George Washington* carries more aviation fuel and weapons for embarked aircraft than the *Kitty Hawk*. The result will be a more powerful and responsive U.S. maritime task force stationed permanently in the western Pacific.

Production of the navy version of the F-35 Joint Strike Fighter, a fifth-generation tactical aircraft, will begin in 2013. Although the deployment locations of the new aircraft have not been announced, the carrier air wing in Japan attached to the *George Washington* will have a high priority. This aircraft will be superior to any aircraft in Asian air forces. In addition, in 2013 the navy will introduce a new maritime patrol aircraft to replace the venerable P-3. This aircraft will modernize wide-area antisubmarine and antisurface warfare capabilities.

Air and missile. Deployments of B-52 and B-2 bombers to Guam have been nearly continuous in recent years, and Guam's logistic support capability has been uniformly increased. A wing of F-22 fighters is now stationed in Alaska and another is scheduled to be stationed in Hawaii. This fifth-generation fighter is the most advanced in the world.

Ground. U.S. ground force power projection capability is unmatched in Asia, and current plans are for both the army and the marines to grow in size and flexibility. Army units will be able to deploy more quickly in Asia given that the army's Stryker medium brigades are positioned in Alaska and Hawaii. One U.S. brigade has left the Korean Peninsula, and Marine Corps staff and support personnel are moving from Okinawa to Guam. These redeployments of personnel do not diminish overall U.S. ground power projection capability, however, as troops can be moved quickly by air. Amphibious lift shipping and bulky supplies remain forward-deployed in the western Pacific. The assault range of amphibious task groups will be greatly extended with the introduction of the V-22 tilt-rotor aircraft to the Marine Corps' inventory. Furthermore, with an amphibious task group homeported in Sasebo, Japan, the United States will continue to be able to deploy and sustain a quick forcible entry capability throughout the region. These same forces form the basis for humanitarian response and peacekeeping participation throughout the region.

Future U.S. power projection policy. Since the end of the Vietnam War, Washington has been judicious and restrained in employing the dominance in power projection capability that the United States enjoys. Although the unilateral U.S. invasion of Iraq has raised suspicions regarding long-term U.S. intentions in the Middle East, the same has not been true in Asia. In recent dealings with North Korea, for example, the United States has relied exclusively on multilateral diplomacy supported by economic sanctions and rewards. In 2004, leading the military component of the international response to the Indian Ocean tsunami, the United States was welcomed in Indonesia, and, according to polls, in a few weeks U.S. prestige in that country was restored to pre-Iraq levels.[8] With the greatest military capability available for humanitarian operations and a tradition of responding to these events, the United States would be expected to play a leading role in the military response either to natural disasters or to a large-scale terrorist attack in the region. Continued U.S. military engagement in the region and occasional use of U.S. power projection capabilities in cooperation with

---

[8] "A Major Change of Public Opinion in the Muslim World: Results from a New Poll of Indonesians," Terror Free Tomorrow, 2005, http://www.terrorfreetomorrow.org/upimagestft/Full%20Report.pdf.

other countries and for purposes that are shared by other Asian nations is likely to continue to be welcomed. The most controversial use of U.S. power projection in the region would be in the case of a Taiwan crisis, in which support for U.S. action would vary. Most countries would try not to take a position on the crisis and would call for a negotiated settlement. Most would privately prefer that the United States prevent a Chinese takeover of Taiwan but would not like to see China humiliated in the course of such a crisis.

Two potential developments could change this relatively stable picture. The first development would be the withdrawal of U.S. forward-based power projection capability from the region. Should the U.S. navy, air force, and marines leave Korea or Japan, either because they were no longer welcomed by the host nations or because the United States decided to shift to a homeland-based posture, the changes in the Asian security landscape would be profound. Although periodically deploying to Asia for exercises or for crises, naval task groups and aircraft detachments would not be the ubiquitous presence that they are now. The gaps in the U.S. presence would provide opportunities for other nations to assert greater influence or even to conduct power projection operations without opposition.

The second potential development that could diminish U.S. power projection dominance would be the development of strong naval task groups by Japan, India, or China and the unilateral deployment of these groups to crisis locations. When crises occurred in the eastern Mediterranean during the Cold War, both the United States and the Soviet Union would routinely deploy task groups. The U.S. task groups were always more powerful and could project power ashore through air strikes or amphibious landings. The Soviet task groups could not project power ashore but could damage U.S. ships, especially if the Soviet navy could take the first shot. The result was that U.S. options were limited, and Soviet interests needed to be taken into account in resolving crises. In a similar fashion, Japan, India, and China could all develop the ability to limit U.S. power projection options in a crisis through the deployment of maritime task groups, even before these states have developed the capabilities to project power ashore themselves.

China

China's power projection capabilities today are focused almost entirely on coercion of Taiwan. Nevertheless, China has sent small numbers of navy ships on symbolic goodwill cruises to distant regions, deployed small contingents of peacekeepers around the world, and deployed troops in Central Asia in battalion strength during Shanghai Cooperation

Organization (SCO) exercises. China's defense budget is growing rapidly, and the country's modernization program includes many elements of an expanded power projection capability.

Maritime. China's naval modernization to date has been dominated by missions focused on Taiwan. The weight of the country's efforts has been devoted to submarines and frigates. As explained in the previous section, the use of submarines can limit another country's maritime power projection forces. Submarines themselves, however, play only a small role in power projection operations. The PLAN's new frigates would be useful in protecting oil tankers against low-level threats in straits and coastal waters. To conduct convoy operations, however, on the coasts of Africa, in the Indian Ocean, or in the Strait of Malacca against more capable threats, China would need stronger antisubmarine forces and defenses against antiship cruise missiles. China would also need access agreements for naval support bases in these regions as well as to increase the size of its replenishment fleet. The obvious first step for the PLAN would be to participate in the many international maritime security exercises and operations. Through these activities, China would gain the experience to build PLAN capabilities. In 2007 then chief of naval operations Admiral Mullen, explained the "thousand-ship navy" concept of collective international maritime security to Admiral Wu, the chief of the Chinese navy.[9] Though Admiral Wu engaged in lively and serious discussions of the concept during his visit to the United States, China has yet to take positive steps to join these activities.[10]

China's heavily publicized interest in aircraft carriers has not yet translated into a serious program to build a prototype of either a smaller ship with the capability for helicopter or short take-off and landing flight operations or a large ship with catapults and arresting gear for fixed-wing aircraft.[11] Development of a class of aircraft carriers and the additional surface combatants and logistics support for a carrier task force would mean that China intends to project power thousands of miles from the country's borders. There is no other military purpose for aircraft carrier task forces. Aircraft carriers have a unique symbolic allure, however. For nations without a maritime tradition, aircraft carriers signify a serious maritime capability. Chinese authors and officials discuss building aircraft carriers not for their

---

[9] Shirley A. Kan, "U.S.-China Military Contacts: Issues for Congress," CRS Report for Congress, RL32496, February 1, 2008, 61, http://www.fas.org/sgp/crs/natsec/RL32496.pdf.

[10] Eric A. McVadon, "U.S.-PRC Maritime Cooperation: An Idea Whose Time has Come?" Jamestown Foundation, China Brief 7, no. 12, June 13, 2007, 10–12, http://www.jamestown.org/china_brief/article.php?articleid=2373469.

[11] China purchased the laid-up small Russian carrier *Varyag* in 1998. In the ten years since, China has not followed the path of India, which purchased another Russian carrier, the *Admiral Gorshkov*, then contracted with Russia to refurbish and return the carrier to service.

military purposes but as a way of proving that China has become a major maritime power, showing little appreciation of the balanced battle group and extensive complex support capabilities that give an aircraft carrier military usefulness beyond displaying the flag.[12] Even without the full capabilities of a carrier task force, a Chinese carrier would be useful for symbolic shows of force and could be used in unopposed power projection operations such as peacekeeping and humanitarian responses.

The PLA is building a Type 081 landing craft in the 20,000-ton category that might form the core of a future amphibious landing task force capable of operating far from China.[13] Current Chinese exercises include amphibious landings, but these are largely short-range. A true long-range power projection capability would include a robust supply fleet, armed helicopters or fixed-wing close air support aircraft operating from carriers, and worldwide communications and ISR systems. PLA sustainment capabilities for maritime task force operations are limited to a small number of relatively primitive replenishment ships, and there have been no indications that China is seeking military basing or access rights overseas to support naval deployment.[14]

Although there is no current indication of a concerted program to build a maritime power projection capability, China will soon be able to assemble and deploy a task force that could challenge U.S. dominance in a crisis situation. For example, if the United States deployed a large naval task force in the Sea of Japan during a confrontation with North Korea, China could deploy and sustain a substantial force of surface ships and submarines, supported by long-range aircraft. China could then announce that the force was to support Chinese interests in the resolution of the crisis. At a minimum this force would give Beijing a seat at the table and at a maximum could prevent Washington from using the deployed U.S. forces to coerce North Korea.

Ground. China's army heritage is one of an infantry-centered force fighting by the precepts of "people's war." The only time since its founding

---

[12] For scholarship related to China's carrier development, see Andrew S. Erickson and Andrew R. Wilson, "China's Aircraft Carrier Dilemma," *Naval War College Review* 59, no. 4 (Autumn 2006): 13–45, http://www.nwc.navy.mil/press/review/documents/NWCRAU06.pdf; and Ian Storey and You Ji, "China's Aircraft Carrier Ambitions: Seeking Truth from Rumors," *Naval War College Review* 57, no. 1 (Winter 2004): 77–93.

[13] Ronald O'Rourke, "China Naval Modernization: Implications for U.S. Navy Capabilities— Background and Issues for Congress," CRS Report for Congress, RL33153, February 4, 2008, 26, http://www.fas.org/sgp/crs/row/RL33153.pdf.

[14] For a discussion of China's overseas sustainment capabilities, see Roy D. Kamphausen and Justin Liang, "PLA Power Projection: Current Realities and Emerging Trends," in *Assessing the Threat: The Chinese Military and Taiwan's Security*, ed. Michael D. Swaine et al. (Washington, D.C.: Carnegie Endowment, 2007), 111–52.

that the army has operated for longer than a month outside of China's borders was when China sent forces to the Korean War in 1950. In the past decade the PLA has adopted the concept of fighting "local wars under high-technology conditions."[15] Though substantially improving the army's mobility, the PLA shows no sign of developing the full range of capabilities necessary for large, sustained operations beyond China's borders. In 2007 China forward-deployed an air-ground task force of battalion strength to an SCO exercise in Russia. Commenting on the exercise, Chen Xueli of the Academy of Military Sciences noted that "the Chinese Army's long-range strategic deployment is still relatively weak...the lack of large-scale Chinese military transport equipment and long-range delivery capability are great constraints."[16] This statement is typical of the sober assessments of China's own capability that Chinese officers publish in professional journals. As described previously, the PLA has dramatically increased participation in UN-sponsored peacekeeping operations around the world. Though these operations provide some experience in long-range operations, these missions are not sufficient to prepare units for power projection operations into hostile environments.

As with any large army, China has elite forces capable of short-duration raids to rescue hostages, conduct sabotage, and undertake similar missions. Though China has developed the skills for these missions and trained the personnel in preparation for a conflict with Taiwan, these capabilities are transferable to other locations.

Air and missile. China has the largest ballistic missile force in Asia and is in the middle of a major modernization of its arsenal at all ranges, from short-range missiles targeted on Taiwan to intercontinental ballistic missiles that range the United States. Improvements include increased survivability, accuracy, and stockpiles. In addition to these ballistic missiles, China is developing a long-range cruise missile. Launched from a long-range bomber, this missile has a range that includes virtually all of Asia.[17]

With this formidable array of missiles, China has the military ability to coerce any country within Asia. This coercion is most relevant to Taiwan. Beijing has made clear that China will not hesitate to attack should Taiwan take certain steps toward independence. The missiles also give pause to any country within range that is contemplating a confrontation that threatens

[15] Information Office of the State Council of the People's Republic of China, *China's National Defense in 2006* (Beijing, December 29, 2006), section II, http://www.fas.org/nuke/guide/china/doctrine/wp2006.html.

[16] "Comments on PLA Capability for Long Range Force Projection," Xinhua, December 16, 2007.

[17] "Annual Report to Congress: Military Power of the People's Republic of China 2008," Office of the Secretary of Defense, Report to Congress, March 2008, 5, http://www.defenselink.mil/pubs/pdfs/China_Military_Report_08.pdf.

China's core interests. Short of such a serious confrontation, however, the political usefulness of China's long-range strike capability is limited. Just as the United States has found that overwhelming military superiority cannot easily be translated into political advantage on every issue, so it is with China. Suppose, for example, that China decided to support Chinese nationals being mistreated during a period of civil violence in a Southeast Asian state. The threat of missile strikes would not be credible and therefore would be of little use either in coercing that country to take action or in punishing it. A situation such as this would require Chinese maritime and ground power projection forces on the scene to protect and punish.

Future Chinese power projection policy. Chinese writings do not provide a consistent explanation of the country's intentions to develop serious power projection capabilities. A widely noted section of China's 2006 defense white paper describes the future developments of the services as follows:

> The Army aims at moving from regional defense to trans-regional mobility, and improving its capabilities in air-ground integrated operations, long-distance maneuvers, rapid assaults and special operations. The Navy aims at gradual extension of the strategic depth for offshore defensive operations and enhancing its capabilities in integrated maritime operations and nuclear counterattacks. The Air Force aims at speeding up its transition from territorial air defense to both offensive and defensive operations, and increasing its capabilities in the areas of air strike, air and missile defense, early warning and reconnaissance, and strategic projection. The Second Artillery Force aims at progressively improving its force structure of having both nuclear and conventional missiles, and raising its capabilities in strategic deterrence and conventional strike under conditions of informationization.[18]

These sentences can be interpreted as a veiled statement of intent to develop a future power projection capability that can be used well beyond China's borders or as a blueprint for a flexible strategy for the defense of China's ground and air space as well as its maritime frontier.

The great majority of articles on the subject in the Chinese press refute commentary from foreigners that China is developing a power projection capability.[19] Though it is tempting to dismiss such writings as propaganda in support of the current Chinese "peaceful development" line, these articles are also read by members of the PLA and therefore cannot be completely disingenuous. There are many articles by Chinese naval authors arguing for China to develop a blue water maritime capability.[20] These authors argue that China must be able to protect its ships carrying essential resource

---

[18] *China's National Defense in 2006*, section II.

[19] See, for example, "China's Military Power No Threat to Any Country: Senior PLA Officer," Xinhua, March 5, 2008; and "China Firmly Opposes U.S. Military Report," Xinhua, March 4, 2008.

[20] See discussion in Erickson and Wilson, "China's Aircraft Carrier Dilemma," 13–45.

imports, especially petroleum, and cite the importance of defending China's maritime frontier against U.S. naval task forces at a distance of many thousands of kilometers. The naval forces required for these missions are submarines, long-range naval aircraft with missiles, surface combatants with helicopters, and ocean surveillance satellite systems, and these are the weapons systems now being pursued by the PLAN. Chinese naval authors do not argue for a power projection capability at these distances in order to support China's interests in regional issues. The types of naval forces required for these missions would be fixed-wing aircraft carrier task groups and amphibious landing ship task groups, supported by resupply shipping and regional base access agreements. The PLAN is not currently developing these forces.

China is very much committed to developing the maritime power to isolate Taiwan and to engage U.S. naval forces hundreds of miles from the Chinese coast. A navy for these purposes would be able to make symbolic shows of force throughout Asia and beyond and could offset traditional U.S. displays of force during crises. On balance, it seems probable that China has not yet decided whether the military will develop a serious power projection capability to support the country's regional and worldwide interests. Should China do so, the clearest signs would be (1) the construction of a class of fixed-wing aircraft carriers, as well as the cruisers and antisubmarine warfare systems of a carrier task group; (2) the development of a robust afloat logistics capability; (3) the pursuit of port and airfield basing and use agreements in Southeast Asia and the Middle East; and (4) the routine operation of balanced aircraft carrier task groups in these regions.

Japan

Japan's security strategy, organizations, and operations are evolving away from their traditional modes, which were entirely defensive. The end of the Cold War marked the beginning of Japan's "lost decade," a period in which Japanese security strategy drifted. North Korea's launch of a Taepodong missile across Japan in 1998 served to jolt Japanese public opinion, and the country's defense outlook began to shift. Following September 11, Japan sent logistics and reconstruction forces into the North Arabian Sea and Iraq as a contribution to fighting the global war on terrorism. Then, in the 2004 National Defense Policy Guidelines, Japan added China to North Korea as the main potential threats to Japanese security.[21] These developments have been controversial within Japan, given that the country has exhibited a strong pacifist strain and has traditionally

[21] Japan Ministry of Defense, *2004 National Defense Program*, section II, http://www.mod.go.jp.

relied on the United States to take the lead in military activities both in the region and globally. Changes in military acquisition programs have been even slower.

Maritime. Japan's most important maritime development program has been the Aegis ballistic missile defense fleet, developed with support from the United States. In December 2007 the JS *Kongo* successfully intercepted a ballistic missile target,[22] and in March 2008 the sixth Aegis cruiser joined the fleet. This increase in ballistic missile defense capability has been widely supported in Japan as a defensive response to the North Korean threat.

More controversial in Japan has been development of the *Hyuga*, a helicopter carrier with an 18,000-ton capacity, capable of embarking eleven CH-47 Chinook-size helicopters. Japan has no program for short take-off and landing fixed-wing aircraft for this carrier, but helicopters alone can provide substantial capability. This *Hyuga*-class vessel will allow the Japanese Maritime Self-Defense Force (SDF) to build a task force that can put ashore and support an air mobile battalion-sized ground force. A task force of destroyers and frigates accompanying the *Hyuga*, supported by land-based maritime patrol aircraft, would be able to defend itself against aircraft, missiles, and submarines much more capably than, for example, any PLAN joint task force supporting the Type 081. The developing Japanese satellite reconnaissance system would provide wide-area intelligence support to the task force. Furthermore, long-range Japanese electronic warfare aircraft, the RC-121, would also provide intelligence support if the aircraft could find a base from which to operate within a thousand miles. The Japanese navy has deployed squadrons of ships for extended periods and has the replenishment ships, communications, and experience to support a task group throughout the western Pacific and Indian Ocean.

Air and missile. Japan has no surface-to-surface ballistic or cruise missiles; however, a new tanker fleet extends the range of Japanese aircraft strike capability. Japan's planned tanker fleet consists of four KC-767 tankers, the first of which has been delivered. With this fleet of tankers, Japanese fighter aircraft will be able to launch air strikes against North Korea, China, and most of Southeast Asia. Current Japanese fighters have large radar cross sections and would be vulnerable to advanced air defense systems such as those in parts of China and in Singapore. Japan is committed to developing or buying from the United States a fifth-generation fighter that will have the ability to penetrate all but the most advanced air defense networks. Despite problems in the development of space systems, Japan is also committed to

[22] Audrey McAvoy, "Japan Completes Missile Intercept Test," Associated Press, December 17, 2007.

building satellite reconnaissance systems that could provide the targeting intelligence for precision air strikes.

Ground. The Japanese Ground SDF has the inherent capabilities for peacekeeping operations. These operations have been controversial within Japan, however, and the few units that have been sent to join peacekeeping coalitions have been so limited by political guidance that they have contributed little. Japanese elite ground forces have the ability to carry out specialized long-distance raids and hostage rescue operations, but Japan has never used these forces.

Future Japanese power projection policies. Japan's traditionally limited interpretation of the role of military forces in its security policies is changing, but Japan is far from adopting a policy of aggressive power projection to support the country's interests abroad. Since World War II, when Japanese citizens or interests were threatened around the world, Japan has turned not to military force but to diplomacy, a checkbook, and the United States. There seems little likelihood of a major change in this approach. Increased military capability enjoys strong public support only if such a capability is clearly defensive, while systems with even potential power projection capability are controversial and acceptable only to a small number of citizens. This popular attitude is the best barometer of future Japanese policies; popular opinion would have to change drastically in order for Japan to develop a more assertive power projection strategy.

The initial emphasis of Japan's new but still defensive security policy is on North Korea and China. Maintaining the military capability—ballistic missile defense and air and naval forces—to deal with missile or maritime aggression by these two countries enjoys widespread support in Japan, but the use of military force to support more distant interests is controversial. The military deployments for the global war on terrorism—most notably refueling ships in the North Arabian Sea—have been started and stopped as the politics of the issue shifted.

The most probable area of expansion in overseas deployments is peace operations. Japanese contingents in UN peacekeeping coalitions have been limited to non-combat roles and have even been precluded from providing their own defense. Commanders have been under strict orders to avoid even a single casualty. More robust SDF peacekeeping contingents, capable of handling tougher sectors, would be a welcome development. As long as Japanese projection capability is used for international purposes, sanctioned by the United Nations, and not for unilateral advantage, there seems to be little for Japan's neighbors to fear and much to welcome.

India

India's defense budgets are increasing at a moderate pace, and the government is attempting to reach a goal of 3% of GDP.[23] Indian defense policy is dominated by the Pakistan threat, and the country's traditional aspirational goal has been military superiority throughout South Asia and the Indian Ocean region. Security priorities further abroad are discretionary and include peacekeeping around the world as well as naval operations in East Asia as a way of countering Chinese pressure on Indian interests. Indian power projection capabilities are being modernized, but dramatic new capabilities are not expected.

Maritime. India operates a single small carrier with vertical/short take-off and landing aircraft. The navy has plans for two more carriers— the *Admiral Gorshkov*, acquired from Russia, and another to be built in India.[24] Both these programs have experienced delays and cost overruns but if completed will deliver a limited capability to provide air support to troops ashore and to bomb lightly defended land targets. To carry troops ashore at long distances, the Indian navy has one old U.S. amphibious ship that can carry less than a battalion in a single load. With this capability India can support its interests in South Asia, where the threat environment is low, but no Indian naval task group could survive conflict in the Persian Gulf or in East Asia where antiship cruise missiles and submarines would inflict heavy damage.

Air and missile. India has a strong missile development program, including both ballistic and cruise missiles. The Indian Air Force, which includes a squadron of tankers, is well equipped and trained. With this force, India can conduct precision strikes throughout South Asia. In addition to Japan, India is the only country in Asia developing ballistic missile defenses. These capabilities will give India the most capable forces in South Asia for punitive attack or coercion by air strikes.

Ground. Comprising 80% of the country's armed forces, the Indian army has the bulk of the responsibility for the country's most important military tasks—confronting Pakistan and China over disputed territories and patrolling Kashmir. The army's long-range mobility, however, is very limited. Though the army has a proud tradition of participating in international peacekeeping operations and has special forces and airborne units that can carry out raids, India is not developing the capability to

---

[23] International Institute for Strategic Studies, *The Military Balance 2008* (London: Routledge, 2008), 334.

[24] Ibid., 329–31.

both move and sustain substantial ground units into distant hostile threat environments.

Future Indian force projection policies. India's ambitions for power projection forces center on South Asia. In a May 2007 official publication, *Freedom to Use the Seas: India's Maritime Military Strategy,* the Indian navy chief of staff wrote "our primary maritime military interest is to ensure national security, provide insulation from external interferences, so that the vital tasks of fostering economic growth and undertaking development activities can take place in a secure environment."[25] India's international military activities in recent years have expanded greatly, especially naval activities. India has sponsored multilateral naval exercises in the Indian Ocean with the United States, Japan, Australia, Indonesia, and Singapore and has participated in an exercise with the United States and Japan in the western Pacific. Though these exercises have drawn sharp criticism from China, India has also conducted bilateral naval exercises with that country. India has additionally undertaken friendship cruises in the Persian Gulf, including port visits in Iran. New Delhi's plan seems to be to continue India's traditional military dominance of the countries of South Asia but in addition to foster more multilateral activities in the Indian Ocean and extend and widen the country's symbolic presence east of Malacca and west of Hormuz. India has recently concluded that the major security threats the country faces are not the military forces and government-sponsored actions of its neighbors or more distant countries but instability in the region. New Delhi fears civil unrest and violent minority groups in South Asia will spawn minority unrest and even terrorist tactics in India itself. Conventional military power projection forces have little capability to deal with these threats.

Table 2 summarizes the current inventories of several key types of power projection forces for the United States, China, Japan, and India.

Flashpoints of Power Projection Conflict

This chapter has defined power projection as political influence at a distance through the use or threat of military force. The most serious threats to the peace in Asia—the flashpoints—occur where two major countries are projecting power in support of conflicting interests.

The most dangerous flashpoint in Asia is Taiwan, where China and the United States are supporting opposing interests. In fact, the clash in interests is so serious that conflict would most likely result in war—whether

---

[25] International Institute for Strategic Studies, *The Military Balance 2008,* 330.

local or all-out war—between the United States and China rather than the limited confrontation more generally characteristic of conflicting power projection. The trajectories of U.S. and Chinese capability development will not fundamentally alter the military essentials of a confrontation over Taiwan. Though increasing faster than that of the United States or Taiwan, China's military capability is growing from a much smaller base and is facing a much more difficult mission: the seizure and subjugation of a well-defended, large island 70 miles offshore. For the next several decades, China will be able both to inflict increasing levels of damage on Taiwan and to cause increasing levels of damage to U.S. forces supporting Taiwan but will not be able with any degree of confidence to conquer and subjugate the island with military force. China—like Taiwan and the United States—is further restrained by the economic consequences of a major conflict in East Asia.

Another potential flashpoint is oil and gas development in the East and South China seas. With conflicting economic claims, there is potential for military confrontation between Japan and China, as well as between China and several of the smaller nations of Southeast Asia. The most likely use of power projection forces would be symbolic—e.g., naval patrols in disputed waters—to underline the seriousness of a contending state's claim. There is also the potential for encounters at sea to lead to short naval engagements in disputed areas, as has occurred in the past. It is unlikely, however, that these engagements would lead to full-scale naval wars between the disputing parties because military force cannot achieve the objective of making a disputed sea area safe for unilateral oil and gas drilling. The weaker contending party can simply withdraw from the disputed area while the stronger party is present and return during the times that the stronger party must rest, repair, and resupply. If the stronger country actually sets platforms for exploration or exploitation, these platforms are very vulnerable to maritime sabotage, even by much weaker countries.

It is prohibitively expensive for even a major maritime nation to protect oil rigs far from home against harassment, sabotage, or attack from even a weak maritime nation. Only minimal self-defense systems can be mounted on an oil platform; to establish a robust defense perimeter around an oil or gas rig would take two or three ships of frigate class or larger with embarked helicopters. Keeping two or three ships on station would require seven to ten ships dedicated only to that mission. Even with such a commitment, it would be difficult to defeat a determined attack by a small number of missile patrol boats at night or in poor weather, especially with other fishing or merchant traffic in the area. It would also be difficult to prevent

TABLE 2 Relative power projection capabilities by service

	China	Japan	India	United States	
				Asia-Pacific[4]	Total
Ground Forces[1]	Airborne: • 1 corps (manned by Air Force, ~35,000) • 2 (naval infantry) brigades (6,000–10,000) Helicopters: • ~30 attack • ~10 assault	Airborne: • 1 brigade (~3,000–5,000) Helicopters: • ~85 attack	Airborne: • 5 battalions (~2,500–4,000) Helicopters: • ~20 attack (operated by the air force) • ~12 assault	Airborne: • 4th Brigade, 25th Infantry Division (~5,000) • Marine Expeditionary Force I MEF & III MEF (~100,000) Helicopters: • ~175 attack • ~375 assault	Airborne: • 9 brigade combat teams (~45,000) • U.S. Marine Corp (~175,000) Helicopters: • ~1,225 attack • ~3,000 assault
Air Force	Advanced fighters: • ~115 Su-27 SK (J-11) Flanker • ~75 Su-30MKK Flanker • ~60 J-10 Air transport: • 18 Il-76MD Candid B • 30 Il-76TD Air refueling: • ~10 HY-6, 8 Il-78M on order	Advanced fighters: • ~150 F-15 Eagle • ~40 Mitsubishi F-2 (F-16 variant) Air transport: • ~20 C-1 • ~10 C-130 H Hercules Air refueling: • 1 KC-767A (first of four)	Advanced fighters: • ~50 Su-30 MKI Flanker • ~35 M-2000H/E Mirage • ~100 MiG-27ML Flogger J2 • ~50 MiG-29B Air transport: • 25 Il-76 Candid Air refueling: • 6 Il-78 Midas	Advanced fighters: • ~130 F/A-18A/B/C/D Hornet • ~120 F/A-18E/F Super Hornet • ~110 F-15A/B/C/D Eagle • ~110 F-16C/D Fighting Falcon • ~40 F-22A Raptor Air transport: • 80 C-17 Globemaster III • 25 C-5A/B/C Galaxy Air refueling: • 25 KC-10A Extender • 25 KC-130J/R Hercules • 50 KC-135A/R/T Stratotanker	Advanced fighters: • ~990 F/A-18A/B/C/D Hornet • ~270 F/A-18E/F Super Hornet • ~520 F-15A/B/C/D Eagle • ~220 F-15E Strike Eagle • ~1280 F-16C/D Fighting Falcon • ~90 F-22A Raptor Air transport: • ~150 C-17 Globemaster III • ~125 C-5A/B/C Galaxy Air refueling: • ~60 KC-10A Extender • ~65 KC-130F/J/R/T Hercules • ~530 KC-135A/R/T Stratotanker

Table 2 continued.

	China	Japan	India	United States Asia-Pacific[4]	United States Total
Navy[2]	60 submarines (7 nuclear) 1 aircraft carrier (not commissioned), Varyag • ~75 small landing ships • ~160 landing craft	16 submarines 1 helicopter-carrying destroyer, Hyuga • ~5 small landing ships • ~18 landing craft	16 submarines 1 aircraft carrier, Viraat (ex-UK Hermes) • 1 large landing ship • 10 small landing ships • 6 landing craft	25 submarines (all nuclear) 6 aircraft carriers • ~19 large landing ships • ~75 landing craft	57 submarines (all nuclear) 11 aircraft carriers • ~30 large landing ships • ~330 landing craft
Missiles	• ~35 intermediate-range ballistic missiles (IRBM) • ~725 short-range ballistic missiles (SRBM)	None	• ~12+ IRBM • ~30 SRBM	Tomahawk missiles	Tomahawk missiles
Satellites[3]	43 (17 commercial, 13 military, 13 other)	39 (23 commercial, 4 military, 12 other)	16 (8 commercial, 1 military, 7 other)	N/A	~400+ (82 military, 320+ other)

SOURCE: International Institute for Strategic Studies, The Military Balance 2008; U.S. Pacific Fleet, U.S. Navy; U.S. Air Force; U.S. Marine Corps; U.S. Army; and the Union of Concerned Scientists satellite database, http://www.ucsusa.org/assets/documents/global_security/UCS_Satellite_Database_4_07_08.xls.

[1] Ground forces include units uncommitted in the Asia-Pacific and available for contingency missions. Attack helicopters refer to helicopters equipped with integrated fire control and aiming systems for the purpose of delivering munitions on a target. Assault helicopters are armed helicopters designed to deliver troops to the battlefield.

[2] Submarine numbers do not include SSBNs (ballistic missile submarines).

[3] "Other" means that it is unclear whether the satellite is used for commercial or military purposes.

[4] Data includes operational hardware stationed both at bases on the Pacific coast of the United States and at U.S. bases in Asia.

special forces in raiding craft from planting charges that would damage key equipment on the rig.[26]

It is unlikely that conflicting development claims will lead to prolonged and serious conflict between major countries in Asia. The much more likely pattern is symbolic shows of force, short engagements, and negotiations leading to joint development without prejudice to conflicting claims—a model that has been used in the Gulf of Thailand and more recently in an agreement between China and Japan in the East China Sea.

A third flashpoint for the major Asian nations might be power projection by two or more countries supporting opposing sides in a struggle for power or civil war in a third country. This form of conflict ravaged Asia during the second half of the last century—the Korean War and the post-colonial wars of Southeast Asia were all of this type. In part because the searing memories of these wars are alive in the Asian consciousness, such conflicts are less likely in the future. Though the "Asian way" is less of a prominent theme than in years past, the region's aversion to interference in the internal affairs of other countries remains strong.

It is theoretically possible to imagine a struggle for power in a smaller Asian country in which the United States supports the government and China supports the insurgents, or in which India and China support opposite sides. It is difficult, however, to think of a specific country in which such a situation might occur. For many years Pakistan might have been the focal point for that type of rivalry, and the United States unsuccessfully attempted gunboat diplomacy in support of Pakistan in the 1971 Indo-Pakistani conflict. Yet, in the most recent India-Pakistan confrontation—the conflict in Kargil in 1999—neither the United States nor China supported Pakistan. Now that both India and Pakistan have nuclear weapons, the basic policies of other countries will be to restrain conflict between the two. Burma and Bangladesh are the only countries that might produce unstable and violent internal conditions that could invite conflicting outside power involvement, but in both cases this seems unlikely. Internal conditions would have to grow unexpectedly worse and more violent, and the rivalry among the United States, China, and India would have to grow much sharper before proxy confrontations or wars there are imaginable. In fact, in the most recent case of violence in Burma, rather than searching for unilateral advantage, the United States, China, and India all shared common objectives in urging restraint and a peaceful transition of power within Burma.

---

[26] For examples of the use of oil platforms in the Persian Gulf during the Iran-Iraq War, see Crist, "Joint Special Operations," 15–22.

Conclusion

As Asia moves into the early decades of the 21st century, the region does not appear on the verge of a scramble for power and influence in which power projection forces are used to press for national influence abroad. Although the rise of China is often compared to the rise of Germany in the late nineteenth century, the differences are more compelling than the similarities. China is far more concerned than was Germany with internal economic and social development. Kaiser Wilhelm II was obsessed with carving out his country's place in the sun and sent forces to Africa and Asia. In contrast, Chinese leaders are focused on raising the income of their still mostly poor citizens through economic development and sending troops to assist in disaster relief at home. In the late nineteenth century, European wars provided advantages to the countries that started and won them, and military force seemed to be a controllable and predictable tool of national advantage. In the late twentieth century, however, wars seldom produced lasting advantages for the countries that started them, and even victors did not always gain clear returns from their efforts. In the 21st century economic development is considered to bestow the greatest national advantage, and the greatest economic development has been achieved by countries that take advantage of the international economy: military tension and wars are bad for international business. For all these reasons and more, China, India, and Japan are unlikely to use their power projection capabilities in an assertive, unilateral manner to gain political advantage.

A more likely scenario is competition among the major powers of Asia for influence—primarily economic and commercial advantage—and political deference to their most important national interests. To achieve most of their national purposes and ambitions Asia's major states need only enough military influence to avoid a power vacuum; to pursue an aggressive policy of asserting military influence with power projection forces is more likely to arouse opposition and undermine—rather than enhance—political and economic influence.

The smaller countries of Asia, the fields on which these great power games would be played, do not wish to be dominated and have thus become adept at playing larger countries off against one another while maintaining their own autonomy. These smaller states are skilled at accepting economic largesse and military assistance while giving away little control and keeping offsetting ties to other major countries intact. When tensions rise or crises occur, Asia's smaller countries invariably call for restraint and peaceful resolution of major power differences.

There are developments that could alter this optimistic outlook, the most dramatic of which are internal changes of sentiment within the great powers. Should the United States—wearied by past overseas involvement and deciding to set military defenses at the nation's own borders—withdraw from the region, an intense scramble for power and influence in Asia would ensue, and China, Japan, and India would use their power projection forces in ways that are now inconceivable. The voices in the United States that do call for such policies are scattered well outside the mainstream. Should intense nationalist sentiment come to dominate the security policies of China, Japan, or India, nationalism could fuel a drive for regional dominance and the aggressive use of power projection military force that would throw off sparks of competition and conflict with the other major powers. All three of these countries have political parties or factions that favor such policies, but they are currently small—if often vocal—minorities that demonstrate little likelihood of coming to power. The official policies of all three governments emphasize defensive military policies, restraint in the use of military force, and respect for the integrity of other countries.

On balance, the prospects in Asia are that major power competition in the region will be primarily economic and diplomatic. The military power projection capabilities of major nations will grow but their use will be generally restrained—primarily symbolic, occasionally coercive or punitive, and often cooperative.

EXECUTIVE SUMMARY

This chapter summarizes how major Asian powers see the Iranian nuclear crisis and outlines options for the U.S. to reverse or contain the Iranian nuclear threat.

MAIN ARGUMENT:
The U.S. alone cannot stop Tehran from continuing to expand Iran's capacity to enrich uranium and, ultimately perhaps, to produce nuclear weapons. The cooperation of the major Asian powers is necessary to cause Iranian leaders to reconsider the costs and benefits of continuing not to comply with IAEA and UN Security Council demands.

POLICY IMPLICATIONS:
All major Asian states would oppose U.S. policies of coercive regime change or military strikes against Iran. This leaves three basic alternative policies:

- Accepting uranium enrichment in Iran, under negotiated limits, conditioned on Iranian steps to reassure Israel and other regional states. This option may appeal most to Asian states, given that it would reduce prospects of further sanctions.

- Acknowledging Iran's refusal to comply with UN Security Council demands, withdrawing the positive inducements that have been offered for Iran to cease enrichment, building support among partners for long-term sanctions, and "fortifying" a red line that holds Iran to its commitment not to build nuclear weapons.

- Inviting Iran to engage the U.S. on non-nuclear issues in hopes of building the political will later to comply with a temporary nuclear suspension.

- To shape the environment for any of these policies, the U.S. could work with Asian powers and Iran's neighbors either to create a forum for regional cooperation if Iran moves to comply with IAEA and UN resolutions or to coordinate containment if Iran is belligerent.

The Iran Nuclear Challenge: Asian Interests and U.S. Policy Options

George Perkovich

The November 2007 U.S. National Intelligence Estimate (NIE) on Iran's nuclear activities famously concluded that Iran had "halted its nuclear weapons program" in 2003.[1] Less famously, the NIE noted that Iran had continued to expand its capacity to enrich uranium, the most difficult step in producing nuclear weapons. This expansion raises warning signs. In violation of nonproliferation obligations, Iran has in the past conducted clandestine nuclear work that Tehran has not fully explained, despite legally binding UN Security Council (UNSC) demands for full transparency and cooperation. Iran will pose a security challenge as long as it continues seeking to produce nuclear materials while both refusing to accede to UNSC demands and threatening other states.

It is not the United States primarily, or even alone, that is threatened by Iran's quest to acquire the technical capacity to make nuclear weapons. Iran's Arab neighbors and Israel are most adversely affected by the perception that Iran could wield nuclear weapons. Like its Persian antecedents in previous centuries, Iran possesses the size, resources, ambition, and talent to exert major influence in Southwest Asia—from Pakistan to the periphery of Central Asia, Turkey, and the Levant (including Israel and Palestine). Iran could be either a force for instability and insecurity within and among these states or an engine of regional dynamism and wary cooperation.

George Perkovich is Vice President for Studies–Global Security and Economic Development and Director of the Nonproliferation Program at the Carnegie Endowment for International Peace. He can be reached at <gperkovich@carnegieendowment.org>.

[1] "Iran: Nuclear Intentions and Capabilities," National Intelligence Council, November 2007, 1, http://www.dni.gov/press_releases/20071203_release.pdf.

The main challenge facing the United States arises from the effects Iran's nuclear activities and general behavior might have on the U.S. capacity to ensure the security, well-being, and cooperation of Iran's neighbors. If they feel threatened and believe Iran could deter the United States from intervening on their behalf, some of these neighboring countries will be inclined to hedge their positions by accommodating Tehran in ways that could diminish Washington's influence in the region. The United States also has led efforts to strengthen the global nuclear nonproliferation regime. If Iran were to get away with breaking nonproliferation rules and defying the efforts of the International Atomic Energy Agency (IAEA) and UNSC to enforce those rules, the risks of a more anarchic nuclear order would grow dramatically, threatening a top U.S. national security priority.

The United States alone cannot reduce this threat by inducing Tehran to alter Iran's nuclear activities. To change Iran's strategy and behavior, the United States will need the cooperation of the European Union (EU), Russia, China, Japan, India, and leading Arab states. Indeed, dating from the 1953 overthrow of Mossadegh, Iranians and many outside Iran have regarded U.S.-Iran relations as exhibiting an almost pathological character. Yet when the international community passes judgment on Iran for transgressing international standards, Iranians question their own government.[2] In addition, UN sanctions—which bind all states—become possible when China, Russia, and Japan join with the United States and Europe. Even though the United States has the power to destroy countless targets in Iran unilaterally, such an action would be self-defeating as long as the other major powers are opposed and will not cooperate in establishing the legal and diplomatic preconditions. Any real prospect of persuading Iran to alter its nuclear policies thus depends on international cooperation.

This chapter considers the technical and political evolution of the Iranian nuclear crisis and the feasible options among which the next U.S. administration could choose to contain or reverse the Iranian nuclear threat. The chapter then surveys how Russia, China, Japan, India, Indonesia, and Pakistan view their interests vis-à-vis Iran and the nuclear issue specifically as well as what types of U.S. policies these countries are likely to support or oppose.

---

[2] For example, penalties endorsed by major Asian powers such as China, India, Japan, and Indonesia can stimulate internal debate in Iran as few other external factors can.

The Story So Far: Iran's Nuclear Activities and the International Response

In August 2002 the IAEA discovered that Iran was building two undisclosed nuclear facilities: a uranium enrichment plant at Natanz and a heavy-water production plant at Arak. Iran's work on these facilities pointed to an interest in producing fissile materials for which there was no apparent peaceful need.

Through an intense investigation over the ensuing six years the IAEA established that in 1985, during the war with Iraq, Iran had started a secret program to procure the capability to enrich uranium.[3] The Iranian nuclear program violated disclosure requirements from 1985 to 2003. Several of the violations involved activities that made more sense as building blocks of a nuclear weapons option than as necessary elements of a civilian energy-production program.[4] In early 2008 the United States and other states provided intelligence to the IAEA regarding alleged studies as well as procurement and R&D activities by Iranian military-related institutes that could indicate efforts to develop nuclear weapons.[5]

Over this six-year period, Iran adopted various tactics for engaging with the IAEA, countering the United States, and diverting the UNSC. Iran was initially defensive. Iranian diplomats sought to dissuade the IAEA secretariat and Board of Governors from reporting Iran's noncompliance to the UNSC as the IAEA statute requires.[6] Among other things, Tehran feared that the United States would use a UNSC judgment against Iran as a basis for coercion or perhaps even attacks. Fearing the same outcome, IAEA Director General Mohammed ElBaradei and key European leaders welcomed an initiative by the leaders of France, Germany, and the United

---

[3] "Implementation of the NPT Safeguards Agreement in the Islamic Republic of Iran," International Atomic Energy Agency (IAEA), Report by the Director General, November 10, 2003, 19, http://www.iaea.org/Publications/Documents/Board/2003/gov2003-75.pdf. During the devastating Iran-Iraq War, Iraq had attacked Iran with chemical weapons. At the time the world did nothing to stop or even acknowledge Iraq's use of chemical weapons.

[4] These activities included: clandestine import and testing of centrifuges; undeclared importation of uranium metal; undeclared extraction of plutonium; experiments with polonium, an isotope typically used to trigger chain reactions in weapons; and possession of blueprints for manufacturing uranium metal spheres, whose only known use is for nuclear weapons.

[5] "Implementation of the NPT Safeguards Agreement and Relevant Provisions of Security Council Resolutions 1737 (2006), 1747 (2007) and 1803 (2008) in the Islamic Republic of Iran," IAEA, Report by the Director General, May 26, 2008, available at http://www.isis-online.org/publications/iran/IAEA_Iran_Report_26May2008.pdf.

[6] Article XII.C of the IAEA Statute states that "the inspectors shall report any non-compliance to the Director General who shall thereupon transmit the report to the Board of Governors" and that "the Board shall report the non-compliance to all members and to the Security Council and General Assembly of the United Nations." The text of the IAEA Statue is available at http://www.iaea.org/About/statute_text.html#A1.12.

426 • Strategic Asia 2008–09

Kingdom (the EU-3) to negotiate a way forward. In October 2003 Iran and the EU-3 agreed on reciprocal suspensions: states on the IAEA Board of Governors would suspend efforts to report Iran to the UNSC, and Iran would "voluntarily" suspend "all uranium enrichment and processing activities as defined by the IAEA."[7]

In 2004, however, Tehran refused to provide full transparency and to cooperate fully with the IAEA. Iran subsequently resumed manufacturing centrifuge components, assembling and testing centrifuges, and producing feed material for the enrichment of uranium.[8] The EU-3, the United States, and other countries responded by threatening to report Iran to the UNSC, and on November 15 Iran and the EU-3 reached the Paris Agreement. Under this agreement Iran voluntarily and temporarily "decided…to continue and extend its suspension to include all enrichment related and reprocessing activities," which were then duly specified.[9]

Iran's confidence grew in early 2005, as the United States appeared to be weakened by exertions and losses in Iraq. As the Iranian presidential campaign was intensifying in late April, lame-duck president Mohammad Khatami reiterated that—contrary to the consistent and shared demand of the EU-3, the United States, and others—Iran would not negotiate a complete or indefinite halt to uranium enrichment. Instead, headed by Supreme Guide Ayatollah Khamenei, the collective leadership had adopted the position that Iran would not forswear uranium enrichment formally or for any duration that seriously impeded technical development of this capability.

With the presidential contest nearing the first round of balloting in May 2005, officials announced plans to resume uranium conversion operations (though not enrichment) at the Isfahan plant. On May 24 EU negotiators warned that Iran would be reported to the UNSC if it resumed conversion operations. Although Iran initially agreed to postpone these plans until Tehran received new negotiating proposals (including incentives) from Europe at the end of July, departing president Khatami announced on July 26 that Iran would resume operations at Isfahan regardless of the European offer. On August 8, six days after Mahmoud Ahmadinejad was elected president, Iran resumed uranium conversion at Isfahan, a decision that was collective and not driven by the new president.

---

[7] "Statement by the Iranian Government and Visiting EU Foreign Ministers," October 21, 2003, http://www.iaea.org/NewsCenter/Focus/IaeaIran/statement_iran21102003.shtml.

[8] "Implementation of the NPT Safeguards Agreement in the Islamic Republic of Iran," IAEA, Board of Governors Resolution, September 18, 2004, http://www.iaea.org/Publications/Documents/Board/2004/gov2004-79.pdf.

[9] The full text of the "Paris Agreement" is available at http://www.armscontrol.org/country/iran/ParisAgreement.asp.

This preemptive rejection of the EU offer in the summer of 2005 ended even the appearance that Iran was willing to negotiate an end to its nuclear activities. Tehran rejected the very premise of these negotiations: that owing to Iran's long and extensive pattern of noncompliance and the suspect nature of some of the country's activities, a suspension of further fuel-cycle activities was required to build international confidence that Iran's nuclear aspirations are purely peaceful. Whereas the EU-3 sought to find terms under which Iran would durably suspend fuel-cycle-related activities, Iran refused to cease such activities under any conditions.[10]

Faced with Iran's defiance, the UNSC in July 2006 passed a resolution demanding that Iran halt all uranium enrichment and plutonium production and processing. Iran refused to comply with the resolution—perhaps emboldened by the relative success of Hezbollah forces in the summer 2006 war with Israel. The UNSC imposed its first sanctions resolution (1737) in December 2006, followed by a second resolution (1747) on March 27, 2007.

On December 3, 2007, the United States released a summary of a National Intelligence Estimate produced by the sixteen agencies that compose the U.S. intelligence community. The first sentence shocked Washington and the rest of the world: "We judge with high confidence that in fall 2003, Tehran halted its nuclear weapons program; we also assess with moderate-to-high confidence that Tehran at a minimum is keeping open the option to develop nuclear weapons."[11]

Properly understood, the NIE did not say that the most serious material threat posed by the Iranian nuclear program had dissipated; to the contrary, Iran continued to enrich uranium. Tehran was now enriching uranium openly, however, instead of through clandestine activities (which would have fit part of the NIE definition of a weapons program). Similarly, Iran continued to develop ballistic missiles suitable to deliver nuclear weapons. According to the NIE, the only activity that Tehran had suspended was work on the design and non-nuclear elements of a nuclear weapon. In other words, the NIE held that Iran was no longer engaged in a narrow, legalistically defined nuclear weapons program.

The NIE had the effect of defanging the threat of U.S. military attacks on Iran for engaging in nuclear activities. This threat could have been leveraged to increase non-military pressure on Iran to comply with the UNSC resolutions. Fearing that stronger coercive diplomacy could be a

---

[10] Iran's approach was revealed in a long, remarkable interview that its principal negotiator, Hasan Rowhani, gave to *Keyhan*, a leading conservative newspaper, days before the presidential run-off election between Hashemi Rafsanjani and Mahmoud Ahmadinejad. Mehdi Mohammadi, interview with Dr. Hasan Rowhani, *Keyhan*, July 23, 2005.

[11] "Iran: Nuclear Intentions and Capabilities."

prelude to war, the IAEA director general, Mohammed ElBaradei, and states such as Russia and China had been chary of such an approach. The NIE could have relaxed that fear and removed an argument against tougher sanctions. This outcome was not the near-term effect, however, even though the UNSC did surprise some observers by proceeding in March 2008 to adopt a third sanctions resolution (1803). As of this writing, it remains to be seen how the UNSC will respond to Iran's refusal to fully answer IAEA requests for clarification on evidence (presented in the director general's May 2008 report) of military-related projects and procurement and R&D activities.

The Range of U.S. Policy Objectives on Iran

Before exploring how key Asian states view the Iranian nuclear challenge and how those states could aid or impair the achievement of U.S. policy aims, it is first necessary to suggest what the United States might want to accomplish. As politics and policy are the art of the possible, this section of the paper seeks to identify a feasible menu of strategic approaches.

Clearly, what is most desirable is for Iran to eschew uranium enrichment and plutonium separation forever (or at least for the long term). This essentially has been the demand of the United States, the EU-3, and the UNSC, although UNSC Resolution 1747 does envision Iran's resumption of enrichment at some point. Israel insists that the international community should not accept an Iranian enrichment program. For substantive and political reasons the new U.S. administration will be reluctant to move indefinite suspension into the diplomatic background and to instead negotiate over how Iran would continue fuel-cycle activities. Washington and close U.S. partners in international security regard the capacity of a belligerent Iran to enrich uranium (or separate plutonium) as too close to development of nuclear weapons to accept.

Yet as of this writing there appears to be little likelihood that Iran will be politically and economically coerced into forgoing enrichment of uranium. Neither the costs of continuing enrichment activities nor the benefits offered for ceasing are high enough to dissuade Iranian leaders. As the former chief nuclear negotiator Ali Larijani put it, Iran was offered "bonbons" for a "pearl."[12]

To manage the Iranian nuclear challenge, the next U.S. administration would need to develop diplomatic approaches on at least two levels. One

---

[12] "Dr. Strangelove in Iran," Radio Free Europe/Radio Liberty, RFE/RL Reports 7, no. 41, November 23, 2004, http://www.rferl.org/reports/iran-report/2004/11/41-231104.asp.

might be called "text" and the other might be called "context." That is, strategy and accompanying policies must be selected to deal specifically with Iran (text) as well as with the broader region that shapes and is shaped by what Iran says and does (context).

The incoming U.S. administration will likely consider five alternative strategies for dealing directly with Iran. Each strategy could initially seek to impose stronger UNSC-authorized sanctions on Iran as well as offer Iran greater and clearer benefits for compliance. These sanctions could include further inhibitions on financial transactions with Iranian entities, reductions of or bans on import and export guarantees for entities trading with Iran, and reductions of or bans on investment in the Iranian energy sector. If Iranian actions became more threatening, the U.S. could seek UNSC sanctions on arms exports.[13] Although the EU and the UNSC already have offered a great deal in the way of benefits and Iran has not negotiated for improvements of such offers, the most important benefit to Iran that the United States could add would be a security guarantee—a commitment to respect Iran's territorial integrity and to deal peacefully with whatever government is empowered by the Iranian constitution. Such a guarantee would in effect take military strikes and regime change off the table.

Five Alternative Strategies toward Iran

Foster regime change. Every U.S. administration (and the governments of many other states) would like to see Iran's government become more democratic and less militant. The strategic issue is whether the United States should emphasize and foster regime change through direct action—such as subversion, support of ethnic minorities, and covert or overt assistance to dissident groups—or instead take a hands-off approach to Iran's political evolution. The unpredictability (even to Iranian elites) of Iranian politics raises difficult questions as to how a distant, largely uninformed U.S. government could affect the direction of Iranian politics.[14]

Asian states, whose cooperation the United States seeks to gain, would regard a regime-change strategy as only marginally less objectionable than military attacks. Chinese and Russian resistance to U.S. foreign policy, for example, is partly based in concerns that Washington seeks regime change in China and Russia. These countries thus want to discourage, not encourage, U.S. proclivities to interfere in the internal affairs of other countries. Likewise, India, though not defending the Iranian theocratic

---

[13] Domestic political-economic realities will prevent states from embargoing Iranian energy exports.

[14] Few outsiders and Iranians predicted Khatami's election as president in 1997 or Ahmadinejad's in 2005.

regime, categorically opposes U.S. interventionism. Overall the prospects of Asian cooperation with an active regime-change strategy are so low that the country analyses in the next section do not consider this option.

Take military action. The United States (or Israel) could still pursue the zero-enrichment objective through military means. Most analyses of the nature, anticipated effectiveness, and consequences of military action conclude that such action would not cause a long-term or permanent suspension of Iranian enrichment and plutonium separation activities. Military action, short of land invasion, also would not likely achieve regime change.[15] This strategy, therefore, would not solve the problem. Although military action could delay the most acute nuclear dangers, many analysts conclude that the value of this outcome would not outweigh the costs of unilateral military strikes.

None of the major Asian states would support U.S. military strikes on Iran. Although not able to stop the United States from taking this action, these states can refuse to lend the international legitimacy and cooperation in isolating Iran that would be needed both before and after U.S. (or Israeli) military strikes. The sharp opposition of Asian states to military strikes could change if the IAEA were to discover clear evidence that Iran is seeking to acquire nuclear weapons. Such a scenario, however, cannot be foreseen at this point.

Accept limited enrichment. The United States could go along if other UNSC members urged accepting some ongoing enrichment activity in Iran. International diplomacy would then concentrate on negotiating terms for limiting and monitoring this activity with inducements such as nuclear cooperation, trade normalization, and security guarantees. The focus would be on the issue of nuclear weapons development and Iran's threat to the security of Iraq and Israel. This option (in effect if not formally) drops the UNSC's legally binding requirement that fuel-cycle activities be suspended during negotiations held to establish how Iran can build international confidence that these nuclear activities are exclusively for peaceful purposes. Tactically, this strategy would increase the positive incentives offered to Iran while rallying UNSC members to increase sanctions and political pressure if Iran continues to refuse to negotiate.

Pull back incentives, maintain sanctions, make weaponization the red line. The United States could encourage UNSC members both to acknowledge that Iran is not willing to negotiate on suspension of fuel-

---

[15] See, for example, Anthony Cordesman, "Covering US Military Options for Dealing with Iran," CSIS Report, April 30, 2008; James Fallows, "Will Iran Be Next?" *Atlantic Monthly*, December 2004, http://www.theatlantic.com/doc/200412/fallows; and Reuel Marc Gerecht, "To Bomb, or Not to Bomb: That is the Iran Question," *Weekly Standard*, April 24, 2006, http://www.weeklystandard.com/Content/Public/Articles/000/000/012/100mmysk.asp?pg=1.

cycle-related activities for a meaningful period and to cease negotiating among themselves and chasing after Iran with more incentives. The focus of UNSC diplomacy would be on reaching a long-term agreement for a sanctions regime. This would include agreeing on further measures if Iran were to reduce cooperation with the IAEA, continue to violate safeguards requirements, or attempt to withdraw from the Treaty on the Non-proliferation of Nuclear Weapons (NPT). This approach would send a message to Iran to in effect "call us if you ever change your mind and want to negotiate."

Without retracting its demands, under this option the UNSC would acknowledge that Iran has not engaged in genuine negotiations since 2005—let alone complied with UN resolutions. This option takes into account that even if Tehran were to break repeated commitments not to build nuclear weapons, it would take two or more years for Iran to succeed, given past difficulties in mastering enrichment technology. Rather than believe that Iran would uphold any agreement on limited-scale enrichment, the P5+1 would state that, though it is Iran's choice to defy UNSC demands, the rest of the world will cease offering bribes designed to induce Iranian compliance.[16] Considering that Iran already has acquired the capability the original inducements were meant to forestall, the P5+1 would instead concentrate on establishing the durability of sanctions. If Iran were to newly violate its nonproliferation requirements and norms and seek to weaponize its nuclear capabilities, contrary to Tehran's unambiguous commitments not to do so, crossing this red line would trigger tougher sanctions, including, for example, an arms embargo. Under this strategy, the UNSC would hold Iran to the commitment not to build nuclear weapons while seeking international cooperation to bolster preparations for deterrence and containment if Iran were to acquire those weapons.[17]

Engage Iran directly on other issues. The United States could invite Iran to engage directly on issues independent of the demands for nuclear suspension—including mutual security guarantees, Iraq, Afghanistan, terrorism, the Israeli-Palestinian-Arab diplomatic process, and models of international and domestic justice. Either party could express how progress on the nuclear issue (however defined) would help build confidence, but in this forum the United States would not negotiate on the nuclear issue. This strategy would not foster unrealistic expectations of a "grand bargain" but instead would aim simply to open all possible channels for constructive dialogue. The premise would be that progress on the nuclear issue is more

---

[16] The P5+1 is composed of the five permanent members of the UN Security Council (China, France, Russia, the United Kingdom, and the United States) plus Germany.

[17] On this point please see the two options below.

likely to come after, rather than before, the United States and Iran build confidence in their basic intentions toward each other.

Two Alternative Strategies toward the Region

Whatever strategy toward Iran the U.S. government chooses should be complemented by a broader strategy to enhance the security of Iran's neighbors and therefore of the United States and the larger international community. Two alternative approaches will be considered.

Classic containment. The U.S. administration would seek to deter Iran from building nuclear weapons and to contain Iran's power projection—both military and political—through aggressive mobilization of the combined resources of the United States and neighboring countries.

This approach might be called a "hard" containment strategy. Such a strategy would aim to prevent Iran from bullying its neighbors in disputes over the United Arab Emirates (UAE) islands, oil transit through the Strait of Hormuz, relations with Shiite populations, or defense ties with the United States. The United States could mobilize Arab and perhaps Turkish fears of Iranian power, including its Shiite character, in a sectarian balance-of-power campaign. Alternatively, and more wisely, Washington could downplay sectarian sensibilities while still emphasizing traditional interstate competition between Iran and its neighbors. In either case, defense and intelligence cooperation between the United States and Iran's neighbors would figure prominently into a hard containment strategy.

Cooperative security. A cooperative security strategy would seek to develop a regional security framework in which states could negotiate a "treaty pledging the inviolability of the region's borders, arms control pacts proscribing certain categories of weapons, a common market with free-trade zones, and a mechanism for adjudicating disputes."[18] Under this approach, the United States would aim to ameliorate Sunni-Shia and Arab-Persian tensions by fostering regional cooperation and confidence-building.

This strategy is more idealistic than realistic in today's environment. Key states do not even agree on the composition of the region: Should the region be limited to the Gulf? Would the Gulf include Yemen? Given Iran's involvement with Lebanon, Syria, and Palestinian rejectionist groups, should a cooperative security strategy aim to develop a wider regional framework? If key states refused to participate in dialogue with Israel, should Israel be included in a security framework and those states excluded? Would outside powers be invited to participate and by what criteria? To provide a materially

[18] Vali Nasr and Ray Takeyh, "The Costs of Containing Iran," *Foreign Affairs* 87, no. 1 (January/February 2008): 93.

meaningful contribution to security, a cooperative security strategy should aim to help resolve outstanding disputes over territory and sovereignty, thereby reducing potential causes of conflict. Is there any basis for thinking that Iran and the UAE could reach a mutually acceptable and stable resolution to their dispute over the Greater and Lesser Tunb and Abu Musa islands? Would a regional dialogue address Kurdish issues in Iraq and Iran? The logic of cooperative security could be pursued in a more modest way by encouraging reassurance among Iran and its neighbors not to interfere in each other's domestic affairs. This reassurance could come through bilateral negotiations or Gulf Cooperation Council (GCC) discussions, perhaps initiated by Qatar. The objective and tone of such a strategy would diverge sharply from an aggressive containment approach. Instead of firmly pushing in attempt to shape Iran's behavior—such as by rallying Iran's neighbors to build and flex their muscles and to refuse Iranian entreaties—a cooperative security strategy would try to guide behavior by embracing Iran.

Most of the foregoing options—textual and contextual—are not mutually exclusive or unrelated. Both variants of a regional strategy would seek to channel Iranian policy and power in more accommodating directions and are consistent with a strategy to open diplomacy with Iran on all issues.

Asia's Interests and Roles in Affecting International Outcomes

Iran's relations with key Asian states will significantly affect the prospects of success or failure for any U.S. strategy. Major Asian powers have eventually joined the United States in supporting the three rounds of UNSC sanctions against Tehran. These sanctions, however, have been relatively mild and limited in scope. More robust sanctions—the type that would be necessary to give Iranian leaders greater pause on their nuclear course—would likely prove a greater test of U.S. relations with major Asian powers. Asian states will prefer "softer" approaches as long as Iran continues to mix cooperation with the IAEA with relatively tempered defiance of UNSC demands. If Iran becomes less cooperative, commits new breaches of safeguard obligations, threatens to withdraw from the NPT, or becomes more bellicose, Asian states could grow more amenable to tougher U.S. approaches.

Russia

Russia and Iran do not share civilizational attraction or warm historical memories. They do, however, enjoy a tradition of tolerable relations. In the nineteenth century imperial Russia wrested the Caucasus from Persia. Soviet troops later occupied northern Iran as part of the Allied takeover during World War II. Stalin, however, agreed to a withdrawal, and Russia and Iran have since lived in peace. Distant neighbors rather than friends, the two states do not trust or expect any favors from one another; yet neither does either state see the other as a mortal threat.

To be sure, the Iranian Revolution was harshly anti-Communist, surpassing the Shah's general dislike of the Soviet system. Iranians also will not forget Russia's closeness to Saddam Hussein's Iraq during the Iran-Iraq War. Tehran has been willing to forgive Russia, however, in order to gain badly needed cooperation. In 1989 Iran's speaker of the Majlis and soon-to-be-president, Hashemi Rafsanjani, traveled to Moscow to initiate arms sales and nuclear cooperation with then Soviet Russia. Russia's interest in building businesslike ties with Iran grew following the 1991 UN-authorized invasion of Iraq. The Persian Gulf War in effect displaced Russia from the region and left Moscow in search of a way to re-establish its place. Iran shared with Russia an interest in balancing the growing U.S. power projection in the region and did not let pride or bitterness stand in the way of this goal. Moreover, Russia was willing to sell Iran military and nuclear technology that other states would not.

Russia has evinced numerous interests vis-à-vis Iran in recent years. For example, Russia has successfully induced Iran not to abet the Chechen struggle and to help contain conflict in Tajikistan. Russia also has appreciated Iran's de facto siding with pro-Moscow Armenia in the latter's conflict with Shiite-majority Azerbaijan.[19] In Afghanistan, Russia and Iran jointly supported the Northern Alliance against the Taliban. The two states also have pursued patient, low-key diplomacy to manage competing interests in the Caspian Sea and Caspian basin. Although differing on the principle by which resources beneath the Caspian Sea should be allocated to littoral states, Iran and Russia agree that this issue should be resolved through negotiation, not threats. Each state would like to gain a greater share of pipeline distribution of energy resources from Central Asia and the Caspian basin. These competitive interests, however, are dwarfed by a shared interest in blocking U.S. efforts to exclude both Russia and Iran.

---

[19] Iranian Azeris comprise 25% of Iran's population, and Tehran seeks to prevent the Azeri irredentism that could be abetted by Azerbaijan.

Russia and Iran thus play for time on this issue and do not pursue zero-sum outcomes in the near term.

Russia has a historic interest in obtaining a significant role in the Persian Gulf and broader Middle East. Russia's role declined radically during the latter days of the Soviet Union, to the advantage of the United States. Moscow now sees Iran as an invaluable re-entry point to the region. If Moscow can establish a durable, beneficial relationship with Iran, this relationship would give Russia a better position than the one the Soviet Union had enjoyed in Iraq until the 1990s. Russia sees potential gains in the gas and oil sector, in defense contracting, and in nuclear cooperation with Iran. Even though the latter two sectors would not assume great absolute importance in Russia's overall economy, Iran could be an important customer.[20] Gazprom, whose interests are exceptionally close to those of top Russian leaders, has significant investment stakes in developing Iran's South Pars and North Kish offshore gas fields and in building oil and natural gas pipelines in the Caspian area. These business ties were reaffirmed just days after the then president Vladimir Putin visited Iran in late 2007.[21]

For its part, Iran has perceived Russia as a valuable partner in limited spheres, if not as an abiding friend. Russia cooperated with the Iranian nuclear program when no one else was willing to do so licitly (Pakistan's A.Q. Khan helped Iran illicitly). After the breakup of the Soviet Union, Russia and Iran expanded their 1989 nuclear cooperation agreement. In 1992–93 Russia and Iran contracted to complete the Bushehr nuclear power plant, whose construction by German firms had been aborted after the Iranian Revolution. The Russian-Iranian contract contained a secret protocol—discovered in 1995—that included Russian promises to supply Iran with 2,000 tons of natural uranium and a gas centrifuge uranium enrichment facility, to provide assistance in construction of a uranium mine in Iran, and to train Iranian scientific personnel. Acceding to U.S. pressure, Russia ultimately cancelled these elements of the agreement.[22] Throughout the 1990s and into the early 2000s, however, Russia maintained a commitment to complete and fuel the Bushehr power plant. Iran has been frustrated by Russian delays and efforts to leverage this nuclear cooperation to pressure Iran into compliance with IAEA and UNSC demands. Russia

---

[20] Russia could be willing to "trade" business in Iran for more lucrative deals in the Gulf Arab states, as discussed below.

[21] "Moscow Deepens Ties to Iran's Energy Sector," *International Herald Tribune*, February 21, 2008.

[22] Russian-Iranian Nuclear Cooperation Accord, trans. Natural Resources Defense Council, January 8, 1995, reprinted in Brenda Shaffer, *Partners in Need: The Strategic Relationship of Russia and Iran*, (Washington, D.C.: Washington Institute for Near East Policy, 2001), 72.

has nonetheless moved to complete the project and began shipping fuel to Iran in late 2007 and early 2008.

Russia also has been Iran's leading supplier of conventional armaments, including potentially advanced anti-aircraft systems. From 1995 to 2005 Russia supplied 70% of Iran's arms imports.[23] In 2006 Russia sold Iran 29 Tor-MI (SA-15) air-defense systems. Reports emerged in 2007 that Russia had agreed to sell Iran more sophisticated, long-range anti-aircraft/anti-missile systems (S-300PMU-1s).

In recent years Russia's greatest value to Iran has been as an inhibitor of the U.S.-led drive to isolate and coerce Iran through the UNSC. Moscow slowed Washington's effort to shift the Iranian nuclear case from the IAEA to the UNSC. Once the matter was sent to the UNSC, Russia slowed and eased moves to ratchet up sanctions. Moscow has made clear that Russia will not support military action against Iran. At the same time, Russia has insisted that Iran suspend fuel-cycle activities and discontinue the national enrichment program on Iranian territory, proposing instead that Iran join in a collaborative enrichment enterprise in Russia. Yet Moscow has neither indicated what international measures Russia would support to pressure Iran to accept this proposal nor imposed a deadline on Iran, leaving the impression that Tehran can put off a decision indefinitely while continuing illegal fuel-cycle activities.

Russia's core perceptions and intentions have been difficult to discern. On the one hand, Russia clearly does not want Iran to acquire nuclear weapons. A nuclear Iran would devalue the currency of Russia's own nuclear status and would badly complicate Russia's long-term security. For example, emboldened by nuclear weapons Iran could support subversive groups in Russia or on Russia's periphery either for ideological or tactical reasons or to extort Russian concessions on Caspian basin issues. Additionally, a nuclear Iran could become a target of U.S. or Israeli military attacks, which could heighten Muslim extremism and increase instability on the Russian periphery. A nuclear Iran would also augment international receptivity to U.S. missile-defense deployments, including deployments in Europe—a situation that Russia would prefer to avoid or at least make politically costly to the United States.

On the other hand, Russian leaders might judge the costs of preventing Iran from acquiring nuclear weapon capability to be greater than the dangers of an Iranian bomb. A U.S.-led war against Iran could yield some benefits for Russia: higher oil prices, heightened regional and global animosity toward

---

[23] Stockholm International Peace Research Institute, *SIPRI Yearbook 2007: Armaments, Disarmament and International Security* (Oxford University Press, 2007), 396–99. Much of these arms imports consisted of armored vehicles such as T-72 tanks and BMP-2 infantry fighting vehicles.

the United States, and a greater Russian stake in Iran (following a war). Nonetheless, Russian analysts seem genuinely alarmed by the prospect of further regional disorder and extremism. A U.S.-led war would deepen U.S. long-term involvement in the region. Additionally, if war or some other form of disorder led to regime change in Iran, the United States could gain ground in the region at Russia's expense. For these reasons, Russian analyst and former defense official Alexei Arbatov concludes that the majority of the Russian elite "would prefer a nuclear Iran to war."[24] Russia also would not welcome the strengthening of UN sanctions to the point that Iran might be compelled to capitulate to U.S.-European–sponsored sanctions that would exclude either Russian arms sales to Iran or Russian investments in the Iranian energy sector. Russia would not welcome this apparent victory of U.S. (and European) power, which would encourage coercive use of sanctions according to U.S.-shaped norms in the future.

The broader strategic consideration is that Russia and Iran have shared a basic interest in resisting U.S. hegemony and the combined power of the United States and the EU. Moscow and Tehran both seek greater multipolarity in the international system to balance U.S. power. Russia also would prefer an Iranian regime that is estranged from rather than reconciled with Washington. An Iranian-U.S. rapprochement could undermine Russian economic and geostrategic interests in Iran.

The foregoing analysis indicates that Russia is not disposed to pressure Iran with the greatest leverage available—by voting for strong UNSC sanctions (or military action) or by withholding arms sales. Although there may be nothing the United States can do to change Russian calculations, the next U.S. administration could explore these issues with Russia early on.

To engage Moscow on these issues, the incoming administration could pose several questions: Under what conditions would Russia commit to more extensive cooperation with the United States and the EU on Iran? Would Russia cooperate more fully if Washington were to agree not to support military action against Iranian nuclear installations as long as Iran did not take new actions to develop nuclear weapons? Would Russia increase its level of cooperation if Washington were to assure Iran that the United States will not take actions to overthrow the government in Tehran?

---

[24] Alexei Arbatov, "Russia and the Iranian Nuclear Crisis," Carnegie Endowment for International Peace, Proliferation Analysis, May 23, 2006, http://www.carnegieendowment.org/publications/index.cfm?fa=view&id=18363&prog=zgp&proj=znpp.

What other U.S. policies that now preclude Russia's full cooperation on Iran would, if changed, elicit corresponding adjustments in Moscow?[25]

Russia's larger interests in the Gulf raise questions for U.S. analysts to consider. In late 2007 Putin became the first Russian (or Soviet) head of state to visit Saudi Arabia and the UAE. Putin welcomed arms sales and defense cooperation with the wealthy Arab states, indicating Russia's interest in helping the GCC develop nuclear energy. U.S. officials and exporters naturally would not welcome Russian competition in a sphere in which the United States has become the dominant external player. Russian cooperation with the southern Gulf states, however, could have important benefits in shaping Iran's behavior and Russian policies toward Iran. The Arab Gulf states offer potentially more lucrative markets for Russian exporters than Iran does, and these states are easier to deal with than Tehran is. A Russia with greater stakes in the smaller Gulf states could be more inclined to press Iran to comply with UNSC demands regarding nuclear activities that genuinely concern Russian officials. By exerting pressure on Iran, Russia could also further endear itself to the smaller Gulf states, which in turn would make displeasing Tehran more affordable for Moscow. Ultimately, both Russia and Iran would prefer to avoid a zero-sum competition. The potential of such competition, however, could not only motivate Iran to be more accommodating both to UNSC and to Russian demands but also motivate Russia to be more cooperative with the United States.

In sum, Russia will not cooperate with U.S. policies that Moscow thinks will lead to military conflict or coercive regime change in Iran. Therefore, Moscow's willingness both to exert pressure on Iran through strengthened UNSC sanctions and to increase positive incentives for Iranian compliance will depend on Washington's willingness to accommodate Russia's broad interests.

China

China and Iran did not welcome each other's twentieth-century revolution. The Shah of Iran cut off diplomatic relations immediately after the emergence of the People's Republic of China (PRC) in 1949. It was not until Beijing broke with Moscow in the mid-1960s that the Shah warmed to China as the lesser of the Communist evils. Relations grew better still after President Richard Nixon, close ally of the Shah, opened ties with China in 1971. Following suit, Iran resumed diplomatic relations with China.

---

[25] These policies might include the timeline and operational plans for U.S. ballistic missile defenses in Europe, the future extension of North Atlantic Treaty Organization (NATO) membership to states bordering Russia, and a possible role for Russia in diplomacy and trade that could create a regional security order in the Persian Gulf.

Iran's revolution posed some ideological awkwardness, but the two states remained pragmatic. China welcomed Iran's departure from the U.S. orbit. Iran welcomed China's preference for Iran over Iraq, which Beijing saw as a Soviet client state. During the Iran-Iraq War, China supported Iran by providing arms and often backing Iran's position in the UNSC.

China and Iran share three enormously important interests. First, both countries resist U.S. hegemony and seek a world in which Chinese or Iranian influence grows while U.S. influence shrinks. Second, China and Iran both zealously guard the principle and practice of state sovereignty and strongly oppose international intervention in each other's internal affairs.[26] Third, China and Iran see each other as exceptionally valuable economic partners, primarily in the energy sector, which is vital to the future of both countries.

Although China and Iran also differ, the importance of their differences is much smaller than the value of their shared interests. China does not want Iran to acquire nuclear weapons or the international nonproliferation regime to fail. China has hoped that Iran could be diplomatically persuaded to comply first with IAEA demands for transparency and cooperation and later with UNSC resolutions. Since 2006 Beijing has slowed but not blocked the successive implementation of sanctions. In April 2008, however, reports emerged that Beijing had supplied the IAEA with intelligence on Iranian nuclear activities.[27] This action may reflect China's growing interest in buttressing the global nonproliferation regime.

Yet China, even more than Russia, sees great risks both in war and in strong sanctions on Iran. As of 2005, oil imports from Iran composed 11.1% of China's total crude oil imports, and this figure is rising. Anything that threatens to disrupt the supply of Iranian (or other regional) oil and gas and thus raise prices would increase pressure on a Chinese government already stressed with many enormous domestic and external challenges.

The Chinese government generally disapproves of international sanctions as an instrument of statecraft. The norms and rules on which sanctions tend to be based are often products of U.S. and Western interests, values, and power, and China—as a one-party, developing Asian state—does not share these norms. Beijing views sanctions as interference in internal affairs, an attitude that has not stopped China from voting for sanctions against Iran but does inform Beijing's preferences.

---

[26] Both China and Iran oppose democratic regime change and the use of international bodies to promote what are seen as duplicitous Western norms. Note that Russia also shares these interests.

[27] George Jahn, "Nuclear Watchdog Gets China's Iran Intel," Associated Press, http://ap.google.com/article/ALeqM5jHz-Bz3Pa0Ivga_oNIvTbrBoIN7QD8VPV9Q80.

China has no reason to support the international militancy of President Ahmadinejad or Iran's arming of Hezbollah. By undermining regional stability, such activities upset the Chinese preference for an environment calm enough to allow Chinese leaders to concentrate on internal development. China's deployment of troops in the UN peacekeeping mission in Lebanon may deepen Beijing's interest in avoiding UNSC or unilateral U.S. actions that might provoke Iran to further encourage the militancy of Hezbollah.

China feels little urgency to use its leverage with Iran and much anxiety over the consequences of doing so. The most obvious source of leverage is China's permanent vote in the UNSC. Additionally, China accounts for roughly 13% of all Iranian exports and more than 11% of Iranian imports, and the volume of trade is rapidly rising. One reason why Beijing will not vote to impose sanctions on Iranian energy exports is that oil comprises the bulk of such exports to China. Furthermore, a significant share of Chinese exports to Iran have replaced European goods held back due to political considerations; thus if Chinese goods were held back under UN sanctions, the effect on the Iranian economy would be significant. According to data collected by the American Enterprise Institute, 6% of Chinese business transactions in Iran since 2000 have been in banking, finance, and export credit, and most of these transactions were administered by the Chinese National Export Credit Agency.[28] Were Chinese institutions to join U.S. and European financial institutions in withholding such credit, the political and economic pressure on Iran would increase. Yet, for reasons adduced above, Beijing is clearly reluctant to exercise this leverage.

The net effect for U.S. policy is that China will oppose actions that might lead to the use of force against Iran—including the use of force to effect regime change. Beijing also will oppose economic sanctions against Iran's energy sector, at least absent significantly greater provocations by Iran than have occurred thus far. Instead, Beijing will insist that efforts to increase pressure on Iran be balanced both by offers of more positive incentives and by a willingness to compromise in allowing Iran some form of enrichment activity. Thus, China should not be expected to play a major role in diplomatic initiatives to deter and contain Iran's nuclear activities, either through hard pressure or soft cooperation. China would likely defer to the United States, the EU, and Russia, whose historic roles and geographic proximity give them greater stakes and capabilities in helping shape a regional order. China's response to Iran's bid to join the Shanghai

---

[28] "Global Business in Iran: Interactive," American Enterprise Institute, Iran Project, http://www.aei.org/IranInteractive.

Cooperation Organization (SCO) will be an indicator of how Beijing wishes to balance relations with Iran and the United States.

Japan

Japan began a durable economic relationship with Iran in the aftermath of World War I. In 1933 the Mitsubishi Trading Company established a trading company in Iran. Soon Japan became the second largest exporter of merchandise to Iran, trailing only Russia.[29] After World War II Japan moved quickly to re-establish diplomatic and trade ties with Iran. Following the Mossadegh government's nationalization of the Iranian economy and the ensuing British blockade of Iranian oil exports, Japan attempted to defy British pressure by purchasing oil from Iran. Though Japan ultimately relented, Iranian nationalists appreciated this demonstration of Japanese solidarity.[30] After the U.S.- and U.K.-backed coup against Mossadegh, Iran reopened oil exports and soon became a major source of energy to fuel Japan's rapid economic growth.

The 1973 oil embargo dramatically raised Japan's energy costs and elicited alarms over energy security. Japanese leaders responded by adopting a pro-Arab and pro-Iranian foreign policy, and the Shah of Iran reciprocated with assurances that Iran would not impose embargoes on oil exports to Japan. The two countries negotiated an investment and development agreement highly favorable to Iran. In December 1973 the Organization of Arab Petroleum Exporting Countries (OAPEC) rewarded Japan with an exemption from an ongoing oil ban imposed on the United States and the Netherlands.[31]

The Iranian Revolution and ensuing oil crisis caused major dislocations for the Japanese economy, yet the new Iranian government, mindful of Japan's friendship, offered to revive the Iran-Japan Petrochemical Company (IJPC) and exempted the company from the wave of nationalization undertaken by the revolutionary regime. Though the project proved to be an economic boondoggle and a source of much consternation in Japan, Tokyo continued to invest in the IJPC as a way to earn Iranian favor and secure uninterrupted oil supplies. Japan's determination to cement ties with Iran grew after the Soviet invasion of Afghanistan. Tokyo feared the possibility of Soviet sway over the energy supplies in the Persian Gulf. As Japan agreed to invest further in the IJPC—by then a favorite project of Ayatollah Khomeini—Iran responded by agreeing to increase oil shipments

---

[29] Bean, "A Historical Perspective," 6.

[30] Ibid., 11.

[31] Ibid., 18.

to Japan by 30%.[32] Japan dismayed the United States by taking a relatively equidistant approach to the hostage crisis then embroiling U.S. politics. Additionally, Tokyo rejected U.S. requests to halt funding of the IJPC and to boycott Iranian oil. Japan had become Iran's largest trading partner.

This history is recounted to show Japan's determination to preserve economic (and therefore political) relations with Iran. Japanese officials do not hide their interest in preserving access to Iranian energy supplies. Japan refused to join U.S. sanctions against Iran in 1995 and 1996, although Tokyo did end yen loan development assistance to Iran. Japan reduced oil imports from Iran in 2006 in order to buttress international pressure on Tehran, but Japan's imports from Iran grew 3.5% in 2007 and again in 2008.[33] Iran is Japan's third largest supplier of oil, providing about 10%.

Japan is a stalwart supporter of the global nuclear nonproliferation regime and categorically opposes the acquisition of nuclear weapons by any other state, including Iran. Japan supported all IAEA resolutions calling on Iran to suspend activities related to uranium enrichment and reprocessing and supported all UNSC sanctions resolutions against Iran. To support U.S. and European pressure on Iran, in October 2006 Japan's INPEX Holdings Inc. withdrew all but a 10% stake of what had been a 75% share of a $2 billion agreement to help develop the giant Azadegan oil field in southwestern Iran.[34] Japanese officials at the highest levels have remonstrated privately with Iranian counterparts to urge compliance with UN demands.

Yet Japanese officials have publicly and privately emphasized their determination to preserve friendly relations with Iran. Some officials have expressed doubt that an international policy centering on coercion will succeed.[35] On balance, Japan will follow but not lead international policy toward Iran. Japan will join in if consensus emerges among the permanent members of the UNSC. Japanese financial institutions will join other major economic powers by disinvesting from projects with Iranian counterparts as needed to protect larger Japanese interests in U.S. and European markets but will not take the lead in this direction. Given the facts of Iran's noncompliance with the IAEA and with legally binding UNSC resolutions, Tokyo could communicate to Tehran that Japan is merely upholding the rules of the global nonproliferation regime and UN system and that Iran's compliance would allow the two states to pursue full cooperation. In any

[32] Bean, "A Historical Perspective," 23.

[33] "Increase in Japan Oil Imports from Iran," *Shana*, April 1, 2008, http://www.shana.ir/newsprint.aspx?lang=en&newsid=128525.

[34] The original deal, which was completed in 2004, had been a major element of Japan's effort to secure energy imports.

[35] Author discussion with Japanese foreign ministry officials, Washington, D.C., April 3, 2008.

event, Japan would not play a major role in broader regional strategies to shape Iranian behavior, either through hard or soft containment.

India

Though their history has not always been happy, India and Iran have important civilization ties and experience no fundamental animus toward each other. Both states see opportunities for mutually beneficial cooperation. The period between the Iranian revolution of 1979 and the U.S. invasion of Iraq in 1991 was particularly tense. Iran's militant Islamist ideology and ardor alarmed India, and India's close relationship with Iraq offended Iran. Yet in longer geostrategic terms, Iran offers a potential bridge for exchange of natural resources from the Caspian basin and Central Asia to India as well as a potential market for Indian goods. Iran's energy resources have strategic significance to energy-starved India. The two states also share interests in preventing or containing Taliban-like Sunni influence in Afghanistan and Pakistan; India and Iran cooperated in backing the Northern Alliance against the Taliban. India has also appreciated Iran's remarkably moderate stance on the Kashmir issue, especially since 1989 when the Pakistan-backed insurgency began. India generally welcomes Islamabad's consternation over Indian ties with Iran. The 2003 New Delhi Declaration outlining aspirations for a "strategic partnership" between India and Iran was, therefore, a natural step in relations between the two states.

There are limits, however, to Indo-Iranian mutual interests. India values ties with the southern Gulf states, which are wary of Iran. More than four million Indians work in the Arab Gulf states. The remittances of these workers are invaluable to the Indian society and economy, and the security of Indian workers—and therefore of their host states—is important to India. The Arab Gulf states also are an invaluable source of energy for India and an increasingly important destination for Indian investment and service exports. India seeks energetically to avoid involvement in zero-sum competitions between Iran and neighboring Arab states but would probably favor the richer and easier-to-deal-with Arab states if forced to choose.

India also cares deeply about relations with the United States, Europe, and Israel. India's relationship with Israel entails sensitive defense and strategic cooperation, as evident most recently in January 2008 when India launched the Israeli Tescar spy satellite, over Iranian protests. In each of these bilateral relationships India's clear interest is to avoid zero-sum choices between adhering to requests to join coercive diplomacy vis-à-vis Iran and maintaining good ties with Tehran.

The general features of the Indo-Iranian relationship are reflected in recent nuclear diplomacy between the two states. India has steadfastly defended Iran's "right" to benefit from atomic energy while insisting that Iran comply with a non–nuclear weapon state's obligation to use atomic energy exclusively for peaceful purposes. India played a leading role in establishing the IAEA, and Indian officials express a strong interest in protecting the agency's role. As evidence of Iran's noncompliance with IAEA safeguards mounted, and when Iran failed to provide the full transparency demanded by the IAEA, India defended the agency's position. Dilemmas have arisen, of course, between India's interests in upholding nonproliferation rules and building better relations with Iran and the United States. When the U.S. government publicly demanded Indian support in IAEA board deliberations on reporting Iran to the UNSC—as a condition of supporting the proposed U.S.-India nuclear cooperation agreement—elements in the Indian polity bristled at the apparent coercion. Iran seized on this discord to press India to defend Tehran's position. Even though India ultimately joined many other IAEA members in reporting Iran to the UNSC, the public U.S. pressure made the decision more difficult than it would have otherwise been.

India clearly does not want Iran to acquire nuclear weapons, given that a nuclear Iran would increase regional insecurity and complicate India's relations with the Arab Gulf states. To prepare for possible conflicts, India would need to make contingency plans to protect and evacuate Indian nationals in the Gulf states. Like other nuclear weapon states, India would see Iran's acquisition of nuclear weapons as a devaluation of the nuclear currency India has obtained. Iran's proximity would force strategic planners in India, more than those in other nuclear weapon states, to address how military operations in areas within range of Iranian missiles would be affected. To the extent that the United States and other states, particularly the Arab Gulf states, might seek to contain and deter Iran through closer countervailing security arrangements, India could be asked to contribute in ways it would rather avoid, especially given that Iran does not otherwise pose a military threat to India.

India will not support or participate in military action to stop Iran's nuclear activities. Nor should India be expected to support sanctions on Iranian energy exports. India would view an energy embargo or a war with Iran as more a threatening prospect than Iran's illegal acquisition of nuclear weapons. India also would not support coercive efforts to bring about a change in the Iranian regime. Though valuing democracy at least as much as any other state, India also values the principle of non-interference in the internal affairs of other countries. As a result of its own struggle for independence and a deep anti-colonial sensibility, India favors self-determination over coercive promotion of democracy. Indians believe that democracy cannot be bestowed by others but must be self-generated.

These perspectives and interests lead India to support only diplomatic efforts to change Iran's behavior—in particular by persuading Iran to comply fully with all IAEA demands and by resolving outstanding doubts that Iran's nuclear activities are exclusively for peaceful purposes. Indians argue that patient, quiet diplomacy and face-saving options are the only way to persuade Iran to comply with international demands. U.S. efforts to push India to support more coercive strategies would likely fail. Public demands on India would be especially counter-productive. Instead, India can be most helpful as a political and moral leader of the Non-Aligned Movement: when the facts warrant, and especially when Iran is belligerent, New Delhi can be an important leader in politically demonstrating that Iran has gone too far and risks global isolation. India's willingness to play such a role would be greater if threats of military force and regime change were off the table and Iran's refusal to negotiate and compromise were the central issue of discussion.

Indonesia

Although not factoring heavily in Iran's calculus, Asian middle powers are not irrelevant either—and Indonesia, the world's most populous Muslim country, is perhaps the most important of these powers. Iran courts Indonesia out of a lingering desire to be the leading voice of Muslims and a major player of the non-aligned world. Neither Persian-Arab tensions nor Sunni-Shia rivalries obtain in Iran's relations with Indonesia. For its part, Indonesia welcomes potential energy cooperation with Iran.

These interests have been reflected in recent Iranian-Indonesian diplomacy. In May 2006 Ahmadinejad visited Indonesia with much fanfare. Though details of the visit were vague, Ahmadinejad displayed his characteristic economic largesse (which critics in Iran find fiscally counter-productive) by offering economic deals valued at more than $4 billion. A reciprocal visit was planned for Indonesian president Susilo Bambang Yudhoyono. Perhaps not accidentally, the Indonesian leader's trip to Iran occurred shortly after the March 2008 UNSC vote on Resolution 1803, in which Indonesia was the only state to abstain.

Post-colonial and Muslim solidarity partially explain Indonesia's position on the Iranian nuclear issue, as does Indonesia's own vague interest in developing nuclear energy. More prosaic economic considerations also exist. Indonesia is both deeply troubled economically and undermined by corruption. With its oil and natural gas field production dropping,

Indonesia struggles to meet export obligations and is hard-pressed to meet domestic energy needs. Indonesia has been compelled to import crude oil and refined products to meet domestic demand. The pinch between export obligations and import needs hurts all the more because the contractual prices obtained for the former are lower than the spot market cost of the latter. Seeing Iran as an important source of imports, Indonesia is inclined to curry favor to affect prices. Displaying sympathy for Iran in international forums addressing the nuclear issue is an obvious way for Indonesia to seek Iran's favor. Moreover, by working to prevent further sanctions, Indonesia might avoid increases in spot market price that would hurt the country's economy.

Unsurprisingly, then, Indonesia abstained in the February 4, 2006, IAEA vote to report Iran to the UNSC. Although Indonesia did vote for UNSC Resolution 1747 in March 2007, this decision provoked public and editorial outcry. Indonesia again chose to abstain from the March 2008 vote on Resolution 1803. Skeptical that sanctions would resolve the issue, Indonesia's UN representative instead promoted greater trust-building and cooperation as a solution. Iran lavishly praised Indonesia for this position.

Absent much greater resolve by the entire UNSC to tighten sanctions on Iran, it is difficult to see how Indonesia could be induced to cooperate more closely with coercive U.S. policy toward Iran. Even with a more resolved international community, Indonesia probably would not reverse its position without seeing clearer national economic benefits, particularly in favorable energy imports.

Pakistan

Pakistan and Iran have wary relations. Iranians are offended by the idea that the international community has "allowed" Pakistan—a country with no great history—to acquire nuclear weapons, while denying Iran cooperation on an avowedly peaceful nuclear program. Remembering the Taliban's murder of nine Iranian diplomats in western Afghanistan in 1998, Iranians also express bitterness and some genuine fear over Pakistan's role in nurturing the Wahhabi extremism of the Taliban.

Pakistan is slightly more charitable toward Iran. Neither Pakistanis nor Iranians see A.Q. Khan's clandestine and long-denied assistance to Iran's enrichment (and perhaps even nuclear weaponization) activities as Pakistan's state policy. Staunchly anti-American Pakistani military figures have in the past spoken of Pakistani-Iranian cooperation as a way to balance U.S. influence in southwest Asia. Yet Sunni-Shia conflict within Pakistan has limited the potential for close cooperation. Pakistan's military dictator

Mohammed Zia ul-Haq fomented Sunni consciousness and militant action within Pakistan in the late 1970s as a way to solidify his power. In 1979 the new revolutionary government in Iran rallied to the Shiite cause in Pakistan by providing clandestine support to violent Shiite groups. This tactic inclined Saudi Arabia to do the same for Sunni groups in Pakistan, thereby adding a proxy layer to growing indigenous Sunni-Shia violence in the country.[36] Pakistan, Iran, and Saudi Arabia, however, took care not to allow their subterranean competition to rise prominently to the surface of interstate relations.

Pakistan and Iran would welcome better relations with each other. Both have interests in developing a natural gas pipeline from Iran through Pakistan and continuing on to India. South Asia badly needs the gas, and Iran would benefit from an eastern market for energy exports. Many factors, however, prevent the project from going forward. The economic value of the pipeline depends heavily on Indian participation; yet India has held back due to concerns over price, security, and U.S. reactions. Pakistan and Iran could undertake the project alone and build a pipeline to the Indian border—thus enabling Pakistan either to buy all the supply or to sell some to India. Yet, as with many deals involving Iran, the parties have been unable to agree on a price. Security concerns, including the ongoing violent unrest in Baluchistan (through which a pipeline would pass), remain highly problematic as well. Ultimately, U.S. support—or non-resistance—appears necessary to make the pipeline feasible. At the same time, such support would not be sufficient because the security and pricing roadblocks to the project are beyond U.S. control. The key point is that changing the politics of the pipeline could become a positive incentive for greater Iranian cooperation.

Pakistan is also generally resistant to tightening the international rules regulating nuclear technology. Pakistan wishes to improve its reputation—so badly damaged by the Khan affair—but at the same time continues to rely on imports to maintain a peaceful and military nuclear infrastructure. Many observers believe Pakistan still has not made available all information regarding the dealings of the Khan network. This perception puts Pakistan in a tenuous position and makes Islamabad generally reluctant to support the strengthening and enforcement of nonproliferation rules.

---

[36] Husain Haqqani, *Between Mosque and Military* (Washington, D.C.: Carnegie Endowment for International Peace, 2005).

Conclusion

Iran's ongoing uranium enrichment and plutonium production activities pose a combination of threats, especially when these activities violate IAEA and UNSC demands. The refusal to heed legally appropriate international demands is itself an act of belligerence. Yet when paired with menacing policy and rhetoric toward Israel and support of organizations that use terrorist tactics, Iran's nuclear fuel production clearly threatens regional and international peace and security.

Iran has its own set of concerns. Iran started its nuclear program during a war in which it was attacked with chemical weapons while the world did nothing to help. U.S.-led initiatives to deny nuclear technology to Iran raised the profile of the nuclear program as an emblem of Iranian nationalism and modernity. The symbolic and political potency of this nuclear program has grown as Iranian leaders successfully defined the contest over the program's future as a matter of "rights." As Iran's power in the Persian Gulf and broader Middle East has increased, so has the country's frustration at being denied recognition as the indispensable actor in the region. Iran, like other countries throughout the greater Middle East, rejects U.S. characterizations of Hezbollah and Hamas as terrorist organizations. Iran feels that U.S. policy in all its dimensions reflects imperialistic ambitions and unjust favoritism of Israeli policies, especially regarding Israeli settlements. The Iranian government seeks reassurance that no adversary can threaten its rule or deny Iran's centrality in all Middle Eastern affairs. Yet Iran's quest for reassurance through the pursuit of nuclear capability makes its neighbors, the United States, and other countries feel vulnerable. These comparatively stronger actors also seek reassurance, which the Iranian regime cannot imagine is necessary; Tehran cannot see beyond its own needs. Each side thus wants reassurance but, feeling aggrieved, is unwilling to offer it to the other. Both sides have a need to save face, and neither side is prepared to offer a reassuring compromise.

The past five years have shown that the United States cannot alone compel Iran to suspend enrichment permanently—or even for the short term. The foregoing analysis suggests real limits to what Asian powers will support in the way of coercing Iran. There appears to be no limit to the positive incentives the Asian states would support to gain Iranian compliance. Working backward from measures that major Asian powers (including P5 members Russia and China) would support, however, makes policy options clearer, albeit more limited than is desirable (especially in Washington). That is, instead of saying "We want an optimal outcome, how much do we have to pay?" the approach would be to ask "We have the following means, what can we get?"

Inducing Iran to forgo all nuclear weapon fuel-production capability would be optimal. Yet if viable threats of military attack or coerced regime change would be necessary means to this end, the world's major powers do not think they can afford this solution. Thus, the realistic question is what can these players get for increased diplomatic pressures and sanctions (on financial transactions with Iran, on investment in the Iranian energy sector, and possibly an arms embargo)?

In return, of course, major Asian states would want the United States to offer more to Iran. Security guarantees against military attacks on Iran and a willingness to deal directly and respectfully with Iran's constitutional government would be high on this list. Asian states also would want Washington's leadership to shape a regional security order through multilateral diplomacy with Iran. This security order would need to recognize Iran's prominence while protecting neighboring countries from Iranian interference or blackmail.

These are strategic considerations as well. Tactically, major Asian powers probably would welcome an approach that focuses on the nuclear issue and accepts some limited ongoing enrichment activity in Iran, with special monitoring and inspection provisions. The Asian powers also might be open to a "pull back" approach that acknowledges Iran's refusal to negotiate without removing sanctions on unceasing Iranian fuel-cycle activities. Such an approach instead would concentrate on shoring up a long-term sanctions regime while withdrawing offers of exceptional incentives to Iran. Finally, major Asian powers would support a U.S. effort toward setting the nuclear issue to the side, without abandoning UNSC demands, and inviting Iran to join the United States and others in addressing regional security issues, including terrorism.

There is a complementary approach that the United States and other P5 members could pursue to deter other states from copying Iran's quest for a nuclear weapon option. As suggested by Pierre Goldschmidt, the former deputy director general of the IAEA Department of Safeguards, in order to prevent future crises the UNSC should pass a non-country-specific resolution under Chapter VII imposing conditions on any state found in noncompliance with NPT safeguards agreements.[37] These conditions would include providing the IAEA immediate access to locations, facilities, individuals, documents, and equipment. The resolution would also require the immediate suspension of all activities related to uranium and plutonium

---

[37] Pierre Goldschmidt, "Expanded Authority for the IAEA in Case a State Is Found to Be in Non-compliance with Its Safeguards Agreements," (unpublished manuscript, 2008).

conversion and reprocessing until the IAEA is able to verify a state's declarations to the IAEA. If a state does not comply with these demands, the UNSC resolution should pre-authorize an international suspension of military sales and cooperation as long as the state remains noncompliant.

Finally, the United States will need to recognize that the way Washington has approached Iran for the past 29 years does not work. John Limbert, a retired U.S. diplomat who served in Iran, has offered fifteen guidelines for negotiation with the Islamic Republic. Among these guidelines are recommendations to "be aware of Iran's historical greatness, its recent weakness, and its grievances from decades or centuries earlier," and to "understand that the Islamic Republic's priority is survival."[38] Iranians will frame issues in terms of justice, even as they may "appear to discard calculation of advantage and disadvantage and become captives of unrealistic, rigid positions and extremist rhetoric."[39] The condescending, righteous, punitive, and Cartesian style often associated with U.S. "diplomacy" toward Iran is designed almost perfectly to fail with such a country. By adopting more of the manner of Asia's major powers, Washington might win stronger support for diplomacy toward Iran and, at the same time, make it harder for Iranian officials to resist diplomacy. With the cooperation of Asia's major powers, there is a chance that the international community can induce Iran to stop short of building nuclear weapons; without cooperation, there is no chance.

[38] John W. Limbert, "Negotiating with the Islamic Republic of Iran: Raising the Chances for Success—Fifteen Points to Remember," United States Institute of Peace, Special Report, no. 199, January 2008, http://www.usip.org/pubs/specialreports/sr199.pdf, 4, 8.

[39] Ibid., 13.

STRATEGIC ASIA 2008−09

INDICATORS

TABLE OF CONTENTS

Strategic Asia
by the Numbers

The following twenty pages contain tables and figures drawn from NBR's Strategic Asia database and its sources. This appendix consists of 23 tables covering: economic growth, economic sectors, R&D, trade, and foreign investment; population size and growth, urbanization, and unemployment levels; politics and international relations; energy consumption; and armed forces, defense spending, conventional military developments, and WMD. The data sets presented here summarize the critical trends in the region and changes underway in the balance of power in Asia.

The Strategic Asia database contains additional data for all 37 countries in Strategic Asia. Hosted on the program's website (http://strategicasia.nbr.org), the database is a repository for authoritative data for every year since 1990 and is continually updated. The 70 strategic indicators are arranged in ten broad thematic areas: economy, finance, trade and investment, government spending, population, energy and environment, communications and transportation, armed forces, WMD, and politics and international relations. The Strategic Asia database was developed with .NET, Microsoft's XML-based platform, which allows users to dynamically link to all or part of the Strategic Asia data set and facilitates easy data sharing. The database also includes additional links that allow users to seamlessly access related online resources.

The information for Strategic Asia by the Numbers was compiled by Next Generation research fellow Andrew David with the assistance of NBR intern Marc Miller.

Economies

Asia's economy grew at a rate of 8.7% in 2007, the highest level in almost twenty years. The growth rate is forecast to slow to 7.6% in 2008 but to then take a slight upturn in 2009. Though not immune to the global slowdown, Asia will likely remain on a strong trajectory as a result of continuing growth in productivity. Rising prices are having an impact, however, and inflation could hit a decade-long regional high.

- China's and India's economies grew at rates of 11.4% and 8.7% in 2007 but are expected to slow to 10% and 8% respectively in 2008.

- Growth in Southeast Asia is expected to slow to a level of 5.8% in 2008 as the global slowdown affects exports. Vietnam has been particularly hard-hit so far with a rising trade deficit and inflation over 25%.

- Rising oil and natural resource prices spurred economic growth of 11.6% in Central Asia in 2007, but deceleration is projected for 2008 as a result of weaker expansion in Kazakhstan.

- In Russia high commodity and oil prices provide economic support, though inflation, nearing 13% in early 2008, remains a problem.

TABLE 1   Gross domestic product

	GDP ($bn constant 2000)				Rank	
	1990	2000	2006	2005–06 growth (%)	1990	2006
United States	7,055.0	9,764.8	11,314.7	3.3	1	1
Japan	4,111.3	4,667.4	5,087.8	2.2	2	2
China	444.6	1,198.5	2,095.9	10.7	4	3
Canada	535.6	724.9	845.4	2.8	3	4
India	269.4	460.2	703.3	9.2	8	5
South Korea	283.6	511.7	671.3	5.0	6	6
Australia	280.5	399.6	481.6	2.4	7	7
Russia	385.9	259.7	373.2	6.7	5	8
Taiwan	–	303.2	312.2	4.6	–	9
Hong Kong	108.4	169.1	221.1	6.9	10	10
Indonesia	109.2	165.0	219.3	5.5	9	11
Thailand	79.4	122.7	165.0	5.0	11	12
Singapore	44.7	92.7	121.6	7.9	14	13
Malaysia	45.5	90.3	118.4	5.9	13	14
Philippines	55.8	75.9	99.6	5.4	12	15
World	23,996.7	31,876.3	37,868.9	4.0	N/A	N/A

SOURCE: World Bank, *World Development Indicators, 2008*; and Central Bank of China, 2006.
NOTE: These values show GDP converted from domestic currencies using 2000 exchange rates. Figures for Taiwan are calculated using the average exchange rate for 2000. Dash indicates that no data is available.

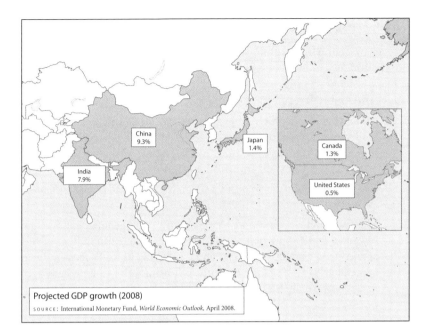

Projected GDP growth (2008)

SOURCE: International Monetary Fund, *World Economic Outlook*, April 2008.

TABLE 2   GDP growth and inflation rate

	Average GDP growth (%)			Average inflation rate (%)		
	1990–99	2000–04	2005–07	1990–99	2000–04	2005–07
United States	2.6	3.0	3.1	3.0	2.5	2.8
Japan	1.5	1.3	2.5	1.3	-0.5	0.0
China	9.3	8.4	10.3	7.4	0.8	2.7
Canada	2.1	3.0	2.8	2.1	2.4	2.2
India	4.8	5.7	8.2	10.0	5.0	5.2
South Korea	6.2	5.7	4.6	5.6	3.0	2.5
Australia	3.4	3.9	3.1	2.6	2.1	3.2
Russia	-6.6	5.7	7.0	34.8	15.9	10.9
Taiwan	5.8	3.4	4.6	3.2	0.6	1.7
Hong Kong	3.5	4.6	6.3	6.8	0.4	1.7
Indonesia	3.6	4.1	5.7	19.3	9.1	10.0
Thailand	5.1	4.7	4.6	5.1	1.8	3.9
Singapore	6.9	3.8	7.1	2.0	1.0	1.9
Malaysia	6.6	5.0	5.5	10.5	1.5	3.0
Philippines	2.7	4.2	6.0	9.2	4.5	5.5

SOURCE: Central Intelligence Agency, *The World Factbook*, 1990–2008.

The Changing Nature of the Asian Economy

Asian countries continue to produce low-cost goods for export to Europe and the United States, but there are indications that the composition of many Asian economies is changing as countries move up the technological ladder and higher-level education expands.

- Japan spends the highest proportion of GDP on R&D, with the United States, second; South Korea, third; and Singapore fourth. High tech exports increased in most Southeast Asian countries, but these countries—with the exception of Singapore—spend little on R&D.

- Indian prime minister Manmohan Singh announced plans to increase R&D spending to 2% of GDP by 2012.

- Chinese policymakers are emphasizing indigenous innovation, research, and production, as witnessed by a quadrupling of patent applications from 2003 to 2006 and a doubling of R&D spending as a percentage of GDP. China remains well behind the United States and Japan, however, in both categories.

TABLE 3 GDP by sector

	GDP by sector (%)					
	Agriculture		Manufacturing		Services	
	1990	2005	1990	2005	1990	2005
Australia	3.6	3.3d	14.5	12.4d	66.4	69.6d
Canada	2.9	2.2c	17.2	17.9c	65.3	66.4c
China	27.0	12.5	32.9	33.3	31.3	40.1
Hong Kong	0.2	0.1	16.7	3.4	73.4	90.7
India	31.3	18.3	17.1	15.7	41.1	54.4
Indonesia	19.4	13.1	20.7	27.5	41.5	42.0
Japan	2.6	1.7d	23.3b	21d	57.9	68.1d
Kazakhstan	26.7a	6.8	8.9a	14.6	28.7a	53.8
Malaysia	15.2	8.7	24.2	30.6	42.6	40.0
Philippines	21.9	13.6	24.8	23.3	43.6	53.4
Russia	–	5.6	–	17.9	–	56.4
Singapore	0.4	0.1	27.3	28.0	64.9	66.1
South Korea	8.9	3.4	27.3	28.4	49.5	57.2
United States	2.1	1.3d	19.4	14.2d	70.1	76.7d
Vietnam	38.7	20.9	12.3	20.7	38.6	38.2

SOURCE: World Bank, *World Development Indicators*, 2008.
NOTE: *a* indicates data from 1992, *b* indicates data is from 1996, *c* indicates data is from 2002, and *d* indicates data is from 2004. Dash indicates that no data is available.

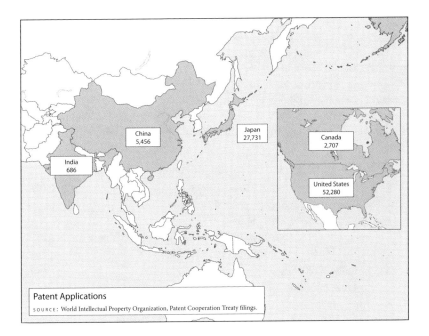

Patent Applications

SOURCE: World Intellectual Property Organization, Patent Cooperation Treaty filings.

TABLE 4 R&D expenditures and high tech exports

	R&D expenditures (% GDP)		High tech exports (% of manufacturing exports)	
	1996	2004	1990	2005
Australia	1.7	1.7i	11.9	12.7
Canada	1.7	1.9	13.7	14.4
China	0.6	1.4	6.1	30.6
Hong Kong	0.4f	0.6i	12.1	33.9
India	–	0.8g	2.4	4.9k
Indonesia	–	0.1h	1.2b	16.3
Japan	2.8	3.2j	23.8	22.5
Kazakhstan	0.3d	0.2h	4.5c	2.3j
Malaysia	0.2	0.7i	38.2	54.7
Philippines	–	0.1	32.5a	71.0
Russia	1.0	1.2	9.4d	8.1
Singapore	1.4	2.3	39.7	56.6
South Korea	2.4	2.6k	17.8	32.3
United States	2.6d	2.7	33.7	31.8
Vietnam	–	0.2i	2.2e	5.6j

SOURCE: World Bank, *World Development Indicators,* 2008.

NOTE: *a* indicates data is from 1991, *b* indicates data is from 1992, *c* indicates data is from 1995, *d* indicates data is from 1996, *e* indicates data is from 1997, *f* indicates data is from 1998, *g* indicates data is from 2000, *h* indicates data is from 2001, *i* indicates data is from 2002, *j* indicates data is from 2003, and *k* indicates data is from 2004. Dash indicates that no data is available.

Trade

Owing to concerns over an economic slowdown in the United States and the global impact of the sub-prime loans crisis, many Asian countries have begun exploring ways to reduce dependence on U.S. and European markets. Asia is unlikely to dramatically decouple from the U.S. and European markets, however, because product components destined for these markets comprise much of the growth of intraregional trade.

- As a region East Asia had a growing current account surplus in 2007, while South Asia's current account deficit continued.

- In June 2007 the United States and South Korea concluded negotiations on an FTA to expand trade and investment ties. Unresolved issues in both states, however, especially over imports of U.S. beef, have delayed the agreement's approval and implementation and have undermined support for the new South Korean government.

- The growth of intra-Asian trade and domestic demand has diminished the effect of declining exports to developed countries. Asian exports to China are growing rapidly, and China's total trade recently surpassed that of Japan and South Korea combined for the first time.

TABLE 5   Trade flow

	Trade flow ($bn constant 2000)				Rank	
	1990	2000	2006	2005–06 growth (%)	1990	2006
United States	1,159.6	2,572.1	3,649.9	6.5	1	1
China	129.9	530.2	1,914.5	17.9	6	2
Japan	649.4	957.6	1,403.2	6.4	2	3
Canada	296.3	617.4	890.4	4.6	4	4
Hong Kong	197.3	475.3	758.1	9.3	5	5
South Korea	118.0	401.6	757.0	7.9	7	6
Russia	305.9	176.8	544.3	11.7	3	7
India	39.8	130.5	429.2	8.1	13	8
Malaysia	67.0	206.7	330.6	8.4	10	9
Australia	88.1	178.0	324.8	4.5	8	10
Thailand	68.3	153.3	298.5	6.8	9	11
Indonesia	66.2	117.9	210.5	16.8	11	12
Philippines	42.8	82.7	112.5	3.6	12	13
Vietnam	4.1	35.1	75.2	19.0	15	14
New Zealand	21.6	36.6	62.8	2.2	14	15
World	8,328.2	15,957.1	29,038.4	7.4	N/A	N/A

SOURCE: World Bank, *World Development Indicators*, 1990–2008.
NOTE: Data for Vietnam is for 2005 rather than 2006. World total for 2006 is an estimate. No comparable data from the World Development Indicators is available for Singapore or Taiwan.

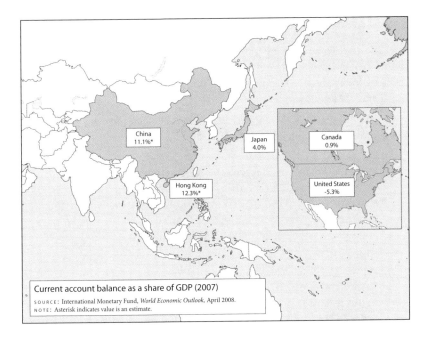

Current account balance as a share of GDP (2007)

SOURCE: International Monetary Fund, *World Economic Outlook*, April 2008.
NOTE: Asterisk indicates value is an estimate.

TABLE 6 Export partners

	Exports ($bn) 2007	Export destinations (top three partners in 2006 with percentage share of total exports)
United States	1,140.0	Canada (22%), Mexico (13%), Japan (6%)
China	1,221.0	U.S. (21%), Hong Kong (16%), Japan (10%)
Japan	665.7	U.S. (23%), China (14%), South Korea (8%)
Canada	440.1	U.S. (82%), UK (2%), Japan (2%)
Hong Kong	353.3	China (47%), U.S. (15%), Japan (59%)
South Korea	371.5	China (22%), U.S. (13%), Japan (7%)

SOURCE: Central Intelligence Agency, *The World Factbook*, 2008.
NOTE: Values for South Korea are for 2007.

TABLE 7 Import partners

	Imports ($bn) 2007	Import origins (top three partners in 2006 with percentage share of total imports)
United States	1,987.0	Canada (16%), China (16%), Mexico (10%)
China	917.4	Japan (15%), South Korea (11%), Taiwan (11%)
Japan	571.1	China (21%), U.S. (12%), Saudi Arabia (6%)
Canada	394.4	U.S. (55%), China (9%), Mexico (4%)
Hong Kong	371.3	China (46%), Japan (10%), Taiwan (8%)
South Korea	356.8	China (18%), Japan (16%), U.S. (11%)

SOURCE: Central Intelligence Agency, *The World Factbook*, 2008.
NOTE: Values for South Korea are for 2007.

Investment

FDI inflows are strong across much of Asia. FDI outflows have also increased in developed and developing countries. Asia is much more resilient today than a decade ago due both to broad economic reforms in the corporate and financial sectors and to improved monetary policies.

- FDI inflows to Canada, Russia, India, New Zealand, and Kazakhstan more than doubled between 2005 and 2006.

- China and Hong Kong accounted for 53%–68% of total FDI inflows to Asia over the past decade. The ADB reports that FDI to China and Hong Kong is positively correlated to other Asian economies. In 2006 East Asia attracted the greatest inflow of FDI at $119.3 billion, followed by Southeast Asia at $83.6 billion, Central Asia and Russia at $42.9 billion, and South Asia at $22.3 billion.

- China's FDI outflows—focused on Asia and Africa—increased from an average of $2.2 billion between 1990 and 2000 to $16.1 billion in 2006. China's outward FDI is only 23% of China's total inward FDI, however, and is significantly less than outward FDI from the United States ($216.6 billion) and Japan ($50.3 billion) in 2006.

TABLE 8   Flow of foreign direct investment

	FDI inflows ($bn)				FDI outflows ($bn)	
	1990–2000 annual avg.	2006	2005–06 growth (%)	2006 rank	1990–2000 annual avg.	2006
United States	109.5	175.4	73.6	1	92.0	216.6
China	30.1	69.5	-4.1	2	2.2	16.1
Hong Kong	13.8	69.0	27.6	3	20.4	43.5
Canada	15.7	42.9	138.7	4	15.8	45.2
Russia	2.4	28.7	125.1	5	1.6	18.0
Singapore	9.2	24.2	61.3	6	4.8	8.6
Australia	7.0	24.0	N/A	7	3.2	22.3
India	1.7	16.9	152.9	8	0.1	9.7
Thailand	3.2	9.8	8.9	9	0.4	0.8
New Zealand	2.3	8.1	383.5	10	0.5	1.2
Malaysia	4.7	6.1	52.8	11	1.6	6.0
Kazakhstan	1.0	6.1	210.7	12	0.0	-0.4
Indonesia	1.5	5.6	-33.4	13	0.6	3.4
South Korea	3.1	5.0	-29.8	14	3.1	7.1
Pakistan	0.5	4.3	94.1	15	0.0	0.1
World	495.4	1,305.9	38.1	N/A	492.6	1,215.8

SOURCE: United Nations Conference on Trade and Development, *World Investment Report*, 2007.
NOTE: Dash indicates that no data is available; net FDI inflows for Australia were negative in 2005.

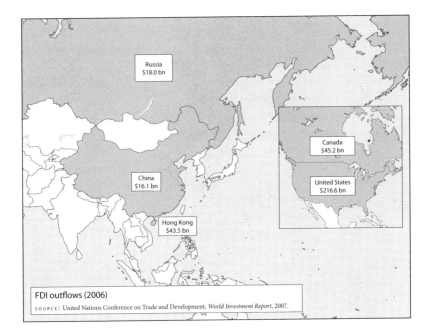

FDI outflows (2006)
SOURCE: United Nations Conference on Trade and Development, *World Investment Report*, 2007.

TABLE 9 Origins of FDI

	Origins of FDI (leading countries of origin for inward investment in 2006)
United States	UK, France, Netherlands
China	Hong Kong, Japan, South Korea
Hong Kong	China, Virgin Islands, Bermuda
Canada	France, Netherlands, Switzerland
Russia	UK, Cyprus, Netherlands
Singapore	U.S., EU, Japan
Australia	U.S., UK, Japan
India	UK, U.S., Netherlands
Thailand	Japan, U.S., Netherlands
New Zealand	Australia, United Kingdom, Canada
Malaysia	Japan, Germany, Iran
Kazakhstan	Netherlands, U.S., Japan
Indonesia	Singapore, UK, South Korea
South Korea	Netherlands, U.S., Japan
Pakistan	U.S., UK, Netherlands

SOURCE: Economist Intelligence Unit, 2007; and U.S. Department of Commerce, *Country Commercial Guides*, 2008.
NOTE: Since data for FDI by country is not reported in a consistent form and varies across sources, this table shows only the main countries of origin for FDI and omits the values and percentage share. Data for Kazakhstan is from 2005.

Population and Society

Asia's population is expected to grow from 4.1 billion in 2007 to 4.8 billion in 2025 and to 5.3 billion in 2050. The percentage of people living in urban areas is likely to increase from 40% in 2005 to 55% by 2030, with growth highest in small and medium-sized cities.

- An influx of young workers and a surplus of unskilled labor are transforming the workforce in Asia's developing countries. Nearly half the population in countries such as Cambodia, Laos, Pakistan, Vietnam, and India is under the age of 20. China's population, however, is less young than that of other developing Asian nations— only 31% are under the age of 20.

- Japan's population is declining and over 40% of its population is at least 50 years old. Russia's population has declined by 0.5% and is expected to fall to 128 million by 2025.

- The number of people in Asia living on less than a dollar a day decreased from approximately 930 million in 1990 to 650 million in 2002. In developing countries, however, regional and class inequalities are rising.

TABLE 10   Population

	Population (m)				Rank	
	1990	2000	2006	2005–06 growth (%)	1990	2006
China	1,135.2	1,262.6	1,311.8	0.6	1	1
India	849.5	1,015.9	1,109.8	1.4	2	2
United States	249.6	282.2	299.0	0.9	3	3
Indonesia	178.2	206.3	223.0	1.1	4	4
Pakistan	108.0	138.1	159.0	2.1	7	5
Bangladesh	104.0	128.9	144.3	1.8	8	6
Russia	148.3	146.3	142.4	-0.5	5	7
Japan	123.5	126.9	127.6	-0.2	6	8
Philippines	61.1	75.8	84.6	1.8	10	9
Vietnam	66.2	78.5	84.1	1.2	9	10
Thailand	54.6	61.4	64.7	0.8	11	11
Myanmar	40.8	47.7	51.0	0.9	13	12
South Korea	42.9	47.0	48.4	0.6	12	13
Canada	27.8	30.8	32.6	0.8	14	14
Nepal	19.1	24.4	27.7	1.9	15	15
World	5,256.3	6,059.5	6,517.8	1.1	N/A	N/A

SOURCE: World Bank, *World Development Indicators*, 2008.

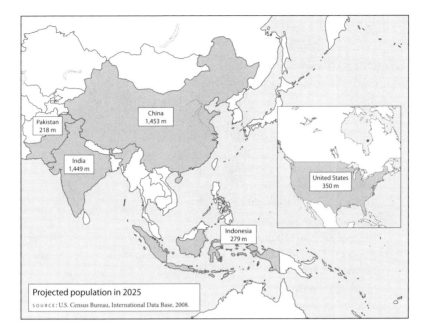

Projected population in 2025

SOURCE: U.S. Census Bureau, International Data Base, 2008.

TABLE 11 Urbanization and unemployment rate

	Urban population (m)			Unemployment (%)		
	1990	2000	2006	1990	2000	2005
China	311.0	452.0	541.8	2.5	3.1	4.2
India	216.6	281.4	321.6	–	4.3	5.0
United States	188.0	223.2	242.5	5.6	4.0	5.1
Indonesia	54.5	86.6	109.8	–	6.1	10.3
Pakistan	33.0	45.7	56.2	2.6	7.2	7.7
Bangladesh	20.6	29.9	36.9	1.9	3.3	7.9
Russia	108.8	107.4	103.8	–	9.8	–
Japan	78.0	82.7	84.2	2.1	4.8	4.4
Philippines	29.8	44.3	53.7	8.1	10.1	2.1
Vietnam	13.4	19.1	22.6	–	–	7.4
Thailand	16.1	19.1	21.1	2.2	2.4	1.3
Myanmar	10.1	13.4	15.9	0.0	–	–
South Korea	31.6	37.4	39.2	2.5	4.1	3.7
Canada	21.3	24.4	26.1	8.2	6.8	6.8
Nepal	1.7	3.3	4.5	–	–	–

SOURCE: World Bank, *World Development Indicators*, 2008.
NOTE: Unemployment figures are calculated by percentage of total work force. Dash indicates that no data is available.

Politics and International Relations

2007–08 was a momentous year of political change in the Asia-Pacific, with leadership transitions in many countries. There are indications that some newly elected leaders will break with the policies of their predecessors.

- President Ma Ying-jeou returned the KMT to power in Taiwan, promising to take a less confrontational and more pragmatic approach toward China as well as to focus on the economy.

- The LDP in Japan lost its upper house majority in parliament for the first time ever. The new prime minister, Yasuo Fukuda, backed away from his predecessor's proposal to create an "arc of freedom and prosperity" with India and Australia.

- Former Pakistani prime minister Benazir Bhutto was assassinated in December 2007 after returning from exile to run in parliamentary elections. Her Pakistan Peoples Party now leads a four-party governing coalition that includes Nawaz Sharif's Pakistan Muslim League.

- In Russia President Vladimir Putin's handpicked successor, Dmitry Medvedev, was easily elected and appointed Putin as prime minister.

TABLE 12   Political leadership

	Political leader	Date assumed office	Next election
Australia	Prime Minister Kevin Rudd	December 2007	2010
Canada	Prime Minister Stephen Harper	February 2006	2009
China	President Hu Jintao	March 2003	N/A
India	Prime Minister Manmohan Singh	May 2004	2009
Indonesia	President Susilo Bambang Yudhoyono	October 2004	2009
Japan	Prime Minister Yasuo Fukuda	September 2007	2009
Kazakhstan	President Nursultan Nazarbayev	December 1991	2012
Malaysia	Prime Minister Abdullah bin Ahmad Badawi	October 2003	2013
Pakistan	President Pervez Musharraf	June 2001	2012
Philippines	President Gloria Macapagal-Arroyo	January 2001	2010
Russia	President Dmitry Medvedev	May 2008	2012
South Korea	President Lee Myung-bak	February 2008	2012
Taiwan	President Ma Ying-jeou	May 2008	2012
Thailand	Prime Minister Samak Sundaravej	January 2008	2011
United States	President George W. Bush	January 2001	2008

SOURCE: Central Intelligence Agency, *The World Factbook*, 2008. Table shows next election year in which the given leader may lose or retain his position. In some countries elections may be called before these years.

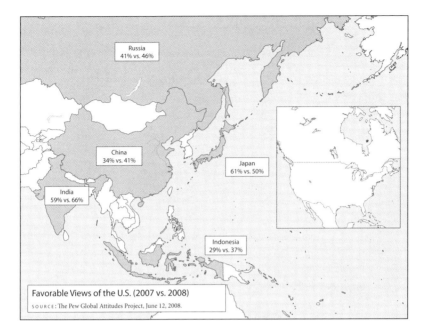

Favorable Views of the U.S. (2007 vs. 2008)

SOURCE: The Pew Global Attitudes Project, June 12, 2008.

TABLE 13   Political rights, corruption, and globalization rankings

	Political rights score		Corruption score		Globalization index	
	2000	2007	2000	2007	2001	2007
Australia	1	1	8.3	8.6	23	13
Canada	1	1	9.2	8.7	10	8
China	7	7	3.1	3.5	47	66
India	2	2	2.8	3.5	48	71
Indonesia	3	2	1.7	2.3	38	69
Japan	1	1	6.4	7.5	29	28
Kazakhstan	6	6	3.0	2.1	–	–
Malaysia	5	4	4.8	5.1	20	23
Pakistan	6	6	–	2.4	–	63
Philippines	2	4	2.8	2.5	33	38
Russia	5	6	2.1	2.3	44	62
South Korea	2	1	4.0	5.1	31	35
Taiwan	1	2	5.5	5.7	–	37
Thailand	2	6	3.2	3.3	30	53
United States	1	1	7.8	7.2	12	7

SOURCE: Freedom House, *Freedom in the World*, 2001 and 2008, Transparency International, *Corruption Perceptions Index*, 2001 and 2007; and A.T. Kearney/Foreign Policy, *Globalization Index*, 2001 and 2007.
NOTE: Political rights = ability of the people to participate freely in the political process (1=most free/7=least free). Corruption = degree to which public official corruption is perceived to exist (1=most corrupt/10=most open). The globalization index tracks changes in economic integration, technological connectivity, personal contact, and political engagement (rank of countries, 1=most globalized, number of countries increased from 62 to 72 in 2007). Dash indicates that no data is available.

Energy and Environment

Driven by soaring energy prices and a nascent environmental movement, Asian states are prioritizing access to and protection of natural resources across the globe. The 2007 UN Climate Change Conference in Bali and 2008 G-8 Summit advanced dialogue on climate change, though disagreements persist between developed and developing countries.

- Beijing set up an energy commission and a new energy bureau in 2008. Both are run by the National Development and Reform Commission rather than by a separate energy ministry.

- Russian oil production has slumped for the first time in a decade. Officials and oil companies argue that the country must utilize the untapped expanses of East Siberia to ensure future growth, but the lack of infrastructure, new legislation limiting foreign investment, and harsh operating conditions will complicate expansion.

- By 2025 Asia is expected to contribute 35% of world carbon emissions. From 1990 to 2004 carbon emissions in Northeast Asia increased by 93% and in South Asia by 100%, though South Asian emissions are only 36% those of Northeast Asia.

TABLE 14   Energy consumption

	Energy consumption (quadrillion Btu)				Rank	
	1990	2000	2007	2006–07 growth (%)	1990	2007
United States	78.0	91.7	93.7	1.7	1	1
China	27.2	38.4	73.9	7.7	2	2
Russia	–	25.2	27.5	0.6	–	3
Japan	17.2	20.4	20.5	-0.9	3	4
India	7.7	12.7	16.0	6.8	5	5
Canada	9.8	11.5	12.8	0.5	4	6
South Korea	3.6	7.6	9.3	3.0	6	7
Australia	3.5	4.4	4.8	-1.6	7	8
Taiwan	2.0	3.8	4.6	2.8	9	9
Indonesia	2.1	3.8	4.5	2.9	8	10
Thailand	1.2	2.4	3.4	3.5	10	11
Kazakhstan	–	1.6	2.4	0.8	–	12
Malaysia	1.0	1.8	2.3	-1.2	12	13
Pakistan	1.1	1.6	2.3	3.0	11	14
Uzbekistan	–	2.0	2.0	5.5	–	15
World	322.7	369.4	444.0	2.4	N/A	N/A

SOURCE: BP plc., "BP Statistical Review of World Energy," 2007.
NOTE: Dash indicates that no data is available.

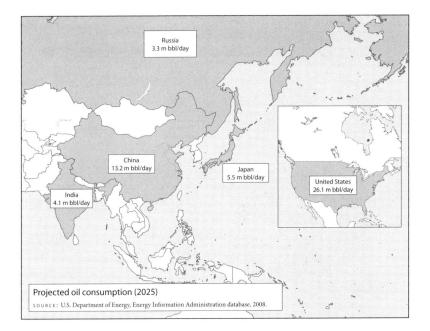

Projected oil consumption (2025)

SOURCE: U.S. Department of Energy, Energy Information Administration database, 2008.

TABLE 15   Energy consumption by fuel type

	2007 energy consumption by fuel type (%)				
	Oil	Gas	Coal	Nuclear	Hydro
United States	39.9	25.2	24.3	8.1	2.4
China	19.7	3.3	70.4	0.8	5.9
Russia	18.2	57.1	13.7	5.2	5.9
Japan	44.2	15.7	24.2	12.2	3.7
India	31.8	8.9	51.4	1.0	6.8
Canada	31.8	26.3	9.5	6.6	25.9
South Korea	46.0	14.2	25.5	13.8	0.5
Australia	34.7	18.6	43.6	0.0	3.1
Taiwan	45.6	9.2	35.7	8.0	1.5
Indonesia	47.5	26.5	24.3	0.0	1.7
Thailand	50.3	37.2	10.4	0.0	2.2
Kazakhstan	17.6	29.6	49.8	0.0	3.0
Malaysia	41.1	44.3	12.1	0.0	2.5
Pakistan	30.7	47.5	7.9	0.9	12.9
Uzbekistan	11.6	82.8	2.8	0.0	2.8

SOURCE: BP plc., "BP Statistical Review of World Energy," 2007.
NOTE: Due to rounding, some totals may not add up to exactly 100%.

Defense Spending

Most major countries are modernizing their militaries and increasing defense capabilities. The rate of defense spending increases, however, generally does not exceed the rate of GDP growth accross the region.

- Russian defense expenditures increased from $58 billion in 2005 to $70 billion in 2006 but fell as a share of GDP. Budget increases enabled engagement in military exercises and the resumption of long-range strategic bomber flights.

- China's officially stated 2008 increase in defense spending was 17.6%, which includes a focus on improving personnel, salaries, and benefits.

- The leading arms importers in Asia in 2006 were China ($2.9 bn), Taiwan ($1 bn), and India ($0.8 bn). The United States ($14 bn), Russia ($5.8 bn), and China ($0.7 bn) were leading arms suppliers.

- Indonesia, Malaysia, Singapore, and Thailand made purchases in 2007 that enhanced traditional war-fighting abilities. Singapore purchased combat and early-warning aircraft, and Malaysia received previously ordered combat aircraft.

TABLE 16   Total defense expenditure

	Expenditure ($bn)				Rank	
	1990	2000	2006	2005–06 growth (%)	1990	2006
United States	293.0	300.5	536.0	8.2	1	1
China	11.3	42.0	121.9	17.9	3	2
Russia	–	60.0	70.0	20.7	–	3
Japan	28.7	45.6	41.1	-6.3	2	4
South Korea	10.6	12.8	24.6	14.5	4	5
India	10.1	14.7	22.4	3.2	6	6
Australia	7.3	7.1	17.2	10.7	8	7
Canada	10.3	8.1	15.0	13.1	5	8
Taiwan	8.7	17.6	7.7	-3.0	7	9
Myanmar	0.9	2.1	6.9	-0.3	13	10
Singapore	1.7	4.8	6.3	13.3	11	11
Pakistan	2.9	3.7	4.2	2.6	9	12
Indonesia	1.6	1.5	3.6	27.0	12	13
Vietnam	–	1.0	3.4	9.1	–	14
Malaysia	1.7	2.8	3.2	3.1	10	15
World	954.0	811.4	1,297.8	7.8	N/A	N/A

SOURCE: International Institute for Strategic Studies, *The Military Balance*, various editions; and (data for World in 1990) SASI Group and Mark Newman, "Military Spending 1990," 2006.
NOTE: Estimates for China vary widely. Dash indicates that no data is available.

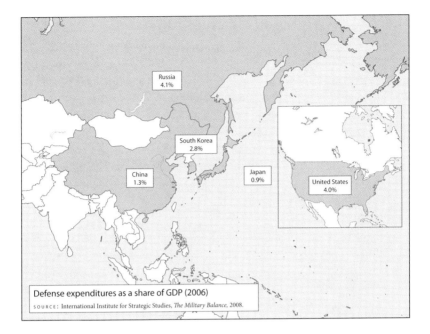

Defense expenditures as a share of GDP (2006)

SOURCE: International Institute for Strategic Studies, *The Military Balance*, 2008.

TABLE 17　Defense expenditure as share of GDP and CGE

	Defense expenditure as a share of GDP (%)			Defense expenditure as a share of CGE (%)		
	1990–99	2000–04	2006	1990–99	2000–04	2006
United States	4.2	3.4	4.0	18.5	17.3	19.5
China	5.2	3.9	2.1	28.3	19.4	–
Russia	7.6	4.5	3.6	26.1	18.4	20.5
Japan	1.0	1.0	1.0	5.7	–	–
South Korea	3.5	2.7	2.5	16.8	13.9	–
India	2.9	2.9	2.7	13.7	14.4	17.7
Australia	2.3	2.2	1.9	9.0	7.2	7.5
Canada	1.6	1.2	1.2	6.3	6.3	6.5
Taiwan	5.0	2.1	2.0	30.6	7.8	–
Myanmar	5.5	5.8	–	99.8	–	–
Singapore	5.1	5.0	4.7	21.9	29.3	–
Pakistan	6.8	4.1	3.2	26.9	25.3	24.9
Indonesia	1.6	2.7	1.3	7.4	–	–
Vietnam	6.7	7.2	–	11.2	–	–
Malaysia	2.5	2.2	2.2	13.0	10.9	–

SOURCE: International Institute for Strategic Studies, *The Military Balance*, various editions; Department of State, "World Military Expenditures and Arms Transfers," 2003; World Bank, *World Development Indicators*, 2008; and SIPRI Military Expenditure Database, 2008.

NOTE: Data for some countries over certain periods is partial. Dash indicates that no data is available.

Conventional Military Developments

Increased defense spending in Asia has not significantly increased the size of armed forces but has contributed to their modernization. States have increased security cooperation and joint exercises to improve regional trust and their abilities to respond to nontraditional security threats.

- China has committed more resources to its navy, including new ships, weapons, and 35 new submarines over the past fifteen years. The PLA's response to the 2008 earthquake was rapid, even as it revealed ongoing challenges with shortages of helicopters and engineer equipment.

- Improvement in Taiwan's self-defense capabilities has supported the status quo political arrangement.

- India and China took steps to increase defense cooperation in 2006–07, but New Delhi remains concerned over China's growing activity in the Indian Ocean region and relationships with Pakistan and Myanmar.

- In September 2007 Australia, India, Japan, Singapore, and the United States participated in the biggest joint naval exercise to date in the Indian Ocean.

TABLE 18   Manpower

	Armed forces (th)				Rank	
	1990	2000	2008	2007–08 change (th)	1990	2008
China	3,030	2,470	2,105	-150	2	1
United States	2,118	1,366	1,498	-8	3	2
India	1,262	1,303	1,288	-28	4	3
North Korea	1,111	1,082	1,106	0	5	4
Russia	3,988	1,004	1,027	0	1	5
South Korea	750	683	687	0	7	6
Pakistan	550	612	619	0	8	7
Vietnam	1,052	484	455	0	6	8
Myanmar	230	344	406	31	13	9
Thailand	283	301	306	-1	10	10
Indonesia	283	297	302	0	10	11
Taiwan	370	370	290	0	9	12
Japan	249	237	240	0	12	13
Sri Lanka	65	–	151	0	15	14
Bangladesh	103	137	150	23	14	15
World	26,605	22,237	19,801	-169	N/A	N/A

SOURCE: International Institute for Strategic Studies, *The Military Balance*, various editions.
NOTE: Active duty and military personnel only. Data value for Russia in 1990 includes all territories of the Soviet Union. Dash indicates that no data is available.

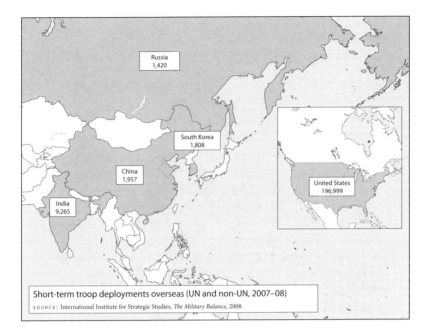

Short-term troop deployments overseas (UN and non-UN, 2007–08)

SOURCE: International Institute for Strategic Studies, *The Military Balance*, 2008.

TABLE 19 Conventional warfare capabilities, 2007

	Tanks, APCs/ LAVs, artillery	Combat aircraft	Principal surface combatants	Submarines
China	30,010	2,554	75	62
United States	35,995	4,191	106	71
India	16,366	599	48	16
North Korea	24,460	590	8	63
Russia	59,171	1,981	62	67
South Korea	15,584	563	44	12
Pakistan	8,018	360	6	8
Vietnam	6,355	219	11	2
Myanmar	968	125	3	0
Thailand	4,343	165	20	0
Indonesia	2,004	94	29	0
Taiwan	4,596	478	26	4
Japan	3,610	360	53	16
Sri Lanka	1,242	22	0	0
Bangladesh	951	76	4	0

SOURCE: International Institute for Strategic Studies, *The Military Balance*, 2008.

Weapons of Mass Destruction

The six-party talks have seemingly advanced the prospect of a nuclear weapons–free North Korea, but concern over Iran's ambitions has heightened. Leadership changes in Asia introduced new views on long-standing nuclear proliferation and WMD issues.

- In a symbolic gesture North Korea destroyed a cooling tower at the Yongbyon nuclear reactor in June 2008 to signal its intention to dismantle the reactor and cease plutonium production.

- Despite indications that the country might be amenable to nuclear negotiations with Western powers, Tehran's test of a new version of the Shahab-3, a long-range missile potentially capable of striking Israel, called into question Iran's interest in diplomatic engagement.

- Wary of closer bilateral relations, left-wing opposition to the U.S.-India civilian nuclear agreement in India's governing coalition has delayed New Delhi's approval of the agreement.

- Australian prime minister Kevin Rudd reversed his predecessor's decision to sell uranium to India because India has not signed the NPT.

TABLE 20 Nuclear weapons

	Nuclear weapons possession				Warheads
	1990	1995	2000	2007	2007
Russia	✓	✓	✓	✓	~16,000
United States	✓	✓	✓	✓	~10,300
China	✓	✓	✓	✓	410
India	✓	✓	✓	✓	70–110
Pakistan	–	–	✓	✓	50–110
North Korea	?	?	?	✓	~5–10

SOURCE: Carnegie Endowment for International Peace; and Monterey Institute of International Studies.
NOTE: Table shows confirmed (✓) and unknown (?) possession of nuclear weapons. Dash indicates that no data is available.

TABLE 21 Intercontinental ballistic missiles

	Number of ICBMs			
	1990	1995	2000	2007
Russia	1,398	930	776	508
United States	1,000	580	550	500
China	8	17+	20+	46
India	–	–	–	–
Pakistan	–	–	–	–
North Korea	–	–	–	?

SOURCE: International Institute for Strategic Studies, *The Military Balance*, various editions.
NOTE: Dash indicates that no data is available. Question mark indicates unconfirmed possession of ICBMs.

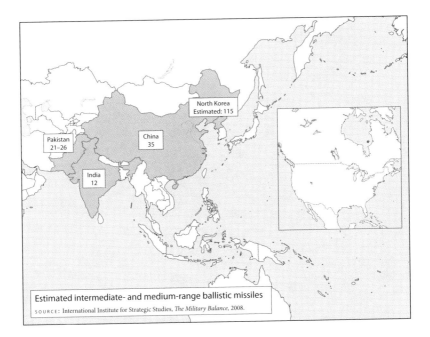

Estimated intermediate- and medium-range ballistic missiles

SOURCE: International Institute for Strategic Studies, *The Military Balance*, 2008.

TABLE 22   Nonproliferation treaties

	NPT	Additional Protocol	CTBT	CWC	BTWC
Russia	Ratified	Signatory	Ratified	Ratified	Ratified
United States	Ratified	Signatory	Signatory	Ratified	Ratified
China	Ratified	Ratified	Signatory	Ratified	Ratified
India	–	–	–	Ratified	Ratified
Pakistan	–	–	–	Ratified	Ratified
North Korea	Withdrew	–	–	–	Acceded

SOURCE: Nuclear Threat Initiative; and Monterey Institute of International Studies.
NOTE: NPT = Nonproliferation Treaty, CTBT = Comprehensive Test Ban Treaty, CWC = Chemical Weapons Convention, BTWC = Biological and Toxic Weapons Convention, Additional Protocol = IAEA Additional Protocol. Dash indicates non-participation.

TABLE 23   WMD export control regimes

	Nuclear Suppliers Group	Australia Group	Wassenaar Arrangement	Zangger Committee	MTCR
Russia	Member	–	Member	Member	Member
United States	Member	Member	Member	Member	Member
China	Member	–	–	Member	–
India	–	–	–	–	–
Pakistan	–	–	–	–	–
North Korea	–	–	–	–	–

SOURCE: Nuclear Threat Initiative; and Monterey Institute of International Studies.
NOTE: Dash indicates non-participation.

About the Contributors

Richard K. Betts (PhD, Harvard University) is the Arnold A. Saltzman Professor and Director of the Saltzman Institute of War and Peace Studies at Columbia University. He has taught at Harvard University and at the Johns Hopkins University's Nitze School of Advanced International Studies (SAIS), and he was formerly Senior Fellow at the Brookings Institution and Director of National Security Studies at the Council on Foreign Relations. Dr. Betts has served on the staffs of the original Senate Select Committee on Intelligence (the Church Committee) and the National Security Council. During the 1990s he served for six years on the National Security Advisory Panel of the Director of Central Intelligence, and in 1999–2000 he was a member of the National Commission on Terrorism. Dr. Betts has published numerous articles on U.S. foreign policy, military strategy, intelligence operations, security issues in Asia and Europe, and terrorism. He is the author of five books—*Enemies of Intelligence* (2007), *Military Readiness* (1995), *Nuclear Blackmail and Nuclear Balance* (1987), *Surprise Attack* (1982), and *Soldiers, Statesmen, and Cold War Crises* (1977 and 1991)—and is editor of several volumes including *Conflict After the Cold War* (3rd ed., 2007) and *Paradoxes of Strategic Intelligence* (co-edited with Thomas G. Mahnken, 2003).

Dennis C. Blair holds the John M. Shalikashvili Chair in National Security Studies at The National Bureau of Asian Research (NBR). From 2003 to 2006 Admiral Blair was President and Chief Executive Officer of the Institute for Defense Analyses (IDA), a federally funded research and development center based in Alexandria, Virginia. Prior to retiring from the navy in 2002, he served as Commander in Chief, U.S. Pacific Command, which is the largest of the combatant commands. During his 34-year navy career, Admiral Blair served on guided missile destroyers in both the Atlantic and Pacific fleets and commanded the *Kitty Hawk* Battle Group. Ashore, he served as Director of the Joint Staff and as the first Associate Director of Central Intelligence for Military Support. He has also served in budget and policy positions on the National Security Council and on several major navy staffs. Admiral Blair has been awarded four Defense Distinguished

Service medals and has received decorations from the governments of Japan, Thailand, Korea, Australia, and Taiwan.

Elizabeth Economy (PhD, University of Michigan) is C.V. Starr Senior Fellow and Director for Asia Studies at the Council on Foreign Relations. Dr. Economy has taught at Columbia University, the Paul H. Nitze School of Advanced International Studies (SAIS) at Johns Hopkins University, and the Henry M. Jackson School of International Studies at the University of Washington. She serves on the board of the China-U.S. Center for Sustainable Development and is a member of the World Economic Forum's Global Agenda Council on the Future of China. Dr. Economy's most recent book, *The River Runs Black* (2004), won the 2005 International Convention of Asia Scholars award for best study in the field of social sciences. Her writings appear often in publications such as *Foreign Affairs*, the *New York Times*, the *Washington Post,* and the *International Herald Tribune*, and she is a frequent radio and television commentator on U.S.-China relations. Dr. Economy regularly testifies before Congress and consults for U.S. government and corporations on Chinese environmental issues.

Richard J. Ellings (PhD, University of Washington) is President and Co-founder of The National Bureau of Asian Research (NBR). He is also Affiliate Professor of International Studies at the Henry M. Jackson School of International Studies, University of Washington. Prior to serving with NBR, from 1986–89 he was Assistant Director and on the faculty of the Jackson School, where he received the Distinguished Teaching Award. He served as Legislative Assistant in the United States Senate, office of Senator Slade Gorton, in 1984 and 1985. Dr. Ellings is the author of *Embargoes and World Power: Lessons from American Foreign Policy* (1985); co-author of *Private Property and National Security* (1991); co-editor (with Aaron Friedberg) of *Strategic Asia 2003–04: Fragility and Crisis* (2003), *Strategic Asia 2002–03: Asian Aftershocks* (2002), and *Strategic Asia 2001–02: Power and Purpose* (2001); co-editor of *Korea's Future and the Great Powers* (with Nicholas Eberstadt, 2001) and *Southeast Asian Security in the New Millennium* (with Sheldon Simon, 1996); and the founding editor of the *NBR Analysis* publication series. He established the Strategic Asia Program and AccessAsia, the national clearinghouse that tracks specialists and their research on Asia.

Evelyn Goh (PhD, University of Oxford) is Reader in International Relations at Royal Holloway, University of London. Prior to joining Royal Holloway, she was University Lecturer in International Relations and

Fellow of St. Anne's College, University of Oxford. Her research interests are Asian security, Sino-U.S. relations, and international relations theory. Dr. Goh's recent publications include *Rethinking Security Cooperation in the Asia-Pacific: Competition, Congruence, and Transformation* (co-edited with Amitav Acharya, 2007), *Developing the Mekong: Regionalism and Regional Security in China-Southeast Asia Relations*, Adelphi Paper, no. 387 (2007), and *Constructing the U.S. Rapprochement with China, 1961–74* (2004).

Mercy Kuo (PhD, University of Oxford) is Director of the Strategic Asia Program and Senior Project Director at The National Bureau of Asian Research (NBR). In these positions, she creates and pursues business opportunities for the Strategic Asia Program and NBR, determines significant and emerging issues in the field, manages project teams, and is responsible for the success of research projects. Dr. Kuo joined NBR in 2006 as Director of the Southeast Asia Studies Program. From 2000 to 2006 she served with the Central Intelligence Agency, Directorate of Intelligence, as an analyst on Northeast and Southeast Asian affairs. Her research specialties and interests include modern Chinese history, Chinese foreign policy, political Islam in Asia, and scenario planning. Her select publications include "Defense Policymaking in Strategic Asia," in *Politics of Defence: International and Comparative Perspectives*, ed. Isaiah Wilson and James J.F. Forest (co-authored with Michael Wills, forthcoming); "China in 2020: Bridging the Academic-Policy Gap with Scenario Planning," *Asia Policy*, no. 4 (co-authored with Andrew D. Marble, 2007); and *Contending with Contradictions: China's Policy toward Soviet Eastern Europe and the Origins of the Sino-Soviet Split, 1953–1960* (2001).

Andrew Marble (PhD, Brown University) serves as Editor at The National Bureau of Asian Research (NBR), where he is responsible for all editorial and managerial aspects of publications at NBR. He has helped launch NBR's peer-reviewed academic journal, *Asia Policy*, which promotes bridging the gap between academic research and policymaking. Before joining NBR in January 2005, Dr. Marble was the Editor of *Issues & Studies: A Social Science Quarterly on China, Taiwan, and East Asian Affairs*. Special issues of *Issues & Studies* that he edited include "Studies of Taiwan Politics" (September/ December 2004), "The State of the China Studies Field" (December 2002/ March 2003), "The Taiwan Threat?" (March 2002), "The 'China Threat' Debate" (March 2000), and "The Clash of Civilizations" (October 1998). Dr. Marble has spent eight years in Asia, having studied, worked, researched, and traveled in Taiwan, China, Hong Kong, Singapore, Malaysia, and Thailand. His research interests include Chinese politics and foreign affairs,

Taiwanese politics, and the interplay of ideas, interests, and institutions in politics and policymaking.

Rory Medcalf is Director of the International Security Program at the Lowy Institute for International Policy in Australia. He has worked as a diplomat, intelligence analyst, and journalist. From 2003 to 2007 Mr. Medcalf was a senior strategic analyst in the Australian government's intelligence analysis organization, the Office of National Assessments, with a focus on Asia. His service in the Australian Department of Foreign Affairs and Trade included a posting to New Delhi, a secondment to the Japanese foreign ministry, truce monitoring in Bougainville, policy development on the ASEAN Regional Forum, and extensive work on nonproliferation, including assisting the 1996 Canberra Commission and the 1999 Tokyo Forum. His journalism has been commended by Australia's premier media awards, the Walkleys. Mr. Medcalf's research interests include reassessing Australian defense capability requirements, the potential of India and China as international security contributors, and the prospects for a nuclear arms restraint regime in Asia.

Polly Nayak is an independent consultant. A long-time South Asia specialist, Ms. Nayak retired from government in 2002 as a senior executive. From 1995–2001, as DCI-appointed Director of the inter-agency South Asia Executive Board, she was the most senior official and expert on South Asia in the U.S. intelligence community, directly informing deliberations at the White House and in Congress. Since 2002 Ms. Nayak has consulted for government and private-sector clients on diverse substantive and security issues, drawing on her experience on Latin America and Africa as well as South Asia. Ms. Nayak serves as a "greybeard" advisor for several organizations, including Sandia National Laboratories. In 2001–02 she was a Federal Executive Fellow at the Brookings Institution. She lectures often on South Asia, U.S. foreign policy, and analytic methods at universities and government agencies. Ms. Nayak's recent publications include the report "U.S. Crisis Management in South Asia's Twin Peaks Crisis" (co-authored with Michael Krepon, 2006) and several articles on South Asia. She is currently working on an interview-based book that examines how relations between senior U.S. appointees and government experts shape foreign policy.

T.J. Pempel (PhD, Columbia University) is Professor of Political Science at the University of California–Berkeley, where his research and teaching focus on comparative politics, political economy, contemporary Japan, and

Asian regionalism. He joined Berkeley in 2001 and served as Director of the Institute of East Asian Studies from 2002 to 2006. Previously Dr. Pempel was the Boeing Professor of International Studies in the Henry M. Jackson School of International Studies and Adjunct Professor in Department of Political Science at the University of Washington. He has also held faculty appointments at Cornell University, the University of Colorado, and the University of Wisconsin. Dr. Pempel serves on the editorial boards of several professional journals as well as on committees of the American Political Science Association, the Association for Asian Studies, and the Social Science Research Council. His most recent books include *Crisis as Catalyst: Asia's Dynamic Political Economy* (co-edited with Andrew MacIntyre and John Ravenhill, forthcoming 2008), *Remapping East Asia: The Construction of a Region* (2004), and *Beyond Bilateralism: U.S.-Japan Relations in the New Asia-Pacific* (co-edited with Ellis S. Krauss, 2003). In addition he has published over one hundred scholarly articles and chapters in books.

George Perkovich (PhD, University of Virginia) is Vice President for Studies–Global Security and Economic Development and Director of the Nonproliferation Program at the Carnegie Endowment for International Peace. Dr. Perkovich also oversees both the South Asia Project and the Trade, Equity, and Development Program at the Carnegie Endowment for International Peace. Dr. Perkovich's expertise includes U.S. foreign policy, nonproliferation, global governance, non-governmental actors, South Asia, and Iran. He is the author of *India's Nuclear Bomb* (2001), which received the Herbert Feis Award from the American Historical Association and the A.K. Coomaraswamy Prize from the Association for Asian Studies. He is also co-author of "Universal Compliance: A Strategy for Nuclear Security," a report that is a blueprint for rethinking the international nuclear nonproliferation regime. From 1990 to 2001 he was Director of the Secure World Program at the W. Alton Jones Foundation, where he also served as Deputy Director for Programs. He was a speechwriter and foreign policy advisor to Senator Joe Biden in 1989–90. Dr. Perkovich is currently developing a project on fairness in the international system.

Jonathan D. Pollack (PhD, University of Michigan) is Professor of Asian and Pacific Studies and Chairman of the Asia-Pacific Studies Group at the U.S. Naval War College, where he also served as Chairman of the Strategic Research Department. Prior to joining the Naval War College faculty, Dr. Pollack worked at the RAND Corporation, serving in a variety of research and management positions. He has taught at Brandeis University, the RAND Graduate School of Policy Studies, University of California–Los Angeles, and the Naval War College. Dr. Pollack's research focuses on East Asian security, politics, and military development, with particular attention to China, the Korean Peninsula, and U.S. foreign policy and defense strategy. His recent publications include *Asia Eyes America: Regional Perspectives on U.S. Asia-Pacific Strategy in the 21st Century* (2007), *Korea: The East Asian Pivot* (2006), and *Strategic Surprise? U.S.-China Relations in the Early 21st Century* (2004). He also contributes frequently to professional journals and edited volumes, and he is a regular media contributor in the United States and abroad.

Eugene B. Rumer (PhD, Massachusetts Institute of Technology) is a Senior Fellow at the Institute for National Strategic Studies at the National Defense University in Washington, D.C. Previously he held positions at the Department of State, on the staff of the National Security Council, and at RAND. He has written extensively on Russia and other former Soviet states.

Teresita C. Schaffer is Director of the South Asia Program at the Center for Strategic and International Studies (CSIS). Prior to joining CSIS in 1998, she served for 30 years in the U.S. Foreign Service, including several years as U.S. Ambassador to Sri Lanka (1992–95) and as Deputy Assistant Secretary of State for the Near East and South Asia (1989–92). Ambassador Schaffer has also been Director of the Foreign Service Institute, and her earlier diplomatic assignments included Israel, Pakistan, India, and Bangladesh. She has taught at American University and Georgetown University. Ambassador Schaffer's recent writings include *Kashmir: The Economics of Peacemaking* (2005), *Pakistan's Future and U.S. Policy Options* (2004), and *Rising India and U.S. Policy Options in Asia* (2002), as well as several reports and chapters in edited volumes. She is currently working on a book on the future of U.S.-India relations.

S. Frederick Starr (PhD, Princeton University) is Founding Chairman of the Central Asia-Caucasus Institute at the School of Advanced International Studies (SAIS), Johns Hopkins University. He began his career in American and Turkish archaeology and went on to study the Soviet Union, founding the Kennan Institute for Advanced Russian Studies at the Woodrow Wilson International Center for Scholars. Subsequently he served as Vice President of Tulane University and President of Oberlin College and the Aspen Institute. More recently he has helped plan both the three-campus University of Central Asia and the Azerbaijan Diplomatic Academy. The author of twenty books and 200 articles, he is currently writing a volume on the golden age of Central Asia and Afghanistan, AD 750–1050. Dr. Starr has advised four U.S. presidents on regional affairs and holds four honorary degrees. He also founded the Greater New Orleans Foundation and is co-founder, clarinetist, and leader of the Louisiana Repertory Jazz Ensemble of New Orleans.

Michael D. Swaine (PhD, Harvard University) is Senior Associate with the China Program at the Carnegie Endowment for International Peace. He came to the Carnegie Endowment after twelve years at the RAND Corporation, where he was named the first holder of the RAND Center for Asia Pacific Policy Chair and served as Research Director for the center. Dr. Swaine specializes in Chinese security and foreign policy, U.S.-China relations, and East Asian international relations. He spearheaded and currently co-directs a multi-year collaborative project with a Beijing-based think-tank on key aspects of Sino-U.S. crisis management. He has also produced several seminal studies both on the Chinese military and its role in national security decisionmaking and on Taiwan's national security decisionmaking process. Dr. Swaine has contributed chapters on Taiwan, China, and ballistic missiles to three previous volumes in the *Strategic Asia* series. His most recent edited books include *Assessing the Threat: The Chinese Military and Taiwan's Security* (with Andrew Yang, Evan Medeiros, and Oriana Mastro, 2007) and *Managing Sino-American Crises: Case Studies and Analysis* (with Tuosheng Zhang and Danielle Cohen, 2006).

Ashley J. Tellis (PhD, University of Chicago) is Senior Associate at the Carnegie Endowment for International Peace, specializing in international security, defense, and Asian strategic issues. While on a recent assignment to the U.S. Department of State as Senior Advisor to the Undersecretary of State for Political Affairs, he was intimately involved in negotiating the civil nuclear agreement with India. He is Research Director of the Strategic Asia Program at NBR and co-editor (with Michael Wills) of *Strategic Asia 2007–08: Domestic Political Change and Grand Strategy* (2007), *Strategic Asia 2006–07: Trade, Interdependence, and Security* (2006), *Strategic Asia 2005–06: Military Modernization in an Era of Uncertainty* (2005), and *Strategic Asia 2004–05: Confronting Terrorism in the Pursuit of Power* (2004). Previously he was commissioned into the Foreign Service and served as Senior Advisor to the Ambassador at the U.S. embassy in New Delhi. He also served on the National Security Council staff as Special Assistant to the President and Senior Director for Strategic Planning and Southwest Asia. Prior to his government service, Dr. Tellis was Senior Policy Analyst at the RAND Corporation and Professor of Policy Analysis at the RAND Graduate

School. He is the author of *India's Emerging Nuclear Posture* (2001) and co-author (with Michael D. Swaine) of *Interpreting China's Grand Strategy: Past, Present, and Future* (2000). His academic publications have also appeared in many edited volumes and journals.

About Strategic Asia

The **Strategic Asia Program** at The National Bureau of Asian Research (NBR) is a major ongoing research initiative that draws together top Asia studies specialists and international relations experts to assess the changing strategic environment in the Asia-Pacific. The Strategic Asia Program transcends traditional estimates of military balance by incorporating economic, political, and demographic data and by focusing on the strategies and perceptions that drive policy in the region. The program's integrated set of products and activities includes:

- an annual edited volume written by leading specialists
- an executive summary tailored for public and private sector decisionmakers and strategic planners
- an online database that tracks key strategic indicators
- briefings and presentations for government, business, and academe that are designed to foster in-depth discussions revolving around major, relevant public issues

Special briefings are held for key committees of Congress and the executive branch, other government agencies, and the intelligence community. The principal audiences for the program's research findings are the U.S. policymaking and research communities, the media, the business community, and academe.

The Strategic Asia Program's online database contains an unprecedented selection of strategic indicators—economic, financial, military, technological, energy, political, and demographic—for all of the countries in the Asia-Pacific region. The database, together with previous volumes and executive summaries, are hosted on the Strategic Asia website at http://strategicasia.nbr.org.

Previous Strategic Asia Volumes

Over the past eight years this series has addressed how Asia is increasingly functioning as a zone of strategic interaction and contending with an uncertain balance of power. *Strategic Asia 2001–02: Power and Purpose* established a baseline assessment for understanding the strategies and interactions of the major states within the region—notably China, India, Japan, Russia, and South Korea. *Strategic Asia 2002–03: Asian Aftershocks* drew upon this baseline to analyze the changes in these states' grand strategies and relationships in the aftermath of the September 11 terrorist attacks. *Strategic Asia 2003–04: Fragility and Crisis* examined the fragile balance of power in Asia, drawing out the key domestic political and economic trends in Asian states supporting or undermining this tenuous equilibrium. Building upon established themes, *Strategic Asia 2004–05: Confronting Terrorism in the Pursuit of Power* explored the effect of the U.S.-led war on terrorism on the political, economic, social, and strategic transformations underway in Asia. *Strategic Asia 2005–06: Military Modernization in an Era of Uncertainty* appraised the progress of Asian military modernization programs and developed a touchstone to evaluate future military changes to the balance of power. *Strategic Asia 2006–07: Trade, Interdependence, and Security* addressed how increasing levels of trade and changing trade relationships are affecting the balance of power and security in Asia. Turning to focus on the factors that motivate states' choices, *Strategic Asia 2007–08: Domestic Political Change and Grand Strategy* examined internal and external drivers of grand strategy in Asia and evaluated their impact on Asian foreign policymaking.

Research and Management Team

The Strategic Asia research team consists of leading international relations and security specialists from universities and research institutions across the United States. A new research team is selected each year. The research team for 2008 is led by Ashley J. Tellis (Carnegie Endowment for International Peace). General John Shalikashvili (former Chairman of the Joint Chiefs of Staff), Aaron Friedberg (Princeton University, and Strategic Asia's founding research director), and Richard Ellings (The National Bureau of Asian Research, and Strategic Asia's founding program director) serve as senior advisors. Advising the program is the executive committee, composed of Herbert Ellison (University of Washington), Donald Emmerson (Stanford University), Francine Frankel (University of Pennsylvania), Mark Hamilton (University of Alaska), Kenneth Pyle (University of Washington), Richard Samuels (Massachusetts Institute of Technology), Robert Scalapino

(University of California–Berkeley), Enders Wimbush (Hudson Institute), and William Wohlforth (Dartmouth College).

The Strategic Asia Program depends on a diverse funding base of foundations, government, and corporations, supplemented by income from publication sales. Major support for the program in 2008 comes from the Lynde and Harry Bradley Foundation and the National Nuclear Security Administration at the U.S. Department of Energy.

Attribution

Readers of *Strategic Asia* and visitors to the Strategic Asia website may use data, charts, graphs, and quotes from these sources without requesting permission from NBR on the condition that they cite NBR and the appropriate primary source in any published work. No report, chapter, separate study, extensive text, or any other substantial part of the Strategic Asia Program's products may be reproduced without the written permission of NBR. To request permission, please write to:

NBR Editor
The National Bureau of Asian Research
1215 Fourth Avenue, Suite 1600
Seattle, WA 98161
nbr@nbr.org

The National Bureau of Asian Research

The National Bureau of Asian Research is a non-profit, nonpartisan research institution dedicated to informing and strengthening policy. NBR conducts advanced independent research on strategic, political, economic, globalization, health, and energy issues affecting U.S. relations with Asia. Drawing upon an extensive network of the world's leading specialists and leveraging the latest technology, NBR bridges the academic, business, and policy arenas. The institution disseminates its research through briefings, publications, conferences, Congressional testimony, and email forums, and by collaborating with leading institutions worldwide. NBR also provides exceptional internship opportunities to graduate and undergraduate students for the purpose of attracting and training the next generation of Asia specialists. NBR was started in 1989 with a major grant from the Henry M. Jackson Foundation.

Index